S0-BPZ-531

The Journals and Miscellaneous Notebooks

of

RALPH WALDO EMERSON

VOLUME IX

1843–1847

EDITED BY

RALPH H. ORTH   ALFRED R. FERGUSON

THE BELKNAP PRESS

OF HARVARD UNIVERSITY PRESS

Cambridge, Massachusetts

1971

ARCHBISHOP ALEMANY LIBRARY
DOMINICAN COLLEGE
SAN RAFAEL, CALIFORNIA

B
Em 34
v. 9

© Copyright 1971 by the President and Fellows of Harvard College
All rights reserved

CENTER FOR EDITIONS OF
AMERICAN AUTHORS
AN APPROVED TEXT
MODERN LANGUAGE
ASSOCIATION OF AMERICA
®

Library of Congress Catalog Card Number: 60–11554
SBN 674–48471–1

Typography by Burton J Jones
Printed in the U.S.A. by the Harvard University Printing Office
Bound by Stanhope Bindery, Inc., Boston, Massachusetts

84256

Preface

Both editors independently established the text of the journals printed in this volume, both did research for the notes, and both analyzed the journals descriptively and recovered as much as they could of erased pencil passages. Mr. Orth has been responsible for the preparation of the text for the press, the writing of the notes, and the introductory material. Each editor has had opportunity to contribute to and review his coeditor's work.

The editors wish to thank a number of institutions and foundations for help of various kinds. The Ralph Waldo Emerson Memorial Association has continued to provide regular grants-in-aid which have been indispensable to the progress of the edition. The University of Vermont provided support for Mr. Orth through a Faculty Research Grant and a sabbatical leave. The Center for Editions of American Authors of the Modern Language Association of America provided generous financial support for the work of both editors from grants made by the National Endowment for the Humanities of the National Foundation on the Arts and the Humanities.

Among individuals who have given invaluable help in the preparation of this volume are Mrs. John A. Leermakers, Mrs. Dorothy C. Bates, Mrs. Richard G. Bennett, Mrs. Hans D. Kellner, Linda Allardt, Mrs. Mary Anne Stewart, Mrs. Raul Hilberg, and Marjorie Zeuch. Frances Pringle transcribed the manuscript journals. Professor Brady B. Gilleland of the University of Vermont helped with quotations from the classics.

For other assistance and courtesies, the editors wish to thank Miss Carolyn Jakeman, Professor William H. Bond, and the staff of Houghton Library; Mrs. Marcia Moss of the Concord Free Library; and the staffs of the libraries of Ohio Wesleyan University and the University of Vermont.

Unless otherwise noted, translations of classical quotations are from the Loeb Classical Library and are reprinted by permission of Harvard University Press and the Loeb Classical Library.

All the editors named on the edition title page have responsibilities of various kinds for the edition as a whole. The Chief Editor has the primary responsibility for the edition, and for certification of individual volumes.

W. H. G.

Contents

Illustrations

Foreword to Volume IX

THE JOURNALS FROM 1843 TO 1847

At one point in the journals which comprise this volume, Emerson notes to himself that he "pound[s] . . . tediously" on "the exemption of the writer from all secular works." It was not an observation made in an idle moment. Although he felt as a man and as a writer that his essential calling was to be independent and disinterested, he was frequently enjoined during this period to take part in public activities in which he often took a merely intellectual interest and for which he felt little aptitude. The demands of the abolitionists, the experiments of the utopian societies, the great national crises over slavery, Texas, and the Mexican War continually threatened to warp him from his true perspective and involve him in the tumult and enthusiasms of the day. During much of this period he struggled to formulate the true attitude of the scholar to this vexed question of involvement.

In the early part of 1844, Emerson might have congratulated himself upon a release from a public task which had become increasingly onerous, the editorship of *The Dial*. He had taken over the editorship from Margaret Fuller in the spring of 1842, unwilling to see the journal die, but reluctant "to be its life." Despite his best efforts, the magazine's prospects became increasingly gloomy over the next two years, and he was forced to halt publication with the issue of April, 1844. Emerson was not allowed to retreat to the study, however, for he had become by this time a central figure in the literary and intellectual life of New England, and received numerous calls to public service.

Most of these calls had to do in one way or another with the reformist syndrome of the 1840's, which took a number of forms of expression. The Temperance movement aimed at eliminating the demoralizing effects of Demon Rum; the Peace Society called for an end to all wars; Horace Mann and other progressives worked diligently for universal free education. The Shakers opted for celibacy to avoid the taint of sin, and Henry Thoreau entered upon a one-man experiment in self-reliance at Walden Pond. For those who despaired of the renewal of human society altogether, a final "reform" was forecast by the followers of William Miller, who predicted that the world would come to an end sometime between March, 1843, and March, 1844. But the most noteworthy of these movements were those which, considering reform within the society as unlikely, chose to begin new communities built on other and higher principles.

Emerson's response to the most celebrated of these communities, Brook Farm, in West Roxbury, was typical of his sympathetic skepticism. Although respecting the high-minded goals of the community, founded by George Ripley and kindred spirits in April, 1841, Emerson refused to join. The communal nature of the enterprise offended his belief in individualism, nor was he yet willing to give up the existing society as a lost cause. As Brook Farm came more and more under the influence of the socialist ideas of Fourier, Emerson became less and less satisfied with it. He predicted that as a phalanstery it would become "culinary & mean" and abandon the high principles with which it had started. Also, with his pronounced distaste for French civilization, which was "devoid of all religion & morality," Emerson noted several times that the sexual freedom Fourier advocated — a freedom which could hardly be charged to Brook Farm — would lead to a drastic weakening of the social fabric. Yet he could not hide his admiration for the Farm itself and its participants, visited it frequently, and encouraged it as he could.

Another community whose fortunes Emerson followed closely was that involving his neighbor and frequent companion Bronson Alcott near Harvard, Massachusetts. Alcott and two English disciples, Charles Lane and Henry Wright, had gathered a small group around themselves, bought land, established "Fruitlands," and worked diligently through the summer and fall of 1843. The principles on which Fruitlands was founded forbade the use of animals for labor or the products of animals for clothing or food. Lane, for instance, refused to wear clothes made from wool and dressed in linen instead. These restrictions, in addition to a mismanaged harvest and a severe winter, led, as Emerson had feared, to the dissolution of the community in January, 1844. Alcott was overwhelmed by the failure, which was only the latest in a series of calamities, and Emerson had to see "this modern Prometheus," as he called him, through his time of trouble.

Emerson saw that these communities had one great virtue. They often accomplished what the great world, with all its resources, seldom did: demonstrate that simplicity, mutual help, and a reliance on the moral sentiment could be the basis of a society. The Shakers, for instance, whose community at Harvard Emerson visited several times, were uniformly courteous, humble, and sincere, despite the fact that Emerson found them "stupid people" with a "nasty religion"; and the Brook Farmers, he observed, made of their farm "the pleasantest of residences." Incapable of joining any such community himself, he understood the value they had for their members, who usually struck some chord of virtue because of their devotion to a special social theory. And to society at large, the communities served as a reproach and an example.

The reform question which eventually overshadowed every other was, of course, the abolition of slavery. In the beginning, the genial temper of Emerson's mind was repelled by the "fanaticism" of people like William Lloyd Garrison, Wendell Phillips, and Parker Pillsbury. Their flaw was that they saw the American experience through very special lenses, in terms of the subjection of black men by white, and would agree to no compromise of their views. Emerson could not be the captive of some one "Idea." The world was too complicated to admit of partial solutions. Yet paradoxically, when he met these men personally or saw them on the lecture platform, he could only admire them. Their wholehearted adherence to their view of things, their contempt for any harm or opprobrium that might come to them, seemed to embody everything he believed about those men whom he labeled "great." They acted out of deep personal conviction and imposed their ideas on other men and on society through force of character.

A number of events conspired to make him more sympathetic toward the advocates of the elimination of the South's "peculiar institution." One was the frequent attempts to silence the abolitionists, as when the Reverend Barzillai Frost and others attempted to prevent Phillips from speaking at the Concord Lyceum in 1845, a move Emerson and Thoreau helped thwart. Another was the cynical use of power by the advocates of slavery in the Congress of the United States, and the moves to annex Texas and to instigate war with Mexico. The most immediately personal event, however, was the insult and actual threat of physical harm that had been offered to the Honorable Samuel Hoar, Concord's most prominent citizen, in Charleston, South Carolina, where he had gone to protect the rights of colored citizens of the state of Massachusetts who were in danger of being detained and sold into slavery. Hoar left South Carolina under mob pressure without accomplishing his mission, but the event served to galvanize public opinion in New England against the South. Indignation meetings were held in various parts of Massachusetts, including Concord, where Emerson, despite his dislike of public assemblies of this sort, apparently delivered a stinging rebuke to the "Alsatia" that was South Carolina.

Emerson skirted as best he could the controversy that arose over the admission of Texas to the Union. Because Texas asked for admission as a slave state, the question crystallized all the fears of the North about the extension of the slave power, while the South saw it as a necessary move if the national balance between North and South was to be preserved. Emerson followed the annexation debate with interest — he notes that he attended the Texas Convention in Boston in January, 1845 — and felt, with most of his New England neighbors, that the proposed statehood was a disgrace. But his equanimity eventually conquered his repugnance, and he was able to see the acquisition of Texas as a "historical" event which future ages would not agitate themselves over.

The war with Mexico, which began in May, 1846, partly as a result of the annexation of Texas, increased Emerson's awareness of the scabrous state of the nation. The flag-waving and patriotic bullying of the Concord *Freeman*, a Democratic organ, repelled him, and he thought of Mexico as perhaps the "arsenic" which would eventually poison the country. Significantly, as with the incident involving Samuel Hoar, it was a close personal event that agitated him most:

Thoreau's refusal to pay his poll tax, partly because of the war and partly because of slavery. When Sam Staples, Concord's jovial jailer, put Thoreau in jail, Emerson was horrified — not at Staples's action, but Thoreau's. He used half a dozen pages in his journal to confide that he found Thoreau's action misguided. Emerson maintained that the state, far from being some kind of abstract menace, is "our neighbors," a mere beast, a "poor cow," and Thoreau's kind of attack diverted attention from the possibility of real reform. The act was trivial, useless, perverse. Emerson was finally able to console himself by ascribing it to Thoreau's well-known cantankerousness and penchant for idiosyncrasy.

The events of these years led Emerson to some bitter conclusions about the state of the country. In February, 1844, he had been able to deliver before the Mercantile Library Association in Boston an optimistic lecture on "The Young American," full of the glory of the national conquest of the continent and celebrating the triumphs that were yet to come. He welcomed wholeheartedly the railroad when, in 1843, it intruded into the peaceful pastures of Concord, hailing it as the representative of "American power & beauty." Trade, which Alcott and Thoreau were so contemptuous of, he saw as "the principle of liberty," providing the ferment which would eventually solve social ills, even slavery, and lead to the spread of culture and taste. But these optimistic attitudes existed side by side with others which, under the impulse of reform, abolition, Texas, and the Mexican War made Emerson despair for the country and for New England. In literature America was an "incapable giant," full of "inaction & whining"; the cultivated classes were afflicted with "the American disease of aimlessness"; the law, as exemplifed by the maneuvering and pettifogging in the Phoenix Bank case, was a "sad game"; the churches and the colleges served the ends of State Street, not Olympus or Parnassus; New England was "cautious, calculating," anxious to avoid all threats to its prosperity, a "debating-society"; the hypocritical North and the unspeakable South both contributed to the "American blight," which Emerson defined as "great strength on a basis of weakness."

The political life of the country, especially, filled him with disgust. It seemed to be given over either to "snivelling nobodies" more interested in compromise than justice, or to cynical, self-serving "master[s] of the brawls," who hid under labels like Texas, Tariff, Temperance, Antimasonry, and the like. Emerson's often pyrotechnic language, much stronger than any he was accustomed to use in public, demonstrates the depth of his disgust. Each of the political groups comprising the Republic was rotten to him. The Whigs, the solid, conservative, property-owning, law-abiding minority, were weak and cowardly; the Democrats, composed of "hordes of ignorant & deceivable natives & the armies of foreign voters" led by "unscrupulous editors & orators," were venal and vulgar; and on the margins of political life lived the abolitionist radicals on the one hand, and groups like the Native American party, with its hatred of immigrants, on the other. The South, of course, was given over to the slaveholders, but the North was hardly better, controlled as it was by the Websters and the Briggses and the Winthrops. "Party" and "interest" and an empty "parliamentariness" seemed to be the order of the day.

The answer to all these manifestations of cultural and political rot, in Emerson's view, was the strong, self-reliant individual, able to listen to his inner voice no matter what the shouts from the world outside. Such a man could be the scholar as Emerson had already described him, reading the timeless patterns of human life in the shifting events of the day. It was for this that Emerson asked for himself "exemption . . . from all secular works." Or, if "secular works" were his meat and drink, the self-reliant individual would have the power to persuade legions of men to listen to and follow him through sheer force of character. It is no accident that at the same time that Emerson is bemoaning the nature of the times, he is preparing a lecture series on "Representative Men," devoted to men who shaped their age fully as much as their age shaped them. In terms of the lectures, these men are historical figures like Plato or Goethe or Napoleon; in terms of contemporary times, they are Garrison and Phillips and Carlyle. They present a healthy contrast to the embalmed dignity of conventionally respectable men like Edward Everett and Henry Ware, Jr. They cannot by their nature be "respectable." Yet it is only by the existence of such men that society can see the standards by which it must be judged.

Especially satisfying to Emerson were those men whose orator-
ical gifts allowed them to sway multitudes. Although he was in
disagreement with Parker Pillsbury, for instance, over the abolitionist's belief in political action, he saw the strength of the man,
whom he called "a tough oak stick . . . not to be silenced or
insulted or intimidated by a mob, because he is more mob than
they." Wendell Phillips "keeps no terms with sham churches or
shamming legislatures, and must & will grope till he feels the
stones." Edward Taylor's chaotic preaching he excused and justified
because he was "mighty nature's child . . . trusting heartily to her
power . . . and arriving unexpectedly every moment at new &
happiest deliverances."

Emerson weighed himself in the same balance and found himself wanting. Especially rueful to him was his lack of what he called
"animal spirits." He was reserved with those who, like Margaret
Fuller, wanted more emotional warmth than he was prepared to
give; even Lidian complained of the coldness of his letters. This
coldness, he was aware, carried over into his public appearances. He
was usually described as "serene," "Olympian," "philosophical." He
moved his audience on intellectual levels, but not on emotional ones,
and he regretted the incompleteness of his effect. It was clear to him
that, although he could outline for others what the "orator" should
be, he was far from being one himself.

Thus much of the material in the journals of this period touches
upon public questions of the time and Emerson's desire to formulate
the most desirable response to them. He does of course in his reading pursue more strictly intellectual or philosophical questions,
especially in the writings of the Orient. He becomes acquainted with
Hafiz, the *Vishńu Puráńa*, and the *Akhlāk-I-Jalāly*. Thomas Taylor
remains a favorite guide to Plato, Plotinus, Proclus, and classical
philosophy in general. At other times, Emerson reads Schelling,
Böhme, and Swedenborg, dips into Robert Chambers's *Vestiges of
Creation*, struggles with Machiavelli's *Florentine Histories*, and
spends lighter moments with the novels of George Sand and Countess
Ida von Hahn-Hahn.

The poetic impulse also persists, encouraged by the prospect
of his first volume of poetry, published in December, 1846. Dozens

x v

of pages in these journals are given over to poetry, including first drafts which Emerson later erased or transcribed. Among the poetry are versions of parts of "Uriel," "Merlin," "Ode to Beauty," "May-Day," and the "Daemonic Love" section of "Initial, Daemonic, and Celestial Love." He also composed a number of short poems which were affixed as mottoes to the appropriate essays in the second edition of *Essays* [*First Series*], published in October, 1847.

Toward the end of this period Emerson received indications of how far his fame had spread. Alexander Ireland wrote from England that he and other admirers wanted to arrange a lecture tour of British cities which would bring Emerson's ideas on man and society to a new, large, eager audience. At first hesitant, Emerson nevertheless began outlining a series of lectures on "Mind and Manners of the Nineteenth Century." In July, 1847, he wrote Ireland that he had decided to accept the challenge of bringing to the Old World his observations on the nature of the age.

Volume IX consists of five regular journals, U, V, W, Y, and O, using the somewhat irregular alphabetical system Emerson began in December, 1833, with Journal A. They cover the period from August, 1843, to February, 1847, usually in consecutive chronological sequence, although there are some inconsistencies.

Editorial technique. The editorial process follows that described in volume I and the modifications introduced in subsequent volumes of the edition. Where substantial portions of erased pencil writing have been recovered, or where the recovered material has a special interest, as in the case of first drafts of poems, it has been printed using the special techniques devised for volume VIII. Unrecovered words are indicated by a bracketed number or numbers and *w* (for "word(s)") in italics; where it is not possible to conjecture as to the number, "[*words*]" is used. Unrecovered letters are represented by hyphens when the number can be estimated; when it cannot, three close dots are set centered on a letter. An unrecovered line in poetry is shown as "[*unrecovered*]." Doubtful readings are shown by the conventional bracketed question mark. Where a printed or copied version exists of a passage in erased or overwritten pencil writing, the editors have first recovered as much as possible without aid and have then consulted another version. They have printed only what they have been able to see.

In certain instances, line numbers of poems as printed in *Poems*, *W*, IX, are supplied in brackets, by fives, except when the manuscript lines are not in the printed order, or where the line number cannot be deduced with certainty from other line numbers. A bracketed "x" means the line does not appear in the poem; a bracketed question mark means uncertainty as to the line number, or as to whether the line is used. No line of poetry in the manuscript is necessarily unchanged in *Poems*. Where an identification is made by means of Emerson's index to the journal at hand, the note does not mention the journal; where it is made by means of another journal or notebook, the manuscript volume is named. Except in a few special instances, punctuation which Emerson added is reported only to account for an otherwise illogical situation, as for example, when Emerson writes a main clause, begins another one, cancels it, and adds a period after the first one.

Whenever one of Emerson's hyphens coincides with the compositor's end-of-line hyphenation, two hyphens have been set, one at the end of the line and one at the beginning of the following line. When the text is quoted in the notes, no silent emendations are made; hence there are occasional variations between notes and text.

Numbering of "Fragments on Nature and Life" and "Fragments on the Poet and the Poetic Life" follows that assigned by Edward Emerson or by George S. Hubbell, *A Concordance to the Poems of Ralph Waldo Emerson*.

As in the previous volumes, use marks are carefully described and references made to places in lectures and essays where journal passages are used, often with help from the locations supplied by Edward W. Emerson in the manuscripts. Because several of the lectures for which these journals were sources have not yet been printed, notes identifying such use give only the title of the lecture and, in the first reference, the date of first delivery.

In accordance with the policies of the Center for Editions of American Authors, a list of silent emendations has been prepared; copies are to be deposited in the Rush Rhees Library of the University of Rochester, the Library of Congress, Houghton Library, Huntington Library, and Newberry Library. The following statement describes the silent or mostly silent emendations. These range from numerous — as with punctuation of items in a series, supplying periods at the ends of sentences if the next sentence begins with a capital, or expansion of contractions — to occasional, as with supplying quotation marks, dashes, or parentheses missing from intended pairs.

Emendation of prose. A period is silently added to any declarative sentence lacking terminal punctuation but followed in the same paragraph by a sentence beginning with a capital letter. If a declarative sentence lacking a period is followed by a sentence beginning with a small letter, either a bracketed semicolon is supplied, or a bracketed period is supplied and the small letter is silently capitalized. In the second instance the reader will automatically know that the capital was originally a small letter. If a direct question lacking terminal punctuation is followed by a sentence in the same paragraph beginning with a capital the question mark is silently added. Punctuation of items in a series, since Emerson habitually set them off, is silently inserted. Small letters at the beginning of unquestionable paragraphs or of sentences which follow a sentence ending with a period are silently capitalized. Where indispensable for clarity a silent period is added to an abbreviation. Quotation marks, dashes, and parentheses missing from intended pairs have been silently supplied; so have quotation marks at the beginning of each of a series of quotations. Apostrophes have been silently inserted or normalized in possessives and contractions. Superscripts have been lowered and double or triple underscorings have been interpreted by small or large capitals. Common Emersonian contractions like y^t for *that*, y^e for *the*, *wh* for *which*, *wd* and *shd* for *would* and *should*, and *bo't* for *bought*, are silently expanded. His dates have been regularly normalized by the silent insertion of commas and periods.

Emendation of poetry. On the whole, Emerson's poetry has been left as it appears in the manuscripts; apostrophes and some commas, periods, and question marks have been supplied, in accordance with the rules for emending prose, but only where Emerson's intention was unmistakable.

Certain materials are omitted, either silently or with descriptive annotation; these will not be reported in the list of emendations. Omitted silently are slips of the pen, false starts at words, careless repetitions of a single word, and Emerson's occasional carets under insertions (assimilated into the editors' insertion marks). Underscoring to indicate intended revisions is not reproduced. Omitted, but usually with descriptive annotation, are practice penmanship, isolated words or letters, and miscellaneous markings.

CHRONOLOGY 1843–1847

1843: August 25, Emerson makes the first of several visits to observe the building of the railroad in Concord; October, he oversees the appearance of another issue of *The Dial*; November 15, he lectures at the Concord Lyceum on the New England character; late November or early December, Henry Thoreau returns to Concord from New York where he had been tutor to William Emerson's children; December 5 and 6, Emerson lectures at Woonsocket and Providence.

1844: January 8–19, Emerson delivers four lectures from the "New England" series at the Franklin Lyceum in Providence; mid-January, Alcott's community at Fruitlands breaks up; also in January, the next-to-last issue of *The Dial* appears; February 7, Emerson delivers his lecture "The Young American" before the Mercantile Library Association in Boston; March 3, he addresses the Non-Resistance Meeting in Amory Hall, Boston, on the topic "New England Reformers"; March 10, he addresses the congregation of the Second Church of Boston, where he was once pastor, on the closing of the old building; April, the last number of *The Dial* appears; June, trains begin running between Concord and Boston; also in June, Emerson makes one of several visits to the Shaker community at Harvard, Mass.; July 10, Edward Waldo Emerson is born; August 1, Emerson delivers an address on "Emancipation in the West Indies" in the Court House in Concord; September, he buys fourteen acres of land on the north shore of Walden Pond;

October, *Essays, Second Series* is published; October 12–November 28, he delivers four lectures at the Nantucket Athenaeum; November, Ellery Channing leaves Concord for New York to work on Horace Greeley's *Daily Tribune*.

1845: January, Emerson takes part in the meeting at Concord to protest the expulsion of Samuel Hoar from South Carolina; January 20, he goes to Boston to hear the speeches in the Texas Convention; March 1, President Tyler signs into law the congressional resolution for the annexation of Texas to the United States; March 5, Emerson is instrumental in getting the Concord Lyceum to let Wendell Phillips speak on slavery; also in March, Ellery Channing returns to Concord from New York; April 2, Emerson delivers a lecture on Napoleon before the Concord Lyceum; April or May, he first makes the acquaintance of James Elliot Cabot; June 23, he hears Edward Taylor preach to a large assembly in Concord; July 4, Thoreau begins his stay at the cabin he has built on Emerson's land at Walden Pond; July 22, Emerson delivers a discourse at Middlebury College on the role of the scholar (and repeats it at Wesleyan University on August 6); the early part of September, he attends the trial in Concord of William Wyman for embezzlement; September 22, he attends the Middlesex County convention of the opponents of the annexation of Texas, held in Concord; October, Hawthorne gives up the Old Manse and leaves Concord; November 5, Emerson meets Robert Owen at Alcott's house; November 17, he refuses to lecture before the New Bedford Lyceum because it excludes Negroes from membership; December 11 to January 22, 1846, he delivers seven lectures in the series "Representative Men" in Boston; December 31 to April 29, he delivers the same lectures in Concord.

1846: January 13 to March ?, he delivers seven lectures in the "Representative Men" series at the Lowell Mechanics' Association; January 23 to February 28, he delivers six lectures in the same series at Worcester; March, Ellery Channing sails for Europe on funds raised by Emerson; April 30, Emerson attends the inauguration of Edward Everett as president of Harvard; May 12, Congress declares war on Mexico after American and Mexican forces clash on the Rio Grande; also in May, the Emerson family become boarders in their own house under the care of Mrs. Marston Goodwin in an arrangement which lasts until September, 1847; July, Ellery Channing returns from Europe; July 4, Emerson lectures to the Massachusetts Anti-Slavery Society at Dedham; July 6, American naval forces capture Monterey, California; July 23 or 24, Thoreau spends a night in the Concord jail for refusing to pay his poll tax; August 27, Emerson meets with his college class at its twenty-fifth reunion and hears Charles Sumner deliver the Phi Beta Kappa Address; September 21–23, American forces under General Zachary Taylor defeat the Mexicans at Monterrey, Mexico; October 6–15, Emerson delivers five lectures in the "Representative Men" series at the Bangor, Maine, Lyceum; December 25 or 26, Emerson's first volume of poetry is published.

1847: January, Emerson arranges to purchase from Cyrus Warren three acres of land adjoining his property on the east; February 10, he reads a lecture on "Eloquence" before the Mercantile Library Association in Boston; February 22–23, American forces defeat the Mexicans at the battle of Buena Vista as the Mexican War continues.

SYMBOLS AND ABBREVIATIONS

⟨ ⟩	Cancellation
↑ ↓	Insertion or addition
/ /	Variant
‖ … ‖	Unrecovered matter, normally unannotated. Three dots, one to five words; four dots, six to fifteen words; five dots, sixteen to thirty words. Matter lost by accidental mutilation but recovered conjecturally is inserted between the parallels.
⟨‖ … ‖⟩	Unrecovered canceled matter
‖msm‖	Manuscript mutilated
[ ]	Editorial insertion
[…]	Editorial omission
⟦ ⟧	Emerson's square brackets
⌐ ⌐	Marginal matter inserted in text

[ ]   Page numbers of original manuscript

n   See Textual Notes

--   Two hyphens are set when the compositor's end-of-line hyphen coincides with Emerson's.

^   Emerson's symbol for intended insertion

[R.W.E.]   Editorial substitution for Emerson's symbol of original authorship. See volume I, plate vii.

*   Emerson's note

epw   Erased pencil writing

☞
☜
🖐
    Hands pointing

For special symbols, not shown here, see p. 73, n. 198; for bracketed numbers after lines of poetry, see p. 12, n. 21.

ABBREVIATIONS AND SHORT TITLES IN FOOTNOTES

CEC   *The Correspondence of Emerson and Carlyle*. Edited by Joseph Slater. New York: Columbia University Press, 1964.

E t E   Kenneth W. Cameron. *Emerson the Essayist*. Raleigh, N.C.: The Thistle Press, 1945. 2 vols.

J   *Journals of Ralph Waldo Emerson*. Edited by Edward Waldo Emerson and Waldo Emerson Forbes. Boston and New York: Houghton Mifflin Co., 1909–1914. 10 vols.

JMN   *The Journals and Miscellaneous Notebooks of Ralph Waldo Emerson*. William H. Gilman, Chief Editor; Alfred R. Ferguson, Senior Editor; Harrison Hayford, Ralph H. Orth, J. E. Parsons, A. W. Plumstead, Editors (Volume I edited by William H. Gilman, Alfred R. Ferguson, George P. Clark, and Merrell R. Davis; volumes II–VI, William H. Gilman, Alfred R. Ferguson, Merrell R. Davis, Merton M. Sealts, Jr., Harrison Hayford, General Editors). Cambridge: Harvard University Press, 1960–

L   *The Letters of Ralph Waldo Emerson*. Edited by Ralph L. Rusk. New York: Columbia University Press, 1939. 6 vols.

Lectures   *The Early Lectures of Ralph Waldo Emerson*. Volume I, 1833–1836, edited by Stephen E. Whicher and Robert E. Spiller; volume II, 1836–1838, edited by Stephen E. Whicher, Robert E. Spiller, and Wallace E. Williams. Cambridge: Harvard University Press, 1959–

Life   Ralph L. Rusk. *The Life of Ralph Waldo Emerson*. New York: Charles Scribner's Sons, 1949.

W   *The Complete Works of Ralph Waldo Emerson*. With a Biographical Introduction and Notes, by Edward Waldo Emerson. Centenary Edition. Boston and New York: Houghton Mifflin Co., 1903–1904. 12 vols. I — *Nature Addresses and Lectures*; II — *Essays, First Series*; III — *Essays, Second Series*; IV — *Representative Men*; V — *English Traits*; VI — *Conduct of Life*; VII — *Society and Solitude*; VIII — *Letters and Social Aims*; IX — *Poems*; X — *Lectures and Biographical Sketches*; XI — *Miscellanies*; XII — *Natural History of Intellect*.

YES   *Young Emerson Speaks*. Edited by Arthur C. McGiffert, Jr. Boston: Houghton Mifflin Co., 1938.

The Journals

U

1843–1844

Journal U is a regular journal covering nine months of Emerson's life; its first dated entry is August 25, 1843, and its last, May 8, 1844. In addition to a number of passages reflecting Emerson's role as editor of *The Dial,* and others on the Utopian reform movements, it contains many passages for "The Young American," delivered on February 7, 1844; for *Essays, Second Series,* especially "Nominalist and Realist," "Experience," and "The Poet"; and a few early and tentative passages for the lecture series on Representative Men, first given in the 1845–1846 season.

The covers of the copybook bear a red and blue mottled design and measure 17.1 x 21 cm. The spine strip, of light brown leather, is embossed with three pairs of horizontal gold lines and edged with a thin gold design. Triangles of leather, similarly edged, appear at the top and bottom corners of both covers. The spine bears the designation "U". On the front cover is written "U 1843"; a smaller "U" also appears in the triangular leather patch at the top corner.

Originally there were 164 lightly ruled pages, plus two flyleaves at both front and back, but the leaf bearing pages 99–100 has been torn out. The leaves measure 16.8 x 20.4 cm. Most of the pages are numbered in ink, but pages 53, 96, and 150 are numbered in pencil, and twelve pages are unnumbered: 2, 51, 75, 113, 142, 143, 151, 165, and 167–170. Pages 118–120 and 122–124 were first numbered in pencil, then in ink. Page 141 was originally numbered 142. Six pages are blank: 2, 9, 113, 143, 155, and 169.

A sheet of blue unlined paper measuring 12.6 x 20 cm bearing on one side jottings in Emerson's hand is laid in between pages 74–75; it has been numbered 74a–74b.

[front cover]   U

U
1843

[front cover verso] [1]
  Engaged to
  _____

        Woonsocket ⟨Dec 7 5⟩
        Providence ⟨Dec 6⟩ Jan ⟨8, 9,⟩ 15, ⟨18,⟩ 19
        Newburyport ⟨Dec 8⟩
        Cambridge 17 Jan   Wednesday
        Waltham
        Boston M[ercantile]. L[ibrary]. A[ssociation]   Wednesday
           7 Feby
        Salem ⟨10 Jan⟩ Wednesday
        Dorchester 16 Jan Tuesd. and 22
        Cabotville &c ⟨23, 24, 25 Jan⟩   Feb 13 14 15
        Fall River 18 ⟨?⟩
        Tuesday — Billerica

[i] [Index material omitted]   R. W. Emerson
                                                          1843
                    U.

      "Apparent imitations of unapparent natures." [2]
                    U 144

      Victurus Genium debet habere liber. [3]
                    Martial. [Epigrams, VI, lxi]

   [1] The entries on the front cover verso are in pencil. As Emerson's own records
show, the list of towns outlines lecture engagements for the 1843–1844 winter
season. See William Charvat, *Emerson's American Lecture Engagements: A Chronological List* (New York, 1961). Four vertical lines in pencil are struck through the
list from "Woonsocket" to "Fall River 18 ⟨?⟩". "Tuesday — Billerica" is enclosed in a box.
   [2] Quoted by Thomas Taylor in "Collection of the Chaldaean Oracles," *Monthly Magazine and British Register*, III (1797), 520. The quotation also occurs on
p. [144] below (in context); in Journal Y, p. [260]; and in Journal O, p. [i]. It
is used in *English Traits*, W, V, 242, and "Poetry and Imagination," W, VIII, 19–20.
   [3] "A book, to live, must have a genius."

4

[ii] [4]

	Lecturers
B[arzillai]. Frost	J[ohn]. M[ilton]. Cheney
J[ames]. Means	E[benezer] R[ockwood] Hoar
[Addison Grant] Fay	H[enry]. D[avid]. Thoreau
	M[oses]. Prichard Jr
	S Jarvis
	Horace Mann
	Sampson Reed
Jan 17	Wendell Phillips
Nov 8	C[harles] T[homas] Jackson
	G[eorge] P[artridge] Bradford
	F[rederic]. H[enry]. Hedge
	Henry Giles
	Charles Eames
Dec 22	O[restes]. A[ugustus]. Brownson
	G[eorge]. Bancroft
	J[ames]. F[reeman]. Clarke
	Prof. [Edward?] Hitchcock
	G[eorge]. S[tillman]. Hillard
	G[eorge] B[arrell] Emerson

[1] pd for Lyceum 3 Nov letter

to Dr C[harles] T[homas] J[ackson]	12
to O[restes] A[ugustus] Brownson	6
to W[endell]. Phillips	6
to answer of C[harles] T[homas] J[ackson]	6

[Index material omitted]

[2] [blank]

[4] The entries on this and the following page are in pencil. The list of lecturers pertains to the Concord Lyceum in the winter season of 1843–1844, when Emerson was one of three curators. Frost, Means, and Fay, listed separately to the left, were president, vice-president, and secretary respectively. Of the nineteen persons mentioned as prospective lecturers, seven eventually appeared before the Lyceum. See Kenneth W. Cameron, "Early Records of the Concord Lyceum," *Transcendental Climate: New Resources for the Study of Emerson, Thoreau, and their Contemporaries*, 3 vols. (Hartford, Conn., 1963), III, 697–698. Here as elsewhere in this volume, full names of persons mentioned have been provided in the text when identification seems necessary and reasonably certain.

[3] I wish to speak with all respect of persons, but sometimes ⟨I find⟩ it needs much heedfulness to preserve the due decorum, they melt so fast into each other, that they are like grass, or trees, and it needs an effort to treat them as individuals. A metaphysician, a saint, a poet of God has nothing to do with them[;] he sees them as a rack of clouds or as a fleet of ripples which the wind drives over the surface of water: but the uninspired man in household matters finds persons a conveniency[.] [5]

[4] ↑Medal engraved at Moscow, "Dieu au ciel et Napoleon sur la terre."↓[6]

"The ⟨intention of⟩ project of universal monarchy revealed by this medal is that which shows most sense in the views of Bonaparte. But on this point as on every other he shows himself an abortion, a halfgreat man, a *Simplist* who confined himself to meditating the conquest of the world & knew not that he must provide for the conserving of conquests.

"Never man since the existence of societies has possessed like Napoleon the means of conquering & conserving the sceptre of the world. He would have succeeded, if he had not been checked by the French spirit. France has reproached him with the education she gave him: He had reason to reproach France with the education he had received from her. Would you make an abortion of one whom nature has moulded for a great man? ॥ It suffices to rear him in France, to fashion him on the taste of the arbitrary, of confusion, of imprudence & other vices which constitute the national character of the French."

Fourier
Theorie de l'Unité Universelle.
Tome IV. [*Oeuvres Complètes*, V,] p. 407

"l'extran↑e↓omanie ou l'esprit anti-national des Parisiens." Fourier

[5] "I wish . . . water:" is struck through in ink with a vertical use mark; the entire paragraph is used in "Nominalist and Realist," *W*, III, 235–236.

[6] Quoted in Charles Fourier's *Théorie de l'unité universelle*, *Oeuvres complètes de Ch. Fourier*, 2d ed., 6 vols. (Paris, 1841–1845), V, 406, cited directly below.

6

En France le cri public est *"Panem et derisores."*[7]

[5] ↑August 25.↓

The railroad whose building I inspected this P.M. brings a multitude of picturesque traits into our pastoral scenery. This bold mole carried out into a broad meadow silent & almost unvisited since the planting of the town, the presence of forty or fifty sturdy labourers, the energy with which they strained at their tasks, & the vigour of the superintendent of the gang, the character of the work itself which reminded one of miners & of negro drivers[,] the near shanties in and around which their wives & daughters & infants were seen, the villages of shanties at the water's edge & in the most sequestered nooks of the town and the number of laborers men & women whom now one encounters singly in the forest paths, the blowing of rocks, explosions all day, & now & then a painful accident, as lately ∧, and the indefinite promise of what the new channel of trade may do & undo for the town hereafter,—are all noticeable. In the process of roadbuilding, to sink the hill & fill the hollow, they make ⟨the⟩use all the way of little railroads, [6] which reminded me of Swedenborg's doctrine that the lungs are made up of lunglets, the liver of little livers, & so on.[8]

There is nothing in history to parallel the influence of Jesus Christ. The Chinese books say of Wan Wang one of their kings "From the west from the east from the south & from the north there was not one thought not brought in subjection to him."[9] This can be more truly said of Jesus than of any mortal.

[7] For this and the preceding quotation, see *JMN*, VI, 353.

[8] Work in Concord on the rail line from Boston to Fitchburg began in the spring of 1843 and continued for over a year. The line was officially opened to Concord on June 17, 1844 (*L*, III, 256). For "Swedenborg's doctrine," see *Angelic Wisdom Concerning the Divine Love and the Divine Wisdom*, sections 190–192. The concept is mentioned in "Napoleon," *W*, IV, 223. This paragraph is struck through in both pencil and ink with single vertical use marks on p. [5]; all but the last sentence is used in "The Young American," *The Dial*, IV (April 1844), 486, but omitted from the text as printed in *Nature, Addresses, and Lectures*. See *W*, I, 453.

[9] *The Chinese Classical Work Commonly Called The Four Books*, trans. Rev. David Collie ([Malacca], 1828), "Shang Mung," p. 44. The first three books are the "Memoirs of Confucius," paginated separately; the fourth book is "Memoirs

Mencius says, "A lover of fame will resign a country of one thousand chariots, while a plate of rice or a dish of soup will show his disposition."[10]

Mencius says, "A sage is the instructor of an hundred ages. When the manners of Pih E are heard of, the stupid become intelligent & the wavering determined."

[7] I think we are as often deceived by being over wise & imputing too much character to individuals of whom we have heard, as by underestimating them. This young C.[,] after he has turned the heads of so many, and been heard of so far, turns out to be the very youth he seemed when years ago I saw him.

Fourier carries a whole French revolution in his head, & much more. This is arithmetic with a vengeance. His ciphering goes where ciphering never went before, stars & atmospheres, & animals, & men, & women, & classes of every character. It is very entertaining, the most entertaining of French romances and will suggest vast ↑& numerous↓ possibilities of reform to the coldest & least sanguine.[11]

[8] To Genius everything is permitted.[12]

In the points of good breeding, ⟨I⟩what I most require & insist upon is deference. I like that every chair should be a throne & hold a king. And what I most dislike is a low sympathy of each with his neighbor's palate & belly at table, anticipating without words what he wishes to eat & drink. If you wish bread, ask me for bread, & if you wish anchovies or lobster, ask me for ⟨an⟩them, & do not hold out your plate as if I knew already. I respect cats, they seem to have so much else in their heads besides their mess. Yet every natural

---

of Mencius," divided into vol. I, "Shang Mung," and vol. II, "Hea Mung," also paginated separately. Emerson acquired this work in early 1843 (L, III, 179), and excerpted it in *The Dial* for October of that year.

[10] This quotation and the following entry, which is a paraphrase, are from *The Chinese Classical Work* . . ., 1828, "Hea Mung," pp. 177 and 130. The second is used in "Uses of Great Men," *W*, IV, 14.

[11] This paragraph is used in "Historic Notes of Life and Letters in New England," *W*, X, 348.

[12] See p. [84] below.

function can be dignified by deliberation & privacy. ⟨Let us⟩ I prefer a tendency to stateliness to an excess of fellowship. In all things I would have the island of a man inviolate. No degree of affection is to invade this religion. Lovers should guard their strangeness. As soon as they surrender that, they are no more lovers.[13]

[9] [blank]
[10] The charge which a lady in much trust made to me against her companions was that people on whom beforehand all persons would put the utmost reliance were not responsible. They saw the necessity that the work must be done, & did it not; and it of course fell to be done by herself and the few principals. I replied, that, in my experience good people were as bad as rogues, that the conscience of the conscientious ran in veins, & the most punctilious in some particulars, were latitudinarian in others. ↑And, in Mr Tuttle's opinion, "Mankind is a damned rascal."↓[14]

Society always values inoffensive people susceptible of conventional polish. The clergyman who would live in Boston must have taste. ⟨The new gospel is, By taste are ye saved.⟩[15]

H. D. T. sends me a paper with the old fault of unlimited contradiction. The trick of his rhetoric is soon learned. It consists in substituting for the obvious word & thought its diametrical antagonist. He praises wild mountains & winter forests for their domestic air; snow & ice for their [11] warmth; villagers & wood choppers for their urbanity[;] and the wilderness for resembling Rome & Paris. With the constant inclination to dispraise cities & civilization, he yet can find no way to honour woods & woodmen ⟨than⟩ except by paralleling them with towns & townsmen. W[illiam] E[llery]

[13] This paragraph, struck through in ink with a vertical use mark, is used in "Manners," W, III, 136–138.
[14] Emerson listed this entry under "Brook Farm" in his index to this journal. All but the quotation from John L. Tuttle, a farmer of Concord, is used in "Historic Notes of Life and Letters in New England," W, X, 366. The quotation is used in "Montaigne," W, IV, 154. See p. [44] below.
[15] The canceled sentence, struck through in ink with a diagonal use mark, is used in *English Traits*, W, V, 223.

C[hanning] declares the piece is excellent: but it makes me nervous & wretched to read it, with all its merits.[16]

The thinker looks for God in the direction of the consciousness,[n] the churchman out of it. If you ask the former for his definition of God, he would answer, "my possibility;" for his definition of man, "my actuality."

In Rhode Island ↑all↓ the cocks in the ⟨country⟩ ↑state↓ can hear each other crow & all the dogs can hear each other bark.

"Stand up straight[,]" said the stagecoachman, "& the rain won't wet you a mite."

[12] We like the strong objectiveness of Homer & of the primitive poems of each country, Ballads, & the (She King) ⟨&⟩ Chinese & Indian sentences, but that cannot be preserved in a large & civilized population. The scholar will inevitably be detached from the mechanic, will not dwell in the same house, nor see his handiworks ⟨as⟩so nearly, & must adopt new classification & a more metaphysical vocabulary. Hawthorne boasts that he ⟨was⟩ lived at Brook Farm during its heroic age: ⟨|| ... ||⟩then all were intimate & each knew well the other's work: priest & cook conversed at night of the day's work. Now they complain that they are separated & such intimacy can not be. — There are a hundred souls.

It seems as if we had abundance of insight & a great taste for writing in this country: only the describers wanted subjects. But that is deceptive. The great describer is known hereby, that he finds topics [⟨in the obscure & supposed insignificant.⟩]

Fame of voice or of rhetoric will carry people a few times to hear a speaker but after many times he will be deserted. A good upholder[n] [13] of what they believe or a business or fact speaker

<hr />

[16] Thoreau's paper, "A Winter Walk," was subsequently published in *The Dial*, IV (Oct. 1843), 211–226. Emerson chided Thoreau in similar language for "the trick of his rhetoric" in a letter on September 8, 1843, but noted that by "pretty free omissions, I have removed my principal objections" and "mean to send [it] to the printer tomorrow" (Franklin B. Sanborn, "The Emerson-Thoreau Correspondence," *Atlantic Monthly*, LXIX, [May 1892], 593). Portions of this paragraph are used in "Thoreau," *W*, X, 479.

of any kind they will follow, but the pause in character is very properly a loss of attraction. ↑All audiences are just.↓[17]

It was a noble thought of Fourier to distinguish in his Phalanx a class as the Sacred Band ⟨to⟩ ↑by↓ whom whatever duties were disagreeable ⟨of p⟩& likely to be omitted were assumed. G[eorge]. P. B[radford] thought it still better that this should be a voluntary than a legal class.[18]

The farmer whom I visited this P.M. works very hard & very skilfully to get a good estate, & gets it. But by his skill & diligence & that of thousands more his competitors, the wheat & milk by which I live are made so cheap that they are within reach of my scanty monies, and I am not yet forced to go to work ⟨mysel⟩& produce them for myself. Tuttle told me that he had once carried 4⟨0⟩1 cwt of hay to Boston ⟨in⟩& received 61.50 for the load.
But it is no part of T.'s design to keep down the price of hay or wheat or milk.

[14] If our friends at Fruitlands should lose their confidence in themselves, —— [19]

The more Fatima boiled & heated herself with anxiety lest things should not go well, the more mischances were sure to befall; and the redder Fatima grew, the cooler seemed the old Sultana Nevada to keep her powers of observation & criticism. Always fresh as the morning and searching as the sun was the judgment of the Sultana, never blown or agitated by any labour. The poor Fatima[,] jaded by care & mortification, it was plain, stood no even chance.[20]

[17] This paragraph, struck through in pencil with two vertical use marks on p. [12] and one on p. [13], and in ink with a vertical use mark, is used in "Eloquence," W, VII, 94. For "All audiences are just.", see JMN, VIII, 335.
[18] Bradford, who had been a fellow student of Emerson at the Harvard Divinity School, was a lifelong friend. "It was a noble . . . assumed.", struck through in ink with a vertical use mark, is used in "The Young American," W, I, 382.
[19] Fruitlands, established by Bronson Alcott and three English disciples near Harvard, Massachusetts, in June, 1843, lost much of its crop at harvest time because of poor weather and the incompetence of the principals.
[20] Emerson indexed p. [14] under House and Housekeeping. "Fatima" is probably Lidian Emerson and the "Sultana Nevada" Emerson's mother, Ruth Haskins Emerson, who lived with them until her death in 1853.

[15] How long shalt thou stay! thou devastator of thy
friend's day. Each substance & relation In nature's operation
Hath its unit & metre; [5] and the new compounds are mul-
tiples of that. [x] But the unit of the visit [9]

> Or ^{n} the meeting of friends   [x]
> Is the meeting of their eyes   [12]
> Nature poureth into nature
> Through the channels of that feature
> And the term of parle and countenance   [24]
> Is the duration of a glance   [23]
>> With the speed of river   [x]
>> Horsed upon the ray of light   [15]
>> Hearts to hearts their errands shew   [18]
>> And exchange intelligence   [20]
>> ⟨A⟩Sum their swift experience   [19]
>> In a moment all confessed   [22]
>> In a moment drained the breast   [21]
>> If another moment stay   [29]
>> Repulsions play   [30]
>> Hatred's swift repulsions play   [30]
>> Speeding Nature cannot halt   [27]
>> Linger thou shalt rue the fault
>> If Love one moment overstay
>> Hat⟨e⟩red's swift repulsions play.[21]   [30]

[21] For the published version of "The Visit," see W, IX, 12–13. The entire poem
is struck through in pencil with a vertical use mark, and in ink with a vertical and
a wavy diagonal use mark from "or the meeting of friends"; the three lines "If another moment stay . . . repulsions play" are struck through in ink with two vertical
lines, perhaps to delete them. A pencil version of this poem, later erased, occurs on
p. [14]. Differences in wording still visible are "Devastator of the day" for "thou
devastator of thy friend's day."; "Is the term of countenance" for "Is the duration
of a glance"; "In a moment years confessed" for "In a moment all confessed"; and
"Single || . . . || drained the breast" for "In a moment drained the breast". See
pp. [128]–[129] below for another erased pencil version.

Here and in certain other instances in this volume, line numbers of the poem as
printed in Poems, W, IX, are supplied in brackets, by fives, except when the manuscript lines are not in the printed order, or where the line number cannot be deduced
with certainty from other line numbers. A bracketed "x" means the line does not
appear in the poem; a bracketed question mark means uncertainty as to the line
number, or as to whether the line is used. (Note continued on next page.)

[16] The founders of Brook Farm ought to have this praise[,] that they have made what all people try to make, an agreeable place to live in. All comers & the most fastidious find it the pleasantest of residences[.] [22]

If you look at these railroad labourers & hear their stories, their fortunes appear as little controuled as those of the forest leaves. One is whirled off to ⟨Ohio⟩ ↑Albany↓[,] one to Ohio, one digs on the levee at New Orleans & one at Walden Pond; others on the wharves in Boston, or the woods in Maine, and they have too little foresight & too little money to leave them any more election of whither ↑to go↓ or what to do ↑than↓ the poor leaf which is blown into this dike or that brook to perish. "To work from dark to dark for fifty cents the day[,]" as the poor woman in the shanty told us, is ⟨|| ... ||⟩but pitiful wages for a married man.[23]

The uniform terms of admission to the advantages of civilized society, are,— You shall have all as a member, nothing as a man.[24]

[17][25] In society, high advantages are set down to an individual as disadvantages.

Emerson noted in a letter to Elizabeth Hoar on August 31, 1843, that "Caroline S[turgis]. is here since last Monday until next Monday" (L, III, 203). For further details of her visit, see pp. [20]–[21] and [28] below.

[22] This paragraph is used in "Historic Notes of Life and Letters in New England," W, X, 364.

[23] This paragraph, struck through in pencil with a diagonal use mark, is used in "The Young American," The Dial, IV (April 1844), 486–487, but omitted from the text as printed in Nature, Addresses, and Lectures. See W, I, 454.

[24] This sentence is struck through in pencil with a diagonal use mark.

[25] Partially erased pencil writing covers most of this page, much of it earlier versions of passages which also occur in ink. Recovered or conjecturally recovered words, phrases, and sentences are "pourvir"; "All as a member[?] nothing as a man" (in ink, p. [16]); "Webster has[?] the propriety of fashion"; "In this country the love of gardens should[?] be a fine art & will be; which makes landscape;" (cf. p. [27]); "The beauty of wealth is power without pretension[?] a gentle despotism under the plainest garb neither rich nor[?] poor fine furniture and[?] equipages" (also in ink, with changes); "Book of Job a poem"; "Ellery's poetry shows this art. A great Engine like Daguerre's has[?] been invented, but these first pictures are grim things" (also in ink, with changes); "vis[?] superba formae" (cf. p. [21]); "Animal spirits for the Present. Its results as incredible as a pyramid

Few people know how to spend a large fortune. A beauty of wealth is power without pretension, a despotism under the quietest speech & under the plainest garb neither rich nor poor. The pride of England is to rule the world in the little unpretending chamber called the House of Commons and the money-lord should have no fine furniture or fine equipage but should open all doors, be warm, be cool, ride, fly, execute or suspend execution at his will & see what he willed come to pass.[26]

Ellery's Poetry shows the Art, though the poems are imperfect, as the first Daguerres are grim things yet show that a great engine has been invented[.]

Animal Spirits belong to the Present. Its results incredible as a pyramid of old Karnac. Its result is a lord.[27]

   Niagara nearer than 500 miles
House better than tree
Horse the complement of his rider, & Wesson the hunter's apology for shooting partridges with his zealous dog [28]

[18][29] *Svend Vonved*.[30] Northern poets no propriety. China is the other extreme; all Etiquette.

---

of old Karnac" (also in ink); "↑High↓ advantages are set down as disadvantages" (also in ink); and "There is that which cannot be caressed" (in ink, p. [21]).

[26] "The pride of England . . . Commons", struck through in ink with three vertical use marks, is used in "Culture," *W*, VI, 153.

[27] See p. [25] below.

[28] These four lines are in pencil. Thomas Wesson operated a tavern in the Middlesex Hotel in Concord and was a devoted hunter. For the remark about Niagara, see p. [29] below.

[29] Erased pencil writing, consisting of a number of separate entries, covers most of this page. The following significant words and phrases have been recovered or conjecturally recovered: "magnificence[?]"; "Centres of Painters"; "Memory is the badge of a"; "things said for conversation ‖ . . . ‖ eggs" (also in ink); "small room; having always"; "a single"; "as history"; "People are ‖ . . . ‖ the whole thing through them" (in ink, p. [19]); "Families ‖ . . . ‖ — to bless you?" (in ink, p. [19]); "Svend Vonved Northern poets no propriety China all etiquette" (also in ink); and "architect".

[30] Emerson quotes several lines from this Danish ballad, translated by George

Superiority of "Vathek" over "Vivian Grey." [31]

Is life a thunderstorm that we can see now by a flash the whole horizon, and then cannot see our right hand?

Things said for conversation are chalk eggs.[32]

Which beat?   of the bears
Never strike a king unless you are sure you shall kill him.

[19] life should lie in masses in white marble palaces[,] not in a tub

      The power of face
      O'Connel becomes moral
      "husbands for their daughters"
      Earthquake sleeps
      Coral precipices
      deep sea fish
      which beat of the bears
Sect lines do not indicate opinions
Never strike a king ⟨till⟩ ↑unless↓ you are sure you shall kill him [33]

People are glass, I see the whole thing through them.
Families should be formed on a higher method than by the Intelligence Office.[34] A man will come to think it as absurd to send[n] thither for his nurse or farmer, as for a wife. Domestics pass in silence through the social rooms & recover their tongues at the kitchen door — to bless you?

I would live in a house ⟨whose history I⟩which I did not build, &

Borrow in *Romantic Ballads, translated from the Danish; and Miscellaneous Pieces* (London, 1826), pp. 61–81, in "Success," *W*, VII, 287.
  [31] William Beckford's *Vathek* was published in 1786, Benjamin Disraeli's *Vivian Grey* in 1826.
  [32] This sentence is used in "Social Aims," *W*, VIII, 96.
  [33] The entries on the page to this point are in pencil. "The power of face . . . daughters' " is erased; see pp. [30]–[31] below.
  [34] An intelligence office was an employment bureau for domestic servants and farmhands.

whose history I d⟨id⟩o not know; in a large house occupying small room; having always more than I show.

[20] September 3, 1843.   ↑*Representative*↓
We pursue ideas[,] not persons, the man momentarily stands for the thought, but will not bear the least examination. And a society of men will cursorily represent well enough a certain culture & state of thought, as e.g. a beauty of manners, but it is only in their congregation: detach them, & there is no gentleman, no lady in the group[.] [35]

My friend came hither and satisfied me in many ways, and, as usual, dissatisfied me with myself.[36] She increased my knowledge of life, and her sketches of manners & persons are always valuable, she sees so clearly & steadily through the veils. But best of all is the admonition that comes to me from ⟨so⟩ a demand of beauty so naturally made wheresoever her eye rests, that our ways of life, our indolences, our indulgences, our want of heroic action are shamed. Yet I cordially greet the reproof. When that which is so fair & noble passes I seem enlarged; all my thoughts are spacious[;] the chambers of the brain & the lobes of the heart are bigger. How am I [21] cheered always by traits of that "vis superba formae" [37] which inspires art & genius but not passion: there is that in beauty which cannot be caressed, but which demands the utmost wealth of nature in the beholder properly to meet it.[38]

[22] We cannot quite pull down & degrade our life ⟨or⟩& divest it of poetry. The ↑day-↓labourer is popularly reckoned as standing at the

---

[35] This paragraph, struck through in ink with a vertical use mark, is used in "Nominalist and Realist," *W*, III, 225.

[36] The friend was Caroline Sturgis (see p. 12, n. 21 above). For further details of her visit, see p. [28] below.

[37] "tyranny of beauty" (Ed.). Quoted from Johannes Secundus by Goethe in *Maximen und Reflexionen*. See Goethe's *Werke*, 55 vols. (Stuttgart and Tübingen, 1828–1833), XLIX, 83, in Emerson's library. The phrase is used in "Beauty," *W*, VI, 305. See *JMN*, VI, 201.

[38] "But best of all . . . meet it." is struck through in ink with a vertical use mark.

foot of the social scale: yet talk with him, he is saturated with the beautiful laws of the world. His measures are the hours, the morning & the night, the solstice and   the geometry, the astronomy, and all ⟨our⟩ ↑the↓ lovely accidents of nature play through his mind continual music. Property keeps the accounts of the world, and always reveals a moral cause. The property will be found where the labor, where the wisdom, where the virtue have been, in nations, in classes, and, (a life taken together & the compensations considered) in the individual also. How wise looks the world when in detail the laws & usages of nations are examined, & the completeness of all the provisions is considered. Nothing is left out. If you go into [23] the markets & the customhouses, the insurance & notary offices, offices of ⟨inspection⟩ ↑sealers↓ of weights & measures, of inspection of provisions, it will appear as if one man had made it all; wherever you go, a wit like your own has been before you & has realized his thought.[39]

Any form of government would content me in which the rulers were gentlemen, but it is in vain that I have tried to persuade myself that Mr Calhoun or Mr Clay or Mr Webster were such; they are underlings, & take the law from the dirtiest fellows. In England it usually appears as if the power were confided to persons of superior sentiment, but they have not treated Russia as they ought in the affair of Poland. It is time these fellows should hear the truth from other quarters than the antislavery papers and Whig papers & Investigators & all other committed organs." We have allowed them to take a certain place in private society as if they were at the head of their countrymen[:] ⟨m⟩they must be told that they have dishonoured themselves & ⟨no⟩ it can be allowed no longer[;] they are not now to be admitted to the society of scholars.[40]

[24] A man should carry nature in his head, should know the hour of the day & the time of the year by the ⟨a⟩sun & the stars, should know the solstice & the equinox, the quarter of the moon, & the daily

---

[39] This paragraph, struck through in ink with a vertical use mark, is used in "Nominalist and Realist," *W*, III, 231–232.

[40] This entry is in pencil.

tides. The Egyptian pyramids, I have heard[,] were square to the points of the compass, & the custom of different nations has been to lay the ⟨bo⟩dead ⟨in⟩ with the feet to the east. It testifies a higher civilization than the want of regard to it.

The relation of parents & children is usually reversed. The children become at last the parents of their parents.

I am in the habit of surrendering myself to my companion, ⟨more⟩ so that it may easily happen that my companion finds himself some what tasked to meet the occasion. But the capital defect of my nature for society, (as it is of so many others) is the want of animal spirits. They seem to me a thing incredible, as if God should raise the dead. I hear of what others perform by their aid, with fear. It is as much out of my possibility as the prowess of Coeur de Lion or an Irishman's [25] day's work on the railroad. Animal spirits seem the power of the Present, and their feats equal to the Pyramids of Karnac. Before them what a base mendicant is Memory with his leathern badge.[41]   I cannot suddenly form my relation to my friend[,] or rather can very slowly arrive at its satisfaction. I make new friendships on the old; we shall meet on higher & higher platforms until our first intercourse shall seem like an acquaintance of tops, marbles, & ball-time. I am an architect & ask a thousand years for my probation. Meantime I am very sensible to the deep flattery of omens.

[26] Has the South European more animal spirits than we, that he is so joyous a companion? I well remember my stay at the *Hotel Giaccheri*, in Palermo, where I listened with pleasure to the novelty of the ↑melo-↓dramatic conversation of a dozen citizens of the world. They mimicked in telling a story the voice & manner of the persons they described. They crowed like cocks, they ⟨barked like dogs,⟩ hissed, cackled, ⟨hollooed⟩ ↑barked↓, & screamed, and were it only by the physical strength they ⟨spent⟩ exerted in telling the story, kept the table in sympathetic life.[42]

[41] "But the capital . . . badge." is used in "Society and Solitude," *W*, VII, 12–13. For "Animal spirits . . . Karnac.", see p. [17] above.
[42] Emerson visited Palermo in March, 1833, on his first trip to Europe. See

A visit to the railroad yesterday, in Lincoln, showed ⟨the grand traits⟩ me the labourers — how grand they are; all their postures, their air, & their very dress. They are men, manlike employed, and the art of the sculptor is to take these forms & set on them a cultivated face & head. But cultivation never except in war makes such forms & ⟨m⟩ carriage as these.

[27] "Germans who love their country with understanding must know," says Borne, "that it is not so much the Leipsic Battle as the Leipsic Fair Catalogue which raises us above the French." [43]

I think it will soon become the pride of this country to make gardens & adorn country houses. That is the fine art which especially fits us. Sculpture, painting, music, architecture do not thrive with us, but they seem as good as dead, & such life as they show, is ⟨secondary,⟩ a sort of second childhood. But land we have in greater extent than ever did any people of the same power, and the new modes of travelling are making it easy to cultivate very distant tracts & yet remain in strict intercourse with the great centres of ⟨p⟩ trade & population. ⟨Ga⟩And the whole force of all the arts goes to facilitate the decoration of ⟨p⟩ lands & ⟨|| . . . ||⟩dwellings. A garden has this advantage, that it makes it indifferent where you live. If the landscape around you is pleasing, the garden shows it: if tame, it excludes it. A little grove which any farmer can find or ⟨mak⟩ cause to grow, will in a few years so fill the eye & mind of the inhabitant, as to make [28] cataracts & chains of mountains quite unnecessary, and he is so contented with his alleys, his brook, his woodland, his orchard, his baths, & his piazza, that Niagara and the Notch of the White Hills and Nantasket Beach are superfluities. The other day came C[aroline]. S[turgis]. with eyes full of Naushon & Nahant & Niagara[,] dreaming by day & night of canoes, & lightning, & deer-parks, & silver waves, & could hardly disguise her disdain for our poor cold low life in Concord, like rabbits in a warren. Yet the interiors of our woodland[,]

JMN, IV, 138–140. This paragraph, struck through in ink with a vertical use mark, is used in "Eloquence," W, VII, 69.

[43] This quotation from Ludwig Börne (1786–1837), German political writer and satirist, is used in "Humboldt," W, XI, 458. See JMN, VI, 372.

which recommend the place to us, she did not see. And the capital advantage which we possess here, that the whole town is permeable, that I can g⟨r⟩o through it like a park, distinguishes it above towns built on three or four ⟨hills⟩ New Hampshire hills, having each one side at 45 degrees & the other side perpendicular. Then as the Indians dwell where they can find good water, so my wife values her house because of the pump in the kitchen above all palaces. The great sun equalizes [29] all places, — the sun & the stars. The grand features of nature are so identical that whether in a mountain or a waterfall or whether in a flat meadow, the presence of the great agents makes the presence or absence of the inferior features insignificant. With the sun, with morning & evening, we[n] are nearer to Niagara than 500 miles: Niagara is in every glance at the heavens & earth. Mr Perkins, W E C says, built a house such as you need never go out of: bath, well, woodhouse, barn, ↑conservatory,↓ offices, it had all under cover. ⟨Well, I should add to this, grounds that should never require the tenant to take a journey[.]⟩[44]

"For Love is dead to me
And Hope has left my breast
And Memory like a bird
Wails round her ruined nest."

I dreamed, I dreamed, but sad & dark
The thoughts that o'er me came,
And welcome was the note of lark,
And ruddy eastern flame.
No faery form of hope & joy
Held vigil near my head,
Nor blindfold cherub Boy
My roaming fancy led.   *E.B.Emerson.*

[44] This paragraph is struck through in both pencil and ink with two vertical use marks to the bottom of p. [27], and on p. [28] in ink with two vertical use marks to "superfluities."; in pencil with a vertical use mark to "life in Concord,"; and in pencil with a vertical use mark to "like a park,". "I think it will . . . superfluities." is used in "The Young American," *W*, I, 367–368. The words "we are nearer . . . 500 miles:" also occur on p. [17] above. In addition to being canceled, "Well, I should . . . journey" is struck through in ink with a vertical use mark and is repeated on p. [56] below. With the remark about Concord and the towns of New Hampshire, cf. *JMN*, VIII, 384–385.

[30] The difference between men[,] if one could accept exterior tests[,] is in power of face. A man succeeds because he has more power of countenance than the other & so coaxes or commands or confounds him. These swindlers are novices at their trade. A greater power of carrying the matter loftily & with perfect assurance, would confound not only merchant & banker[,] police & judge, but men of influence & power, the poet & the president, & might head any party & unseat any sovereign, & abrogate any constitution in Europe or America. It was said that a man has already at one step attained vast power who has ⟨abdicated⟩ renounced his moral sentiment, & settled it with himself that he will no longer stick at any thing.[45]

That is true so far as it is natural, not calculated. But it is easy to see that as soon as one acts for large masses, the moral element will & must be allowed for, will & must work. Daniel O'Connell is no saint, yet at this vast meeting on the hill of Tara 18 miles from Dublin, of 500 000 persons, [31] he almost preaches; he goes for temperance, for law & order, & suggests every reconciling, gentilizing, humanizing ⟨th⟩consideration. There is little difference between him & Father Matthew, when the audience is thus enormously swelled.[46] So I notice that an Emperor in his robes is dressed almost in feminine attire, because the supreme power represents woman as well as man, the moral as ↑well as↓ the intellectual principle.[47]

Sept. 13. In town yesterday I talked with S[amuel]. G[ray]. W[ard]. on the American disease of aimlessness in the cultivated class and suggested concentration as likely to serve a partial remedy.[48] He agreed to the truth of the picture, added that the class were regarded with jealousy & with contempt at the same time, that they were of no use in the community except as furnishing husbands to the daugh-

---

[45] This paragraph, struck through in ink with a vertical use mark, is used in "Eloquence," *W*, VII, 77–78.

[46] The largest and most famous of the meetings held by O'Connell, the Irish nationalist leader, in support of home rule for Ireland took place on Tara Hill on August 15, 1843. Father Matthew was a Catholic priest who conducted a service on the hilltop before O'Connell spoke.

[47] The words "well as" were inserted in pencil, then traced in ink.

[48] Ward, a Boston businessman, literary and artistic patron, and contributor to *The Dial*, remained a close friend of Emerson for many years.

ters of rich men: being esteemed very good & safe young men; and
said that with all this dubious feeling with which these were regarded
the rich practical men were doing all they could to train up their
children in the same way.ⁿ It was a competition between ideal aims,
⟨a⟩on the one part[,] & *savings* on the other. Janissaries. Coming home
I resume with E[lizabeth]. H[oar] the question whether it is wise
⟨to⟩ or simply selfish to provide for good [32] neighborhood. Selfish,
is it? Well we do a good many selfish things every day. Among them
all, let us do one thing of enlightened selfishness. It were fit to
forbid concert & calculation in this, if that were our system, if we
were up to the mark of selfdenial & ⟨divine⟩ faith in our general
activity. But to be prudent in all ⟨our daily⟩ the particulars of life,
and in this one thing alone religiously forbearing,—prudent in
securing ourselves competitors, conventional people, degrading examples, & enemies, & only abstinent when it is proposed to provide
ourselves with guides, examples, lovers.⁴⁹

It will no doubt appear after 20 years that the circle of friends
with whom we stand connected, was a sort of masonic ⟨ass⟩fraternity
strictly bound,ⁿ only we are impatient of the slow introductions of
Destiny and a little faithless, & think it worth while to venture some-
thing.⁵⁰

Ellery says that at Brook Farm they keep Curtis & Charles
Newcomb & a few others as decoy-ducks.⁵¹

Our writing is the complement to our character, instead of being as
it should a superfluity.

[33] Life. A great lack of vital energy: excellent beginners, in-

---

⁴⁹ This paragraph is struck through in ink from the top of p. [32] with two
vertical use marks, one of which extends through the next entry; "Well we do . . .
lovers." is used in "A Letter," *W*, XII, 395–396.
⁵⁰ This paragraph, struck through in ink with two vertical use marks, is used
in "A Letter," *W*, XII, 397.
⁵¹ George William Curtis, a young disciple of Emerson, left Brook Farm at just
about this time (the autumn of 1843) because he found its doctrines too confining;
Charles King Newcomb was a sensitive, idiosyncratic mystic whom Emerson respected for his insights (see Journal W, p. [84] below).

firm executors. I should think there were factories above us which
⟨‖ ... ‖⟩stop the water; ⟨they⟩ ↑the upper people↓ must have raised
their dams an inch. Or is not a man[,] as we talked the other day[,]
a bit of Labrador spar which must be turned round until you come
to the exact angle, then only will you see the deep & beautiful
colours.[52]

God will have life to be real, we will be damned but it shall be
theatrical.

Fear haunts the building railroad but it will be ⟨power⟩ American power & beauty, when it is done. And these peaceful shovels are
better, dull as they are, than pikes in the hands of these Kernes;
and this stern day's work of 15 or 16 hours[,] though deplored by
all the humanity of the neighborhood & though all Concord cries
shame! on the contractors, is a better police than the Sheriff & his
deputies to let off the peccant humours[.] [53]

[34] The appeal to the public indicates infirm faith, like people
whose heads are not clear, & must see a house built before they can
comprehend the plan of it. It is not a great character. Fountains,
fountains, the self moved, the absorbed, the commander because he
is commanded, the assured, the primary, that is what is beautiful
& holy to us, touching all the springs of wonder in us by suggesting
the Infinite, the Wild Wisdom which here before our sight has moved
— is moving a man.[54]

Yet this must be said in defence of Alcott & Lane, that their appeal
to the public is a recognition of mankind, a proof of abiding interest
in other men, of whom they wish to be saviours[.] [55]

---

[52] This paragraph is struck through in ink with a diagonal use mark. "I should
think . . . inch." and "Or is not . . . colours." are used in "Eloquence," *W*, III,
46, 57.
[53] "And these peaceful . . . humours", struck through in ink with a vertical
use mark, is used in "The Young American," *The Dial*, IV (April 1844), 487, but
omitted from the text as printed in *Nature, Addresses, and Lectures*. See *W*, I, 455.
[54] This paragraph, struck through in ink with a vertical use mark, is used in
"Character," *W*, III, 100.
[55] Charles Lane, an English follower of Alcott, was a cofounder of the Fruitlands community. See Emerson's estimate of him on pp. [37]–[38] below.

⟨Tennyson's⟩ ↑Sterling's↓ verses to Daedalus
Sculpture [56]

A poet in his holidays, or vacations rather, should write Criticism.

[35] It is in vain to tell me that you are sufficient to yourself but have not anything to impart. I know & am assured that whoever is sufficient to himself will, if only by existing, suffice me also.

↑Autob[iography].↓

Let others grumble that they see no fairies nor muses, I rejoice that my eyes see the erect eternal world, always the same & erect, without blur or halo[.] [57]

When the
'Tis a great convenience to be educated for a time in a countingroom or attorney's business[;] then you may safely be a scholar the rest of your life & will find the use of that partial thickening of the skin every day ⟨like your⟩ as you will of your shoes or your hat. What mountains of nonsense will you have cleared ⟨away⟩ your brain of forever!

I reckon the inaction & whining of the literary class debility of course, & when I admit ⟨its⟩the existence of this grief, it is only as I hear with their ears & see with their eyes.

We want, we say, some steep antagonism to draw an articulate sound or a great act from this incapable giant whose long arms hang so listless[.]

[36] Pruning: so many of our best youth must die of consumption, so many of despair, & so many be dunces or insane before the one

---

[56] These two lines are in pencil. Four lines from John Sterling's "Daedalus" are quoted in "Uses of Great Men," *W*, IV, 21; "Sculpture" may refer to the concluding section of Sterling's *Poetical Works* (Philadelphia, 1842), which contains several poems on Florentine sculpture.

[57] This paragraph, struck through in pencil with a curving vertical use mark, is used in "The Superlative," *W*, X, 166.

shoot which they all promised to be can force its way upward to a thrifty tree[.] [58]

I fell today upon the sentence which I have often searched in Montaigne, in vain, to find. It is this.[n] "I will say a prodigious thing, but I will say it however. I find myself in many things more curbed & retained by my manners than my opinion, & my concupiscence less debauched than my reason."

Essay on Cruelty. Vol. II p 152 [59]

⟨The objection of men of the world to the socalled Transcendentalists, is not ⟨th⟩ a hostility to their truth, but that they unfit their children for business in their statestreet sense, & do not qualify them for any complete life of a better kind.⟩ [60]

I who was President of the Roanoke River Company must now be glad of a bit of cheese.

[37] Consciousness
We admire the tendency, but the men who exhibit it are grass & waves, until they are conscious of ⟨it⟩ that which they share: then it is still admirable in them, as out of them; yea, how much more dear!

There is no chance for the aesthetic village. Every one of the villagers has committed his blunders, his ⟨g⟩Genius was good, his fortunes fair, but he the marplot was too swift or too slow. And though the recuperative force is also perfect, may be relied on infinitely, yet until he has expiated this error, the after-nature does not betray its resources. Whilst he has the old sin, he will keep the old misfortune.[61]

---

[58] This sentence, struck through in ink with fourteen vertical use marks, is used in "A Letter," *W*, XII, 404.

[59] *The Essays of Michael Seigneur de Montaigne*, trans. Charles Cotton, 3 vols. (London, 1700). Emerson owned this edition of volume 2 of the Cotton translation; his copies of volumes 1 and 3 were in the edition of 1693. See *JMN*, VI, 143.

[60] This paragraph, which also occurs in Journal V, p. [31] below, is used in "Discourse at Middlebury College," July 22, 1845, and "The Scholar," *W*, X, 280.

[61] This paragraph, struck through in ink with one vertical and five diagonal use marks, is used in "A Letter," *W*, XII, 397.

Sept. 26. This morning Charles Lane left us after a two days' visit. He was dressed in linen altogether, with the exception of his shoes, which were lined with linen, & he wore no stockings. He was full of methods of an improved life: valued himself chiefly just now on getting rid of the animals; thinks there is no economy in using them on a farm. He said, that they could carry on their Family at Fruitlands in many respects better, no doubt, if they wished to play it well. He said that the clergy for the most part opposed the Temperance Reform, [38] and conspicuously this simplicity in diet, because they were alarmed, as soon as such nonconformity appeared, by the conviction that the next question people would ask, would be, "Of what use are the clergy?" In the college he found an arithmetic class, Latin, German, Hebrew classes, but no Creative Class. He had this confidence, namely, that Qui facit per alium facit per se:[62] that it was of no use to put off upon a second or third person the act of serving or of killing cattle, as in cities, for example, it would be sure to come back on the offending party in some shape, as in the brutality of the person or persons you have brutalized[.]

[39][63]   I drank at thy fountain
            Remediless thirst
            Thou intimate stranger
            Thou latest & first
            Thy dangerous glances
            Make women of men
            We long to be buried
            In Nature again [64]

            And drunken be buried

            We would slumber /unconscious/unknowing/
            In ⟨Nature⟩

The poet should walk in the fields drawn on by new scenes supplied

---

[62] "What a man does through another, he does through himself" (Ed.).
[63] The entries on this page are in pencil.
[64] "Ode to Beauty," ll. 13–20, *W*, IX, 87.

each with ⟨ner⟩ vivid pictures & thoughts until insensibly the recollection of his home was crowded out of his mind & all memory
obliterated & he was led in triumph by nature[.]

⟨The stars⟩ When he spoke of the stars, he should be innocent of
what he said; for it seemed that the stars[,] as they rolled over him,
mirrored themselves in his mind as in a deep well, & it was their
image & not his thought that you saw.

[40] It is of no importance to real wisdom how many propositions you add on the same platform, but only what new platforms.
I knew somewhat concerning the American Revolution, the action
at Bunker hill, the battle of Monmouth, of Yorktown, &c. Now
today I learn new particulars of Gen. Greene, of Gen Lee, of Ro-
chambeau. But now that I think of that event with a changed mind
and see ⟨how⟩ what a compliment to England is all this ⟨g⟩ self
glorification, and betrays a servile mind in us who think it so ⟨gr⟩
overgreat an action, makes the courage & the wit of the admirers
suspected, who ought to look at such things as things of course.

Let us shame the fathers ⟨& not⟩ by the virtue of the sons, & not
belittle us by brag.

A great deal of laughing & minute criticism but it helps not, but the
austere impracticable unavailable man who is a firebrand in society,
whom society cannot let pass in silence, but must either worship or
hate, and to whom all people feel drawn, both the leaders and the
obscure & eccentric, he puts the entire America & entire Europe into
doubt & destroys [41] the Skepticism which says, "Man is a poltroon,
let us eat & drink, 'tis the best we can do,"—by intimating the un-
tried & unknown.[65]
We ought to thank the nonconformist for every thing good he does.
Who has a right to ask him why he compounds with this or that
wrong?
Certainly the objection to Reform is the Common sense of Mankind,

[65] This paragraph, struck through in ink with a vertical use mark, is used in
"Character," W, III, 100.

which seems to have settled several things; as traffic, and the use of the animals for labor & food. But it will not do to offer this by way of argument, as *that* is precisely the ground of dispute.

Read Montaigne's Journey into Italy[,] which is an important part of his biography.[66] I like him so well that I value even his register of his disease — Is it that the valetudinarian gives the assurance that he is not ashamed of himself?[n] Then what a treasure, to enlarge my knowledge of his friend by his narrative of the last days & the death of Etienne de la Boetie. In Boston when I heard lately Chandler Robbins preach so well the funeral sermon of Henry Ware, I thought of Montaigne[,] who would also have felt how much this surface called Unitarianism admits of being opened & [42] deepened, and that this was as good & defensible a post of life to occupy as any other.[67] It was a true cathedral music & brought chancels & choirs, surplices, ephods, & arks & hierarchies into presence. Certainly Montaigne is the antagonist of the fanatic reformer. Under the oldest mouldiest conventions he would prosper just as well as in the newest world. His is the common sense which though no science is fairly worth the seven.[68] In his "Journey," I am much struck with the picture of manners. His arrival in each place is an event of some importance[,] the arrival of a gentleman of France. Wherever he goes, he calls upon whatever Prince or gentleman of note, as a duty to himself & to civilization. When he leaves any house in which he has lodged a few weeks, he ⟨p⟩causes his arms to be painted & hung up as a perpetual sign to the house, as was the custom of gentlemen.[69] He looks as he enters each town to see whether the lilies of France appear

---

[66] The "Journey into Italy" first appeared in English in *The Complete Works of Michael de Montaigne; comprising; the Essays, translated by Cotton; the Letters; the Journey into Germany and Italy, now first translated; a life by the editor; notes . . .*, ed. William Hazlitt (London, 1842).

[67] Henry Ware, Jr., Emerson's predecessor as pastor of the Second Church in Boston, died September 22, 1843. The discourse by Chandler Robbins, pastor of the church at the time, was not delivered at the funeral but at a commemorative service on October 1 (*L*, III, 209n).

[68] Pope, *Moral Essays*, IV, 43–44, slightly misquoted. See *JMN*, VI, 30.

[69] "Certainly Montaigne . . . gentlemen." is struck through in ink with a vertical use mark; "In his 'Journey,' . . . gentlemen." is used in "Manners," *W*, III, 136.

⟨in⟩on the houses & public squares. The wines he drunk appear in every page. His house, Ellery says, looks like a powder mill.

[43] A newspaper lately called Daniel Webster "a steam engine in breeches" and the people are apt to speak of him as "Daniel," and it is a sort of proverb in New England of a vast knowledge — "if I knew as much as D. W." Os oculosque Jovi par.[70]

Henry Ware with his benevolence & frigid manners reminded men how often of a volcano covered with snow. But there was no deep enthusiasm. I think his best eulogy was Dr Beecher's remark on his "Formation of Xn [Christian] Character,"[n] that "it was the best counterfeit he had met with."[71] All his talent was available & he was a good example of the proverb no doubt a hundred times applied to him of "a free steed driven to death." He ought to have been dead ten years ago, but hard work had kept him alive. In the post mortem examination his lungs were found healed over & sound & his disorder was in the brain. A very slight & puny frame he had, & the impression of size was derived from his head. Then he was dressed with heroical plainness. I think him well entitled to the dangerous style of Professor of Pulpit eloqu[enc]e[,] [44] none but W E Channing so well & he had ten times the business valour of Channing. This was a soldier that flung himself into all risks at all hours, not a solemn martyr kept to be burned once & make the flames proud.
In calm hours & friendly company, his face expanded into broad simple sunshine; and I thought le bon Henri a pumpkin-sweeting.[72]

Plato paints & quibbles & by & by a sentence that moves the sea & land.[73]

---

[70] "A mouth and eyes equal to Jove" (Ed.).

[71] Ware's *On the Formation of the Christian Character*, 1831, went through some fifteen editions and was republished abroad. "Dr Beecher" is probably Lyman Beecher, former minister of the Hanover Street Church in Boston and at this time president of Lane Theological Seminary in Cincinnati. See *JMN*, VIII, 355.

[72] A Pumpkin Sweeting is a variety of apple. See *JMN*, VIII, 548.

[73] This sentence, struck through in ink with a diagonal use mark, is used in "Plato; or, the Philosopher," *W*, IV, 60.

⟨Ah! if our Genius was a little more of a genius!⟩[74]

G[eorge]. B[arrell]. E[merson]. ⟨|| ... ||⟩read me a criticism on Spenser[,] who makes twenty trees of different kinds grow in one grove, wherein the critic says it was an imaginary grove. G. B. E., however, doubts not it was after nature, for he knows a piece of natural woodland near Boston, wherein twentyfour different trees grow together in a small grove.[75]

Mr John L. Tuttle of Concord, said that ⟨Mankind was a damned rascal.⟩[76]

[45] New England cannot be painted without a portrait of Millerism with the New Advent Hymns[.][77]

> "You will see the Lord a coming
> To the old church yards
>   With a band of music &c
>
> "He'll awake all the nations
> In the old church yards
>
> "We will march into the city
> From the old church yards"

Misses A & E C Fellows   Corner of Tremont & Common ↑(?)↓ St. Boston. Direction for orphan girls & boys.

F. of Groton says that he ⟨is⟩means to be as honest as the times admit of.

The Age
  Millerism
  Homoeopathy

[74] This entry is used in "Experience," *W*, III, 46.

[75] Emerson's second cousin, a noted teacher, was an amateur botanist.

[76] This sentence is struck through in ink with two diagonal use marks. See p. [10] above.

[77] The followers of William Miller (1782–1849), known as Millerites or Adventists, believed that the Second Coming of Christ would occur in 1843 or 1844.

Association,   Joint stock companies
Cheap Press,   Newspapers
Roads & locomotives
America preternatural irritability
Cheapness of fire (in friction matches) & of alcohol

[46] Hard clouds, & hard expressions, & hard manners, I love.

↑*Aristocracy*↓

In Salem, the aristocracy is of the merchants, even the lawyers are a second class. In Boston is aristocracy of families which have inherited their wealth & position, and of lawyers & of merchants. In Charleston, the Merchants are an inferior class, the Planters are the aristocracy. In England the aristocracy[,] incorporated by law & education[,] degrades life for the unprivileged classes. Long ago they wrote on placards in the streets "Of what use are the lords?" And now that the misery of Ireland & of the English manufacturing counties famishes & growls around the park fences of Lord Shannon, Lord Cork, & Sir Robert Peel, a park and a castle will be a less pleasant abode. The only compensation to the embittered feeling of ⟨the⟩ ↑a↓ proud commoner, is in the reflection that the ⟨lord⟩ worthless lord who by the magic of a title paralyzes his arm & plucks from him half the graces & rights of a man, is himself also an aspirant excluded with the same ruthlessness[n] [47] from higher circles, for there is no end to the wheels within wheels of this spiral heaven. Philip II of Spain rated his Ambassador for neglecting business of great importance in Italy, whilst he debated some *pundonore* with the French Ambassador, "How have you left a business of importance for a ceremony!" The Ambassador replied, "How? for a ceremony? Your majesty's self is but a ceremony." In the East[,] where the religious sentiment comes in to the support of the aristocracy, & in the Romish Church also, there is a grain of sweetness in the tyranny, but in England the fact seems to me intolerable that no man of letters is received into the best society except as a lion.[78] I must nevertheless

---

[78] "The only compensation . . . lion.", struck through in ink with a vertical use mark, is used in "The Young American," *W*, I, 393–394, as is "In England . . . unprivileged classes.", earlier in the paragraph.

respect this *Order* as "a part of the order of Providence," as my good
Aunt used to say of the rich, when I see, as I do everywhere, a class
born with these attributes of rule.[79] The class of officers I recognize
everywhere in town or country. They come ~~These gallants come~~
into the world to ruffle it & by rough or smooth to find their way to
the top. When I spoke to N[athaniel]. H[awthorne]. of the class who
hold the keys of State street & are yet excluded from the best Boston
circles, he said "Perhaps he has a heavy wife."

[48]   The Reformer. (after the Chinese)
There is a class whom I call the thieves of virtue. They are those
who mock the simple & sincere endeavourers after a better way
of life, & say, these are pompous talkers; but when they come to act,
they are weak, nor do they regard what they have said. These
mockers are continually appealing to the ancients. And they say,
Why make ourselves singular? Let those who are born in this age,
act as men of this age. — Thus they secretly obtain the flattery of the
age.
    The inhabitants of the village & of the city ↑all↓ praise them.
Wherever they go they are attentive & generous. If you would blame
them, there is nothing to lay hold of. They accord with prevailing
customs & unite with a polluted age. They appear faithful & sincere,
& act as if sober & pure. The multitude all delight in them but they
confuse virtue.

[49] Chin Seang praised Heu Tsze to Mencius as a prince who taught
& exemplified a righteous life. "A truly virtuous prince, he added,
will plough along with his people & while he rules will cook his own
food.
Mencius. Does Heu Tsze sow the grain which he eats?
⟨Y⟩*Seang* Yes[.]
M.   Does Heu Tsze weave cloth & then wear it[?]
S.   No: Heu Tsze wears coarse hair-cloth.
M.   Does Heu Tsze wear a cap?
S.   Yes.

[79] The "good Aunt" is Mary Moody Emerson (M.M.E.).

M   What sort of cap?
S   A coarse cap.
M   Does he make it himself?
S   No: he gives grain in exchange for it.
M   Why doesn't he make it himself?
S   It would be injurious to his farming.
M   Does he use earthen ware in cooking his victuals or iron utensils
     in tilling his farm?
S   Yes.
     Does he make them himself?
S   No, he gives grain in barter for them.
M   Why does not Heu Tsze act the potter, & take everything from
     his own shop he wants to use. Why should he be in the confused
     bustle exchanging articles with the mechanics? He is not afraid
     of labor surely?
S.   The work of the mechanic & that of the husbandman ought not
     to be united.
M.   O then the government of the Empire & the labor of the hus-
     bandman are the only [50] employments that ought to be
     united. Were every man to do all kinds of work, it would be
     necessary that he should first make his implements, & then use
     them: thus all men would constantly crowd the roads. Some
     men labor with their minds, & some with bodily strength. Those
     who labor with their strength, are ruled by men. Those who
     are governed by others, feed others. This is a general rule
     under the whole heavens."
     [*The Chinese Classical Work* . . ., 1828, "Shang Mung,"
                                                    pp. 78–79]

Mencius proceeds to instance Yu, who, after the deluge, was eight
years abroad directing the opening of channels to let off the inundation
into the sea, & the burning of forests & marshes to clear the land of
beasts of prey, so that he had no time to go home even, but passed
his own door repeatedly without entering; and asks if he had leisure
for husbandry, if he had been inclined? Yu & Shun employed their
whole ⟨time⟩minds in governing the empire, yet they did not plough
the fields. [*Ibid.*, pp. 80–81]

33

The antagonist urges again the levelling principles of Tsze, — saying that if these were followed, there would not be two market prices, nor any deceit in the country. Cloth of the same length would be of the same price. &c &c. [51] Mencius replies; Things are naturally unequal in value. [*Ibid.*, pp. 82–83]

Afterwards the defender of Tsze adduces for praise the ⟨ex⟩ behaviour of Chung as an example of moderation (the highest virtue)[.]

Was not, he says[,] Chin Chung Tsze a moderate scholar? When in Ling, he was three days without food, till his ear heard not, nor did his eye see. On the side of the well was a Le (a sort of plum), which the Tsaou had more than half eaten: he crawled to it, attempted to eat it, &, after three efforts, managed to swallow it, after which his ear heard & his eye saw.

Mencius replied; I must consider Chung as chief among the scholars of Tsze, but I cannot deem him moderate. Were he to act up to his own principles, he ought to become an earthworm. Then he might be considered moderate. The worm above eats dry earth, & below, drinks muddy water. Was the house which Chung lived in built by Pih E (a sage) or by Taou Chih, (a robber some say)? Was the grain he eat sown by Pih E, or by Taou Chih? This he could not know.

What ⟨injury⟩harm can be in that⟨;⟩? said the other.[n] He made shoes, & his wife prepared hemp, & gave these in exchange for food.

[52] Chung's brother had ten thousand chung of salary. He deemed it unjust, & would not eat of it. He considered his brother's house unjust, & would not live in it. He avoided his ⟨mother⟩ brother, left his mother, & dwelt in Woo Ling. Having afterwards returned, some one presented a live goose to his brother, on seeing which he gathered up his brows, & said, Why use that cackling thing? Another day his mother killed this same goose, & gave it him to eat. His brother happening to come in, said, "You are eating the flesh of that cackling thing." On which he went out, & spewed out what he had eaten. Had he become an earthworm, then would he have acted up to his own tenets?

[*Ibid.*, pp. 95–96]

Yang taught that we should love ourselves only,

34

Mih taught that we should love all men alike.
Confucius taught the law of the Golden Mean,
Tsze taught not to be dependent on any other.

See also the quotation
in *R.* p 123,[80]

[53] Gonzalo in the "Tempest" anticipates our Reformers.

Gonzalo. "Had I plantation of this isle, my lord,
         And were the king of it, what would I do?
         In the commonwealth I would by contraries
         Execute all things; for no kind of traffic
         Would I admit; no name of magistrate;
         Letters should not be known; no use of service,
         Of riches, or of poverty; no contracts,
         Successions; bound of land, tilth, vineyard, none:
         No use of metal, corn, or wine, or oil;[n]
         No occupation; all men idle, all;
         And women too; but innocent & pure,
         No sovereignty;
Sebastian   And yet he would be king on't.
Gon   All things in common, nature should produce
         Without sweat or endeavour; treason, felony,
         Sword, pike, knife, gun, or need of any engine,
         Would I not have; but nature should bring forth
         Of its own kind all foizon, all abundance,
         To feed my innocent people.
         I would with such perfection govern
         To excel the golden age."
                              Act II Scene 1 [ll. 143–168,
                                   with some omissions]

Queenie thinks the Fruitlands people far too gross in their way of
living. She prefers to live on snow.[81]

[54] ↑*Aristocracy*↓

Let me live in America, & until I am very good or very able
not creep into England to cast another foolsweight to the side of

[80] See *JMN*, VIII, 410.
[81] "Queenie" is Lidian Emerson, also referred to as "the Queen" and "the Queen
of Sheba."

flattery & servility. Yet am I sure that worth & personal power must sit crowned in all companies[,] nor will Lord Herbert of Cherbury, or Daniel Webster or Edward Taylor or Bronson Alcott, so long as they are themselves, be slighted or affronted in any company of civilized men.[82] Our people creep abroad that they may ruffle it at home. But one part of their apprenticeship, their compliances to the foreign great, they quite omit to report in their book of travels. In solitude, — in the woods, for example, every man is a noble, and we cannot prize too highly the staid & erect & plain manners of our farmers.

[55] Nature seems ⟨to delight⟩ a little wicked & to delight in mystifying us. Every thing changes in ourselves & our relations, and for twenty or thirty years I shall find some old cider barrel or well known rusty nail or hook or rag of dish clout unchanged[.]

The only straight line in nature that I remember is the spider swinging down from a twig.
The rainbow & the horizon seen at sea are good curves.
    The hair on a cat's back is a straight line[.]
The last luxury Fin Chin gave up in his economizing was ⟨the⟩ his giving.[83]

    "For Laughter never looked upon his brow"
            Giles Fletcher ["Christ's Victory and Triumph
                        on Earth," stanza 12]

[56] In this country where land is so cheap & the disposition of the people so pacific every thing invites to the ⟨making⟩arts of domestic architecture & gardening. In this country we have no garden such as the Boboli Garden in Florence or the Villa Borghese in Rome. Such works make the land dear to the citizen & ⟨e⟩inflame patriotism. A noble garden makes the face of the country where you live, of no account; low or high, noble or mean, you have made a beautiful abode worthy of man. It is the fine art which is left for us now that

[82] "Let me live . . . men." is struck through in ink with a vertical use mark.
[83] These four sentences, and the quotation from Giles Fletcher directly below, are in pencil.

sculpture & painting & religious & civil architecture have become
effete & have a second childhood.

In this climate what ↑a↓ joy to build! The south side of the house
should be almost all window for the advantage of the winter sun.
The house should be built so as that one should never need to go out
⟨& th⟩of doors, & the grounds should be so richly laid out that one
should never need to take a journey to see better orchards, mills,
woods, [57] & waters. Marble baths, a turret for a library like Montaigne, or a cave for a summer study, like   (See Aubrey)[84]

And yet the selection of a fit houselot is the same thing as the
selection of a man of genius for a particular work. All the culture of
means & years will never make the most willing scholar his equal; no
more will gardening give grandeur to a house in a fen.[85]

Our hero decided to go [to] N.Y. & edit the Dayspring[,] a
semimonthly Journal. Accordingly he wrote to H. that all was now
clear to him which had been cloudy, that he esteemed it a privilege
to exist in the world at the same time with H. and intended after six
months to go to the borders of Seneca ⟨t⟩Lake to live. If editing "The
Dayspring" had taught him to live on a pound & a half of food per
day instead of two pounds [86]

[58] In Saadi's Gulistan, I find many traits which comport
with the portrait I drew.[87] He replied to Nizari; — "It was rumoured

---

[84] These two paragraphs are struck through in ink with a vertical use mark;
the first is used in "The Young American," W, I, 367–368. In the lecture as
originally printed in The Dial, Emerson fleshed out the reference to Aubrey: "[He]
has given us an engaging account of the manner in which Bacon finished his own
manor at Gorhambury." See Letters Written by Eminent Persons in the Seventeenth
and Eighteenth Centuries: to which are added, Hearne's Journeys to Reading, and to
Whaddon Hall, . . . and Lives of Eminent Men, by John Aubrey, Esq. . . . , ed.
John Walker, 2 vols. in 3 (London, 1813), II, 228–235, in Emerson's library.

[85] This paragraph, struck through in ink with three vertical use marks, is used
in "The Young American," W, I, 368.

[86] This entry is in pencil.

[87] The Gulistan, or Flower-Garden, of Shaikh Sadī of Shīraz . . . , trans.
James Ross (London, 1823). Emerson's "portrait" is his poem entitled "Saadi," W,
IX, 129–135.

abroad that I was penitent & had forsaken wine but this was a gross calumny for what have I to do with repentance?" [p. 36][88] Like Montaigne, he learns manners from the unmannerly and he says "there is a tradition of the prophet that poverty has a gloomy aspect in this world & in the next!" [p. 402] There is a spice of Gibbon in him when he describes a schoolmaster so ugly & crabbed that the sight of him would derange the ecstasies of the orthodox[.] [pp. 377–378][89]

⟨It is to⟩Like Homer and Dante & Chaucer, Saadi possessed a great advantage over poets of cultivated times in being the representative of learning & thought to his countrymen. These old poets felt that all wit was their wit, they used their memory as readily as their invention, & were at once the librarian as well as the poet, historiographer as well as priest of the muses.[90]

[59] Saadi[91]   "If conserve of roses be frequently eaten it will cause a surfeit whereas a crust of bread eaten after a long interval will relish like conserve of roses." [p. 260]

"Ardishir Babagan asked an Arabian physician what quantity of food ought to be eaten daily. He replied Thirteen ounces. The king said What strength can a man derive from so small a quantity. The physician replied So much can support you but in whatever you exceed that, you must support it." [p. 257]

"I heard of a dervish who was consuming in the flame of want, tacking patch after patch upon his ragged garment & solacing his mind with verses of poetry. Somebody observed to him Why do you sit quiet while a certain gentleman of this city ⟨is so⟩ has girt up his loins in the service of the reli-

---

[88] This quotation is used in "Shakspeare," *W*, IV, 216.

[89] "There is a spice . . . orthodox", struck through in ink with a vertical use mark, is used in "Beauty," *W*, VI, 298–299.

[90] This paragraph, struck through in pencil with a vertical use mark, is used in "Shakspeare," *W*, IV, 196–197.

[91] Of the following seventeen excerpts from *The Gulistan . . . of Shaikh Sadī* . . . , 1823, the first three are struck through in both pencil and ink with vertical use marks, and the fifth through the tenth in ink with a vertical use mark; all of those struck through, with the exception of the sixth, appear in "Ethnical Scriptures," *The Dial*, IV (Jan. 1844), 404. The fourth is used in "Discourse at Nantucket," May 8, 1847, the eighth is used in "Old Age," *W*, VII, 317–318, and the tenth is used in "The Fugitive Slave Law (New York)," *W*, XI, 236.

gious independents & seated himself by the door of their hearts? he would esteem himself obliged by an opportunity of relieving your distress. He said, be silent, for I swear by Allah it were equal to the torments of hell to enter into paradise through the interest of a neighbour." [pp. 254–255]

"The blow of our beloved has the relish of raisins" [p. 350]

[60] "Any foe whom you treat courteously will become a friend, excepting lust; which the more civilly you use it, will get the more perverse." [p. 398]

"It is not every man that is apt at argument that is expert in business: — many is the gracious form that is covered with a veil; but on withdrawing this, thou discoverest a grandmother." [pp. 438–439]

"The dervish in his prayer is saying, O God! have compassion on the wicked for thou hast given all things to the good in making them good." [p. 470]

Saadi found in a mosque at Damascus an old Persian of an hundred & fifty years, who was dying, & was saying to himself "I said I will enjoy myself for a few moments, alas! that my soul took the path of departure: alas! at the variegated table of life, I partook a few mouthfuls, & the fates said, Enough!" [pp. 360–361]

Saadi was troubled when his feet were bare & he had not wherewithal to buy shoes; "but soon after meeting a man without feet, I was thankful for the bounty of Providence to me & submitted cheerfully to the want of shoes." [p. 272]

[61] "Take heed that the orphan weep not; for the throne of the Almighty is shaken to & fro when the orphan sets a-crying." [p. 6]

Saadi was long a Sacayi or Water-drawer in the Holy Land, "till found worthy of an introduction to the prophet Khizr, Elias or the Syrian & Greek Hermes, who moistened his mouth with the water of immortality." Somebody doubted this, & saw in a dream a host of angels descending with salvers of glory in their hands. On asking †one of↓ them for whom those were intended, he answered, "for Shaikh Saadi of Shiraz, who has written a stanza of poetry that has met the approbation of God Almighty." [pp. 17–18]

— "Khosraw of Delhi asked Khizr for a mouthful of this inspiring beverage; but he told him, that Saadi had got the last of it." [p. 19]

"It was on the evening of Friday in the month *Showal*, of the Arabian year 690, that the eagle of the immaterial soul of Shaikh Saadi shook from his plumage the dust of his body." [p. 50]

[62] ↑altered↓
He who hung two arms from thy shoulders & ten fingers from thy arms will not forget to add a piece of bread in thy hand[.] [p. 384, paraphrased]

fireworks from a house of straw. [Cf. pp. 390–391]

"The angel who presides over the storehouse of the winds, feels no compunction though he extinguish the old woman's lamp." [p. 452]

"Nothing is so good for an ignorant man as silence and if he knew this, he would no longer be ignorant." [p. 436]

[63] Yankee
John Richardson got a living by buying odd bits of land near good dwelling houses & removing on to them some old crazy barn or wretched shop & ⟨then⟩ keeping it there until the proprietor of the house paid him a round sum for the land.[92]

↑Representative↓
Every man can do a feat or two, but has no universality, and his mastery consists in keeping where & when that turn shall be oftenest done. But life is not worth the having to do tricks in. Eli Robbins liked to have lectures, churches, & other "amusements" kept up.[93] I cannot find a man who is not a dummy in his turn. ↑[Bottom cannot play all the parts; work it how we will.ⁿ]↓ There will be somebody else, and the world will be round.[94]

[92] Richardson was the owner of a woodlot which bordered Emerson's property at Walden Pond.
[93] Robbins was a Lexington furrier, tavern keeper, and local wit. See *JMN*, VIII, 91.
[94] This paragraph is struck through in pencil with a vertical use mark. "Every man . . . tricks in." and "I cannot find . . . turn." are used in "Experience," *W*, III, 57; "Eli Robbins . . . kept up." is used in "New England Reformers," *W*, III, 268; "[Bottom cannot . . . round." is used in "Nominalist and Realist," *W*, III, 236. The heading and "[Bottom cannot . . . we will,]" are in pencil.

No wonder the farmer is so stingy of his dollar. A dollar is no waif to him. He knows how many strokes of labor it represents; how much land, how much rain, how much frost, & sunshine. He knows that in the dollar he gives you so much patience, so much hoeing, & threshing. Try to lift his dollar[:] you must lift all that heavy weight [64] which holds it down to him. In the city the farmer is cheated by the sleight of the gamesters with whom he plays, & there money comes to be looked upon as light, because it came lightly. I wish the farmer held it dearer than he does, & would spend it only for real bread, — force for force.[95]

Yankee   is like a goose in a deluge.

In Montaigne, man & thinker are inseparable: you cannot insert the blade of a pen knife betwixt the man & his book.[96]

Young people ⟨value⟩ ↑admire↓ talents or particular excellences. But as we grow older, we only value total powers & effects, as, the impression, the spirit, the quality or genius of the man.[97]

Ellery says, Wordsworth writes like a man who takes snuff.

"Was this a coloured person you speak of?" said M.M.E. to my story of the mystic.

[65] Criticism may go to great fineness. Tennyson is a master of metre but it is as an artist who has learned admirable mechanical secrets. He has no woodnotes. Great are the dangers of education — skepticism. Tennyson a cosmetic poet. No man but is so much a skeptic as ↑not↓ to f⟨ind⟩eel a grateful surprise now & then at finding himself safe & sound & things as he thought them[.]

---

[95] This paragraph, struck through in ink with a vertical use mark which extends through the next entry, is used in "Wealth," *W*, VI, 101–102.

[96] This entry is struck through in ink with a vertical use mark.

[97] This paragraph, struck through in ink with two vertical use marks, is used in "Nominalist and Realist," *W*, III, 228.

Would you have property, stick where you are: then shingle: put dollars to dollars, & let them beget sons & daughters[.] R. 12 [98]

I will say it again today, — I am very much struck in literature by the appearance that one person wrote all the books. As if the Editor of the Journal planted his body of reporters in different parts of the field of action & ⟨at different⟩ relieved some by others ⟨at⟩ from time to time[,] but there is such equality & identity in the story that it is plainly the production of one all[-]seeing[,] all[-]hearing person. ↑See R 14↓[99]

A man on whom words made no impression [100]

The noble river Jumna
    "Her bed is India; — there she lies — a pearl." [101]

[66] Immense benefit of Party I feel today in seeing how it reveals faults of character in such an idol as Webster which the intellectual force in the persons, if in equilibrium, & not hurled to its aphelion by hatred, could not have seen. What benefit, since the world is so stupid, that there should be *two stupidities!* It is the same brute advantage, so essential to astronomy[,] in having the diameter of the earth's orbit for a base of its triangle.[102] The great men dull their palm by entertainment of those they dare not refuse. And lose the tact of greeting the wise with sincerity, but give that odious brassiness to those who would forgive coldness, silence, dislike, — everything but simulation & duping.

Society a machine   P. office. Roads

---

[98] This entry was written first in pencil, with "Property:" for "Would you have property,". See *JMN*, VIII, 354.
[99] This paragraph, struck through in ink with a vertical use mark, is used in "Nominalist and Realist," *W*, III, 232. See *JMN*, VIII, 355. With "I am very . . . books.", cf. p. [97] below.
[100] This entry was first written in pencil, beginning "P. was a man . . ."
[101] *The Gulistan . . . of Shaikh Sadī . . .* , 1823, p. 72.
[102] "Immense benefit . . . triangle.", struck through in ink with a vertical use mark, is used in "Nominalist and Realist," *W*, III, 239–240.

In Helena
    Ants & pigmies
    drama a good way to say contradictions & leave them so
    It was a bright thought to take the same liberty with time as
    Enchantment had done with space —
        The only question for time to decide is whether
        this play is cold.[103]

[67] In Goethe, is that sincerity which makes the value of
literature and is that one voice or one writer who wrote all the good
books (see above p. 65). In Helena, ⟨the⟩Faust is sincere & represents
actual cultivated strong natured Man;[n] the book would be farrago
without the sincerity of Faust. I think ⟨Helena⟩ the second Part of
Faust the grandest enterprise of literature that has been attempted
since the Paradise Lost. It is a philosophy of history set in poetry.
It is the work of a man who found himself the master of histories,
mythologies, philosophies, sciences, & national literatures[,] in the encyclopaediacal manner in which modern erudition[,] aided by the
wonderful mechanical aids of modern time such as international intercourse of the whole earth's population,[n] researches into Indian &
Etruscan & all Cyclopaean arts; geology; astronomy; &c   and
every one of these deep kingdoms assuming a certain aerial & poetic
character from the circumstance of the multitude. One looks at a
king with devotion, but if one should chance to be at a congress of kings
the eye would take liberties with the [68] peculiarities of each.
It labours with the *fault*, if you please, at all events, with the fact,
that these are not wild miraculous songs but profoundly thought and
elaborated designs ⟨in⟩to which the poet has confided the results of
his life & eighty years of observation. ⟨But still he is a poet &⟩ But
this reflective & critical wisdom only makes the poem more truly
the result & flower of this time. It dates itself. Still he is a poet,
possesses the highest poetic talent of all his contemporaries, & *under*
this genius of microscopes (his eyes are microscopes) strikes the harp
with a man's strength, variety, & grace,
But the wonder of the book is its superior intelligence. It enlarges

[103] "Society a machine . . . is cold." is in pencil.

the known powers of the human mind, as was said of Michael's
Sistine Chapel. What a strong menstruum was this man's wit! how
the ages past & the present century & their religions & politics & modes
of thinking lie there dissolved into archetypes & Ideas. What new
mythologies sail through [69] his head[!] They said that Alexander
got as far as Chaos. Goethe got, only the other day as far, & one step
farther he hazarded, & brought himself back[.][104]

Ben Jonson ——————— See below, p. 94

Fame
"Her house is all of echo made
Where never dies the sound
And as her brows the clouds invade
Her feet do strike the ground"

Ben Jonson
Masque of Queens
Vol III, p 393

See as specimens of his admirable songs
Ben Jonson's Works   Vol I p 286, 381,
                      III p 302, 443, 394, 187,
                      IV. p. 292
                      V. p 150   344–5–6,
                      VI. 393, 45 69, 72, 73

Gipsy Songs

Vol 5, 382, 383,

Equal skill is shown in his Epitaph on S[alomon] P[avy] Vol 3, p. 164:
& p 166 [105]

---

[104] "It is a philosophy . . . himself back", struck through in ink with a vertical
use mark, is used in "Goethe," *W*, IV, 271–273.
[105] All of Emerson's page references are to *The Works of Ben Jonson*, 6 vols.
(London, 1716). This edition, except for vol. 2, is in Emerson's library. The title
actually reads "*The Works of Ben. Johnson.*" Page numbers 443, 394, and 292 were
first written in pencil, then traced in ink; "IV. p." and "V. p 150 . . . Vol 5, 382,
383," are in pencil only.

[70] The skeptic says,[n] how can any man love any woman except by delusion & ignorance? Brothers do not wish to marry sisters because they see them too nearly[,] and all attractiveness[,] like fame[,] requires some distance. But the lover of nature loves nature in his mistress or his friend; he sees the faults and absurdities of the individual as well as you↑.↓ ⟨but⟩ No familiarity can exhaust the charm. It is not personalities but universalities that draw him.
The like is true of life. It seems to me that he has learned its lesson who has come to feel ↑so↓ assured of his well being ⟨of⟩as to hold lightly all particulars of today & tomorrow, & to count death amongst the particulars. He must have such a grasp of the whole as to be willing to be ridiculous and unfortunate[.]

See V, p. 82

[71][106] Men have a puzzled look as if they did these things from not knowing what is better[.]

Literature is the only art that is ashamed of itself. The poet should be delivered as much as may be from routine, to increase his chances. It is a game of luck that he plays, & he must be liberated & ready to use the opportunities. Every one of them has been a high gambler[.]

Interesting people are selfish. S is good by merit and serves: the old primary sort; less interesting than the class of Appearers; they serve nobody but charm all.

Ellery says, that Writers never do any thing: they are passive observers. Some of them seem to do, but they do not; H ⟨|| ... ||⟩will never be a writer[;] he is as active as a shoemaker.[107]

[72] The noble ↑G[iles].↓ W[aldo].'s zeal for his friend reminds me of the brave man that stood in the street opposite ⟨Somerset⟩Northumberland House & gazing at the figure of ⟨St George⟩ ↑the Lion↓ on the roof, ⟨of the house,⟩ cried, "By heaven! he wags his head!"[n] The

---

[106] The entries on this page are in pencil.
[107] Emerson indexed p. [71] under H. D. T[horeau].

crowd gathered & gazed ⟨‖ ... ‖⟩until each man could take his Bible oath that he saw it ↑wag↓ also.[108]

It is in vain to attempt to get rid of the children by not minding them, ye parents dear! for the children measure their own life by the reaction, and if purring & humming is not noticed, then they begin to squeal; if that is neglected, to ⟨hoot & howl⟩ ↑screech↓; then, if you chide & console them, they find the experiment succeeds, & they begin again. The child will sit in your arms if you do nothing, contented; but if you read, it misses the reaction, & commences hostile operations: "pourvu seulement qu'on s'occupe d'eux," is the law.[109]

↑Inspiration↓

Contagion, yeast, "*emptins*," anything to convey fermentation, import fermentation, induce fermentation into a quiescent mass, inspiration, by virtue or by vice, by friend or fiend, angels or "gin." [110]

↑See next page↓

[73] I thought yesterday as I read letters of M M E that I would attempt the arrangement of them.[111] With a little selection & compiling and a little narrative thinly veiled of the youth of E↑llen↓ & C↑harles↓ ⟨it⟩&ⁿ if brought far enough with letters from C. and later letters from my sweet saint, there should be a picture of a New England youth & education so con⟨c⟩nected with the story of religious opinion in N. England, as to be a warm & bright life picture.

↑*Autobiography*.↓

My great grandfather was ↑Rev.↓ Joseph Emerson of Malden,

[108] Emerson himself is probably the friend. Waldo, whom he had first met in Washington in January, 1843, became an ardent disciple and wrote many letters to Emerson in 1843 and 1844.

[109] "It is in vain . . . misses the reaction," is struck through in ink with a vertical use mark; "It is in vain . . . operations:" is used in "Emancipation in the British West Indies," *W*, XI, 118.

[110] This paragraph, struck through in ink with a vertical use mark, is used in "Power," *W*, VI, 60.

[111] Emerson had first entertained the idea of using Aunt Mary's letters as a basis for "the interior & spiritual history of New England" in May, 1841 (*JMN*, VII, 446). His current interest may have been prompted by the near-fatal illness she suffered in late September, 1843 (*L*, III, 208–209).

son of [Edward] Emerson, ↑Esq.↓ of Newbury(port). I used often
to hear that when William, son of Joseph, was yet a boy walking
before his father to church, on a Sunday, his father checked him,
"William, you walk as if the earth was not good enough for you."
"I did not know it, sir," he replied with the utmost humility. This
is one of the household anecdotes in which I have found a relation-
ship. ↑'Tis curious but the same remark was made to me, by Mrs
Lucy Brown, when I walked one day under her windows here in
Concord.↓[112]

↑*Inspiration*↓
It is sufficient to set me in the mood of writing verses at any time,
to read any original poetry.

[74] ↑Such is the advantage of a firm front, that,↓ even[n] if a
man have anything disgusting in his appearance or habits, as happens
to sickness & old age, let him not know that it disgusts & he takes
away half its ugliness —

"invisible solids & solvents" [113]

Lord Herbert's hospitality

I am a painter. C[?] N[?] has a task[,] a great felicity. Society mistook
me[.][114]

Mr Palmer's yoke of ox & cow [115]

the great brooding man[,] magnificent dreamer[,] reappearing to
plague society with his schemes to redeem it

[112] Lucy Jackson Brown was Lidian Emerson's sister.
    [113] From this line on, the entries on p. [74] are in pencil. "Lord Herberts hos-
pitality", "I am a painter . . . mistook me", and "the great brooding . . . redeem it" were later erased.
    [114] See p. [78] below.
    [115] This may be a reference to Edward Palmer, an itinerant preacher of idealism
who visited Emerson in 1842 (see *JMN*, VIII, 216), or Joseph Palmer, a member of
the Fruitlands community.

⟨For digging potatoes I know but one rule & that is Bishop Oradici's counsel to Philip II concerning the Moors; "The more you ⟨kill⟩ ↑take↓, the fewer will remain."⟩[116]

milksop. Man is made of milk.

The scholar a bachelor

[74a][117] Back of the torso Venus
music accidental
What confidence can I have in a fine behaviour & way of life that requires riches to bear it out? ⟨|| . . . ||⟩Shall I never see a greatness of carriage & thought combined with a power that actually earns its bread & teaches others to earn theirs?[n]

[74b] [blank]
[75][118] a gun is a liberalizer [119]

We come down with freethinking into the dear institutions & at once make carnage amongst them. We are innocent of any such fell purpose as the sequel seems to impute to us. We were only smoking a cigar, but it turns out to be a powder mill that we are promenading[.]

[76] If one could have any security against moods! If the profoundest prophet could be holden to his words & the hearer who is ready to sell all and join the crusade, could have any certificate that tomorrow his prophet shall not unsay his testimony! But the Truth sits veiled there on the Bench & never interposes an adamantine Syllable: and the most sincere & revolutionary doctrine[,] put as if the ark of God were carried forward some furlongs and planted

---

[116] See Robert Watson, *History of the Reign of Philip the Second, King of Spain* (New York, 1818), p. 137. Emerson knew this story as early as 1821, probably from Watson's book. See *JMN*, I, 57, 264, and VI, 22.

[117] A sheet of blue unlined paper measuring 12.6 x 20 cm, laid in loose at this point, has been numbered [74a]–[74b] by the editors. The entries on it are in pencil.

[118] The entries on this page are in pencil.

[119] See Journal Y, p. [74] below.

there for the succour of the world, shall in a few weeks be coldly set aside by the same speaker as morbid: "I thought I was right, but I was not," and the same immeasureable credulity demanded for new audacities.[120]

[77] *The best yet, or T T's last.*
My divine Thomas Taylor in his translation of Cratylus (p 30 (note)) calls Christianity "a certain most irrational & gigantic impiety," αλογιστος και γιγαντικη ανοσιουργια[.][121]

[78] People came, it seems, to my lectures with expectation that I was to realize the Republic I described, & ceased to come when they found this reality no nearer. They mistook me. I am & always was a painter. I paint still with might & main, & choose the best subjects I can. Many have I seen come & go with false hopes & fears, and dubiously affected by my pictures. But I paint on. I count this distinct vocation[,] which never leaves me in doubt what to do but in all times, places, & fortunes, gives me an open future, to be the great felicity of my lot. Dr C[harles].T.J[ackson]. too, was born to his chemistry & his minerals.[122] See p 135

Yet what to say to the sighing realist as he passes & comes to the vivid painter with a profound assurance of sympathy[n] ↑saying,↓ "he surely must be charmed to scale with me the silver mountains whose dim enchantments he has so affectionately sketched." The painter does not like the realist: sees his faults: doubts his means & methods: in what experiments [79] they make, both are baffled: no joy.[n] The painter is early warned that he is jeopardising his genius in these premature actualisations.

Very painful is the discovery we are always making that we can only give to each other a rare & partial sympathy: for, as much time as we have spent in looking over into our neighbor's field & chatting with him is lost to our own, & must be made up by haste & renewed solitude.

---

[120] This paragraph, struck through in ink with a vertical use mark, is used in "Nominalist and Realist," *W*, III, 247.

[121] *The Cratylus, Phaedo, Parmenides, and Timaeus of Plato*, trans. Thomas Taylor (London, 1793), in Emerson's library.

[122] Jackson, brother of Lidian Emerson, was a noted chemist and mineralogist.

La nature aime les croisements.[123] *Fourier.*

"L'esprit est une sorte de luxe qui détruit le bon sens, comme le luxe détruit la fortune."

Un auteur *apud Fourier.*

[80] The condition of participation ⟨of⟩ in any man's thought, is, entering the gate of that life. No man can be intellectually apprehended. As long as you see only with your eyes, you do not see him. You must be committed, before you shall be entrusted with the secrets of any party.

The sanity of Society is a balance of a thousand insanities[.] [124]

A[lcott]. came, the magnificent dreamer, brooding as ever on the renewal ⟨of⟩ or reedification of the social fabric after ideal law, heedless that he had been uniformly rejected by every class to whom he has addressed himself and just as sanguine & vast as [n] ever; — the most cogent example of the drop too much which nature adds of each man's peculiarity. To himself he seems the only realist, & whilst I & other men wish to deck the dulness of the months with here & there a fine action or hope, he would weave the whole a new texture of truth & beauty. Now he spoke of marriage & the fury that would assail him [81] who should lay his hand on that institution, for reform: and spoke of the secret doctrines of Fourier. I replied, as usual, — that, I thought no man could be trusted with it; ⟨T⟩the formation of new alliances is so delicious to the imagination, that St Paul & St John would be riotous; and that we cannot spare the coarsest muniment of virtue.——Very pathetic it is to see this wandering emperor from year to year making his round of visits from house to house of such as do not exclude him, seeking a companion, tired of pupils.

The stealing is not to be determined by the law of the land, as,

[123] This quotation is used in "Inspiration," *W*, VIII, 289. Cf. "Nature loves to cross her stocks" in "Works and Days," *W*, VII, 162, and "Nature loves mixtures" in "Natural History of Intellect," *W*, XII, 25–26. Cf. Journal O, p. [23] below.
[124] This sentence, struck through in ink with a vertical use mark, is used in "Nominalist and Realist," *W*, III, 237.

whether this property is mine or another's, but by the spirit in which it is taken. The rich man steals his own dividends.

[82] Let us not europize — neither by travel, neither by reading. Luckily for us[,] now that steam has narrowed the Atlantic to a strait, the nervous rocky West is intruding a new & continental element into our national mind, & we shall have an American genius.[125] We early men at least have a vast advantage: We are up at 4 o'clock in the morning, & have the whole market: We Enniuses & venerable Bedes of the empty American Parnassus. "Wish not a man from England."

The Shakers do not exclude any body yet have no difficulty in excluding. Disinclination excludes without bolts.   The Shakers — but the Shaken.[126]

It is hardly rhetoric to speak of the guardian angels of children. How beautiful they are, so protected, from all infusions of evil persons, from vulgarity & second thought.[127] Well-bred people ignore trifles & unsightly things; but heroes do not see them through an attention preengaged to beauty.

[83][128] "That is musk, which discloses itself by its smell, & not what the perfumers impose upon us," said Saadi[.][129]

———————

William Lorris the beginner of the Roman de la Rose (AD 1250) wrote 4150 verses of this poem; and Jean de Meung surnamed Clopinel (AD 1300) wrote more than 18000 verses and ended the poem.

———————

[125] This sentence, struck through in pencil with a vertical use mark, is used in "The Young American," *W*, I, 369–370.

[126] This entry is in pencil.

[127] "It is hardly . . . thought.", struck through in pencil with a vertical use mark, is used in "Uses of Great Men," *W*, IV, 29.

[128] Erased pencil writing covers the upper third of this page, of which the only significant words recovered are "figure whose".

[129] *The Gulistan . . . of Shaikh Sadī . . .* , 1823, p. 447.

Amir Khosraw, Saadi's contemporary[,] wrote between 400 & 500,000 verses.

I began to write Saadi's sentence above as a text to some homily of my own which muttered aloud as I walked this morning, to the effect, that the force of character is quite too faint & insignificant. The good are the poor, but if the poor were ↑but↓ once rich, how many fine scruples would melt away; how many blossoming reforms would be nipped in the bud. I ought to see that you must do that you say, as tomato vines bear tomatos & meadows yield grass. But I find the seed comes in the manure, and it is your condition[,] not your genius[,] which yields all this democratical and tenderhearted harvest.

[84] November 5. To Genius everything is permitted, & not only that, but it enters into all other men's labours. A tyrannical privilege to convert every man's wisdom or skill as it would seem to its own use or to show for the first time what all these fine & complex preparations were for. See how many libraries one master absorbs. Who hereafter will go gleaning in those contemporary & anterior books, from each of which he has taken the only grain of truth it had, & has given it tenfold value by placing it? The railroad was built for him; for him history laboriously registered; for him arms & arts & politics & commerce waited, like so many servants[,] until the heir of the manor arrived, which he quite easily administers[.]

See K 53

Genius is a poor man & has no house but see this proud landlord who has built the great house & furnished it so delicately opens it all to him & beseeches him respectfully to make it honourable by entering there & eating bread.[130]

[85] Some philosophers went out of town, founded a community in which they proposed to pay talent & labor at one rate, say, ten cents

---

[130] These two paragraphs, struck through in ink with a vertical use mark, are used in "Discourse at Middlebury College." The passage "for him arms . . . bread." is used in "The Scholar," W, X, 270. "To Genius everything is permitted," also occurs on p. [8] above. For the reference to Journal K, see JMN, VIII, 219.

the hour! But not an instant would a dime remain a dime. In one hand, it became an eagle as it fell, & in the other hand a copper cent. The whole difference is in knowing what to do with it. One buys a land title with it of an Indian which makes his posterity princes; or buys corn enough to feed the world; or pen, ink, & paper; or a painter's brush & colours,[n] by means of which he can communicate himself to the human race as though he were fire; and in the hand of the other it is as paltry & useless as the same piece of metal would be in the paw of a baboon or a wolf in the desart. Money is of no value, it cannot spend itself. All depends on the skill of the spender.[131]

[86] The true romance[,] not which will be written but which the progress of life & thought will realize, will be the transformation of genius into practical power. The symbol of this is the *working King* like Ulysses, Alfred, Czar Peter; [132]

[87] Your criticism of reformers and your abstaining to confess your own trials do not impose on me, or persuade me that you do not feel the ridicule of life. When I think of ridiculous men so aspiring, & nourished by so mean arts, I do not except you.

———

Punctuality. On the dinnerbell was written, "I laughed on them & they believed me not." [132a]

———

The sect is the stove, gets old, worn out[.] There are a hundred kinds but the fire keeps its properties. Calvinism is a fine history to show you how peasants, paddies, & old country crones may be liberalized & beatified.[133]

[88] The Reformers wrote very ill. They made it a rule not to bolt their flour & unfortunately neglected also to sift their thoughts.

[131] This paragraph, struck through in both pencil and ink with single vertical use marks, is used in "The Young American," *W,* I, 383.
[132] The first sentence, struck through in ink with two vertical use marks, is used in "Experience," *W,* III, 86. With the second, cf. *JMN,* VIII, 370.
[132a] Cf. Job 29:24.
[133] This paragraph was first written in pencil at the top of the page and later erased.

But Hesiod's great discovery ⟨P⟩Πλεον ημισυ παντος [134] is truest in writing, where half is a great deal more than the whole. Give us only the eminent experiences.

A↑lcott↓ & L↑ane↓ want feet; they are always feeling of their shoulders to find if their wings are sprouting; but next best to wings are cowhide boots, which society is always advising them to put on.[135]

⟨Women⟩ Married women uniformly decided against the communities. It was to them like the brassy & lackered life in hotels. The common school was well enough, but the common nursery they had grave objections to. Eggs might be hatched in ovens, ⟨& the chicken might come out⟩ but the hen on her own account greatly preferred the old way. A hen without chickens was but half a hen.[136]

[89] I sometimes think the health of the sick is the best health: they value it & husband it. Rude health is wasted.

Ellery says that Hawthorn agrees with him about Washington [Allston?] that he is the extreme of well dressed mediocrity.[137]

[90] 9 November. I have written much in prose & verse on the Poet but neither arrive at nor tend to any conclusion. This morning I think that the right conclusion of the Essay is a man, the poet that shall be born, the new religion, the Reconciler, for whom all things tediously wait.[138]

[91] 12 November. The "Community" of socialism is only the continuation of the same movement which made the joint stock com-

---

[134] "How much more the half is than the whole," *Works and Days*, l. 40. See *JMN*, VI, 138.

[135] The words "want feet; they" are canceled in pencil, perhaps by Edward Waldo Emerson.

[136] In the third sentence, the word "to" is deleted in pencil and inserted before "the common nursery" in pencil, perhaps by Edward Waldo Emerson. This paragraph is used in "Historic Notes of Life and Letters in New England," *W*, X, 365.

[137] If it is indeed Allston whose talent is in question here, Emerson's own reservations are pertinent; see *JMN*, V, 195, 210–211.

[138] This paragraph is struck through in ink with a vertical use mark; "the poet that shall . . . wait." is used in "The Poet," *W*, III, 37.

panies for manufactures, mining, insurance, banking, & the rest. It has turned out cheaper to make calico by companies, & it is proposed to bake bread & ↑to↓ roast mutton by companies, & it will be tried & done. It is inevitable[.] [139]

[92] It is wiser to live in the country & have poverty instead of pauperism. Yet citizens or cockneys are a natural formation also, a secondary formation, and their relation to the town is organic — but there are all shades of it and we dwellers in the country are only half countrymen. As I run along the yard from my woodpile I chance to see the sun as he rises or as he hangs in beauty over a cloud & am apprised how far off from that beauty I live, how careful & little I am. He ⟨summons⟩calls me to solitude[.]

———

The Italians have a good phrase to express the injury of translations; *traduttore traditore*.[140]

⟨One of our chief sins is the deference to a false aristocracy. The lawful heir humbles himself before the bastard.⟩

See Plotinus p 285, 363 [141]

The wise lassitude

Where does the light come[n] from that shines on things[?]
From the soul of the sufferer of the Enjoyer[.]

Minerva & Telemachus Plot[inus,
Select Works, 1817, p.] 452

[93] Wisdom is the knowledge of real being. Spiritual is that which is its own evidence. All which ⟨it⟩ we can with dignity ask or

[139] This paragraph, struck through in both pencil and ink with single vertical use marks, is used in "The Young American," *W*, I, 383.
[140] This sentence, struck through in ink with three vertical use marks, is used in "Books," *W*, VII, 204.
[141] *Select Works of Plotinus*, trans. Thomas Taylor (London, 1817), in Emerson's library. "See Plotinus . . . Plot 452" is in pencil.

say is selfasserted. The Immortality of the Soul in the popular sense is not a truth but a dogma.

See p 97

Every thing divine partakes the selfexistence
See how this bears on *Ecstasy*.[142]

[94] I have known a person of extraordinary intellectual power on some real or supposed imputation of weakness of her reasoning faculty from another party, enter with heat into a defence of the same by naming the eminent individuals who had trusted & respected her genius. The moment we quote a man to prove our sanity, we give up all. No ⟨|| ... ||⟩authority can stablish it & if I have lost confidence in myself I have the Universe against me.

Ben Jonson writes to ⟨his⟩the Muse, [*Works*, 1716,] Vol. III p 137

"Get him the time's long grudge, the Court's ill will;
And, reconciled, keep him suspected still;
Make him lose all his friends; &, which is worse,
Almost all ways to any better course.
With me thou leav'st a happier muse than thee,
And⟨,⟩ which thou broughtst me, welcome Poverty." [143]
                              [Epigram LXV, "To my Muse"]
See above, p. 69.

[95] Let us make the moments of this day solid. Let us not postpone our existence. Five minutes of today, as I used to preach, are worth as much to me as five minutes a million years hence.   This I add in correction of my own remark, that, the shortness of life considered, it mattered not whether we were sprawling in want, or sitting high. But that I say not. Let us be poised, & wise, & our own, today. Let us even treat the men & women well; treat them as if they were real.[144]

---

[142] These two lines are in pencil.
[143] These lines, struck through in ink with a vertical use mark, are used in "Culture," *W*, VI, 161–162.
[144] "This I add . . . real." was added in pencil, then erased. "Let us make . . .

[96][145] We fathers of American nations should not set the bad example of Repudiation to the Centuries. The Years are the moments of the life of this Nation[.]

Common sense knows its own & so recognizes the fact at first sight in chemical experiment. The commonsense of Dalton, Davy, Black is that commonsense which made these arrangements which now it discovers[.] [146]

Life— fidelity. Each religion has served

Nature— coactive

Subjective— in the eye. Yet[,] yet is the eye wiser than I am & surprises me

political economy & wealth a bigger knapsack[;] 'tis a great blunder to go overloaded

[97]   *Eternity of the World.*
The different ages of men in Hesiod's Works & Days signify the mutations of human lives from virtue to vice & from vice to virtue. There are periods of fertility & of sterility of souls: sometimes men descend for the benevolent purpose of leading back apostate souls to right principles. ⟨‖ . . . ‖⟩Hades signified the profound union of the soul with the present body.   See Taylor's Cratylus[,*Phaedo, Parmenides, and Timaeus of Plato* . . . , 1793].
The world is superfluously omnihabently rich. ⟨It keeps⟩ It is a plenum. It keeps a passage open for souls, only by the divine method of concealing all the furniture & persons which do not concern a particular soul from the senses of that soul. Through the solidest eternal things, he finds his path as if they did not exist, & does not suspect

---

hence." is struck through in ink with a vertical use mark; "Five minutes . . . real." is used in "Experience," *W*, III, 60.
[145] The entries on this page are in pencil.
[146] This paragraph is used in "Nature," *W*, III, 183–184.

their being. As soon as he needs them, he sees them, & takes another way.[147]

Euclid, Plato, and the multiplication table are spheres in your thought. Bale up with a spoon & you shall get Mrs Glass or the newspaper; bale up with a bucket & you shall have purer water[;] dive yourself & you shall come to the immortal deeps[.]
Therefore we feel that one man wrote all the books of literature. It will certainly so appear at a distance. Neither is any dead[,] neither Christ nor Plato, see R 112.[148]   See also ⟨p⟩above, p 9⟨o⟩3

[98] "The power of the kings of India was unlimited; & when, for example, the⟨re⟩ question was to collect imposts, the ministers chimed in (préconisaient) and employed the quite oriental maxim:[n] The people is like a grain of sesame, which does not yield its oil until you press it, until you pound it or roast it." Eugene Burnouf.[149]

Each man reserves to himself alone the right of being tedious.

There are many audiences in every public assembly, each one of which rules in turn. If any thing frivolous & comic appears, & coarse, you shall see the emergence of the boys & the rowdies: they are so loud & vivacious that you would think the house was filled with them. If new topics are started, graver, higher, these people recede: a more chaste & wise attention takes place: you would think the boys all slept, & the men had any degree of profoundness. If the speaker utters a noble sentiment, the attention deepens: a new & highest audience [150] [99]–[100] [leaf torn out] [151]

[101] Goethe is the poet who alone has in the recent ages thrown

[147] "It is a plenum . . . way.", struck through in ink with a vertical use mark, is used in "Nominalist and Realist," W, III, 243–244.
[148] JMN, VIII, 402. With "Therefore we . . . literature.", cf. p. [65] above.
[149] Cf. Introduction à l'histoire du buddhisme indien (Paris, 1844), pp. 145–146. Enough discrepancies exist to suggest that Emerson used an intermediary source.
[150] This paragraph, which is struck through in ink with a vertical use mark, is used in "Eloquence," W, VII, 66, where it is completed with "now listens, and the audiences of the fun and of facts and of the understanding are all silenced and awed."
[151] Emerson indexed p. [99] under Age, Criticism, Homoeopathy, Neurology, and Science, and p. [100] under C[harles]. Lane and Woman.

into the world a new organic figure which remains & will remain. Mephistopheles is as real as Prometheus. In the Second Part of Faust he seems to have proposed to himself great & present problems, namely, the antique life, the modern civilization, & the passage of the first into the last.[152]

The abstaining to chaunt our own times & private & social circumstance is a confession of sin. If we filled the day with grandeur we should not shrink from celebrating it.[153]

[102] ↑25 Dec.↓ At the performing of Handel's Messiah I heard some delicious strains & understood a very little of all that was told me. My ear received but a little thereof. But as the master overpowered the littleness & incapableness of the performers, & made them conductors of his electricity, so it was easy to see what efforts nature was making through so many hoarse, wooden, & imperfect persons to produce beautiful voices, fluid & soulguided men & women.[154] The genius of nature could well be discerned. By right & might we should become participant of her invention, & not wait for morning & evening to know their peace, but prepossess it. I walked in the bright paths of sound, and liked it best when the long continuance of a chorus had made ⟨‖ . . . ‖⟩the ear insensible to the music, made it as if there was none, then I was quite solitary & at ease in the melodious uproar. Once or twice in the solos, when well sung, I could play tricks, as I like to do, with my eyes, darken the whole [103][155] house & brighten & transfigure the central singer, and enjoy the enchantment.

This wonderful piece of music carries us back into ⟨a⟩the rich

[152] This paragraph is struck through in ink with a vertical use mark; "Goethe is . . . Prometheus." is used in "Goethe," W, IV, 277.

[153] This paragraph, struck through in ink with a vertical use mark, is used in "The Poet," W, III, 37.

[154] This sentence, struck through in ink with a vertical use mark, is used in "Nominalist and Realist," W, III, 233.

[155] Erased pencil writing, apparently a number of separate entries, covers the lower half of this page. The following significant words and phrases have been recovered or conjecturally recovered: "be tabulated & the results"; "as to be hardly observable"; "the continual"; "of the better"; "itself"; "The Community[?] makes a ‖ . . . ‖ community"; and "terms of admission U 16".

historical past[.] It is full of the Roman Church & its hierarchy & its architecture. Then further it rests on & requires so deep a faith in Christianity that it seems bereft of half & more than half its power when sung today in this unbelieving city.

———

We love morals until they come to us with mountainous melancholy & grim overcharged rebuke: then we so gladly prefer intellect, the light mocker. Dear sir, you treat these fantastical fellow men too seriously, you seem to believe that they exist.

———

The solid earth exhales a certain permanent average gas which we call the atmosphere; & the spiritual solid sphere of Mankind emits the volatile sphere of literature[,] of which books ↑are↓ single & inferior effects.

———

[104] 31 December. The year ends, and how much the years teach which the days never know! The individuals who compose our company converse, & meet, & part, & variously combine, and somewhat comes of it all, but the individual is always mistaken. He designed many things, drew in others, ⟨repelled⟩ quarrelled with some or all, blundered much, & something is done; all are a little advanced; but the individual is always mistaken.[156]

[105] In the progress of the character there is an increasing faith in the moral sentiment, and a decreasing faith in propositions.[157]

The Ayes & the Nays — The Nays have it

Ivo bishop of Chartres [158]

[106] At the Convention of Socialists in Boston last week, Alcott was

---

[156] This paragraph, struck through in ink with a vertical use mark, is used in "Experience," *W*, III, 69–70.

[157] This and the following entry are struck through in ink with a vertical use mark; the first is used in "Worship," *W*, VI, 227.

[158] Ivo is mentioned in a lengthy quotation from Jeremy Taylor in a footnote to chap. V of Coleridge's *Biographia Literaria* (New York and Boston, 1834), p. 64, in Emerson's library. This entry is in pencil.

present & was solicited to speak, but had no disposition, he said, to do so.[159] Although none of the representatives of the "Communities" present would probably admit it, yet in truth he is more the cause of their movements than any other man. He feels a certain parental relation to them without approving either of their establishments. His presence could not be indifferent to any speaker, & has not been nothing to any of them in the past years.

[107] A true course of English literary history would contain what I may read the Wartons & not learn; [160]
e.g. of Marlow's mighty line;
    of Crashaw's Musician & Nightingale
    of Ben Jonson's visit to Drummond
    of Wotton's list of contemporaries
    of the history of John Dennis
    of [George Villiers'] the Rehearsal
    of [Richard Sheridan's] the Critic
    A history of Bishop Berkeley
    Of the Scriblerus Club
    Of [Anthony à] Wood, and [John] Aubrey,
    Of Shakspeare at the last dates.
    Of Cotton's Montaigne
    Of the translators of Plutarch.
    Of the ⟨F⟩forgeries of Chatterton, Lander, & Ireland.
    Of Robert of Gloucester
    Of the Roxburgh Club
    Of Thomas Taylor

[108] We rail at trade, but the historian of the world will see that it was the principle of liberty, that it settled America, & destroyed

---

[159] This convention, held the last week of December, 1843, and the first week of January, 1844, was reported by Elizabeth Palmer Peabody in "Fourierism," *The Dial*, IV (April 1844), 473–483.

[160] Thomas Warton's *The History of English Poetry, from the Close of the Eleventh to the Commencement of the Eighteenth Century*, ed. Richard Price, 4 vols. (London, 1824), had been one of Emerson's main sources for his lectures on English literature in 1835–1836.

feudalism, and made peace & keeps peace, that it will abolish slavery[.] [161]

Belief & Unbelief [162]

Kant, it seems, searched the Metaphysics of the Selfreverence which is the favourite position of modern ethics, & demonstrated to the Consciousness that itself alone exists[.]

The two parties in life are the believers & unbelievers, variously named. The believer is poet, saint, democrat, theocrat, free-trade⟨r⟩, no-church, [n] no capital punishment,   idealist,

The unbeliever supports the church, education, the fine arts, &c as *amusements*, [163]

Horace Mann urges the Education of the State as a defence; to keep the fingers of the poor from our throats. I see it plainly that a man has not much to say when he speaks for an hour.

But the unbelief is very profound: [109] [164] who can escape it? I am nominally a believer: yet I hold on to property: I eat my bread with unbelief. I approve every wild action of the experimenters. I say what they say concerning celibacy or money or community of goods and my only apology for not doing their work is preoccupation of mind. I have a work of my own which I know I can do with some success. It would ⟨prejudice⟩ leave that undone if I should undertake with them and I do not see in myself any vigour equal to such an enterprise. My Genius loudly calls me to stay where I am, even with the degradation of owning bankstock and seeing poor men suffer whilst the Universal Genius apprises me of this disgrace & beckons me to the martyr's & redeemer's office.

This is belief too, this debility of practice, this staying by our work. For the obedience to a man's genius is the *particular* of Faith: by & by, shall come the *Universal* of Faith.

---

[161] This paragraph, struck through in pencil with a vertical use mark, is used in "The Young American," *W*, I, 378.

[162] This heading is enclosed by two wavy lines.

[163] See p. [63] above.

[164] Erased pencil writing covers most of this page, of which only "wanted, but" and "high price" have been recovered.

I take the law on the subject of Education to read thus, *the Intellect sees by moral obedience.*

[110][165] Alypius in Iamblichus had the true doctrine of money.[166] C[harles]. L[ane]. describes the action of the Shakers in reference to all their daily ⟨|| . . . ||⟩arrangements as nervous. Without any formal communication they coincide, and when one is ready, others are,[n] and the cart & the horse also.[167]

For the matter of marriage, it is falsified to the common sense as all other doctrines are, by emphasis or detachment, but it is honest & intelligible to say, (Shaker or Hermit) I am clear that in the state of prayer I neither marry, nor vote, nor buy, nor sell: I have experiences that are above all civil or nuptial or commercial relations: and I wish to vow myself to those. If you ask how the world is to get on, &c. &c. I have no answer. I do not care for such cattle of consequences. It is not my question, it is your own; answer it who will: I am contented with this new & splendid revelation of the One, and will not dispute.

[111][168] A man should not go where he cannot carry his whole sphere or society with him, — not bodily, the whole circle of his friends, but atmospherically; [n] ⟨or in⟩ I mean he should preserve in a new company the same attitude of mind and reality of relation which his daily associates call out, else he is shorn of his best beams,

---

[165] Erased pencil writing, apparently a number of separate entries, covers this page. The following significant words and phrases have been recovered: "a demonstration"; "Aristocracy disintegrates"; "comfortable"; and "bandit & brigand || . . . || strings up the merchant & manufacturer".

[166] Emerson is probably referring to the question Alypius asks of Pythagoras in Thomas Taylor's Introduction to *Iamblichus' Life of Pythagoras* (London, 1818), p. xiii: "Tell me, O philosopher, is either the rich man unjust, or the heir of the unjust man? For in this case there is no medium."

[167] This paragraph is struck through in ink with a vertical use mark. For use of the remark about the Shakers, cf. "Worship," *W*, VI, 203.

[168] Erased pencil writing, apparently all one paragraph, covers the upper third of this page. The following words and phrases have been recovered or conjecturally recovered: "These are the representatives[?] of"; "grow[?] the luxury"; "they must"; and "left".

and will be an orphan & a mourner in the merriest club. ⟨Better be an ⟨honest⟩honoured blacksmith than a despised lord.⟩ "If you could see Vich ian Vohr with his tail on!" But Vich ian Vohr must always carry his belongings in some fashion; if not added as honour, then severed & made a disgrace. What is mine & not appropriated by me is noxious to me.[169]

but spring will come again with lilacs & ⟨epigaeas &⟩ willows.

[112][170] There is an immense interval between all that is to be prescribed and all that is to be done.
He said he had treated the ox well, & it was sound. I asked the ox.

[113] [blank]
[114] Jan. 26[, 1844] There is no expression in any of our poetry, state papers, lecture-rooms or churches, of a high national feeling. Only the conventional life is considered. I think the German papers greatly more earnest & aspiring. "Conventional worth is intolerable, where personal is wanting," said Schlegel. Who announces to us in Journal or pulpit or lecture room
                    "Alone may man
                    Do the Impossible"[?] [171]

[169] "A man should not . . . disgrace.", struck through in ink with a vertical use mark, is used in "Manners," W, III, 132–133. For the remark about Vich Ian Vohr, see Sir Walter Scott, Waverley, chap. xvi.
[170] Erased pencil writing, apparently a number of separate entries, covers the middle of this page. The following words, phrases, and sentences have been recovered or conjecturally recovered: "Church irritable officers[?]"; "The Abolitionists have[?] ‖ . . . ‖ the right we all the wrong"; "I do not & can not forsake my vocation for abolitionism but to oppose them would call crime"; "State" (a heading for the following); "I asked the ox" (also in ink); "I hate the cant about our Union"; "The abolitionists[?] have all the reason & all the eloquence: dog cheap:" (cf. p. [120]); and "Mrs Kneeland".
[171] These two lines are a translation of Goethe's "Das Göttliche," ll. 37–38. This entry is struck through in pencil with a vertical use mark; in addition, there is no expression . . . considered." and "Who announces . . . Impossible' " are struck through in ink with vertical use marks and used in "The Young American," W, I, 388–389. "Whiggism" is written vertically in ink in the right margin from " 'Conventional worth" to "lecture room".

Napoleon said he was child of circumstances B 276, also [what he Irishman's country a wheelbarrow   said of crime] Nature has her favourites however, men of genius 103 [172]

Finish each day before you begin the next, ⟨one⟩ and interpose a solid wall of sleep between two. This you cannot do without temperance.

[115] ↑30 Jan[uary 1844]↓
I wrote to M[argaret] F[uller] that I had no experiences nor progress to reconcile me to the calamity whose anniversary returned the second time last Saturday.[173] The senses have a right to their method as well as the mind; there should be harmony in facts as well as in truths. Yet these ugly breaks happen there, which the continuity of theory does not compensate. The amends are of a different kind from the mischief. Then
But the astonishment of life is the absence of any appearance of reconciliation between the theory & practice of life. Our sanity, our genius, the prized reality, the law, is apprehended now & then for a serene & profound moment amidst the hubbub of cares & works which have no direct bearing on it; is then lost for months or years, & again found for an interval, to be lost again. If we compute it in time, we may in fifty or seventy years — ⟨But what is life, what are these cares & work⟩have half a dozen such happy & noble hours. But what are these cares & works the better for it? A method in his world he does not see, but this parallelism of great & little, which never react on each other or discover the smallest tendency to converge. His experiences, his fortunes, his reading or writing [116][174] are nothing to the purpose[,] as when a man comes into the room it does not appear whether he has been fed on yams or ⟨potatoes⟩ ↑⟨beans⟩↓ ↑oatmeal↓, ⟨on lemons or apples,⟩ — he has contrived to get so much azote & ammonia as he

[172] These four lines are in pencil. For the reference to Journal B, p. [276], see *JMN*, V, 226. Both statements by Napoleon appear in "Napoleon," *W*, IV, 231–232. See also *JMN*, V, 473.
[173] The death of Waldo Emerson occurred January 27, 1842. For Emerson's letter to Margaret Fuller, see *L*, III, 235–239.
[174] Erased pencil writing covers the lower two-thirds of this page, of which only the numeral "88" has been recovered.

wants, out of venison or out of snow. So vast is the disproportion between the vaulting sky of the law, and the motes & feathers of the performance, that whether he is man of worth or sot, is not so great a matter as we say.[175]

If we were not of all opinions; if we did not in any moment shift the platform on which we stand, & look & speak from another, if[n] there could be any regulation[,] ⟨that a man⟩any one hour rule, that a man should never leave his point of view oftener than once in 15 minutes, or never without sound of trumpet! I am always insincere, as always knowing there are other moods.[176]

Introvert your eye & your consciousness is a taper in the desart⟨s⟩ of Eternity. It is the Channel though now diminished to a thread through which torrents of light roll & flow in the high tides of spontaneity & reveal the landscape of the dusky Universe[.]

That idea which I approach & am magnetized by,—is my country.

[117][177] We read in youth a great many true proverbs concerning the narrowness & inconsistency of men but we are very tardy in verifying ⟨of⟩them[n] on our own respectable neighbors of whom they are accurately descriptive. I knew a Dr S.[,] a pious Swedenborgian in the country, from whom I heard much truth. He is now a tippler. ⟨I⟩We have accustomed ourselves to respect our dignified fellow citizens so much that their exceeding narrowness & selfishness puzzles us & we are slow at calling it by its proper name.

How we love to be magnetised! Ah ye strong iron currents, take me in also! We are so apologetic[,] such waifs & straws ducking & imi-

[175] This paragraph, struck through in ink with a vertical use mark on p. [115] and two vertical use marks on p. [116], is used in "Montaigne," W, IV, 178–179.

[176] This paragraph, struck through in ink with a vertical use mark, is used in "Nominalist and Realist," W, III, 247.

[177] The entries on this page were first written in pencil, then partially erased when they had been copied in ink. The pencil version of the first entry had "heard much good" for "heard much truth."; "I have accustomed myself" for "We have accustomed ourselves"; "selfishness puzzles me, & I am slow" for "selfishness puzzles us & we are slow"; and other minor differences.

tating[,] & then the mighty thought comes sailing on a silent wind
& fills us also with its virtue & we stand like Atlas on our legs & uphold
the world.

The magnetism is alone to be respected: the men are steel filings.
Yet we say, O steelfiling number One! What heart drawings I feel
to thee! What prodigious virtues are these of thine: how constitutional to thee & impartible! Whilst we speak, the loadstone is withdrawn: down falls steelfiling in a heap with the rest, & we continue
our mummery to the dead undistinguishable thing.[178]

[118] It is impossible to write a sentence with malice prepense. I sit
hours in vain over the correction of a bad paragraph in a proof —
And nothing is easier than to write well with the favouring gales.

The greatness of the centuries is made out of the paltriness of
the days & hours. See with what motives & by what means the
railroad gets built, and Texas annexed or rejected,

I am sorry to say that the Numas & Pythagorases have usually a spice
of charlatanism & that abolition Societies & Communities are dangerous fixtures. The manliness of man is a frail & exquisite fruit which
does not keep its perfection twenty four hours. Its sweet fragrance
cannot be bottled or barreled or exported. Carlyle is an eloquent
writer but his recommendations of emigration & education appear
very inadequate. Noble as it seems to work for the race, & hammer
out constitutions for phalanxes, it can only be justly done by mediocre
thinkers, or men of practical, not theoretic faculty. As soon as a
scholar attempts it, I suspect him. [119][179] ↑Good physicians have
least faith in medicine. Good priests the least faith in church-forms.↓ [180]

[178] This paragraph, struck through in ink with a vertical use mark, is used in
"Nominalist and Realist," *W*, III, 228.

[179] Erased pencil writing, apparently two separate entries or more, covers this
page. The following significant words and phrases have been recovered or conjecturally recovered: "knowledge"; "his own"; "ones"; "but this at least we are
found"; and "sure he will join me in a vote of thanks to a philanthropist abolitionist[?]".

[180] All but the added sentences was written first in pencil at the top of p. [118]
and later erased. There are some minor differences between the two versions. "To
make the earth a garden", also in pencil and erased, is written directly below the

That bread which we ask of Nature is that she should entrance us, but amidst ⟨the m⟩ her beautiful or her grandest pictures, I cannot escape the *second thought.* I walked this P.M. in the woods, but there too the snow banks were sprinkled with tobacco juice. We have the wish to forget night & day, father & mother, food & ambition, but we never lose our dualism. Blessed wonderful Nature nevertheless! without depth but with immeasureable lateral spaces. If we look before us,[n] if we compute our path, it is very short. Nature has only the thickness of a shingle or a slate; we come straight to the extremes: but sidewise & at unawares ⟨to⟩the[n] present moment opens into other moods & moments, rich, prolific, leading onward without end. Impossible to bring her, the goddess, to parle: coquettes with us, hides herself in coolness & generalities; pointed & personal is she never[.]

[120][181] The dead.

Ζωμεν τον εκεινων θανατον, τεθνηκαμεν δε τον εκεινων βιον.[182]
Heraclitus. [On the Universe, LXVII]

———

The fair magnetic lady whom I saw thought that every person in the room was as clairvoyant as herself if only they knew it.
↑No doubt of it.↓

The Daguerrotype of the Soul   "The oracles assert that the impressions of characters & other divine visions appear in aether."
Τους τυπους των χαρακτηρων και των αλλων θειων φασματων εν τω αιθερι φαινεσθαι τα λογια λεγουσιν.

Simplic. in Phys. p. 144 ap. T. Taylor
["Collection of the Chaldaean Oracles,"]
in Monthly Magazine [*and British Register,*]
Vol III [1797,] p. [522]

———

pencil version. The added sentences, to which attention is directed at the bottom of p. [118] by a capital X and a hand sign pointing right, are written at the bottom of p. [119] and separated from the paragraph on that page by a long rule.

[181] Erased pencil writing covers most of this page. Almost all of it is an early inscription of the paragraph about Swedenborg and Brook Farm on p. [121], with no discernible significant differences.

[182] "One living the other's death and dying the other's life."

Chip chop chain,
Give a thing & never take it back again.

Eloquence at Antislavery Conventions is dog cheap[.] [183]

Rattlesnake & wild cat banks

[121] [184] A debate is a game at cross purposes. Each of the speakers expresses himself very imperfectly. No one of them hears much that another says, such is the preoccupation of mind of every speaker. And the audience[,] who have only to hear & not to speak[,] judge very wisely & superiorly how wrongheaded & unskilful is each of the debaters to his own affair. [185]

⟨I dwell today amid a cloud of pictures.⟩

Swedenborg should not be reduced to a category. Why not have a new man, & a new region of life & power?ⁿ Why should the attractive depths of nature be vulgarised by the foot of ignorant conjurers, mesmerisers, & phrenologists,

                                                ↑See p 99↓ [186]

"And fools rush in where angels fear to tread."
                                    [Pope, *Essay on Criticism*, 1. 625]

So say I of Brook Farm. Let it live. Its merit is that it is a new life. Why should we have only two or three ways of life & not thousands & millions? [187] This is a new one so fresh & expansive that they are all homesick when they go away. The shy sentiments are there

---

[183] This and the following entry are in pencil; the first is used in "Emancipation in the British West Indies," *W*, XI, 138.

[184] Erased pencil writing, apparently two separate entries or more, covers the upper half of this page. The following significant words and phrases have been recovered or conjecturally recovered: "world of society"; "they must be allowed to speak till they have"; and "ourselves[?] we must be patient".

[185] This paragraph, struck through in ink with a vertical use mark, is used in "Nominalist and Realist," *W*, III, 226.

[186] This cross-reference is in pencil.

[187] "Its merit . . . millions?", struck through in ink with a vertical use mark, is used in "Nominalist and Realist," *W*, III, 240.

expressed. The *correspondence* of that place would be a historiette of the spirit of this age. They might see that in the arrangements of B[rook]. F[arm]. as out of them it is the person not the communist that avails.

[122][188]   Of Succession.
It is not enough to say that we are bundles of moods, for we always rank our mental states. The graduation is exquisite. We are not a bundle but a house.

Ellery Channing is quite assured that he has a natural music of expression, which is wanting in all the so called poets of the day. He is very good natured, & will allow them any merit you choose to claim; but this he always feels to be true. It is infinitely easy to him, as easy as it is for running water to warble, but at the same time impossible to any to whom it is not natural.

Every act of man has the ground tone and the high treble. Nothing but is dual, or goes through the gamut.

The Highest should alternate the two states of the contemplation of the fact in pure intellect, and the total conversion of intellect into ⟨the action⟩ energy: angelic insight alternating with bestial activity: sage & tiger.

[123] When I address a large assembly, as last Wednesday, I am always apprised what an opportunity is there: not for reading to them as I do, ⟨many⟩ lively miscellanies, but for painting in fire ⟨your⟩ ↑my↓ thought, & being agitated to agitate. One must dedicate himself to it and think with his audience in his mind, so as to keep the perspective & symmetry of the oration, and enter into all the easily forgotten secrets of a great nocturnal ⟨audience⟩ ↑assembly↓ & their relation to the speaker. But it would be fine music & in the

---

[188] Erased pencil writing, apparently three separate entries or more, covers most of this page. The following significant words and phrases have been recovered: "What is the Lyceum for?"; "yet we have"; "present"; "Middlesex"; "instantly exerted"; and "conspiracy where we are the victim".

present well rewarded; that is, he should have his audience at his devotion and all other fames would hush before his. Now eloquence is merely fabulous. When we talk of it, we draw on our fancy. It is one of many things which I should like to do, but it requires a seven years' wooing.[189]

Now when at any time I take part in a public debate, I wish on my return home to be shampooed & in all other ways ⟨p⟩ aired & purified[.]

[124][190] Precisely what the painter or the sculptor or the epic rhapsodist feels, I feel in the presence of this house, which stands to me for the human race, the desire, namely, to express myself fully, symmetrically, gigantically to them, not dwarfishly & fragmentarily. H.D.T., with whom I talked of this last night, does not or will not perceive how natural is this, and only hears the word Art in a sinister sense.[191] But I speak of instincts. I did not make the desires or know anything about them: I went to the public assembly, put myself in the conditions, & instantly feel this new craving, — I hear the voice, I see the beckoning of this Ghost. To me it is vegetation, the pullulation & universal budding of the plant man. Art is the path of the creator to his work. The path or methods are ideal and eternal, though few men ever see them: not the artist himself for years, or for a lifetime, unless he come into the conditions. Then he is apprised with wonder what herds of daemons hem him in. He can no more rest: he says, 'By God, it is in me & must go forth of me.'   I

[189] The "address [to] a large assembly . . . last Wednesday" was probably Emerson's lecture "The Young American," read February 7, 1844, before the Mercantile Library Association in Odeon Hall, Boston. "what an opportunity . . . wooing." is struck through in ink with a wavy vertical use mark. Beneath "One must dedicate . . . assembly & their" is erased pencil writing, apparently all one paragraph, of which "Let us be nobler", "magnetism[?]", and "p 114" have been recovered or conjecturally recovered.
[190] Erased pencil writing, apparently a number of separate entries, covers the upper two-thirds of this page. The following significant words and phrases have been recovered or conjecturally recovered: "The farm[?]"; "happen in"; "Brook farm"; and "Let them be[?] working kings".
[191] "Precisely what . . . sense." is struck through in ink with a vertical use mark; "Precisely what . . . fragmentarily." is partially used in "The Poet," W, III, 3 –39.

go to this place [125]¹⁹² and am galvanized, and the torpid eyes of my sensibility are opened. I hear myself speak as a stranger — Most of the things I say are conventional; but I say something which is original & beautiful. That charms me. I would say nothing else but such things. ⟨W⟩ In our way of talking, we say, that is mine, that is yours; but this poet knows well that it is not his, that it is as strange & beautiful to him as to you; he would fain hear the like eloquence at length.

Once having tasted this immortal ichor, we cannot have enough of it. Our appetite is immense. And, as "an admirable power flourishes in intelligibles," according to Plotinus, ⟨so that⟩ "which perpetually fabricates," it is of the last importance that these things get ⟨c⟩spoken. What a little of all we know, is said! What drops of all the sea of our science are baled up! And by what accident it is that these are spoken, whilst so many thoughts sleep in nature!

Hence the oestrum of speech: hence these throbs & heart beatings at the door of the assembly" to the end, namely, that the thought may be ejaculated as Logos or Word.¹⁹³   ↑See p. 131↓

[126] Some men have the perception of difference predominant, and are conversant with surfaces & trifles, with coats & coaches, & faces, & cities; these are the men of talent. Hence Paris ↑city↓ & the western European, and New York & New England. And other men ⟨ha⟩ abide by the perception of Identity; these are the Oriental⟨i⟩s, the philosophers, the men of faith & divinity, the men of genius. These men[,] whose contempt of *soi disant* conservatism cannot be concealed[,] which is such a conserving as the Quaker's, who keeps in his garments the cut of Queen Ann's time but has let slip the fire & the love of the first Friends, are the real loyalists.

A strong
a vigorous monad refreshed by prosperity¹⁹⁴

---

¹⁹² Erased pencil writing, apparently a number of separate entries, covers most of this page. Only the cross-reference "p 57" has been recovered.

¹⁹³ "Art is the path . . . go forth of me.'" and "Most of the things . . . or Word.", struck through in ink with single discontinuous vertical use marks, are used in "The Poet," *W*, III, 38–40.

¹⁹⁴ These two lines are in pencil.

[127] The children are not quite at the mercy of such poor educators as we adults, for if we huff & chide them, they soon come not to mind it, & get a selfreliance; & if we respect & indulge them to an excess, yet they keep the love & learn the renunciation elsewhere.[195]   ↑See p 82↓

It was then I discovered the secret of the world[,] that all things subsist, and do not die, but only retire a little from sight & afterwards return again.[196]

⟨|| ... ||⟩ The text of our life is accompanied all along by this commentary or gloss of dreams.

Henry⟨'s⟩ ↑T's↓ lines which pleased me so well were

> "I hearing get, who had but ears,
> And sight, who had but eyes before;
> I moments live, who lived but years,
> And truth discern who had but learning's lore" [197]

[128]
To -ove   The Visit [198]
                     Askest, how long thou shalt stay?
                     Devastator of the day

---

[195] This paragraph, struck through in ink with two vertical use marks, is used in "Uses of Great Men," *W*, IV, 29. "See p 82" is in pencil.

[196] This paragraph, struck through in ink with a vertical use mark, is used in "Nominalist and Realist," *W*, III, 242–243.

[197] "Inspiration," ll. 25–28. The lines occur in "Friday," *A Week on the Concord and Merrimack Rivers*, first published in 1849. Emerson quoted them in "Thoreau," *W*, X, 477.

[198] This version of "The Visit" was inscribed in pencil and later partially erased. Both headings are encircled by a line. For another version of the poem, see p. [15] above.

Here, as with other concentrations of erased and/or overwritten pencil writing in this volume, special symbols are used to convey as precisely as possible the completeness or incompleteness of the transcription and the degrees of uncertainty about readings. Unrecovered words are indicated by a bracketed number or numbers and *w* (for "word(s)") in italics. Unrecovered letters are represented by hyphens when the number can be estimated; when it cannot, three close dots are set centered on a letter. An unrecovered line in poetry is shown as "[*unrecovered*]." Doubtful readings are shown by the conventional bracketed question mark. Where a printed or copied version exists of a passage in erased or overwritten pencil writing, the editors

Know, each substance & relation
In nature's opera⋯
Hath its unit, ---nd, metre   [5]
And /each/every/ new compound

A

[*1–2 w*] product & repea⋯
[*2 w*] product of the early found
But [*1 w*] unit of the visit
The encounter of the wise,   [10]

Say [⟨*1 w*⟩]

What other metre is it
Than the meeting of the eyes?
Nature poureth into nature
Through th-- channel of that feature.
[*2–3 w*] ray of lig--   [15]
[*1 w*] fleet [*1–2 w*] or whirlwind go
[*unrecovered*]   [?]
[*1–2 w*] swift experience   [19]
And exchange intelligence   [20]

Single

⟨A⟩ [*3–4 w*] confessed   [22]
⟨–⟩ [*1 w*] look has [*2 w*] breast   [21]
The durat⋯ a [*1 w*]   [23]
[*1 w*] the term of c⋯en-n⋯   [24]
[*2–3 w*] cannot halt   [27]
[*1 w*] thou shalt rue the fault
If love one moment overstay,
Hatred's swift repulsions play   [30]

The question of the annexation of Texas is one of those which look very differently to the centuries and to the years. It is very certain that the strong British race which have now overrun so much of this continent, must also overrun that tract, & Mexico & Oregon also, and it will in the course of ages be of small import by what particular occasions & methods it was done. It is a secular question. It is quite necessary & true to our New England character that we should consider the question in its local & temporary bearings, and resist the annexation with tooth & nail.

---

have first recovered as much as possible without aid, and have then consulted another version. They have printed only what they have been able to see.

It is a measure which goes not by right nor by wisdom but by feel-ing.[199]

It would be a pity to dissolve the union & so diminish immensely every man's personal importance. We are just beginning to feel our oats.

[129] What a pity that a farmer should not live three hundred years.[200]

We fancy ⟨p⟩ that men are individuals; but every pumpkin in the field goes through every point of pumpkin history. The rabid democrat[,] as soon as he is senator & rich man, has ripened beyond the possibility of sincere radicalism and unless he can resist the sun he must be conservative the rest of his life. Lord Eldon said in his old age, that "if he were to begin life again he would be damned but he would begin as Agitator." [201]

Most of the world lives by humbug, & so will I, is the popular conclusion.[202]

> [*unrecovered*]
> [*2–3 w*] thy [*2–3 w*] state
> Frugal ⋯tiples of that[203]

[130] I cannot often enough say that a man is only a relative & representative nature, that each is a hint of a truth, but is far enough from being himself that truth which yet he quite newly & inevitabl⟨e⟩y suggests to us. If I seek it in him I shall not find it. We ⟨‖ ... ‖⟩have such exorbitant integrating ⟨o⟩eyes that ⟨an arc⟩ the smallest arc of a curve being shown us we instantly complete the curve, & when the

[199] See p. [142] below.
[200] Cf. *JMN*, VII, 476.
[201] This paragraph, struck through in ink with a vertical use mark, is used in "Nominalist and Realist," *W*, III, 246.
[202] This sentence, struck through in ink with a vertical use mark, is used in "Montaigne," *W*, IV, 154.
[203] These three lines of erased pencil writing, visible directly after the last entry, are part of "The Visit." The last two appear as ll. 25–26, *W*, IX, 13.

curtain is lifted from the diagram which we saw, we are vexed to find that no more was drawn than just that fragment of an arc which we first beheld. We are greatly too liberal in our construction of each other's faculty & promise. Exactly what they have already done they shall do again, but that which we inferred from their nature & inception, they shall not do. That is in nature but not in them. That is in us.

Ah if any man could conduct into me the pure stream of that which he pretends to be. Long afterwards, I find that quality elsewhere which he promised me.[n] Intoxicating is to me the genius of Plotinus or of Swedenborg [133] [204] yet how few particulars of it can I glean from their books. My debt to them is for a few thoughts. They cannot feed that appetite they have created. I should know it well enough if they gave me that which I seek of them.[205]

[131] Continued from p 125
Say, it is in me & shall out; stand there baulked & dumb, stuttering & stammering, hissed & hooted, stand & strive until at last ⟨indignation⟩ rage draw out of thee that *Dream*-power which every night shows thee to be thine; a power transcending all limit & privacy, and ↑by virtue↓ of which the man is the conductor of the whole universe of electricity. Nothing walks or creeps or grows or exists, which must not in turn arise & walk before him as exponent of his meaning. Comes he to that power, his genius is no longer exhaustible: all the ⟨world⟩ ↑creatures by pairs & by tribes↓ pour⟨s⟩ into his mind ⟨like⟩ ↑as into↓ a Noah's Ark, to come out again and people a new world. This is like ⟨our magazine⟩ ↑the stock↓ of air for my respiration or the combustion of my hearth[,] not a measure of gallons but the entire atmosphere for each one if wanted,[n] or like the credit by which the great merchant takes up first & last the total property of the ↑civil↓ world into his operations. And [132] therefore the rich poets as Homer, Chaucer, Shakspeare, & Raphael, have obviously no limits to their works, except the limits of their life-time, and resemble a

---

[204] Emerson wrote *"over* to p. 133" at the bottom of p. [130] and "from p 130" at the top of p. [133].

[205] These two paragraphs are struck through in ink with single discontinuous vertical use marks; all but the last three sentences are used in "Nominalist and Realist," *W*, III, 225–226.

mirror carried through the street ready to render an image of every created thing.[206]

[134]   ↑Otherness↓

H.D.T. said, he knew but one secret ⟨an⟩which was to do one thing at a time, and though he has his evenings for study, if he was in the day inventing machines for sawing his plumbago, he invents wheels all the evening & night also; and if this week he has some good reading & thoughts before him, his brain runs on that all day, whilst pencils pass through his hands. I find in me an opposite facility or perversity, that I never seem well to do ⟨this⟩ a particular work, until another is due. I cannot write the poem though you give me a week, but if I promise to read a lecture day after tomorrow, at once the poem comes into my head & now the rhymes will flow. And let the ↑proofs of the↓ Dial be crowding on me from the printer, and I am full of faculty how to make the Lecture.

[135] Men who in the present life knew the particular deity from whom they descended, and gave themselves always to their proper employment, were called by the ancient, *divine men.* See Taylor's *Cratylus.*   See ⟨p⟩above p. 78
↑Taylor p 32↓ [207]

⟨Poetry⟩   ↑Skeptic↓

Pure intellect is the pure devil when you have got off all the masks of Mephistopheles. It is a painful symbol to me that the index or forefinger is always the most soiled of all the fingers.

↑The two Histories↓

The question whether the trilobites or whether the gods are our grandfathers; and whether the actual existing men are an amelioration or a degradation, arises from ↑the↓ contingence whether we look from the material or from the poetic side.

---

[206] This paragraph, struck through in ink with a vertical use mark, is used in "The Poet," *W,* III, 40–41. Page [133] is printed at the end of the preceding entry.
[207] *The Cratylus, Phaedo, Parmenides, and Timaeus of Plato . . . ,* 1793. This entry is struck through in ink with a vertical use mark.

Railroads make the country transparent.

[136] Somebody said of me after the lecture at Amory Hall within hearing of A. W., "The secret of his popularity is, that he has a *damn* for everybody."[208]

I tell the Shakers that the perfect unit can alone make a perfect member.

12 March. On Sunday evening, ↑10th inst.↓ at the close of the fifteenth year since my ordination as minister in the Second Church, I made an address to the people on the occasion of closing the old house[,] now a hundred & twenty three years old, and the oldest church in Boston. Yesterday they begun to pull it down[.]

[137] Love shows me the opulence of nature by disclosing to me a world in my friend hidden from all others, & I infer ⟨the⟩an equal depth of good in every other direction.[209]

↑Bohemian.↓
Intellect is a piratical schooner cruising in all ⟨companies⟩ ↑latitudes↓ for its own pot.

It is not the intention of Nature that we should live by general views. We fetch fire & water, run about among the shops & get our boots mended, day by day, and are the victims of these details, and once in a fortnight we arrive perhaps at a general remark. If we were not thus infatuated, if we saw the real from hour to hour, we could not preserve a due regard to the sensible world but should surely be burned or frozen.[210]

[138][211] Make haste home, Uncle, & tell your nieces all you saw.

[208] The lecture was "New England Reformers," read March 3, 1844.
[209] This entry, struck through in ink with a vertical use mark, is used in "Nominalist and Realist," *W*, III, 244.
[210] This paragraph, struck through in ink with a vertical use mark, is used in "Nominalist and Realist," *W*, III, 237.
[211] In the left margin beside "This, mainly, that . . . record his own." is written "no Law but has a law behind it."; beside "Every man says . . . foolish things,"

This, mainly, that the game of the world is like that of two boys trying on the sidewalk ⟨to see⟩ which can push the other ↑off↓. Every thing in nature is alternately mover & moved, or first, *law*, & then *subject* or culprit, and there is no law that will not come to the bar in due time: this also, that ↑it is as much↓ an honest function of the poet ⟨is⟩ to ⟨keep⟩ ↑record↓ the good things that are said in the street, as to record his own. Every man says wise things as well as he: the difference is, that the others say a good many foolish things, & do not know when they have spoken wisely, he discerns their wisdom from their folly.[212] Consuelo, as E[lizabeth]. H[oar]. remarked[,] was the crown & fulfilment of all the tendencies of literary parties in respect to a certain Dark Knight who has been hovering about in the purlieus of heaven & hell for some ages. The young people have shown him much kindness for some time back. Burns advised [139] him to "take advice & mend"; Goethe inclined to convert him & save his soul in the second part of Faust. He has here in America been gaining golden opinions lately & now in Consuelo he actually mounts the shrine & becomes an object of worship under the name & style of "He to whom wrong has been done."[213]

A capital merit of Consuelo [is] the instant ⟨|| ... ||⟩mutual understanding ⟨of⟩ between the great,[n] as between Albert & Consuelo[.]

[140][214] Art seems to me to be in the artist a steady ⟨eye⟩ ↑respect↓ to the whole, by an eye loving beauty in details. Proportion

is written "Saadi"; and beside "Consuelo, as E.H. remarked . . . some ages." is written "Devil".

[212] "this also, that . . . folly." is struck through in pencil with two vertical use marks; "Every man says . . . wisely," is used in "Shakspeare," *W*, IV, 197.

[213] For Burns's remark, see "Address to the Deil," l. 122; see *JMN*, III, 304. The Satanic figure in George Sand's *Consuelo* (1842) is Count Albert de Rudolstadt, a nobleman threatened with insanity. Emerson apparently read *Consuelo* in January, 1844 (see *Letters from Ralph Waldo Emerson to a Friend, 1838–1853*, ed. Charles Eliot Norton, Boston and New York, 1899, p. 54).

[214] Erased pencil writing, apparently all one paragraph, covers the middle of this page. The following significant words and phrases have been recovered or conjecturally recovered: "⟨it is a suicidal⟩"; "↑stealing↓"; "& tardy"; "preoccupied"; "the common"; "need of"; "is our chief disease, the"; "opinion   Good in"; "good mixture[?]"; "the wrongdoer[?]   It is to balance[?] a vicious"; and "is made entire".

is almost impossible to human beings[;] there is no one who does not exaggerate. In all conversation each man manages well enough until the story comes within gunshot of his personality[;] then he talks too much. In modern sculpture & picture & poetry, the beauty is miscellaneous, the artist works here & there & at all points, adding and adding, instead of developing the unit of his thought. Beautiful details we must have or no artist[,] but they must be means divinely subordinated to his great purpose. All lively boys write poetry to their ear & eye, & the cool ⟨observ⟩ reader finds nothing but sweet jingles in it: As they grow older, they respect the argument of the poem.[215]

To this point I quote from old MS. A man is an exaggerator. In every conversation see how the main end is lost sight of by all but the best & with slight apology or none a digression [141][216] made to every creaking door or buzzing fly. What heavenly eloquence could hold the ear of an audience if a child cried?[n] A man with a truth to communicate is caught by the beauty of his own words & ends by being a rhymester or a critic[,] & genius is sacrificed to talent every day.[217]

[142][218] Art
Symmetry. He shall do well who can keep his judgment so even as to see the whole through all the particulars. Most lovers of beauty are dazzled by the details. To have seen many beautiful details cloys us & we are better able to keep our rectitude[.]

The straight line is better than the Square[:] a man is the one; horse the other.

[215] This paragraph, struck through in ink with a vertical use mark, is used in "Nominalist and Realist," *W*, III, 234.

[216] Erased pencil writing, apparently all one paragraph, covers the upper third of this page. The following significant words and phrases have been recovered: "I shall not go"; "our national"; "↑crime,↓"; "to you for redemption   It is not"; "complain"; "fear"; and "that it will succeed   Stealing is a suicidal business".

[217] The "old MS" is the lecture "Reforms," first delivered January 15, 1840. This paragraph is struck through in ink with a vertical use mark. See *JMN*, VIII, 66. With "genius is sacrificed to talent", cf. *JMN*, VIII, 108.

[218] The entries on this page are in pencil; the third and sixth have been erased.

The measure goes not by right nor by wisdom, but by feeling, as Texas[.] [219]

I do not feel myself a poet but a scribe. I write when I have thoughts & when my friends have thoughts.

Orders have arrived in Concord & Amesbury & Brook Farm for a hundred poems, two hundred Tales, & fifty or sixty Lectures[.]

Wm Green came here[?] &[?] disproved his dogmas for it was at once manifest that we had nothing between us[.] [220]

[143] [blank]
[144] *Poet.*
Among the ↑"Chaldaean↓ Oracles which were either delivered by Theurgists under the reign of Marcus Antoninus or by Zoroaster," Taylor inserts the following.
"Rulers who understand the intelligible works of the Father. These he spread like a veil over sensible works & bodies. *They are standing transporters, whose employment consists in speaking to the Father & to matter;* in producing apparent imitations of unapparent natures, & in inscribing things unapparent in the apparent fabrication of the world."

Concerning the universe —
"It is an imitation of intellect, but that which is fabricated possesses something of body."

Concerning the light above the empyrean world
"In this light things without figure become figured."

See [Thomas Taylor, "Collection of the Chaldaean Oracles,"] Monthly Magazine [*and British Register,*] Vol III p[p.] 509[-526] (A D. 1797) [221]

---

[219] See p. [128] above.

[220] Emerson's reference may be to William Greene, whom he met in New York in March, 1842, and described as "a devout man who seems to read nothing but Boehmen & Madame Guion" (*L*, III, 23). See p. [158] below.

[221] The passages Emerson quotes occur on pp. 520–521 of Taylor's article. The phrase "apparent imitations of unapparent natures" also occurs on p. [i] above, in

[145][222] It is curious that intellectual men should be most attractive to women. But women are magnetic; intellectual men are unmagnetic: therefore as soon as they meet, communication is found difficult or impossible. Various devices are tried in the villages to *wont* them, such as candy parties, nut-crackings, ↑picnics↓, sleighrides, charades, but with slender success.

Quotation is good only when the writer goes my way & better mounted than I, and "gives me a cast," as we say; but if I like the gay equipage so well as to go out of my road, I had better have gone a-foot.[223]

[146][224] It was a good saying, Age gives good advice when it is no longer able to give a bad example. ⟨As far as I observe, it is⟩ By ⁿ acting rashly ⟨that⟩ we buy the power of talking wisely. People who know how to act are never preachers.

I have always found our American day short. The constitution of a Teutonic scholar with his twelve, thirteen, or fourteen hours a day, is fabulous to me. I become nervous & peaked with a few days editing the Dial, & watching the stagecoach to send proofs to printers. If I try to get many hours in [a] day, I ⟨have⟩shall not ⟨any⟩have any.

We work hard in the garden and do it badly & often twice or thrice over, but "we get our journey out of the curses," as Mr H's Brighton drover said of his pigs.

[147] Allston is adamas ex veteri rupe; [225] chip of the old block;

Journal Y, p. [260], and Journal O, p. [1] below. "*They are standing* . . . world.' " is used in "Poetry and Imagination," *W*, VIII, 19.

[222] To the right below the last entry on this page is a pencil drawing of a bell within an arch.

[223] This paragraph is used in "Quotation and Originality," *W*, VIII, 189.

[224] Erased pencil writing covers the upper half of this page, of which the following significant words and phrases have been recovered: "So do we"; "give the less lively"; and "thereby indicate that".

[225] In *JMN*, III, 219, Emerson quoted a fuller form of the Latin from Sir Thomas Browne's *Hydriotaphia* (*Tracts* [London and Edinburgh, 1822], p. ix):

boulder of the European ledge; a spur of those Appennines on which Titian, Raphael, Paul Veronese, & Michel Angelo sat — cropping out here in this remote America ⟨&⟩ unlike anything around it, & not reaching its natural elevation. What a just piece of history it is that he should have left this great picture of Belshazzar *in two proportions!* The times are out of joint, & so is his masterpiece.[226]

Allston & Irving & Dana are all European[.]

[148] There is a genius ⟨to⟩ of a nation as of individuals which is not to be found in the numerical men but characterises the society. England, strong, practical, punctual, well-spoken England, I should not find, if I should go to the island to seek it; in parliament or in the play house or at dinner tables, I should see a great number of rich, ignorant, or book-read, conventional, proud men, many of them old women, and not the Englishman who made the good speeches, combined the accurate engines, & did the bold persistent deeds.[227]

But in America I grieve to miss the strong black blood of the English race: ours is a pale diluted stream. What a company of brilliant young persons I have seen with so much expectation! the sort is very good, but none is good enough of his sort. Every one ↑an↓ imperfect specimen,[n] respectable not valid. Irving thin, & Channing thin, & Bryant & Dana[,] Prescott & Bancroft. ⟨Then the youth as I said⟩There is Webster, but he cannot do what he [149] would; he cannot do Webster.[228] Then the youth, as I said, are all promising failures. No writing is here[,] no redundant strength, but declamation, straining, correctness, & all other symptoms of debility.

"Adamas de rupe veteri praestantissimus" — "a most excellent gem of the old rock" (Ed.). See *JMN*, IV, 434.
    [226] Allston, who died on July 9, 1843, left his giant canvas "Belshazzar's Feast" unfinished, although he had worked on it for over twenty years. It has *"two proportions"* in that Allston began, but never finished, a sweeping revision of its perspective. For "The times are out of joint," see Shakespeare, *Hamlet*, I, v, 189.
    [227] This paragraph, struck through in ink with a vertical use mark, is used in "Nominalist and Realist," *W*, III, 229–230.
    [228] This sentence, struck through in ink with two vertical use marks, is used in "Nominalist and Realist," *W*, III, 230.

The orientals behave well, but who cannot behave well who has nothing else to do? The poor Yankees who are doing the work, are all wrinkled & vexed.

The Shaker told me they did not read history not because they had not inclination for there were some who "took up a sound cross in not reading." Milton's "Paradise Lost," he knew, was ⟨in⟩among Charles Lane's books, but he had never read it.[229] Most of them did not know it was there; he knew. There would be an objection to reading it. They read the Bible & their own publications. They write their own poetry. "All their hymns & songs of every description are manufactured in the society."

[150][230]   The fervent class
How stands the grim question

As soon as a man comes to say, I am good, but you have not goodness enough to see me, the game is up.

⟨Rich man's dividend s⟩ [231]

Each man a tyrant in tendency, because he would impose his idea on others, and their *vis inertiae* is their natural defence. Jesus would else absorb the race: but Tom Paine & the coarsest blasphemer helps humanity by resisting this overpowering.[232]

Solitude of solitude

I suppose the money is only the costume of the thing, & that the evil ⟨exists⟩ would exist in another shape where money was not. If I see the state, I am guilty of the state[.] [233]

---

[229] After the collapse of Fruitlands, Lane lived for a time in the Shaker community at Harvard. The entry to this point is used in "Address at the Opening of the Concord Free Public Library," *W*, XI, 505.

[230] The entries on this page are in pencil. The fourth and fifth have been erased.

[231] See p. [81] above.

[232] This paragraph is used in "Nominalist and Realist," *W*, III, 239.

[233] Cross-hatching separates the two sentences of this entry, perhaps to cancel something.

In the most of men's parsimony or covetousness, so-called, it is the fact speaks, not they. They have just counted up their sums of income & expense & see the need of austere answers.

[151] There are no such men as we fable. No Jesus nor Caesar nor Angelo nor Washington nor Pericles such as we have made. And yet Plato's book is a greater reality than most men.[234]

[152] In the actual world, the population, we say, is the best that could yet be.[235] Its evils[,] as war & property, are acknowledged, which is a new fact, & the first step to the remedying of them. But the remedying is not a ⟨thing⟩work for society, but for me to do. If I am born to it, I shall see the way. ⟨Where there is a will, there is a way.⟩ If the evil is an evil to you, you are party, chief party to ⟨you⟩it. Say not, you are not covetous⟨n⟩, if the chief evil of the world seem to you covetousness. I am always environed by myself: what I am, all things reflect to me. The state of me makes Massachusetts & the United States out there. I also feel the evil, for I am covetous and I do not prosecute the reform ⟨|| ... ||⟩because I have another task nearer. I think substantial justice can be done maugre or through the money of society, and though it is an imperfect system & noxious, yet I do not know how to attack it directly, & am assured that the directest attack which I can make on it, is to lose no time in fumbling & striking about in all directions, but ⟨in⟩to mind ⟨my⟩ ↑the↓ work that is mine, and accept the facilities & openings which [153] my constitution affords me.

[154] Dante's praise is that he dared to write his auto-biography in colossal cipher & make it universal.
Genius is able to see through its milkpans, rent-roll, & tailor's bills, and ⟨ar⟩know that there is a law which dignifies these facts, and so it dares to use them as universal ciphers. It is too plain that we have had no genius yet in America; for our ⟨|| ... ||⟩shops, pastures, & fishing trade are all unsung.[236]

[234] This entry, in pencil and erased, is struck through in pencil with a vertical use mark.
[235] Cf. *JMN*, VIII, 362, and "Fate," *W*, VI, 16.
[236] These two paragraphs are struck through in pencil with two diagonal use

The Peace Society speaks civilly of Trade, in its attacks on
War. Well, let Trade make hay whilst the sun shines; but know
very well that when the war is disposed of, Trade is the next object
of incessant ⟨‖ ... ‖⟩attack[n] and has only the privilege of being last
devoured.[237]

[155] [blank]
[156] Very sad indeed it was to see this halfgod driven to the
wall, reproaching men, & ⟨a⟩hesitating whether he[n] should not reproach the gods.[238] The world was not, on trial, a possible element
for him to live in. A lover of law had tried whether law could be
kept in this world, & all things answered, NO. He had entertained
the thought of leaving it, & going where freedom & an element could
be found. And if he should be found tomorrow at the roadside, it
would be the act of the world. We pleaded guilty to perceiving the
inconvenience & inequality of property & he said "I will not be a
convict." Very tedious & prosing & egotistical & narrow he is, but a
profound insight, a Power, a majestical man, looking easily along
the centuries to explore *his contemporaries* with a painful sense of
being an orphan & a hermit here. I feel his statement to be partial
& to have fatal omissions, but I think I shall never attempt to set
him right any more. It is not for me to answer him: though I feel
the limitations & exaggeration of his picture, and the wearisome
personalities. [157] His statement proves too much: it is a *reductio
ad absurdum*. But I was quite ashamed to have just revised & printed
last week the old paper denying the existence of tragedy, when this
modern Prometheus was in the heat of his quarrel with the gods.[239]

Alcott has been writing poetry, he says, all winter. I fear there

marks, and in ink with a vertical use mark. The first paragraph is used and the second is paraphrased in "The Poet," W, III, 37-38.
    [237] The American Peace Society, founded in 1828, was the leading pacifist or-
ganization of the time.
    [238] Emerson indexed p. [156] under Alcott. The Fruitlands community had bro-
ken up in mid-January, 1844.
    [239] Emerson's "old paper," "The Tragic," *The Dial*, IV (April 1844), 515-
521, had originally been a lecture in the series on Human Life, first delivered in the
1838-1839 season.

is nothing for me in it. His overpowering personality destroys all poetic faculty[.]

It is strange that he has not the confidence of one woman. He would be greater if he were goodhumoured but such as he is he "enlarges the known powers of man," as was said of M. Angelo.[240]

A man sends to me for money ⟨to⟩that he may pursue his studies in theology; he wants fifty or sixty dollars, & says he wants it the "last of this week or fore part of next." —

[158] The man, — it is his system.

We do not consider ⟨the⟩ ↑a↓ word or act of a man, but only the legitimate results of his system. The acts which you praise, I praise not, since they are departures from his faith & law, & are mere compliances to the tyranny of another mind.[241]

What you say only distributes you in your group & class & section[.]

W[illiam]. G[reene?]. dreamed that he had disposed of books & the world in his fontal peace of mind — but did not well know what to do with the reply that the past has a new value every moment to the advancing mind.

W.G. came here & disproved his dogmas, for it was at once manifest that ⟨there was nothing⟩ ↑we had↓ little for each other.[242]

[159] I find it settled that while many persons have attraction for me, these styles are incompatible. Each is mine, but I love one, because it is not the other. What skepticism is like this? Hence the philosophers concluded that the Turk was right: Mahomet was right & Jesus was wrong.

I wish to have rural strength & religion for my children & I wish city facility & polish. I find with chagrin that I cannot have both.[243]

---

[240] This remark is used in "Michael Angelo," W, XII, 228.

[241] This and the following entry, struck through in ink with a vertical use mark, are used in "Nominalist and Realist," W, III, 228, 236.

[242] See p. [142] above.

[243] This entry is in pencil.

Carlo. I spent the winter in the country. Thickstarred Orion was my only companion. I preferred the forest, dry forest. Water made me feel forlorn.[244]

↑Inextinguishableness.↓[245]
Unhappily no knife is long enough to reach to the heart of any enemy we have. If what we hate was murderable, that would be some comfort.

[160] *Criticism.* The temperature of the day is determined by considering whether the basis of the temperature is cold or warm. We ↑have↓ warm winds with a cold basis, & cold gusts on a warm day. So it is in criticism: one has to determine first whether the basis of a speech or writing be living or dead. Coleridge & Dr [William Ellery] C[hanning]. & so many more men of celebrity are nothing but the Dr Porters & Dr Wares under warm & favorable exposures with all the Porterisms & Warisms carefully scraped off, so as to look as much like geniuses as they can.[246] But their popularity convicts them. The men of the generation have an instinct which indicates who threatens the stability of stocks.

Writers are so few that there are none: writing is an impossibility, until it is done. A man gives you his paper & hopes there is something in it, but ⟨he⟩does not know. There is nothing in it: do not open it. ⟨I⟩When a man makes ↑what he calls an↓ answer to a ↑speculative↓ question, he commonly changes the phrase of the question. But the only conversation we wish to hear is two affirmatives, and again two affirmatives, & so on.

[161] Able men ⟨‖ ... ‖⟩do not care ⟨that⟩ in what work a man is able, so only he is able. Men of talents think their work the best, ⟨as⟩ ↑whether↓ a geologist, a musician, a sportsman, a merchant, a

---

[244] In Notebook OP Gulistan, p. [101], Emerson identifies "Carlo" as Charles King Newcomb. "I spent . . . dry forest." is struck through in ink with a vertical use mark; "I spent . . . companion." is used in "Worship," *W*, VI, 235, where it is attributed to "Benedict," not "Carlo."

[245] This heading is enclosed above, below, and to the right by a continuous line.

[246] Ebenezer Porter (1772–1834) was the first president of Andover Theological Seminary; Henry Ware, Sr. (1764–1845) was professor of theology at Harvard.

preacher, but a master requires a master, & does not ask whether it be in a mill wright, a cutler, or an ideologist.[247]

I have read a proverb somewhere "— the cards beat all ↑the players↓ at last,"[n] which is as good a text as Eripitur persona, manet res, for my piece on the Genius of Life.[248]

An example of the prevailing genius over all wilfulness is the veracity of language which cannot be debauched. Proverbs, words, & grammar inflections are wiser than the wisest man.[249]

Character brings to whatever it does a great superfluity of strength which plays a gay accompaniment, the air with variations. Hear D[aniel] W[ebster] argue a ⟨petty⟩ ↑jury↓ cause. He imports all the experience of the senate & the state & the man of the world into the county court.

[162] C[aroline]. [Sturgis?] inquired why I would not go to B[erkshire?]? But the great inconvenience is sufficient answer. If I could freely & manly go to the mountains, or to the prairie, or to the sea, I would not hesitate for inconvenience: but to cart all my pots & kettles, kegs, & clothespins, ⟨over the mountains⟩ & all that belongs thereunto, over the mountains seems not worth while. I should not be nearer to sun or star.

The Genius is friendly to the noble and in the dark brings them friends from far. I had fancied my friend was unmatchable and now a stone is cut out from the mountain without hands, of miraculous virtues.[250]

---

[247] This paragraph, struck through in ink with a vertical use mark, is used in "Goethe," W, IV, 268.

[248] This sentence is struck through in ink with a wavy vertical use mark. In JMN, VI, 94, Emerson quotes a fuller version of the "proverb" from Abraham Tucker ("Edward Search"), perhaps from The Light of Nature Pursued; it is used in "Nominalist and Realist," W, III, 241. The Latin quotation is from Lucretius, De Rerum Natura, III, 57: "The mask is torn off, the man remains." See JMN, VI, 43.

[249] This paragraph, struck through in ink with a vertical use mark, is used in "Nominalist and Realist," W, III, 230–231.

[250] This paragraph occurs in an earlier pencil version, later erased, at the bot-

"My dear sir," said my friend to her suitor, "I cannot realize you." [251]

[163] Sunday, April 14, 3 P.M. After more than a week of finest weather, the mercury stands now at 82° in the shade.

May ⟨9⟩8. This morn the air smells of vanilla & oranges[.] [252]

Let us guard our strangeness, & if our relations lose something of tenderness let them gain in nobility[.]

Let us sit apart as the gods talking from peak to peak all round Olympus.

[164] [253] Our people are slow to learn the wisdom of sending character instead of talent to Congress. Again & again they have sent a man of great acuteness, a fine scholar, a fine forensic orator, and some master of the brawls has crunched him up in his hand like a bit of paper. At last they sent a man with a back and he defied the whole southern delegation when they attempted to smother him & has conquered them. Mr Adams is a man of great powers, but chiefly he is a sincere man & not a man of the moment and of a ↑single↓ measure. And besides the success or failure of the measure there remains to him the respect of all men for his earnestness. [254] When Mr Webster argues the case there is the success or the failure, and the admiration of the unerring talent & intellectual nature[,] but no respect for an affection to a principle. Could Mr Webster have given

---

tom of p. [163], with "I concluded" for "I had fancied" and "fitness" for "virtues". The first sentence, struck through in ink with a vertical use mark, is used in "Worship," *W*, VI, 231.

[251] This sentence occurs in pencil, later erased, on p. [163], above the entry beginning "Let us sit apart as the gods . . ."

[252] This line is in pencil, as are the two following entries, which were later erased.

[253] The entries on this and the following page are in pencil. The one at the bottom of p. [165] was later erased.

[254] John Quincy Adams's long fight for the repeal of the "gag rule," which forbade any discussion of the issue of slavery in the House of Representatives, ended with repeal of the rule in 1844.

himself to the cause of Abolition of Slavery in Congress, he would
have been the darling of this continent[,] of all the youth, all the
genius, all the virtue in America. Had an angel whispered in his
young ear,[n] Never mind the newspapers, ⟨Give yourself⟩ Fling yourself on this principle of freedom, Show [165][255] the legality of freedom[;] though they frown & bluster they are already half convinced
& at last you shall have their votes[;] the tears of the love & joy
& pride of the world would have been his[.]

George B[ancroft]'s conundrums

> Why is sympathy like blindman's buff
> Why was Charles I's execution consented to
> Why was Neptune like an alchemist
> Why was Noah like a bad mouser

It is perfectly natural that men of feeble intellect & faltering
virtue should roar[?] [1–2 w] for the union as their[?] only safe-
guard[;] they owe their safety to the joint stock of virtue[,] to the
virtue of all the others[,] not to their own. But not so the wise &
the just[;] they always protect themselves[,] they need never exaggerate the importance of any particular law for they give it all
its strength[,] & if it falls tomorrow they remain & can give their
strength to a new & better one. What is the meaning of this distrust
of the people[?]

[166][256] What I would ask of every man is, Is there method in
your consciousness? Does the taper light of the present moment

---

[255] Erased pencil writing, apparently three separate entries, covers most of this
page. Of the first two entries, the following significant words and phrases have been
recovered or conjecturally recovered: "very well"; "derision and contempt[?]"; "a
right to their opinion"; "blaspheme"; "truth"; "to expose falsehood"; "to supply
the deficiency of the"; "this state is drowsy &"; "enough"; "because he under";
"gentleman"; and "the law". The third, beginning "It is perfectly natural . . .", is
printed below.

[256] Erased pencil writing, apparently two separate entries, covers this page. The
following significant words and phrases have been recovered: "Brook Farm" (a
heading); "shed a ray over"; and "be a deluge of dulness".

shed a ray over proportion or over stupefaction? Can you even see tendency?

God, the moral element[,] must ever be new, an electric spark, then it agitates & deifies us. The instant ⟨there is too much of it, the instant⟩ when it is fixed & made chronic, it is hollowness & cant. It is the difference between poets & preachers.[257]

"I was always used to quick people," said Mrs H.; and Aunt M[ary]. said with such bitter emphasis, "I am tired of fools." [258]

Wherever a squirrel or a bee can go with security, I can go, said Robin[.] [259]

Belinda Randall's music taught us what a song should be: how slight & thin its particular meaning.[260]

[167][261]
[168] [Index material omitted]
[169] [blank]
[170][262]
[inside back cover] [Index material omitted]

[257] "there is too much of it, the instant" is canceled in pencil.
[258] For Aunt Mary's remark, see *JMN*, VII, 30.
[259] Emerson referred to himself at least once as "Robin"; see *JMN*, VIII, 33. This sentence is used in "Worship," *W*, VI, 235.
[260] In a letter of May 10, 1844, George William Curtis wrote "For the last three evenings I have been in the village, hearing Belinda Randall play and sing . . . Last night I saw her at Mr. Hoar's, only herself and Miss E. Hoar, G. P. Bradford, Mr. and Mrs. Emerson, and myself and Mr. Hoar. She played Beethoven, sang the 'Adelaide Serenade,' 'Fischer Madchen,' 'Amid this Green Wood' " (*Early Letters of George Wm. Curtis to John S. Dwight*, ed. George Willis Cooke (New York and London, 1898), pp. 185-186.
[261] Erased pencil writing, consisting of at least two separate entries, covers the upper half of this page. The following significant words and phrases have been recovered or conjecturally recovered: "Belinda Randall's music taught me ↑better than the↓ what a song ‖ . . . ‖ slight & thin its particular meaning" (in ink, p. [166]); "of the people"; "instead of"; "curious[?] mob shall speak[?] up"; "cut all our throats & fire all our houses"; "charitable"; "Brothers of Charity preferred"; "oppressed But"; "we all know"; "the people"; and "dissolved[?]".
[262] A preliminary index, in pencil and erased, covers this page.

V

1844–1845

Journal V covers the period from May, 1844, to March, 1845, but its chronology is irregular, material from the two years overlapping frequently. Interior evidence shows that it was used very heavily in January, 1845, when Emerson was involved in a number of concurrent projects: fighting to allow Wendell Phillips to speak at the Concord Lyceum; attending the Texas Convention in Boston; preparing a speech for a meeting protesting the expulsion of Samuel Hoar from South Carolina; and reading and writing extensively for his lecture on Napoleon, first delivered in the spring of 1845 and later included in the Representative Men series. It also contains lengthy passages used in Emerson's address "Emancipation in the British West Indies," delivered August 1, 1844.

The copybook is of the same type used for Journal U, except that its spine strip is dark green instead of light brown. The letter "V" is written on the spine, and the notations "V V 1844" appear on the front cover.

Originally there were 164 lightly ruled pages, plus two flyleaves at both front and back, but the leaves bearing pages 33–36, 97–98, 127–128, 145–146, and 163–164 are missing. Most of the pages are numbered in ink, but sixteen pages are numbered in pencil: 1, 3, 9, 56, 74, 77, 140, 144, 148, 154, 157, 158, 160, and 168–170, and thirteen pages are unnumbered: 2, 13, 38, 69, 75, 79, 121, 141, 143, 149, 155, 156, and 159. Pages 84, 90, and 142 were first numbered in pencil, then in ink. Page 131 was originally numbered 132. Three pages are blank: 85, 148, and 149.

A sheet of faintly lined blue paper measuring 12.6 x 20.2 cm and bearing jottings in Emerson's hand is laid in between pages 156–157; it has been numbered 156$_a$–156$_b$.

[front cover]   V   V
                                  1844

[front cover verso] [1]
1845. Tuesday, 22 July, Middlebury College
       Wednesday, 6 August Wesleyan University, Harrington, Ct.[2]

[Index material omitted]

[i]   R. W. Emerson.
                           V

          But Jove was the eldest born & knows most.
                         Homer. [*Iliad*, XIII, 355][3]

                         1844

          "How finely dost thou times & seasons spin,
          And make a twist chequered with night & day!
          Which, as it lengthens, winds, & winds us in;
          As bowls go on, but turning all the way."
                         Herbert. ["Providence," ll. 57–60]

                         —

          "Concordia res parvae crescunt." [4]

                         —

[ii][5] [Index material omitted]

    [1] A list of lecture engagements for the 1844–1845 season, written in pencil and
later erased, is still visible on parts of the front cover verso. A circle of red sealing
wax in the upper left-hand corner indicates that something was once attached thereto — perhaps a calendar, as on the front cover verso of Journal O.
    [2] Emerson read the same address, on the role of the scholar, on both of these
occasions. Never printed, "Discourse at Middlebury College" was later mined for
various lectures and essays. The major portion survives in "The Scholar," prepared
by James Elliot Cabot for delivery at the University of Virginia in 1876 and printed
in *W*, X, 259–289.
    [3] Quoted by Thomas Taylor in *The Works of Plato* . . . , trans. Floyer Syden-
ham and Thomas Taylor, 5 vols. (London, 1804), V, 700, and in *The Commentaries of Proclus on the Timaeus of Plato* . . . , trans. Thomas Taylor, 2 vols.
(London, 1820), II, 426. Both works are in Emerson's library. See Journal W,
p. [80] below.
    [4] "Harmony makes small states great." Sallust, *The War with Jugurtha*, X, 6.
    [5] The poetry on this and the next page is in pencil.

⟨To & fro the Genius ⟨flies⟩ hies⟩
⟨A light now hovering⟩

[1]   To & fro the Genius hies
⟨The genius comes & goes⟩
A light which ⟨dances⟩ plays & hovers
Over the loved head
And dips sometimes so low as to her eyes

⟨Weakness⟩
Of her faults I take no note
⟨Weakness⟩ ↑Fault↓ & folly ⟨‖ ... ‖⟩ ↑are not↓ mine
Comes the Genius all's forgot
Replunged again into that upper sphere
She scatters wide & wild its lustres here [6]

[Index material omitted]

[2] Taylor adduces Archimedes as a Platonist because of Plutarch's account of him in life of Marcellus, "that A. considered the being busied about mechanics & in short every art which is connected with the common purposes of life as ignoble & illiberal, & that those things alone were objects of his ambition, with which the beautiful & the excellent were present unmingled with the necessary." See "Gen. Introd." [*The Works of Plato,* 1804,] Vol I. p. lxxxv.

"I conduct the reader thro' novel & solitary paths, solitary, indeed, they must be, since they have been unfrequented from the reign of the Emperor Justinian to the present time; & novel, doubtless, to readers of every description, & particularly to those who have been nursed, as it were, in the bosom of matter, the pupils of *Experiment,* darlings of sense, & legitimate descendants of the earthborn race that warred on the Olympian Gods." p. lxx⟨x⟩ix ↑Lamb↓[7] These

[6] The first four uncanceled lines occur as ll. 35–38 of the second section ("The Daemonic Love") of "Initial, Daemonic, and Celestial Love," *W*, IX, 110. All nine uncanceled lines occur in "Fragments on Nature and Life," XVI, *W*, IX, 352.

[7] This word is written above the Roman numerals in pencil, probably by Emerson.

are [3]⁸ they, in Taylor's mind, whose whole life is a sleep, "a transmigration from dream to dream, like   men passing from bed to bed." He contrasts ever the knowledge of Experiment, with that of abstract Science: the former is the cause of a mighty calamity to the soul, extinguishing her principal & brightest eye, the knowledge of divinity. One makes piety, the other atheism.

There can be no ↑other↓ remedy for this enormous evil, than the philosophy of Plato.——[*Ibid.*, I, lxxix, lxxxiii–lxxxiv]

—"The fellows of New College (Oxford) with whom I resided for three weeks, & from whom I experienced even Grecian hospitality" [*Ibid.*, I,] p cxi
"With respect to the faults of this translation I might plead as an excuse that the whole of it has been executed amidst severe endurance from bodily infirmity & indigent circumstances, & that a considerable part of it was accomplished amidst other ills of no common magnitude, & other labours inimical to such an undertaking. But whatever be my errors, I will not fly to calamity as an apology. Let it be my excuse, that the mistakes I may have committed in lesser particulars, have arisen from my eagerness to seize & promulgate [4]⁹ those great truths in the philosophy & theology of Plato, which, tho' they have been concealed for ages in oblivion, have a subsistence coeval with the universe, & will be again restored, & flourish for very extended periods thro' all the infinite revolutions of time." [*Ibid.*, I,] p cxi.

Then follow Taylor's rich apostrophes to the stupid & experimental — "Abandon, then, ye grovelling souls," &c &c[.] [*Ibid.*, I, cxiv]

Thomas Taylor died at Walworth near London 1 Nov. 183⟨7⟩5 aged 77. He was born in London in 1758, & learned the rudiments of Latin & Greek at St Paul's School. His publications comprize

---

⁸ Erased pencil writing, consisting of a number of separate entries, covers the upper two-thirds of this page. The following significant words and phrases have been recovered or conjecturally recovered: "Essays" (perhaps a heading); "Poets,"; "Life" (perhaps a heading); "In our recipe the ingredients are"; "we drink the"; "exquisitely"; "nourished, & without"; "repentance"; and "Temperament is the last form this most poetic" (see p. [24] below).

⁹ "Thomas Taylor died . . . p. cvii of Taylors Introd." actually occurs first on this page and is separated by a long rule from the conclusion of the passage on p. [3].

23 vols 4to & 40 vols. 8vo. He translated Aristotle, Plato, Proclus, Plotinus, Pausanias, Iamblichus, Porphyry,[10]

"Of the ten dialogues translated by Dacier I can say nothing with accuracy, because I have no knowledge whatever of the French language." [*Ibid.*, I,] p. cvii of Taylor's Introd.[11]

[5] Taylor tilts against some notable windmills, as, e.g., the Copernican theory.

Man is that noble endogenous plant which grows from within outwards, but nature also has pleased herself in modern ages with the production of dicotyledonous creatures[.] [12]

T. Taylor & his works — See J 80   K 121 [13]

"though I have from lonely youth laughed at what others cry" M.M.E.[14]

↑Tom Appleton Beckford↓[15]

Beckford's Italy & Spain is the book of a Sybarite of the Talleyrand, Brummel, Vivian Grey school written in 1787–9,[16] and much of the humor consists in the contrast between the volume of this Johnson-&-Gibbon ⟨style⟩ sentence ⟨with⟩ and the ball-room petulance it expresses. He delights in classic antiquity; in sunsets as associated with that mythology; in music[;] in picturesque nature. He is only a dilettante, and before the humblest original worker would feel the

---

[10] "Thomas Taylor . . . St Paul's School." is struck through in pencil with a diagonal use mark.

[11] This entry is struck through in pencil with a diagonal use mark.

[12] This entry is in pencil. "Man is that . . . outwards," is used in "Uses of Great Men," *W*, IV, 6. See p. [12] below.

[13] *JMN*, VIII, 171 and 243.

[14] This entry is in pencil.

[15] Thomas Gold Appleton (1812–1884), a Boston wit whom Emerson got to know well in the 1850's when both were members of the Saturday Club, toured Europe with the same kind of exuberant dilettantism Emerson detected in Beckford.

[16] William Beckford, *Italy, with Sketches of Spain and Portugal*, 2 vols. (London, 1834), was withdrawn from the Boston Athenaeum February 13–24, 1845. The statements about the Duomo in Florence and Veronese's *Cana in Galilee* occur in I, 106–107, and 180–181.

rebuke of a solid domestic being as of a creator of that classic world, which he only gazes at, but lays no stone of ⁿ ↑it.↓ He would affect contempt, but his confidence would be the great foolish multitude, [6] and that steads him not; for when a man has once met his master, that is a secret which he cannot keep. Yet the travellers why should we blame any more than the thousands who stay at home to do less, or worse?

He loves twilight, & sleep.

Many of his criticisms are excellent. He says of the Duomo at Florence that the architect seems to have turned his church inside out, such is the ornate exterior & so simple is the interior. He says ⟨|| . . . ||⟩of Paul Veronese's Cana in Galilee, that the people at the table seem to be decent persons accustomed to miracles.

In sleeping figures he likes sculpture best.

[7] Ole Bull a dignifying civilizing influence. Yet he was there for exhibition, not for music; for the wonders of his execution, not as St. Cecilia incarnated, who would be there to carry a point, & degrading all her instruments into meekest means. Yet he played as a man who found a violin in his hand, & so was bent to make much of that; but if he ↑had↓ found a chisel or a sword or a spyglass or a troop of boys, would have made much of them. It was a beautiful spectacle. I have not seen an artist with manners so pleasing. What a sleep as of Egypt on his lips in the midst of his rapturous music! [17]

We are impressed by a Burke or a Schiller who believes in embodying in practice ideas; because literary men, for the most part, who are cognisant of ideas, have a settled despair as to the realization of ideas in their own times.

In Boston, I trod the street a little proudly, that I could walk from ↑Allston's↓ *Belshazzar's Feast* to the sculpture Gallery, & sit before

---

[17] In a letter to Margaret Fuller on June 3, 1844, Emerson writes that he was "very glad to hear the wonderful [Norwegian] violinist", who held several concerts in Boston in late May (*L*, III, 252). This entry and the two others on p. [7] were written first in pencil and later erased when they had been copied in ink. A few minor differences are discernible between the two versions.

Michel Angelo's "Day & Night,"[18] & the Antiques; then into the Library; then to Ole Bull.

[8] We want deference and when we come to realize that thing mechanically we want acres. Scatter this hot ⟨&⟩ crowded population at respectful distances each ⟨man⟩ from ⟨the rest⟩ ↑each↓, over the vacant world. Lane & his friends thought the cattle made all this wide space necessary, and that if there were no cows to pasture, less land would suffice. ⟨But my eyes need more land than a cow between me & my neighbour.⟩ But a cow does not need so much land as my eyes require between me & my neighbour.[19]

The poorer class encrusts itself over with vulgarity to deaden the force of those insults & wrongs it has to suffer, as the cuticle of the foot thickens itself to a callus to bear the continual rude friction ⟨to⟩ which ⟨it⟩ falls to its share.

[9] Our solemn church music, I am told, is often made by the common street tunes like "Molly put the kettle on," or "Get out, old Dan Tucker," played to a slow time. So is there ⟨sentence⟩ no admirable sentence, the last result of the subtlest mind, but is already current in some foul adage in the market.

For economy it ⟨needs⟩ is not sufficient that you make now & then a sharp reduction, or that you deny yourself & your family to meanness things ⟨in⟩within their system of expense; but it needs a constant eye to the whole. You yourself must ⟨‖ ... ‖⟩be always present throughout your system. You must hold the reins in your own hands, & not trust to your horse. ↑The farm must be a system, a circle, or its economy is naught; and the fantastic farmers piece out their omissions with cunning.↓

The effect of these calamitous pictures of Pauperism which

[18] The exhibition of sculpture and painting in the Boston Athenaeum's art gallery on Pearl Street included Horatio Greenough's reproductions of Michelangelo's statues of "Day" and "Night" on the tomb of Giuliano de' Medici in Florence. See *JMN*, VII, 284.
[19] "Lane & his friends . . . neighbour." is used in "Country Life," *W*, XII, 148.

obtrude every where[,] even in the comic literature, in Punch & Judy, in Hood & Dickens suggests an admonition not so much to charity as to economy, that we may be selfcontained & ready, when the calamity comes nearer, to do our part.

[10]²⁰ Fourier is a French mind, destitute of course of the moral element. Brisbane, his American disciple, is also a French mind. The important query is *what will women say to the Theory?* Certainly not Brisbane but Channing must propose it to them. These are military minds, and their conversation is always insulting; for they have no other end than to make a tool of their companion.

I think Genius alone finishes.

Classifying words outvalue many arguments; upstart, cockney, granny, pedant, prig, precisian, rowdy, niggers,

[11]²¹ Goethe with his extraordinary breadth of experience & culture, the security with which, like a great continental gentleman, he looks impartially over all literatures of the mountains, the provinces, & the sea, and avails himself of the best in all, contrasts with the rigour of the English, & superciliousness & flippancy of the French. His perfect taste, the austere felicities of his style.
It is ⟨‖ . . . ‖⟩ delightful to find our own thought in so great a man.

[12]   Here lies Sir Jenkin Grout
         who loved his friend and tormented his enemy

²⁰ Erased pencil writing, consisting of three or more separate entries, covers the upper two-thirds of this page. The following significant words and phrases have been recovered or conjecturally recovered: "Manichee" (a heading); "Life", "talent to", and "falls asleep" (apparently all one entry); "I think Genius alone finishes" (traced in ink); "I think the Catholic" and "he thinks the Church have that which the member has not" (apparently one entry); and "A few", "many arguments[?]", "granny, small", and "precisian[?]" (apparently a version of the last ink entry on the page).

²¹ Erased pencil writing, apparently a number of separate entries, covers most of this page. The following significant words and phrases have been recovered or conjecturally recovered: "Bruiser &[?] bully" (perhaps a heading); "true; I will bleed"; "The true gentleman"; "exclude"; "excluded"; "men, cannot be"; "it is[?] in[?] vain[?] to fortify against him; he has the"; "myself[?] as him"; and "Gentleman respects the[?] beautiful".

What his mouth ate his hand paid for
What his followers robbed he restored [22]

↑*Life*↓

All we have to do, said B., is to draw in the breath, & then to blow it out again.[23]

Men are excellent in their own way by means of not apprehending the gift of another.

It is the unhappy necessity of man that he cannot look at any one object without looking from all other objects in the universe[.]

———

You have faith, for you are fearless.[n]

———

Man is that noble endogenous plant which grows from within outwards, but nature also has pleased herself in modern ages with the production of dicotyledonous creatures.[24]

[13] "There is in every man a feeling agreeing with this, that he has been what he is from all eternity, & by no means first become such in time." *Schelling.*[25]

[14][26] ⟨His⟩ ↑H[enry]. [Thoreau]'s↓ conversation consisted of a con-

———

[22] These lines were written in pencil and later erased. They are used in "Manners," *W*, III, 145.

[23] This sentence, struck through in ink with two vertical use marks, is used in "Considerations by the Way," *W*, VI, 247.

[24] See p. [5] above.

[25] Emerson may have found this statement in James Elliot Cabot's translation of Schelling's *Philosophische Untersuchungen über das Wesen der menschlichen Freiheit*, the manuscript of which he kept for well over a year. It does not appear that the translation was ever published, despite Emerson's efforts in its behalf (*L*, III, 293, 343, 345, 346). The quotation, struck through in ink with two vertical use marks, is used in "Fate," *W*, VI, 13.

[26] An apparently consecutive passage in erased pencil runs from the top of p. [14] through the first line on p. [17]. The following significant words and phrases have been recovered or conjecturally recovered: on p. [14], "fair picture"; "with its less"; "I have"; "find[?] a private effect"; "effect on[?] months & years in"; "not annoyed"; "superabundance[?]"; "my body"; "The first day"; "overran"; on p. [15], "contemplate[?]"; "life, and"; "I think; I"; "But I have not found that much was gained by manipular attempts to realize the"; "& all make themselves rides"; "history of"; "example of success. I own this is a base way to prejudge our

tinual coining of the present moment into a sentence & offering it ↑to↓ me. I compared it to a boy who from the universal snow lying on the earth gathers up a little in his hand, rolls it into a ball, & flings it at me.

In January 184⟨3⟩5 arose the question again in our village Lyceum whether we should accept the offer of the Ladies who proposed to contribute to the Course a Lecture on Slavery by Wendell Phillipps. I pressed the acceptance on the part of the Curators of this proffer, on two grounds; 1. because the Lyceum was poor, & should add to the length & variety of their Entertainment by all innocent means, especially when a discourse from one of the best speakers in the Commonwealth was volunteered; 2. because I thought in the present state of this country the particular subject of Slavery [15] had a commanding right to be heard in all places in New England in season & sometimes out of season, that[,] as in Europe the partition of Poland was an outrage so flagrant that all European men must be willing once in every month or two to be plagued with hearing over again the horrid story; so this iniquity of Slavery in this country was a ghost that would not down at the bidding of Boston merchants, or the best democratic drill-officers; but the people must consent to be plagued with it from time to time until something was done, & we had appeased the negro blood so.[27]

The proposition was later made to have a Lyceum supplied by enthusiasts only.

---

own experiment, by adducing experience against the Law, & so speaking the words of despair; I speak this only polemically, in"; on p. [16], "reply to the inquiry 'Why not realize your"; "Curiosity"; "You must"; "weighing the"; "eat or to sleep"; "conceive[?] a hope[?]"; "the light"; "which keep"; "never converge. We split[?]"; "our dinners[?]"; "but these"; "on us, are"; "but in the solitude"; "every man"; "has a sanity &"; "his passage"; "world"; on p. [17], "will carry with him."

[27] The records of the Concord Lyceum show that on March 5, 1845, Phillips, who had lectured on slavery in the two previous seasons, was again invited to speak, by a vote of 21 to 15. Two curators, Barzillai Frost and John S. Keyes, resigned in protest, and Emerson, Thoreau, and Samuel Barrett were chosen to replace them. Phillips delivered his lecture on March 11. "Out of place" is written above this entry, with a hand sign pointing downward, and in the left margin, both times in pencil.

We want a Lyceum just as much as a shoe-shop. It must be boundless in its hospitality.

Aristo compared lectures to baths[.] [28]

[16] The finest women have a feeling we cannot sympathize with in regard to marriage. They cannot spare the exaltation of love & the experiences of marriage from their history. But shall a virgin descend & marry below her? Does she not see that Nature may be trusted for completing her own circle?[n] The true Virgin will raise herself by just degrees into a goddess admirable & helpful to all beholders.

[17] H.D.T. said that the other world was all his art; that his pencils would draw no other; that his jackknife would cut nothing else. He does not use it as a means.[29]

⟨H.⟩ ↑Henry↓ is a good substantial childe, not encumbered with himself. He has no troublesome memory, ⟨but⟩ no wake, but lives extempore, & brings today a new proposition as radical & revolutionary as that of yesterday, but different. The only man of leisure in the town. He is a good Abbot Samson: & carries counsel in his breast. If I cannot show his performance much more manifest than that of the other grand promisers,[n] ⟨I⟩at least I can see that with his practical faculty, he has declined all the kingdoms of this world. Satan has no bribe for him.[30]

[18][31] In America we are such rowdies in church & state, and

[28] See *JMN*, VIII, 357, where Emerson copied the text of Aristo's statement as given by Montaigne in "Of Vanity," *Essays of Michael Seigneur de Montaigne . . .*, 1693, III, 339.

[29] This paragraph, an earlier erased pencil version of which is still discernible under the ink version, is struck through in pencil with a diagonal use mark and used in "Thoreau," *W*, X, 464.

[30] This paragraph is struck through in pencil with two diagonal use marks; "He has no . . . breast." is used in "Historic Notes of Life and Letters in New England," *W*, X, 356–357. Abbot Samson, a sturdy, simple monk, is the hero of Carlyle's *Past and Present* (1843).

[31] Erased pencil writing occurs at the top of the page, of which the following significant words and phrases have been recovered or conjecturally recovered: "I do

the very boys are so soon ripe, that I think no philosophical skepticism will make much sensation. Spinosa pronounced that there was but one substance; — yea, verily; but that boy yonder told me yesterday he thought the pinelog was God, & that God was in the jakes. What can Spinoza tell the boy? [32]

Even Dickens is doubtless of much use to this country, though in so humble a way as to circulate into all towns & into the lowest classes the lesson which is pasted in the waterclosets of public houses, — *Do not spit, & please close the covers.*

In America, fusion.

What a mistake is the universal usage of statesmen here to make long papers, as the Presidents' & Governors' messages, Addresses of Conventions, &c. What care our rowdy people for a constitutional argument? Cannot you give a short reason?

[19] Poetry has never dived. It hovers opaline about the brighter surfaces, but ⟨never⟩ ↑rarely↓ ventures into the real world. How pungent are the words that once in an age or two record those experiences.[33]

Fourier has the immense merits of originality & hope. Whilst society is distracted with disputes concerning the negro race, he comes to prescribe the methods of removing this mask & caricature of humanity, by bringing out the true & real form from underneath.

———

not live with people in ideal relations yet I"; "often"; "happiness[?]"; and "should depart[?]".

[32] An earlier pencil version of this entry, later erased, covers the upper half of p. [19]. The pencil version began "I hear this clatter[?] of opinion & hear of Spinoza & Hegel & Kant. But in America . . . " and had "will ever make much" for "will make much" and "What can Spinoza add[?]" for "What can Spinoza tell".

[33] An earlier pencil version of this entry, later erased, occurs in the middle of p. [19]. The pencil version had "into the world ventures never" for "rarely ventures into the real world."

In America, we drag a pine-log to a mill, turn a crank, & it comes out at the other end chairs & tables.[34]

———

[20][35] Whenever Heaven sends a great man into the world, it whispers the secret to one or two confidants.[36]

↑In↓ ⟨T⟩the woods with their ever festal look I am ever reminded of ⟨by⟩ that parable which commends the merchant who, seeing a pearl of great price, sold all to buy that:[37] so I could not find it in my heart to chide the Yankee who should ruin himself to buy a patch of heavy-timbered oak-land. I admire the taste which makes the a⟨c⟩venue to a house[,] were ⟨it⟩ ↑the house↓ ever so small, through a wood, as it disposes the mind of guest & host alike to ↑the↓ deference due to each. Hail vegetable gods!

[21][38] I observe two classes very easily among those capable of thought & spiritual life, namely, those who are very intelligent of this matter, & can rise easily into it on the call of conversation, & can write strongly of it, & secondly those who think nothing else & live on that level & are conscious of no effort or even variety in experience.

Life is made up of the interlude & interlabor of these two amicable worlds. We are amphibious & weaponed to live in both. We have two sets of faculties[,] the particular & the catholic[,] like a boat furnished with wheels ⟨in⟩ for land & water travel[.]

It is never strange[,] an ⟨odd⟩ ↑unfit↓ marriage, since man is the child of this most impossible marriage[,] this of the two worlds.

[34] This sentence is struck through in ink with a diagonal use mark.
[35] Erased pencil writing covers the upper half of this page. It consists of an earlier inscription of the entry on p. [54] beginning "In every profound conversation", an entry containing the word "judge", and the notation "The *farm*   The Brighton drover" (see Journal U, p. [146] above).
[36] This sentence, struck through in ink with a vertical use mark, is used in "Uses of Great Men," *W*, IV, 32.
[37] Cf. Matt. 13:45–46.
[38] The entries on this page are in pencil.

[22] It is strange that Jesus is esteemed by mankind the bringer of the doctrine of immortality. He is never once weak or sentimental: he never preaches the personal immortality; whilst Plato & Cicero had both allowed themselves to overstep the stern limits of the Spirit & gratify the people with that picture.[39]

The Lyceum gives opportunity for Mr Hudson & other writers to read their impatient thoughts; [40] but it also immediately ⟨makes⟩ constitutes a mark at which young men write: a mark or rather a market. The Lyceum should refuse all such pieces as w⟨ri⟩ere written *to* it.

I.S. wrote to L. that the Lord gives but never takes away.

[23]   Von Raumer   Goethe Nachg. Werke vol 5 p 415 [41]

↑*Behmen*↓

I read a little in Behmen.[42] In reading there is a sort of half & half mixture. The book must be good, but the reader must also be active. I have never had good luck with Behmen before today. And now I see that his excellence is in his comprehensiveness, not like Plato in his precision. His propositions are vague, inadequate, & straining. It is his aim that is great. He will know not one thing, but all things. He is like those great swaggering country geniuses that come now & then down from New Hampshire to college & soon demand to learn not Horace & Homer but also Euclid and Spinoza, and Voltaire, and Palladio, & Columbus, & Bonaparte, and Linnaeus.

[39] This paragraph, struck through in pencil with a vertical use mark, is used in "Immortality," *W*, VIII, 348.

[40] Henry Norman Hudson, later a famous Shakespearean scholar, read a lecture on *Macbeth* in Concord on January 1, 1845.

[41] This line is in pencil. Goethe's review of Friedrich von Raumer's *Geschichtliche Entwicklung der Begriffe von Recht, Staat und Politik* appears in volume 45 of the *Werke*, 1828–1833, volumes 41–55 of which are volumes 1–15 of the *Nachgelassene Werke*.

[42] Emerson's library contains *The Works of Jacob Behmen, the Teutonic Philosopher . . . With figures, illustrating his principles, left by the Reverend William Law . . .*, 4 vols. (London, 1764–1781), and *Aurora . . .* (London, 1656).

wheat & rye   railroads & cocks & hens [43]

I read in him today this sentence[:] "Men do with truths as children
with birds, either they crush them or they let them fly away."
    again[:] "This new wine made the bottle new."
Of Adam — "His bones were strengths."
"Thus hath this rose of Sharon perfumed our graves." [44]
See an important mystic sentence p 166 [177 Theos. Quest.]
Of *Woman.* "The temptation might take hold of her most readily
being herself a kind of temptation."

[24] Jacob ↑Behmen↓ is a great man, but he accepted the accommo-
dations of the Hebrew Dynasty.
Of course he cannot take rank with the masters of the world. His
value like that of Proclus is chiefly for rhetoric.

The Imagination is central. Fancy is superficial. The Imagination
joins what God has joined, or uses a necessary classification. The
Fancy joins by accidental resemblance and surprises & amuses the
vacant. It is silent in the presence of the great. [45]

                    ↑Theory & Practice↓
Life. In our recipe, the ingredients are separately named, but in the
cup ↑which↓ we drink, the elements are exquisitely mixed; the
heart & head are both nourished, & without fumes or repentance. [46]
    ↑Copied in *S.* [p. 86]↓

Temperament is the last form this most poetic spirit took[,] the self-
imposed limitation. [47]

---

[43] This line is in pencil.
[44] See p. [28] below.
[45] This paragraph, struck through in pencil with two vertical use marks, is used
in "Poetry and Imagination," *W*, VIII, 28–29.
[46] This paragraph is struck through in pencil with a diagonal use mark. "Theory
& Practice" and "Copied in *S.*" are in pencil.
[47] After the word "took" has been added ", — " in pencil, perhaps by Emerson.

[25] Religion must always be a crab: it cannot be grafted & keep its wild beauty.[48]

———

Our greatest debt to Woman is of a musical character, & not describable. Harriet Martineau solved the problem of Woman by describing a man! [49]

Society is babyish[.] [50]

"Many demands makes Destiny on ↑a↓ Prince⟨s⟩ which are only to be answered by his humanity: are these heeded, there follow higher demands which are to be answered by his princeliness; and on these mounts the genius of humanity & makes demands which his divinity must answer." Bettine [51]

Woman. It is the worst of her condition that its advantages are permissive. Society lives on the system of money and woman comes at money & money's worth through compliment. I should not dare to be woman. Plainly they are created for that better system which supersedes money. But today, ——— In our civilization her position is often pathetic. What is she not expected to do & suffer for some invitation to strawberries & cream. Mercifully their eyes are holden that they cannot see.[52]

[26] Pythagoras was right who used music as a medicine.[53] I lament my want of ear, but never quite despair of becoming sensible to this discipline. We cannot spare any stimulant or any purgative, we lapse

[48] This sentence, struck through in ink with a vertical use mark, is used in "Worship," *W*, VI, 214. See p. [51] below.

[49] See *JMN*, VIII, 381.

[50] This sentence, struck through in ink with a vertical use mark, is used in "Discourse at Middlebury College," "Wealth," *W*, VI, 92, and "The Scholar," *W*, X, 280. See p. [45] below.

[51] Emerson's library contains two editions of Bettina von Arnim's *Goethe's Correspondence with a Child* . . . , 3 vols. (London, 1839) and 2 vols. (Lowell, 1841); two editions of *Die Gunderöde* . . . (Boston, 1842, an incomplete translation by Margaret Fuller), and 2 vols. (Grünberg and Leipzig, 1840); and *Dies Buch Gehört dem König* (Berlin, 1843). This entry is in pencil.

[52] With the last sentence, cf. Luke 24:16.

[53] Cf. *Iamblichus' Life of Pythagoras*, 1818, pp. 43–44 and 80, and *JMN*, VII, 424–425.

so quickly into flesh & sleep. We must use all the exalters that will bring us into an expansive & productive state, or to the top of our condition. But to hear music, as one would take an ice-cream or a bath, & to forget it the next day, gives me a humble picture.

"Those men occupy my place." [54]

Of what use is genius, if ⟨it is too⟩ the organ is too convex or too concave, & cannot find a focal distance within the actual horizon. Of what use if the brain ⟨it illuminates,⟩ is too cold or too hot, and the man does not care enough for results to stimulate him to experiment, & hold him up in it,[n] or if he is too finely woven & irritable by pleasure & pain, so that life becomes a reception without equivalent [27] energy?[n] Of what use to make good resolutions, if the resolution is to be kept by the old law-breaker? Once more, how disgusting are the inferences of the phrenologist ⟨I draw a⟩that a man's fortune is told in the back of his head. I draw a veil over these things. A man of wit whom I knew, used to say that the Calvinists were those whose liver was diseased, & the sound were unitarians.[55] I ⟨d⟩am silent on such facts. I appeal from them. They are effects subject to higher causes which alone it consoles us to consider. How sad to consider each man the victim of that other who knows his law, & by such cheap signboard means as the colour of his beard or the ⟨outline⟩ ↑slope↓ of his occiput, to hold the key to all his fortune & character.[56]

↑Jan. ⟨2⟩30.↓ In Boston to hear the debates of the Texan Convention with the hope that I might catch some ⟨volcanic⟩ sparks of the Typhonic rage. But I was unlucky in my visits to the house & heard

[54] Credited to Talleyrand in Charles Maxime Catherinet de Villemarest, *Life of Prince Talleyrand*, 4 vols. (London, 1834–1836), II, 218. Emerson withdrew all four volumes of this work from the Boston Athenaeum in January and February, 1845.

[55] In *JMN*, VI, 77–78, and VIII, 173, Emerson credits this statement to Dr. Gamaliel Bradford, superintendent of Massachusetts General Hospital.

[56] This paragraph, struck through in ink with a vertical use mark, is used in "Experience," *W*, III, 51, 53. The word "outline" is circled and struck through in pencil with a horizontal line, and "slope" is inserted in pencil.

only smooth whig speeches on moderation, &c. to fill time. The poor mad people did not come.

[28] The Unitarian the milk & water era, the day of triviality & verbiage. Once "the rose of Sharon perfumed our graves," as Behmen said; [57] but now, if a man dies, it is like a grave dug in the snow, it is a ghastly fact abhorrent to nature, & we never mention it. Death is as natural as life, and should be sweet & graceful.[58]

> God only knew how Saadi dined
> Roses he ate, & drank the wind
>
> And thou Kereef from year to year
> Companion of my noblest dream
>
> Nor found in mortal pair
> ⟨Type⟩ The pattern of a faith so rare
> But sought among the graceful fables
> The lovers at the Elysian tables [59]

[29] And this one thing is certain[,] that the benefactor of his country shall not propose to himself models, nor content himself with outstripping his neighbors & contemporaries in the race of honor, pausing when he is the best in his little circle; that leads to atheism and despair. New Hampshire & Vermont will in six months let loose some young savage from their wilds who ↑shall↓ take this petit maitre of virtue & culture like a doll in their hands & shatter the pretty porcelain. All reference to models ⟨& reputations⟩, all comparison with neighboring abilities ⟨‖ ... ‖⟩& reputations is ⟨an infallible means of securing⟩ ↑the ⟨sure⟩ road⟨s⟩ to↓ mediocrity. But the generous soul on arriving in a new port makes instant preparation for a new voyage. He has the distant & unseen heroes ⟨always⟩ present to his imagination. By ⟨vast⟩ excursions, by original studies, by secret obedience,

---

[57] See p. [23] above.

[58] A faint pencil sketch of a cloaked figure underlies this entry.

[59] All three verse entries are in pencil. For the first, see *JMN*, VIII, 467–468, and "Fragments on the Poet and the Poetic Gift, V," ll. 13–14, *W*, IX, 325.

by incessant power, by rivalry not with men, but with the planets
& elemental forces in the ⟨vastness⟩ ↑scope↓ of his designs & attempts,
[30] he has taken hold of the heart of the world; stands there a
real & substantial and unprecedented person: and when the great
come by, as always there are angels in the ⟨world⟩ ↑earth↓, they know
him at sight, as one who gives character to a region of the earth &
whole generations who inhabit there. Calm pure effectual service
distinguishes him from ⟨all⟩ the vulgar great. He is one who without
phrase does what was hitherto impossible[.] [60]

In general, I am pained by observing the indigence of nature
in this American Commonwealth. E↑llen↓ H[ooper]. said she sympathized with the Transcendental movement, but she sympathized
even more with the objectors.[61] I replied that when I saw how little
kernel there was to that comet which had shed terror from its flaming
hair on the nations, how few & what cinders of genius, I was rather
struck with surprize ⟨in⟩at the largeness of the effect, & drew a
favorable inference as to the intellectual & spiritual tendencies of
⟨|| . . . ||⟩our [31] people. ⟨If⟩For there had not yet appeared one
man among us of a great talent. If two or three persons should come
with a high spiritual aim & with great powers the world would fall
in to their hands like a ripe peach.

The objection of Men of the world to the socalled Transcendentalists, is not a hostility to their truth, but that they unfit their children for business in their state-street sense & do not qualify them for
any complete life of a better kind.[62] [See U 161]

Go & hear a great orator to see how presentable truth & right
are, & how presentable are common facts. As we read the newspapers,

[60] "All reference to . . . attempts," is struck through in pencil with three vertical use marks; "he has taken hold . . . ⟨world⟩ earth," is struck through in pencil
with two vertical use marks; and "as one who gives . . . inhabit there." is struck
through in ink with five vertical use marks. "All reference to . . . vulgar great."
is used, with several omissions, in "Aristocracy," W, X, 61.
    [61] Ellen Sturgis Hooper (1812–1848) was Caroline Sturgis's sister and a con-
tributor to The Dial.
    [62] See Journal U, p. [36] above.

and as we see the effrontery with which money & power carry their
ends, and ride over honesty & good-meaning, morals & religion seem
to become mere shrieking & impotence. We will not speak for them,
because to speak for them seems so weak & hopeless. But a true orator
will instantly show you that all the states & kingdoms in the world,
all the senators, lawyers, & [32] rich men are ⟨|| ... ||⟩caterpillars'
webs & caterpillars, when seen in the light of this same despised &
imbecile truth. Grand grand truth! the orator himself becomes a
shadow & a fool before this light which lightens through him. It shines
backward & forward; diminishes, annihilates everybody, and the
prophet so gladly[,] so sublimely feels his personality lost in this
gaining triumphing godhead.[63]

See above. p. 7 ↑and, below, p 52, 71↓

> "He'd harpit a fish out of saut water,
> Or water from a stone,
> Or milk out of a maiden's breast
> That bairn had never none." [64]

"O I did get the rose water
Whair ye wull neir get nane,
For I did get that very rose-water
Into my mither's wame."

[33]–[36] [leaves missing] [65]
[37] Every man has his own courage, and is betrayed because he
seeks in himself the courage of other persons, which is not there.[66]

All reading is a kind of quotation[.]

[63] This paragraph, struck through in pencil with a vertical use mark, is used in
"Discourse at Middlebury College" and "The Scholar," *W*, X, 281–282.
[64] Jamieson's Scottish Ballads, I, 93, as quoted in the Editor's Preface in Warton's *History of English Poetry* . . . , 1824, I, (66). See *JMN*, V, 90, and VII, 146.
These lines, struck through in pencil with a vertical use mark, are used in "Eloquence," *W*, VII, 71.
[65] Emerson indexed p. [33] under Ballad and Tennyson; p. [34] under
E[dward] W[aldo] E[merson]; p. [35] under Ballad; and p. [36] under Character, Demonology, Times, and Transition.
[66] This sentence is struck through in pencil with a diagonal use mark; cf.
"Courage," *W*, VII, 270.

Whoever can write something good himself, is thenceforward by law of the Muses' Parliament entitled to steal at discretion.[67]

The gradual submerging of the eastern shore of America, and so of all the continents, & the correspondent rise of the western shore; the continual formation of new edge to the teeth of mastodons, &c.; the new races rise all predivided into parties ↑ready↓ armed & angry to fight for they know not what: Yet easy it is to see that they all share to the rankest Philistines, the same idea; that the drygoods--men & brokers are idealists; and only in quantity differ, — only differ in the degree of intensity. The idea rides & rules like the sun. Therefore, thou philosopher, rely on thy truth; bear down on it with all thy weight; add the weight of thy town, thy country, & the whole world: triumphantly, thou shalt see, it will bear it all like a scrap of down.[68]

[38] I think the best argument of the conservative is this bad one; that he is convinced that the angry democrat who wishes him to divide his park & chateau with him, will, on entering into the possession, instantly become conservative, & hold the property & spend it as selfishly as himself. For a better man, I might dare to renounce my estate; for a worse man, or for as bad a man as I, why should I? All the history of man with unbroken sequence of examples establishes this inference. Yet is it very low & degrading ground to stand upon. We must never reason from history, but plant ourselves on the ideal.

I.S. 18 July 6 AM

[39] Men are edificant or otherwise. Samuel Hoar is to all men's eyes conservative & constructive: his presence supposes a well ordered society, agriculture, trade, large institutions & empire. If

---

[67] This sentence, struck through in ink with a vertical use mark, is used in "Shakspeare," *W*, IV, 198.

[68] "the new races . . . intensity." is struck through in pencil with two vertical use marks; "the new races . . . scrap of down." is used in "Instinct and Inspiration," *W*, XII, 81–82; "the drygoods-men . . . intensity." is used in "Discourse at Middlebury College" and "The Scholar," *W*, X, 269.

these things did not exist, they would begin to exist through his steady will & endeavours. Therefore he cheers & comforts men, who feel all this in him very readily. The reformer, the rebel, who comes by, says all manner of unanswerable things against the existing republic, but discovers to my groping Daemon no plan of house or empire of his own. Therefore though Samuel Hoar's ⟨plan & prosperity⟩ town & state are a very cheap & modest commonwealth men very rightly go for him & flout the reformer.[69]

[40] June 1⟨6⟩5. A second visit to the Shakers with Mr Hecker.[70] Their family worship was a painful spectacle. I could remember nothing but the Spedale dei Pazzi at Palermo;[71] this shaking of their hands like the paws of dogs before them as they shuffled in this dunce-dance seemed the last deliration. If there was anything of heart & life in this it did not appear to me: and as Swedenborg said that the angels never look at the back of the head so I felt that I saw nothing else.[72] My ⟨The⟩fellow[n] men could hardly appear to less advantage before me than in this senseless jumping. The music seemed to me dragged down nearly to the same bottom. And when you come to talk with them on their topic, which they are very ready to do, you find such exaggeration of the virtue of celibacy, that ⟨it⟩ you might think you had come into a ⟨class⟩ ↑hospital-ward↓ of invalids afflicted with priapism. Yet the women were well dressed and appeared with dignity as [41] honoured persons. And I judge the whole society to be ⟨very innocent⟩ ↑cleanly↓ & industrious but stupid people. And these poor countrymen with their nasty religion fancy themselves *the Church* of the world and are as arrogant as the poor negroes on the Gambia river.

The lords of [*1 w*] the lords of life

[69] This paragraph, struck through in pencil with a spiraling vertical use mark and in ink with a vertical use mark, is used in "Montaigne," *W*, IV, 170–171.

[70] Isaac Hecker had spent time at both Brook Farm and Fruitlands and was currently living in the Thoreau household doing private study. He was shortly to become a convert to Roman Catholicism.

[71] For Emerson's repugnance at his visit to this Sicilian insane asylum in March, 1833, see *JMN*, IV, 139.

[72] In *JMN*, VI, 315, Emerson cites Swedenborg's statement from *A Treatise Concerning Heaven and its Wonders, and also Concerning Hell*, section 144.

I saw them pass
[1–2 w] grand & grim   [5]
[1 w] & Dream   [7]
[1 w] & Surprise   [6]
[1 w] Right[?] & [1 w]   [?]
To ···t without a tongue   [9]
S··· to see some to guess   [12]
And [1 w] omnipresent without name   [11]
Poor man [1 w] walked   [14]
Among the [1 w] of his high guardians   [15]
With [↑1 w↓] puzzled look
Dear nature [2–3 w] the hand [1 w]
& said, My darling, never mind   [1 w]   [19]
Tomorrow they will [1 w] new faces [73]   [20]

Fourier said, Man exists to gratify his twelve passions: and ↑he↓ proposes to remove the barriers which false philosophy & religion & prudence have built against indulgence. Some of the old heroic legislators proposed to open public brothels as safety-valves to defend virtuous women from the occasional extravagances of desire in violent persons & to yield a resort ⟨to⟩ of less danger to young men in the fury of passion. And in Amsterdam & other cities, the governments have authorized the stews. Well, Swedenborg too wandered through the Universe and found not only heavenly societies but horrid ⟨re⟩[n] cavernous regions where imps & dragons delighted themselves in all bestialities and he said these too enjoyed their condition[n] [42] & recreations, as well as the cherubim theirs. Fourier too has a sacred Legion and an order called sacred, of ⟨A⟩Chastity, Virgins & bachelors; a lower order of husband & wife; a lower of free companions & harlots. In having that higher order he gives all up. For the vulgar world not yet emancipated from prejudice replies to his invitation, Well, I will select only that part from your system, and leave ⟨out⟩ the sty to those who like it. I have observed that indulgence always effeminates. I have organs also & delight in pleasure, but I have experience also that this pleasure is the bait of a trap.

_____

[73] These lines were inscribed in pencil under the entry which follows and later erased. Revised and expanded, they became the epigraph to "Experience," *W*, III, 43.

↑*The long life.*↓

We must infer ⟨f⟩ our destiny from the preparation. We are driven by instincts to hive innumerable experiences which are of no ↑visible↓ value, and which we may revolve through many lives in the eternal whirl of generation before we shall assimilate & exhaust.

It is the rank of the spirit makes the merit of the deed. Les attractions sont proportionelles aux destinées.[74] Yes, cries the angel, but my attractions transcend all your system.

[43] Normal virtue is totally unaffecting in history, but vigour is in the highest degree liberating & electric & radiant. Napoleon is strong, self denying, self postponing, firm, sure, well-informed, sacrificing everything to his aim, not mistaking, as common adventurers, a bright means for the end. "Incidents ought not to govern policy, but policy incidents." "To be hurried away by every event, is to have no political system at all." Unhappily, his ends were egotistic.[75]

I ate whatever was set before me. I touched ivy & dogwood. I kept company with every man in the road for I knew that my evil & my good did not come from these but from the spirit whose servant I was, for I could not stoop to be a circumstance as they did who put their life into their fortune & their company.[76]

↑Mrs↓ S↑now↓ confessed[,] when the phrenologist found love of approbation, that "*she did like to suit.*"[77]

[44][78] If I made laws for Shakers or a School, I should gazette

[74] Emerson used English versions of this sentence in "Montaigne," *W*, IV, 183, 184, and "Poetry and Imagination," *W*, VIII, 41–42.

[75] The two quotations, which are repeated on p. [94] below, are from *Memoirs of the History of France during the Reign of Napoleon, Dictated by the Emperor at Saint Helena* . . . , 4 vols. (London, 1823–1824), IV, 277, 281. "Napoleon is strong . . . egotistic.", struck through in ink with two vertical use marks, is used in "Napoleon," *W*, IV, 233.

[76] This paragraph, struck through in ink with two vertical use marks, is used in "Worship," *W*, VI, 235.

[77] According to Edward Emerson, Mrs. Snow was "a kind and comforting old-fashioned nurse" (*J*, VI, 525n).

[78] Erased pencil writing, apparently a number of separate entries, covers this

every Saturday all the words they were wont to use in reporting religious experience as 'Spiritual life,' 'God,' 'soul,' 'cross,' &c. and if they could not find new ones next week they might remain silent.

Be an opener of doors for such as come after thee and do not try to make the Universe a blind alley.

Form is the mixture of matter & spirit[;] it is the visibility of spirit[.]

↑*The right Dandies.*↓

We have, it is true, a class of golden young men & maidens, of whom we say that for practical purposes they need a grain or two of alloy to make them good coin. If society were composed of such, the race would speedily be extinct by reason of bears & wolves who would eat them up. Granted. But perhaps it is in the great system that society shall have always some pensioners & pets and how much better that [45]⁷⁹ such musical souls as these, worshippers of true beauty, objects of friendship, and ⟨votaries⟩ monks & vestals in sacred culture, should be the exempts than the present *muscadins* of civilized society the dandies, namely, who inherit an estate without wit or virtue.

Society is babyish. Talleyrand's question is the main one to be asked; not, is he honest? is he rich? is he committed? is he of the movement, or, is he of the establishment? but, "Is he any body?" We want fire; a little less mutton and a little more genius.⁸⁰

[46] Novels make us skeptical by giving such prominence to wealth & social position, but I think them to be fine occasional stimu-

---

page. The following significant words and phrases have been recovered: "selves"; "keep"; "the plenitude of"; and "life,".

⁷⁹ Erased pencil writing, consisting of at least two separate entries, covers this page. The following significant words and phrases have been recovered: "Yet there were"; "N. H is"; and "offer".

⁸⁰ Talleyrand's question, repeated on p. [159] below, is quoted from Villemarest's *Life of Prince Talleyrand*, 1834–1836, IV, 202–203. "Society is babyish." also occurs on p. [25] above. "Talleyrand's question . . . genius." is struck through in ink with a vertical use mark; "Talleyrand's question . . . any body?' " is used in "Discourse at Middlebury College" and "Goethe," *W*, IV, 268.

lants, and, though with some shame, I am brought into an intellectual
state. But great is the poverty of their inventions. The perpetual
motive & means of accelerating or retarding interest is the dull device
of persuading a lover that his mistress is betrothed to another.
D'Israeli is well worth reading; quite a good student of his English
world, and a very clever expounder of its wisdom & craft: never quite
a master. Novels make us great gentlemen whilst we read them.
How generous[,] how energetic should we be in the crisis described,
but unhappy is the wife, or brother, or stranger who interrupts us,
whilst we read: nothing but frowns & tart replies from the reading
gentleman for them. Our novel reading is a passion for results, [47]
we admire parks & the love of beauties, & the homage of parliaments.[81]

Government
A fire ⟨in⟩breaking out in a village makes immediately a natural
government. The most able & energetic take the command, and are
gladly obeyed by the rest. The feebler individuals take their place
in the line to hand buckets, & the boys pass the empty ones.

In Demonology — the insurance ↑of life↓ which an unfinished design
springing from the Genius intimates.[82]

———

It is by means of my vices that I understand yours.

———

Agriculture is grown homoeopathic.

———

"Qui bien chante et bien danse, peu ⟨ad⟩ avance."

———

There came an orator excellent to melt all sorts of hearers into
perfect fusion: and he did not inspire ⟨a⟩the smallest wish to know
anything of his mind.

[48] I cannot make any exceptions. The only pardonable persons
are those who lead the sensual life & know not that they lead it, but

———

[81] "Novels make us . . . social position,"; "But great is . . . to another.";
and "Our novel reading . . . parliaments." are used in "Books," *W*, VII, 216–217.
[82] This entry is struck through in ink with a vertical use mark.

all philosophers & cultivated persons are cripples. Beauty has departed from them. Bishops & martyrs, saints & poets, sages & prophets,
I dare not believe that one was pure. No matter what asceticism nor
what elevation they attained, they all accepted all the accommoda-
tions of the Hotel Royale of this world; and ⟨it⟩ ↑the question↓ seems
to me trifling ⟨that question⟩ whether their compromise was only for
a few shillings or, like the bigger traders, for a thousand pounds of
pollution. It is all with ⟨me⟩ ↑them↓ as with men of sentiment. I can
well hear a stranger converse on mysteries of love & romance of
character; can easily become interested in his private love & fortunes; but as soon as I learn that he eats cucumbers, or hates parsnep,
values his luncheon, and eats [49] his dinner over again in his talk,
I can never thenceforward hear that man talk of sentiment.

Judge Fay shot a swallow on the wing & took off his head. The
Fitchburgh cars run at the rate of one mile in one minute, 45 seconds.
E H says "Try me on leather, & I'm your man." Hathaway said
of his fishing party at Plymouth, that he lived two years in that trip.
"There are all sorts of meat in a turtle." "Only one man of any sense
in the jury,ⁿ & he believed that Sam Hoar made him." [83] The two
sorts of fools, the natural & the d——d. I rode with a merry ↑sea↓
Captain, between whom & the stagecoachman was a continual banter.
We stopped at the poorhouse. "Mr Winchester," said the Captain,
"your passengers say you ought to stop at the poor-house every day."ⁿ
The driver replied, "If we should both stop there, Captain Davis, we
should only stop where we started from."
The Fitchburg Road cost $1,100 000, 50 miles. The Worcester
$3,000 000, forty miles.
New Church in Hanover st cost $65,000.[84]

[50] People seem to me often sheathed in their tough organization.[85] I know those who are the charge each of their several Daemon,

[83] Beside this sentence are two vertical lines in ink in the left margin and one
vertical line in ink in the right margin.

[84] See Journal W, p. [47] below.

[85] This sentence, struck through in ink with a diagonal use mark, is used in
"Fate," W, VI, 9.

and in whom the Daemon at intervals appears at the gates of their eyes. They have intervals, God knows, of weakness & folly like other people. Of these I take no heed: I wait the⟨se⟩ reappearings of the Genius, which are sure and beautiful.

[51] The abolitionists with their holy cause; the Friends of the Poor; the ministers at large; the Prison Discipline Agents; the Soup Societies, the whole class of professed Philanthropists, — it is strange & horrible to say — are an altogether odious set of people, whom one would be sure to shun as the worst of bores & canters. Religion must be a crab, not a cultivated tree.[86]

I wish the man to please himself, then he will please me.

[Ellery] C[hanning?]. is very sagacious for himself, he leaps at results, and sits down in them, very heedless as to the means. Of course, mother & father & wife & brother are shocked at the cold selfishness; but the philosophic observer is much inclined to absolve him, and even praise the courage & genius of the choice.

[52] A man should be ↑a↓ guest in his own house, and a guest in his own thought; he is there to speak for truth, but who is he? Some clod the truth has snatched from the ground & with fire has fashioned to a momentary man: without the truth he is a clod again.[87]

↑p 7, 52, 32,↓

Do not lead me to question whether what we call science, is help or hurt. Yet unluckily in my experience of the scientific, it is a screen between you & the man having the science. He has his string of anecdotes and rules⟨,⟩ as a physician, which he must show you, & you must endure, before you can come at the colour & quality of the man. Phrenology too, I hate. C. adapts his conversation to the form of the head of the man he talks with! Alas! I dreamed that the value of life lay in its inscrutable possibilities: that I never know in

---

[86] See p. [25] above. Erased pencil writing, none of which has been recovered, underlies this entry.

[87] This paragraph is used in "The Sovereignty of Ethics," W, X, 194.

addressing myself to a new individual what may befall me. I carry ever the keys of my castle in my hand ready to throw them at the feet of my lord whenever & in whatever disguise [53] in this great carnival, I may encounter him. But the assurance that he is in the neighborhood, hidden among these vagabonds[,] consoles me. And shall I preclude my fortune & my future by setting up for graduate & doctor & kindly adapting my conversation to the shape of heads? When I come to that, you shall buy me for a cent.[88]

Presently the railroads will not stop at Boston ⟨w⟩but will tunnel the city to communicate with each other. The same mob which has beat down the Bastille will soon be ready to storm the Thuilleries.

[54] Henry described Hugh as saving every slip & stone & seed, & planting it.[89] He picks up a peach stone & puts i⟨n⟩t in his pocket to plant. That is his vocation in the world, to be a planter of plants. Not less is a writer to heed his vocation of reporting. Whatever he beholds or experiences, he is to daguerrotype. It is all nonsense that they say that some things rebuke literature, & are undescribable; he knows better, & would report God himself or attempt it. Nothing so sudden, nothing so broad, nothing so subtle, nothing so dear, but it comes therefore commended to his pen, & he will write. In his eyes a man is the faculty of reporting, & the universe is the possibility of being reported.

In every profound conversation ⟨in⟩he saw plainly that all he had yet written was exoteric[,] was not the law, but gossip on the eternal politics[;] but true to his art he instantly endeavoured to record the conversation that so by some means he might yet save some one word of the heavenly language.[90]

[55] The vice of Swedenborg's mind is its theologic determination. Nothing with him has the liberality of universal wisdom but

---

[88] "C. adapts his . . . cent.", struck through in ink with a vertical use mark, is used in "Experience," *W*, III, 53–54.

[89] Hugh Whelan was Emerson's gardener and man-of-all-work.

[90] This and the preceding entry, struck through in ink with a vertical use mark, are used in "Goethe," *W*, IV, 262–264.

every sentence respects the Bible or some church. But a rose, a sun-beam, the human face do not remind us of deacons[.] [91]

[56]   Life [92]
Life which finishes & enjoys
    I do not exculpate my contemporaries
Life is so affirmative that I can never hear of personal vigour of any kind, great power of performance, without lively sympathy & fresh resolutions.

———

The power of a straight line is a square,[93] and wisdom is the power, or rather the powers, of the present hour.

[57] We have no prizes offered to the ambition of generous young men. There is with us no Theban Band, no stern exclusive Legion of Honor to be attained only by long & real service [n] and patient climbing year by year up all the steps. We have a Brummagem aristocracy, O plenty of cambrichandkerchief nobles, & grocer gentle-men, cake, cigars, & champagne, musty parlours & irritable women. But a grand style of culture, a supreme class which without injury an ardent youth can propose to himself as a pharos through long dark years, does not exist, & there is no substitute. The youth[,] having got through the first thickets which oppose his entrance into life[,] having got into decent society, is left to himself and falls abroad with too much freedom.[94]

[58] If the orator addressing the public assembly should attempt to make people wise in that which they already know, he would fail; but by making them wise in that which he knows, he has the ad-vantage of the whole assembly every moment, & astonishes them. Napoleon's famous tactics of marching on the angle of an army, &

[91] "The vice . . . church.", struck through in ink with a vertical use mark, is used in "Swedenborg," *W*, IV, 134.
    [92] This word, and the line "I do not exculpate my contemporaries" below, are in pencil.
    [93] See p. [111] below.
    [94] This paragraph, struck through in ink with a discontinuous vertical use mark, is used in "Aristocracy," *W*, X, 59.

so always presenting a superiority of numbers, is the orator's secret also.[95]

Our mass meetings are a sad spectacle: they show great men put to a bad use, men consenting to be managed by committees, & worse, consenting to manage men. The retribution is instant, diminution & diminution, bereavement of ideas & of power, of all loveliness & ↑of all↓ growth. It is in vain to bawl "Constitution" and "patriotism"[;] ⟨once⟩those words repeated once too often have a most ironical hoarseness.

In common with all boys, I held a river to be good, but the name of it in a grammar hateful.

[59] Ah! how different is it to render account to ourselves of ourselves & to render account to the public of ourselves.

———

> "Tis the most difficult of tasks to keep
> Heights which the soul is competent to gain"
> [Wordsworth, *The Excursion*, IV, 138–139][96]

Granted; sadly granted, but the necessity by which Deity rushes into distribution[,] into ⟨particles⟩ variety & particles, is not less divine than the unity from which all begins. Forever the Demiurgus speaks to the junior gods as in the old tradition of the Timaeus, "Gods of gods that mortal natures may subsist & that the Universe may be truly all, convert [or distribute] yourselves according to your nature to the fabrication of animals" &c &c[.][97]

[60] The use of geology has been to wont the mind to a new chronology. The little dame school measures by which we had gauged[n] everything, we have learned to disuse, & break up our European & Mosaic & Ptolemaic schemes for the grand style of nature & fact. We

[95] This paragraph is used in "Eloquence," *W*, VII, 84. For the source of Napoleon's maxim, see p. [119] below.

[96] See *JMN*, IV, 87.

[97] Taylor, *The Works of Plato* . . . , 1804, II, 504. See Journal Y, p. [160] below.

knew nothing rightly for want of perspective. Now we are learning
the secularity of nature; & geology furnishes us with a metre or clock,
a coarse kitchen clock, it is true, compared with the vaster measures
which astronomy has to make us acquainted with! Now first we learn
what weary patient periods must round themselves ere the rock is
formed, then ere the rock is broken, & the first lichen race has dis-
integrated the thinnest [n] external plate into soil, & opened the door
for the remote Flora, Fauna, Pomona, & Ceres, to come in. How far
off yet ⟨ar⟩is the trilobite: how far the quadruped: how inconceivably
remote is man. All duly arrive, & then race after race. It is a long
way from granite to a woodpecker, farther yet to ⟨the⟩Plato [61]
& the preaching of the immortality of the soul. Yet all must come,
as surely as the first atom has two sides.[98] The progress of physics &
of metaphysics is parallel[;] at first it is lowest instinctive life loath-
some to the succeeding tribes ⟨it is⟩like the generation of sour paste.
It is animalcules, earwigs, & caterpillars writhing, wriggling, devour-
ing, & devoured. As the races advance & rise order & rank appear,
& the aurora of reason & of love. Who cares how madly the early
savages fight[,] who sides with one or another[:] their rage is organic
and has its animal sweetness. The world goes pregnant with Europe
& with better than Europe.
Nothing interests us of these or ought to. We do not wish a world of
bugs or of birds. Neither afterwards do we respect one of Scythians,
or Caraibs, or Feejees. As little interests us the crimes of the recent
races, the grand style of nature & her periods is what they show us,
but they are not for permanence[,] her foot will not rest. Onward
& onward that evergoing progression. That breathless haste what god
can [62] tell us whither? Who cares for the crimes of the past, for
oppressing whites or oppressed blacks, any more than for bad dreams?
These fangs & eaters & food are all in the harmony of nature: & there
too is the germ forever protected, unfolding⟨,⟩ gigantic leaf after leaf,
a newer flower, a richer fruit in every period. Yet its next is not to be
guessed. ⟨|| ... ||⟩It will only save what is worth saving & it saves not
by compassion but by power. It saves men through themselves. It
appoints no police to guard the lion but his teeth & claws, no fort or

[98] "The use of geology . . . two sides.", struck through in ink with a vertical
use mark, is used in "Nature," *W*, III, 179–180.

city for the bird but his wings, no rescue for flies & mites but their
spawning numbers, which no ravages can overcome. It deals with
men after the same manner. If they are rude & foolish down they
must go. When at last in a race a new principle appears[,] ⟨a h⟩an
idea, that conserves it. Ideas only save races. If the black man is feeble
& not important to the existing races, not on a par with the [63] best
race, the black man must serve & be sold & exterminated. But if the
black man carries in his bosom an indispensable element of a new &
coming civilization, for the sake of that element no wrong nor
strength nor circumstance can hurt him, he will survive & play his
part. So now it seems to me that the arrival of such men as Toussaint
if he is pure blood, or of Douglas if he is pure blood, outweighs all
the English & American humanity. The Antislavery of the whole
world is but dust in the balance, a poor squeamishness & nervous-
ness[;] the might & the right is here. Here is the Anti-Slave. Here
is Man; & if you have man, black or white is an insignificance. Why
at night all men are black. ⟨I esteem⟩ The[n] intellect, that is miraculous, who has it has the talisman, his skin & bones are transparent,
he is a statue of the living God, him I must love & serve & perpetually
seek & desire & dream on: and who has it not is superfluous. But a
compassion for that which is not & cannot be useful & lovely, is degrading & maudlin[,] this towing along as by ropes that which cannot
go itself. Let us [64] not be our own dupes; all the songs & newspapers & subscriptions of money & vituperation of those who do not
agree with us will avail nothing against eternal fact. I say to you, you
must save yourself, black or white, man or woman. Other help is
none. I esteem the occasion of this jubilee to be that proud discovery
that the black race can begin to contend with the white[;] that ⟨they
have⟩ in the great anthem of the world which we call history, a piece
of many parts & vast compass, after playing a long time a very low
& subdued accompaniment they perceive the time arrived when they
can strike in with force & effect & take a master's part in the music.
The civilization of the world has arrived at that pitch that their moral
quality is becoming indispensable, & the /genius/quality/ of this race
is to be honoured for itself. For this they have been preserved in
sandy desarts, in rice swamps, in kitchens & shoeshops so long. Now
let them emerge clothed & in their own form. I esteem [65] this

jubilee & the fifty years' movement which has preceded it to be the announcement of that fact & our antislavery societies[,] boastful as we are, only the shadow & witness to that fact. The negro has saved himself, and the white man very patronisingly says, I have saved you. If the negro is a fool all the white men in the world cannot save him though they should die.[99]

The light of the public square must at last test the merit of every statue.[100]

——

All ↑our↓ literature is a quotation, our life a custom or imitation, and our body is borrowed like a beggar's dinner from a hundred charities.[101]

——

But I am struck in George Sand with the instant understanding between the great; and in I Promessi Sposi with the humiliation of Fra Cristoforo; & in Faustina with the silent acquiescence of Andlau in the new choice of Faustina; for truth is the best thing in novels also.[102]

[66] Does not he do more to abolish Slavery who works all day steadily in his garden, than he who goes to the abolition meeting & makes a speech? The antislavery agency like so many of our employments is a suicidal business. Whilst I talk, some poor farmer drudges & slaves for me. It requires a just costume then, the office of agent or speaker, he should sit very low & speak very meekly like one

---

[99] "Nothing interests us [p. [61]] . . . the recent races, [p. [61]]" and "Who cares for the crimes [p. [62]] . . . should die. [p. [65]]" are each struck through in ink with a vertical use mark; "like the generation [p. [61]] . . . their own form. [p. [64]]" is used, with a number of omissions, in "Emancipation in the British West Indies," *W*, XI, 143–145. Page [64] is reproduced in Plate I.

[100] In *JMN*, IV, 369, Emerson credits this to Michelangelo, as quoted in Thomas Roscoe's "The Life of Michael Angelo Buonaroti," in *Lives of Eminent Persons* (London, 1833), p. 72. This volume is in his library.

[101] "our life . . . charities." is used in "Quotation and Originality," *W*, VIII, 188.

[102] For the reference to George Sand's *Consuelo*, see Journal U, p. [139] above. Fra Cristoforo is a saintly Capuchin who shelters the heroine in Manzoni's novel, an edition of which Emerson owned; Andlau and Faustina are characters in Countess Ida von Hahn-Hahn's *Faustina*, published in 1841.

64

not be our own dupes, all the songs & newspapers & subscriptions of money & vituperation of those who do not agree
with us will avail nothing against
eternal fact. I say to you, you must
save yourself, black or white, man
or woman. Other help is none.
I esteem the occasion of this jubilee
to be that proud discovery that the
black race can begin to contend with
the white that ~~they have~~ in the great
anthem of the world which
we call history, a piece of many
parts & vast compass, after playing
a long time a very low & subdued
accompaniment they perceive
the time arrived when they can
strike in with force & effect & take
a master's part in the music.
The civilization of the world has
arrived at that pitch that their
moral quality is becoming indispensable, & the genius capacity of this race
is to be honoured for itself.
For this they have been preserved
in sandy desarts in rice swamps
in kitchens & shoe shops so long
now let them emerge clothed
& in their own form. I esteem

Plate I   Journal V, page 64   Text, page 125
The Negro's role in history

compelled to do a degrading thing. ⟨It is very easy to⟩ Do not then,
I pray you, talk of the work & the fight, as if it were any thing more
than a pleasant oxygenation of your lungs. It is easy & pleasant to
ride about the country amidst the peaceful farms of New England
& New York[n] &[,] sure every where of a strict sympathy from the
intelligent & good, argue for liberty, & browbeat & chastise the dull
clergyman or lawyer that ventures to limit or qualify our statement.
This is not work. It needs to be done but it does not consume heart &
brain, does not shut out culture, does not imprison you as the farm
& the shoeshop & the forge. There is really [67] no danger & no
extraordinary energy demanded[;] it supplies what it wants. I think
if the witnesses of the truth would do their work symmetrically, they
must stop all this boast & frolic & vituperation, & in lowliness free
the slave by love in the heart. Let the diet be low, & a daily feast of
commemoration of their brother in bonds. Let them eat his corn cake
dry, as he does. Let them wear negro-cloths. Let them leave long
discourses to the defender of slavery, and show the power of true
words which are always few. Let them do their own work. He who
does his own work frees a slave. He who does not his own work, is
a slave-holder. Whilst we sit here talking & smiling, some person is out
there in field & shop & kitchen doing what we need,[n] without talk
or smiles. Therefore, let us, if we assume the dangerous pretension of
being abolitionists, & ⟨ag⟩make that our calling in the world, let us do
it symmetrically. The world asks, do the abolitionists eat sugar? do
they wear cotton? do they smoke tobacco? Are they their own servants? Have they managed to put that dubious institution of servile
labour on an agreeable & thoroughly intelligible & transparent foundation? [n] [68] It is not possible that these purists accept the accom-
modations of hotels, or even of private families[,] on the existing
profane arrangements? If they do, of course, not conscience, but mere
prudence & propriety will seal their mouths on the inconsistences of
churchmen. Two tables in every house! Abolitionists at one & *servants*
at the other! It is a calumny that you utter. There never was, I am
persuaded, an asceticism so austere as theirs,[n] from the peculiar emphasis of their testimony. The planter does not want slaves: give him
money: give him a machine that will provide ⟨|| ... ||⟩him with as
much money as the slaves yield, & he will thankfully let them go:

he does not love whips, or usurping overseers, or sulky ↑swarthy↓ giants creeping round his house & barns by night with lucifer matches in their hands & knives in their pockets. No; only he wants his luxury, & he will pay even this price for it.[103] It is not possible then that the abolitionist will begin the assault on his luxury, by any other means than the abating of his own. A silent ⌈69⌉ fight without warcry or triumphant brag, then, is the new abolition of New England ⟨num⟩ sifting the thronging ranks of the champions, the speakers, the poets, the editors, the subscribers, the givers, & reducing the armies to a handful of just men & women. Alas! alas! my brothers, there is never an abolitionist in New England[.]

15 October, 1844.

I send my New Essays to	Margaret Fuller √
	Caroline Sturgis √
My Mother √	Sarah [Freeman] Clarke √
Lidian √	S[amuel]. G[ray]. Ward √
M[ary]. M[oody]. Emerson	W[illiam]. Emerson √
Samuel Ripley √	G[eorge] B[arrell] Emerson √
Elizabeth Hoar √	N[athaniel]. L[angdon]. Frothingham √
W[illiam] H[enry]. Furness √	W[illiam]. H[enry]. Channing √
Ogden Haggerty √	W[illiam]. E[llery]. Channing √
Benjamin Rodman √	A[bel] Adams √
Horace Greeley √	C[hristopher] P[earse] Cranch √
L[ucy]. C[otton] Brown √	H[enry]. W[adsworth]. Longfellow
Giles Waldo √	C[harles]. T[homas]. Jackson √
W[illiam]. A[spinwall]. Tappan √	G[eorge]. P[artridge]. Bradford √
W[illiam]. M[ackay]. Prichard √	H[enry] D[avid] Thoreau √

---

[103] "The planter does not . . . let them go:" and "No; only he . . . for it." are used in "Emancipation in the British West Indies," *W*, XI, 118.

C[hristopher]. P[earse].   A[mos] B[ronson] Alcott ✓
  Cranch ✓
C[harles]. K[ing]. New-   G. Bemis ✓
  comb ✓
R[ufus]. W[ilmot]. Gris-   J[ames]. R[ussell]. Lowell ✓
  wold ✓
W[illiam]. H. Dennett ✓   W[arren]. Burton ✓
[70]¹⁰⁴ Mrs L[ydia] M[aria]   H[arriet] Martineau
  Child ✓
C[harles]. C[reighton].   J. W. Morgan
  Hazewell ✓
C[hristopher]. G[ore].   T[homas]. Carlyle
  Ripley ✓

Mrs [Caroline Neagus]   J[ohn]. Sterling
  Hildreth ✓
Miss Lydia Jackson
                                  Cornelius Mathews
Mrs W[illiam]. Pope ✓
Mrs [Mary?] Larkin
Miss M[ary]. C. Adams
N[athaniel]. Hawthorne ✓
⟨Warren Burton⟩   J[ohn]. G[reenleaf]. Whittier
B[enjamin]. P[eter].
  Hunt
Charles Lane

Our relations to fine people are whipped cream & not necessary
bread.¹⁰⁵

    Cities to me are rifled rocks
    ⟨And⟩ ↑The↓ houses are fallen limbs of pine ¹⁰⁶

---

¹⁰⁴ Erased pencil writing, apparently a number of separate entries, covers the
upper two-thirds of this page. Portions of three entries have been recovered: "of
life"; "in our" and "the judge" (an earlier inscription of the sentence beginning
"We must not be parties" on p. [71]); and "Society".
¹⁰⁵ A pencil version of this entry, later erased, underlies the ink version.
¹⁰⁶ These two lines are in pencil.

Hafiz, b. 1300   beginning of fourteenth cent.
Saadi b 1175

[71] For the fine things, I make poetry of them; but the moral sentiments make poetry of me[.] [107]

We must not be parties in our dealing with our friends, but the judge.

There are beggars in Iran & Araby
Said was hungrier than all
⟨Men⟩ ↑Hafiz↓ said he was a fly
That came to every festival
Also he came to the Mosque
⟨And followed the⟩ ↑In the trail of↓ camel & caravan
↑Out↓ from[n] Mecca to Ispahan
↑North↓ he[n] went to snowy hills
He sat in the grave divan
Was never form & never face
So sweet to him as only grace
Which did not last like a stone
But gleamed ↑in sunlight↓ & was gone
⟨That⟩ ↑Beauty↓ /he followed/chased he/ everywhere
In flame in storm in clouds of air
He smote the lake to feed his eye
With the precious green of the broken wave
He flung in pebbles well to hear
The moment's music which they gave
⟨He⟩ Loved[n] ⟨flowers⟩ ↑harebells↓ nodding on a rock
⟨And⟩ A[n] cabin topped with curling smoke
⟨But⟩ ↑Nor loved he less↓ stately men in palaces
Guarded by ceremonies
⟨Better when the in her lo⟩ More he revered in mountain land
Men built ⟨up⟩ with power & grace to stand
⟨Slo⟩ Like castles [108]

---

[107] This sentence, struck through in ink with a vertical use mark, is used in "Swedenborg," *W*, IV, 93–94.

[108] This poetry is in pencil. "Was never form . . . which they gave" occurs,

[72][109] Marshal Lannes said "Know, Colonel, that none but a poltroon will boast that he never was afraid." Bourrienne [110]

There is a certain pleasure in getting on to the lowest ground of politics; because there is plain dealing & no cant.[111]

"I have seen more than 20 000 men seized with fear fly helterskelter at the cry of a coward   There are the Cossacks! I have seen them filled with alarm interrupt the calm & tranquil march of 4000 warriors of the Imperial Guard who still bearing their arms marched steadily on without troubling themselves to inquire whether the sun still existed &c"

Bausset p. 365 [112]

[73][113] The sun & moon are in my way when I would be solitary[.]

There are many topics which ought not to be approached except in the plenitude of health & playfully.

---

somewhat changed, as ll. 1–10 of the epigraph to "Beauty," *W*, VI, 279. "There are beggars . . . grave divan" and "⟨He⟩ loved ⟨flowers⟩ . . . ceremonies" occur in "Fragments on the Poet and the Poetic Gift, I," ll. 1–6, 8–10, 21–22, 25–26, 28, *W*, IX, 320–321.

[109] Erased pencil writing, apparently a number of separate entries, covers the upper two-thirds of this page. The following significant words and phrases have been recovered or conjecturally recovered: "Slave", "5", and "a day" (one entry); "There is a certain" (part of an entry also inscribed in ink); "as this injury" and "on his sword or foot[?]" (one entry); and "The intense selfishness in the most", "↑dress↓", and "in utter dishabille" (one entry).

[110] Louis Antoine Fauvelet de Bourrienne, *Private Memoirs of Napoleon Bonaparte, During the Periods of the Directory, the Consulate, and the Empire,* 4 vols. (London, 1830), II, 72n. Emerson borrowed all four volumes of this work from the Boston Athenaeum in January, 1845. The quotation, struck through in ink with two vertical use marks, is used in "Culture," *W*, VI, 139.

[111] This sentence, struck through in ink with two vertical use marks, is used in "Napoleon," *W*, IV, 227.

[112] Louis François Joseph de Bausset, *Private Memoirs of the Court of Napoleon, and of Some Publick Events of the Imperial Reign, from 1805 to the First of May 1814* . . . (Philadelphia, 1828), borrowed from the Boston Athenaeum January 16–February 11, 1845.

[113] Erased pencil writing covers the upper two-thirds of this page, of which the following significant words and phrases have been recovered or conjecturally recovered: "In this cause[?] we must renounce our temper &"; "who will[?] not so much as part with his[?] ice cream to save them from the"; "his ice cream is"; "he will be likely to get more"; "↑them↓"; and "resemblance[?]".

It is a great happiness to escape a religious education. ⟨It⟩ ↑Calvinism↓ destroys religion of character.[114]

The beautiful creature persuaded me that all his ways & conditions & employments were the best not only for him but for me. I reconsidered my whole economy, and revolved in my head, as I lay in bed before daybreak,[n] what means of saving & of earning would put large sums at my disposal for expenditure on my house, on grounds, on collections of art. I soon woke from this ridiculous humour to a wiser judgment.[115]

In Maine they have not a summer but a thaw.

[74][116] I understand very well in cities how the Southerner finds sympathy. The heat drives every summer the planter to the north. He comes from West & South & Southwest to the Astor & the Tremont Houses. The Boston merchant ⟨calls at the Tremont &⟩ bargains for his cotton at his counting house, then calls on him at the hotel, & ↑politely↓ sympathizes ⟨as the custom is,⟩ with all his modes of thinking. 'He never sided with those violent men, — poor Garrison[,] poor Phillips are on the coals': well, all that is very intelligible, but the planter does not come to Concord. Rum comes to Concord but not the slave driver & we are comparatively safe from his infusions. I hardly understand how he persuades so many dignified persons, — who were never meant ⟨to be his⟩ ↑for↓ tools, — to become his tools.

[75] Intense selfishness which we all share. Planter will not hesitate to eat his negro, because he can. We eat him in milder fashion by pelting the negro's friend. We cannot lash him with a whip, because we dare not. We lash him with our tongues. ⟨W⟩ I like the southerner the best; he deals roundly, & does not cant. The northerner is surrounded with churches & Sunday schools & is hypocritical. How gladly[,] how gladly, if he dared, he would seal the lips of these

---

[114] This entry, struck through in ink with a vertical use mark, is used in "Worship," *W*, VI, 214.

[115] Emerson indexed p. [73] under Samuel Gray Ward, presumably the "beautiful creature."

[116] The entries on this and the following page are in pencil.

poor men & poor women who speak for him. I see a few persons in the church, who, I fancy, will soon look about them with some surprise to see what company they are keeping.

I do not wonder at feeble men being strong advocates for slavery. They have no feeling of worthiness which assures them of their own safety. In a new state of things they are by no means sure it would go well with them. They cannot work or facilitate work or cheer or decorate labour. No[,] they live by certain privileges which the actual order of the community yields them. Take those and you take all. I do not wonder that such would fain raise a mob for fear is very cruel.

[76] ↑Instinct of Whigs may shudder at Napoleon. But↓ ⟨W⟩what does Webster, or Andrew Jackson, or what does Crocker, or Belknap, or the Hosmers ⟨care for⟩ ↑fear from↓ the elevation of Irish or ne-groes? They know they can defy competition from the best whites or Saxons. They should be abolitionists.[117]

Imbecility of ordinary kings & governors. They do not know what to do. The weavers strike for bread, & they[,] not knowing what to do, meet them with bayonets: Bonaparte knew what to do. An immense satisfaction to have a real king.[118]

[77][119] A gentleman may have many innocent propensities but if he chances to have the habit of slipping arsenic into the soup of whatever persons sit next him at table he must expect some inconvenience. He may call it his peculiar institution, a mere way of his, he never puts

[117] Alvah Crocker, president of the Fitchburg railroad, and Sewel F. Belknap are included in a list of successful men in Journal O, p. [271] below; the Hosmers were a numerous and prosperous family of Concord. A pencil version of this entry, later erased, underlies the ink version. The pencil version has "Such should be abolitionists" for "They should be abolitionists."

[118] This paragraph, struck through in ink with a diagonal use mark, is used in "Napoleon," W, IV, 232–233. Cf. p. [79] below. Erased pencil writing underlies this entry and extends to the bottom of the page. It apparently consists of a number of separate entries, of which the following significant words and phrases have been recovered: "gentlemen in" and "persons" (one entry); "England" and "civilization" (one entry); and "having", "nobler", "intellect", and "party" (one entry).

[119] The entries on pp. [77]–[79] are in pencil. The first three on p. [79] were later erased.

it in his own soup[,] only in the soup of his neighbour[,] & even only in some of his neighbours', ↑for example he is partial to light hair, & only spices the dish of such as have black hair,↓ & he may persuade his chaplain to find him a text & be very indignant & patriotic & quarrelsome & moral & religious ⟨&⟩on the subject & swear to die in defence of this old & strong habit he has contracted[.]

Our N[ew] E[ngland] Christianity is Whiggism.

[78] It is the history of civility.

The conscience of the white & the improvement of the black cooperated, & the Emancipation became inevitable. It is a great deed with great sequel & cannot now be put back. The same movement goes forward with advantage[;] the conscience is more tender & the black more respectable. Meantime the belly is also represented & the ignorant & sensual feel the danger & resist, so it goes slower. But it gains & the haters of Garrison have lived to rejoice in that grand world-movement which every age or two casts out so masterly an agent of good. I cannot speak of that gentleman without respect. ⟨He⟩ I found him the other day in his dingy office

I have no doubt there was as much intense selfishness, as much cowardice, as much paltering then as now[;] many held back & called the redeemers of their race fanatics & methodists[;] there were many who with the utmost dignity & sweetness gave such peppercorn reasons. There were church carpets ⟨& parish⟩ then too. And many an old aunt in man's clothes that would nail up her pew to keep ⟨the⟩ Clarkson out.[120]

[79] The moral sense is always supported by the permanent interest of the parties. Else I know not how in our world any good thing would get done. England had an interest in abolishing slavery & pushed it.[121]

---

[120] Thomas Clarkson (1760–1846) was one of the most famous English abolitionists.

[121] "The moral sense . . . get done." is used in "Emancipation in the British West Indies," *W*, XI, 125.

The stream of human affairs flows its own way & is very little affected by the activity of legislators[.] [122]

The new revolution is not ⟨of⟩ political but social. It is not power & title & privilege men want, but bread[.]

Our politics very superficial. The poor in despair of Bread cry out for Bread & become unruly[.] They are met by bayonets. ⟨A⟩ Kings & presidents know not what to do.[123] There are no dragons or monsters described in mythology so dreadful as the real monster that is at this hour eating Europe & laying his curse on this country, — pauperism.

[80₁] Buonaparte was sensible to the music of bells. Hearing the bell of a parish church, he would pause & his voice faltered as he said, "Ah! that reminds me of the first years I spent at Brienne, I was then happy." [124]

Bonaparte by force of intellect is raised out of all comparison with the strong men around him. His marshals[,] though able men, are as horses & oxen. He alone is a fine tragic figure related to the daemons, & to all time. Add as much force of intellect again to repair the immense defects of his *morale*, and he would have been in harmony with the ideal world.[125]

[81] Dr Lowell said, "Mr Moderator. The gentleman says that he has been ⟨this for many⟩ ↑by adoption now for several↓ years a citizen here: But I, sir, was freeborn. In this city, my eyes first saw the light. Here lie the bones of my fathers, and here is laid the dust of my children. I know the people well, they are my friends & companions,

---

[122] This sentence is used in "Emancipation in the British West Indies," *W*, XI, 139.

[123] "Our politics . . . to do." is struck through in pencil with two vertical use marks; with "The poor . . . to do.", cf. p. [76] above.

[124] Bourrienne, *Private Memoirs of Napoleon Bonaparte* . . . , 1830, II, 33–34, paraphrased.

[125] "Bonaparte by force . . . all time." is struck through in ink with a vertical use mark.

and I know ⟨well⟩ their strong aversion to any sectarian interference. I know that they will not consent to trust their contributions ⟨t⟩for the necessities of these widows & orphans to this Convention, so long as they see it controlled for the purposes of a sect or party. They will withdraw [80₂]¹²⁶ their contributions, and these pensioners must suffer. Gentlemen will do as they please. But I ↑feel it my duty to↓ warn you, ⟨and⟩ ↑that↓ the moaning of the widows may not disturb my slumbers, ⟨&⟩ ↑nor↓ the blood of these orphans, if they must perish, ⟨shall not⟩ stain the skirts of my garments."¹²⁷

[82]¹²⁸ The lover transcends the person of the beloved; he is as sensible of her defects & weaknesses as another: he verily loves the tutelar & guiding Daemon who is at each instant throwing ⟨him⟩↑it↓self into the eyes[,] the air & carriage of his mistress, & giving to them this unearthly & insurmountable charm.

↑See above p 50,↓   ↑See U p. 70↓

Time is the great assistant of ⟨the⟩ criticism. We see the gallery, & the marble imposes on us. We cannot tell if it be good or not.ⁿ But long after the truly noble forms reappear to the imagination & the inferior are forgotten.¹²⁹

I wish that Webster & Everett & also the young political aspirants of Massachusetts should hear Wendell Phillips speak, were it only for the capital lesson in eloquence they might learn of him. This,

¹²⁶ Emerson directed attention to the close of this entry at the bottom of p. [80] by the notation "◀▯ (continued at bottom of p. 80," at the bottom of p. [81]. A long rule separates the conclusion from the other entries on p. [80].

¹²⁷ In Notebook S (Salvage), p. [57], Emerson quotes this same speech with the prefatory explanation: "At the ↑Massachusetts↓ ⟨Congre⟩Convention of Congregational Ministers, in ⟨Boston⟩ the Court House, in Boston, May ⟨1844 or 1845⟩ on a proposition of Rev Dr Wisner (Orthodox,) to ⟨throw⟩ ↑apply↓ (I believe) the contributions of the Boston Churches ⟨in⟩to the ⟨contribution⟩ ↑benefit↓ of all the churches of the State, [this was the reply of the] ↑Rev.↓ Dr Charles Lowell . . ." Dr. Wisner's motion was subsequently rejected.

¹²⁸ Erased pencil writing covers most of this page, of which the following significant words and phrases have been recovered or conjecturally recovered: "It is a"; "as another"; "new day[?] not"; "discuss"; "to be tempted"; and "wish done will".

¹²⁹ This paragraph is struck through in pencil with a diagonal use mark.

namely, that the first & the second & the third part of the art is to keep your feet always firm on a fact.[130] They talk about the Whig party. There is [83][131] no such thing in nature. They talk about the Constitution. It is a scorned piece of paper. He feels after a fact & finds it in the money-making, in the commerce of New England, and in the devotion of the Slave states to their interest[,] which enforces them to the crimes which they avow or disavow, but do & will do. He keeps no terms with sham churches or shamming legislatures, and must & will grope till he feels the stones. Then his other & better part, his subsoil, is the *morale*, which he solidly shows. Eloquence, poetry, friendship, philosophy, politics, in short all power must & will have the real or they cannot exist.

The ground of Hope is in the infinity of the world, which infinity reappears in every particle. I know, against all appearances, that there is a remedy to every wrong, and that every wall is a gate.

[84][132]
[85] [blank]
[86] Dumont's Mirabeau.[133] Mirabeau said of Barnave, "He is a tree growing to become some time the mast of a line of battle ship." [p. 200n]
Target was said to be "drowned in his talents." [134] [p. 201]
"I could not puncture his dropsical eloquence," says D↑umont.↓ [p. 201]

[130] Cf. "Eloquence," *W*, VII, 93.
[131] Erased pencil writing, apparently a number of separate entries, covers the upper two-thirds of this page, of which the following significant words and phrases have been recovered: "then state &"; "It is a"; and "far".
[132] Erased pencil writing, apparently a number of separate entries, covers p. [84]. The following significant words and phrases have been recovered or conjecturally recovered: "What[?] great", "of men", "will be", and "they wish it not from freak" (one entry); "It only shows[?]" and "way" (one entry); "There is", "ground", and "& absence" (one entry); "All the[?] people[?] in the" and "not" (one entry).
[133] Emerson may have used either the London, 1832, or the Philadelphia, 1833, edition of Etienne Dumont's *Recollections of Mirabeau, and of the Two First Legislative Assemblies of France.* Page references in this volume are to the London edition.
[134] This sentence is used in "Discourse at Middlebury College" and "The Scholar," *W*, X, 279.

Of Insurrection of Versailles, 5 & 6 October,[n] Mirabeau said, "Instead of a glass of brandy, a bottle was given." [p. 141]
⟨He said o⟩Of Duke of Orleans he spoke favorably of his natural talents; for in morals, he said, that nothing must be imputed to the duke, who had lost his taste, & could not therefore distinguish ⟨between⟩ good ⟨&⟩from evil." [pp. 137–138] Of him, Talleyrand said, "The duke of Orleans is the slop pail into which is thrown all the filth of the revolution" [p. 145]
The mob cried, "Let our little mother Mirabeau speak."[135] [p. 147]
"Madame le Jay," said Mirabeau, "if probity did not exist, it should be invented as a means of growing rich."[136] [p. 99]
Barnave cased in armour [p. 226]
[87] "A man like me, he said, might accept a hundred thousand crowns, but I am not to be bought for that sum." [p. 231]
Talleyrand said of Mirabeau that he dramatised his death. [p. 251]
"Let us follow upon the Atlantic that ship laden with captives, or rather that *long coffin*." *Mirabeau*. [p. 252n]

Barrere was the coffeehouse wit of the revolution. When a woman expressed her horror of the murders, he exclaimed, "We must oil the wheels of the revolution."[137]

[88]   ↑Napoleon↓
Napoleon's opinion of medicine. "Believe me we had better leave off all these remedies; life is a fortress which neither you nor I know anything about. Why throw obstacles in the way of its defence? its own means are superior to all the apparatus of your laboratories. Corvisart candidly agreed that all your filthy preparations & mixtures are good for nothing. Medicine is a collection of uncertain prescriptions which kill the poor, & sometimes succeed with the rich; & the results of which, ⟨are⟩ collectively taken, are more fatal than useful to mankind."[n]   *Antommarchi*. Vol. 1. p[p]. 180[–181][138]

---

[135] This quotation is used in "Art and Criticism," *W*, XII, 287.
[136] See Journal O, p. [198] below.
[137] Bourrienne, *Private Memoirs of Napoleon Bonaparte* . . . , 1830, I, 105, paraphrased.
[138] Francesco Antommarchi, *The Last Days of the Emperor Napoleon*, 2 vols. (London, 1825). Emerson withdrew volume 1 from the Boston Athenaeum January

"Water, air, & cleanliness were the chief articles in my pharmacopoeia."

[*Ibid*., I, 182]

[89] A Pantheon course of lectures should consist of heads like these

Plato	⟨Thomas Taylor⟩ ↑Philosopher↓
Montaigne	Skeptic
Shakspeare	Poet
Swedenborg	Mystic
⟨Napoleon⟩	
Goethe	Writer
Bonaparte	Man of the World

Jesus should properly be one head, but it requires great power of intellect & of sentiment to subdue the biases of the mind of the age, and render historic justice to the world's chief saint.

[90]¹³⁹   ↑Napoleon↓

Gen Laharpe was shot by his own soldiers who mistook him for an enemy, in Italy, in 1796. "It was remarked, says Napoleon, that during the action of Fombio, throughout the evening preceding his death, he had seemed very absent & dejected, giving no orders, appearing as if he were deprived of his usual faculties, & entirely overwhelmed by a fatal presentiment." Nap. Mem[*oirs*, 1823–1824,] Vol III, p. 172.

"In all battles a moment occurs when the bravest troops ⟨feel⟩after having made the greatest efforts feel inclined to fly. That terror proceeds from a want of confidence in their own courage, & it only requires a slight opportunity, a pretence, to restore ⟨courage⟩ ↑confidence↓ to them. The art is to give rise to the opportunity & to invent the pretence. At Arcole, I won the battle with 25 horsemen, I seized that moment of lassitude," &c. "You see that two armies are two bodies which meet & endeavour to frighten each other: a moment of panic occurs, & that moment must be t⟨‖ … ‖⟩urned to advantage. When a man has been present in many

---

1–8, 1845. This and the following entry, struck through in pencil with a vertical use mark, are used in "Napoleon," *W*, IV, 251.

¹³⁹ Erased pencil writing, consisting of at least two separate entries, covers most of this page. The following significant words and phrases have been recovered or conjecturally recovered: "world"; "the people[?]"; "foreign"; and "should depart".

actions, he distinguishes that moment without difficulty; it is as easy as
casting up of an addition." [140]

Antommarchi, vol 1, p[p]. [168–]170,

[91][141]   ↑Memoirs of Napoleon
                                                  dictated by himself↓

"The French," said the prelates at Rome, hearing the rapid submission of the papal cities to Napoleon, "do not march, but run." [142]

[*Memoirs*, 1823–1824, IV, 15]

Sieyes was alarmed at rumours of the plots of the Jacobins to assas-
sinate the consuls. "Let them alone," said Napoleon; "in war as well
as in love, we must come to close quarters to make an end of it. Let
them come; it may as well be settled one day as another."

[*Ibid.*, I, 119]

Napoleon was France[.] [143]

"The Arabs lie in ambuscade behind the dikes, & in the ditches on their
excellent little horses, & woe to him who straggles a hundred yards from
the columns. Brigadier General Muireur notwithstanding the remon-
strances of the grand guard, through a fatality which I have often observed to attend those whose last hour is at hand, would go alone to a
mount about two hundred paces from the camp. Behind it were three
Bedouins who assassinated him."

[*Ibid.*,] Vol 2 p[p. 350–]351

[92] ⟨"Soldiers, from[n] the tops of those pyramids forty centuries
look down on you."⟩[144] [*Ibid.*, II, 246]

A man of Napoleon's stamp almost ceases to have a private speech &
opinion. He is so largely receptive & is so posited that he comes to be
an office for all the light, intelligence, wit, & power of the age &

---

[140] These two paragraphs, struck through in both pencil and ink with vertical
use marks, are used in "Napoleon," *W*, IV, 248–249.

[141] "Napoleon" is centered at the top of the page.

[142] This quotation is struck through in pencil with a vertical use mark.

[143] These three words, struck through in pencil with a diagonal use mark, are
used in "Napoleon," *W*, IV, 223. See p. [92] below.

[144] This sentence, struck through in ink with a vertical use mark, is used in
"Napoleon," *W*, IV, 246.

country. He makes the code, — the system of weights & measures. All distinguished engineers, savans, statists, report to him[;] so likewise do all good heads in every kind. He catches not only the best measures & adopts them, sets his stamp on them, but also every happy & memorable expression[n] (as illustrated by Mirabeau & Dumont). Every line of Napoleon's therefore deserves reading as it is the writing of France, & not of one individual. Napoleon was truly France[.]

He was nicknamed *Cent mille hommes*[.] [145]

[93][146] ↑Vide Vol 3 p. 137 Mem[*oirs*]. of Nap[*oleon*]. [1823–1824]↓

Napoleon looking down from Montezemoto on Piedmont & back on the Alps, said, Hannibal forced the Alps, & we have turned them. [*Ibid.*, III, 150, 151] The object of the expedition to ⟨the Nile⟩ ↑Egypt↓ was to make the Mediterranean a French lake.[147]

Napoleon was citizen before he was emperor, & so has the key to citizenship. He is not a baby like a hereditary monarch, but all his remarks & estimates discover the information & justness of measurement of the middle class. ⟨Murad Bey⟩ "The Grand Master of Malta's palace was the house of a gentleman with 100 000 livres a year." [*Ibid.*, II, 201] "The patriarch of Alexandria lives in a convent at Old Cairo in the style of a head of a religious order in Europe with 30 000 francs per annum." [*Ibid.*, II, 225] & the like. I often notice in A[bel]. A[dams]. the skill & detail he learned as a grocer.[148]

Proclamation at Cherasco — Apr 1796

"Soldiers, you have in 15 days gained six victories, taken 21 stand of colours, 55 pieces of cannon, & several fortresses, & conquered the richest part of Piedmont. You have taken 15,000 prisoners, & killed or

---

[145] This sentence and the preceding paragraph are struck through in both pencil and ink with vertical use marks; the paragraph is used in "Napoleon," *W*, IV, 227, and the sentence in "Considerations by the Way," *W*, VI, 250. For "Napoleon was truly France", see p. [91] above.

[146] "Napoleon" is centered at the top of the page.

[147] This sentence, struck through in ink with a vertical use mark, is used in "Works and Days," *W*, VII, 167–168. See Journal O, p. [355] below.

[148] This paragraph is struck through in both pencil and ink with vertical use marks; "Napoleon was citizen . . . middle class." is used in "Napoleon," *W*, IV, 239. Abel Adams was Emerson's lifelong friend and financial advisor.

wounded upwards of 10 000 men. You have gained battles without cannon, passed rivers without bridges, performed forced marches [94][149] without shoes & bivouacked without brandy & often without bread."

[*Ibid*.,] Vol III p 158

K[ing]. of Sardinia is Porter of the Alps. [*Ibid*., III, 136]

Napoleon took from a mantelpiece a porcelain vase which Count Cobentzel prized as a present from the empress Catherine; "Well said Napoleon, the truce then is at an end, & war is declared; but remember that before the end of autumn, I will shatter your monarchy as I shatter this porcelain. Saying this, he dashed it furiously down & the carpet was covered with its fragments. He then saluted the Congress, & retired." [*Ibid*.,] Vol. IV. p[p]. 251[−252]

"She who has borne the greatest number of children." [150] [*Ibid*., IV, 272]

"Incidents ought not to govern policy, but policy incidents." [*Ibid*., IV, 277]
"To be hurried away by every event is to have no political system at all." [*Ibid*.,] Vol 4. p 281 [151]

"The[n] grand principle of war, says Napoleon, is, that, an army be every day & at all hours in readiness to fight." [152] [*Ibid*., IV, 318, paraphrased]

[95][153] It is an axiom that "an army ought always to be ready by day by night & at all hours to make all the resistance it is capable of making." [*Ibid*., IV, 321]

"The Austrians in general do not know the value of time." [154] [*Ibid*., IV,] p 324

[149] *"Napoleon"* is centered at the top of the page.
[150] This is given as Napoleon's answer to a question by "a celebrated woman" (Madame de Staël) who "addressed him in the midst of a numerous circle, demanding who was, in his opinion, the first woman in the world, dead or alive."
[151] These two quotations are struck through in ink with a vertical use mark. See p. [43] above.
[152] This quotation, struck through in ink with a vertical use mark, and the following one, struck through in pencil with a vertical use mark, are combined into one statement in "Napoleon," *W*, IV, 235–236.
[153] *"Napoleon"* is written at the top of the page toward the left.
[154] This quotation, struck through in pencil with a vertical use mark, is used in "Napoleon," *W*, IV, 247.

"Their calculations would have been clever had they not forgotten the proverb that 'although mountains are motionless, men walk & meet together.'" [*Ibid.*, IV,] p 319

I myself can easily translate, not without some terror, the maxim, "that an army should never have more than one line of operations;" and the principle of "never joining your columns before your enemy, or near him." [*Ibid.*, IV, 333]

⟨‖ . . . ‖⟩See Bonaparte's letter to the Directory May 1796 [Mem. Nap. Vol. 4. p. 472] "I have conducted the campaign without consulting any one: I should have done no good if I had been under the necessity of conforming to the notions of another person. I have gained some advantages over superior forces, & when totally [96][155] destitute of every thing, because in the persuasion that your confidence was reposed in me, my actions were as prompt as my thoughts." &c. &c. &c.[156] [*Ibid.*, IV,] ↑p 473↓

[*unrecovered*]
Thyself [*2–3 w*] diffuse
All the [*1 w*] of the coast
[*4–5 w*] ghost
[*1–2 w*] colours eve-- fl-w--   [5]
Thine [*1 w*] leaf [*2–3 w*]
[*2–3 w*] badg-- [*1–2 w*] fa--u--
In [*3–4 w*] their [*1 w*]
⟨The⟩ Every moth with painted wing
Every [*2–3 w*] ···ling   [10]
The wood boughs [*2 w*] manners ···d
The rocks[?] [*1 w*] thy name engraved
The sod ---obb··· [*2–3 w*]
And [*3–4 w*] thee was [*1 w*]
The saffron [*3–4 w*]   [15]
Studied [*3–4 w*] thy [*1 w*]

[155] "Napoleon" is centered at the top of the page.

[156] This quotation, struck through in pencil with a vertical use mark on p. [95] and in both pencil and ink with vertical use marks on p. [96], is used in "Napoleon," *W*, IV, 232.

[*1 w*] in [*2–3 w*] be···
[*4–5 w*] design
[*unrecovered*]
To gaz- [*2–3 w*] -ori··· edge   [20]
To search [*1 w*] now thy beauty glowed
And made w··· [*1 w*] p···s [*1 w*] [157]

The Corsicans ↑in 1769↓ fought resolutely at the passage of the Golo. Not having had time to cut down the bridge, which was of stone, they made use of the bodies of their dead to form a↑n↓ ⟨re⟩entrenchment.[158]
[*Memoirs*, 1823–1824,] Vol 4. p 47.

"How could you, Desaix," said Napoleon, "put your name to the capitulation of El Arisch?" "I did it," replied Desaix, "because the Commander in chief was unwilling to remain in Egypt, & because in an army at a distance from home, & beyond the influence of Govt, the inclinations of the Commander in chief are equivalent to those of five sixths of the army." [*Ibid.*,] Vol. 1, p. 290. [pp. 285–286]

The winter is not the most unfavorable season for the passage of lofty mountains. The snow is then firm, the weather settled, & there is nothing to fear from avalanches the real & only danger to be apprehended in the Alps. On those high mountains [159] [*Ibid.*, II, 65] [97]–[98] [leaf torn out]

[99][160] so heartily bent he was on his objects. It is plain that in Italy he did what he could, & all he could; he came within an inch of ruin several times, & his own person was all but lost. He was flung into the marsh at Arcola: the Austrians were between him & his troops in the melée, & he was brought off with desperate efforts. So at Lonato & other points he was on the point of being taken prisoner.[161]

---

[157] "Lines to Ellen," *W*, IX, 387–388. These lines, inscribed in pencil and later erased, underlie the ink entries on p. [96].

[158] This quotation is used in "Resources," *W*, VIII, 145.

[159] This quotation, struck through in ink with a vertical use mark, is used in "Napoleon," *W*, IV, 248, where it is concluded, as in Emerson's source, "there are often very fine days in December, of a dry cold, with extreme calmness in the air."

[160] "Napoleon" is centered at the top of this page. The page is struck through in ink with a vertical use mark.

[161] This entry, struck through in pencil with a vertical use mark, is used in "Napoleon," *W*, IV, 236.

He was a man who knew what to do next. Few men have a next, they are ever at the end of their line, & must have their impulse from abroad.[162]

How many unemployed Napoleons stand around!

There shall be no Alps[.] [163]

He would shorten a straight line[.]

Cambacères said no government could be carried on without good dinners.[164] In Italy, "he sought for men & found none." "Good God, said he, how rare men are! There are 18 millions in Italy, & I have with difficulty found two, — Dandolo & Melzi." *Bourrienne* Vol. 1, p. 72. In Italy, he left his letters three weeks in a basket.[165] [*Ibid.*, I, 73]

"Men," said Napoleon, "deserve the contempt with which they inspire me. I have only to put some gold lace on the coats of my virtuous republicans, & they immediately become just what I wish them." *Bourrienne.* Vol. 2 p 334 [166]

[100] Alcott does not do justice to the merits of labour: The whole human race spend their lives in hard work from simple & necessary motives, and feel the approbation of their conscience; and meet with this talker at their gate, who, as far as they see, does not labour himself, & takes up this grating tone of authority & accusation against them. His unpopularity is not at all wonderful. There must be not a few fine words, but very many hard strokes every day, to get what even an ascetic wants.

Putnam[n] pleased the Boston people by railing at Goethe in his

---

[162] This paragraph, struck through in pencil with a vertical use mark, is used in "Napoleon," *W*, IV, 233.

[163] This and the following line, struck through in pencil with a vertical use mark, are used in "Napoleon," *W*, IV, 235, 233. The first is repeated on p. [117] below.

[164] Bourrienne, *Private Memoirs of Napoleon Bonaparte* . . . , 1830, II, 257.

[165] This paragraph is struck through in pencil with a vertical use mark. The remarks about Dandolo and Melzi and Napoleon's letters are used in "Napoleon," *W*, IV, 243, 238–239.

[166] This quotation, struck through in pencil with a vertical use mark, is used in "Napoleon," *W*, IV, 243.

ΦBK oration because Goethe was not a New England Calvinist.[167] If our lovers of greatness & goodness after a local type & standard could expand their scope a little they would see that a worshipper of truth and a ⟨s⟩most subtle perceiver of truth like Goethe with his impatience of all falsehood & [101] scorn of hypocrisy was a far more useful man & incomparably more helpful ally to religion than ten thousand lukewarm churchmembers who keep all the traditions and leave a tithe of their estates to establish them. But this clergyman should have known that the movement which ⟨he calls⟩ in America created these Unitarian dissenters of which he is one, begun in the mind of this great man he traduces; that he is precisely the individual in wh⟨ich⟩om the new ideas appeared & opened to their greatest extent & with universal application[,] which more recently the active scholars in the different departments of Science, of State, & of the Church have carried in parcels & thimblefuls to their petty occasions. Napoleon I join with him as being both representatives of the impatience & reaction of nature against the morgue of convention↑s↓[,] two stern realists.[168] They want a third peer who shall stand for sentiment as they for truth & power.

[102] S[arah]. A[lden]. R[ipley] [169] is a person externally very successful[,] [⟨well⟩ ↑respectably↓ married & well provided for,] with a most happy family around her by whom she is loved & revered, & surrounded too by old & tried friends who dearly cherish her. She has ⟨a lively interest⟩ quick senses and quick perceptions and ready sympathies which put her into just relations with all persons, and a tender sense of propriety which recommends her to persons of all conditions.

---

[167] For George Putnam's strictures on Goethe in his oration on "The Connection between Intellectual and Moral Culture," see *An Oration delivered at Cambridge before the Phi Beta Kappa Society in Harvard University, August 29, 1844* (Boston, 1844), pp. 16–20. At the bottom of p. [100], in reference to Emerson's defense of Goethe as a "worshipper of truth," someone has written in pencil "Did he manifest his love of Truth and scorn of falsehood — to the women whose hearts he broke?"

[168] This sentence, struck through in ink with a vertical use mark, is used in "Goethe," *W*, IV, 289.

[169] Sarah Alden Bradford Ripley was the wife of Samuel Ripley, Emerson's half uncle.

Her bias is intellectual. It is not her delicacy of moral sentiment that sways her, but the absence of all motive to vice in one whose passion is for the beauty of laws. She would pardon ⟨as much⟩ ↑any↓ vice in another ⟨as⟩ ↑which↓ did not obscure his intellect or deform him as a companion. She knows perfectly well what is right & wrong, but it is not from conscience that she acts, but from sense of propriety in the absence too of all motives to vice. ⟨‖ ... ‖⟩She has not a profound mind, but her faculties are very muscular, and she is endowed with a ⟨a⟩certain restless & impatient [103] temperament, which drives her to the pursuit of knowledge not so much for the value of the knowledge but for some rope to twist, some grist to her mill. For this reason it is almost indifferent to her what ⟨the object is⟩ she studies, languages, chemistry, botany, metaphysics, with equal zeal, & equal success, grasping ever all the details with great precision & tenacity, yet keeping them details & means, to a general end which yet is not the most general & grand.

I should say that her ⟨in⟩ love of ends is less than her ↑impartial↓ delight in all means; ⟨her⟩ delight in the exercise of her faculties, ⟨is her⟩ and not her love of ⟨knowledge⟩ truth[,] is her passion. She has a wonderful catholicity, not at all agreeable to precisians[,] in her creed & in her morality. She sympathizes with De Stael, & with Goethe, as living in this world, & frankly regrets that such beings should die as had more fitness to live in this world than any others in her experience. In like manner, whilst she would rapidly appreciate all the objections which speculative men would offer to the actual society among us, [104] she would deprecate any declaration or step which pledged ⟨the⟩ one of her friends to any hostility to society, fearing much more the personal inconvenience to one she loved, than gratified by his opportunity of spiritual enlargement.

This delight in detail, this pleasure in the work, & not in a result, appears in her conversation, wherein she does not rest for the tardy suggestions of nature & occasion, but eagerly recalls her books, her studies, her newest persons, and recites them with heat & enjoyment to her companion.

extreme gentleness

147

excels in what is called using philosophy against the hurts of life. She follows nature in many particulars of life where others obtrude their own will & theory. She leaves a dunce to be a dunce, & rather observes & humours than guides a scholar. She is necessitarian in her opinions, & believes that a loom which turns [105] out huckabuck can never be talked into making damask. This makes her very despondent in seeing faults of character in others, as she deems them incurable. She however has much faith in the maturation & mellowing of characters, which often ⟨completes⟩ ↑supplies↓ some early defect.

She will by no means content a↑n↓ absolutist by her reliance on principles. She has too much respect to facts. She delights in French science for its precision & experiment[n] and its freedom from English convention.

Very little taste in the fine arts, not at all disposed to hazard a judgment on a picture, or a statue, or a building, and only a secondary taste in music, & even in poetry, — admiring what those whom she loves & trusts admire, & so capable of pleasure, that she can easily be pleased by what she is assured by those she trusts is pleasing. ↑If they say 'tis good, 'tis good; if they say 'tis bad, 'tis bad.↓[170]

[106][171] She is feminine in her character, though she talks with men. She has no disposition to preach, or to vote, or to lead society. She is superior to any appetites or arts. She wishes to please & to live well with a few, but in the frankest, most universal & humane mode: but in her unskilfulness & inattention to trifles, likes very well to be treated as a child & to have her toilette made for her by her young people, too confident in her own legitimate powers of engaging the best, to take any inferior methods.

An innate purity & ⟨loftiness⟩ ↑nobility↓ which releases her once for all from any solicitudes for decorum, or dress, or other appearances. She knows ⟨well that⟩ her own worth, & that she cannot be soiled by a plain dress, or by the hardest household drudgery.

[170] Cf. *JMN*, VII, 364.
[171] This page is struck through in pencil with two vertical use marks.

She is a pelican mother, and though one might not say of her what was said of the Princess [107]¹⁷² Vaudemont, "ask any beggar the way to her house; they all know it;"¹⁷³ yet of her house & her husband's, it is certain that every beggar & every guest ⟨will⟩ who has once visited it, will never forget it. It is very certain that every young man of parts remembers it as the temple of learning & ideas.

After all, we have not described her, for she is obviously inspired by a great bright ⟨daemon⟩ fortunate daemon.

She is of that truth of character that she torments herself with any injustice real or imagined she may have done to another.

Eloquence needs no constable[.]
One orator makes many.
    Conservatism, poverty, frugality, memory
    Creation, Wealth, ⟨‖ ... ‖⟩forgetful squandering

↑*Demonology*↓   ↑*Mesmerism*↓

"Extasi omnia praedicere." ¹⁷⁴

[108] The critic knows very well that ⟨the wisest writer, as Plato or Spinoza though his wit were keen as the lightning cannot on that⟩ Nature will outwit the wisest writer, though it were Plato or Spinoza, and his book will fall into this dead limbo we call literature; else the writer were God too, & his work another nature.

February 26. A thaw for more than a week & three days of heavenly weather bringing all mythology on their breezy dawns. Down falls the water from the steeps; up shoots the northern-light after sunset from the horizon. But nature seems a dissipated hussey. She seduces

---

¹⁷² This page is struck through in pencil with a vertical use mark to "done to another."

¹⁷³ Talleyrand is credited with this statement in Villemarest, *Life of Prince Talleyrand*, 1834–1836, III, 327, as noted on p. [160] below.

¹⁷⁴ In *JMN*, VII, 311, Emerson quotes this from Robert Burton's *The Anatomy of Melancholy*, 3 vols. (London, 1804), I, 12; volume 1 is in his library. Burton's translation is "answer all questions in an extasis."

us from all work, listen to her rustling leaves, — to the invitations which each blue peak, and rolling river, & fork of woodland road offers, & ⟨all⟩we should never wield the shovel or the trowel.

March 15. How gladly, after three months sliding on snow, our feet find the ground again! [175]

[109] ⟨A man has too many enemies than that he can afford to be his own.⟩ [176]

Venus or Beauty, ⟨|| ... ||⟩author of sport & jest, cheerer & rejoicer of men by the illuminations of beauty, was worshipped as the mother of all things. What right have you scholars & thinkers to pretend to plans of philanthropy, who freeze & dispirit me by that selfish murderous hang-dog face?[n]

Proclus. I not only do not think he has his equal among contemporary writers, but I do not know men sufficiently athletic to read him. There is the same difference between the writings of these Platonists & Scotch metaphysics as between the sculptures of Phidias & the statues of Tam o'Shanter & My Uncle Toby. They abound in personification. Every abstract idea, every element, every agent in nature or in thought, is strongly presented as a god, in this most poetic philosophy, so that the universe is filled [110] with august & exciting images. It is imaginative & not anatomical. It is stimulating.

[111] "The soul is intellect in capacity but life in energy."
↑P[lato]. in Tim[aeus]. Vol 2 p 448↓ [177]

"The parts in us are more the property of wholes & of things above us, than they are our property."   [*Ibid.,*] ↑Vol II p 435↓

Why fear to die
At death the world receives its own [178] [*Ibid.,* II, 435, paraphrased]

---

[175] This sentence, struck through in ink with two vertical use marks, occurs in a versified form on p. [143] below.

[176] This sentence is used in "Montaigne," *W,* IV, 160. See p. [137] below.

[177] *The Commentaries of Proclus on the Timaeus of Plato* . . . , 1820.

[178] These two lines are in pencil.

"For the universe uses them as irrational animals" [*Ibid.*,] ↑Vol 2 p 400↓

The Demiurgus, as Orpheus says, was nurtured indeed by Adrastia, but associates with Necessity, & generates Fate. [*Ibid.*, II, 397]

A right line i⟨n⟩s in power a square   Scholia [179]

[112] Very great was the inconvenience in the country of finding domestics, but the darker the night the nearer the dawn[.] When at last ⟨night[?]⟩we could absolutely get none, our deliverance was suddenly achieved: we instantly simplified in good earnest our modes of living: we disused fifty luxuries and our health & wealth & morals were improved.[180]

———

In the ideal republic, of course, no man should ever do one thing but once.

———

↑Producer & Consumer.↓
Luckily in the contingency of glutted markets, every man who is a producer is also able to throw himself on his reserved rights as a consumer. An iron bar is not only a bolt but also a conductor.[181]

[113] It is curious how incidental the best things are. A nation is dedicated to trade for some centuries[;] that occupies the vast majority of men ⟨al⟩every day for all that long duration. Yet the last day it is not more elevated than the first day & cannot command our respect. But as they grow rich, some men of leisure & study are formed, some men of taste appear; by the very indignation at the general meanness & hurry, some souls are driven into a secluded & sublime way of thinking; these invent arts & sciences[;] these pray & sing & carve & build. Incidentally too on all this vast grocery business floating all over the world, ↑books & letters go[,]↓ a passenger is carried from one country who inoculates hundreds & thousands in the new land with the opinions & ⟨aspirations⟩ ↑hopes↓ cherished by a handful of men in the old. This new influence[,] quite incidental to

[179] See p. [56] above.
[180] Erased pencil writing underlies most of this entry. Only the words "excellent" and "but" have been recovered.
[181] See p. [117] below.

151

trade, lets loose new thoughts on trade & politics & religion ⟨in the⟩ⁿ among the traders which go to revise & ⟨modify⟩ revolutionize all their modes of living & ⟨ac⟩conduct.

[114] The history of Buonaparte is the commanding romance of modern times because ⟨it⟩ every reader studies in it his own history. ⟨It⟩ He is a good average man because he was a citizen like his reader who arrived by very intelligible merits at such a free position that he could indulge & did indulge all those tastes which the reader possesses but is obliged to conceal and deny. Good society, good books, fast travelling, personal weight, the execution of his ideas, the standing in the attitude of a benefactor to all persons, the refined enjoyment of pictures, statues, music, ⟨ar⟩ palaces, & conventional honours, precisely what is agreeable to the heart of every man in the 19th Century this powerful man possessed.[182]

An extraordinary genius governed him which seemed the genius of a hundred men or of a nation.[183] A scope of magnificence is visible in all his schemes & words. He is a ⟨c⟩founder of colonies, a ⟨legislator⟩ lawgiver, and a patriarch in every new place. Yet he is thoroughly modern & has the spirit of the [115] newspapers. & is "no Capuchin, not he."[184]

What events, what circumstances aided his inspirations! his carousals, his cups of coffee, his opium-eating were the spying the Alps by a sunset in the Sicilian sea, or drawing up his army for battle in sight of the Pyramids or ⟨cr⟩fording the Red Sea or wading in the gulf by the Isthmus of Suez. "On the shore of Ptolemais gigantic projects agitated him." "Had St Jean d'Acre fallen I should have changed the face of the world."

---

[182] This paragraph, struck through in pencil with a vertical use mark, is used in "Napoleon," *W*, IV, 225–226.

[183] This sentence is struck through in pencil with a vertical use mark.

[184] This quotation, and the incidents and quotations in the following entry, are from Bourrienne, *Private Memoirs of Napoleon Bonaparte* . . . , 1830, I, 188–189, 221, 241–242, 289, 291, and 325. "Yet he is . . . of the world.' ", struck through in pencil with a vertical use mark, is used in "Napoleon," *W*, IV, 225, 246.

Talleyrand replied to Cambaceres who said that Sieyes was profound; "Profound! yes a cavity, a perfect cavity."[185]

At Montebello, "I ordered Kellermann ↑(said Napoleon)↓ to attack with 800 horse, & with these he separated the 6000 Hungarian grenadiers before the very eyes of the Austrian cavalry. This cavalry was half a league off & required quarter of an hour to arrive on the field of action; & I have observed that it is always those quarters of an hour that decide the fate of a battle."[186] Antommarchi [*The Last Days of the Emperor Napoleon*, 1825, I, 167]

"Love, said Napoleon, is merely a silly infatuation; depend on it." *Duc de Vicenza*[187]

[116] "Caulincourt," said Napoleon ↑in 1813,↓ "you see that none but my poor soldiers & officers who have not yet obtained the rank of Princes, Dukes, & Counts, are worth anything. It is melancholy to say this, but it is the truth. I will tell you what I ought to do. I ought to send all these newly created nobles to repose on their down beds, or to strut about in their chateaux. I ought to rid myself of these growlers, & recommence the war with an army formed of the young & uncorrupted; of men who would look neither before nor behind them, but who would inscribe on their banners as in 1793 the words, 'Conquer or Die!' With that device in my heart, I overran Egypt, subjugated Italy, & raised the French eagles to a height to which none will raise them after me." Mem. of Duc de Vicenza Vol 1 p 163

In 1814, Talleyrand said to Alexander; "Sire, only one of two things is possible. We must either have Bonaparte or Louis XVIII. Bonaparte if you can support him; but you cannot, for you are not alone. We will not have another soldier in his stead. If we want a soldier, we will keep the one we have he is the first in the world. After him, any other who may be proposed would not have ten men to support him. I say again, Sire, either Bonaparte or Louis XVIII. Any thing

[185] Bourrienne, *Private Memoirs of Napoleon Bonaparte* . . . , 1830, I, 461, paraphrased.
[186] This quotation, struck through in pencil with a vertical use mark, is used in "Napoleon," *W*, IV, 238.
[187] Armand Augustin Louis de Caulaincourt, *Recollections of Caulincourt, Duke of Vicenza*, 2 vols. (London, 1838), I, 135. Emerson withdrew both volumes from the Boston Athenaeum in January, 1845. The quotation, struck through in pencil with a vertical use mark, is used in "Napoleon," *W*, IV, 254.

else is an intrigue." *Bourrienne* [*Private Memoirs of Napoleon Bona-parte* . . . , 1830,] ↑Vol. 4↓ [p. 297]

Louis XVIII is a principle.[188] [*Ibid.*, IV, 321]

[117] Shall we say that the best physical fact is the porosity of all bodies? An iron bar is not so much a barrier, as it is a ⟨conductor⟩ road & a conductor when we have skill. And when we have sat before a mountain of obstruction for a time gleams & flashes of light begin to play and by & by it grows transparent. There shall be no Alps. We can turn them. We surrender the field to these Vandal mobs of selfishness & brutality & under their very breasts & animalism suddenly a conscience glows.[189]

———

Marshal Ney said to the Emperor before Lutzen, "Sire, give me some of those young & valiant conscripts, I will lead them whither you please. Our old warriors know as much as we do; they judge of position & difficulties; but these brave youths are afraid of nothing, — they look neither to the right nor the left, but always forward."

Duroc, at Dresden, after the death of Bessiéres, said, "We have had rather too much of this; we shall all be carried off."

[118] "During the night, said Bonaparte, enter my chamber as seldom as possible. Do not awake me when you have any good news to communicate; with that there is no hurry. But when you bring bad news, rouse me instantly, for then there is not a moment to be lost."[190] Bourrienne   Vol 2 p 22

He was very fond of talking of religion. He readily yielded up all that was proved against religion as the work of men & time, but he would not hear of materialism. One fine night on deck with some persons arguing in favor of materialism, Bonaparte raised his hand to heaven, & pointing to the stars, said, You may talk as long as you please, gentlemen, but who made all that? Bourrienne   Vol 2 p 38 [191]

---

[188] This entry is in pencil.
[189] For "An iron bar . . . a conductor", see p. [112] above; for "There shall be no Alps.", see p. [99] above.
[190] This quotation, struck through in pencil with a vertical use mark, is used in "Napoleon," *W*, IV, 238.
[191] This and the following quotation, struck through in pencil with a vertical use mark, are used in "Napoleon," *W*, IV, 249–250.

On the voyage to Egypt, one of Bonaparte's greatest pleasures was after dinner to fix upon three or four persons to support a proposition & as many to oppose it. He always gave out the subjects which were to be discussed & they most frequently turned on questions of religion, the different kinds of government, & the art of war. One day he asked whether the planets were inhabited[;] on another what was the age of the world[;] then he proposed to consider the probability of the destruction of our globe either by water or by fire[;] at another time the truth or fallacy of presentiments, & the interpretation of dreams.

Bourrienne   Vol 1 p[p. 221–]222

[119] On the road from the Tuilleries to Notre Dame Lannes & Augereau wished to alight from the carriage as soon as they saw that they were being driven to mass, & it required an order from the First Consul to prevent their doing so. They went therefore to Notre Dame. The next day Buonaparte asked Augereau what he tho't of the ceremony? "O it was all very fine," replied the general, "there was nothing wanting except the million of men who have perished in ↑the↓ pulling ⁿ down of what you are setting up."

Bourrienne, Vol. II. p. 273[–274]

Bonaparte showed that very often the best means of defence consists in attacking, & that the art of conducting a war on a large scale lies chiefly in being able to regain the liberty of option when it has been lost by the first success of the enemy.[192]

Antommarchi [*The Last Days of the Emperor Napoleon*, 1825,] Vol 1. 304

"With an inferior army the art of war consists in always having more forces than the enemy on the point where the enemy is attacked or where he attacks."[193] Bonaparte ap. Bourrienne Vol 1 p 98

[120] The Gentleman regards only beauty; so that it is almost ungenerous to report of him any thing else than his most outside action. But it is a pleasure to know the leaders of our time. Horace Walpole knows the first men & women of his time. Every man should know the great ⟨who⟩ among his contemporaries.

K[ing]. of Sweden had a camp printing press for ↑bulletins.↓[194]

---

[192] "Bonaparte showed . . . attacking,", struck through in ink with a vertical use mark, is used in "Napoleon," *W*, IV, 237.

[193] This quotation, struck through in ink with a vertical use mark, is used in "Napoleon," *W*, IV, 229–230. Cf. also p. [58] above and *English Traits*, *W*, V, 56.

[194] Bourrienne, *Private Memoirs of Napoleon Bonaparte* . . . , 1830, III, 296.

⟨The journals received⟩ Articles[n] for insertion in the journals were received on the bayonets of grenadiers or the lances of cossacks[.]

At Milan, Napoleon put on his head the iron crown of Lombardy, saying, "Dieu me l' a donnée gare à qui la touche!"[195]

Here let me pause a moment on the illustration he gives to the universality of this gift of genius. He delighted in every play of invention in a romance, in a recitation, in a bon-mot, as well as in a stratagem or a campaign. He delighted to entertain & to affright Josephine & her ladies in a dimlighted apartment by the terrors of a fiction to which his voice & dramatic power lent every assistance.[196]

[121] I believe our political parties have nothing fantastic or accidental in their origin, but express very rudely some lasting relation. ⟨But⟩ We cannot ⟨therefore⟩ quarrel with the parties with more reason than with the east wind, or the winter; for, on the whole, no option is made, but the men stand for the defence of those interests in which they find themselves. Our quarrel with them is when they quit this deep ↑natural↓ ground at the bidding of some leader, &, altogether from personal considerations, throw themselves into the defence & maintenance of points nowise belonging to their system. A party is perpetually corrupted by personality, and, whilst we absolve the party from all wilfulness or dishonesty, we cannot extend the same charity to the leaders. They ⟨are persons who⟩ reap the rewards of the fidelity & [122] zeal of the ⟨party⟩ masses they direct, and no party was ever without adroit & unscrupulous guides who turned their docility & ardour to a private account.[197]

Bonaparte delighted in tasting his ⟨f⟩good fortune. Raguideau[,] who had dissuaded Mme Beauharnois from "marrying a soldier with nothing but his cloak & his sword," was sent for on the day of

---

[195] *Ibid.*, III, 192.
[196] This paragraph, struck through in ink with a vertical use mark, is used in "Napoleon," *W*, IV, 252.
[197] This entry is struck through in ink with discontinuous vertical use marks. "I believe . . . they direct," is used in "Politics," *W*, III, 208–209.

the Coronation of the Emperor, and asked "Well, have I nothing but my cloak & my sword?" [198]

When Bourrienne stated the difficulty of getting acknowledged by the old reigning families of Europe, Bonaparte said, "If it comes to that I will dethrone them all, & then I shall be the oldest sovereign among them." [199]

"Courage," said he to Caulincourt, "may defend a crown, but infamy never." [200]

"Gentlemen" said he in 1814, "You may say what you please but in the situation in which I stand my only nobility is the rabble of the faubourgs, & I know of no rabble but the nobility whom I have created." *Bourrienne* [201] [IV, 256]

[123] I neither think our democratic institutions dangerous to the citizen, nor on the other hand do I think them better than those which preceded them. They are not better but only fitter for us. We may be wise in asserting the advantage in modern times of the democratic form, but to other states of society in which religion consecrated the monarchical, that & not this was expedient. The democracy is better for us, because the religious sentiment of the present time accords better with it. ⟨We must not⟩ We are in our whole ⟨h⟩ education & way of thinking & acting, democrats, & are nowise qualified to judge of monarchy, which to our fathers living & thinking in the monarchical idea was just as exclusively right.[202]

As a pendant to the Corsican anecdote (p. 96), and to the story, in Aubrey, of ———— who covered himself with dead bodies to

---

[198] Bourrienne, *Private Memoirs of Napoleon Bonaparte* . . . , 1830, III, 167–168. This entry is struck through in ink with a vertical use mark.

[199] *Ibid.*, III, 181. This paragraph is struck through in ink with a vertical use mark. See Journal W, p. [26] below.

[200] *Ibid.*, IV, 262.

[201] This quotation is struck through in ink with a vertical use mark; " 'Gentlemen . . . faubourgs," is used in "Napoleon," W, IV, 243.

[202] This paragraph, struck through in ink with a vertical use mark, is used in "Politics," W, III, 207.

keep himself warm on a battle field, I read in Bentley magazine
of a soldier at Borodino who crept into the carcass of a horse to
sleep.[203] At Nantucket, I saw a ⟨m⟩ship master who had eaten a man
and at New Bedford one who had been in the mouth of a whale.

[124] [204] "Before he fought a battle Bonaparte thought little ⟨of⟩about
what he should do in case of success, but a great deal about what he
should do in case of a reverse of fortune." [205]

Bourrienne Vol 2 p 27

He risked everything & spared nothing[.] [206]
What he had determined to do he did thoroughly[:] on any point
he poured hosts: he rained grape & cannon shot.[207]
He ⟨declared⟩ promised the troops in his proclamation at Austerlitz
that he would not expose his person, the reverse of the ordinary
declaration of generals & sovereigns in their proclamations.[208]

The idol of common men because he had in transcendant degrees
the qualities & powers of common men. This terrific ciphering[,] this
just expectation from gold & iron, from earth & water, from wheels
& ships, from troops & cabinets[,] that each should do after its kind
& not the folly of expecting that from them which in ordinary experience they do not. Herein resembling Luther a little. ⟨He⟩

---

[203] Aubrey's story is told about Sir Adrian Scrope in *Letters Written by Eminent Persons . . . and Lives of Eminent Men, by John Aubrey*, 1813, III, 379.
The magazine article was Bayle St. John's "The Gates of Death. A Revelation of
the Horrors of the Battle-field," *Bentley's Miscellany*, XVI (1844), 501–511, in
which the incident is related on p. 504.

[204] In addition to the use marks struck through individual entries, this page is
struck through in pencil with a vertical use mark. Erased pencil writing, apparently
a number of separate entries, covers this page. The following significant words and
phrases have been recovered or conjecturally recovered: "necessity"; "democrat";
"better"; "But good as"; "Nor has any state"; "state[?] corrupt"; "necessity";
"practical defect"; and "tell of it".

[205] This quotation, struck through in pencil with a vertical use mark, is used in
"Napoleon," *W*, IV, 238.

[206] This sentence, struck through in pencil with a vertical use mark, is used in
"Napoleon," *W*, IV, 235.

[207] This sentence is struck through in pencil with a vertical use mark; "on any
point . . . cannon shot." is used in "Napoleon," *W*, IV, 236.

[208] This paragraph, struck through in pencil with a vertical use mark, is used
in "Napoleon," *W*, IV, 241.

He was moreover entitled to his crowns. He won his victories in his head before [125] he won them on the field. He was not lucky only.[209]

But this ciphering is specially French. Fourier is another arithmetician. Laplace, Lagrange, Berthollet walking metres & destitute of worth. These cannot say to men of talents, I am that which these express, as Character always seems to say.[210]

Yet ⟨Napoleon⟩ man always feels that Napoleon fights for him; these are honest victories: this strong steam-engine does our work.[211]

"a⟨z⟩ssez de Bonaparte" 1814 [212]

On hearing of the execution of the Duc d'Enghien Mr Pitt said "Bonaparte has now done himself more ⟨injury⟩mischief than we have done him since the last declaration of war." [213]

⟨"The air is full of poniards," said Fouché⟩ [214]

"God made Bonaparte & rested;" said M. de la Chaise, prefect of Arras. Count Louis de Narbonne remarked, "that, it would have been well had God rested a little sooner." *Bourrienne* [*Ibid.*, III, 148]

French are skeptics & French history makes skeptics[.] [215]

---

[209] This and the preceding paragraph are struck through in pencil with a vertical use mark; "The idol of . . . common men.", "This terrific . . . do not.", and "he won . . . field." are used in "Napoleon," *W*, IV, 227, 229, and 232. For "He was moreover . . . field.", see *JMN*, VIII, 68.

[210] See *JMN*, VI, 353. Three lines of erased pencil writing, of which nothing has been recovered, underlie this paragraph.

[211] This sentence, struck through in pencil with a vertical use mark, is used in "Napoleon," *W*, IV, 245.

[212] This entry, struck through in ink with two vertical use marks, is used in "Napoleon," *W*, IV, 258.

[213] Bourrienne, *Private Memoirs of Napoleon Bonaparte* . . . , 1830, III, 35.

[214] *Ibid.*, III, 99. This entry, struck through in ink with a diagonal and two vertical use marks, is used in "Culture," *W*, VI, 132.

[215] See *JMN*, VI, 352.

[126] B⟨u⟩onaparte said to Bourrienne, "My power would fall were I not to support it by new glory & new victories. Conquest has made me what I am, & conquest alone can maintain me." [*Ibid.*, II, 25] We did not need that confirmation to teach that for conservation as much life is needed as for creation. We are always in a bad box, — just on the edge of ruin, — & to be saved only by invention & ⟨resolution⟩ courage. The politicians speak the truth who begin all their speeches by saying "We are arrived at a crisis."[216]

People who take care of ⟨chil⟩ young children say that their preservation is a perpetual miracle[;] so is it with old children[;] so is it with a man who splits wood, with a sailor, with an engineer, with all men.

Buonaparte was singularly destitute of generous sentiments. He is not a gentleman. He is unjust to all his generals, egotistic & monopolizing, meanly stealing the credit of their great actions — from Kellermann, from Bernadotte. He is a boundless liar. All his bulletins were proverbs and his ⟨new⟩ moniteurs for saying what he wished to be believed, and, what is ⟨ex⟩most ex[217] [127]–[128] [leaf torn out]

[129] A despair has crept over the Whig party in this country. They the active, enterprizing, intelligent, well meaning, & wealthy part of the people[,] the real bone & strength of the American people[,] find themselves paralysed & defeated everywhere by the hordes of ignorant & deceivable natives & the armies of foreign voters who fill Pennsylvania, N. Y., & New Orleans, and by those unscrupulous ⟨‖ . . . ‖⟩editors & orators who have assumed to lead these ⟨people.⟩ masses. The creators of wealth and conscientious, rational, & responsible persons, those whose ⟨sta⟩ names are given in as fit for jurors, for referees, for offices of trust, those whose opinion is public opin-

---

[216] "B⟨u⟩onaparte said . . . courage.", struck through in pencil with a vertical use mark, is used in "Napoleon," *W*, IV, 236–237.

[217] This entry, struck through in pencil with a vertical use mark, is used in "Napoleon," *W*, IV, 253–254, where it is concluded "and worse, — he sat, in his premature old age, in his lonely island, coldly falsifying facts and dates and characters, and giving to history a theatrical *éclat*."

ion, find themselves degraded into observers, & violently turned out
of all share in the action & counsels of the nation.
[See, below, p 137]

How many degrees of power! That which we exert[,] political, social,
intellectual, moral[,] is most superficial. We talk & work half asleep.
Between us & our last energy lie terrific social & then sublime solitary
exertions. Let our community rise en masse[,] the undrilled original
militia; or let the private man [130] put off the citizen, & awake the
hero; then is one a match for a nation[.]   ↑See p 139↓

The position of Massachusetts seems to me to ⟨have gained
⟨|| ... ||⟩an adva⟩ be better for Mr Hoar's visit to S. Carolina, in this
point, that one ⟨d⟩illusion is dispelled.²¹⁸ Massachusetts was dishonoured before; but she was credulous in the protection of the
Constitution & either did not believe or affected not to believe that
she was dishonoured. Now all doubt on that subject is removed, &
every Carolina boy ⟨&⟩ will not fail to tell every Massachusetts boy,
whenever they meet, how the fact stands. The Boston merchants
would willingly salve the matter over, but they cannot hereafter
receive Southern gentlemen at their tables, without a consciousness
of shame. ↑I do not like very well to hear a man say he has been in
Carolina. I know too well what men she suffers in her towns. He
is no freeman.↓

In every government there are wild lawless provinces where
the constituted authorities are forced to content themselves with
such obedience as they can get. Turkey has its [131] Algiers &
Morocco, ⟨Italy⟩ ↑Naples↓ its Calabria, Rome its Fondi, London its
Alsatia, & Bristol County its Slab Bridge, where the life of a man
is not worth insuring. South Carolina must be set down in that in-

---

²¹⁸ Samuel Hoar, an agent of Massachusetts, had gone to South Carolina in
December, 1844, to take measures for the protection of Negro seamen who were
citizens of Massachusetts and faced imprisonment and sale when they entered the
port of Charleston. On a request to the governor from the legislature of South
Carolina, Hoar was expelled. An indignation meeting apparently was held in Concord in January, 1845 (L, III, 275), for which Emerson prepared remarks here
and on pp. [154]–[157] and [168]–[169] below.

famous category, and we must go there in disguise & with pistols in our pockets leaving our pocketbooks at home,[n] ↑making our wills before we go.↓[219]

Literature is resorted to as consolation, not as decalogue[;] then is literature defamed & disgraced.

Lord Edward Fitzgerald[,] after travelling amongst barbarous nations, said "I have seen human nature in all its forms; it is everywhere the same, but the wilder it is, the more virtuous."
⟨Ap⟩ See *Fitzgerald's letters.*   ⎫   ap. W L Fisher
                                    ⎬   Hist. of Sabbath
                                    ⎭   p 167 [220]
See in Fisher's book also p 134 the remark of Lord Brougham concerning perjury & bishops[.] [221]

[132] I talked yesterday with the Shaker Elders Joseph Myrick & Grove Blanchard and stated my chief objection to their community as a place of education, that there was too much interference. In heaven, a squadron of angels would be a Squadron of Gods, with profoundest mutual deference; so should men live.

It is true that ⟨t⟩a community cannot be truly seen from the outside. If deep sympathy exists, what seems interference, is not, being justified by the heart of the suffering party. ↑See U 80↓ And in Lane's representation of their society, they appear well. He thinks them open to the greatest improvement & enlargement on every side, even of science, learning, & elegance: only not suddenly. In that case, one can well enjoy their future, and leave them as an order of American monks & nuns, and willingly release from nuptial vows a class of Virgins & Children of light, who would dedicate [133] themselves to austerity & religion, labor, & love.

Lane thought that they looked on their speech, their dress, & even

---

[219] The last six words are added in pencil.

[220] William Logan Fisher, *The History of the Institution of the Sabbath Day, Its Uses and Abuses* . . . (Philadelphia, 1845). The quotation, struck through in ink with a diagonal use mark, is used in "Worship," *W*, VI, 214.

[221] This entry is struck through in ink with a vertical use mark; "p 134" is circled. For Brougham's words, see Journal W, p. [45] below.

their worship as not sacred, ⟨but⟩ nor even the best, but as open to revisal, & though not rashly ⟨yet⟩ alterable, yet ⟨‖ ... ‖⟩modifications were ⟨probable⟩ likely to be received. Elder Grove had said, that their ↑mode of↓ worship was once spontaneous; now it was only preserved as a condition for exciting the spirit.

I told him they seemed peasants, with a squalid contentment.

> John B. Webster
> New Market, N.H.
> Martin W. Damon.   Hanover Mass

[134] The aim of writers is to tame the Holy Ghost, & produce it as a show to the city. But the sole terms on which the Infinite will come to cities, is the ⟨absolute⟩ surrender of ⟨all things⟩ ↑cities↓ to its Will. And yet Nature seems sometimes to coquette with great poets, and, in its ⟨tendency⟩ ↑willingness↓ to be expressed, suffers them to be knowing men of the world, ⟨without⟩ yet does not withdraw its inspirations.

The Daemons lurk & are dumb: they hate the newspapers.

> And willing to be God the worm
> Flees through all the /round/spire/ of form [222]

[135] Let us however, says Prudence, attempt some what practicable: why should we call meetings to vote against the law of gravitation, or organize a society to resist a revolution round the sun?

In the Antislavery Conventions, & in most other meetings, I am forced to remember the clock, & regret how much time is passing, and if I spend any hour upon any history of facts, I think on this loss; but if you bring me a thought; if you bring me a law[;] if I contemplate an idea, I no longer count the hours. This is ⟨the⟩ of the Eternity which is the generator of time.[223]

---

[222] These two lines are in pencil. They occur, with some changes in wording, as ll. 5–6 of the epigraph to *Nature*, W, I, 1, and as ll. 81–82 of "May-Day," W, IX, 166.

[223] "In the Antislavery . . . the hours", struck through in ink with two ver-

The only defence I can think of for the fanatic who lives without labour, is that of Mirabeau quoted above, p. 87.

[136] Good manners require a great deal of time, as does a wise treatment of children. Orientals have time, the desart, & stars; the occidentals have not.

⟨The⟩ No man passes for that with another, which he passes for with himself. The respect & the ⟨slight⟩ censure of his brother are alike injurious or misplaced. We see ourselves, we lack organ to see others, & squint at them.

The state is our neighbors; our neighbors are the state. It is a folly to treat the state as if it were some individual arbitrarily willing thus and so. It is the same company of poor devils we know so well, of William & Edward & John & Henry, doing as they are obliged to do, & trying hard to do conveniently what must & will be done. They do not impose a tax. God & the nature of things imposes the tax, requires that the land shall bear its burden, of road, & of social order, & defence; & [137] I confess I lose all respect for this tedious denouncing of the state by idlers who rot in indolence, selfishness, & envy in the chimney corner.

Commonsense is the wick of the candle.
A flake of snow brought the avalanche down.

Eve softly with her womb
Bit him to death

Lightly was woman snared, herself a snare[.]

⟨Dicke⟩ [224]

---

tical and three diagonal use marks, is used, considerably altered, in "Uses of Great Men," *W*, IV, 21–22.

[224] This fragment, and the three lines directly above it, are in pencil.

A man has t⟨‖ ... ‖⟩oo many enemies than that he can afford to be his own.[225]

What is the difference between the abolitionist & the ⟨democrat⟩ ↑loco foco↓? this only, that the one knows the facts in this iniquity, & the other does not. One has informed himself of the slave laws of the Southern states, & the other has not; but both suffer the whole damnable mischief to go on. (See p. 129)

Waiting to be last devoured.[226]

[138] Alas! our penetration increases as we grow older, and we are no longer deceived by great words when unrealized or unembodied. Say rather we detect littleness in expressions & thoughts that once we should have taken & cited as proofs of strength.

↑At the time↓ when ⁿ Bonaparte appeared ↑military↓ men believed there was nothing new to be done in war. They think the same today of letters, property, labor, & all the rest[.] [227]

Voltaire called the soldiers, "Alexanders at five sous a day." [228] [*Epistles*, XXXVII, 11–12]

Legion of honour, "These are the rattles by which men are led," ⁿ said Napoleon.

Friends to me are frozen wine
I wait the sun shall on them shine [229]

[139] We do not ⟨leave⟩ live an equal life but one of contrasts & patchwork; now a little joy[,] then a sorrow, now a sin[,] then a generous or brave action. We must always be little whilst we have

[225] See p. [109] above.
[226] Cf. Journal U, p. [154] above.
[227] This paragraph, struck through in ink with a vertical use mark, is used in "Napoleon," *W*, IV, 247.
[228] This and the two following entries are in pencil.
[229] "Fragments on Nature and Life," XIV, *W*, IX, 352.

these alternations. Character is regular & homogeneous. Our world, it is true, is like us: it has many weathers, here a shade & there a rainbow; here gravel, & there a diamond; polar ice, then temperate zone, then torrid; now a genius[,] then a good many mediocre people[.]

H.D.T. said that the Fourierists had a sense of duty which led them to devote themselves to their second best.[230]

"What has posterity done for us that we should do so much for posterity?"[231]

Every parish steeple will be the standard of a troop[.]

[140][232]   I went to the woods
To^n see the forest Anakim
Toss from their limbs the snow

The silver trees
Jingle^n & ring
With myriad bells
Of the falling icicles
Every tree
Seemed a fountain ⟨in full playing⟩ ↑foaming↓ free
And in this day of jewelry
Nothing was forgot
Justice was done
To^n the tiniest leaf & straw
Every form ⟨was⟩

[230] A pencil version of this sentence, later erased, underlies the ink version; there are no significant differences between the two. The sentence is used in "Historic Notes on Life and Letters in New England," W, X, 356.

[231] A pencil version of this sentence, later erased, is still visible in the space between this and the previous entry: "Dr J[?] tells the story of the man who said he should like to know what posterity had done for us that we should do so much for them".

[232] The entries on this and the following page are in pencil. Four lines of erased pencil writing, possibly poetry, are visible in the space between "Toss from their limbs the snow" and "The silver trees" on p. [140]. The last three of the four lines are struck through in pencil with a vertical use mark. No significant words have been recovered.

Was pranked in glass,[233]
The impartial storm
Dealt alike with every form
To ⟨every one⟩ lowly & to lordl⟨y⟩iest one
Was justice done
The aged oak, the blade of grass
⟨Were pranked in perfect case of glass⟩
Was pranked in ⟨living⟩ suit of living glass

[141]   He shall know
             The noble forest laws

                    Free of the forest laws

        I go discontented thro' the world [234]   [x]
        Because I cannot strike   [x]
        The harp to please my tyrannous ear   [1–2]
        Gentle ⟨strokes will not content me⟩ ↑touches↓ are not
              wanted   [x]
        These the yielding gods had ⟨sent me⟩ granted   [x]
        It shall not tinkle a guitar   [x]
        But strokes of fate   [16]
        Chiming with the ample winds
        With the pulse of human blood   [21]
        With the voice of mighty men
        With the din of city arts
        With the cannonade of war
        With the footsteps of the brave   [25]
        And the /prophecies/sayings/ of the wise   [x]
        Chiming with the forest ⟨boughs⟩ tone   [17]
        When they buffet ⟨each other⟩ ↑boughs↓ in ⟨storms⟩ ↑the
              windy↓ wood
        Chiming with the gasp & ⟨the⟩ moan

[233] This and the preceding three lines are struck through in pencil with a vertical
use mark.
[234] A number of the following lines, considerably changed, occur in "Merlin,"
W, IX, 120–121.

Of the ↑ice-↓imprisoned ⟨lake⟩ flood   [20]
I will not read a pretty tale   [x]
To pretty people in a nice saloon   [x]
Borrowed from their expectation   [x]
But I will sing aloud & free   [x]
From the heart of the world   [x]

[142][235] Men do blunder into victories. The compromise which
prevails every day, is the accepting of other people's aims for our
own, through these treacherous sympathies, and so this expedient
civilization subsists & gets on, which pleases nobody and ⟨which⟩
torments the sincere. Yet it seems of little consequence at last whether
we move on other people's tactics or on our own. Experience is the
only teacher, & we get his lesson indifferently in any school. I speak
to A's state of mind; I write on a hint of B's learning; I enjoy myself in C's genius & tendency; E. comes & says all this is wrong. Be
it so, but I have always been thus facile, and here I am with prodigious
enjoyments & hopes.

————

↑*Poverty*↓
The worst thing I know of poverty is that if a man is dead, they
call him *poor fellow.*

So I will sing my song
By the help of nature dear
Under all impediments
⟨Until⟩ Evil times & wayward men
Frivolous and sensual
Until I melt the obstruction
And pour myself ⟨in music⟩ like a bird
And as I speak am heard

[235] The upper half of this page is covered by at least two separate prose entries in
pencil, later erased, of which no words have been recovered. The lower half bears
fifteen lines of poetry in pencil, the first seven of which are partially erased and the
rest of which are printed in the text. The following significant words and phrases
in the first seven lines have been recovered: "Rolls"; "winter through"; "Until its";
and "case".

[143][236]   Do not ⟨judge⟩ tell the age of souls
               By bended ⟨for⟩ backs or whitening polls
               Some of those you see are young
               New released from ⟨b⟩Chaos strong
               Unskilled to live and brutal still
               With the vegetable will

               Nature in your garden grown
               But she better likes her own

                         The feet which slid for months on snow
                         Ar⟨g⟩e glad at last to feel the ground [237]

               Winter builds
               Sudden cathedrals in the wilds [238]

                    frozen wine [239]

                         stone-cleaving cold [240]

                              The air is full of whistlings [241]
               She stately in the garden paced
               She stately on the sunset gazed

               The wood is soberness with a basis of joy

               Sober with a fund of joy [242]

[144]   I found this
               That of goods I could not miss

[236] The entries on this and the following page are in pencil. Page [143] is reproduced in Plate II.
    [237] These two lines occur, somewhat changed, as ll. 280–281 of "May-Day," W,
IX, 173. The prose passage from which they are drawn occurs on p. [108] above.
    [238] Cf. "May-Day," ll. 47–48, W, IX, 164.
    [239] See p. [138] above.
    [240] Cf. "Monadnoc," l. 57, W, IX, 62.
    [241] Cf. "May-Day," l. 7, W, IX, 163.
    [242] Cf. "Waldeinsamkeit," ll. 19–20, W, IX, 249.

If I /served within/fell into/ the line,
Once a member, all was mine,
Houses, ⟨ga⟩banquets, gardens, fountains,
Fortune's delectable mountains,
But if I would walk alone
Was neither cloak nor crumb my own.

And thus the high muse treated me
Directly never greeted me
But when she spread her ↑dearest↓ subtle spells
⟨Seemed⟩ ↑Feigned↓ to speak to some one else
I was free to overhear
Or was welcome to forbear
But that idle word
Thus at random overheard
Was the song of all the spheres
And ⟨burden⟩ ↑proverb↓ of the following years
All the planets with it shone
A livery all events put on
It fell in rain it grew in grain
It wore flesh in friendly forms
It frowned in enemies
It spoke in Tullius Cicero
In Milton & in Angelo
I travelled & found it at Rome
Eastward it filled all Heathendom
And lay on my hearth when I came home [243]

[145]–[146] [leaf missing] [244]
[147]   The ste-- [*1 w*] ↑war↓ gods shook their heads   [27]
            And[?] [*2–3 w*] th··· [*1 w*]   [?]
            [*unrecovered*]   [?]
            ↑I know not↓ [*1–2 w*] ↑if doomed↓ [*2–3 w*] to g···s
                [*1 w*]   [39]

----

[243] "Fragments on the Poet and the Poetic Gift, IV," ll. 7–34, *W*, IX, 323–324.
[244] Emerson indexed p. [146] under Fourier.

Do not judge till the age of souls
By bended backs or whitening polls
Some of those you see are young
new released from Chaos strong
Unskilled to live and brutal still
With the vegetable will

Nature in your garden grown
But she better likes her own

The feet which slid for months on snow
Are glad at last to feel the ground

Winter builds
Sudden Cathedrals in the wild

frozen wine
stone-cleaving
stone-cleaving cold

The air is full of whistlings
The stately in the garden paced
She stately on the funeral gazed

The wood is soberness with a basis of joy

Sober with a fund of joy

Plate II   Journal V, page 143   Text, page 169
Poetic jottings

In the sea of generation   [40]
And their lip- the secret kept   [45]
If [⟨2–3 w⟩] [4–5 w]   [?]
But now & then truth speaking things   [47]
Shames the angels veiling wings
And ⟨in⟩ ↑shrilling out of↓ the ⟨curve[?] of projection⟩
     solar course
Or ↑fruit of↓ a chemic [⟨1 w⟩] ↑force↓   [50]
⟨Or the⟩ procession of a soul in matter
Or [1 w] speeding change of water
Or ⟨in⟩ ↑out of↓ good [1 w] evil born
Came ⟨…o's⟩ ↑Uriel's↓ voice of angel scorn
And [1–2 w] tinged the upper sky   [55]
And gods looked[?] scarce knew why   [56]

[3–4 w] too bright   [41]
    To hit the nerve of feebler sight

A forgetting wind
Stole over the Olympian kind [245]   [44]

it may be conceded to him that there will be rowdies & there will be vixens. Capt Chandler at the Farm School said to me "I want no good boys: the worse rogues they are, the better for my purpose." [246]

Fourier is a virile mind. His system is a military one, military without war. It is a Sparta[.]

[148]–[149] [blank]
    [150] Once you saw phoenixes, and now you see such no longer, but the world is not therefore disenchanted. The vessels on which

[245] The recovered lines in this erased pencil entry appear, with changes, in "Uriel," W, IX, 14–15.
[246] Daniel Chandler was, from 1835 to 1839, superintendent of the Boston Asylum and Farm School for Indigent Boys, located on Thompson's Island in Boston Harbor. The sentence is used in "Considerations by the Way," W, VI, 258–259. See JMN, VIII, 186. This and the following entry are inscribed in ink on top of the first seven lines of erased poetry on the page.

you read sacred emblems have turned out to be common pottery, but the sacred pictures are transferred to the walls of the world. You no longer see phoenixes; ⟨but⟩ men are not divine individuals; but you learn to revere their social & representative character. They are not gods, but the spirit of God sparkles on & about them.[247]

After this generation one would say mysticism should go out of fashion for a long time. It makes now the stereotype turn & return of all poems & poetic prose, "In thyself," &c[.]

Men are weathercocks & like nothing long. We are disgusted with history because it is precise, [151] external, & indigent. But take up Behmen or Swedenborg or Carlyle even or any other who will write history mystically, & we wish straightway for French science and facts recorded agreeably to the common sense of mankind.

———

God's ways are parabolic projections that do not return into themselves[.]

———

The good Fourier does not go for virtue beyond his nose. The highest word I find in his vocabulary is the Aromal, under which, spiritual distinctions such as he can recognize, should fall.

[152] Dr [Charles T.] J[ackson]. invented Morse's Magnetic Telegraph; told the Legislature of Maine the value of the Aroostook Country for wheat; so that they sent 7000 men to take possession of the country & made the war[.] [248]

Mr How's shuffling reasons.[249]

---

[247] This paragraph, struck through in ink with a vertical use mark, is used in "Uses of Great Men," *W*, IV, 34–35.

[248] Jackson, Emerson's brother-in-law, claimed to have pointed out to Samuel F. B. Morse the basic principles of the telegraph. As state geologist of Maine, he surveyed the soil of the state's northern lands, then disputed with Canada; his reports contributed to the war scare of 1838–1839.

[249] Phineas How was a partner in the firm of How & Hidden, general merchants of Concord.

We cannot spare the coarsest guard of virtue. We are disgusted by gossip, yet it is of the utmost importance to keep the angels in their proprieties[.] [250]

Was it fit after such sacrifices as France had made in the Revolution, to adopt again the ⟨old⟩ musty garments of the old civilization? Was it pathetic to see Napoleon in St Helena turn his green coat: it was sadder to see Europe turn its old coat.

And see the story of Augereau *V* p 119
how appl⟨|| . . . ||⟩icable to Louis Napoleon! [n] June 1852 [251]

[153] Of what use is it that I should take the chair, and glibly rattle off theories of society, religion, & nature, when I know so well that three or four of my worthy neighbors will each of them pin me to my ⟨chair⟩ ↑seat↓ & reduce me to silence by objections & arguments unanswerable by me? [252]

[154] [253] We pretend indignation & hold indig[nation] meetings. The truth is stronger than the fa⟨ct⟩ble. We ⟨do⟩ are very cool: The people *do not care a damn*, to use their phrase. S[outh]. C[arolina]. has placed itself in a foolish position & we are willing she should[.]

It is a jail[,] an Alsatia. Leave it to itself[.]

It has excluded every gentleman, every man of honour, every man of humanity, every freeman from its territory. Is that a country in which I wish to walk where ⟨every man's⟩ I am assured beforehand

---

[250] This paragraph, struck through in ink with two diagonal use marks, is used in "Worship," *W*, VI, 222.

[251] Louis Napoleon, a liberal who applauded the Revolution of 1848 in Paris, culminated his increasingly autocratic measures as president of the Republic by making himself dictator through a coup d'état in December, 1851.

[252] This paragraph, struck through in pencil with a diagonal use mark and in ink with a vertical and a wavy vertical use mark, is used in "Montaigne," *W*, IV, 156–157.

[253] The entries on pp. [154]–[157] are in pencil.

that I shall not meet a great man; that all the men are cottongins; where a great man cannot live, where the people are degraded for they go with padlocked lips, & with seared consciences.

I am far from wishing that Mass should retaliate. If we could bring down the N. Eng culture to the Carolina level[,] if we were cartwhip gentlemen[,] it might be possible to retaliate very effectively, and to the apprehensions of Southerners. Shut up Mr Calhoun and Mr Rhett when they come to Boston as hostages for the mulattoes & negroes [155] they have kidnapped from the caboose & the cabin of our ships. But the N. Eng. culture is not so low. Ours is not a brutal people, but intellectual & mild. Our land is not a jail[;] ⟨but a⟩ ⟨we live with open door⟩ ↑we↓ keep open house[;] ⟨our doors are taken off⟩ we have taken out the bolt & taken off the latch & taken the doors off the hinges. Does S.C. warn us out & turn us out, and then come hither to visit us? She shall find no bar. We are not afraid of visiters. We do not ring curfews nor give passes nor keep armed patroles[;] from Berkshire to the sea our roads are open[;] from N.H. to Connecticutt the land is without a guard[;] we have no secrets[,] no fears. For her flying slave & for his ⟨unhappy⟩ ↑degraded↓ master here is rest & plenty and wisdom & virtue which he cannot find at home[.]

We don't expect a sovereign state to treat us like a footpad. But S.C. does so treat us[.]

The doctrine of S.C. proves too much[.]

[156] But new times have come & new policy subtler & nobler & more strong than any before. It is the inevitable effect of culture [—] it cannot be otherwise [—] to dissolve the animal ties of brute strength, to insulate, to make a country of men[,] not one strong officer but a thousand strong men[,] ten thousand. In all S.C. there is but one opinion[,] but one man[:] Mr Calhoun. Its citizens are but little Calhouns. In Massachusetts there are many opinions[,] many men. It is coming I hope to a pass when there shall not be /an/the/ Atlas and /a/the/ ⟨Morning⟩ Post[,] the Daily Advertiser & the Courier[,]

but these voices shall lose their importance in a crowd of equal & superior men.

And such shall their influence be. Every one a new & finished man whom the rogue shall have no increased skill to meet by his dealing with his predecessor but here is a new accuser with new character & all the majesty of wisdom & virtue[.]

[156ₐ]²⁵⁴ 'Tis always time to do right
and perhaps at a time of disaster which certainly grows out of our social wrongdoing
(a wrongdoing to which↓ we have made ourselves parties)
is the very hour when we should throw in a noble expiation[.]

We in Massachusetts see the Indians only as a picturesque antiquity.
          Masstts
          Shawmut, Samoset,
          Squantum,
     Nantasket, Narraganset,
     Asabet, Musketaquid
But where are the men?
          "Alas for them! their day is o'er" ²⁵⁵

[156ᵦ] Well this feeling still honors the race
Hiawatha Wyoming
We thank them for names
Indian relics   arrowheads
He is the oldest man
What real merits —
          Knowledge as naturalist,
          Skill to make bow, tent, sledge, canoe
          to find his ⟨way⟩ north
          wise as a hound

²⁵⁴ A sheet of blue, faintly lined paper measuring 12.6 x 20.2 cm, laid in loose at this point, has been numbered [156ₐ]–[156ᵦ] by the editors.
²⁵⁵ Charles Sprague, "Ode Pronounced at the Centennial Celebration of the Settlement of Boston, September, 1830," stanza 19.

```
            bottom of a tree
            north of a rock & west
            can call a moose
                        muskrat
                    swimming
His virtues
            Red Jacket        ⟨M⟩Parker
```

[157] An

Let us not pretend an union where union is not. Let us not ⟨say th⟩ cowardly say that all is right where all is damnable. Let us not treat ⟨a⟩ with fawning hospitalities ⟨as if he were a gentleman⟩ & deceive others by harbouring as a gentleman a felon & a manstealer but let us put all persons on their guard & say this dog will bite. Come not into his company[,] he will kidnap & burk you[.]

[158] Talleyrand (born 1754) [256]

"The use of speech was to disguise the thought" [257] [I, 53, paraphrased]

"Speech was given to man for the purpose of disguising his thoughts." [*Ibid.*, paraphrased]

To Louis XVIII on his return to France Talleyrand said "Sir, there is something in me which bodes no good to ↑those↓ governments which neglect me." [II, 316]

Bertrand Barrere said, "They are really extraordinary with their honest people. A man may undoubtedly be honest & wish for power; but the moment he has attained it, he must make a choice, & either cease to be an honest man, or give up the idea of governing." [I, 259]

---

[256] The twelve entries under this heading are all taken from Villemarest's *Life of Prince Talleyrand*, 1834–1836.
   [257] This and the two following entries are struck through in ink with a diagonal use mark.

"That lame rascal," said Chenier, "without any respect for epis-
copacy, resembles a spunge which imbibes every liquid into which
it is dipped, with this difference, that when the spunge is pressed, it
returns the liquid it has taken, whilst our limping friend makes it
his own." [II, 184–185]

[159] When the Pope had interdicted Talleyrand the latter wrote
to M. de Biron; "You know the news: come & console me & sup
with me. Everybody is going to refuse me fire & water; we shall
therefore have nothing this evening but iced meats, & drink nothing
but wine." [I, 346–347]

Lannes said of T. "If any one gave him a kick on the posteriors,
it would not make him change countenance." [258] [III, 235]

He condescended to court those generals of the Army "who had
formerly figured in other stations, & could stand on the polished floor
without slipping." [*Ibid.*]

Mme Hammelin reproached M. de Montrond, Talleyrand's most
intimate friend, with being too much attached to Talleyrand. "In
God's name," replied M. de Montrond with naiveté, "⟨how⟩who
can help liking him, he is so vicious." [IV, 41]

"This *people*, this somebody who is cleverer than everybody," —
said Talleyrand[.] [IV, 123]

"D⟨r⟩octor Bourdois, an odd notion strikes me I wish to give you a
pension; yes, I am serious, a pension of 6000 francs; but, let us understand each other, it will not be for your life, but for mine." [IV, 44]

"Is he any body?" asked T. of one who desired a place for his
friend.[259] [IV, 202–203]

[160] Napoleon is immersed in things,[n] in the land, fruits,
forests, arts, money, & so forth of the world; he does not say anything

---

[258] See Journal W, p. [119] below.
[259] See p. [45] above.

of himself, but he says what they say, or rather, they always give some tincture to his speech. That is a very different sort of speech from any thinker's. There are men enough immersed in things, farmers, smiths, truckmen, &c. who have the strength of this sphere, but who cannot speak, who cannot organize and arrange. Napoleon stands at the confluence of the two streams of thought & of matter, and derives thence his power.[260]

"I am convinced I shall have as much pleasure in reading your work as I have had in receiving it,"[n] wrote Talleyrand to every author.[261]

Where does ⟨M⟩the Princess of Vaudemont live? "Rue St Lazare but really I have forgotten the number. You have only to ask the first beggar you meet; — they all know her house," replied Talleyrand.[262]

[161] The use of all books is suggestional or critical and who reads Swedenborg will be struck with its spirit of true science. It shames literature by hugging things so closely. One would say there never was a book before. The others were pert[,] were false inasmuch as they were detachments & declarations of independence,[n] false by being ⟨|| ... ||⟩fragmentary, as nature or things never are; whilst Swedenborg is systematic & respective of the world in every sentence & in every word. This is no writer of sentences, weak because they are bon mots, & not parts of natural discourse; mere childish expressions of surprise[n] or pleasure in nature, or, worse, owing their brief notoriety to their petulance or aversion from the order of nature, being some curiosity or oddity, designedly not in harmony with nature, & so framed as to excite surprise & attention, as jugglers do by concealing the means. In Swedenborg all the means are evenly given without any trick or defect. This[n] admirable writing is ⟨no⟩ ↑pure from all↓ pertness or egotism[.] [263]

[260] This paragraph, struck through in both pencil and ink with vertical use marks, is used, considerably altered, in "Napoleon," *W*, IV, 228–229.
[261] Villemarest, *Life of Prince Talleyrand*, 1834–1836, IV, 204.
[262] *Ibid.*, III, 327. See pp. [106]–[107] above.
[263] This paragraph is struck through in ink with a vertical use mark; "The others were pert . . . egotism" is used in "Swedenborg," *W*, IV, 103.

[162] That Plato is philosophy, & philosophy Plato, is the stigma of mankind. Vain are the laurels of Rome, vain the pride of England in her Newton, Milton, & Shakspeare, whilst neither Saxon nor Roman have availed to add any idea to the categories of Plato.[264]

Of course, I do not wish the formation of "mutual admiration societies," but I do not think the sterility of periods is to be ⟨too⟩ rashly inferred from the ⟨wa⟩absence[n] of eminent talent ↑in a town↓. A divine soul, I can easily ⟨see⟩ ↑believe↓, would content itself with the society of illustrious minds which this very hour would afford it, (for such exist, pure, true, faithful amidst the faithless, seeing amidst the blind,) although no person exists among these with a talent sufficient to realize & establish his ideas. Not to be bruised by the bruisers is now a mark of merit; not to despond in cities; to look at the lower powers, viz. of demonstration, realization, edification, as at salt, & lime, & granite, — materials & agents as indispensable as light & fire[,] though lower in the scale of energy. ↑Besides, remember Sir H. Davy's "My best discovery was the discovery of Michael Faraday."↓[265]

[163]–[164] [leaf missing][266]
[165] So many men whom I know are degraded only by their sympathies. Their native aims or genius being high enough, but their relation all too tender to the gross people about them. A poet is so rare because he must be exquisitely fine & vital in his tissue, & at the same time immoveably centred.

A true melody like Ben Jonson's good songs & ↑all↓ Milton's is of eternity already. ⟨&⟩Verses of true poets are hickory nuts so fresh & sound.

---

[264] This paragraph, struck through in ink with a vertical use mark, is used in "Plato; or, the Philosopher," *W*, IV, 40.

[265] With "faithful amidst the faithless," cf. Milton, *Paradise Lost*, V, 897. The remark by Davy, struck through in ink with a diagonal use mark, is used in "Greatness," *W*, VIII, 306.

[266] Emerson indexed p. [163] under Nature, Poet, Religion, and Solitude, and p. [164] under Demonology, M M E, Farmers, Love, Lover, Man, and Plato.

Criticism misleads like Bonaparte's quartermaster, if we listen to him, we shall never stir a step. The part you have to take, none but you must know. The critic can never tell you.[267]

The annexation of Texas looks like one of those events which retard or retrograde ↑the↓ civilization of ages. But the World Spirit is a good swimmer, and storms & waves cannot easily drown him. ⟨He makes small account of laws.⟩ He snaps his finger at laws.[268]

"As we grow old," said ↑A[lcott].,↓ "the beauty steals inward."

[166] New Hampshire is treacherous to the honor, honesty, & interest of New England: is & has been. I do not look at the Massachusetts democrats in the same light. Theirs is a sort of fancy politics. I have a better opinion than to believe they would vote as they do, if the question depended on them. But as the proverb goes, "You may well walk if you ⟨lead⟩ hold the bridle of your horse in your hand," so I interpret the caprice of & tactics of our compatriots in this Commonwealth on the subject of Texas. They know that the great & governing sentiment of the State is anti-slavery & anti-Texas, and whilst it is so, they can safely indulge a little flirting with the great Mother Democracy at[n] ⟨Washington⟩ Tammany Hall or at Washington which has made Texas the passport to its grace.

The constitutional argument is ever trivial for the *animus* of the framers is not a fixed fact but a Proteus. The Constitution was an arrangement, not an organic somewhat, and in S. Carolina means one thing, in Massachusetts another. In [167] such a case, nothing avails but morals & might:—'You hurt me, and I will blow your brains out, but I will put an end to this.' I do not see why the two states cannot immediately settle the dispute by a treaty. Let them appoint commissioners to meet at Philadelphia, & fix a rule of conduct to which both states will agree.

---

[267] In the left margin beside this paragraph is a wavy vertical line in ink. For Napoleon's remark, see Journal W, p. [24] below.

[268] This paragraph, struck through in ink with a vertical use mark, is used in "Montaigne," *W*, IV, 185.

[168]²⁶⁹ Position of Mass. better
    1. that is explained
    2. that S.C. is selfpunished by the Exclusion of
       every virtuous man from Alsatia

I infer this not only ↑1.↓ from my own feeling but 2. from the fact that there is no indignation. S.C. ⟨‖ ... ‖⟩ has not even been able to excite wrath. We make believe indignation but nobody cares[.]

At Erfurt, N↑apoleon↓ said to Talma, "a pitfull of Kings." ²⁷⁰

[169] If any one will look at the S C papers he will see that her mind is as exhausted & sterile as her cotton fields, — that a country which once produced really able men, now vapors & screams in tumid & feminine vehemence & weakness[.]

[170] [Index material omitted] ²⁷¹
[inside back cover] [Index material omitted]

---

²⁶⁹ The entries on this and the following page are in pencil. Between the second and third entries on p. [168] are four lines of erased pencil writing, of which only the first has been recovered: "Napoleon's prudence".

²⁷⁰ Villemarest, *Life of Prince Talleyrand*, 1834–1836, IV, 146. Napoleon's remark to Talma, an actor of the Comédie Française, was prompted by the distinguished audience at one of his performances.

²⁷¹ A preliminary index, in pencil and erased, covers this page.

W

1845

Journal W covers a period of six months, from March to September, 1845. Much of it consists of passages which were later used in the lecture series Representative Men, especially the lecture on Plato, and in Emerson's address on the role of the scholar, delivered at Middlebury College on July 22.

The copybook is of the same general type used for Journals U and V, with the following slight variations: the covers bear a green, black, and white mottled design and measure 17.2 x 21.1 cm, and the spine strip is red leather and lacks a gold edging. On the spine is the designation "W". "W 1845" is written on the front cover.

Originally there were 144 lightly ruled pages, plus two flyleaves at both front and back, but the leaf bearing pages 77–78 has been torn out. The leaves measure 16.9 x 20.6 cm. Most of the pages are numbered in ink, but pages 79, 144, 145, and 146 are numbered in pencil ("144" was subsequently erased). Seven pages are unnumbered: 25, 41, 63, 89, 93, 113, and 143. Page 70 was first numbered in pencil, then in ink. Two pages, apparently overlooked in Emerson's initial pagination, were later numbered 127 1/2 and 127 2/3. Blank pages total thirteen: ii, iv, 5–8, 15, 25, 37, 59, 88, 89, and 143.

The bottom of the leaf numbered 99–100 has been cut away, with the loss of three lines on each side; the top of the leaf numbered 101–102 has been cut away, with the loss of six lines on each side. A pressed tree leaf is laid in between pages 68 and 69.

[front cover]   W
                                     1845

[front cover verso] [1] Lowell Institute   after 1 Feb
                    Salem Lyceum
                    Waltham Institute

[Index material omitted]

          Nec deus intersit, nisi dignus vindice nodus
              Inciderit [2]   [Horace,] Ars Poet. 191[–192]

[i] [Index material omitted]   R. W. Emerson
                                                March, 1845
                              W
                            1845

          χαλεποι δε θεοι φαινεσθαι εναργεις.[3]
              [Homer,] Iliad. Book 20 Verse 131

[ii] [blank]
[iii] Mackintosh   Wordsworth
      Jeffrey   Coleridge
      Hallam   Scott
      Brougham   Landor
      Playfair   Carlyle
      Smith   Byron [4]
      Herschel
      Mitchell
      Macaulay
      DeQuincey

[iv] [blank]

---

[1] The entries on the front cover verso are in pencil, except for an isolated "37"
in ink in the upper left-hand corner. The first three lines refer to lecture engagements for the 1845–1846 winter season.
    [2] "And let no god intervene, unless a knot come worthy of such a deliverer."
    [3] "For hard are the gods to look upon when they appear in manifest presence."
    [4] In this list, the names of Hallam, Herschel, Macaulay, Wordsworth, Coleridge,
and Scott are struck through in ink with vertical lines.

[1] Plato. The fine laid on the just if they refuse to govern is the punishment of being governed by a base person.[5]

Is it not strange that the transcendent men[,] ⟨Plato⟩Homer, Plato, Shakspeare, confessedly unrivalled, should have questions of identity & of genuineness raised respecting their writings?[n 6] Was there such a man as Homer? Here a Scholiast on Plato avers that Homer learned all his epic of some ↑Creophilus of Chios whose daughter he married.↓ Several of Plato's pieces are reckoned spurious. Who knows who wrote the book of Job, or of Genesis, or the Gospel of St Matthew? Of Shakspeare, we have many dubious remains, & ⟨‖ ... ‖⟩touching him many questions. The architect who designed the Cathedral of Cologne, has left his plans, but not his name.   ↑See p[p.] 140–142↓

[2] A terrific motive power, he touches things & they spin: the solar system is fast becoming a fine transparency.
   Yet to women his book is Mahometan.

Republic Book III, Plato declares that his "Guardians" shall not ⟨use⟩handle gold or silver, but shall be instructed that there is gold & silver in their souls, which will make men willing at all times to give them without money that which they want.[7] A coinage not corruptible, for with this organic gold we can buy bread & garments & tools, but cannot make an ill use of it, to buy comfits & brandy.

Pherecydes ⟨of⟩Syrus wrote, "Jove is a circle, triangle, & square, centre & line & all things before all,"[n 8] which indicates profoundness of perception. We say then of a Jove[-]like soul like Plato, that he at once shows the evanescence & the centrality of things. Things are in

---

[5] *Republic*, Bk. I, in Taylor, *The Works of Plato* . . . , 1804, I, 125. This entry, struck through in ink with three vertical use marks, is used in "Plato; New Readings," *W*, IV, 84, and "Eloquence," *W*, VII, 62. See Journal Y, p. [28] below.
   [6] This sentence, struck through in ink with a vertical use mark, is used in "Plato; or, the Philosopher," *W*, IV, 41.
   [7] Taylor, *The Works of Plato* . . . , 1804, I, 258. This sentence is used in "Plato; New Readings," *W*, IV, 84.
   [8] Taylor, "General Introduction to the Philosophy and Writings of Plato," *The Works of Plato* . . . , 1804, I, xxvii.

a flood and fixed as adamant: The Bhagavat Geeta adduces the illustration of the sphered, mutable, yet centred air or ether.[9]

[3] "You may place me likewise, said Adimantus, among those who are of that opinion." [Plato, *Republic*,] B. IV.[10]

Plato has always finished his thinking before he brings it to the reader and abounds in the surprises of a literary master.

Ammianus said, Jupiter himself would not speak otherwise, if he were to converse in the Attic tongue.[11]

[4] Floyer Sydenham translated,
1. First Alcibiades
2. Second Alcibiades
3. Greater Hippias
4. Lesser Hippias
5. The Banquet (except
    Speech of Alcibiades)
6. Philebus
7. Meno
8. Io
9. Rivals.

Thomas Taylor translated thirty three.

⟨10⟩   Republic Ten Books.   10
         Laws Twelve Books   12 [12]

[5]–[8] [blank]

[9] The English nation is full of manly clever men[,] well--bred[,] who write these pungent off-hand paragraphs in ↑the↓ literary

---

[9] Emerson acquired a copy of *The Bhăgvăt-Gēētă, or Dialogues of Krēēshnă and Ărjŏŏn* . . . , trans. Charles Wilkins (London, 1785), in September, 1845 (*L*, III, 303).

[10] Taylor, *The Works of Plato* . . . , 1804, I, 266.

[11] Taylor, "General Introduction . . . ," *The Works of Plato* . . . , 1804, I, ci. This and the preceding entry, struck through in ink with a vertical use mark, are used in "Plato; or, the Philosopher," *W*, IV, 59, 57.

[12] Emerson has miscalculated Taylor's own breakdown in "General Introduction . . . ," *The Works of Plato* . . . , 1804, I, cvi. Taylor says he translated the ten books of the *Republic*, the twelve books of the *Laws*, and twenty-four other dialogues, while Sydenham translated the rest, which he gives as Emerson lists them.

& political journals expressing clearly & courageously their opinion on any person or performance, & so far very satisfactory to read. In all this wide America littered with newspapers, there is not a solitary writer of this sort, so common in England. They do this, & they write poetry[,] as they box[:] by education. The Praeds & Freres & Milneses & Hoods & Cannings ↑& Macaulays↓ seem to me ⟨all poets who⟩ to make poems as they make speeches in Parliament or at the hustings or as they shoot and ride. It is a *coup de force*. All this is convenient & civilized: But I had rather take very uncultured, ⟨poe⟩inornate, irregular, very bad poetry with the chance of now & then an urgent fiery line like threads of gold in a mass of ore.[13]

We ↑in America↓ have the comfort of ↑the↓ wretched, that out of this zone of clever mediocrity, ⟨in England,⟩ [10] England is as indigent ⟨in⟩as America in great writers[.]

Ah we busybodies! Cannot we be a little abstemious? We talk too much, & act too much, & think too much. Cannot we cease doing, & gravitate only to ⟨‖ . . . ‖⟩our ends? Cannot we let the morning be?

The only use which the country people can imagine of a scholar, the only compliment they can think of to pay him, is, to ask him to deliver a Temperance Lecture, or to be a member of the School Committee.

A few foolish & cunning managers ride the conscience of this great country with their Texas or Tariff or Democracy or other mumbo jumbo, & all give in & are verily persuaded that that is great, — all else is trifling. And why? Because there is really no great life; not one demonstration in all the broad land of that which is the heart & the soul of every rational American Man[:] the mountains walking, the light incarnated, reason & virtue clothed in flesh, — he does not see.[14]   See p. 58

[11] Friends have nothing to give each other; nothing to with-

[13] "The English nation . . . civilized:" is struck through in ink with a vertical use mark; "The English nation . . . shoot and ride." is used in *English Traits*, *W*, V, 262.
[14] This entry was written first in pencil, with "Democracy or some other" for "Democracy or other", then in ink.

hold; nothing to ask for, or that can be refused: such liberty would infer imperfect affinity. All that behoves them is clearness, or, not to miscall relations. Truth forevermore & love after that.

Men of talent create a certain artificial position, a camp in the wilderness somewhere, about which they contrive to keep much noise, ⟨&⟩ firing of guns, & running ⟨to & fro⟩ⁿ of boys & idlers with what uproar they can. They have talents for contention, & they nourish a small difference into a loud quarrel, & persuade the surrounding population that it is the cause of the country & of man. But the world is wide; nobody will go there after tomorrow; the gun can defend nothing but itself; nor itself any longer than the man is by. But Genius flings itself on real elemental ⟨powers⟩ things, which are powers, self-defensive, which first subsist, & therefore resist, unweariably forevermore all that opposes. Genius loves truth & clings to it, so that what it says & does is not in a wilderness or a by road, visited for curiosity or forgotten, but on the great highways of nature which were before [12] the Appian was built, which all men & angels travel, and he ⟨keeps⟩ holds fast there, a cement & comfort of the social being of men.

The scholar does not fall into the existing forms & professions: They may fall into him; but guided ⟨by⟩ in his selection by religion & necessity,

Sea = shore, an imaginative man with a good hand. The imaginative = practical. Imagination is suspected, the mechanical is despised; unite the solid ⟨&⟩*and* the ethereal, for the divine. Lord Bacon & Swedenborg & Plato have this superb speculation as from a tower over nature & art without ever losing the sequence of things.[15]

[13] Yet can he explain Life? Can he unfold the theory of this particular Monday? Can he uncover the living ligaments, concealed from all but poets, which attach the dull men & things we converse with, to the splendor of the First Cause? to the awe of eternity, intelligence, & strength? These present fifteen minutes are time, not

[15] The last sentence is struck through in ink with a vertical use mark.

eternity; are low & subaltern; are but hope or memory, — that is, the way *to* or the way *from* welfare; but not welfare. Then shall he ascend from a menial & eleemosynary existence into riches & stability, into repose; then he dignifies the present hour & the place where ↑he↓ is; Beauty is at home: this mendicant America[,] this curious peering ⟨travelling⟩itinerant imitative ⟨Greece & Rome⟩ America, studious of Greece & Rome[,] studious of England, will take off its dusty shoes, will take off its glazed traveller's cap, & sit at home with repose & deep joy on its face. The world has no such landscape; the aeons of history no such hour; the future no ⟨grander⟩ ↑/second/equal/↓ opportunity ⟨than is here⟩. Now let poets sing! now arts unfold! The Iliad is no more foreign & old, Shakspeare no *book*. Now these are easy & inevitable as the breathing of the lungs.[16]

↑Printed in "Society & Solitude."↓

[14] I have found a subject, *On the use of great men*; which might serve a Schleiermacher for monologues to his friends. But, in the first place, there should be a chapter *on the distribution of the hand into fingers*, or on the great value of these individuals as counterweights, checks on each other. What a satisfaction, a fortress, a citadel I find in a new individual who is undoubtedly of this class. How much now Schelling avails, and how much every day Plato! What storms of nonsense they silently avert.

[15] [blank]

[16] It is but a few years ago that Swedenborgism was exhibited to our people in a pamphlet of garbled extracts from Swedenborg's writings as ↑a↓ red rag of whoredom. Dr Ripley lived & died in the belief that it was a horrible libertinism.[17] Now Fourier is represented in the same light by the Swedenborgians, who get their revenge so.

It is easy to see what must be the fate of this fine system in any

[16] This paragraph is struck through in ink with a discontinuous vertical use mark; "Can he unfold . . . arts unfold!" is used in "Works and Days," *W*, VII, 179–180. "Printed in 'Society & Solitude.'" refers only to the last two sentences, as Emerson made clear by an enclosing line.

[17] The Reverend Ezra Ripley (1751–1841), Emerson's stepgrandfather, had been suspicious of all religious unorthodoxy.

very serious & comprehensive enterprise to set it on foot in this
country. As soon as our people got wind of the doctrine of sexual
relations of this master, it would fall at once into the hands of the
rowdies, who would flock in troops & gangs to so fair a game. "Who
would see fun must be on hand!" And like the dreams of poetic
people on the first outbreak of the old French Revolution they must
disappear in a ⟨hideous⟩ slime of mire & blood.

[17] Fourier is of the opinion of St Evremond's philosopher,
Bernier, who confided to St E. a secret, that, "abstinence from plea-
sure⟨s⟩ appeared to him a great sin." [18]

No, it is not the part & merit of a man to make his stove with
his own hands, or cook & bake his own dinner: Another can do it
better & cheaper; but it is his essential virtue to carry out into action
his own dearest ends, to dare to do what he believes & loves. If he
thinks a sonnet the flower & result of the world, let him sacrifice all
to the sonnet; if he loves the society of one or of several friends,
more than life, let him so arrange his living & make everything yield
to the procuring him that chief good. Now, we spend our ⟨br⟩money
for that which is not bread, for paint & floor-cloths, for newspapers,
& ↑male and↓ female servants that yield us the very smallest fraction
of direct advantage. The friction of this social machine is grown
enormous, & absorbs almost all the power applied.

[18] We have no land to put our words on, yet our words are
true[.]

Every thing is my cousin[.] [19]

Our civilization is the triumph of talent.[20] The poet seeks the civilization which is the growth of genius. Unity for miscellany, grandeur
for trifles, beauty for expense, freedom for wealth,

[18] This sentence is used in "Historic Notes of Life and Letters in New England,"
W, X, 354. See JMN, VI, 363.
[19] This line is in pencil.
[20] Cf. "Plato; or, the Philosopher," W, IV, 52. See Journal Y, pp. [201] and
[202] below.

We are bound hand & foot with our decorums & superstitions. England has achieved respectability at what a cost! America with a valet's eyes admires & copies in vain.

Talent bankrupts us: We become forlorn in our poverty of thought & power. We are like manufacturers of buckles thrown out of employment by the fashion of wearing shoestrings, or of carriages by the invention of railroads. Every thing has been sacrificed to the demonstration of our talent: we are become vain, and the plain homestead & the hour without audience & without event is dull. We are solitary in the midst of throngs unseen. We have cut in twain all the ties that bound us to the Universe but one, & that is become false & superfluous.

[19] Art requires a living soul. The dunces believe, that, as it must, at any one moment, work in one direction, an automaton will do as well, or nearly; & they beseech the Artist to say, "In what direction?" "In every direction," he replies, "in any direction, or in no direction, but it must be alive."

[20] Surfaces are safe. There are no improprieties, no perturbations, no risks, no questions hard to be solved. ↑Ah!↓ Let us live there.

Love has that temperance which asks for nothing which is not already on the moment granted.

[21] "You have, ↑O↓ Socrates, said he, like a statuary, made our governors all-beautiful." "And our governesses likewise, Glauco," said I. "For do not suppose that I have spoken what I have said any more concerning the men, than concerning the women, — such of them as are of a sufficient genius."

Republic. end of the B. VII.
[Taylor, *The Works of Plato* . . . , 1804, I, 385]

"The female sex is another kind of men, more occult & fraudulent than we are through the imbecility of its nature." *The Laws*   B. VI Taylor [*Ibid.*,] Vol II p 174

[22] Does the same skepticism exist at all times which prevails at present in regard to the powers of performance of the actual population? Edm[und]. H[osmer]. thinks the women have degenerated in strength. He can find no Matron for the else possible community.[21] The men think the men are less, a puny race.

↑& G. Minott thinks the cows are smaller.↓[22]

Every work repeats in small the nature of the workman, ⟨thus⟩as a house is a sort of statue o⟨f⟩r mask of the builder, the underpinning being the feet; the cellar⟨;⟩ the abdomen; the kitchen, the stomach; the windows the eyes; the chimney the nose; the sitting room, the heart; the library the brain; and the lower members with their uses are not wanting in the vents & vaults of the house —

[23] Conservatism has in the present society every advantage. All are on its side. Of those who pretend to ⟨lib⟩ ideas, all are really & in practice on the side of the state. ⟨If⟩ They know that, if they should persist in actualising their theories, it would be all convulsion & plunging. Their talk is the mere brag of liberalism. Yet, yet, they like to feel their wings. The soul with Plato in Phaedrus[n] likes to feel its wings; [23] and they indulge themselves with this religious luxury, assured, that, though the lion is as yet only half disengaged from the soil, the dream of today is prophetic of the experience of tomorrow.

Fourier, in his talk about women, seems one of those salacious old men who are full of the most ridiculous superstitions on this matter. In their head, it is the universal rutting season. Any body who has lived with women will know how false & prurient this is; how serious nature always is; how chaste is their organization, & how lawful ⟨women⟩ a class of people women are.[24]

[21] Hosmer was a neighboring farmer and Emerson's "agricultural adviser and executor," according to Edward Emerson (J, IV, 394, n. 2).

[22] George Minott, a small farmer, lived across the road from Emerson. This sentence is in pencil.

[23] Cf. Taylor, "General Introduction . . . ," The Works of Plato . . . , 1804, I, 1: "For, as Plato says in the Phaedrus, when the winged powers of the soul are perfect and plumed for flight, she dwells on high . . ." — a reference to Phaedrus 246C.

[24] Portions of this paragraph are used in "Historic Notes of Life and Letters in New England," W, X, 354.

[24]²⁵ The Native American party resembles a dog which barks at all strangers.²⁶

Bonap[arte] represents the Business Men's Party against the Morgue[.]
But the Morgue is only the Bu[siness] M[en's] Party gone to seed[.]

The lesson he teaches is that which vigour always teaches, that, there is always room for it. He would not take No for an answer. When he was born there could be nothing new in war. And he found impediments that would have stopped anybody else, but he saw what gibbering quaking ghosts they were, & he put his hand through them. If you listen to your commissary[,] he said[,] an army would never move[.] ²⁷

[25] [blank]
    [26] Bonaparte is a confutation of heaps of cowardly doubts. When he appeared it was the belief of all military men in Europe that "there could be nothing new in war." As it is always the belief of society that the world is used up. But Genius always sees room for one ↑man↓ more.²⁸

↑*Practical Man*↓
There is always room for a man of force, and not only so, but he makes room for many. There is always room for a man of force, if it were only as Buonaparte replied to Bourrienne when he showed the difficulty of getting acknowledged by the old reigning families of Europe, "If it comes to that, I will dethrone them all, & then I shall be the oldest sovereign among them." For really society is at any time only a troop of thinkers, and the best heads among them

²⁵ The entries on this page, with the exception of the first, are in pencil.
²⁶ The Native American Party (originally the American Republican Party), founded in 1843, was anti-Catholic and anti-immigrant.
²⁷ This paragraph, struck through in pencil with a vertical use mark, is used in "Napoleon," *W*, IV, 247–248. See Journal V, p. [165] above.
²⁸ This paragraph, struck through in ink with a vertical use mark, is used in "Napoleon," *W*, IV, 247. The first sentence is repeated in somewhat different form on p. [40] below.

take the best seats. It is with the prizes of power & place as it is with estates. A feeble man can only see the farms that are fenced & tilled; the houses that are built. At the end of the town, he is at the end of the world. The strong man sees [27] not only the actual but the possible houses & farms. His eye makes estates & villages, as fast as the sun breeds clouds.[29]

There is always room for a man of force as I think even swindlers & impostors show. A man of more talent than Cagliostro or Monroe Edwards would take the wind out of the sails of kings & governors, cotton-lords & Rothschilds and make asses of the heads of Society. For, as these are the slaves of appearance also, & not of truth, they have not an intrinsic defence to make, but only stand on opinion. But the lover of truth is invulnerable[.]

Yet a bully cannot lead the age[.]

[28] Another distinction should be made. It is obvious that the two Parties I describe as dividing modern society — conservative & democratic, — differ only as young & old. The democrat is a young conservative, & conservative is an old democrat. It is then not two Parties but one, and Bonaparte represents the whole history of this Party, — its youth & its age, — and needs a counterpart who has not yet appeared, in the shape of a lover and a transcendentalist[.] [30]

"Beauty without grace is a hook without bait," said Ninon[.] [31]

"The figures of rhetoric," said St Evremond, "are very insipid after those of Aretin."

Jung Stilling seems ever to have prayed Heaven to lend him a thaler.[32]

---

[29] This paragraph, struck through in ink with a vertical use mark, is used, with the omission of "There is always room for a man of force, if it . . . them.' ", in "Power," *W*, VI, 58–59. For the source of the omitted passage, see Journal V, p. [122] above.

[30] This paragraph, struck through in ink with a vertical use mark, is used in "Napoleon," *W*, IV, 256–257.

[31] This quotation is used in "Beauty," *W*, VI, 299.

[32] Cf. "Fate," *W*, VI, 6: "And now and then an amiable parson, like Jung Still-

Poetry must be as new as foam, & as old as ↑the↓ rock.

"Railroad & ↑Dr Bragg's↓ resurrection pills, through direct." [33]

[29] T. Taylor (Gen. Introduc. to Plato p. lxxxiv) calls Bacon's Novum Organon the baseless fabric of a vision[.] [34]

[30] The puny race of Scholars in this country have no counsel to give, and are not felt. Every wretched partisan, every village brawler, every man with talents for contention, every clamourous place hunter makes known what he calls his opinion, all over the country, that is, as loud as he can scream. Really, no opinions are given, only the wishes of each side are expressed, of the spoils party, that is, & of the malcontents.[n] But the voice of the intelligent & the honest, of the unconnected & independent, the voice of truth & equity is suppressed. In England, it is not so. You can always find in their journals & newspapers, a better & a best sense as well as the low coarse party cries.

[31] ⟨For I say to you that⟩ I have now arrived ⟨on⟩at a perfect selfishness on the most enforced consideration. For I am constrained by many lapses & ⟨dismaying⟩ failures to proportion my attempts to my means. Now I receive daily just so much vital energy as suffices to put on my clothes, ⟨to tie my shoes,⟩ to take a few turns in my garden & in my study with a book or a pen in my hand. If I attempt anything beyond this, if I so much as stretch out my hand to help my neighbor in his field, the ⟨good⟩ stingy Genius leaves me faint & sprawling; and I ⟨am farther to⟩ ↑must↓ pay for this vivacity by a prostration for two or three days following. These are costly experiments to try, I cannot afford two or three days when I count how many days it requires to finish one of my tasks; so I grow circumspect

---

ing . . . , believes in a pistareen-Providence, which, whenever the good man wants a dinner, makes that somebody shall knock at his door and leave a half-dollar" — a trait of the German mystic noted several times by Goethe in *Dichtung und Wahrheit*.

[33] "Dr Bragg's" is written at the right margin above the quotation and linked to it by a line at the top and to the left.

[34] *The Works of Plato* . . . , 1804, I. Cf. Shakespeare, *The Tempest*, IV, i, 151. This entry is in pencil.

& disobliging beyond the example of all the misers. My kings &
exemplars are St Hunks & St Elwes —[.] [35]
↑See CD 78 [36]
O 115↓

[32] ↑*Degrees*↓
Do you think nobody would be the poet if he could be the hero?
And do you think the painter cares to be the subject which he paints? [n]
I cannot even find that a woman wishes to be her lover, though she
wishes to be united to him. There are steps & limitations in the Uni-
verse, & not a huddle of identity only.[37]

I ⟨walked⟩ ↑stood↓ methought in a city of beheaded men, where
the decapitated trunks continued to walk. Purposeless, ⟨st|| . . . ||⟩con-
founded, and to seek, were all the parties. Is it the odours of a city[,]
so mnemonical in their properties[,] which degrade & jade the mind
of a countryman? I have in Boston a disease of skepticism, hunger,
& miscellany.[38]

[33] What argument, what eloquence can avail against the
power of that one word *niggers?* The man of the world annihilates
the whole combined force of all the antislavery societies of the world
by pronouncing it.[39]

I have charged the Abolitionist sometimes with stopping short
of the essential act of abstaining from all products of slave-labour.
The apology for their use is not comfort & self indulgence, but, I
doubt not, the same feeling which I & others insist on, that we will
not be headlong & abandoned to this one mania.

————

↑These things go to-
gether[:]↓ Cultivated people cannot live in a shanty, nor sleep at night

[35] "Hunks" is a slang term for a miser (cf. *L*, III, 214); John Elwes was a
notorious English miser of the eighteenth century.
[36] Journal CD will be published in a future volume.
[37] This paragraph is struck through in ink with a wavy diagonal use mark.
[38] "I ⟨walked⟩ stood . . . parties." is struck through in ink with a wavy diagonal
use mark.
[39] This paragraph is struck through in ink with three vertical use marks.

as the poor do in a bag[.] [40]

Whilst we thought here was a good government & a good people with good usages it seems there is a man in the midst of us who carries with him a better government, better people, & better manners.

---

[34] There is a certain heat in the breast which attends the perception of a primary truth which is the shining of the spiritual sun down the shaft of the mine.[41] ↑See Y. 34↓   ↑printed↓

[35] A journal might find its resources in Calvert, Ward, M. Fuller, Channing, Thoreau, Cabot, Hunt, Tappan, Wendell Holmes, Whipple. Dr Frothingham should contribute his treatise on the Augustan Astronomy. Alcott should be made effective by being tapped by a good suction-pump. Hawthorne, Tuckerman the botanist, Parker, Hedge, Lane, George Curtis, El[len]. H[ooper], J. F. C[larke].[42]

[36] I do not see but the dunces must have their joke & glass of wine, & the sharpers their bargain, for an age or two more.[n]

In reading books as in seeing men, one may well keep, if he can, his

[40] This and the following entry are in pencil.

[41] This sentence, struck through in ink with a vertical use mark, is used in "Discourse at Middlebury College" and "Goethe," W, IV, 264–265.

[42] Persons mentioned here not previously identified or easily recognizable are: George Henry Calvert, minor poet, essayist, and translator of works from the German; James Elliott Cabot, a recent acquaintance of Emerson, much later his biographer and literary executor; Benjamin Peter Hunt, contributor to The Dial, businessman in Haiti, and later scholar on the West Indies; William Aspinwall Tappan of New York, later the husband of Caroline Sturgis; Edwin Percy Whipple, essayist and critic; Nathaniel Langdon Frothingham, pastor of the First Church of Boston at this time, translator of the Phaenomena of the Greek poet Aratus which enjoyed a high reputation among the Romans; Edward Tuckerman, brother of Frederick Goddard Tuckerman the poet, and later professor of botany at Amherst; Theodore Parker, Unitarian clergyman, antislavery agitator, and frequent contributor to The Dial; Frederic Henry Hedge, Unitarian clergyman and German scholar, at this time minister of the Independent Congregational Society of Bangor, Maine; and James Freeman Clarke, Unitarian clergyman, founder and pastor of the Church of the Disciples, Boston.

first thoughts; for they will soon be written over by the details of
argument & sentiment in the book, and yet they are a juster judgment of the book than a digest of the particular merits can yield.
As W[illiam]. T[appan] said of the first impression of a face[,] that
after your friend has come & gone many times & now is long absent that first seen face comes back to the memory & not the more
intimate knowledge of recent days.[43]

Is it not good that the muse should not govern; that men of thought
& of virtue should be at leisure, and ridiculously vacant, & to seek,—
rambling ingloriously in woods & by seashores; — that things should
be left to themselves, as now in America all goes to a merry prosperous tune,—good & bad is done, government is not felt, & the
governers have an idle time of it?

[37] [blank]
        [38] Society at all times has the same want ⟨of⟩, namely, of
one sane man with adequate powers of expression to hold up each
new object of monomania in its ↑right↓ relations. The ambitious &
the mercenary bring their last new mumbo-jumbo, whether it be
Tariff or Texas or Mesmerism or Phrenology or Antimasonry or
Trade in Eastern lands or Puseyism, and by detaching this one object from its relations easily succeed in making it seen insanely: and
a great multitude go suddenly mad on the subject; and they are
not to be reproved or cured by the opposite multitude, who are
kept from this particular insanity only by an equal frenzy on another
crotchet. But let one man have so ⟨much⟩ comprehensive an eye that
he can replace this isolated wonder in its natural ⟨pla⟩neighborhood
& relations, it loses instantly all illusion, and the returning reason
of the community thanks the reason of the monitor.[44]

[39] The eager Shaker charged Adam with the capital sin of generation, and all his posterity with the same, compromising the exis-

[43] In the left margin beside the last sentence are two vertical lines in ink.
[44] This paragraph, struck through in both pencil and ink with vertical use
marks, is used in "Discourse at Middlebury College" and "Goethe," W, IV, 265.

tence of Mother Ann, and of the accuser himself with sincere absurd-
ity. And most of our criticism is of the same web.

[40][45] I had rather stand charged in your eyes with the melancholy
& weakness of Skepticism, than with the meanness of an untruth. I
will not lie for the truth.

All the arguments are against literature yet one verse of a poem
will blow them & me away[.]

Ballads show the indifferency of subjects, times, styles, & manners.

I woke this morn with a dream which perchance was true that I was
living in the morning of history amidst barbarians, that right &
truth had yet no voice, no letters, no law, every one did what he
would & grasped what he could[.]

To how many cowardly ⟨law⟩doubts was this man's life an
answer.[46]

[41] A jersey wagon does not go by my gate, but from a motive &
to an end as little contemplated by the ⟨rider⟩ ↑driver↓ as by his
horse.[47]

[42] Take away their wineglass & nuts, and they do not believe
there is anything.[48]

Are we to make believe think & feel? If any one stood for the sentiments, the man & the landscape would be divine. But on certain
occasions a poetical person stands up & makes a sort of parade speech

[45] The entries on this page, with the exception of the first, are in pencil. The
first is struck through in ink with a vertical use mark; its first sentence is used in
"Montaigne," W, IV, 182.
[46] See p. [26] above.
[47] A pencil version of this entry, later erased, is visible in the space above the ink
version.
[48] This sentence is struck through in ink with a vertical use mark.

for virtue & beauty, and there is the end of it; for, if we buy & sell, poetic & unpoetic alike make a truce with the sentiments, and do lie & steal. Only the religious can expect the succour of religion.[49] ↑It is the old story of the preacher to the Wreckers. My Brethren wait till I come down from the pulpit & let us start fair.↓

⟨To me it   Why⟩

Strange superfluity of nature, that so little account is made of multitudes of men. The masses, from the dawn of history down, are food for powder. The idea dignifies a few leaders in whom is sentiment, opinion, love, self devotion, and they make war & death sacred, but the wretches whom they hire and kill, remain the wretches whom they hire & kill.[50]

We have received the opinion, let us hope unjustly, that the men who surround us value a long life, and do not esteem life simply as a means of expressing the sentiment. But [43] Beauty belongs to the sentiment & is always departing from those who depart out of that. The hero rises out of all comparison with contemporaries & with ages of men, because he scorns old age & lands & money & power, and will brave all mankind just as readily as a single ⟨highwayman⟩ ↑enemy↓ at the call of that private & perfect Right & Beauty in which he lives.

↑"Man is a torch borne in the wind"↓
[Chapman, *Bussy D'Ambois*, I, i, 18]

————

Is there only one courage & one warfare?[n] I cannot manage sword & rifle, can I not therefore be brave? I thought there were as many courages as men, and as many weapons as men. Is a man only the breech of a gun or a ⟨pendant⟩ ↑hasp↓ to a bowie knife?[n] I think the reason why men fail in fighting giants, is because they wear Saul's armour instead of their own. The shepherd boy very sensibly fought with a sling & a pebble.[51] I decline henceforward (ah would God

[49] This sentence is used in "Discourse at Nantucket." See p. [44] below.
[50] This paragraph, struck through in both pencil and ink with vertical use marks, is used in "Uses of Great Men," *W*, IV, 30–31.
[51] Cf. I Sam. 17:38–40.

it were so!) foreign methods & foreign courages. I will do that which
I can do: I will fight by my strength, not by my weakness.[52]

"Not dead but living are ye to account those who are slain in the
way of God."

Mahomet.[53]

[44] Only the religious can expect the succour of religion.[54]

When we come into the world a ⟨secret⟩ ↑wonderful↓ whisper
gives us a direction for the whole road (much as ⟨o⟩if one should
hear from a skilful guide at setting out on a journey, that to come
at the point he sought, he should keep always to the northeast.)
This whisper is wonderfully impressed on us, and is temperament,
taste, bearing, talent.* But ⟨as⟩ having made & moulded the constitution, the Counsellor contents himself, and is ever dumb. ⟨It⟩ He
that made the world lets that speak, & does not also employ a town
crier. Beauty forbids. But the man[,] having received this plastic
counsel to which he alone is privy, never ⟨hears it or⟩ can hear it
from any other person. On the contrary, all persons whom he meets
have a different & contrary counsel to offer. Society is unanimous
against his project. And he never hears it as he knows it. It happens
to most men that they listen to these opinions of men, & forsake their
own, and attempt to work in other men's work[,] which ↑is↓ as if
cripples should attempt to dance and harelipped men should be
orators. [45] But he who listens to this counsel is called religious,
for he alone worships, and he may rightly expect virtues & beauties

*It is like the ⟨mariner's⟩ ↑card of the↓ compass ⟨in which the ⟨needle⟩
↑card↓ is fastened to the needle, so that the whole plate ⟨turns⟩ or
card is a compass, &⟩ ↑which↓ arranges itself with the poles of the
world.[55]

[52] This and the preceding entry are used in "Discourse at Middlebury College"
and "The Scholar," *W*, X, 274–275.
[53] Quoted in *Practical Philosophy of the Muhammadan People, exhibited in its
professed connexion with the European, so as to render either an introduction to the
other; being a translation of The Akhlāk-I-Jalāly, the most esteemed ethical work of
middle Asia, from the Persian of Fakīr Jāny Muhammad Asäad*, trans. W. F.
Thompson (London, 1839), pp. 94–95. See Journal Y, p. [81] below.
[54] See p. [42] above.
[55] This footnote occurs in the middle of p. [45] after "he is consonant." and before the quotation from Brougham.

& powers consonant with the whole frame of things; to which also he is consonant.

"How will the reverend bishops of the other house be able to express their due abhorrence of such a crime (perjury), who solemnly declare in the presence of their God, that, when they are called to accept a living perhaps of £ 4000 a year, at that very instant they are moved by the Holy Ghost to accept the office & administration thereof, & for no other reason whatever." ⟨Lord⟩ Brougham   Speech on Irish elective Franchise bill, Apr. 27, 1825 [56]

[46] The wise Queen of Sheba affirmeth that our life is like that of an ass led to market by a bundle of hay being carried before him. He sees nothing but the bundle of hay. [57]

"May you likewise find the means better to employ time, which is only truly precious to more highly organized natures!" *Goethe.*

Understand me, O Charles, when I speak of miracles, I am never thinking of dead men. [58]

Vice of the age that the integrating power which belongs to an idea is imputed by the grossness of men to a multitude of men; and politicians cry "a majority" and churchmen cry "The Church." ↑Skin heals at the first intention. We are made of hooks & eyes & do exceedingly tend to coalesce & cohere. We are born to be educated & to be governed.↓ [59]

⟨Are⟩ Do the Shakers appear to you a society of lovers? No, but of doers.

[56] Quoted in Fisher, *The History . . . of the Sabbath Day . . .* , 1845, p. 134. This quotation, struck through in ink with a vertical use mark, is used in *English Traits, W*, V, 227. See Journal V, p. [131] above.

[57] The "Queen of Sheba" is Lidian Emerson; see p. 35, n. 81 above. This paragraph, struck through in pencil with a vertical use mark, is used in "Montaigne," *W*, IV, 154.

[58] "Charles" is probably Charles King Newcomb.

[59] This and the three following entries are in pencil. For the first, see Journal Y, p. [183] below.

The girl likes the ice cream but does not wish therefore to marry the confectioner[.]

↑*Degrees*↓

There are not one or two but many things in the world and un-like, as mutton, & vowel sounds, & heathen gods, & the nine solids, & uncles, & many other things[.]

[47] And the question now is whether Mr. B[erkeley]. actually thought this thought, or whether he embezzled it.[60]

Bishop Berkeley,[n] in the "Minute Philosopher," compared southern wits to cucumbers, "which are commonly all good in their kind; ⟨while the northern geniuses are like melons of which not one in fifty is good."⟩ but at best are an insipid fruit; while the northern geniuses are like melons, of which not one in fifty is good."[61]

↑Eloquence↓

"Every bullet will hit the mark, which is first dipped in the marks-man's blood."[62]

The new "Second Church" in Hanover street cost $65,000.⟨00⟩[63]

[48] Give me bareness & poverty, so that I know them as the sure signs of the coming Muse. Not in many things[,] not in a thriving well-to-do condition she delighteth. He that would sacrifice at her altar, must sacrifice orchards & gardens, convenience & prosperity; he may live on a heath without trees; a little hungry, & a little rheumatic with cold: the fire retreateth & concentrateth within into

---

[60] This sentence, a comment on the entry which follows it, is in pencil.

[61] *Alciphron or the Minute Philosopher*, Fifth Dialogue, 26. See *The Works of George Berkeley, Bishop of Cloyne*, ed. A. A. Luce and T. E. Jessop, 9 vols. (London, 1948–1957), III, 205.

[62] Emerson copied this sentence into Notebook S (Salvage), p. [31], and commented, "a superstition of hunters." It is used in "Eloquence," *W*, VII, 93. See *JMN*, VIII, 331 and 520.

[63] See Journal V, p. [49] above.

a pure flame, pure as the stars to which it mounts. The solitude of the body is the populousness of the soul.[64]   ↑See p 57↓

It is easy to hide for something, — to hide now, that we may draw the more admiration anon. Easy to sit in the shade, if we have a Plato's Republic teeming in the brain, which will presently be born for the joy & illumination of men, easy to withdraw & break somewhat morosely the bienseances of society, visit not, & refuse visits, if we can make good to others & to ourselves a rare promise. But how if you have no security of such a result; how if the fruit of your brain is abortive, if cramp & mildew, if dreams & the sons of dreams, if prose & crotchets & cold trifles, [49] matter unreadable by other men & odious to your own eyes be the issue? ⁿ How if you must sit out the day in thoughtful attitude & experiment, & return to the necessities & conversation of the household without the support of any product, and they must believe & you may doubt ⟨whether⟩ ↑that↓ this waste can ↑not↓ be justified? ⁿ I call you to a confidence which surmounts this painful experience. You are to have a selfsupport which maintains you not only against all others, but against your own skepticism. Pain, indolence, sterility, endless ennui have also their lesson for you, if you are great. The Saharas must be crossed as well as the Nile. It is easy to live for others; every body does. I call on you to live for yourselves, so shall you find in this penury & absence of thought, a ⟨gre⟩purer splendour than ever clothed the exhibitions of wit.[65]

You shall not know too much. There is a difference between a judge's & a Deputy sheriff's knowledge of the world, & again between that of the last & a burglar's.

The laborer does not care whether his employer swears, but whether he pays.

[50] When I read poetry in an English journal, as in the "Athe-

---

[64] This paragraph, struck through in pencil with a vertical use mark, is used in "Discourse at Middlebury College" and, without the last sentence, in "The Scholar," W, X, 287–288.

[65] This paragraph is struck through in pencil with a vertical use mark.

naeum," I am relieved, if, on coming to the end of the article, I find it is not American.

What drivelling is this, the examination of all the papers written on both sides in this brawl of the Herald of Freedom to see whether Rogers or ⟨French[?] is⟩Pillsbury is right. Rogers of course, & without or against any or all statements. Is it that we wish once more to know what a society decides, a majority, the reason of fools, the fortress of the weak; or do we want a pamphlet because a genius writes it? [66]

The poet and the citizen perfectly agree in conversation on the wise life. The poet counsels his own son as ⟨the president of the bank does⟩ ↑if he were a merchant↓. The poet with poets betrays no amiable weakness; they all chime in, and are as inexorable as bankers on the subject of real life. They have no toleration for literature: it is all dilettantism and ⟨inexcusable.⟩ ↑disgusts.↓ [51] Not Napoleon hated ideologists worse than they.[67] Art is only a fine word for appearance in default of matter. And they sit white over their stoves and talk themselves hoarse on the mischief of books and the effeminacy of bookmakers[.]

But at a single strain of a flute out of a window, at the dashing among the stones of a brook from the hills, or at the suggestion of a word from an imaginative person all this grave conclusion is blown out of memory, the sun shines & the worlds roll to music, and the poet replaces all this cowardly self-denial & God-denial of the literary class, with the one blazing assurance that to one poetic success the world will surrender on its knees. Instantly he casts in his lot with the pearl-diver or the diamond merchant & joyfully will lose days

---

[66] Nathaniel P. Rogers (1794–1846) had been, until December of 1844, editor of the *Herald of Freedom*, an antislavery magazine published at Concord, New Hampshire, by William Lloyd Garrison. He had been relieved of his post because of his growing belief that slavery should be abolished only through "moral suasion" rather than political action, and that antislavery societies should be dissolved because they placed undue restrictions on the individual beliefs of their members. Parker Pillsbury (1809–1898) was, like Garrison, an activist, and subsequently became editor of the *Herald of Freedom*.

[67] Cf. Bourrienne, *Private Memoirs of Napoleon Bonaparte* . . . , 1830, II, 90, 167, 321. Cf. "Discourse at Middlebury College," "Napoleon," *W*, IV, 228, and "Goethe," *W*, IV, 266.

& months & estates & ⟨rep⟩ credit also in the profound hope that one
restoring, all-rewarding, immense success will arrive at length which
[will] give him at one bound the throne of the universe. And rightly;
for if his wild prayers are granted, if he is to succeed, his achieve-
ment is the piercing of the brass heavens of Boston & Christendom
[52] and letting in one beam of the pure Eternity which instantly
burns up this whole universe of shadows & chimaeras in which we
dwell. Every poet knows the unspeakable hope & represents ⟨the⟩
its audacity by throwing it out of all probability in his conversation.[68]

Mrs [Sarah A.] R[ipley?]. "hated to hear of the opposition of clergymen & others to the Fast Day, for she thought our people had so
few festivals and this was now well established," and the penitential
form of the proclamation gives it a certain zest which the other holidays want.

[53] 1. The first look of the poet
      2. The power to execute

      ⟨First⟩ ↑Today's↓ success depends on executive talent[.]
      Permanent success depends on grandeur of design[.]

      [54] The mountain & the squirrel had a quarrel, and the former
called the latter little prig. Bun replied You are doubtless very big
[5] but all sorts of weather must be taken in⟨to⟩ together to make a
year & a world. And I think it no disgrace [10] to occupy my proper
place   If I am not so large as you,
             You are not as small as I   [13]
             If[n] I cannot carry forests on my back   [18]
             Neither can you crack a nut.[69]   [19]

      In gardening, the new value created is such that the original
price of the land is really of very little importance. One tree yields
the ⟨value⟩ ↑product↓ of an acre of land in farming.

---

[68] These two paragraphs, struck through in pencil with a vertical use mark, are
used in "Discourse at Middlebury College" and "The Scholar," *W*, X, 264–266.
[69] "Fable," *W*, IX, 75. The entry is struck through in ink with a wavy vertical
use mark and three vertical use marks.

H[enry]. [Thoreau] complained that when he came out of the garden, he remembered his work.

Is not a small house best? Put a woman into a small house, and after five years she comes out large & healthy, and her children are so. Put her into a large house, & after the same time, she shall be haggard, sickly, with a sharp voice, & a wrinkled careful countenance, & her children suffer with her.

[55] ⟨The poet knows that⟩ "Only poetry inspires poetry," said Schiller, "& therefore we ought to avoid affairs,"[70] — or something like this he said. True, if he use "poetry" in a liberal sense, but if he mean books of poems, no. For the test of the poet is that he be able to read the poetry of affairs. A whole volume of sermons might be made out of the chips of one sonnet.

A pilgrim wandering in search of a man. This too will plainly be a looking-glass business. Like to like, or, as I wrote in New-York, — ⟨I met no gods, — I harboured none.⟩

Frivolous reasons have allowance with all men & with poets also, but no man says, I was reading Plato & therefore could not come; I had new rhymes jingling in my brain, and would not risk losing them.

[56] Today is carnival in Heaven, the angels almost assume flesh, and repeatedly have been visible. The imagination of the gods is excited, & rushes on every side into forms. Yesterday not a bird peeped, scarcely a leaf was left, the world was thin & barren, peaking & pining. Today it is inconceivably populous, creation swarms.[71]

One would think from the talk of men that riches & poverty were a great matter whilst they are really a thin costume & our life, ⟨is⟩ the life of all of us[,] is identical. For we transcend circumstance con-

[70] See Journal Y, p. [259] below.
[71] This paragraph, struck through in pencil with a wavy diagonal use mark, is used in "Works and Days," *W*, VII, 170.

tinually and taste the real quality of existence; as, in our employments which only differ in the manipulation but express the same laws; or in our thoughts, which wear no coats & taste no ice creams. We see God face to face every hour & know the savour of nature.[72]

[57] The muse demands real sacrifices. I must lose an important advantage by neglect. I must suffer the well of my house to be dug in the wrong place. I must sacrifice a ⟨pear⟩tree.[n]

See p 48

A man shall not be a pond. As the water came in, so it shall go out. I think the charm of rhetoric is still that; the hint or advertisement it gives us of our constitution; the pilgrim[,] the palmer, shell on shoulder, marching fraternity, — we are bound on a long tramp. Before God, why sit ye here? [73]

One man all ligament & another all explosion[.]

Life is a game between God & man. The One disparts himself & feigns to divide into individuals. He puts part in a pomegranate, part in a king's crown, part in a person. Instantly man sees the beautiful things & goes to procure them[.] As he takes down each one the Lord smiles & says It is yourself; and when he has them all, it will be *yourself*. We love & die for a beauty which we wronged ourselves in thinking alien[.]

[58] Writing should be the settlement of dew on the leaf, of stalactites on the wall of the grotto, the deposite of flesh from the blood, of woody fibre in the tree from the sap.

Our virtue runs in a narrow rill: we have never a freshet. We ought to be subject to enthusiasms. One would like to see Boston & Massa-

[72] A pencil version of this paragraph, later erased, is visible in the space between this and the previous entry. The pencil version begins "We transcend circumstance" and apparently omits "which only differ . . . no ice creams." The paragraph, struck through in ink with a vertical use mark, is used in "Illusions," *W*, VI, 323–324.

[73] This and the two following entries are in pencil.

chusetts agitated like a wave with some generosity, mad for learning, for music, for philosophy, for association, for freedom, for art; but now it goes like a pedlar with its hand ever on its pocket, cautious, calculating[.]   ↑See above, p. 10↓

How hard to find a man. It would take as Taylor said the lamp of Diogenes added to the splendour of the noonday sun. Otis talked too much. Webster has no morale. Choate wants weight. Alcott is unlimited & unballasted. Bound, bound, let there be bound! But let there not be too strict bound. Rogers here was handsome but rigid & stupid[.] [74]   ↑See↓

Alcott is a pail of which the bottom is taken out & Whig a pail from which you cannot get off the cover.   ↑See Y↓

[59] [blank]
     [60] These farmers so keen in trade, so cool & solid in their manners, are no fools, and their considerate heads might wag to advantage with those in Congress or the Cabinet. But living as they now do to so humble aims, it seems as if they must on some day & year not far back, have compounded with more generous hopes & have renounced their homage & duty and resolved to get what dirty compensation they could for their right of subscription to wild goodness & beauty, by an unmixed undistracted attention to squalid economies.

A great deal of God in the Universe but not valuable to us until we can make it up into man. Plenty of air but worth nothing until we can get it into a shape to send us for example with our baggage on the railroad. Then it is worth hundreds of thousands ⟨of dollars⟩ ↑of our money↓. Plenty of water but who cares? sea full, sky full;

[74] The remark by Edward Taylor, pastor of Seamen's Bethel in Boston, is repeated on p. [112] below. Harrison Gray Otis had been at various times a member of the House of Representatives, a U.S. Senator, and mayor of Boston; Rufus Choate, a Boston lawyer, was U.S. Senator from Massachusetts at this time. Which Rogers Emerson refers to is not known; perhaps the "Col. Rogers of Boston" who was the prosecutor in the Wyman trial (see p. 249, n. 190 below). This and the following entry are in pencil.

but when we can get it where we want it on our ↑mill↓ wheel or boat paddle we will buy it with millions. Plenty of wild wrath but all nought until we have made it up into pies & tarts. So we find it in our company. How many grand poetic geniuses ⟨I⟩even I alone have seen[:] Homer, Numa, Raphael, & Pericles; and the sexton will [61] presently be the last that shall speak of them, for want of a little talent[.] [75]

What is the use of trying to get that out which is not in? You may ask me as often as you will, & in what ingenious forms, for an opinion concerning the mode of building the wall or sinking the well, or laying out the acre, but always the ball will rebound. These are questions which you & not I will answer. [76]

The scholar passes, like the Russian bathers from hot water to ice--cold, so he from height of honour to that of insult, as he falls into studious or into "practical" company.   ↑See the sentence from Veeshnoo Sarma T 97↓ [77]

Much of the time, he must be, every man must be, his own friend. Let him beware of being an old trifler, ↑& growing older↓ a rich, well-connected, well-reputed trifler[.] [78]   ↑See p 139↓

[62] Mr Briggs's[n] sermon preached to define his position in regard to Mr Parker ⟨is⟩[n] has so much trifling distinction and penurious avowal, accompanied with so much parade of frankness, as to remind one of the common country answer when we ask a farmer

---

[75] This paragraph, which is in pencil, is used in "Discourse at Middlebury College" and "The Scholar," *W*, X, 276.

[76] This paragraph, struck through in ink with two diagonal use marks, is used in "Wealth," *W*, VI, 123.

[77] See *JMN*, VI, 358, for the quotation from *The Hĕĕtōpădēs of Vĕĕshnoŏ-Sărmă, in a Series of Connected Fables, Interspersed with Moral, Prudential, and Political Maxims* . . . , trans. Charles Wilkins (Bath, 1787). The volume is in Emerson's library.

[78] "Much of the time . . . friend" is struck through in ink with two vertical use marks; the entire entry is struck through in "ink with a vertical use mark. "See p 139" is in pencil.

his name; — he replies "My name is Gilbert, and I an't ashamed on't." [79]

Identity
Coarse & fine is a distinction of the most odious persistency in the cosmic arrangements and the mode in which Plato grasps a thought sadly reminds the naturalist of the eldest plesiosaurus snatching at a distance his prey.[n]

Steer well, that's all [80]
End of the Oration to change the course of life in half an hour for many men [81]
Genius is my country
Varying estimate of money earned by self   Mirabeau's sentiment [82]
Can't see a house till 'tis built [83]
[63]   Falling sickness & writing sickness
machine
organism
we dash up to heaven in our brag & down
again to hell in our behaviour and
perform our whole orbit with caracoles
in three weeks

Our frivolous people hear Sealsfield praised in one newspaper paragraph and the press teems with editions of him[.]   Bremer Hahnhahn(?) [84]

---

[79] "Mr Briggs" may be the Reverend Charles Briggs, the Unitarian minister at Lexington, a conventional churchman who might be expected to dislike the radical theology of Theodore Parker.

[80] The entries from this line to the end of p. [62], and all the entries on p. [63], are in pencil.

[81] Cf. "Discourse at Middlebury College" and "The Scholar," *W*, X, 282.

[82] Probably a reference to the statement quoted in Journal V, p. [87] above.

[83] See Journal U, p. [34] above and p. [66] below.

[84] Charles Sealsfield (Karl Anton Postl), Fredrika Bremer, and Countess Ida von Hahn-Hahn all enjoyed popular success with novels, essays, and travel sketches. For a comment on the last-named's novel *Faustina*, see Journal V, p. [65] above.

Why does not society feel the compliment of the existence of philosophers, which fact indicates a high degree of security & refinement[?]

[64]   *Vestiges of Creation*
      What is so ungodly as these polite bows to God in English
books? He is always mentioned in the most respectful & deprecatory
manner, 'that august,' 'that almighty,' 'that adorable providence,'
&c &c. But courage only will the Spirit prompt or accept. Everything
in this Vestiges of Creation is good except the theology, which is
civil, timid, & dull.[85]
These things which the author so well collates, ought to be known
only to few, and those, masters & poets.

> —— —— —— "Cithara crinitus Iopas
> Personat aurata, docuit quae maximus Atlas.
> Hic canit errantem lunam, solisque labores
> Unde hominis genus, et pecudes; unde imber et ignes,
> Arcturum, pluviasque Hyadas, geminosque Triones,
> Quid tantum Oceano properent se tingere soles
> Hiberni, vel quae tardis mora noctibus obstet." [86]
>   [Virgil,] Aeneid. I, 740[–746].

It is curious that all we want in this department is collation[;] [65]
as soon as the facts are stated we recognize them all as somewhere
expressed in our experience or in history, fable, sculpture or poetry.
We have seen men with tails in the Fauns & Satyrs. We have seen
Centaurs, Titans, Lapithae.
      All science is transcendental, or else passes away. Botany is now
acquiring a right theory. And how excellent is this MacLeay &
Swainson theory of animated circles! Symbolic also, as in Kirby &
Spence.[87] The cyclic or encyclopaediacal character that science acquires,

[85] Robert Chambers, *Vestiges of the Natural History of Creation* (New York,
1845), in Emerson's library. "What is so ungodly . . . books", struck through in
ink with a vertical use mark, is used in *English Traits, W*, V, 229.
[86] "Long-haired Iopas, once taught by mighty Atlas, makes the hall ring with
his golden lyre. He sings of the wandering moon and the sun's toils; whence sprang
human kind and the brutes, whence rain and fire; of Arcturus, the rainy Hyades and
the twin Bears; why wintry suns make such haste to dip themselves in Ocean, or
what delay stays the slowly passing nights."
[87] The "theory of animated circles," or Quinary System, was put forward by
William Sharp MacLeay in his *Horae Entomologicae, or Essays on Annulose Animals*

pleases also & satisfies. The avatars of Brahma will presently be text-books of natural history.

Well & it seems there is room for a better species of the genus Homo. The Caucasian is an arrested undertype.

[66] *Persons*
I can't see a house until it is built[.] [88]

Or does any one suppose himself to be without bounds or limits? Perhaps he will defy mesmerism. Does he think that no man can possibly come to him who can persuade him out of his most settled determination ↑e.g.↓ if he is a miser, to give up his money freely for some purpose he now least thinks of: or, if he is a prudent & industrious person, to forsake his work & give up whole days to a new interest? [n] A man who has tastes like mine but in greater power will do that any day, & is like a hill which commands our military ground.[89]

↑pope;↓ Amicus Curiae↑;↓ & right of revolution [90]

> "But in our circumstance & course of thought
> 'Tis heavy with him"
> [Shakespeare, *Hamlet*, III, iii, 83–84]

[67]   ↑*Fame.*↓
⟨What a social⟩ Among our social advantages what a signal convenience is fame! Do we read all authors, to grope our way to the best? no, but the world selects for us the best, & we select from the best, our best.

(1819, 1821), and later popularized by his disciple William Swainson. Once considered a possible key to the system of nature, it compared the relation of created beings to a number of intersecting circles. Emerson was familiar with William Kirby and William Spence, *An Introduction to Entomology* (London, 1816–1826), as early as 1830 (*JMN*, III, 164, 342).

[88] This line and the heading are in pencil. See p. [62] above and Journal U, p. [34] above.

[89] This paragraph, struck through in ink with two vertical use marks, is used in "Eloquence," *W*, VII, 80–81.

[90] The insertions in this line are in pencil. See p. [137] below.

[68] A crop of poets ⟨are⟩ ↑is↓ as inevitable as a crop of violets or anemones, and the asperity or the narrowness or the conceit of any one is of no account in the cycle, being readily compensated not in him, but in the choir. They are all less than the genus, & why not he?

↑Identity↓
Liars also are true. Truth is the moral gravitation, and let a man begin where he will, & work in whatever false direction, he is sure to be found instantly afterwards arriving at a true result.

Is it good to be hospitable & to give one a meal and a night's lodging? and is it not better to be candid & appreciating to a good tendency & good meaning, & give courage to a companion? ↑We must be as courteous to a man as we are to a picture, which we are willing to give the advantage of a good light[.]↓ [91]

In ⟨you⟩good conversation, the parties do not speak to the words, but to the meanings & characters of each other. [92]

———

Black men built the railroads, not blue eyes. [93]

[69] The Whig party is anxious to disembarrass itself of the abolitionists. Does it not know that no injustice can be done except by the help of justice? that its true policy is to take away from the Loco-foco party every right principle & adopt the same itself? then will the ruin be inevitable of the bad. But this boyish policy of becoming bad & rowdy gives strength to the ⟨ene⟩other side.

———

Plato. "We know all things as in a dream, & are again ignorant of them according to vigilant perception." (in *Sophista*) [94]

[91] This paragraph, struck through in ink with a vertical use mark, is used in "Behavior," *W*, VI, 196. See p. [101] below.
[92] This sentence, struck through in ink with a vertical use mark, is used in "Social Aims," *W*, VIII, 99.
[93] See *JMN*, VIII, 525.
[94] Taylor, "General Introduction . . . ," *The Works of Plato* . . . , 1804, I, lxvii.

Plato, the whetstone of wits, the yardstick standard metre of wits[95]

The hint of the dialectic is more valuable than the dialectic. One who has seen one proof ever so slight of the terrific powers of this organ will remember it all the days of his life. The most venerable proser will be surprised with silence. It is like the first hint that the earth moves or that iron is a conductor of fluids, or that granite is a gas. The solids, the centres, rest itself, fly & skip. Rest is a relation and not rest any longer. Ah these solid houses[,] real estates[,] have wings like so many nimble musquitoes, & do exceedingly hop & [70][96] avoid me.

Plato: Republic, [Book IV,] Vol IX
Definition of Courage   p 214
        Justice   p 221
        Temperance   218 [97]

Books are worth reading that settle a principle, as lectures are. All others are tickings of the clock & we have so much less to live; Robbers.

Swedenborg's law of series appears p 226[98] — The character & manners of a state are in each of the individuals who compose it.

Objections made to Repub[lic]. are shallow — He keeps a cobler a cobler but that is only illustration to show that each passion & action should keep its orbit. There is no cobler to the Civitas Dei, which alone he would build[.]

Caution for the sake of emphasis with which he broaches his doctrine that kings should be philosophers.

[95] This entry is in pencil.
[96] The entries on this page, with the exception of "avoid me.", are in pencil. Between "avoid me." and the beginning of the next entry, "Plato" has been erased.
[97] Emerson's volume and page references are to *Oeuvres de Platon*, trans. Victor Cousin, 13 vols. (Paris, 1822–1840), presented to Emerson by a group of appreciative Concord citizens in 1839 (see *L*, II, 207, and *JMN*, VII, 4).
[98] Cousin, *Oeuvres de Platon*, 1822–1840, IX.

Modern Europe in all Plato
Alfieri's plant — man [99]
Swedenborg's doctrine of series: E.g. ↑bad↓ state made up of bad men:
soliform eyes;

Socrates & Plato   the double star which the most powerful instruments will not entirely separate [100]

[71] *Plato.* "O Glaucon, I conjure Adrastia to favor me in that which I am now to do; for I fear that it were a less crime to kill some one involuntarily than to deceive him ⟨on⟩ ↑in regard to↓ the beautiful, the good, the just, & the laws." Rep. B. 5 — [Cousin, *Oeuvres de Platon,* 1822–1840,] Vol IX. p. 254

The naked athlete was a novelty & ridiculous in Greece, it seems[,] some little time before Plato. First the Cretans, then the Lacedaemonians adopted the practice of naked games. [*Ibid.,*] Vol IX p 257

Plato anticipates us (pereant qui ante nos).[101] Every brisk young man who says fine things to each reluctant generation in succession as Rabelais, Erasmus, Rousseau, ↑Alfieri,↓ Goethe, Carlyle, is some reader of Plato translating into the vernacular wittily his good things. E.g. Carlyle's *"Shams"* [102]

↑Swedenborg↓
Measure of merit of a writing — this perpetual modernness,[n] since the

[99] Emerson quotes a remark by Alfieri that "The plant Man grows more vigorous in Italy than in any other country" in "Permanent Traits of the English National Genius," *Lectures,* I, 242.

[100] This entry is used in "Plato; or, the Philosopher," *W,* IV, 70.

[101] The original Latin saying is usually attributed to the Roman grammarian Aelius Donatus: "Pereant qui ante nos nostra dixerent" — "May those who have said our ideas before us perish" (Ed.). See *JMN,* VII, 194.

[102] This reference may have been added later, since Carlyle deals extensively with "Shams" in "The Present Age," *Latter-Day Pamphlets* (1850). "Every brisk . . . good things.", struck through in ink with a vertical use mark, is used in "Plato; or, the Philosopher," *W,* IV, 39.

author has not been misled ever by the shortlived, local, accidental, but has abode by real & abiding traits.[103]

Beauties of "the majority" Vol. 10 p. 22 *Cousin*. [*Oeuvres de Platon*, 1822–1840]
S.H's, & Judge A's jury [104]   & Judge S.'s
People were coaxed & wheedled into the Fed. Constit.
T. said he had the grease out of K.[105]
Beauties of majority. See above *W* p. 50

[72] As I have elsewhere written, it destroys how many originalities, pretended originals, to read Plato. Here is the mountain from which all these detached boulders were torn. Plato was the bible of the learned for 2⟨0⟩200 years, and when Swedenborg or the Xn [Christian] Fathers, or Locke, or Bacon say the same thing as he, we fairly infer, they read it.[106]
Yet how easy to say "My thunder;" "that's new church truth"
Poor little fellows, all our propositions are related.
The broadest generalizer, of course, is found to have anticipated all the particulars comprised in his thesis.[107]

The beautiful is difficult[.] [108]

It is easy to read Plato, difficult to read his commentators[.] [109]

Luther's saying about the inspiration of the prophets would shake down how many modern churches about the ears of their votaries.[110]

---

[103] This paragraph, struck through in ink with a vertical use mark, is used in "Plato; or, the Philosopher," *W*, IV, 45.

[104] See *JMN*, VIII, 360, for comments by Samuel Hoar and Charles Allen on the justice of the jury system.

[105] This line is in pencil.

[106] This paragraph, struck through in ink with a vertical use mark, is used in "Plato; or, the Philosopher," *W*, IV, 39.

[107] This sentence, struck through in ink with a vertical use mark, is used in "Plato; or, the Philosopher," *W*, IV, 40.

[108] Cousin, *Oeuvres de Platon*, 1822–1840, IX, 226. This line is in pencil.

[109] See Journal Y, p. [24] below.

[110] For Luther's saying, see *JMN*, IV, 350, and VI, 349, where it is quoted from

On the advantage of Reputation.

Mr Parkman ⟨looking⟩ groping in the snow for the eloquent part of Henry Ware's sermon.[111]

————

A man afraid of his own razor

[73] There was an ugly rumour went about from London to Boston & in other places a twelvemonth since, that Cousin was dished, & now I owe to him this magnificent "Republic"; and how many scholars will thank him for a century to come for this translation!

There is not the smallest probability that the college will foster an eminent talent in any youth. If he refuse prayers & recitations, they will torment & traduce & expel him though ⟨it⟩he were Newton or Dante.

The Pedlars

H↑orace↓ M↑ann↓ declared that Connecticutt was great in small things, patenting bootstraps, horse-bits, and all manner of knick-knacks[,] never any valuable invention. No Connecticutt man, he affirmed, was ever known to pay for a letter which he put in the mail though it respected his own business, & the legislation, he said, of the state was on a scale as contracted, instancing the law which sent all the N.Y. & Boston trade from New London round Point Judith[.]

[74] Of what use to put one whole thread into a rotten web? The neighbors tax the philosopher with not using his opportunity, if he refuse to serve in the School Committee. But to what end should he serve? Any reform that he might propose is beforehand either wholly inadequate, or else sure of rejection. Because he differs from them in the aim of his teaching; he wishing to make of the ⟨child⟩ pupil a worshipper of truth & goodness, and they to make a lover of gain. The clergymen ⟨use⟩on the committee do not say this, but they also mean it, & aim at it, for the children generally, & for

————

Colloquia Mensalia: or, Dr. Martin Luther's Divine Discourses at his Table . . . , trans. Henry Bell (London, 1652).

[111] This and the following entry are in pencil. For the first, see *JMN*, III, 125.

their own children also. Is it different in regard to political employments?

↑see p 100↓ 112

[75] When one sees that the knaves always win in every political struggle; that society is delivered over from criminals to criminals[,] an endless ⟨series⟩train of felonies, he wonders, how general
ends ever get answered.[113]   ↑see V 165↓

But we have — have we not? — a real relation to markets &
brokers, to currency & coin. The unmentionable money itself has at
last a high origin in moral & metaphysical nature. "Gold & silver
grow in the earth from the celestial gods, an effluxion from them."
Fitchburg stock is not private property, but the quality & essence of
the universe is in that also.[114]

You say that ⟨they⟩we talk of slavery & patriotism but will not
do any thing. Why, but because we have not sufficient insight? In
this new matter of association, are men to blame that they will not
leave their homesteads & try the hazardous experiment of a new
colony in the woods of the west or in Brook Farm or Skeneateles,
perilling the means of living of their families? They wish well to
your Enterprise but it looks to them ⟨ve⟩by no means wise & secure.
They want sight, certainty, thorough knowledge.ⁿ
[76] They are ⟨perfectly commendable,⟩ perfectly right in refusing their contribution & their personal aid to your ⟨cause⟩ ↑project↓.
Better certainly that you should lack their aid, than that they should
do a foolish thing. Then let us have insight before all things.

With our Saxon education & habit of thought we all require to
be first.[115] Each man must somehow think himself the first in his

---

[112] This notation is in pencil.
[113] This paragraph, struck through in ink with a vertical use mark, is used in
"Montaigne," W, IV, 185.
[114] The quotation is from *The Commentaries of Proclus on the Timaeus of
Plato . . .* , 1820, I, 36. This paragraph, struck through in pencil with a vertical
use mark, is used in "The Scholar," W, X, 272.
[115] This sentence is used in "Uses of Great Men," W, IV, 22.

own ⟨line⟩ career: if he find that he is not, he thinks himself cheated; he accuses Nature & Providence. We are born with lotus in our mouths, & are very deceivable as to our merits, easily believing we are the best. But in our present system that is the basis, that I am to be the first of my kind. Meantime we have somewhere heard or dreamed of another order, to wit, purely social, where a social or loving perfection subsisted, blending the proprieties of all, & each found his beatitude in the atmosphere of his club. If an American should wake up some morning & discover that his existence was unnecessary, he would think himself excessively ill-used & would declare himself instantly against the Government of the Universe. We construct all our theories & philosophies so as to show how with many members each member may be best.

[77]–[78] [leaf torn out] [116]
[79]   The moth & miller
            Caddisworm & caterpillar
            ⟨Crawls from form to form⟩
            As creeps from leaf to leaf the worm
            So creeps ⟨|| . . . ||⟩its life from form to form
            And the poor emmet on the ground
            On march of centuries is bound [117]

        Guest in his house   guest in his thought   V 52

Topics
        ____

            What is the use of great men? ↑v. p 14↓
        ____

            On the misuse of men
        ____

            That we should respect men, or Faith, and History should
            be written by Faith
        ____

[116] Emerson indexed p. [78] under Manners.
[117] These lines, apparently a version of the epigraph to *Nature* (see Journal V, p. [134] above and *W*, I, 1), are in pencil, as is the following entry.

Dejection cuts the throat of all philosophy

———

The French genius & the English aversion

———

Swedenborg & Fourier

[80] Jove was the eldest & knows the most.[118] Truth or the connexion of cause & effect alone interests us. A skeptical book which goes to show this fact & then that other, a fool begotten by a hero, a poet born of an ideot, and to dissipate all faith or searching for connexion dispirits us[,] profits nothing[,] & we throw it away. We are invincibly persuaded that the connexion exists[,] seen or not seen. We hire a lawyer: the whole people assemble breathless to listen to the lawyer who puts this & that together; then shows an unobserved third; and then a hidden fourth; which brings ↑us,↓ as it were, underground, to the manifest fifth, & makes the chain of things & our satisfaction complete. Talent makes counterfeit ties. Genius finds the real ones. Wonder is begotten by showing us legitimate series, but suppressing one or more of the terms.[119]
Skepticism profits by suggesting the grander generalization which yet remains to us (as proved by this or that anomaly) after our present religion & philosophy shall be outlived.

[81] We say sometimes of a personage that he spreads his ability over his whole discourse & does not utter epigrams; so eminently does the good Genius of the world and cares little to distil sweetness or sense into moments or persons but ↑by↓ here a little & there a little, with infinite tediousness of apparatus & detail, arrives surely at his ends.

[82] But I will tell you how you can enrich me — if you can recommend today to me.

---

[118] See Journal V, p. [i] above.
[119] This paragraph is struck through in both pencil and ink with vertical use marks; "Truth . . . not seen." and "Talent makes . . . real ones." are used in "Montaigne," *W*, IV, 170.

Is there a book that will not leave us where it found us?
"The Republic," perhaps?
Yes, if there were one to read it with.
What we want, then, is a class.
A class of two.

———

Society is a great boarding house in which people of all characters
& habits meet for their dinner & eat harmoniously together; but, the
meal ↑once↓ over, they separate to the most unlike & opposite employments.

———

On the superlative. The low expression is strong & agreeable. In the
fine scenery on the Hudson river one boy said to another "Come up
here, it looks pretty out of doors." In crossing Mount Holly in
Vermont one of the country girls on the top of the coach said to another "We shall soon come to that rocky spot,"ⁿ which turned out to
be a wild place ⟨that delighted me⟩. The↑y↓ ⟨mou⟩ do not call particular summits as Killington Peak, Camel's Rump, Mansfield Mt.
&c. mountains, but only "*them ⟨a⟩ere rises*" & reserve the [83] word
mountain for the *range* as when they cross the mountain at Mt
Holly or Woodstock or ————— ¹²⁰

I avoid the Stygian anniversaries at Cambridge[,] those hurrahs
among⟨s⟩ the ghosts, those yellow, bald, toothless meetings in memory of red cheeks, black hair, and departed health. Most forcible
Feeble made the only oration that fits the occasion that contains all
these obituary eloquences. ↑Bluebirds celebrate theirs.↓

Animal Spirits. On common grounds as at a feast common people
entirely meet or even blend. Each new comer is only the animal
spirit of the other extended. Instead of carrying the water in a
⟨tho⟩hundred buckets we have a hose, and every hose fits every
hydrant[.] ¹²¹

¹²⁰ This paragraph is struck through in ink with two wavy diagonal use marks
to the bottom of p. [82]; "The low . . . out of doors.' " and "They ⟨mou⟩ . . .
range" are used in "The Superlative," *W*, X, 169–170.
¹²¹ "every hose fits every hydrant" is used in "Swedenborg," *W*, IV, 121, and
"Natural History of Intellect," *W*, XII, 20. See Journal Y, p. [246] below.

[84] ↑1845↓

Saturday, 7 June. I went with C[aroline]. S[turgis]. to see Charles K[ing]. N[ewcomb]. We found him rapt as ever in his great Gothic cathedral of fancies; pained now, it seems, by the doubt whether he should retire to more absolute inward priesthood, or accept the frequent & to him dear solicitations of domestic & varied life. His idea of love, which he names so often, is, I think, only the wish to be cherished. He is too full of his prophecy, ⟨to⟩once to think of friendship. Saints in a convent who all recognize each other, & still retire, — that is his image. A purer service to the intellect was never offered than his, — warm, fragrant, religious, — & I feel, ↑when↓ with him, the pertinency of that Platonistic word, "all-various." Beautiful & dear, God & all his hosts shall keep him.

[85] What shall I say of the friend with whom I have spent so many hours of the past month?ⁿ Very dear & pleasing memories, though the future, it now seems, may be changed. Of all the persons I know, this child, called romantic & insane & exaggerating, is the most real. And it is strange that she should not have that which she wants, somewhat to do.[122]

[86] "If we look at the shadow of a bare head upon a white wall we shall see very distinctly the shadow of a flying smoke issuing from the head & mounting upwards." Winslow

ap A.K. p 415 Vol II [123]

Adaptiveness ☞ [124]

The philosophy we want is one of fluxions & mobility; ☞ not a house, but a ship in these billows we inhabit. Any angular dogmatic theory would be rent to ⟨s⟩chips & splinters in this storm of many elements. No, it must be tight & fit to the form of man, to live at

---

[122] The friend is Caroline Sturgis, who visited in Concord in late May and early June (L, III, 290). The left two-fifths of this entry is struck through in ink with a series of connected vertical lines, perhaps to cancel it.

[123] Emanuel Swedenborg, The Animal Kingdom, considered Anatomically, Physically, and Philosophically, trans. James John Garth Wilkinson, 2 vols. (London and Boston, 1843–1844), in Emerson's library. "Winslow" is Jakob Benignus Winslow, author of Exposition anatomique de la structure du corps humain (1732).

[124] The hand signs in this and the next line point to the last line on p. [87].

all; as a shell is the architecture of a house ⟨for⟩ ↑founded on↓ the sea. The form of man, the soul of man must be the type of our Scheme, just as the body of man is the type after which a dwelling house is built.[125] The Universe & the individual perpetually act & react on each other. Thus all philosophy begins from Nox & Chaos, the Ground or Abyss which Schelling so celebrates. And in every man we require a bit of night, of chaos, of *Abgrund*, as the spring of a watch turns best on a diamond. In every [87] individual we require a *pièce de resistance*, a certain abyss of reliance & fortitude ⟨‖ ... ‖⟩on which to fall back, when worst comes to worst. That continent, that backbone being secure, he may have what variety, what surface, what ornament, what flourish, he will.

For Plato, it would be pedantry to catalogue his philosophy, the secret of constructing pyramids & cathedrals is lost, & not less of Platonic philosophies. But every whole is made of similars and in morals & metaphysics this is specially true. I shall think a grand proposition important. The fables of Plato will reward the ear[.]

Plato philosopher, Swedenborg mystic, affirmer, Montaigne skeptic, ⟨Nap⟩Shakspeare poet, Napoleon practical will make my circle[.]
☞ See ⟨W⟩Y p. 56   Adaptiveness

[88]–[89] [blank]
    [90][126] There is no whim a scholar may not settle into by indulgence if it were that one of his lamps had a friendly influence on his brain & was a counsellor[.]

Scholar is here to affirm
        to know that ⟨under⟩ every word means a thing
        to know that the sentiments make poetry of me
        to feel the affirmative vigor of others' genius
———
        to believe the omnipresence, or the surprise, or, that, flow
            the river how it will, cities will rise

[125] "The philosophy we want . . . built.", struck through in ink with a vertical use mark, is used in "Montaigne," *W*, IV, 160–161.
[126] The entries on this page, with the exception of the first, are in pencil.

that though governors are ever knavish, general ends are
served by states.

———

no knife was ever long enough to reach a heart [126a]
to see that the power of ideas is shared by them who
    oppose them
that we are oppressed by necessity
the sea & the ship are made of one stuff [127]
ploughman & plough & furrow & wheat
to believe wholes, to believe what the years & the centuries say against the Hours

The astronomer is not ridiculous in as far as he is an astron-
omer but inasmuch as he is not [128]
He is insured
Yet let him always speak for the magnetism not needle

Beauty is a leader & draws by being beautiful not by ⟨con-
trivance⟩ taking thought.[129] It is the greatest advantage to
the Universe. What are doers?

[91][130]   ↑Individuality self-defended↓
Nothing strikes me with more force than the powers by which
individuals are protected from individuals in a world where every
benefactor becomes so easily a malefactor only by continuation of
his activity into places where it is not due; and where children seem
so much at the mercy of their foolish parents and where almost all
men are excessively social & interfering[.] [131]

[126a] See Journal U, p. [159] above.

[127] See p. [106] below.

[128] This sentence is used in "Discourse at Middlebury College" and "The
Scholar," W, X, 281. See p. [144] below.

[129] Cf. "Discourse at Middlebury College" and "The Scholar," W, X, 262.

[130] The entries on pp. [91]–[93], with the exception of the first on p. [91], are
in pencil.

[131] This paragraph, struck through in pencil with two vertical use marks and in
ink with a vertical use mark, is used in "Uses of Great Men," W, IV, 28–29.

See how rare is insight by the value I attach to a seer's words though not his words of sight[.] C[harles] K[ing] N[ewcomb]

Always new values; first for self truth[,] then for instrumentality[.]

Perfect system. You cannot hear what I say until it is yours. Who of all of you dare take home to himself this[,] that he need not seek anything. We are protected from the usurpation of individualism. Beauty & Virtue are the two last realities. Great & general ends served by sots. Secret architecture of things is alike & analogous[.] [132]

You may know all the people on earth. Do you know your own Genius? No. Every thought[,] every deed you drag before it that you may have a verdict & know something of itself and it answers from its cloudy seat.
What alone in the history of this world interests us? What but the mystic import of two or three [92] words men use? Genius, Muse, Love, Right,

Men in the present age are not Unitarians but Dualists. They alternate a faith in Love and in Truth. They do not ascend to faith in Being[.]

He will have to answer certain questions which I must plainly tell you cannot be staved off. For ↑all↓ men, ↑all↓ women, time, your country, your condition, the invisible world, are the interrogators —
Who are you?
What do you?
Can you obtain what you wish? [133]

I invite you not to cheap joys, to the fluttered bosom of gratified vanity, to a sleek & rosy comfort[;] no[,] but to bareness, to power, to mountains, to chemistry, to true & natural supremacy, to the society of the great, & to love.[134]

[132] See *JMN*, VIII, 478.

[133] This entry is used in "Discourse at Middlebury College" and "The Scholar," *W*, X, 284.

[134] This paragraph is used in "Discourse at Middlebury College" and "The Scholar," *W*, X, 287.

Not to be a pendant & a pensioner to society but a commander & a friend.

[93] Others may build cities[;] it suffices that he understand them & keep them in awe.[135]

Believe in magnetism[,] not in needles, in the unwearied & unweariable power of Destiny, which, without an effort, brings together like to like, the arrow to its mark, the cause to its effect, the friend to the friend, and the soul to its fortune[,] for though the ⟨summ⟩ bases are divided, the summits are united.[136] Silver to silver.

[94] The Farm once more! The unanimous voice of thoughtful men is for the ⟨f⟩life of labor & the farm. All experience is against it, it being found, 1. that a small portion of the people suffice for the raising of bread for the whole. 2. that men are born with the most positive peculiarities of power ↑as↓ for music, for geometry, for chemistry, for care of animals, &c, &c, 3. that hard labor on the farm untunes the mind, unfits for the intellectual exercises which are the delight of the best men. I suppose that all that is done in ploughing & sowing & reaping & storing is repeated in finer sort in the life of men who never touch the plough handles. The⟨s⟩ essence of those manipulations is subtle & reappears in countinghouses & council boards, in games of cards & chess, in conversations, correspondences, & in poets' rhymes.

The obvious objection to the indulgence of particular talent & refusing to be man of all work is th⟨at⟩e rapid tendency to farther subdivision & attenuation, until there shall be no manly man[.]

The good of doing with [95] one's own hands is the honouring of the symbol. My own cooking, my own cobbling, fencebuilding, digging of a well, building of a house, twisting of a rope, forging of a hoe & shovel, — is poetic.

Poltroonery is in acknowledging an inferiority as incurable. Kohl

---

[135] This sentence, struck through in ink with a vertical use mark, is used in "Swedenborg," *W*, IV, 93.
[136] See p. [106] below.

relates that the Russian traders do. The Indian is said to be unable to stand the gaze of the white.[137]   ↑See also Republic, Book II at the end↓[138]

The only suppression of truth we can forgive is in ↑restraining↓ the confession of inferiority when really felt, because of some trivial advantage. Let the penitent wait & not prematurely poltroonize.

[96] Against low assailants we have also low defenders. As I came home by the brook, I saw the carcass of a snake which the mud-turtles were eating at both ends.

———

Poetry aids itself both with music & with eloquence, neither of which are essential to it. Say rather that music is proper to it, but that within the high organic music proper to it are inferior harmonies & melodies, which it avails itself of at pleasure. Thus in W.E.C.'s piece called "Death," the line

> "I come, I come, ⟨I⟩think not I turn away" [l. 79]

is a turn of eloquence. And Byron, when he writes,

> "For who the fool that doth not know
> How bloom & beauty come & go
> And how disease & pain & sorrow
> May chance today, may chance tomorrow
> Unto the merriest of us all."

enhances the pleasure of the poem by this bit of plaintive music. In like manner,

> "Out upon time who will leave no more
> Of ^{n} the things to come than the things before
> Out upon time who forever will leave
> But enough of the past for the future to grieve

---

[137] Emerson's reference to Kohl is to Johann George Kohl, *Russia. St. Petersburg, Moscow, Kharkoff, Riga, Odessa, the German Provinces on the Baltic, the Steppes, the Crimea, and the Interior of the Empire* (London, 1844), pp. 67–68. In Account Book 3, he notes the purchase of this work in January, 1844. The first sentence is used in "Culture," *W*, VI, 140; the last is used in "Civilization," *W*, VII, 20.

[138] In Bk. II, xii, Plato says that tradesmen are those persons who are useless for any other task. This line is in pencil.

[97]¹³⁹   Relics of things that have passed away
        Fragments of stone reared by creatures of clay."
            [Byron, *The Siege of Corinth*, ll. 499–502, 505–506]

    Scholar goes for faith, but is a skeptic
He is here to say that God is
        Yet he denies all your isms
        Well it is better that he should speak the truth
        He feels the yawning gulf between demand & supply
            between vital power & the perception
                    constructive
                genius   &   talent

    Remedy in a vaster perception
    Scholar a generalizer
                            Vast Skepticism   G 136¹⁴⁰

[98] Persons are a luxury & a convenience like shops. Names
are the only poems which loving maidens will hear. Nearness is the
aim of all love. An exchange of nobleness, is it also. But if you would
sublimate it, I think you must keep it hard & cold, and with a Dantean
leanness. We strangely stand, — souls do, — on the very edges of
their own spheres, leaning tiptoe towards & into the adjoining sphere.
The initial love must be allowed; then the celestial shall follow.
The nuptial love releases each from that excess of influence which
warped each from his own beauty, ⟨so t⟩and gives each again to
himself & herself, so that they acquire their own feature & proportion again, & a new beauty & dignity in each other's eyes. ⟨R⟩Healedⁿ
of the fever, let them beware of a second fever. It is not for lovers
(on a high degree of love) to sue. ⟨Th⟩ Great love has that temperance which asks for nothing which is not already ↑in the moment↓
granted. It is theirs only to be indulgent to the joyful necessity which,
making them coexistent, has also made them cotemporary. They are
only to find each other and to be in each other.

    ¹³⁹ The entries on this page, with the exception of the first two lines, are in
pencil.
    ¹⁴⁰ See *JMN*, VIII, 62.

[99] With what astonishment & reverence would not men listen to music if it were rarely heard & a little at a time! But when they stand by an organ & hear its voluminous voices all day, the natural reverence is abated.

One who wishes to refresh himself by ⟨with⟩ contact with the bone & sinew of society must avoid what is called the respectable portion of his city or neighborhood with as much care as in Europe a good traveller avoids American & English people. The laborers jawing

[100] Shall I say that I am driven to express my faith by a series of skepticisms?ⁿ The lover & philanthropist come to me & propose alliance & cooperation: & I am forced to say, O these things will be as they must be: What can you do? You blow against the wind.

The ⟨go⟩ instinct of man is to take the part of hope: it is the rule of mere comity & courtesy to turn your sentence with something auspicious & not sneering & sinister. Yet Texas & Slavery & Pauperism & Association and "Humanity" & all the other soup societies of the day are such hopeless matters that against all the dictates of good nature he is obliged to say he has no pleasure in them. This he does out of honesty & sincerity of character. Well, the like part he must take in regard to ⟨the⟩any defined dogma of immortality, or of love, & personality. Will any say this is cold & infidel I say that the heart sees that it can afford to grant you all that skepticism without disturbing the ||msm|| [141]

[101] ||msm|| Well, we will remember that Heaven seems to affect low & poor means, as (see above p. 75) the world gets on in the hands of one set of scamps to another. "Most poor matters point to rich ends." By atoms, by trifles, by sots, Heaven operates. The needles are nothing, the magnetism is all. [142]

---

[141] The bottom of p. [100] and the top of p. [101] have been cut away. The unfinished entry and the one above it, struck through in ink with a vertical use mark, are used in "Montaigne," W, IV, 181–182.

[142] This paragraph is struck through in ink with a vertical use mark; most of

Volvox globator has got on so far! He has rolled to some purpose truly.[143]

↑Candor.↓

We must be as courteous to a man ⟨w⟩as we are to a picture, which we are willing to give the advantage of a good light.[144] ↑v. p 68↓

There are days when the ↑angels of the↓ great are near us; when there is no frown on their brow, no condescension even, when they take us by the hand, and we share their thought.[145]

Intoxication with brandy is a remedy sometimes applied in cases of lockjaw to relax excessively the tense muscles.

[102][146] ‖msm‖
⟨‖ . . . ‖S[?] G[?] Fr.⟩[147]

We require that the man should give us tokens that he has not given up the holy ghost, that he knows where to plant his foot again. On that condition, we will indulge him with any length of repose, any quantity of wine or folly. Otherwise, he has the very secret of ugliness, namely, of being uninteresting to us. You shall have the love of a goddess, if you are yet alive: but the husband of yonder beautiful dame does not continue to deserve her: He is not here, & his merit is not here to lead her home; but, in its place, a rope of custom & cowardice.

"There is not anything in this world to be compared with wisdom for purity." Bhagvat Geeta [1785, p. 56]

---

it is used in "Discourse at Middlebury College." " 'Most poor matters point to rich ends.' " is from Shakespeare, *The Tempest*, III, i, 3–4. See *JMN*, VI, 26, 80.

[143] *Volvox globator* is a species of minute organism occurring in spherical colonies which rotate about a central axis. Cf. Journal Y, p. [119] below.

[144] This sentence is struck through in ink with two diagonal use marks.

[145] This sentence, struck through in pencil with a diagonal use mark, is used in "Works and Days," *W*, VII, 170. The insertion "angels of the" is in pencil.

[146] Parts of several letters still visible indicate that an entry was lost when the top of the leaf comprising pp. [101]–[102] was cut away.

[147] This heavily canceled entry of two lines is struck through in ink with a vertical use mark.

[103] All conversation, as all literature, appears to me the pleasure of rhetoric, or, I may say, of metonomy. "To make the great little, & the little great," Isocrates said, "was the orator's part." [148] Well that is what poetry & thinking do. ↑I am a reader & writer, please myself with the parallelism & the relation of thoughts, see how they classify themselves on the more fundamental & the resultant & then again the new ⟨result⟩ & newer result.↓[149] I go out one day & see the mason & carpenters busy in building a house, and I discover with joy the parallelism between their work & my construction ⟨of a sonnet⟩, and come home glad to know that I too am a housebuilder. The next day I go abroad & meet hunters, and, as I return, accidentally discover the strict relation between my pursuit of truths & theirs of forest game. Yet how have I gained in ⟨|| ... ||⟩either comparison ↑or see the seed, the plant, & the tree.↓

[104]   Bhagvat Geeta

"Children only & not the learned speak of the speculative & the practical doctrines as two. They are but one for both obtain the selfsame end, & the place which is gained by the followers of the one is gained by the followers of the other. That man seeth who seeth that the speculative doctrines & the practical are one."   Bhagvat Geeta. [1785,] p. 57 [150]

[105] [151] Eminent Experiences [152]
        Eras   when the Kepler laws were learned
                    when the 47th proposition [153]
                    when the Idealism was known

---

[148] Quoted in "The Lives of Ten Orators: Isocrates," *Plutarch's Morals: . . . Translated from the Greek, by several hands . . .* , 5th ed., 5 vols. (London, 1718), V, 29, in Emerson's library. The quotation is used, with varying wording, in "Eloquence," *W*, VII, 64, and 98. See *JMN*, VI, 133.

[149] This sentence, written at the bottom of the page and enclosed in brackets, is indicated for insertion after "thinking do." by a long-angled line and a caret.

[150] This quotation is used in "Discourse at Middlebury College" and "Goethe," *W*, IV, 267–268.

[151] The entries on this page, with the exception of "Eminent Experiences", are in pencil.

[152] These words are used in "Discourse at Middlebury College," "Goethe," *W*, IV, 262, and "Poetry and Imagination," *W*, VIII, 10. See *JMN*, VIII, 438.

[153] The "famous 47th proposition by Pythagoras" is mentioned in the lecture "The Superlative in Manners and Literature," first delivered in Manchester, England, in November, 1847. See *W*, X, 545.

doctrine of Like to like
doctrine of Compensation
doctrine of symbols or Correspondence

[106] Worship is the height of rectitude. "This world is no place for the man who doth not worship, & where, o Arjoon! is there another?" [*The Bhăgvăt-Gēētă* . . . , 1785, p. 55] Worship, because the sailor & the ship & the sea are of one stuff; worship because though the bases of things are divided yet the summits are united, because not by thy private but by thy public or universal force canst thou share & so know the nature of things.[154] Worship, because that is the difference between genius & talent; between poetry & prose; between Imagination & Fancy. The poet is like
———————— the vaulters in the circus round
Who step⟨s⟩ from horse to horse, but never touch the ground.[155]

↑*Manners*↓   ↑Superlatives↓[156]

Zonamque segnes solvere Gratiae [157]

αιει αριστευειν says Landor [158]

Choate's Thousand-for-one style
⟨H⟩ Choate is a locomotive that runs so readily back & forward that there is perpetual need to scotch the wheels. With so much sail /she/the craft/ should mind her helm well.
The grimace is a part of the superlative, & very bad part. A man fullgrown should not cry in a public place alone[.]

[154] For "the ship & the sea are of one stuff;", see p. [90] above; for "though the bases . . . united,", see p. [93] above.
[155] "Fragments on the Poet and the Poetic Gift," XIX, *W*, IX, 331.
[156] This heading is enclosed on both sides and at the top by straight lines in ink.
[157] Emerson cited an English version of these words in his lecture "The Superlative in Manners and Literature": "the old Latin verse declares that 'the Graces are slow to unbind their zone'" (see *W*, X, 544). Cf. Horace, *Odes*, III, xxi, 22: "segnesque nodum solvere Gratiae" — "the Graces [are] loth to break their bond." See Journal Y, p. [46] below.
[158] The Greek is from Homer's *Iliad*, VI, 208, and IX, 784: "ever to be . . . pre-eminent." This and the following entry are in pencil.

[107] The rich take up something more of the world into man's life; they include the country as well as the town, the ocean-side, Niagara, the far west, and the old European homesteads of man, in their notion of available material; and therein do well.

We owe to every book that interests us one or two words. Thus to "Vestiges of Creation" we owe "arrested development."[159] I remember to have seen three or four important words claimed as the result of Bentham of which I think "International" was one. To Plato we owe a whole vocabulary. I at this moment remember the importance of the words "obstetrical," ⟨of⟩"mania," & "assimilation," in their Platonic sense.

> The orange & the squash
> hammer & the pail [160]

[108] ↑June 23,↓[161]

It was a pleasure yesterday to hear Father Taylor preach all day in our country church. Men are always interested in a man, and the whole various extremes of our little village society were for once brought together. Black & white, poet & grocer, contractor & lumberman, methodist & preacher joined with the regular congregation ⟨with⟩in rare union.

The speaker instantly shows the reason in the breadth of his truly social nature. He is mighty nature's child[,] another Robert Burns trusting heartily to her power as he has never been ⟨|| ... ||⟩deceived by it and arriving unexpectedly every moment at new & happiest deliverances. How joyfully & manly he spreads himself abroad. It is a perfect Punch & Judy affair[,] his preaching. The preaching quite accidental & ludicrously copied & caricatured from the old style, as he found it in some ⟨Y⟩Connecticutt tubs[.] As well as he can he mimics & exaggerates the parade of method & logic of text & argu-

---

[159] In "Poetry and Imagination," *W*, VIII, 7, Emerson credited the English surgeon John Hunter with the "electric word[s] . . . *arrested and progressive development.*"

[160] These two lines are in pencil.

[161] This date is in pencil.

ment[n] [109] but after much threatening to exterminate all gain-sayers by his syllogisms he seldom remembers any of the ⟨parts⟩ ↑divisions↓ of his plan after the first, and the slips & gulfs of his logic would involve him in irreparable ridicule if it were not for the inexhaustible wit by which he dazzles & conciliates & carries away captive the dullest & the keenest hunter. He is perfectly sure in his generous humanity. He rolls the world into a ball & tosses it from hand to hand. He says touching things, plain things, grand things, cogent things, which all men must perforce hear. He says them with hand & head & body & voice; the accompaniment is total & ever varied. "I am half a hundred years old, & I have never seen an un-fortunate day. There are none" ——— "I have been in all ↑the four↓ quarters of the world, and I never saw any men I could not love[.]"

"We have sweet conferences & prayer meetings. We meet every day. There are not days enough in the year for us."

Everything is accidental to him[:] his place, his education, his church, his seamen, his whole system of religion a mere confused rigmarole of refuse & leavings of former generations — all has a grinning ab-surdity, *except* the sentiment of the [110] man. He is incapable of thought[;] he cannot analyse or discriminate[;] he is a singing danc-ing drunkard of his wit — Only he is sure of the sentiment. That is his mother's milk, that he feels in his bones, heaves in his lungs, throbs in his heart, walks in his feet, and gladly he yields himself to the sweet magnetism & sheds it abroad on the people rejoicing in his power. Hence he is an example, — I, at this moment say — the single example, we have of an inspiration; for a wisdom not his own, not to be appropriated by him, which he cannot recall or ever apply, sails to him on the gale of this sympathetic communication with his auditory. There is his closet, there his college, there his confessional, he discloses secrets there, & receives informations there, which his conversation with thousands of men (and he knows every body in the world almost,) and his voyages [111] to Egypt & journeys in Germany & in Syria never taught him. Indeed I think that all his talk with men and all his much visiting & planning for the practical in his "Mariners' House," &c &c, is all very fantastic, all stuff; I think his guardians & overseers & treasurers will find it so. Not the smallest dependence is to be put on his statement of facts. Arithmetic is only one of the nimble troop of dancers he keeps —. No; this free happy expression of himself & of the deeps of human nature, of the happier sunny facts of life, of things connected & lying amassed & grouped in healthy nature, that is his power and his teacher. He is so confident, that his security breathes in all his manners, & gestures, in his tones, & the expressions of his face, & he lies all open to men a man, & disarms criticism & malignity by perfect frankness. We open our arms too & with half closed eyes enjoy this rare sunshine. A wondrous beauty swims all the time over the picture gallery & touches points with an ineffable lustre.

[112] Obviously he is of the class of superior men and every one associates him⟨self⟩ necessarily with Webster, and, if Fox & Burke were alive, with Fox & Burke.

What affluence! There never was such activity of fancy. How wilful & despotic is his rhetoric — "No not ⟨if⟩the blaze of Diogenes's lamp added to the noonday sun would suffice to find it," he said.[162] ⟨Indis⟩Every thing dances & disappears[,] ⟨&⟩changes & becomes its contrary in his sculpturing hands. How he played with the word "lost" yesterday, "the parent who had lost his child." "Lost!" Lost became found in the twinkling of an eye. So will it always be[.]

His whole work is a sort of day's sailing out upon the sea not to any ⟨remote port⟩ voyage, but to take an observation of the sun, & come back again. Again & again & again, we have the whole wide horizon, — how rare & great a pleasure! That is the Iliad, that is picture, that is art, that is music. His whole genius is in minstrelsy. He calls it religion, methodism, Christianity, & other names, it is minstrelsy, he is a minstrel; all the rest is costume. For himself, it is [113] easy to see that though apparently of a moderate temperament he would ⟨sympathize⟩ like the old cocks of the bar-room a thousand times better than their temperate monitors[.]

↑See again on this subject Y 3↓

[162] See p. [58] above.

↑Timaeus↓

The weathers fit our moods. A thousand tunes the variable wind plays[,] ⟨a⟩ ↑ten↓ thousand spectacles brings, and each is the frame or dwelling of a new spirit in our own mind. One must look long before he finds the Timaeus weather. But at last the high cold silent serene morning comes, at early dawn with a few lights conspicuous in the heaven as of a world just created & still becoming[,] and in these wide leisures we ↑dare↓ open that book.[163]

↑printed in↓

There is a little opium in it, tête exaltée, the figures wear the buskin & the grandiose tragic mask: it is all from the tripod, though in admirable keeping[.]

[114] Men go through the world each musing on a great fable dramatically pictured & rehearsed before him. If you speak to the man, he turns his eyes from his own scene, & slower or faster endeavors to comprehend what you say. When you have done speaking, he returns to his private music. Men generally attempt early in life to make their brothers first, afterwards their wives, acquainted with what is going forward in their private theatre, but they soon desist from the attempt on finding that they ↑also↓[164] have some farce or perhaps some ear- & heart-rending tragedy forward on their secret boards on which they are intent, and all parties acquiesce at last in a private box with the whole play performed before himself *solus*.

Even for those whom I really love I have not animal spirits[.]

[115] What an eloquence Taylor suggests! Ah could he guide those grand sea-horses of his with which he ⟨rides &⟩ caracoles on the waves of the sunny ocean. But no, he ⟨sits, &⟩ is drawn up & down the ocean currents by the strong sea monsters, — only on that condition, that he shall not guide. How many orators sit mute there below! They

[163] This paragraph, struck through in pencil with a vertical and a diagonal use mark, is used in "Works and Days," W, VII, 169–170. The words "printed in" are in pencil.
[164] This word is inserted in pencil.

come to get justice done to that ear & intuition which ↑no↓ Chatham & no Demosthenes has begun to ⟨content.⟩ satisfy.[165]

↑Oliver↓ Houghton, Kimball, John Garrison, Belknap, Britten, Weir, & the Methodist preachers, W E Channing, Thoreau, H. Mann, Samuel Hoar, the Curtises, Mrs Barlow, Minot Pratt, Edmund Hosmer, were of ⟨E⟩Taylor's auditory. Nobody but Webster ever assembles the same extremes.[166]

[116] A traveller wants universal presence of mind, a sublime lassitude, or his opportunities avail him nothing.

The ⟨weap⟩scholar ⟨r⟩is very unfurnished who has only literary weapons. He must be spiritual man. He must be ready for bad weather, poverty, insult, weariness, reputation of failure, & many other vexations. He ought to have as many talents ⟨&⟩as he can. Memory, practical talent, good manners, temper, lion-courage are all good things. But these are superficial, and if he has none of them he can still do, if he has the main mast, if he is anything. But he must have the resource of resources, ⟨he⟩ be planted on Being. ⟨If⟩ He^n must ride at anchor and vanquish every enemy whom his small arms cannot reach, by the grand resistance of submission, of ceasing from himself, of ceasing to do. He is to know that he is here not to work but to be worked upon, and is to eat insult, drink insult, be clothed & shod in insult, until he has thoroughly learned that this bitter bread and shameful dress is ⟨wh⟩also wholesome & warm, is in short absolutely indifferent, is of the same chemistry as praise & fat living, that they also[,] *they also* [117] are disgrace & shabbiness to him who has them. I think that much may be said to discourage & dissuade the young scholar from his career. Freely be that said. Dissuade all you can from the lists. Sift the wheat. Blow away the light spirits. But let those who come, be those who cannot but come, and

[165] "How many . . . satisfy.", struck through in ink with a vertical use mark, is used in "Eloquence," *W*, VII, 63.
[166] Houghton, Kimball, Garrison, Belknap, Britton, Weir, Pratt, and Hosmer were all ordinary citizens of Concord, either farmers, shopkeepers, or handymen; George William Curtis and his brother Burrill, after a stay at Brook Farm, were working for a local farmer; Mrs. Almira Penniman Barlow was a family friend.

who see that there is no choice here, no advantage & no disadvantage compared with other careers. For the great Necessity comes bursting in, and distributes sun & shade according to the laws of life, & not of street-laws. Yes, he has his dark days, he has weakness,[n] he has waitings, he has bad company, he is pelted by a storm of petty cares, untuning cares, untuning company, that is the sting of them; they are like some foul beasts of prey, who spoil much more than they devour. Well let him meet them[;] he has not consented to the frivolity nor to the dispersion. ⟨he⟩ The practical aim is forever higher than the literary aim. I shall not submit to degradation but will bear these crosses with what grace I can and I know that with every self truth come mysterious offsets for all that is lost in some pearl of great price which is gained. Self truth[,] then instrumentality[.][167]

[118] We have great neighbors. We can die[.][168]

Oriental sentences
Runic poetry
Edward Taylor's preaching
                    cogent witnesses for reliance
                    on the present resources

I think the scholars who have given so many counsels are too worldly. Scott will have it that they shall not be in false position with "good society," they shall not be insulated. Goethe thinks dealing habitually with men & affairs essential to the health. Both these are worldly moods and most scholars when they talk with their own children are selfish calculators and faithless, because these counsels come not in their illumination but in their disguise & cowardice. But it is all costume. One man is a scholar but ⟨can als⟩ has also inherited from his father or his mother a common sense, an easy address, a facility of dealing; and another man his equal in insight has not this aptness. Time will show whether the facility is not a snare, & do not drag

---

[167] This paragraph, struck through in pencil with a vertical use mark, is used, with some omissions, in "Discourse at Middlebury College" and "The Scholar," W, X, 286–287. For "some pearl of great price," see Matt. 13:46.
[168] These two sentences are in pencil.

him that has it back to the shops from which his genius would remove him. These things are no more to be regarded than is the colour of the coat, or whether I brought my watch with its face turned out or turned in[.]

[119] When somebody adduced the children as examples of the value of a careful education Aunt Mary replied "My good friend, they were born to be educated." It stands just so with this superstition ⟨people have⟩ good whigs have concerning ⟨|| ... ||⟩our debt to good laws, I always wish to answer 'Good friend[,] we are a lawful people.' The law is a mere effect, like their obedience to laws; Men, these men are lawful, & make laws & obey laws.

A cat falls on its feet; shall not a man? You think he has character; have[n] you kicked him? Talleyrand would not change countenance; [169] Edward Taylor, Henry T[horeau], would put the assailant out of countenance.

[120] I am sorry we do not receive the higher gifts justly & greatly. The reception should be equal. But the thoughts which wander through our mind we do not absorb & make flesh of, but we report them as thoughts, we retail them as stimulating news to our lovers & to all Athenians[.]
At a dreadful loss, we play this game; for the secret God will not impart himself to us for teatable talk; he frowns on moths & puppets, passes by us & seeks out a solitary & religious heart[.]

Cephas A. Leach
Middlebury Vt [170]

Thievish manners: in the midst of festivities & genialities these people steal. All crime is comparative. When I consider what a tissue of unspeakable meanness and subterranean calculation makes up the day of these people, it seems to me that suicide would in them be a high act of virtue[.]

[169] See Journal V, p. [159] above.
[170] This entry is in pencil.

[121] ↑Man↓

Literature has been before us, wherever we go. When I come in the secretest recess of a swamp, to some obscure, and rare, & to me unknown plant, I know that its name & the number of its stamens, every bract & awn, is carefully described & registered in a book in my ⟨library.⟩ ↑shelf.↓ So is it with this ⟨new & youthful⟩ ↑young↓ soul wandering lonely, wistful, reserved, unfriended up & down in nature. ⟨All⟩ These[n] mysteries which he ponders, which astonish & entrance him, this riddle of liberty, this dream of immortality, this drawing to love, this trembling balance of motive, and, ⟨much more,⟩ the central↑ity↓ ⟨law⟩ whereof these are ⟨but single facts⟩ ↑rays↓, have all been explored to the ⟨dimmest⟩ recesses of consciousness, to the ⟨very⟩ verge of Chaos & the Néant, by men with grander steadfastness & subtler organs of search than any now alive; so that when this tender philosopher comes from his reverie to literature, he is alarmed (like one whose secret has been betrayed) by the terrible fidelity, with which, men long before his day, have described all & much more than all he has just seen⟨,⟩ as new Continent in the West.

[122] ↑August 19↓

We do not expect the tree to bear but one harvest in the year, but a man we expect to yield his fruit of wit & action every day.

We are the children of many sires, and every drop of blood in us in its turn betrays its ancestor. We are of the party of war & of the peace party alternately, & both very sincerely. Only we always may be said to be heartily only on the side of truth.

↑See-saw↓ [171]

We are as men who by baths & oils seeking to trim their heads, & promote the growth of the hair, & the health of the head, should find their feet ⟨grow⟩becoming numb & palsied; and then converting their attention to the exercise & health of the feet, should find baldness ensuing on the head. Whatever we do, undoes somewhat else. Skepticism is this belief in partiality. And observation of life will

[171] This heading is in pencil.

certainly breed it. But we may well give it space & as much line as we can: The spirit will always return & fill us with enthusiasm: It drives the drivers.[172]

[123] One is not to criticize the Fourier movement with too much severity, nor the genius of Fourier, but to rejoice on so favorable an indication. When in that godless French nation a genuine Frenchman appears, as national a Frenchman as Napoleon himself, and though, like the nation, devoid of all religion & morality, yet goes for philanthropy, solves the problem of human misery in a new & French way, — it is the same auspicious sign as this other, that Punch in London goes for philanthropy, and is a feather blowing the right way at last. Monsieur Kickee also takes the part of the poor & the slave! The good beastie!

↑Novels↓

Sam Ward thought D'Israeli & the Young England very paltry if after so much politics & pretension his only resource for his romantic Sibyl, lay in — two hundred thousand pounds.[173]

———

The world is enigmatical, every thing said & everything known, & done, & must not be taken literally but genially.
W.C is a middleman, ↑dragoman,↓ or graceful translator of ideas into the vernacular understanding[.]

[124] There are always two histories of man ⟨contending⟩ in literature contending for our faith. One is the scientific or skeptical, & derives his origin from the gradual composition, subsidence, & refining, from the negro, from the ⟨monkey⟩ape, ⟨from the⟩ progressive from the animalcule savages of the waterdrop, from volvox globator, up to the wise man of the nineteenth century. The other is the believer's, the poet's, the faithful history, always testified by

---

[172] "And observation . . . drivers." is struck through in ink with two vertical use marks. "But we may . . . drivers." is used in "Worship," *W*, VI, 202.

[173] Disraeli, a member of the parliamentary group known as "Young England," i.e., democratic aristocrats, ends *Sybil* (1845) with the heroine, daughter of one of the Chartist leaders, marrying the wealthy Charles Egremont, a liberal Tory. Cf. "Goethe," *W*, IV, 278. The heading "Novels" is in pencil.

the mystic & the devout, the history of the Fall, of a descent from a superior & pure race, attested in actual history by the grand remains of elder ages, of a science in the east unintelligible to the existing population. Cyclopean architecture in all quarters of the world. In Swedenborg, it is called the "Most Ancient Church" and the nobilities of thought are called "Remains" from this. The height of this doctrine is that the entranced soul living in Eternity will carry all the arts, all art, *in power*, but will not cumber itself with superfluous realizations.[174] ↑The faithful dogma assumes that the other is an optical show, but that the Universe was long already complete through law, and that the tiger & the midge are only penal forms, the Auburn & Sing-sing of nature; men, men, all & everywhere.↓

[125] The nearsighted people have much to say about action. But I can well say that the singing Iopas[175] seems to me as great as the sworded Hector. It is by no means action, which is the essential point, but some middle quality indifferent both to poet & to actor, and which we call reality. So that we have reality & necessity, it is equivalent in a word or in a blow. The election of the will is the crisis; that is celebrated often by Yea or Nay: the following action is only the ⟨baggage-⟩ ↑freight↓ train. Not action, not speculation imports, but a middle essence common to both.   I believe in the sovereign virtue, or, shall I say, virulence, of ⟨moral⟩ probity, against all arithmetic. Arithmetic is the science of surfaces, probity that of essences. The most private will be the most public, if it be only real. I have no defence to set up for the existing philosophers or poets. The rogue ↑or↓ the statesman is not made to feel his insignificance among either divines or literary men; for, at a glance, he sees that it is rogue again under the cassock, or with the manuscripts, and they greet each other; but when he shall see the prophet, he shall be shamed[.]

[126][176] We seek tonics; for the world-old images[,] ⟨the⟩ morning

[174] This sentence, struck through in ink with a vertical use mark, is used in "Montaigne," *W*, IV, 151.

[175] See p. [64] above.

[176] Erased pencil writing covers this page, of which no significant words or phrases have been recovered.

& evening, man & woman, plant & rock, fall on jaded perceptions and do not suggest their secret. To quicken them, what will we not do? We mesmerise ourselves by seeing ⟨them⟩ ↑objects↓ through the senses & minds of other men, insatiable to know if yellow be yellow, & grass grass to another ⟨man⟩ ↑eye↓: Then we ⟨love to⟩ ↑gladly↓ associate with heroic persons, finding that our thoughts & manners very easily become grandiose. Then we ⟨delight⟩ avail ourselves of the road-building of love. We cannot alone find a way to join two far-sundered thoughts; but to express their copula or tie to a friend, is easy & eloquent.[177]

We do not enough consider that every creature is armed, and innocence itself has its fang, as well as its ⟨service⟩ honey. The smallest fly will draw blood: See how powerful a weapon is gossip, which is impossible to exclude from the privatest selectest circle, & which guards & avenges.[178]

[127][179] To the vigilant, the history of the universe is only symptomatic; & life mnemonical.[180]

Lectures are a few reasonable words to keep us in mind of truth amidst our nonsense.

Whiggism hates the relative; it dogmatises, ↑it pounds.↓ To science, there is no *poison*: the word is relative[.]

See how many cities of refuge we have. Skepticism & again skepti-

[177] Between "to another ⟨man⟩ eye:" and "Then we ⟨love to⟩" is the paragraph directly below, set off by a large enclosing circle. The two sections of the separated paragraph are connected by a line in ink in the left margin and are struck through in pencil with a vertical use mark.
[178] "The smallest . . . circle," is used in "Worship," *W*, VI, 222.
[179] Erased pencil writing, apparently a number of separate entries, covers this page. The following significant words and phrases have been recovered or conjecturally recovered: "It is the objective of a"; "Fate"; "against the abolition society, against the philanthropists"; "perfect[?] race, that the"; "friend[?] is a blowing against"; "that[?] he stands a caricature of the pale man beside him to"; "↑sweat↓"; "No the universe is not bankrupt"; "in reply to this one"; "face &"; and "damnable".
[180] This sentence is used in "Uses of Great Men," *W*, IV, 32.

cism? Well, let abyss open under abyss, they are all contained &
bottomed at last, & I have only to endure. I am here to be worked
upon.

We expose our skepticism out of probity. ⟨Well,⟩ We ⁿ meet,
then, on the ground of probity, & not of skepticism.

I am shamed in reflecting on the little new skill the years bring
me, at the power trifles have over me, at the importance of my dinner,
& my dress, & my house, more than at the slenderness of my acquisi-
tions[.]
For we do acquire some patience, some temper, some power
of referring the particular to the general. We acquire perspective
so as to rank our experiences & know what is eminent. Else the term
An old one would have no meaning.

[127½]¹⁸¹ Travelling seems a modern invention since the application of steam.

———

What a luck in teaching! The tutor aims at fidelity, the pupil strives
to learn, but there is never a coincidence, but always a diagonal line
drawn ⟨by⟩ partaking of the genius of the tutor & the genius of the
pupil. This, when there is success, but that how capricious! ↑Two
precious madmen who cannot long conspire[.]↓

———

Honor among thieves, let there be truth among skeptics. Are
any or all the institutions so valuable as to be lied for? Learn to
esteem all things symptomatic, — no more.

But faith, has it not its victories also? Behold these sacred persons,
repulsive perhaps to you, yet undeniably born of the old simple
blood, to whom rectitude is native; see them here[,] ⟨amid gl⟩white

¹⁸¹ In his initial pagination, Emerson overlooked two pages between pp. [127]–
[128], and later numbered them [127½] and [127⅔]. Erased pencil writing covers
p. [127½], of which the following significant words and phrases have been recovered
or conjecturally recovered: "superiority to give to bestow to protect to love to serve";
"powers"; "enlighten[?]"; "nations"; "& generosity"; and "lawful men".

silver amid the bronze population, one, two, three, four, five, six, & I know not how many more, but conspicuous as fire in the night. Each of them can do some ⟨stroke⟩ ↑deed↓ of the impossible. Do you say, our Republic can never be? — I say, But let citizens be born for it & it can.

[127⅔]¹⁸² The Bank is made up of the directors: Every director is also a bank; and the enemies of the bank are enemies only because they also are banks; & the war is a sna⟨rl⟩tching ⟨& biting⟩ for the same bone.

———

Let the flies come; they will only come so long as their food is here.

———

Useless? must there not be a lake as well as a river?

———

We tire to be sure of people saying ten times every day "from bodily causes," yet is Goethe no less absurd in quarrelling with the phrases "upper & lower nature," "within & without." I should as soon deny that a cent had two sides.

———

Nothing but God can give invention; every thing else, one would say, the study of Plato would give; a discipline, it seems, in logic, in arithmetic, in taste or symmetry, in poetry, in longanimity, in language, in rhetoric, in science or ontology, & in morals or practical wisdom[.] ¹⁸³

———

V[ide]. Luther's saying concerning economy & counting puddings[.] ¹⁸⁴

[128] I know that the slaveholding is not the only manstealing

¹⁸² Erased pencil writing covers the upper two-thirds of this page. The following significant words and phrases have been recovered or conjecturally recovered: "house, & the latter in a shed; the one rides a bloodhorse"; "one stroke[?] & the other dies, & tho'[?] this have"; "condition, and all the flowers[?] of nature fight on the other side"; "appear"; "of the black man"; and "never is the planter[?] safe His house is a den".

¹⁸³ This paragraph, struck through in pencil with a vertical use mark, is used in "Plato; or, the Philosopher," *W*, IV, 39.

¹⁸⁴ For this saying, see *JMN*, VI, 349, where it is quoted from *Colloquia Mensalia: or, Dr. Martin Luther's Divine Discourses at his Table*, 1652.

and that white men are defrauded & oppressed as well as black but this stealing is not so gross & is not so legalized & made hopeless[.] [185]

↑Aug. 25.↓

I heard last night with some sensibility that the question of slavery has never been presented to the south with a kind & thoroughly scientific treatment, as a question of pure political economy in the largest sense.

A practical question, you say, is, what are common people made for? You snub them, and all your plans of life & all your poetry & philosophy only contemplate the superior class. ↑—↓This is a verbal question, never practical. Common people, uncommon people, all sorts of people, dispose of themselves very fast, and never wait for the sentences of philosophers. The truth seems to be, there are no common people, no populace, but only juniors & seniors; the mob is made up of kings that shall be; the lords have all in their time taken place in the mob. The appearance in any assembly is of a rapid self-distribution into cliques & sets, and the best are accused [129] of a fierce exclusiveness. Perhaps it is truer & more charitable to say, they separate as children do from old people, as oil does from water, without any love or hatred in the matter. Each ⟨of the⟩ seeking his own like, and any interference with the affinities would produce constraint & stupidity enough. All conversation is a relative power[,] not an absolute quality; like magnetism[,] which does not act on wood or gold or silver but only on iron. You know he can talk eloquently[;] you have heard him. I too know that he can be struck with dumbness & be unable to articulate a reasonable syllable for hours & days.
Each of these persons you implicate, has, no doubt, made the experiment more than once to speak in unfit company, & been baffled. A good heart made him willing to serve everybody. A sacred voice checked him & forbade him to leave his place. ⟨Thy⟩ Go back into thy solitude, ⟨||...||⟩it said, Why shouldest thou be frivolous? [n] Assort, assort your party or invite none. Put Oliver Houghton & Mr Hoar; Ellery Channing & Aunt Betsey; Ellen Emerson & Gazetteer Worcester into pairs and you will make them all wretched. It is an

[185] This entry is in pencil.

extempore Auburn or Sing Sing built in a parlour. Leave them, ⟨at⟩to seek their own mates and they will find them [130] as fast as the flies & the birds do.[186]

The games & amusements of men vary with their work. The soldier's son plays with sword & plume & toy-cannon, the boy nowadays with a ⟨‖ ... ‖⟩mimic locomotive & steamboat; & the girls' dolls dance the Polka: the boys have ⟨‖ ... ‖⟩toy-printing presses. ⟨So is it⟩ As they grow older, the young men's diversions & fancies borrow their color from the despotic Genius of the time, and now, instead of fitting their straps & promenading the fashionable streets, they go to farms, & taking a pruning knife in hand, they affect to learn the country-work. Instead of ⟨getting⟩ ↑managing balls, or↓ aspiring to ⟨be elected captains of military companies⟩ the command of a military corps, they now are found in the committees & rostrums of the Abolition agitators and write melodious prose & verse for this & kindred societies. For abolition & for socialism. You will not exaggerate the depth of this benevolence; it is facility & fashion in great part. You will not expect more justice or magnanimity in his private dealings of an abolitionist or of a socialist than of a politician or soldier of the old school.

[131] Do you think we should be practical? I grieve that we have not yet begun to be poetical. It is after long devotion to austere thought that the soul finds itself only on the threshold, and that truth has steeps inaccessible to any new & profane foot; long noviciate, long purgation, maceration, vigils, enthusiasm, she requires. Human life seems very short to the student. Its practical importance in your sense vanishes like a cloud. They have all eaten lotos alike. — [n]

Over & above all the particular & enumerable list of talents & merits of any distinguished person is their superiority[,] not to be described, but which brought into notice all those talents & merits.

---

[186] "The appearance in . . . stupidity enough.", "You know he can . . . & days.", and "Assort, assort . . . will find them" are struck through in ink with vertical use marks; "The appearance in . . . & days." and "Assort, assort . . . birds do." are used in "Society and Solitude," *W*, VII, 14.

One face of it is a certain eminent propriety, which is taste & reason & symmetry and makes all homogeneous. ⟨W⟩Homer & Milton & Shakspeare ↑all↓ have ⟨all⟩ this atmosphere or garment of fitness to clothe themselves withal and ⟨Webster⟩we sometimes call it their "humanity." In Webster our great lawyer it is a propriety again.[187]

[132] Plato ↑is no Athenian.↓ An Englishman says how English! [n] a German, how Teutonic! an Italian, how Roman & how Greek! It transcends sectional lines[,] the great humane Plato. But we read impatiently, still wishing the chapter or the dialogue at its close. [A trans-national book again is the Bhagvad Geeta] ⟨People⟩ The reader in Plato is soon satisfied that to read is the least part. The whole world may read the Republic & be no wiser than before. It is a chief structure of human wit, like Karnac or the mediaeval cathedrals or Cuma[,] is as broad as man & requires all the variety of human faculty to know it. One man or one generation may easily be baffled ⟨by⟩ in the endeavor to account for it. When we say, It is a fine collection of fables or when we praise his style or his common sense or his logic or his arithmetic we speak as boys. And much of our impatient criticism about the dialectic, I suspect, is no better. The criticism is like our impatience of the length of miles when we are in a hurry. The great[-]eyed Plato proportioned the lights & shades after the Genius of our life.
⟨He is⟩ As they say that every one seemed related to Helen the universal beauty so Plato seems to us an American genius[.] [188]

[133] I lent him my book: it was as if he had lent me a book of logarithms, the wisdom of Plato was still safe & uncommunicated[.]

[134] B[ronson] A[lcott] told me that ⟨he⟩when he saw Cruikshank's

---

[187] This paragraph is struck through in both pencil and ink with single vertical use marks.

[188] These two paragraphs, the second of which is in pencil, are struck through in ink with a vertical use mark; in addition, "Plato is no Athenian . . . its close." and "It is a chief . . . American genius" are struck through in pencil with vertical use marks. "An Englishman says . . . humane Plato." and "As they say . . . American genius" are used in "Plato; or, the Philosopher," *W*, IV, 40–41; "It is a chief . . . to know it." and "When we say . . . our life." are used in "Plato; or, the Philosopher," *W*, IV, 78–79.

drawings, he thought him a fancy caricaturist, but when he went to London he saw that he drew from nature without any exaggeration.

We manage with exquisite awkwardness to get the least benefit from each one by putting him forcibly to work for which he has no genius. A man who hates company is tortured to entertain the strangers to the mutual wretchedness of all parties. To a man who is by temperament mobile, a fagot of nerves, it is as easy to go & to grasp & to originate action, as, to a phlegmatic man it is easy to resist & to rest. Little Weir is all go: great Choate is all go; both need very strong helm.   ↑T 101 [189]

See Proclus; Theol. Plato; Vol 1 p 52↓

What an immense body of nonsense the state must absorb & dispose of to get the simplest ends accomplished by its officers. They cut down a whole palm to get the bud in the top. On plantations with twenty slaves in the house you cannot get a clean plate. If you take a long journey, *you* carry the horse.

[135] I was in the Courthouse a little while to see the sad game.[190] But as often happens the judge & jury[,] the government & the counsel for the prisoner were on trial as much as he. The prisoner's counsel were the strongest & cunningest lawyers in the Commonwealth[;] they drove the attorney for the state from corner to corner taking his reasons from under him & reducing him to silence,

[189] See *JMN*, VI, 361, for the relevant quotation from *The Six Books of Proclus . . . on the Theology of Plato . . .* , trans. Thomas Taylor, 2 vols. (London, 1816), in Emerson's library.

[190] What follows is Emerson's description of the "Wyman Case," held in Concord County Court. This was the third trial of William Wyman, president of the Phoenix Bank of Charlestown, who had been accused of embezzlement. The first trial had ended in a hung jury; in the second, Wyman had been found guilty, but the Supreme Court had set aside the verdict on technical grounds. The "strongest & cunningest lawyers in the Commonwealth" were Webster, Choate, Franklin Dexter, and Rockwood Hoar; the hapless prosecutor, according to the Concord *Freeman* of September 5, 1845, was "Col. Rogers of Boston"; and the beleaguered judge was probably Emory Washburn, later governor of Massachusetts. Wyman was acquitted "upon a legal point raised by Mr. Choate under a recent decision of the Supreme Judicial Court" (Boston *Courier*, September 11, 1845).

but not to submission. When hard pushed, he revenged himself in his turn on the Judge by requiring the Court to define what a Trust was. The Court thus hard pushed tried words, and said every thing it could think of to fill the time; supposed cases, & described duties of cashiers, presidents, & miscellaneous officers that are or might be; but all this flood not serving the cuttle fish to get away in, the horrible shark of district attorney being still there grimly awaiting with his "The Court must define[,]" the poor Court ⟨fled to the⟩pleaded its "inferiority." The superior Court must establish the law for this, — [136] and it read away piteously the decisions of the Supreme Court[,] but to those who had no pity. The Judge was at last forced to rule something, & the lawyers saved their rogue under the fog of a definition. The parts were so well cast & discriminated that it was an interesting game to watch. The Government was well enough represented. It was stupid, but had a strong will & possession, and stood on that to the last. The Judge was no man, had no counsel in his breast, yet his position remained real, & he was there merely as a child might have been to represent a great Reality, the Justice of States, which we could well enough see there beetling over his head, and which his trifling talking nowise affected, & did not impede, since he was innocent & well meaning. There are judges on all platforms, & this of Child-judge, where the position is all, is something.

Three or four stubborn necessary words are the pith & fate of the business; all the rest is expatiating [137] & qualifying: three or four real choices, acts of will of somebody, the rest is circumstance, satellite, & flourish[.] [191]

There was Webster the great cannon loaded to the lips: he told Cheney that if he should close by addressing the jury, he should blow the roof off.[192] As it was, he did nothing but pound. Choate put in the nail & drove it; Webster came after & pounded. The natural grandeur of his face & manners always satisfies; easily great; there

[191] These two paragraphs are struck through in ink with two vertical use marks on pp. [135] and [136] to "& well meaning.", with one vertical use mark from "There are judges" to "& flourish", and with three vertical use marks from "Three or four" to "expatiating". They are used in "Eloquence," *W*, VII, 85–88.
[192] John Milton Cheney, Emerson's classmate at Harvard, was cashier of the Middlesex Institution for Savings in Concord.

is no strut in his voice or behaviour as in the others. Yet he is all wasted[;] he seems like a great actor who is not supported on the boards, & Webster like the actor ought to go to London. Ah if God had given to this Demosthenes a heart to lead New England! what a life & death & glory for him. Now he is a fine symbol & mantel ornament — costly enough to those who must keep it; for the great head aches, & the great trunk must be curiously fed & comforted. G[eorge]. [P.] B[radford?] said, the Judge looked like a schoolmaster puzzled by a hard sum who reads the context with emphasis. The *amicus curiae* doctrine is the right of revolution. Always a loophole.

[138] Hahnemann's hypothesis is that seven eighths of the chronic maladies affecting the human frame are forms of psora, & that *all* such maladies are referable in some sense to three types of skin disease.

> See Wilkinson's Introd to Swedenborg's
> *Animal Kingdom* [1843–1844, I,] p. xxxv.

The apparatus of the Law is large & cumbrous and when one sees to how short an issue it leads it seems as if a judge would be as safe. All is for a vent to these two or three decisive phrases that come leaping out no man knows when, at first or at last in the course of the trial.[193] We go & sit out the tedious hearing for these moments. But at last when we come away we are to eliminate that result for ourselves[;] no reporter except Time will do it for us.

[139] That the thing done, that the quality avails, and not the ⟨momentary⟩ opinion entertained of it[,] is a lesson which all things teach & no man can sufficiently learn. When I come to a selfrelying man in a comedy of Beaumont & Fletcher who breasts the change of fortune with ⟨a selfreli⟩stoutness I pause & read it over again. Landor is attacked savagely in Blackwood yet nothing in the attack is memorable, and in Landor we have still to go back & find again that wise remark, that elegant illustration. ⟨Yet⟩At the same time, this

---

[193] This sentence is struck through in ink with a vertical use mark. See pp. [136]–[137] above.

attack must have been painful enough to Landor, & for the moment he seemed to ⟨me⟩the spectators to be down.[194]

↑See p 61↓   ↑See W. 50↓ [195]

In skepticism remember we meet on a ground of probity[.]

[140] In reading the old mythology how easily we detect the men & women we know, clothed there in colossal masks & stilted on high buskins to go for gods & goddesses.

Old Dr Henry Ware said one day↑, — (I think↓ to Mussey,↑)↓ — that old as he was in preaching, he never prepared to go on Sunday into the pulpit of the College Chapel without a slight peristaltic motion.[196]

It is a rule of war ⟨never⟩not to fight often with the same enemy; for you teach him by every campaign your tactics. Even Buonaparte in time communicated all his art.

The spurious Platonic dialogues are not easily discriminated; nor the ⟨Homeric⟩pseudo-Homeric verses; nor the school of Raffaelle[n] from Raffaelle; nor the genuine Shakspeares truly known[.]

[141] "Some persons are born with almost superhuman memory; others with great activity of the memory, that is with great imaginative power," ——

Swedenborg
A[nimal]. K[ingdom]. [1843–1844,] Vol II p 354

The old dramatists wrote the better for the great quantity of their writing and knew not when they wrote well. The playhouse

---

[194] The attack was made in Edward Quillinan's "Imaginary conversation, between Mr. Walter Savage Landor and the Editor of *Blackwood's Magazine*," *Blackwood's Magazine*, LIII (April 1843), 518–536. "That the thing . . . entertained of it" and "Landor is attacked . . . illustration." are struck through in ink with vertical use marks; "That the thing . . . sufficiently learn." and "Landor is attacked . . . to Landor," are struck through in ink with diagonal use marks. Cf. *English Traits*, *W*, V, 9–10.

[195] These two notations, and the sentence directly below, are in pencil.

[196] Benjamin B. Mussey was a Boston publisher. In the left margin beside this entry is a single vertical line in ink.

was low enough to have entire interests for them; they were proprietors; it was low & popular; and not literary. That the scholars
scorned it, was its saving essence. Shakspeare & his comrades, Shak-
spear evidently thought the mass of old plays or of stage plays
corpus vile, in which any experiment might be freely tried. Had the
prestige which hedges about a modern tragedy or other worthless
literary work existed, nothing could have been done. The coarse but
warm blood of the living England circulated in the play as in ↑street↓
ballads, & ⟨attempered or⟩ gave body to his airy & majestic fancy.
For the poet peremptorily needs a basis which he cannot supply; a
tough chaos-deep soil, or main, or continent, on which his art may
work, as the sculptor a block of stone, and this basis the popular mind
supplies: otherwise all his flowers & ⟨the⟩elegances are transcendental
& mere nuisance.[197]

[142] "Hardly a single drama of Shakspeare can be deemed to
have been of his own original invention." I. D'israeli [198]

See how the translation of Plutarch gets its wonderful excellence
as does the ↑Eng.↓ Bible by being translation on translation: there
never was a time when there was none: and all the truly idiomatic
& nationally generic phrases are kept, & all the others successively
picked out & thrown away[.]
Something like the same process had gone on long before with
the originals of these books. The world takes liberties with world-
-books; [n] Vedas, Aesop's fables, Homer, Arabian Nights, are not the
work of single men. The time thinks for us; the parliament thinks
for us; the market thinks for us; the mason, the carpenter, the merchant, the farmer, the dandy, all think for us. Every book supplies
us with one good word, — every law, every trade, every folly; and
the generic catholic genius who is not afraid or ashamed to owe his

---

[197] This paragraph is struck through in ink with a vertical use mark; "Shakspeare & his comrades . . . fancy." is used in "Shakspeare," *W*, IV, 193–194.
[198] Probably paraphrased from a passage in Isaac D'Israeli's *Amenities of Literature, Consisting of Sketches and Characters of English Literature*, 3 vols. (London,
1841), III, 46. Emerson withdrew volume 3 of this work from the Boston Athenaeum September 16, 1845–January 28, 1846. The entry is struck through in ink with
a vertical use mark. Cf. "Shakspeare," *W*, IV, 195.

originality to the originality of all, [and who perhaps is looked down upon as feeble and a treasuring word-catching student[,]] stands with the next age as the true recorder & embodiment of ⟨this⟩his own.[199]

[143] [blank]
    [144][200] Life is a Spanish play with a threefold or fourfold plot[.]

    Be Firm[.]

    I should like to arm you against the clamour of frivolous, rich, & official people[.] [201]

    Doers! Despise doers; action too strong for actor
    ↑Astronomer not ridiculous inasfar as he is but as he is not astronomer[.]↓[202]
    Spec[ulative] & prac[tical] are one[.]
    Know too that philistines share the ideas[.] [203]

Be on your guard against reforms next after Whigs. Good as hints & as leaves of your tree[.]

But dispose[,] dispose of these things. You are not the candidate for so gross a discipline. Your preoccupied mind has happily made you no slaveholder, no sot, no drone, but given you by privilege of beauty the possession of those things you desire.
You are here to chant the hymn of Destiny, to be worked upon, here for miracle, here for resignation, here for intellect, love, & being[;] here to know ⟨yourselves⟩ the awful secret of genius, here to become not readers of poetry but Dante, Milton, Shakspeare, Homer, Swe-

---

[199] These two paragraphs, struck through in ink with a vertical use mark, are used in "Shakspeare," *W*, IV, 200–201.
[200] The entries on this and the following page are in pencil.
[201] Cf. "Discourse at Middlebury College" and "The Scholar," *W*, X, 267.
[202] See p. [90] above.
[203] See Journal Y, p. [37] below.

denborg, in the fountain through that: here to foresee India [145]
& Persia & Judaea & Europe in the old paternal mind[.]

If I could reach to initiate you, if I could prevail to communicate the incommunicable mysteries, you should see the breadth of
your realm[;] that even as you ascend inward your radiation is immense[;] that you receive the keys of history & of nature[.]
You assimilate the remote, & rise on the same stairs to science & to
piety[.] [204]

here to be the youth of the universe[,] the boy
here to be sobered. How? by terror & famine & poverty, no, but by
the depth of the draughts of the cup of immortality[.] [205]

[146] [206]
[inside back cover] [Index material omitted]

[204] "[You are] here to know . . . through that:" and "If I could reach . . . to
piety" are used in "Discourse at Middlebury College" and "The Scholar," W, X,
288–289.

[205] "here to be sobered . . . immortality" is used in "Discourse at Middlebury
College" and "The Scholar," W, X, 264.

[206] A preliminary index, in pencil and erased, covers this page.

Y

1845–1846

Journal Y runs from September, 1845, to March, 1846. It contains a great many passages for the lecture series on Representative Men, especially the lectures on Plato, Swedenborg, Shakespeare, and Uses of Great Men. Many passages used in Emerson's address on "Eloquence," first delivered in Boston on February 10, 1847, also occur.

The covers of the copybook bear a green rippled design and measure 16.8 x 21.5 cm. The spine strip, of dark brown leather, carries the letter "Y" in gold and eight pairs of horizontal gold lines. "Y 1845" is written on the front cover.

Originally there were 264 lightly ruled pages, plus two flyleaves at both front and back, but the leaves bearing pages 53–54, 59–62, and 103–104 are missing, and that numbered 67–68 has become detached. The leaves measure 16.5 x 21.2 cm. Most of the pages are numbered in ink, but twenty-three are numbered in pencil: 26, 43, 45, 63, 72, 84, 91, 98, 101, 137, 143, 193, 196, 200, 202, 224, 226, 234, 236, 238, 249, 262, and 268. Thirty-four pages are unnumbered: 2, 11, 12, 49, 55, 65, 67, 69, 71, 92, 93, 97, 121, 125, 151, 159, 164, 170, 197, 199, 206, 215, 218, 221, 225, 233, 235, 237, 239, 241, 247, 257, 259, and 261. Nine pages were first numbered in pencil, then in ink: 39, 80, 88, 90, 94, 192, 228, 246, and 248. In his initial pagination Emerson overlooked pages 156 and 157 and numbered page 158 as 156, but returned to correct pagination with page 160; later he numbered the overlooked pages 155 1/2 and 155 2/3. Blank pages total nineteen: ii, iv, 2, 11, 12, 21, 25, 55, 93, 151, 159, 164, 170, 198, 206, 217, 233, 235, and 267.

A clipping from a German-language newspaper is laid in between pages 144 and 145.

[front cover]   Y
                               1845

[front cover verso] [1]
⟨Lowell Institute   Wednesday   Nov 12⟩
⟨Rumford Institute⟩   Saturday   14 Feb
        1st Lecture in Feby counting alternate Saturdays from
        8 Nov.
Fall River ⟨when I go to New Bedford, giving timely notice⟩
                                            18 Feby   Wednesd
⟨New Bedford⟩
⟨Cambridge   1 or 2 Wed⟩   Feb
⟨Warren st Chapel⟩
Lowell Mechanics ⟨Institute⟩ Association   Tuesday 13 Jany
Worcester   Friday 23 ⟨Feby⟩ Jan
Gloucester   25 Feb
Salem   18 March
⟨Dorchester⟩
⟨Newburyport,⟩   6 Feby   Friday   J. C. Randall
⟨Dedham⟩
⟨Beverly   Tuesd 3 March⟩
⟨Saxonville   Feb 12⟩   Thursday
                        Malden   Tuesd.
                        Warren Chapel
Feb 3   Lowell
     4   Cambridge
     5
     6   ⟨Worceste⟩ Newburyport
     7   28
     8   29
     9   1
    10   Lowell   2
    11   Cambridgeport   3   ⟨Boston⟩

---

[1] The entries on the front cover verso, which are in pencil, outline Emerson's lecture engagements for the 1845–1846 winter season. A circle of red sealing wax in the upper left-hand corner indicates that something was once attached thereto — perhaps a calendar, as on the front cover verso of Journal O.

12 Saxonville	4	Boston
13 Worcester	5	Plymouth
14 Waltham	6	
15	7	
16	8	
17 Lowell	9	
18 Fall River	10	Tuesd. Lowell
19 Prov	11	F. River
20 Prov	12	
21	13	
22	14	
23	15	
24	16	
25 Gloucester	17	
26 Prov	18	W Salem
27 Prov		

[i] [Index material omitted]   R. W. Emerson
                                                       1845

The earth is upheld by the veracity of the good.[2]

[ii] [blank]
[iii] [Index material omitted]
[iv] [blank]
[1] Identity[,] identity. If a wise man should appear in our village, he would create in all the inhabitants a new consciousness of wealth by opening their eyes to the sparkle of half concealed treasures that lie in everybody's door-yard; he would establish a sense of immoveable equality, as every body would discern the checks & reciprocities

[2] Cf. *The Vishṅu Puráṅa, a System of Hindu Mythology and Tradition*, trans. H. H. Wilson (London, 1840), p. 312: "The earth is upheld by the veracity of those who have subdued their passions." Emerson noted that "The 'Purana' I carried with me to Vermont, & read with wonder in the mountains" (*L*, III, 293) — apparently on his lecture trip to Middlebury in July, 1845; it is quoted often in this journal. The copy in his library was a later bequest from Thoreau. The entry, struck through in ink with two vertical use marks, is used in "Uses of Great Men," *W*, IV, 3.

of condition, and the rich would see their mistakes & poverty, whilst the poor would behold their ↑town↓ resources.[3]

[2] [blank]

[3] Father Taylor valuable as a psychologic curiosity. A man with no proprium or peculium, but all social. Leave him alone & there is no man: there is no substance, but a relation. His power is a certain mania or low inspiration that repeats for us the tripod & possession of the ancients. I think every hearer feels that something like it were possible to himself if he could consent: he has sold his mind for his soul (soul in the low semi-animal sense, soul including animal spirits). Art could not compass this fluency & felicity. His sovereign security results from a certain renunciation & abandonment. He runs for luck, & by readiness to say everything[,] good & bad, says the best things. Then a new will & understanding organize themselves in this new sphere of no-will & no-understanding, and as fishermen use a certain discretion [4] within their luck, to find a good fishing--ground, or the berry women to gather quantities of whortleberries, so he knows his topics, & his unwritten briefs, and where the profusion of words & images will likeliest recur. ⟨In⟩ ↑With↓ all his ⟨haphazard⟩ ↑volleys of↓ epithets & imagery, ⟨a perfect volley of stones,⟩ he will ever & anon hit the white. He called God in a profusion of other things "a charming spirit"; he spoke of "Men who sin with ⟨ingenuity⟩ ↑invention↓, sin with genius, sin with all the power[n] they can draw," ——————
But you feel this inspiration⟨, low inspiration, all the time⟩. It clothes him like an atmosphere, & he marches into ⟨the most⟩ untried depths with the security of a grenadier.[n] He will weep, and ⟨|| ... ||⟩grieve, & pray, & chide, in ⟨the wildest⟩ ↑a↓ tempest of passionate speech, & never [5] ⟨once⟩ break the perfect propriety with a single false note; and when all is done, you still ask, or I do, "What's Hecuba to him?" [Shakespeare, *Hamlet*, II, ii, 585]

↑September↓
    We sidle towards the problem. If we could ⟨solv⟩speak the

[3] This paragraph, which is in pencil, is used in "Uses of Great Men," *W*, IV, 18–19.

↑direct↓ solving word, it would solve us too; we should die, or be liberated as the gas in the great gas of the atmosphere.

[6] ↑Call it by whatever name,↓ we[n] all believe in personal magnetism, of which mesmerism is a lowest ⟨|| ... ||⟩example. But the magnetisers are few. ↑The best head in the company affects all the rest.↓ We believe that if the angels should descend, we should associate with them easily, & never shame them by a breach of celestial propriety.

[7] ⟨Least⟩ Swedenborg
Essential not apparent resemblances like the resemblance of a house to the man who built it.[4]

[8] How easy to give a poetic analysis of Byron's apostrophe to Nemesis in the 4th Canto of the "Childe Harold," —[n] too good an example of a poetic end dissipated & annihilated through the seduction of the means.[5]   ↑Copied in RT↓ [p. 157]

[9] Dinas Emlinn of Scott, like his Helvellyn, shows how near to a poet he was.[6] All the Birmingham part he had, and what taste & sense! yet ⟨|| ... ||⟩ never rose into the creative region. As a practitioner or Professional Poet, he is unrivalled in modern times. In lectures on Poetry almost all Scott would be to be produced[.]

What was said of the Rainers[,] that they were street singers though good of their kind & that it was a mistake to bring them into concert rooms, the like is true of Scott[.][7]

[10] Platonic studies
Plutarch's Essay on the Procreation of the soul *Morals*: [1718,] *Vol* II [329–369]

[4] This entry, which, like the heading, is in pencil, is used in "Swedenborg," *W*, IV, 123.
[5] This paragraph is struck through in ink with a diagonal use mark.
[6] Dinas Emlinn is the subject of Scott's poem "The Dying Bard."
[7] This entry is in pencil. The Rainers were a Tyrolese minstrel family of two sisters and two brothers whose concert in Concord on February 3, 1841, Emerson had attended (*JMN*, VII, 419).

Plutarch on the Daemon of Socrates [*Ibid.*,] Vol II [379–421]
Plutarch's Symposiacs; an admirable passage concerning
    Plato's expression that God geometrises.[8] See especially p 434
    in Plut. Morals   Vol III [226–483]
Plato first used the word Poem. Stanley [9]

[11]–[12] [blank]
[13] I think the Platonists may be read for sentences, though the
reader fail to grasp the argument of the paragraph or the chapter.
He may yet obtain gleams & glimpses of a more excellent illumination
from their genius outvaluing the most distinct information he owes to
other books. The grandeur of the impression the stars & heavenly
bodies make on us is surely more valuable than our exact perception
of a tub or a table on the ground.
                ↑Where printed?↓
                  ↑No where↓ [10]

[14] The aim of natural philosophy is still to know, as the elder
groping philosophers said, — "what they held concerning the Universe, whether it had a beginning, & whether it is moved at present
wholly or in part according to reason."
              ↑Copied in Naturalist↓ [p. 2₁] [11]

The age intellectual
    Its crimes ⟨intellectual⟩ fraud not force
    Brigand goes to bureau
    Capitalist eats us up
        Age of Commerce
        Age of Tools

[8] See p. [16] below.
[9] See Thomas Stanley, *The History of Philosophy: Containing the Lives,
Opinions, Actions and Discourses of the Philosophers of Every Sect . . .* , 3rd ed.
(London, 1701), p. 163. Emerson withdrew this volume from the Boston Athenaeum
October 18–November 24, 1834. This line is in pencil. "Stanley" is enclosed in a
box.
[10] These two notes are in pencil.
[11] In this notebook, Emerson wrote under the quotation, "I suppose I copied
these lines from Plutarch".

World is mechanized & life is.

Filled with wonder at our own success, we say, Come let us make it perfect & a beehive. See the very awkward relation of men of thought to loaves of bread. Yes & ↑let us have bread enough & sun & sea shall get it[.]↓

But you leave out the first element; — let them have bread that they may be men; but you unman them, that they may have bread.

If they have no bread

[15] ⟨I suppose that⟩ Everything ⁿ good came of private men.

I suppose why men ⟨fail⟩ ↑starve↓ is biographical[.]

I suppose that all the difficulties ⟨are biograph⟩ that skepticism suggests are biographical[,] that

Tools do not much raise us, but men are men, & history alike, & that only intellectual laws obtain. That God geometrises [12]

One rule is certain, that, he should mind his own genius, & not yours, however valuable cooperation may seem: and the penalty of disobedience is maim or mutilation to him (appearing in imbecility or despondency & limitation) and presently ⟨in⟩ the degradation of multitudes to be tools.

Meantime one must look at Fourier & the rest as also true prophets describing a true state of society; one which the tendencies of nature lead unto, but as one [17₁] [13] to which, however desireable, no sacrifice can be made;   as describers of that which is really doing; the large cities are phalansteries, the cheap way is to make every man do what he was born for.

[16] ↑Earnestness↓

"None any work can frame
Unless himself become the same." [14]

---

[12] See p. [10] above.

[13] The notation "[turn to p. 17]" occurs at the bottom of p. [15]. On p. [17₂] the conclusion of the entry occurs between the couplet and the unfinished sentence about Emerson's dream, from both of which it is separated by long rules. Above it is written "from p 15".

[14] These lines are used in "Poetry and Imagination," W, VIII, 43. See p. [230] below. The heading "Earnestness" is in pencil.

⟨Intellect with his interval⟩
Earnestness is Intellect without his interval[.]

———

"God said The heavens, the earth & all that is between them we created not in sport:" Koran [15]

———

"Then think ye we have created ye in jest, & that ye are not to return to us?" *Koran.*

———

Worship   see W 106,
                    120,

———

Earnestness hates Confucius.
                    See Y 162.

"The saint's best blush in heaven is from his heartblood's red." *Koran* [16]

          Y 230
We owe so many fiery sentences to Mahomet!

[172] We are waiting until some tyrannous idea emerging out of heaven shall seize us & bereave us of this liberty with which we are falling abroad[.]   ↑Copied in IL↓ [17] [p. 245]

          "Fooled thou must be, tho' wisest of the wise,
          Then be the fool of virtue not of vice." [18]

I will tell you my dream of last night: I was in the East Indian Heaven & watched the proceeding

[18]   ↑*Metempsychosis*↓
          For this Indian doctrine of transmigration, it seems easy of reception where the mind is not preoccupied. Not more wonderful

[15] This and the following quotation are from *The Akhlāk-I-Jalāly* . . . , 1839, p. 12. The quotations, struck through in ink with a diagonal use mark, are used, in telescoped form, in "Swedenborg," *W*, IV, 94, and "Shakspeare," *W*, IV, 217–218. See p. [80] below.
[16] *The Akhlāk-I-Jalāly* . . . , 1839, p. 96. This quotation is used in the lecture "The Superlative in Manners and Literature" (see *W*, X, 547). See p. [82] below.
[17] This notation is in pencil.
[18] *The Akhlāk-I-Jalāly* . . . , 1839, p. 95. This quotation, struck through in ink with two vertical use marks, is used in "Illusions," *W*, VI, 325. See pp. [81] and [176] below.

than other methods which are in use. And so readily suggested not only by the manners of insects, but by the manners of men. Here is a gentleman who abused his privileges when in the flesh as a gentleman, & curtailed therefore his amount of vital force. We cannot kill him, for souls will not die. ⟨But h⟩His punishment self-imposed, is, that he ⟨must⟩ take such a form as his diminished vital force can ⟨supply⟩ ↑maintain↓. Now it takes to make a good dog, say, half a ⟨pound⟩ ↑grain↓; to make a peacock, ⟨ten ounces⟩ ↑a quarter grain↓; to make a great general, ⟨ten pounds⟩ ↑a pennyweight↓; a philosopher, ⟨fifty⟩ ↑two↓; a poet, ⟨a hundred;⟩ ↑ten;↓ & a good & wise man ⟨a thousand⟩[n] ↑⟨an ounce⟩ a thousand pounds↓. Now our ill behaved man on emerging[n] [19] from his rotten body & a candidate for a new birth ⟨has shamefully reduced his patrimony & is bankrupt, and, as we mortals say on earth, must put his estate of life to nurse. He⟩ has not capital enough to maintain himself as man, & with his diminished means ⟨|| ... ||⟩nothing is left for it, but that he should take a turn through nature this time as monkey. That costs very little, & by careful governance in the monkey form, he shall ↑have saved something &↓ be ready at his return, ⟨to death to have saved something⟩ to begin the world again ⟨with⟩ more decent↑ly↓ ⟨circumstance⟩, say, as dog. There ⟨still⟩ he saves ↑again↓, &, at the end of that period, may drop his tail, & ⟨appear in earth as⟩ ↑come out↓ Hottentot. ⟨If he is⟩ Good[n] Hottentot, he will rise, ⟨& next time,⟩ and one of these ⟨days⟩ ages will be a Massachusetts man. [20][19] What other account is to be given of these superfluous triflers who whisk through nature, whom we are sure we have seen before, and who answer no purpose to the eye while they are above the horizon? They are passing through their grub state, or are expiating their ill economy of long ago.

"Travelling the path of life through thousands of births"[20]

[21] [blank]
[22] It requires for the reading & final disposition of Plato, all sorts of readers, Frenchmen, Germans, Italians, English, & Americans. If

---

[19] "Metempsychosis" is centered at the top of the page.
[20] *The Vishńu Puráńa* . . . , 1840, p. 650. This quotation, struck through in ink with a vertical use mark, is used in "Swedenborg," *W*, IV, 96. See pp. [89] and [160] below.

it were left to apprehensive, gentle, imaginative, Plato-like persons, no justice would be done to his essence & totality, through the excess or ⟨p⟩violence of affection that would be spent on his excellence of reason & imagination. But Frenchmen have no reverence, they seize the book like merchants, it is a piece of goods, and is treated without ceremony after the manner of commerce; and though its diviner merits are lost by their profanation, the coarser, namely, the texture & coherence of the whole, & its larger plan, its French availableness, its fitness to French taste, by comprehending that. Too much seeing is as fatal to just [23] seeing, as blindness is. People speak easily of *Cudworth*, but I know no book so difficult to read as Cudworth proper.[21] For, as it is a magazine of quotations, of extraordinary ethical sentences, the ⟨most⟩ shining summits of ancient philosophy, ⟨the eye of the reader⟩ and as Cudworth himself is a dull writer, the eye of the reader rests habitually on these wonderful revelations, & refuses to be withdrawn; so, that, after handling the book for years, the method & the propositions of Cudworth still remain a profound secret. Cudworth is sometimes read without the Platonism; which would be like reading Theobald's Shakspeare leaving out only what Shakspeare wrote.

I think the best reader of Plato the least able to receive the totality at first, just as a botanist will get the totality of a field of flowers better than a poet.[22]

[24] Platonists: a decline into ornament from the severity of strength. Corinthian, Byzantine, Plato is grand, they are grandiose.
It is easy to read Plato, difficult to read his commentators.[23]

[25] [blank]
[26]   ↑Cement of Inertia↓
Is it not beautiful[,] the wit that inserted this inertia into everything however small?[n] The conserving, resisting, recalcitrating energy; the anger at being waked; the anger at being changed. Altogether in-

---

[21] Ralph Cudworth, *The True Intellectual System of the Universe* . . . , ed. Thomas Birch, 4 vols. (London, 1820), in Emerson's library.
[22] This paragraph was written first in pencil, with "it will" canceled between "just as" and "a botanist", then in ink.
[23] See Journal W, p. [72] above.

dependent of the intellectual force in each is this inexorable Achillean defiance; the pride of opinion, the security that we are right. Not the feeblest old woman, not the dimmest sighted ideot, but chuckles & triumphs in h⟨is⟩er ↑or his↓ opinion over the differences of all the rest; never ↑has a↓ misgiving of being wrong. It was a bright thought that made things cohere with this bitumen, fastest of cements.[24] It is the bulwark of individualism.

[27] Plato & the great intellects have no biography. If he had wife, children, we hear nothing of them[;] he ground them all into paint. As a good chimney burns up all its own smoke, so a good philosopher consumes all his own events in his extraordinary intellectual performances.[25]

Webster says, The curse of this country is eloquent men.[26]

[28] In the convention yesterday it was easy to see the drunkenness of eloquence.[27] As I sat & listened, I seemed to be attending at a medical experiment where a series of patients were taking nitrous oxide gas.[28] Each patient, ⟨as he⟩ ↑on↓ receiv⟨ed⟩ing it in turn, ⟨stood &⟩ exhibited similar symptoms; redness in the face, volubility, violent gesticulation, ↑the oddest attitudes,↓ occasional stamping, a loss of perception of the passage of time, a selfish enjoyment of the sensation, & loss of perception of the suffering of the audience.   Plato says that the punishment which the⟨y⟩ wise suffer who refuse to take part in the government, is to live under the government of worse men.[29] That is the penalty of abstaining to speak in a public meeting, that

---

[24] This paragraph, struck through in both pencil and ink with single vertical use marks, is used in "Uses of Great Men," W, IV, 24.

[25] This paragraph, struck through in pencil with a vertical use mark and in ink with two vertical use marks, is used in "Plato; or, the Philosopher," W, IV, 43.

[26] This sentence, struck through in ink with three vertical use marks, is used in "Eloquence," W, VII, 75.

[27] The Middlesex County convention of the opponents of the annexation of Texas was held at Concord on September 22, 1845 (L, III, 306–307).

[28] In JMN, VII, 531, Emerson reports he saw several persons take "laughing gas" at the office of his brother-in-law, Charles T. Jackson. See p. [247] below.

[29] For the source of Plato's statement, see Journal W, p. [1] above.

you shall sit & hear wretched & currish speakers. I have a bad time
of it on these occasions, for I feel responsible for every one of the
speakers, & shudder with [29] cold at the thinness of the morning
audience, & with fear lest all will fail at every bad speech. ↑Mere
ability & mellowness is then inestimable.↓ Stephen C. Phillips was a
great comfort to me, for he is a good housewarmer with his obvious
honesty & good meaning & his hurra- & universal-scream sort of
eloquence which inundates the ⟨whole⟩ assembly with a flood of
animal spirits & makes all safe & secure so that any & every sort of
good speaking becomes at once practicable.[30] His ⟨is⟩ⁿ animal elo-
quence⟨, and⟩ is as good as a stove in a cold house.[31]

An orator is a thief of belief[.]

[30] Garrison is a /masculine/virile/ speaker; he lacks the feminine
element which we find in men of genius. He has great body to his
discourse, so that he can well afford occasional flourishes & eloquence.
He ⟨seems to be⟩ ↑is↓ a man in his place. He brings his whole history
with him, wherever he goes, & there is no falsehood or patchwork,
but sincerity & unity.

The Americans are easily pleased, the saints also.

> [31] Meno's definition of Virtue is
> "To feel a joy from what is fair,
> And o'er it to have power."

à se plaire aux belles choses, et à pouvoir se les procurer: *Cousin*
[*Oeuvres de Platon*, 1822–1840, VI, 159]
That is very subtle, at least.
In Greek, Χαιρειν τε καλοισι και δυνασθαι. [Plato, *Meno*, 77B]

[32] ↑Proteus↓
    The Proteus is as nimble in the highest as in the lowest grounds,

---

[30] Phillips was a congressman (1834–1838), mayor of Salem (1838–1842),
and Free-Soil candidate for governor of Massachusetts in 1848.

[31] This paragraph, struck through in both pencil and ink with vertical use marks,
is used in "Eloquence," *W*, VII, 62, 67–68.

when we contemplate the One, the True, the Good, as in the surfaces & tendrils of matter.[32]

Keep a thing by you ⟨&⟩seven years & it will come in use, though it were the devil, thought I, when Abaddon came lately into favour.[33] Goethe had remarked that all men liked to hear him named.

Nature has a stratum of cockneys[,] a secondary formation as well as the granitic series[.]
Proteus. Grass is not milk, though swallowed by a cow it becomes milk.

[33] Golden averages, volitant stabilities, compensated or periodic errors, houses founded on the sea, are we.[34]

Volitant endurers we,
Or houses founded on the sea.[35]

[34₁]   ↑Nature↓
Every thought like every man wears at its first emergence from the creative Night its rank ⟨in⟩stamped on it. This is a witticism, and this ↑other↓ is a Power.
see W 34. There is a certain heat in that breast, &c

[35] Health is genius, the higher tone. Potentially all wise enow, wine is what we want, wine of wine, excitement, opportunity, an initiative. Is the solar system good art & architecture? The same wise achievment is in my brain; can you only wile me from interference & marring. The poetic gift we want, but not the poetic profession; — poetic gift, as the health & supremacy of man, but not rhymes & sonneteering, not bookmaking & bookselling, not cold spying & au-

---

[32] This sentence, struck through in ink with a vertical use mark, is used in "Plato; or, the Philosopher," *W*, IV, 49.
[33] Cf. Rev. 9:11: "And they had a king over them, which is the angel of the bottomless pit, whose name in the Hebrew tongue is Abaddon, but in the Greek tongue hath his name Apollyon."
[34] This sentence, struck through in ink with a vertical use mark, is used in "Montaigne," *W*, IV, 161.
[35] These two lines are in pencil.

thorship. A poet who suffers the man to sit in him with the poet, as a charioteer with the hero in the Iliad.

Byron, because his poetic talent was surpassing, could ruin his poem, (see above, p. 8) a human wisdom should have assisted at the birth. Genius consists in health[,] in plenipotence[,] or that "top of condition" which allows of not only exercise but frolic of faculty.

To coax & woo the strong Instinct to bestir itself & work its miracle ⟨that⟩ is the end of all wise endeavour[.]

[34₂] [36] The Instinct is resistless & knows the way, & is melodious, & at all points a god.

The reason we set so high a value on any poetry & the same on a line or phrase as on a poem, is, that it is a new work of nature as a man or a woman is. We admire a new maiden infinitely, and a new verse is as divine. But ⟨we never meet with one⟩ ↑a new verse comes once in 500 years↓[.]

This is the reason why Hafiz & Herrick & Pindar speak so proudly of what seems to the thoughtless a mere jingle[.] [37]

[36] Whiggism, a feast of shells, idolatrous of the forms of legislature; like a cat loving the house[,] not the inhabitant[.]

⟨Child⟩

Science considers the thing in its purity: Children are unripe & defective. Grass is not wheat, nor are the berries of the woodbine grapes.

H.D.T. says "that philosophers are broken down poets"; and "that universal assertions should never allow any remarks of the individual to stand in their neighborhood,ⁿ for the broadest philosophy is narrower than the worst poetry."

But truly philosophers are *poètes manqués*, or, neutral or imperfect poets.

---

[36] The notation "[turn back p 34]", written at the bottom of p. [35] in pencil, directs attention to "The Instinct . . . jingle".

[37] "Health is . . . jingle" was written in pencil, then the passage "The poetic gift . . . at the birth" was written over in ink. In the pencil version, "God" is canceled between "but" and "not rhymes"; "⟨is more than a poet,⟩ a poet who [is ‖ . . . ‖; &]" occurs between "A poet who" and "suffers the man"; and "Byron himself is" is canceled before "Byron, because".

[37] Travelling. Discendi causa ultimas terras lustrasse Pythagoram, Democritum Platonem accepimus.[38] *Cicero.* Tusc. Disp. 4. 19

Love attaches   thought detaches
                 man from his family
                 ⟨man⟩ ↑head↓ from his hands
                 head from his heart [39]

[38] Kosmos [40]
The wonderful Humboldt, with his extended centre & expanded wings, marches like an army, gathering all things as he goes. How he reaches from science to science, from law to law, tucking away moons & asteroids & solar systems, in the clauses & parentheses of his encyclopaediacal paragraphs! [41]
Gibbon has a strength rare with such finish. He built a pyramid, & then enamelled it.

⟨Omnipotence.⟩ ↑*Pantheism.*↓ Sin,[n] & every man thou meetest shall stand up like a god, & judge thee. The God has delegated himself to a thousand deputies, & at every street corner. God-like is yonder youth to those who go by, &, where he halts, lo! the tenth man is a god to him[.]

[39] *Opportunity.* This world was created as an audience for thee. They have so many faculties, they are so keen & thorough in their knowledge, only to appreciate thy profoundness. They are so averse, and they hate thee, only to give thee a fair field & the greatest value to their suffrages, O Coriolanus!

[38] The words "discendi causa" — "for the sake of learning," a common Latin phrase — do not occur in Emerson's source, but his quotation is otherwise accurate: "We have been told that Pythagoras, Democritus, Plato journeyed to the ends of the earth."

[39] These four lines are in pencil.

[40] This heading is in pencil. A pencil version of the two paragraphs which follow, later partially erased, underlies the ink version.

[41] Emerson owned an incomplete set of Baron Alexander von Humboldt's *Cosmos: Sketch of a Physical Description of the Universe,* trans. under the superintendence of E. Sabine [by Mrs. Sabine], 4 vols. (1847 [1845]–?). The paragraph is used in "Humboldt," *W,* XI, 457.

[40] A system there must be in every economy, or the best single expedients avail not. The farm is excellent only when it begins & ends with itself, & does not need a salary or a shop or other resources, to eke it out. If it be not a sphere, it is but a bowl or cup which spills. The farm has the cattle, and it is a material link in the chain-ring. If the Gentoo leaves out the cattle, & does not also leave out of his wants the want which the cattle supply, he must ⟨supply⟩ ↑fill↓ the defect by begging or stealing. The cunning & discoursing of our philosophers is not wilful, but an inevitable resort of weakness. When men now alive were born, the farm yielded everything that was consumed on the farm. Now, ⟨it yie⟩the farmer buys almost all he consumes, cloth, sugar, tea, coffee, fish, coal, railroad-tickets, & newspapers.[42]

[41] New England on each new political event resolves itself into a debating-society. And is the Germany of the U. States.

[42] The moral of science should be a transference of that trust which is felt in nature's admired arrangements in light, heat, gravity, & so on, to the social & moral ⟨na⟩order.[43] Artificial legislation[,] perpetual brazen-faced interference of every rowdy boy into the circles of Law: he will help the Law! Can't he set his shoulder to the earth to assist it to spin on its axis, or to hasten it round the sun. If we had not confidence that the Law provided for every exigency, that not an impulse of absolute freedom could exist, we should rush by suicide ⟨to⟩ ↑out of↓ the door of this staggering Temple.

_____

        ↑Nature↓
    C. Lane says he has found that though he cannot trust men, he can trust their natures.
                            _____
                        ↑See p 44↓

[43][44] I have

_____

[42] This paragraph, struck through in ink with a vertical use mark, is used in "Wealth," _W_, VI, 118–119.
[43] This sentence is struck through in ink with a vertical use mark.
[44] Except for "I have", this page is in pencil.

Reference of preference

He dares not even love or hate but in his mind is ever asking how far his love is allowed by this person & by that person & by that other[.]

It is bad but true that you cannot[,] O Adam[,] eat your cake & have it. Excellent is culture for a savage but as soon as he has read in this book he is no longer able not to think of Plutarch's heroes.[45] You have transformed God's hero into a secondary Plutarch's hero.

[44] Abolition the Scotland of our politics immeasureably higher than Whiggism if——[46]

Every thing indicates the selfbalance of nature; that there can be no waste, only transference: kill here, there is birth elsewhere; burn here, the released elements re-combine in new wood. Why must not the ⟨same⟩ selfequality which makes the proportion of the sexes constant in the births,[47]—& which makes the identity of the composition of air, ⟨whenever &⟩ whencesoever taken,—hold throughout nature's kingdoms? The world is not left like ↑our old shingled towns,↓ a ⟨North end⟩ tinderbox at the mercy of incendiaries. Hence the philosopher denies progress of the species. If a peachtree or an oak tree grows faster by cultivation its fruit & its timber are so much poorer.   See p 42

[45] A great man will not make haste or run, ⟨even⟩ ↑no not↓ though he should be late at the Thursday lecture.[48]

[46]   ↑*Idea of the Time.*↓[49]
There is a ↑XIX-↓Century or secular disease which infects all those who stand on or near the dividing line between conservatism &

---

[45] This sentence is used in "Montaigne," *W*, IV, 158–159.

[46] This entry is in pencil.

[47] In *JMN*, VI, 206, Emerson credits Pierre Simon, Marquis de Laplace, with this idea, as quoted from Dugald Stewart's *The Philosophy of the Active and Moral Powers of Man* in *The Works of Dugald Stewart*, 7 vols. (Cambridge, Mass., 1829), V, 624.

[48] This entry is in pencil.

[49] This heading is added in pencil.

absolutism. Many are born of conservative parents, hedged round
with conservative connexions, & are themselves by genius absolutists.
In proportion to their nearness to this line, the ⟨f⟩ conflict of energies
in them is exasperated, & the distemper acute. You see them without
visible cause or any organic ail, thin, dyspeptic, irritable, melancholy,
& imbecile.

Superlatives [50]

Segnes Zonam solvere Gratias [51]

The common people diminish, as, "a coldsnap," "it blows
fresh," [52]

[47]   ↑Superlatives↓
"I judge by every man's truth of his degree of understanding,"
said Chesterfield.[53] ⟨I⟩And I do not know any advantage more conspicuous which a man acquires by experience in State street than the
caution & accuracy of his report of facts. "Uncle Isaac's news is always
true," for the old head[,] after deceiving & being deceived many
times, thinks, What is the use of having to unlearn today what I
learned yesterday? I will not be responsible[,] I will be as moderate
as the fact & use the same expression without colour which I received and rather repeat it several times than vary it never so little.[54]

You cannot say God, blood, & hell too little. Always suppose God.
The Jew named him not.[55]

Every time Garrison repeats his phrase, "a covenant with death, &

<hr>

[50] This heading and the two entries below it are in pencil.
[51] See Journal W, p. [106] above.
[52] This remark is used in "The Superlative," *W*, X, 169.
[53] This remark is slightly misquoted from Letter 41, September 21, O.S., 1747.
See *The Letters of Philip Dormer Stanhope, Lord Chesterfield*, ed. J. Bradshaw, 3
vols. (London, 1892), I, 59. See *JMN*, VI, 63, and p. [184] below.
[54] This paragraph, struck through in ink with a vertical use mark, is used in
"The Superlative," *W*, X, 168.
[55] This entry, which is in pencil, is struck through in ink with a vertical use
mark.

with hell they are at agreement," I think of Dr Bell's patients.[56]
The superlative in manners too. People with manners of desperation
who ↑go↓ shrieking, tearing, ⟨te⟩convulsed[n] through life[,] wailing,
praying, swearing.[57]

[48] The way from Rome is the way to Rome.

———

A great man is he who answers questions which I have not skill
to put.[58]

One man all his lifetime answers a question which none of his
contemporaries put: he is therefore isolated.

Our quarrel with religion, philosophy, & literature is that they
answer some ↑other↓ question.[59] After much reading, I am not fur-
thered. I want a hammer, you bring me a bucket.

Phedo p 202. Ah, if Cebes & Simmias had now said, Yes the
Reminiscence is well enow but if my future is related to my Present
only as my present to my past, that is no immortality for Cebes &
Simmias. It does for the Universe. That suffers no detriment; but
I have not sufficient property in it to interest me a moment in such
a sky high concern. I wish to be certified that these dear Johns &
Henries[,] Anns and Maries shall keep the traits that are most their
own & make them dear[.] [60]

[49][61] We have all need of charity, for we have all sweethearts.

---

[56] Dr. Luther V. Bell was superintendent of the McLean Asylum for the Insane in
Charlestown.

[57] This paragraph is struck through in ink with a discontinuous use mark.
"People with manners . . . swearing" is used in "The Superlative," *W*, X, 163.

[58] This sentence was written first in pencil, then in ink.

[59] "A great man . . . other question.", struck through in ink with a discontinuous use mark, is used in "Uses of Great Men," *W*, IV, 6–7.

[60] This entry is in pencil. Emerson's page reference is to *The Cratylus, Phaedo,
Parmenides, and Timaeus of Plato* . . . , 1793. In the *Phaedo*, Socrates argues for
the immortality of the soul by discussing its remembrances (or "reminiscences") of
existence before birth with Cebes and Simmias, his interlocutors. See Journal O, p.
[125] below.

[61] The entries on this page are in pencil.

If they are annoyed it is hell at freezing or boiling point[.]

[50] ↑Defining↓

How unskilful definers we are may be seen in the poverty of our speech respecting those traits which our feelings discriminate instantaneously. We say the man has talent, he has character, he has force, or he has none: and then we are at an end. But these words discriminate not well enough: the man is still not described: — we gaze again, & say, there is a great deal of something about him.[62]

[51] "For we should dare to affirm the truth," says Plato, "especially when speaking concerning the truth." Phaedrus [*The Works of Plato* ..., 1804, III] p 323

The Universe is traversed with paths or bridges or stepping stones across all the gulfs of space in every direction. To every soul that is created is its path, invisible to all but to that soul. ⟨He⟩Each soul therefore walking in its own path walks firmly & to the astonishment of all other souls, who see not its path. Yet it goes as softly & effeminately & playfully on its way, as if instead of being a line narrow as the edge of a sword over terrific pits right & left, it were a wide ⟨meadow⟩ prairie[.][63]   ↑printed, I believe↓

[52]   ↑Parallelism↓

We know ⟨that⟩ in one mood ↑that↓ which we are ignorant of in another mood, like mesmerised patients who are clairvoyant at night & in the day know nothing of that which they told.

A man who did not need to economize his strength, but could toil at his desk week after week almost without sleep or exercise —

The scholar is led on by the sweet opium of reading to pallor & squalor, to anxiety & timorousness, to a life as dry & thin as his paper, to coldness & hardness & inefficiency.[64]

---

[62] This paragraph, struck through in ink with a vertical use mark, is used in the lecture "The Superlative in Manners and Literature." "Defining" is added in pencil.

[63] This paragraph, struck through in ink with a vertical use mark, is used in "Natural History of Intellect," *W*, XII, 42.

[64] This entry is in pencil.

[53]–[54] [leaf torn out] [65]
[55] [blank]
[56][66] You cannot do or make any thing that shall not symbolize the soul. Is your house warmed by a furnace, fed by an aquaduct, lighted by a gas reservoir, supplied in all its expenditure from your wealth, distributed, ordered, & made still new & full ⟨by⟩of ↑all↓ varied advantages by your central method & genius

Adaptiveness the peculiarity of human nature. The heavenly bodies are also animals, "but they enjoy not that fluctuating movement — through various steps & in divergent directions, that circum-lation through all the limits of imperfection, that shifting with the revolution of all things, so as to master the whole mass of reality in all its ramifications, — which forms the essential peculiarity of human nature" Ak↑h↓lak-I-Jalaly [1839, p. 16]   ↑See W. 86↓

[57][67] He who writes poetry now, seems to take advantage of the dulness of the times[.]
Aristotle founding on the qualities of matter is the European skeptic[.]
Plato the Believer

We are cast into a situation contemptible & of marked insignificance, of persons nowise parties to that which is done, something is always done or doing but over our heads & under our feet we are made to feel that we are strangers & loafers[.]

Compensation.
The law by which the centrifugence is increased by the increase of centripetence consoles us in the wildest outbreaks of the Spirit.

India repeats the Sects of Greek Philosophy.
Academy

[65] Emerson indexed p. [53] under Greatness and Life and p. [54] under Bible.
[66] The entries on this page are in pencil.
[67] The entries on this page, with the exception of the heading "*Compensation.*", are written in pencil; later, Emerson traced "The law by which . . . Spirit." and "India repeats . . . Philosophy." in ink.

Peripatetics
Stoic
Epicurean
   the man wriggles this way & that[,] then dives to ecstasy
& abandonment & that is Buddism

[58] Vigilance or anxiety is required of us. We do not eat for pleasure. We go to the table at least for necessity, and when there, eat too much, for pleasure; but ⁿ how gladly we would eat exactly enough, if there were a measured & scaled Enough: if a cubic inch of pemmican ⟨wou⟩ per day would keep us ⟨in⟩ at the top of our condition, how gladly we would swallow it & go about our business. But ⟨most of us have⟩ ↑every sane man in turn has↓ tried ⟨the⟩ starving ⟨system⟩, tried parched corn, tried ⟨yams⟩ ↑grass↓, & found that it did not give ⟨us⟩ ↑him↓ blood but that we were faint & dispirited. If it could be settled once for all that coffee & ⟨tea⟩ ↑wine↓ & all stimulus were bad.[68]

[59]–[62] [leaves missing] [69]
[63]   Good Heart that ⟨givest⟩ ↑ownest↓ all   ↑p 79↓
        I ask for what is small
        Not for heaven & earth ⟨to lift⟩ the gift
        But for one ⟨creature⟩ proper form
        Which the eye
        Sweeping the map of earth
        ↑Or↓ of ⁿ the district of New England
        Or of the Bay State
        Could not descry
        Is it much to ask of all thy ↑gay↓ creation
        So minute a part
        One heart
        Yet think me not meanspirited
        Or that ⟨I ask little⟩ a mean demand

[68] This entry is in pencil.
[69] Emerson indexed p. [59] under America, [Luigi] Cornaro, and New England; p. [60] under Opinion and Skeptic; p. [61] under Cornaro and Home; and p. [62] under Nature.

For this is the concentration
And ⟨essence of⟩ ↑worth of all↓ the land
The sister of the sea
The daughter of thy land
Made of wind & light
And the swart earth-force
So little to my prayer
Thou canst spare
And yet if she were gone
The rest were ⟨not worth preserving⟩ ↑better left alone↓ [70]

[64]   "Herbs gladly cure our flesh because that they
            Find their acquaintance there"
                                [Herbert, "Man," ll. 23–24]

This is mystically true. The master can do his great deed[,] the desire
of the world, say to find his way between azote & oxygen, detect the
secret of the new rock superposition, find the law of the curves,
because he has just come out of nature or from being a part of that
thing. As if one went into the mesmeric state to find the way of nature
in some function & then[,] sharing it[,] came out into the normal state
& repeated the trick. He knows the laws of azote because just now he
was azote. Man is only a piece of the universe made alive. Man active
can do what just now he suffered.[71]

[65] [72] Is not this the Montaigne
That Monta↑igne↓ & the skeptics help us as myrrh & fruit against
costiveness.
But there is a platform of health which has its own Energy[,] Energy
only
The problem for health to study is the flowing ⟨life⟩ power ⟨of the
Cause⟩ detected only in results[.] The media or appearances are to be

---

[70] These lines, which are in pencil, are struck through in pencil with wavy and
swirling vertical lines. For an account of their later publication, see p. 284, n. 88
below.
[71] This paragraph is struck through in ink with one straight and two swirling
vertical use marks. Cf. "Uses of Great Men," W, IV, 11–12.
[72] The entries on this page are in pencil.

ignored. ⟨The Poet⟩ All the words of a poet are poems. And days &
years & men are symptomatic only[.]

[66] The greatest man underlies the human nature. The longest
wave quickly is lost in the sea. No individualism can make any head
against the swallowing universality. Plato would willingly have a
Platonism[,] a known & accurate expression for the world, and it
should be adequate: — it shall be — the world passed through the
mind of Plato — nothing less; every atom shall have the Platonic
tinge. Every atom, ⟨you⟩every relation, every quality⟨,⟩ you knew
before, you shall know again, & find here, but now, ordered; not
nature, but art, & you shall feel that Alexander indeed overran with
some men & horses some countries of the planet, — but countries, &
things of which countries are composed, — elements, — planet itself,
& laws of planet, & of men, thoughts, truths, all ⟨possible⟩ actual &
possible things, have [67] passed through this man as ⟨foo⟩ bread into
his body & become no longer bread but body; so all this mammoth
mouthful has become Plato.
Well this is the ambition of Individualism: but the mouthful proves
too great. Boa Constrictor has good will to eat it, but he is foiled. He
falls abroad in the attempt and[,] biting[,] gets strangled, & the bitten
world holds him fast by his own teeth. There he perishes, & the
Unconquered Nature goes on & forgets him. Alas[,] alas[,] Plato
turns out to be philosophical exercitations. He argues now on this
side[,] now on that. The acutest searcher, the lovingest disciple could
never tell what Platonism was; indeed admirable texts can be quoted
on both sides of every great question, from him.[73]

[68] The sea shore; sea seen from shore, shore seen from sea,
must explain the charm of Plato. Art expresses The One, or The
Same, by the Different. Thought seeks to know Unity in unity;
Poetry, to show it by Variety,[n] i.e. always by an object or symbol.
Plato keeps the two vases, one of ⟨water⟩ ↑aether↓ & one of pigment,
always at his side, & invariably uses both. Things added to things, as,

---

[73] These two paragraphs, struck through in ink with a vertical use mark, are
used in "Plato; or, the Philosopher," *W*, IV, 77–78. In addition, "Well this is . . .
strangled," is struck through in pencil with two diagonal use marks.

statistics, geography, civil history, are mere inventories or lists. Things used as language or symbols, are inexhaustibly attractive. Plato is a master of the game, & turns incessantly the obverse & the reverse of the ⟨coin of Jove⟩ ↑medal↓. He prefixes to the science of the naturalists the dogma

"Let us declare the cause which led the Supreme Ordainer to produce & compose the Universe. He was good, & he who is good, has no kind of envy: Exempt from envy, he wished that all things should be as much as possible like himself. Whosoever taught by wise men shall admit this as the prime cause of the origin & foundation of the world, will be in the truth" *Timaeus*.[74]

"All things are for its sake, & it is the [69] cause of every thing beautiful." [75] This dogma animates the whole philosophy[.] [76]

[70] The eloquent man is he who is no beautiful speaker, but who is inwardly & desperately drunk with /his matter.[n]/a certain belief;/ it agitates & tears him, & almost bereaves him of the power of articulation. Then it rushes from him as in short abrupt screams, in torrents of meaning. The possession by the subject of his mind is so entire, that it ensures an order of expression which is the order of Nature itself, and so the order of greatest force & inimitable by any art. And the main distinction between him & other well graced /orators/actors/ is the conviction communicated to the hearer by every word, that his mind is contemplating a whole, and inflamed with the contemplation of the whole, & that the words & sentences uttered by him, however admirable, fall from him as unregarded parts of that terrible whole, which he sees, & means that you shall see.

[71] The hearer[,] occupied with the excellence of the ↑single↓ thoughts & images[,] is astonished to see the inspired man still impatient of the tardiness of words & parts, pressing forward to new parts, and in his prodigality ever announcing new & greater wealth ↑to come↓. Add to this concentration, a certain regnant calmness which

[74] Emerson's language shows this is a close translation of the version in Cousin, *Oeuvres de Platon*, 1822–1840, XII, 119.

[75] *The Six Books of Proclus . . . on the Theology of Plato*, 1816, I, 125. See *JMN*, VIII, 219 and 364.

[76] These three paragraphs are used in "Plato; or, the Philosopher," *W*, IV, 55–57. " 'All things are . . . beautiful.' " is also used in "The Scholar," *W*, X, 271.

(in all the tumult) never ⟨tells⟩ ↑utters↓ one premature ⟨word⟩ ↑syllable↓, but keeps the secret of its means & method, (never gossips, nor lets the hearer sidewise into any gossiping information of arts & studies) and the orator stands before the people as a daemoniacal power to whose miracles they have no key.

It is vanity that gossips; anything to secure your attention to itself. Earnestness[,] with its eye nailed to the argument, has no wish to give you anecdotes[n] about itself & its talents.[77]

[72] [78]   ↑Memory↓
This prolific past never ceases to work. With every new fact a ray of information shoots up from the long buried years. Who can judge the new book? He who has seen many books before. Who the new assertion? He who has heard a thousand like ones. Who the new man? He who has seen men[.]
Plato's Reminiscence is the Apotheosis of the Memory[.]
Plato esteemed a memory, & was jealous of writing, as its enemy. See Phaedrus in Cousin [*Oeuvres de Platon*, 1822–1840,] vol VI p 122
See parijata tree. Y p. 172

[73] Old question[:] which is first[,] egg or bird? I bring you an older question[:] which is the first, — good or true? Answer who can. You shall have a hundred years to think of it and then you will ask a millennium.

[74]   ↑Culture↓ [79]
Love, war, trade, government, are gymnastic, medicinal, & educative; a gun is a liberalizer.[80] See p 103

The scholar's is a position of perfect immunity. The vulgar think

[77] These three paragraphs are struck through in pencil with a vertical use mark; "The eloquent man . . . no key." is struck through in ink with a vertical use mark. "The eloquent man . . . shall see." and "Add to this . . . key." are used in "Eloquence," *W*, VII, 92–93.
[78] The entries on this and the following page are in pencil.
[79] This heading is added in pencil.
[80] See Journal U, p. [75] above.

he would found a sect; he knows better. Society has no bribe for him[.]

Do not give up your thought because you cannot answer an objection to it. Consider only whether it remains in your life the same which it was.[81]

We are waiting until some tyrannous idea emerging out of heaven shall seize us & bereave us of this liberty with which we are falling abroad.[82]
Every intellectual advantage bought at the expense of manhood. The lumpers are manlier than the grocers, more absolute. In the water party, the Skipper of the boat was the only interesting person: The rest made puns.

[75] ↑Conversation.↓
      A convertible proverb, *It is Greek to him.*[83]
Those eastern story tellers whose oily tongues turn day into night, & night to day, who lap their hearers in a sweet drunkenness of fancy so that they forget the taste of meat. Coleridge too[,] who could dissipate the solar system to a thin transparency.

      Are not Lectures a kind of Peter Parley's story of Uncle Plato,[84] and of a puppetshow of Eleusinian Mysteries?

[76] ↑Knowledge↓
      The ⟨theatres &⟩ railroad companies write on their tickets "good for this trip only" but in all action or speech which is good, there is a benefit beyond that contemplated by the doer. ⟨I seem⟩In seeing it, I seem to have learned a new tactics, applicable to all action.[85]

---

[81] This paragraph, struck through in ink with a vertical use mark, is used in "Worship," *W*, VI, 230. See Journal O, p. [34] below.

[82] This sentence is used in "Inspiration," *W*, VIII, 276.

[83] Cf. Shakespeare, *Julius Caesar*, I, ii, 288.

[84] Samuel Griswold Goodrich, a Boston publisher, issued numerous books for the instruction of the young under the pseudonym "Peter Parley."

[85] This paragraph is struck through in pencil with a vertical use mark; "The ⟨theatres &⟩ . . . only' " is struck through in ink with a vertical use mark. Cf.

[77]⁸⁶ World full of tools or machines[,] every one a contrivance to exclude some one error or inconvenience & make a practical thinker. Thus in making coffee many errors are likely to intervene & spoil the beverage. The biggin thinks for us[,] is a practical thinker[,] and excludes this & that other imprudence. It hinders the riling[,] it determines the quantity[.]
What a stroke of genius is each carpenter's tool[.]

[78] It would be so easy to draw two pictures of the literary man, as of one possessed & led by muses, or, as of one ridden by some dragon, or dire distemper. A mechanic is driven by his work all day, but it ends at night; it has an end. But the scholar's work has none. That which he has learned is that there is much more to be learned. He feels only his incompetence. A thousand years, tenfold, a hundredfold his faculties, would not suffice: the demands of the task are such, that it becomes omnipresent; he studies in his sleep, in his walking, in his meals, in his pleasures. ⟨He becomes anxious:⟩ He ⁿ is but a fly or a worm to this mountain. He becomes anxious: if one knock at his door, he scowls: if one intimate the purpose of [79] visiting him, he looks grave.⁸⁷

Good Heart that ownest all,   ↑(See p. 63)↓
I ask for what is small
Not of ⟨heaven & earth⟩ ↑lands & towns↓ the gift
Too large a load for me to lift
But for one proper creature
Which geographic eye
Sweeping the map of earth
Or the ⟨New England⟩ ↑Virginian↓ coast,
⟨Or⟩ ↑And↓ ⟨the Bay state Massasoit's⟩ ↑Powhatan's↓ domain
Could not descry
Is't much to ask in all thy ⟨gay⟩ ↑huge↓ creation

"Uses of Great Men," *W*, IV, 28. The words "or speech" are enclosed by brackets in pencil.

⁸⁶ The entries on this page are in pencil.

⁸⁷ "A mechanic . . . mountain.", struck through in ink with a diagonal use mark, is used in "Immortality," *W*, VIII, 341. The word "more" is enclosed by brackets in pencil.

So mini⟨mum⟩↑ature↓ a part
⟨One heart⟩ A solitary heart?
Yet ⟨think⟩ ↑count↓ me not of spirit mean,
Or mine a mean demand,
For 'tis the concentration
And worth of all the land
The sister of the sea
The daughter of the ⟨land⟩ strand
Composed of ⟨wind⟩ ↑air↓ & light
And of the swart earth ⟨force⟩ might
So little to my prayer
Thou canst well spare
And yet, — if she were gone
Thy world were better left alone.[88]

[80] *Akhlak-I-Jalaly* [. . . , 1839].

God said, *The heavens the earth & all that is between them, we created not in sport*: and again; *Then think ye we have created ye in jest, and that ye are not to return to us?* [89] [p. 12]

Abu Said Abulkhair ⟨&⟩the mystic, & Abu Ali Seena the philosopher, on leaving each other said; the one, "All that he sees, I know," and the other, "All that he knows, I see." [90] [p. 25, paraphrased]

"There are two that I cannot support, the fool in his devotions, & the intelligent in his impieties" Koran [91] [p. 29]

↑*Bias.*↓

"If ye hear that a mountain has changed its place, believe it: but if ye

[88] These lines, which are in pencil, are struck through in ink with a vertical use mark. Emerson indexed p. [79] under Lover's Prayer. The lines were published, with some minor changes, as "Lover's Petition" in the privately printed *Over-Songs* (Cambridge, Mass., 1864), pp. 10–11. They were later reprinted in *May-Day and Other Pieces*, 1867, pp. 90–91, but are not included in *W*, IX.

[89] This entry is struck through in ink with one vertical and four diagonal use marks, and in pencil with two diagonal use marks that reach to the end of the next entry. See p. [16] above.

[90] This entry, struck through in pencil with two diagonal use marks and in ink with a vertical use mark, is used in "Swedenborg," *W*, IV, 95.

[91] This quotation, struck through in ink with a vertical use mark, is used in "Worship," *W*, VI, 240–241.

284

hear that a man has changed his disposition, believe it not." ⟨Koran.⟩ 92 [p. 35]

"He shall assuredly return to that for which he was created." *Koran* [pp. 35–36]

[81]   ↑Idiodynamics↓
"Men have their metal like the metal of gold & silver: those of you who were the worthy ones in the state of ignorance, will be the worthy ones in the state of faith as soon as they embrace it." Koran 93 [p. 37]

"Content is a treasure that never spends" [p. 75]

———

"Haste is of the devil & delay is of the All-giving." Mahomet [p. 75]

———

Wisdom with wealth is waking and with poverty is asleep. [p. 91]

Making money is like carrying a mass of stone to the mountain's head & spending it is like rolling the same down again. [p. 91]

———

Not dead but living are ye to account those who are slain in the way of God. 94 [pp. 94–95]

    Fooled thou must be tho' wisest of the wise
    Then be the fool of virtue not of vice 95 [p. 95]

———

"By the God of Abu Talib's son said the Prophet I swear that a thousand beheadings [82] were easier than one deathbed." 96 [pp. 95–96]

The saint's best blush in heaven is from his heart⟨s⟩-blood's red. 97 [p. 96]

———

Sleeping are men, & when they die, they wake [p. 102]

———

92 This quotation is used in "Eloquence," *W*, VII, 64. A single vertical line in ink is drawn in the left margin from "has changed his disposition," to the end of the following quotation.

93 This quotation, struck through in pencil with a vertical use mark, is used in "Plato; or, the Philosopher," *W*, IV, 66. "Idiodynamics" is added in pencil.

94 This quotation is used in "Immortality," *W*, VIII, 343. See Journal W, p. [43] above.

95 This quotation is struck through in ink with a vertical use mark. See p. [172] above and p. [176] below.

96 This quotation is used in the lecture "The Superlative in Manners and Litera-ture" (see *W*, X, 547).

97 See p. [16] above.

Truly hell is a circle about the unbelieving [p. 102]

———

Verily, the ground of Paradise is extension, & the plants of it are hallelujahs to God's praise.[98] [p. 103]

———

Futurity is our estate. [p. 103]

———

Every scholar has his superior.[99] [p. 160]

———

⟨The gardener's beauty is not of himself,
His hue the rose's, & his form the palm's.⟩[100] [p. 140]

———

Verily worlds upon worlds can add nothing to Him.[101] [p. 301]

What stream could fill the skull with what it craves?
That tilted ewer, where nought abides that enters. [p. 239]

Whoso teaches me a letter renders me his slave. *Ali.* [p. 351]

[83] His very flight is presence in disguise.[102] [p. 364]

———

Men resemble their contemporaries even more than their progenitors. [p. 381]

Five classes of men. 1. Those who are by nature good, ↑& whose goodness has an influence on others.↓ &c This class is the aim of Creation. In fact, the other classes are admitted to the feast of being, only as following in the train of these.

Go boldly forth & feast on being's banquet:
Thou art the called, — the rest admitted with thee [103]
[p. 391, with some omissions]

———

The men of Hind have a saying, "Better justice in the sovereign than

[98] This quotation is used in the lecture "The Superlative in Manners and Literature" and "The Superlative," *W*, X, 177. See Journal O, p. [92] below.

[99] See p. [86] below.

[100] This quotation is struck through in ink with three vertical use marks. See p. [86] below.

[101] This quotation is used in the lecture "The Superlative in Manners and Literature." See Journal O, p. [92] below.

[102] This quotation is used in "Goethe," *W*, IV, 273. See p. [160] and Journal O, p. [92] below.

[103] This entry, struck through in pencil with a vertical use mark, is used in "Swedenborg," *W*, IV, 95.

plenty in the season:" & on certain stones there is an inscription in Syriac,
  "Might to right is friend & brother
          Neither thrives without the other." [p. 457]

―――――

Professions are either noble, mean, or indifferent. Of the noble, 3 kinds. 1 Those which depend on the quality of mind; as with statesmen 2 Those depending on attainment & merit, as book-making, rhetoric, astronomy &c [p. 254, paraphrased]

[84]   ↑Idiodynamics↓

In the doctrine of the ⟨fi⟩ organic character & disposition is the origin of caste. "Such as were fit to govern, into their composition the informing deity mingled gold; military, silver; iron & brass for husbandmen & artisans." *Timaeus* [104] [*Akhlāk-I-Jalāly* . . . , 1839, p. 37]

          The cup of Jam was dug from other mines
          Why overtask the humble vase of clay? [p. 37]

"If mankind were exactly on a[n] par, they must perish altogether." Tusy [p. 320n]

Caste & Culture are Asia & Europe.
Greek philosophy is discipline[.]
I should say again that the East loved infinity, & the West delighted in boundaries.[105]

Plato by his Eastern Education imported these tastes, & joined them to his native ones; but Europe was never his follower, but loved better the Whiggish Aristotle, the king of ⟨|| . . . ||⟩limits, certi denique fines, who declared that ⟨Propriety of [85] Conduct⟩ ↑Virtue↓ always consists in a mean or middle between two vicious extremes.[106]

          In all the ⟨faults⟩[n] ↑crimes↓ of men there's none so great

---

[104] This entry, struck through in ink with a vertical use mark, is used in "Plato; or, the Philosopher," *W*, IV, 66. "Idiodynamics" is added in pencil.

[105] These three sentences, struck through in pencil with a vertical use mark, are used in "Plato; or, the Philosopher," *W*, IV, 52.

[106] This paragraph is struck through in pencil with a vertical use mark to the bottom of p. [84]. The three Latin words are from Horace, *Satires*, I, i, 106: "there are, in short, fixed bounds."

As the least ⟨lapse⟩ⁿ ↑fault↓ in him who might be perfect.
[*Akhlāk-I-Jalāly* . . . , 1839, p. 178, paraphrased]

Men are either learned or learning: the rest are blockheads. *Mahomet*[107]
[p. 179]

⟨Let him reflect how far arrogance befits one who has twice passed thro'
the urinary passage.⟩ [p. 192]

On the day of resurrection those who have indulged in ridicule will be
called to the door of Paradise & have it shut in their faces when they
reach it. Again on their turning back they will be called to another door,
& again on reaching it will see it closed against them, & so on *ad infini-
tum*[108] [pp. 193–194]

[86][109]   ↑*The One*↓
Only the law of God it is, which has no antecedent; the law of
God in which no change is to be discovered. *Koran*[110] [p. 197]

↑Scholar.↓
The world shall live in me, not I in it. [p. 200]

↑Idiodynamics↓[111]
Every class rejoiceth in his own. [p. 238]

Every fort has been taken. [p. 413]

Every scholar has his superior.[112] [p. 160]

↑Identity↓
"The gardener's beauty is not of himself
His hue the rose's, & his form the palm's."[113] [p. 140]

·[87]   ↑*Vishnu Purana*↓
At the moment of the birth of the Budhu Gautama, the hellfire

[107] This quotation is used in "Address at the Opening of the Concord Free
Public Library," October 1, 1873, *W*, XI, 504.
[108] This quotation is used in "Social Aims," *W*, VIII, 98.
[109] "Aklak Y Jalaly" is written at the top of the page to the right.
[110] See p. [203] below.
[111] This word is added in pencil.
[112] See p. [82] above.
[113] See p. [82] above.

suffered a momentary extinguishment; the brutes banished their dread, the salt water of the Ocean became fresh, the sea was adorned with flowers, the flowers were blown on the surface of land & sea; every tree was bent down with flowers; these covered the earth & emerged through stones[.]

Brahma descended from the highest heaven which decayeth not & with the light of his own body illumined the dark abyss which now constitutes this world & walking in the heavens joyed in the possession of his glory[.]

One Brahma & then another from time to time descended & dwelt in the heavens & from the selfinherent virtue of the said Brahmas this world below became sweet as the honey of the honey-bee[.]

One of the Brahmas beholding the earth said to himself What thing [88] is this[?] & with one of his fingers having touched the earth put it to the tip of his tongue & perceived the same to be deliciously sweet: from which time all the Brahmas ate of the sweet earth for the space of 60 000 years. In the meantime, having coveted in their hearts the enjoyment of this world, they began to say one to another, this part is mine; that is thine; & so fixing boundaries divided the earth between them. On this account, the earth lost its sweetness.   then grew a mushroom
                                                          then a creeping plant
                                                          then a tree
                                                          then a grain rice
                                                          then rice grain

Then later, because of the sons of the Brahmas having used substantial food, the light which once shone in their bodies was extinguished[.] [114]

[89] Vishnu Purana

"Man performs all acts for the purpose of bodily fruition, & the

[114] Despite Emerson's heading, this has not been located in *The Vishńu Puráńa.* Since the heading was added at a later time, Emerson may have misremembered his source; nor are pp. [87]–[88] entered under "Vishnu Purana" in Emerson's own index to this journal. "At the moment . . . its sweetness." is struck through in pencil with a vertical use mark; cf. "Uses of Great Men," *W*, IV, 3.

consequence of such acts is another body; so that their result is nothing but confinement to bodily existence." [p. 650]

"Travelling the ⟨wa⟩path of the world for many thousands of births man attains only the weariness of bewilderment & is smothered by the dust of imagination" [115] [p. 650]

"There is no affinity between fire & water but when the latter is placed over ⟨a⟩the former in a cauldron it bubbles & boils & exhibits the properties of fire. In like manner when the soul is associated with Prakriti it is vitiated by egotism & the rest, & assumes the qualities of grosser nature although essentially distinct from them & incorrup[t]" [pp. 650–651]

"There is but one cure of worldly sorrows, the practice of devotion: no other is known" [p. 651]

"The supreme spirit attracts to itself [90][116] him who meditates upon it & who is of the same nature as the loadstone attracts the iron by the virtue which is common to itself & to its products." [p. 651]

↑*Individualism*↓
"The notion that self consists in what is not self & the opinion that property consists in what is not one's own, constitute the double seed of the tree of ignorance" [pp. 649–650]

Aphoristic Literature [117]

[91][118] W E C. said A[lcott]. is made of earth & fire. He wants water & air. How fast all that magnetism would lick up water. He discharges himself in volleys. Can you not hear him snap when you are near him?

"I never find anything which I look for" [119]

He cannot drive a nail[.]

[92] Prometheus is to have a working plan of this fine machine,

---

[115] "Travelling . . . of births" is struck through in ink with a vertical use mark. See p. [20] above and p. [160] below.

[116] "Vishnu Purana" is written at the top of the page to the left.

[117] These two words are in pencil.

[118] The entries on this page are in pencil.

[119] In his notebook OP Gulistan, p. [22], Emerson attributes this sentence to Ellery Channing.

⟨wit⟩ this crystal globe with glass wheels & hooks & teeth within, transparent like that African apple whose seeds are seen[.] [120]

English nobles are active travelled men who have always associated with the most refined people in every nation, have run through every country, seen all that was best in the planet; borne a leading part in ↑counsel & conduct of↓ every important action[.] [121]

[93] [blank]
[94] The Caliph Ali is a fine example of character.
He "possessed a vein of poignant humour which led Soliman Farsy to say of a jest he one day indulged in, This it is which has kept you back to the fourth (Abu Beker, Omar, & Othman having been successively elected before him,) for a reliance on his rights of sovereignty was the ruling feeling of that sacred person, & it is one which gives ascendance to the inner & individual nature in opposition to the suggestions of appearance & the observance of our relations with the many"   *Akhlak I Jalaly*, p 158

"In his consciousness of deserving success, Ali constantly neglected the ordinary means of attaining it" ↑Thompson↓ [122] [*Ibid.*, p. 158n]

↑Idiodynamics↓

Mahomet said, "Various are the Virtues, O Ali, by which men are brought near to their Creator, but thou by thy intellect art created near; and standest before them by many degrees of approach." [*Ibid.*, p. 179]

[95] *Vedanta.* The Internal Check.
"He who eternally restrains this & the other world, & all beings therein, who standing in the earth is other than the earth, whom the earth knows not, whose body the earth is, who interiorly restrains the earth, the same is thy soul, and the Internal Check immortal."
"The internal check is the supreme being." Colebrooke's Essays
p. 341 [123]
From a dialogue in which Yajnyawalcya instructs Uddalaea[.]

[120] This entry is in pencil.
[121] This paragraph, struck through in ink with a vertical use mark, is used in *English Traits, W*, V, 185.
[122] This quotation is used in "Aristocracy," *W*, X, 58.
[123] Henry Thomas Colebrooke, *Miscellaneous Essays*, 2 vols. (London, 1837), I. The copy in Emerson's library is a later bequest from Thoreau. " 'The internal

What he (God) is, I know not; what he is
not, I know. *Socrates* [124]

"Gold is solid light"

↑Nature↓

'Nature is likened to a female dancer exhibiting herself to soul
as to an audience' [& is reproached with shamelessness for repeatedly
exposing herself to the rude gaze of the spectator.] "She desists
however when she has sufficiently shown herself. She does so, because
she has been seen. [96] He desists because he has seen her. There is
no further use for the world: yet the connexion of soul & nature still
subsists." Colebrooke [*Miscellaneous Essays*, 1837, I,] p 259 [125]

"He is great in whom nought else is seen or heard or known. —
⟨b⟩But that wherein aught else is seen, heard, or known, is small." [*Ibid.*,
I, 343]

↑The One↓
"In the midst of the sun is the light, in the midst of the light is truth, in
the midst of truth is the unperishable being."   Vedanta [126]

the sportive sun. [127]

[97] Representative [128]

[98]   The poppy-wreath
Plato well guarded from those to whom he does not belong by a
river of sleep[.] [129]

---

check is the supreme being.' " is enclosed by a large bracket at the left and used in
"Swedenborg," *W*, IV, 140.
      [124] This quotation is used in "Swedenborg," *W*, IV, 140.
      [125] See p. [259] below.
      [126] This and the preceding entry are struck through in pencil and ink with
vertical use marks; the second is used in "Plato; or, the Philosopher," *W*, IV, 48. The
heading "The One" is added in pencil.
      [127] This phrase, struck through in pencil with a vertical use mark, is used in
"Song of Nature," l. 3, *W*, IX, 244. The poem was first published in 1860.
      [128] This word is in pencil.
      [129] This sentence and the heading are in pencil.

"During passion, anger, fury, great trials of strength, wrestling, fighting, &c a large amount of blood is co⟨nn⟩llected in the arteries, the maintenance of bodily strength requiring it & but little is sent into the veins. This condition is constant with intrepid persons, — with those who are animated with what we term heroic valour." Swedenborg: Animal Kingdom. [1843–1844,] Vol. II. p. 205 [130]

[99]   ↑*Budha or he who knows.*↓

Intellect puts an interval: if we converse with low things, with crimes, with mischances, ⟨th⟩we are not compromised, the interval saves us. But if we converse with high things, with heroic actions, with heroic persons, with virtues, the interval becomes a gulf, & we cannot enter into the highest good.

                                        Icy light.

    It is the chief deduction, almost the sole deduction from the merit of Plato (that which is no doubt incidental to this regnancy of the intellect in his work,) that ⟨they⟩his writings have not the vital authority which the screams of prophets & the sermons of unlettered Arabs & Jews possess. There is an interval, & to the cohesion, contact is necessary. Intellect is the king of non-committal.[131]

answers with generalities

He gave me wit instead of love

_____

Bana or sermons [132]

[100]   ↑Only be strong enough↓ [133]

    Landor says of Canning (?) that "he was an understrapper made an overstrapper." The expression is coarse enough, but is true of men of thought also. They are good pupils, & their life would be fair & blooming, if they could continue such; but, in the absence of intellectual men, in the absence of many grades & ranks of power, from the

_____

[130] This quotation, struck through in ink with a vertical use mark, is used in "Power," *W*, VI, 55.

[131] "It is the chief . . . necessary.", struck through in pencil and ink with vertical use marks, is used in "Plato; or, the Philosopher," *W*, IV, 76.

[132] Bana is a warlike foe of Krishna in *The Vishńu Puráńa*, 1840, pp. 593–596. In Notebook RT (Rhetoric), p. [37], Emerson notes that "Bana [means] Sermons" in a list of word derivations.

[133] This heading is added in pencil.

lawful & thoroughly educated king, to the youngest page, — our
scholar, on his first showing of intellectual power, is hurried from
the pupil's desk to the Master's Chair; and by this rude & rapid
change is cheated of those perfections which long training & faithful
abiding in all the intermediate degrees alone can give. A false relation
& false manners & incompleteness of beauty in every part are [101]
the ⟨inevitable⟩ result. The scholar ⟨now⟩ finds himself not excellent
in his own art, ⟨whilst he is⟩ ↑and↓ [134] painfully deficient in the arts
of men around him. He wants security, the unquestionable front of
⟨conscious⟩ power, & feels himself ⟨surrounded by⟩ interrogat⟨ers⟩↑ed↓
⟨& scorners⟩ ↑& defied↓. He wants in this loneliness nerves of ⟨iron⟩
↑a lion↓ & has the nerves of a caterpillar. Sympathy gives health ⟨&⟩
↑but↓ he has not the sympathy of those he can see, & he has not quite
eyes enough to see those whose sympathy he has. The bear comes out
fatter from his hybernation than he went to it, and the great man
should not have less resource in his hybernation.

[102] The boy learns chess & whist & takes lessons in dancing; the
⟨anxious⟩ ↑watchful↓ father observes that another has learned algebra
& geometry, in the meantime. But the first boy has got much more
than those goodfornothing games with the games. He is absorbed
for a month or two in whist & chess, but presently he will find them
tedious & will learn in himself that when he rises from the game ↑too
long played↓ he is vacant & forlorn, & despises himself. Thenceforth
it ⟨falls into its right place,⟩ takes place with other things, & has
⟨perspective & exactly⟩ its ↑one↓ weight in his experience. These
games, & especially dancing, are ⟨inestimable⟩ ↑necessary↓ as tickets
of admission to the commonwealth of mankind, to a class of civilization, & the being master of them enables the youth to judge intel-
ligently of much on which otherwise he would give [135] [103]–[104]
[leaf torn out] [136]

[105] In Spenser [Book III Canto XI p 181] is the Castle of Busy-

---

[134] This word is inserted in pencil.

[135] This paragraph, struck through in ink with a vertical use mark, is used in
"Culture," W, VI, 143, where it is concluded "a pedantic squint."

[136] Emerson indexed p. [103] under Education.

rane on whose gate is writ Be bold,[n] on the second gate, Be bold, be bold,[n] and the inner iron door, Be not too bold.[137]

[106]   ↑*Skepticism.*↓
       There are many skepticisms. The Universe is like an infinite series of planes, each of which is a false bottom, and when we think our feet are planted now at last on the Adamant, the slide is drawn out from under us.[138]

Value of the Skeptic is the resistance to premature conclusions. If he prematurely conclude, his conclusion will be shattered, & he will become malignant. But he must limit himself with the anticipation of law in the mutations, — flowing law.[139]

[107] The scholar blunders along on his own path for a time, assured by the surprise & joy of those to whom he first communicates his results; ⟨new⟩then new solitudes, new marches; but after a time on looking up, he finds the sympathy gone or changed, he fancies himself accused by all the bystanders; the faces of his friends are shaded by grief; and yet no tongue ever speaks of the cause. ⟨He⟩ There is some indictment out against him, on which he is arraigned in many counts, & he cannot learn the ⟨smallest⟩ charge. A prodigious power we have of begetting false expectations. These are the mistakes of others' subjectiveness. The true scholar will not heed them: Jump into another bush, & scratch your eyes in again. He passes on to acquit himself of their charges by developments as surprising [108] as was his first word, by indirections & wonderful *alibis* which dissipate the whole crimination[.]

No wonder a writer is rare. — It requires one inspiration or transmutation of nature into thought to yield him the truth; another inspiration to ⟨direct⟩ write it.

[137] Emerson's page reference is to *The Works of Edmund Spenser. With observations on his Life and Writings* (London, 1844), in his library. This paragraph, struck through in ink with a vertical use mark, is used in "Plato; or, the Philosopher," *W*, IV, 58–59.
[138] The second sentence is used in "The Preacher," *W*, X, 226.
[139] See p. [231] below.

[109] One service which this age has rendered to men, is, to make the life & wisdom of every past man accessible & available to all. Mahomet is no longer accursed; Voltaire is no longer the scarecrow: ⟨&⟩Plato ⁿ is no longer a pagan. Even Rabelais is citable[.] [140]

Economy.
Nobody need stir hand or foot, the custom of the country will do it all. I know not how to build or to plant, how to buy wood, nor what to do with the house lot or the field or the wood lot when bought. Never fear: it is ⟨as⟩all settled how it shall be, long beforehand, in the custom of the country; whether to sand or whether to clay it, when to plough, & how to ⟨manure⟩ ↑dress↓, & whether to grass or to corn: And you can not help or hinder it.[141]

[110]   ↑*Croisements.*↓
Symbols. The seashore, and the taste of two metals in contact, and our enlarged powers in the presence or rather at the approach & at the departure of a friend, and the mixture of lie in truth, and the experience of poetic creativeness which is not found in staying at home, nor yet in travelling, but in ⟨a⟩transitions from one to the other, which must therefore be adroitly managed to present as much transitional surface as possible. "A ride near the sea, a sail near the shore;" said the ancient.[142] So Montaigne travelled with his books, but did not read in them.
La nature aime les croisements, says Fourier.[143]

[111] The poem must be *tenax propositi*, the fable or myth must hold, or it is worth no man's while to read it. If a pilot swings his vessel from the wharf with one intention, &, after letting go, changes

[140] This paragraph, struck through in ink with a vertical use mark, is used in "Character," *W*, X, 110.
[141] This paragraph, struck through in pencil and ink with vertical use marks, is used in "Wealth," *W*, VI, 121.
[142] Cf. "Symposiacs," *Plutarch's Morals: . . . Translated from the Greek, by several hands . . .* , 1718, III, 244 ("That a Voyage near the Land, and a Walk near the Sea, is the best Recreation").
[143] These two paragraphs are used in "Inspiration," *W*, VIII, 289; "The seashore . . . as possible." is used in "Plato; or, the Philosopher," *W*, IV, 55–56. For the quotation from Fourier, see Journal U, p. [79] above, and p. [120] below.

his intention, & a vessel deceived by his first demonstrations is run
afoul of & injured, the pilot loses his branch. Certainly we must hold
the poet to as strict a law.[144]

[112]   ↑Winter apples.↓
The worst day is good for something. All that is not love, is
knowledge, and all that is not good today, is a store laid up for the
wants of distant days.

I am touched with nothing so much as ⟨the⟩ with words like these; —
"Yes, that is an example of a destiny springing from the character."
And again — "I ⟨always⟩ see your destiny hovering before you, but
it always escapes you."[145]

[113] ⟨In t⟩The faerie kingdom stands to men & women not as the
Angelic hierarchy above our heads, & with the same direction as we,
but feet to feet. And, in Faerieland, all things are reversed. Thus the
faeries are small, and they that are more powerful among them are
smaller than the commonalty, their energy increasing with their
parvitude. And the Faerie-king↑'s↓ ⟨is⟩chief title of honor is, *The
smallest of the small.*

Fate is found in the bill of the bird which determines tyrannically
its limits[.][146]

[114] ⟨You⟩ ↑The President of the Temperance Society↓ would think
it ⟨good⟩poetic justice, ⟨O president of the Temperance Society⟩ if
on every unlicensed tavern the word *Rum* should appear scrawled
in vast letters every morning, and ↑on trial it should be found that↓
no rasp or whitewash or paint would obliterate them, but on the first
refusal of the landlord to sell liquor, the letters should fade away,

[144] Cf. *JMN*, VIII, 366. The Latin is from Horace, *Odes*, III, iii, 1: "tenacious
of . . . purpose."
[145] Emerson attributed these observations to Margaret Fuller in *Memoirs of
Margaret Fuller Ossoli*, 2 vols. (Boston, 1852), I, 215. This paragraph is struck
through in ink with a vertical use mark.
[146] This sentence, struck through in ink with a vertical use mark, is used in
"Fate," *W*, VI, 9.

↑& become invisible,↓ and on ⟨the⟩ any attempt of the landlord to renew the sale of poison, R U M should instantly appear in ⟨bloodred⟩ ↑scarlet↓ letters all over the house. But this ⟨really⟩ ↑substantially↓ happens to ⟨certain⟩ ↑good↓ eyes.[147]

[115] Spartans, who wrote to be read, & spoke to be understood; whose laws were not written; ⟨whose⟩ ↑the↓ whole ⟨le⟩business of whose legislation was the bringing up of youth, whose ceilings were wrought with no tool but the axe, & the doors only with the saw. Leotychidas at Corinth asked "Whether trees grew square in that country?" Who planted the human seed in a beauty-bearing soil; whose king offered a sacrifice to the Muses, before a battle, whose aristocracy consisted in the enjoyment of leisure, being forbidden to exercise any mechanic trade; a little statue to the god of laughter in each eating hall; terrific pre-fourierites; bees; "if successful, for the public; if unsuccessful, for ourselves." Alas for the poor Helots with the Cryptia or ambuscade, — the price with ⟨th⟩which this grandeur was bought. The death of lawgivers should have its use, said Lycurgus & in exile & by his own act lay down in the red cloth & with the olive leaves of the dead. Other nations asked of them no other aid than a Spartan General. So Gylippus by the Sicilians, Brasidas by Chalcidians, [116] Lysander, Agesilaus, by the people of Asia[.]

See the excellent Life of Lycurgus in Plutarch[.] [148]

See also of their jaculation of sentences. *Taylor's* [*The Works of*] *Plato*. [1804,] Vol. V. p 136

[117] ⟨*Wisdo*⟩*Knowledge* is the straight line[;]
Wisdom is the power of the straight line, or, the Square;
Virtue is the power of the Square or the solid.

[147] This paragraph is struck through in ink with a vertical use mark.
[148] All of Emerson's statements about the Spartans are drawn from the "Life of Lycurgus" in the edition he owned, *Plutarch's Lives* . . . , trans. John and William Langhorne, 8 vols. (New York, 1822). The entry is struck through in pencil with a vertical use mark to the bottom of p. [115], and is used, down to "leaves of the dead.", in the lecture "The Superlative in Manners and Literature."

Thus my friend reads in the Cultivator on the method of planting & hoeing potatoes, or he follows a farmer ↑hoeing↓ along the row of potatoe hills; that is knowledge. At last, he takes the hoe in his hands & hoes the hills; the first, with care & heed, & pulls up every root of piper grass: as the ⟨gr⟩day grows hot, & the row is long, he says to himself, ⟨well⟩ ↑This is wisdom; but↓ⁿ one hill is like another, I have mastered the art, it is mere trifling to waste my ⟨time⟩ ↑strength↓ⁿ in doing many times the same thing: Why should I hoe more? And he desists.

But the last lesson was still unlearned: the moral power lay in the continuance; in fortitude, in [118] working against pleasure, to the excellent end & conquering all opposition. He has knowledge, he has wisdom, but he has missed Virtue, which he only acquires who endures routine & sweat & postponement of fancy to the achievment of a worthy end.[149]

"He had sharp white teeth, he was of great bulk, irascible, sometimes savage, sometimes mild. He rolled his eyes with rage sometimes he danced, sometimes he laughed aloud, sometimes he stood wrapped in meditation, sometimes he sang, & he was endowed with wisdom, dispassion, power, penance, truth, fortitude, dominion & selfknowledge
he created wealth & influence from the pores of his skin"

[119] ↑Native Americans.↓

I hate the narrowness of the Native American party. It is ⟨a⟩the dog in the manger. It ↑is↓ precisely opposite to all the dictates of love & magnanimity: & therefore, of course, opposite to true wisdom. It is the result of science that the highest simplicity of structure is produced, not by few elements, but by the highest complexity. Man is the most composite of all creatures, the wheel-insect, *volvox globator*, is at the beginning.[150] Well, as in the old burning of the Temple at Corinth, by the melting & intermixture of silver & gold & other metals, a new compound more precious than any, called the Corinthian Brass, was formed so in this Continent, — asylum of all nations, the energy of Irish, Germans, Swedes, Poles, & ⟨the⟩Cossacks,

---

[149] This entry is struck through in pencil with a vertical use mark.
[150] "It is the result . . . beginning." is used in "Goethe," *W*, IV, 290.

& all the [120] European tribes, — of the Africans, & of the Poly-
nesians, will construct a new race, a new religion, a new State, a new
literature, which will be as vigorous as the new Europe which came
out of the smelting pot of the Dark Ages, or that which earlier
emerged from the Pelasgic & Etruscan barbarism.

La Nature aime les croisements.[151]

[121] A dot appears in the wheel animalcule & then it becomes two
⟨new &⟩ perfect animalcules. ⟨w⟩The ever⟨las⟩ proceeding detachment
appears not less in all thought & in society. Children cannot live
without their parents; but long before we or they are aware of it,
the black dot has appeared, & the detachment taken place. Any
accident, any conversation, will now reveal to them their indepen-
dence.[152]

[122] The anger of god is better than the mercy of men.

Fascination of Swedenborg
His brilliant treatment of nat[ural]. phil[osophy].[153]

It is not possible, said Socrates, to cover fire with a garment, or sin
with time.

Swedenborg is like a bear who fattens in the dark & the cold[.][154]

[123] "Any thing, child, that the mind covets, from the ⟨husk⟩
↑milk↓ of a cocoa to the throne of the three worlds, may be obtained
by propitiating Vishnu."[155]   ↑Continued p 127↓

[151] This line is in pencil. See Journal U, p. [79] above and p. [110] above.
[152] This paragraph, struck through in pencil and ink with vertical use marks, is
used in "Uses of Great Men," W, IV, 30.
[153] "Fascination of . . . phil." is in pencil.
[154] This entry is in pencil.
[155] The Vishńu Puráńa . . . , 1840, pp. 88–89, where, however, "from the
. . . three worlds," does not occur. The quotation is used in the lecture "The Superlative in Manners and Literature" and "Poetry and Imagination," W, VIII, 42,
where Emerson ended it differently: "by keeping the law of thy members and the
law of thy mind." See p. [195] below.

I find in Plato the same absence of an energetic national faith which we deplore nowadays. Jupiter and the Olympian family have a quite mythologic air, nowise a modern & affecting character.

[124] Swedenborg perceived the central life of each object & saw the change of appearance as it passed before different eyes. He does not seem to have seen with equal clearness the necessity of progression or onwardness in each creature. Metamorphosis is the law of the Universe. All forms are fluent and as the bird alights on the bough & pauses for rest, then plunges into the air again on its way, so the thoughts of God pause but for a moment in any form, but pass into a new form, as if by touching the earth again in burial, to acquire new energy.[156] A wise man is not deceived by the pause: he knows that it is momentary: he already foresees the new departure, and departure after departure, in long series. Dull people think they have [125] traced the matter far enough if they have reached the history of one of these temporary forms, which they describe as ⟨cl⟩fixed & final. Reminiscence

    Metamorphosis
    Equation or Balance
    Like to Like — Identity
    Inertia

A transient person

[126] A man should not be rich by having what is superfluous, but by having what is essential to him, like a manufacturer or engineer or astronomer who has a great capital invested in his costly apparatus. How to animate all his possessions?[n] If he have any not animated by his quality & energy, let him sell them & convert them into things nearer to his nature. Such a rich man excites no envy. He has no more than he needs or uses.

The reason why I wish to live near Boston, is, because I use Boston.

[156] "as the bird alights . . . in any form," is used in "Poetry and Imagination," *W*, VIII, 15.

Whilst Dhruva⟨'s mind⟩ ↑sat↓ entranced apart
Passed Vishnu into Dhruva's heart [157]

[127]   ↑See p. 123↓
"Whilst ⟨his⟩Dhruva's mind was absorbed in meditation, the mighty
Hari identical with all beings & all natures, took possession of his heart.
Vishnu being thus present in his mind, the earth the supporter of elemental life could not sustain the weight of the ascetic. As he stood upon
his left foot, one hemisphere bent beneath him, & when he stood upon his
right, the other half of the earth sunk down." [*The Vishńu Puráńa . . . . ,*
1840, p. 90]

> See in this short passage the depravation effected by
> simply passing a bold trope into popular use as literal
> fact. A poet describes ⟨a⟩the powers of contemplation;
> a fanatic seizes the words, & goes to standing first on one
> leg, then on the other, a week at a time, to propitiate
> a god. &

[128] One ⟨negative evidence contradicts⟩ ↑dissenter countervails↓ a
thousand assenters. Swedenborg's ⟨doctrine⟩ theology does well as
long as it is repeated to & by those who are wont to accept something
positive, & find this as likely to be true as their own. But when I hear
it, I say, ⟨I⟩All this is nothing to me. ⟨Why do you speak so much⟩
The more coherent & elaborate your system, the less I like it. ↑I say
with the Spartan↓ "Why do you speak so much to the purpose concerning that which is nothing to the purpose?" The intricacy & in-
genuity of your insanity makes you only the harder to be undeceived.[158] This is the excess of form. The fallacy seems to be in the
equivocal use of the term *The Word.* In the high & sacred sense of
that term used ⟨as⟩ by a strong Oriental rhetoric for the energy of
[129] the Supreme Cause [in act,] all that is predicated of it, is true:
it is equivalent to Reason.
But this being granted, theologians shift the ⟨sense of the⟩[n] word
from this grand sense to signify a written sentence of St Matthew

[157] These lines are in pencil. See the quotation directly below for the sentence
from *The Vishńu Puráńa* Emerson is versifying.
[158] "One ⟨negative evidence . . . undeceived" is struck through in pencil with
a vertical use mark; "The more coherent . . . purpose?' " is used in "Swedenborg,"
W, IV, 135–136.

or St John, and instantly assume for this wretched ↑written↓ sentence all that was granted to be true of the Divine Reason.

———

Concerning the sentimentalism of the Unitarians.
Seer of productive forms
The sight of youth is seminal and generative: all its objects are productive.

[130] "All this world is but the transmutation of oblations." [159]

———

↑*Timing*↓
What will we have? This only, a good timing of things. The waters become solid, but not now when we want to cross them. Honey is stored in the flower, & in the hollow tree by bees; but not when I am hungry in my chamber, the road, or the field, do the flowers collect themselves, or do I see the tree. I pass full through a field of corn. The bread moulds in loaded granaries. When I am hungry, I cannot go back so far. When I am in the woods I am warm; when I am cold & wish sticks to burn I have arrived where no trees are. When I am listless, thoughts come crowding on my brain & each hinders the remembrance of the other. So do friends come when I would be [131] alone, & come not when they would refresh me.

"Unseasonable love is like hate"   Socrates ap. Stobaeus

"All things are good & fair to those things wherewith they agree, but ill & deformed in respect of those things with which they agree not."
                    Socrates ap Xenoph. Memorabil[ia]. [III, viii, 7] [160]

———

What is strength? The motion of the soul with the body. *Soc. in Stob.*[161]

[132] [162] ↑Philosophy↓
Unity or Identity, & Variety. The poles of philosophy. It makes

[159] *The Vishńu Puráńa* . . . , 1840, p. 100. This quotation is struck through in ink with two vertical use marks, a diagonal use mark, and a wavy diagonal use mark. See p. [259] below.
[160] See p. [207] below.
[161] This entry is struck through in ink with a diagonal use mark. See p. [207] below.
[162] Erased pencil writing covers the upper half of this page. It is canceled by

haste to develop these two. A too rapid Unity or unification & a too exclusive devotion to parts are the Scylla & Charybdis. A too rapid Unity[:] Yes, for a⟨n⟩ wise Skepticism, a long secular patience that delays & still delays the premature summation[,] is rewarded with truth perhaps in another sphere & cycle. This rashness or partiality is one Vice; the other is confusion, or the misplacing the properties of the planes or spheres of nature.
⟨Y⟩As[n] the mind describes Deity by simple purification of its own self, Indian mythology creates nature from the parts of human body. A gigantic crystal

[133] Every man who would do any thing well must come to it from a higher ground, and a philosopher must be much more than a philosopher. Plato is a poet.

↑Rachel.↓ But Rachel possesses a certain demoniacal power which is worthy of wonder. You feel in her veiled & nowise resonant voice, in her measured & earnest acting, & in her majestic delivery, that she is incessantly brooding on this inward raging fire. But this bursts up at decisive moments[.] [163]

[134][164]   ↑Vishnu Purana.↓
"From thine eyes come the sun; from thine ears the wind; & from thy mind the moon; heaven from thy head; the earth from thy feet. As the bark & leaves of the plantain tree are to be seen in its stem, so thou art the stem of the Universe, & all things are visible in thee." ↑"identical with the atmosphere, pure, illimitable, shapeless, separating all creatures —"↓ "To Vishnu, to that supreme ⟨form⟩being who is one with time, whose first forms, though he be without form are day & evening & night, be adoration" [pp. 94, 108–109]

---

swirling pencil lines which are also erased. The following significant words have been recovered: "daemoniacal"; "earnest"; "moments"; and "misplacing" (perhaps a version of the entry headed "Rachel." on p. [133] below).

[163] This entry, which except for "Rachel." is in pencil, must be later than the surrounding material, since Emerson first saw the French actress Rachel (Elisa Félix) in Paris in May, 1848 (L, IV, 73, 75, 77, 79).

[164] This page is struck through in pencil with a vertical use mark to "Vishnu's attributes p. 109, 144 158".

[Enumeration of Vishnu's attributes p. 109, 144 158]
  Vishnu means *entrance* & *pervading*
See also p 249
        253   flute
        255
        257   you & I
        340   Skepticism

[135₁]¹⁶⁵   Close close to men   [23]
            [*1 w*] undulating [*1 w*] of air
            Right [*3–4 w*]   [25]
            [*2 w*] plain of Daemons spreads
            Stands to each human [*2–3 w*]
            F… watch & ward & furtherance
            [*1–2 w*] snares of …'s dance
            And his[?] lustre [*2–3 w*]   [30]
            [*1 w*] -asci… [*1 w*] youthful ⟨–⟩heart
            B… from [*1–2 w*] ↑count…↓
            T-a… thr… [*1 w*] …ta… [*1 w*]
            Is the D… [*1–2 w*] face
            To [*3–4 w*] …es   [35]
            A [*3–4 w*] hovers
            Over [*2–3 w*] head
            And [*3–4 w*] low as to her eyes

            [*unrecovered*]   [?]
            [*3–4 w*] the Dae… sphere   [40]
            [*2–3 w*] that swiftly [*2–3 w*] go
            Leave no track on the heavenly snow
            Sometimes [*2–3 w*] …ad bends
            And the mighty c… descends
            And the brains of men thenceforth   [45]

---

¹⁶⁵ Printed in continuous sequence here is the erased pencil writing which covers pp. [135]–[137] and an additional line at the top of p. [138]. The ink entries on these pages are printed as pp. [135₂]–[138₂] below. The lines are a version of much of the second section ("The Daemonic Love") of "Initial, Daemonic, and Celestial Love," *W*, IX, 110–112.

[136₁]   In crowded [1–2 w] still[?] resorts
             Teem [2–3 w] ···oughts
             As when [3–4 w] ···eteors
             Cross [1 w] orbit of [1–2 w]
             And lit by f··· air   [50]
             Blaze near & far
             [1 w] the [1–2 w] ···ight
             ···d s··· their sacred bars
             And [2–3 w] men [1 w] night
             [2–3 w] ···nn···g -t···   [?]

             Beauty of[?] [1–2 w] vein[?]   [56]
             Grace [1–2 w] subtler str···
             These [3–4 w] lend
             And the shrinking [1 w] extend
             S··· [3–4 w]   [?]
             [1 w] ···gth [1 w] terror[?] [1–2 w]   [61]

             From[?] [3–4 w] ···ing   [?]
             [unrecovered]   [?]
             The [3–4 w] speaking   [64]
             They [2–3 w]   [?]
             And their votaries[?] unkind   [x]
[137₁]   [3–4 w] not [1 w]   [?]
             The erring [1–2 w] made love blind   [68]
             Love who shines on all
             Him radiant sharpest sighted god   [70]
             None can bewilder
             Whose [1 w] ↑rays↓ pierce [1–2 w]
             The Un···se
             Path find··· [1–2 w]
             Mediator [1–2 w]   [75]
             W··· ever[?] bu··· a ···d   [?]
             [1 w] Daemon [2–3 w]   [?]
             [1–2 w] ···all   [?]
             Himself en··· [2–3 w]   [94]
             Solitude in[?] solitude   [95]

                         306

[*1 w*] like sort [*1 w*] love doth fall
He [*3–4 w*]   [?]
He [*2–3 w*] fame and mark   [?]
He [*2–3 w*]   [?]
of[?] [*3–4 w*]   [?]
[*unrecovered*]   [?]
The [*2–3 w*] fortuna--   [98]
And [*3–4 w*]   [?]
And the souls of ample fate   [100]
[138₁]   [⟨*1 w*⟩] ↑Minions↓ of the morning star   [102]

[135₂] Sublime ethics of the *Vishnu P.* p 132, 135, 136, 137, ⟨158⟩
Thus, p. 137 "Whatever power I possess, said Prahláda, is neither
the result of magic rites nor is it inseparable from my nature it is no
more than that which is possessed by all in whose hearts Achyuta
abides. He who meditates ↑not of↓ wrong to others, but considers
them as himself is free from the effects of sin inasmuch as the cause
does not exist; but he who inflicts pain upon others in act, thought,
or speech, sows the seed of future birth, & the fruit that awaits him
after ⟨future⟩ birth is pain. I wish no evil to any, & do & speak no
offence; for I behold Kesava in all beings as in my own soul." [166]

[136₂] "Om! ⟨|| ... ||⟩Glory to thee, lord who art subtile & sub-
stantial; mutable & immutable; perceptible & imperceptible; divisible &
indivisible; indefinable & definable; subject of attributes & void of attributes; abiding in qualities though they abide not in thee; morphous
& amorphous; minute & vast; visible & invisible; hideousness & beauty;
cause & effect; existence & nonexistence; thou who art both one & many!
large & small," &c   Vishnu Purana p 144

He that plucks a leaf or treads on a worm is guilty of Brahmanicide [167]
[p. 238, paraphrased]

Emancipation from *existence*, they say, is the Indian beatitude. I think
it intends emancipation from *organization*.[168]

---

[166] "for I behold . . . soul.' " is used in "Character," *W*, X, 120.
[167] See p. [161] below.
[168] This entry is struck through in ink with two vertical use marks. Cf. "Plato;
or, the Philosopher," *W*, IV, 51.

[137₂] "he put a pebble in his mouth (i.e. that he might not eat or ⟨drink⟩ speak.) & ↑naked↓ went the way of all flesh" [*Vishṅu*] Purana p 163 [paraphrased]

Emancipation, is that which the sage seeks. He looks upon heavenly fruition as an impediment to felicity. He seeks final emancipation; "He whose mind is devoted to Hari in silent prayer, burnt offering, or adoration, is impatient even of the glory of the King of the gods. Of what avail is ascent to the summit of heaven, if it is necessary to return from thence to earth." [*Ibid.*,] p[p. 210–]211

"Heaven or Swerga is that which delights the ↑pure↓ mind. Hell is that which gives it pain: hence vice is called hell, virtue is called heaven. That which at one time is a source of enjoyment becomes at another the cause of [138₂] suffering. It follows that nothing is in itself either pleasurable or painful & pleasure & pain & the like are merely definitions of various states of mind. That which alone is truth is wisdom but wisdom may be the cause of confinement to existence, for all this universe is wisdom; there is nothing different from it & consequently both knowledge & ignorance are comprised in wisdom" [*Ibid.*,] p 211

> Beauty of a richer vein   [56]
> Grace of a subtler strain
> These to men & wisdom lend
> And the shrinking sky extend
> So is man's narrow path   [60]
> By strength & terror skirted
> Also now may the wrath
> Of the ⟨De⟩Genii be averted
> Thy song the truth unwelcome speaking
> They are self seeking   [65]
> And their sons unkind.[169]   [x]

[139] The Indian widow burns herself on her husband's funeral pile, because she believes in Transmigration; & being born again, i⟨n⟩f faithful, in a form not less than the last, retains enough memory to

---

[169] These lines, the first of which lies under the last line of the previous entry, are in pencil. All but the last line occur in the second section ("The Daemonic Love") of "Initial, Daemonic, and Celestial Love," *W*, IX, 111. An erased pencil version of the lines occurs on p. [136₁] above.

find her husband in his new form, though a dog, or a jackal, or a wolf, &, by affectionate speech recals to him also his memory & ⟨his pr⟩ exhorts him to devest his present unworthy weeds. In the long rotation by fidelity they meet again in worthy forms.[170]

Knowing the heart of the dice

[140] Hari! smallest of the least, & largest of the large; all, & knowing all things;
thou art accentuation, ritual signification, metre, & astronomy
history, tradition, grammar, logic, & law;
without name or color or hands or feet, thou hearest without ears
and seest without eyes
⟨one & multiform⟩
thou movest without feet
thou seizest without hands
atom of atoms
thou whom no acts affect
Thou art the gods, Yakshas, demons, saints, serpents, choristers & dancers of heaven
goblins, men, animals, birds, reptiles, plants, stones, earth, water, fire, sky, wind, sound, touch, taste, colour, flavour, mind, intellect, soul, time, & the qualities of nature
thou art all these & the chief object of them all
Thou art the performance & the discontinuance of acts, the enjoyer & the fruit of all acts & the means by which they are accomplished
[141] All kinds of substances with or without shape here or elsewhere are the body of Vishnu. I am Hari. All that I behold is Janarddana. Cause & effect are from none other than from him[.][171]

[142]   ↑Commercial value.↓
Take away ⟨instantly⟩ those peaches from under ⟨that⟩ ↑the↓ tree. Carry them ⟨only so far as to be⟩ out of sight of the tree, & their

---

[170] Emerson recalls the story of Satadhanu and his queen, Saivya, as told in *The Vishńu Puráńa* . . . , 1840, pp. 342–344. See p. [160] below.
[171] Emerson has amalgamated a number of passages from *The Vishńu Puráńa* . . . , 1840, pp. 495–496, 141, and 159. See p. [203] below.

value is enhanced a thousandfold to all eyes. That is the main consideration in fruit[,] to put the tree out of sight.¹⁷² Drop your penknife or pencil case on the ground: what a ⟨new⟩ costliness it wears in that unaccustomed place! Bread & butter, say housekeepers, ⟨is always⟩ ↑relishes↓ better away from home. "Another's wine," said Diogenes.¹⁷³ Jugglery, or the order of wonder[,] ⟨always⟩ consists in putting the tree out of sight[.]

[143]¹⁷⁴ There were Swedenborgs in those days[,] Missouriums, Mastodons of literature, not to be measured by a whole population of modern scholars[.]¹⁷⁵

Every genius is defended from approach by great quantities of unavailableness. Good only for himself. What property! says the hungry mind as it sees it afar, and swims toward it as a fish to its food[.]¹⁷⁶

We
All atoms have hooks & eyes[.]

People who live together grow alike & if they should live long enough we should not know them apart.¹⁷⁷

[144]¹⁷⁸ Jones Very ⟨was⟩is like the rain[,] plentiful. He does not

¹⁷² "Take away . . . out of sight" is struck through in ink with a vertical use mark; cf. "Wealth," *W*, VI, 87. See Journal O, p. [53] below.
¹⁷³ According to Diogenes Laertius, *Lives of Eminent Philosophers*, Bk. vi, sec. 54, this was Diogenes' answer to the question "what wine he found pleasant to drink."
¹⁷⁴ The entries on this page are in pencil.
¹⁷⁵ This sentence, struck through in pencil with a vertical use mark, is used in "Swedenborg," *W*, IV, 103.
¹⁷⁶ This paragraph is struck through in pencil with a vertical use mark; "Every genius . . . unavailableness." is used in "Uses of Great Men," *W*, IV, 27.
¹⁷⁷ This sentence, struck through in pencil with a vertical use mark, is used in "Uses of Great Men," *W*, IV, 25.
¹⁷⁸ A newspaper clipping measuring 9.3 x 9.3 cm is laid in loose between pp. [144]–[145]. Taken from a German newspaper published in New York (as determined by advertisements on the back), it is datelined "Thorn, 2 April." and describes the deportation of "polnische Insurgenten" from Prussia — perhaps during the Polish uprising against Russian rule in February, 1846.

love individuals: he is annoyed by edge. He likes only community; &
he ⟨|| ... ||⟩likes the lowness also, if it be community. I like sharp salts.
Strength is wonderful. Are the days great? [179] ☞

Some men think their goodness made of themselves, others think the
reverse. See the Indian *Self.*   Y

Once the earth fed them, it was sweet to the taste; now life does not
feed ⟨t⟩Man; the men die therefore; nothing but their bodies lives.[180]

Men think their goodness made of themselves. Others think the
reverse[.] [181]

[145] ↑*Days.*↓
        Every age has its objects & symbol, & every man. Why not then
every epoch of our life its own; & a man should journey through his
own zodiack of signs.[182]

        The flame of the funeral pile is cool to the widow[.]
To this practical doctrine of Migration we have nothing correspond-
ing. Ours is sentimental & literary[.] [183]

Indian mythology a lace veil, clouds of legends, but the old forms
seen through. We should infer a country of sages & devotees; but
there seems no relation between the book & the actual population.
        One thing marks it all, the Fate in the character. As soon as they
confront each other, victory is declared without a struggle. It is by
posts[,] not battles.[184]

---

[179] This entry was written first in pencil, then in ink. In the pencil version,
Emerson used "you" instead of "Jones Very" and "he", with the second person verb
form, and something unrecovered stood in place of "Strength is wonderful." The
hand sign points to the first entry on p. [145].
        [180] This entry was written first in pencil, with "to the taste" omitted, then in ink.
        [181] This entry is in pencil.
        [182] This entry was written first in pencil, then in ink.
        [183] These three sentences are in pencil. "The flame of . . . the widow", which also
occurs on p. [160] below, is used in the lecture "The Superlative in Manners and
Literature" (see *W*, X, 547).
        [184] These two paragraphs were written first in pencil, then in ink. In the pencil
version, "present themselves" is canceled before "confront each other".

[146] Things always bring their own philosophy with them, that is, prudence. England is the country of property & of selfishness. Sensible people[,] it is said[,] are selfish. Sensuous are. In India, — king, courtier, god, are represented as making the most romantic sacrifices, — kingdom, goods, life itself, for knowledge & spiritual power. In France, — wit, science, personal ability, — counts for more than in England. In England possession in every kind counts for more than person.[185]

"To diminish his intensity, Viswakarman placed the sun on his lathe to grind off some of his effulgence, & in this manner reduced it to an eighth: more [147] was inseparable." Vi Purana, p. 267

The sun is bright by the jewel called Syamantaka, ↑quintessence of the worlds.↓ He took it off his neck at the request of Satrajit, who wore it home on his neck. The jewel deposited in his house yielded daily eight loads of gold, & through its marvellous virtue dispelled all fear of portents, wild beasts, fire & famine. It was the peculiar property of this jewel that, whilst it was an inexhaustible source of good to a virtuous person, yet worn by a man of bad character, it was the cause of his death.

V[ishńu]. P[uráńa]. p[p]. [425–]426. [partly paraphrased]
Is the gem power, official power?

Lycurgus, Pythagoras, Plato, all poets, all women believe in the plasticity or Education of man, but the whig world is very incredulous.

[148]   Oct. 27.
In this finest of all Indian summer days it seems sad that each of us can only spend it once. We sigh for the thousand heads & thousand bodies of the Indian gods, that we might celebrate its immense beauty in many ways & places, & absorb all its good.[186]

Trace these colossal conceptions of Buddhism & of Vedantism home, and they are always the necessary or structural action of the human

[185] "Things always bring . . . selfishness." and "In England . . . person." are struck through in ink with vertical use marks; cf. "Montaigne," W, IV, 152.
[186] This paragraph, struck through in pencil with a vertical use mark, is used in "Uses of Great Men," W, IV, 12.

mind. Buddhism ⟨or⟩ ↑read literally is↓ the tenet of Fate; Worship & Morals, or the tenet of freedom[,] are the unalterable originals in all the wide variety of geography, language, & intelligence of the human tribes. The buyer thinks he has a new article; [149] but if he goes to the factory, there is the selfsame old loom as before, the same mordaunts & colours, the same blocks even; but by a little splicing & varying the parts of old patterns, what passes for new is produced.[187]

↑Fate↓

The Indian ⟨‖ . . . ‖⟩system is full of fate, the Greek not. The Greek uses the word indeed, but in his mind the Fates are three respectable old women who spin & shear a symbolic thread, so narrow[,] so limitary is the sphere allowed them[,] & it is with music. We are only at a more beautiful opera ↑or at private theatricals↓. But in India, it is the dread reality, it is the cropping out in our planted gardens of the core of the world: it is the abysmal Force untameable & immense. They who wrestle with Hari, see their doom in his eye before the fight begins[.] [188]

[150]   ↑Skeptic↓
In the V. Purana it is a vice "a man by selfish desires devoted to his family." [189]

[151] [blank]
[152] As for King Swedenborg I object to his cardinal position in Morals that evils should be shunned as sins. I hate preaching. I shun evils as evils. Does he not know — Charles Lamb did, — that every poetic mind is a pagan, and to this day prefers Olympian Jove, Apollo,

---

[187] This paragraph is struck through in pencil with a vertical use mark. "Trace these colossal . . . mind." and "The buyer thinks . . . blocks even;" are used in "Uses of Great Men," *W*, IV, 4–5.
    [188] "it is the dread . . . world:", struck through in ink with a vertical use mark, is used in "Fate," *W*, VI, 19.
    [189] Emerson may be recalling the story of Saubhari, who renounced his excessive fondness for his family and became an ascetic; see *The Vishńu Puráńa* . . . , 1840, pp. 366–368.

& the Muses & the Fates, to all the barbarous indigestion of Calvin & the Middle Ages? [190]

Great King is King Swedenborg. I will not deny him his matchless length & breadth.[191] Such a world of mathematics, metallurgy, astronomy, anatomy, ecclesiastic history, theology, demonology, ouranology, love, fear, terror, form, law, all to come out of that quiet sleepy old gentleman with the gold headed cane, lodging at Mr Shearsmith's!

[153] He is a theoretic or speculative man whom no practical man in the Universe could scorn. Plato is a gownsman; the ⟨purple⟩ robe, though of purple, & almost skywoven, is yet an academic robe, & would hinder the rapid action, if need were, with its voluminous folds. But Swedenborg is awful to Caesar. Lycurgus himself would bow. — [192]

As for "shunning evils as sins," I ⟨like better⟩ prefer the ethics of the Vishnu: see beyond; p. 166   ↑and also, above, p 135,↓ [193]

Too much form, O Swedenborg! too many steps, too much dogma, too much government. I see not that the soul can have need of eloquence, said Confutsee[.] [194]

Addenda to Swedenborg Lecture
p 234, 83
V 73, 132,[195]

[154] We are very clumsy writers of history. We tell the chronicle of parentage, birth, birthplace, schooling, companions, ⟨pr⟩ acquisition of property, marriage, publication of books, celebrity, & death, and when we have come to an end of ⟨tru⟩this external

---

[190] This paragraph is struck through in ink with a vertical use mark; "his cardinal . . . as sins" is used in "Swedenborg," *W*, IV, 137.

[191] These two sentences are struck through in ink with a vertical use mark.

[192] This paragraph, struck through in ink with a vertical use mark, is used in "Swedenborg," *W*, IV, 123–124.

[193] "As for . . . Vishnu:" is struck through in ink with a vertical use mark; cf. "Swedenborg," *W*, IV, 137–138.

[194] See *JMN*, VI, 387, for the original wording of this statement by Confucius as quoted from *The Phenix; A Collection of Old and Rare Fragments* (New York, 1835), p. 101.

[195] These three lines are in pencil.

history, the reader is no whit instructed, no ray of relation appears between all this lumber & the goddess-born, and it really appears as if[,] had we dipped at random into the modern Plutarch ⟨& read⟩ or Universal Biography, & read any other life there, it would have fitted to the poems quite as well. It is the very essence of Poetry to spring like the rainbow daughter of Wonder from the invisible: to abolish the Past, & refuse all history. Dyce & Collier[,] Malone & Warburton have exhausted their life in vain. The builders of the Theatres[,] [155] proprietors of the Covent Garden & Haymarket & Drury Lane[,] of Park & Tremont[,] have wrought in vain. Garrick, Kean, Kemble, & Macready dedicate in various ways their lives to this Genius, him they adorn or would fain help adorn, elucidate, obey, & express. The Genius knows not of them. The moment we come at last to hear one golden word, it leaps out immortal from all this wretched mortality and sweetly torments us with invitations to its own inaccessible homes. I remember I came to the city once to hear Macready's Hamlet and all I now remember of that master was ↑that in which the master had no part,↓ simply the magical expression,

> Revisit'st now the glimpses of the Moon
>   [*Hamlet*, I, iv, 53]

What can any biography biographize the wonderful world into which the Midsummer Night's dream admits [155½₁] me? Did Shakspeare confide to any Notary or Parish Recorder[,] sacristan or surrogate in ⟨t⟩Stratford upon Avon[,] the genesis of that delicate creation?[n] The forest of Arden⟨nes⟩, the air of Scone Castle, the moonlight of Portia's villa; where is the ↑third↓ cousin or grandnephew[,] the prompter's[n] book or private letter that has heard one word of those transcendant secrets? Shakspeare is the only biographer of Shakspeare. And ah[̄ what can Shakspeare tell in any way but to the Shakspeare in us?[n] He cannot any more stoop from off his [155⅔] tripod & give us anecdotes of his inspirations. Read now the laborious results of years of D[yce] & Collier — read, one sentence at a time.
And now

> my delicate Ariel [*The Tempest*, IV, i, 49]

> or

mandragora [*Othello*, III, iii, 330; *Antony and Cleopatra*, I, v, 4]
or

bleak virtue's bones [Cf. *All's Well that Ends Well*, I, i, 114–115]
or

Shackle accident & bolt up change [*Antony and Cleopatra*, V, ii, 6]

In fine it is very certain that the genius draws up the ladder after him when the creative age goes up to heaven, & gives way to a new, who see the works & ask vainly for a history. Your criticism is profane. Shakspeare by Shakspeare. Poet in his interlunatim is a critic.[196]

[155½] Plato shows for example that Realism[,] which ↑proceeds↓ from the idea of the unconditioned Essence or of absolute Unity, ⟨proceeds⟩ is as untenable as ⟨th⟩Dualism[,] which ↑contemplates↓ all in steady formation & alteration ⟨considers⟩, without ↑recognizing↓ a subsisting & firm and true Essence[.] [197]

[156] My dear friend — standing on his mountains of fact[,] whose strata,[n] ⟨of⟩ chemistry, meteors, landscape, counties, towns, meridian magnetism & what not he knows, asks me how all goes with me floating in obscure questions, musing on this & that metaphysical riddle? Well it is even so. I stay where I ↑can &↓ am peaceful & satisfied enough as long as no sentinel challenges me. I use no election of the questions that occupy me. No doubt I should feel a humiliation if I were wont to task myself for men, or to compute in any manner of political economy my day's work, but well assured that this Questioner who brings me so many Problems will bring the answers also in due time. Very rich, very potent, cheerful giver that he is, — he shall have it all his own way for me.[198]

[196] "We are very clumsy [p. [154]] . . . at a time." and "In fine it is . . . a critic." are struck through in ink with vertical use marks; "Did Shakspeare confide [p. [155½]] . . . at a time." and "In fine it is . . . a critic." are struck through in pencil with vertical use marks; all the marked passages are used in "Shakspeare," *W*, IV, 206–208.
[197] This entry, which is in pencil, appears at the top of p. [155½] above the continuation of the entry about Shakespeare.
[198] A partially erased pencil version of this entry underlies the ink version. The pencil version has "I stay where I am, do as I can &" for "I stay where I can &".

[159]¹⁹⁹ [blank]

[160] see p 18

Metempsychosis
Transmigration
Metamorphosis
Proteus

"His very flight is presence in disguise" ²⁰⁰

In India, a practical doctrine full of love. The flame of the funeral pile is cool to the widow. Travelling through the path of the world by birth after birth, if true, she knows her own secret, that it, through what lives she came, & knows through all disguises, the life of her lover. She seeks him, & speaks to him, & makes him ashamed to tarry in unworthy masks: then he dies again, & at last they are both reborn in the right circumstance & caste.²⁰¹

Deity rushing into distribution in Timaeus²⁰²

[161] In its extravagance it becomes, "He that plucks a leaf, or treads on a worm, is guilty of Brahminicide." ²⁰³

[162]   ↑Amalgam↓
The absolutist is good & blessed though he dies ⟨in⟩without the sight of that paradise he journeys after; & he can forgive the earth-worms who remain immersed in matter & know not the felicities he seeks. But not so well can he dispose of the middle man who receives and assents to his theories & yet[,] by habit & talent formed to live in the existing order, builds & prospers among the worldly men, extending his affection & countenance all the time to the absolutists. Ah thou evil two-faced half & half! how can I forgive thee? Evil, evil hast thou done. Thou it is that confoundest all distinctions. If

¹⁹⁹ Emerson inadvertently omitted pp. [157]–[158] in his numbering of this journal.
²⁰⁰ This quotation is struck through in ink with three vertical use marks. See p. [83] above and Journal O, p. [92] below.
²⁰¹ For the source of Emerson's story, see p. [139] above. For the source of "Travelling thro' . . . birth after birth," see p. [20] above; see also p. [89] above. "The flame of . . . the widow." occurs also on p. [145] above.
²⁰² See Journal V, p. [59] above.
²⁰³ See p. [136] above.

thou didst not receive the truth at all, thou couldst do the cause of [163] virtue no harm. But now the men of selfishness say to the absolutist, Behold this man, he has all thy truth, yet lo! he is with us & ours. — Ah thou damnable Half-and-half! choose, I pray you, between God & the whig party, and do not longer strew sugar on this bottled spider.

Yes: But Confucius. Confucius[,] glory of the nations, Confucius[,] sage of the absolute East, was a middleman. He is the Washington of philosophy, the moderator, the Μηδεν αγαν [204] of modern history.

Also, this is not any body's choice, but this double sympathy is born; this hated amalgam comes into the world, a natural & permanent power.

[164] [blank]
[165] Vishnu Purana

"As the young Sal-tree by its beauty declares the excellence of the juices which it has imbibed from the earth, so when the Eternal has taken up his abode in the bosom of any one, that man is lovely amidst the beings of this world." p 288

"Who has been freed from fascination" * [205]

————

Kesava ⟨is most pleased with⟩ ↑approves↓ him who does good to others, who never utters untruth, who is always desirous of the welfare of all creatures, x ⟨x x⟩ — he best worships Vishnu, there is no other mode [*Ibid.*,] p. 291 [paraphrased]

[166] [206] "What wise man would feel hatred towards beings who are objects of compassion? Why should I cherish malignity towards those who are more prosperous than myself? I should rather sympathise with

*We familiarly say every body is a little cracked.   See infra ↑Y.↓ p 171 [207]

[204] "Nothing in excess" — one of the two mottoes in the temple at Delphi.
[205] This quotation is used in "Illusions," *W*, VI, 324.
[206] "Vishnu Purana" is written at the top of the page to the left.
[207] This footnote is in pencil.

318

their happiness; for the suppression of malignant feelings is of itself a reward. If beings are hostile, & indulge in hatred, they are objects of pity to the wise, as encompassed by profound delusion." [*Ibid.*,] p 132

"The whole world is but a manifestation of Vishnu, who is identical with all things, & it is therefore to be regarded by the wise as not differing from but as the same with themselves. Let us therefore lay aside the angry passions of our race, & so strive that we may obtain that perfect, pure, & eternal happiness which shall be beyond the power of the elements or their deities, of fire, of [167] the sun, of the moon, of wind, of Indra, of the regent of the sea," &c &c [*Ibid.*,] p. 133 [208]

"What living creature slays or is slain? What living creature preserves or is preserved? Each is his own destroyer or preserver, as he follows evil or good." [*Ibid.*,] p. 135 [209]

"but I, father, know neither friends nor foes." [210] [*Ibid.*, p. 139]

"that is active duty which is not for our bondage; that is knowledge which is for our liberation; all other duty is good only unto weariness." [*Ibid.*,] p 139 [211]

"What the great end of all is, you shall, monarch, briefly learn from me. It is soul: one (in all bodies) pervading, uniform, perfect, preeminent over nature, exempt from ⟨youth⟩birth, growth, & decay, omnipresent, undecaying, made up of true knowledge, independent, & unconnected with unrealities, [168] [212] with name, species, & the rest, in time past, present, or to come. The knowledge that this spirit which is essentially one, is in one's own & ↑in↓ all other bodies, is the great end or true wisdom of one who knows the unity & the true principles of things. As one diffusive air passing through the perforations of a flute, is distinguished as the notes of a scale, so the nature of the great spirit is single, tho' its forms be manifold, arising from the consequences of acts. When the difference of the investing form, as that of god or the rest, is destroyed, there is no distinction." [*Ibid.*,] p. 253 [213]

[208] " 'The whole world . . . eternal happiness" is struck through in pencil with a vertical use mark; " 'The whole world . . . themselves." is used in "Plato; or, the Philosopher," *W*, IV, 50.

[209] Emerson versified this quotation on p. [266] below.

[210] This quotation is used in "Character," *W*, X, 120.

[211] This quotation, struck through in ink with a vertical use mark, is used in "Swedenborg," *W*, IV, 138.

[212] "Vishnu Purana" is written at the top of the page to the left.

[213] This quotation, struck through in pencil and ink with vertical use marks, is used in "Plato; or, the Philosopher," *W*, IV, 50.

"I neither am going nor coming nor is my dwelling in any one place nor art thou, thou; nor are others, others; nor am I, I." [214] [*Ibid.,* p. 255]

[169] The doctrine of the Triform came from India, as did the poetic horror that the ⟨gods in heave⟩ demons in hell had that tremendous power of vision that they saw through all intermediate regions & worlds the great & happy gods moving in heaven; whilst the heavenly souls were also made to know their own felicity by discerning the infernal spaces. [Cf. *ibid.,* pp. 209–210]

[170] [blank]
[171] [215] "Thou art all bodies. This thy illusion beguiles all who are ignorant of thy true nature, the fools who imagine soul to be in that which is not spirit. The notions that 'I am, — this is mine,' which influence mankind, are but delusions of the mother of the world, originating in thy active agency. Those men who attentive to their spiritual duties, worship thee, traverse all this illusion, & obtain spiritual freedom." [*Ibid.,*] p[p].
[584–]585
It is the sport of thy fascinations that induces men to glorify thee, to obtain the continuance of their race, or the annihilation of their enemies,[n] instead of eternal liberation. Dispel, o lord of all creatures, the conceit of knowledge which proceeds from ignorance. [216] [*Ibid.,* p. 585]

[172] [217] Story of the Parijata tree "the smell of which perfumed the earth for three furlongs & an approach to which enabled every one to recollect the events of a prior existence." [*Ibid.,*] p 589

"Since you, Sankara, have given a boon unto Bana, let him live: from respect to your promises, my discus is arrested. The assurance of safety granted by you is granted also by me. You are fit to apprehend that you are not distinct from me. That which I am, thou art, and that also is this world, with its gods, & demons, & mankind. Men contemplate distinctions because they are stupefied by ignorance" [*Ibid.,*] p 596 [218]

[214] This quotation, struck through in ink with a vertical use mark, is used in "Plato; or, the Philosopher," *W,* IV, 50.
[215] "Vishnu Purana" is written at the top of the page to the left.
[216] "The notions that . . . of the world," and "Dispel, o lord . . . ignorance." are used in "Illusions," *W,* VI, 324.
[217] "Vishnu Purana" is written at the top of the page to the left.
[218] "You are fit . . . ignorance' " is used in "Plato; or, the Philosopher," *W,* IV, 49.

The words "I" & "mine" constitute ignorance. [*Ibid.*,] p. 659 [219]

[173] [220] "I have now given you a summary account of the sovereigns of the earth. — These, & other kings who with perishable frames have possessed this ever-during world, & who, blinded with deceptive notions of individual occupation, have indulged the feeling that suggests 'This earth is mine, — it is my son's, — it belongs to my dynasty, —' have all passed away. So, many who reigned before them, many who succeeded them, & many who are yet to come, have ceased or will cease to be. Earth laughs, as if smiling with autumnal flowers to behold her kings unable to effect the subjugation of themselves. I will repeat to you, Maitreya, the stanzas that were chanted by Earth, & which the Muni Asita communicated to Janaka, whose banner was virtue.

" 'How great is the folly of princes who are endowed with [174] [221] the faculty of reason, to cherish the confidence of ambition when they themselves are but foam upon the wave. Before they have subdued themselves, they seek to reduce their ministers, their servants, their subjects, under their authority; they then endeavour to overcome their foes. "Thus," say they, "will we conquer the ocean-circled earth;" &, intent upon their project, behold not death, which is not far off. But what mighty matter is the subjugation of the sea girt earth, to one who can subdue himself. Emancipation from existence is the fruit of self-control. It is through infatuation that kings desire to possess me, whom their predecessors have been forced to leave, whom their fathers have not retained. [175] [222] Beguiled by the selfish love of sway, fathers contend with their sons, & brothers with brothers, for my possession. Foolishness has been the character of every king who has boasted, "All this earth is mine — every thing is mine — it will be in my house forever;" — for he is dead. How is it possible that such vain desires should survive in the hearts of his descendants, who have seen their progenitor absorbed by the thirst of dominion, compelled to relinquish me whom he called his own, & tread the path of dissolution? When I hear a king sending word to another by his ambassador, "This earth is mine; resign your pretensions to it," — I am at first moved to violent laughter; but it soon subsides in pity for the infatuated fool.'

"These were the verses, Maitreya, which Earth recited & by listening to which ambition fades away like snow before the sun."

[*Ibid.*,] p[p. 487–]488 [223]

[219] This quotation is used in "Plato; or, the Philosopher," *W*, IV, 49–50.
[220] "Vishnu Purana" is written at the top of the page to the left.
[221] "Vishnu Purana" is written at the top of the page to the left.
[222] "Vishnu Purana" is written at the top of the page to the left.
[223] See Emerson's poetic reworking of this quotation in "Hamatreya," *W*, IX, 35–37.

[176]²²⁴   ↑*Abgrund*↓

"The goddess Yoganidra, the great illusory energy of Vishnu, by whom, as utter ignorance, the whole world is beguiled. — To her, Vishnu said, 'Go, Nidra, to the nether regions, & by my command conduct successively six of their princes to be conceived by Devaki,'" &c. &c.
[*Ibid.*,] p. 498 ²²⁵

Illusion,   *Mania*

"Fooled thou must be tho⟨e⟩' wisest of the wise,
Then be the fool of virtue not of vice." ²²⁶

———

[177] The Indian teaching through its cloud of legends has yet a simple & grand religion ⟨like a face of admirable beauty seen through a veil of ⟨wrought⟩ lace wrought all over with figures⟩ like a queenly countenance seen through a rich veil. It teaches to speak the truth, love others as yourself, & ⟨not mind⟩ ↑to despise↓ trifles. The East is grand, — ↑& makes↓ Europe ⟨is⟩ ↑appear↓ the land of trifles. Identity, identity! friend & foe are of one stuff, and the stuff is such & so much that the variations of surface are unimportant. All is for the soul, & the soul is Vishnu; & animals & stars are transient paintings; & light is whitewash; & durations are deceptive; and form is imprisonment and heaven itself a decoy. That which the soul seeks is resolution into Being above form, out of Tartarus & out of Heaven; liberation from existence is its name. Cheerful & noble is the genius of this cosmogony. [178] Hari is always gentle & serene, — he ⟨immortalizes⟩ ↑translates to heaven↓ the hunter who has accidentally shot him in his human form; he ⟨plays⟩ pursues his sports with boors & milkmaids at the cow-pens; all his games are benevolent, and he enters into flesh to relieve the burdens of the world.²²⁷

[179] Wisdom consists in keeping the soul liquid, or, in resisting the tendency to too rapid petrifaction[.]

²²⁴ "Vishnu Purana" is written at the top of the page to the left.
²²⁵ " 'the goddess Yoganidra . . . beguiled.'', struck through in ink with a vertical use mark, is used in "Montaigne," *W*, IV, 178.
²²⁶ These lines are struck through in ink with a vertical use mark. See pp. [172] and [81] above.
²²⁷ For the statements about Hari, see *The Vishṅu Puráṅa* . . . , 1840, pp. 510–511 and 612. "Identity, identity . . . its name.", struck through in ink with a vertical use mark, is used in "Plato; or, the Philosopher," *W*, IV, 49–51.

[180] ↑Contemporaries.↓

We learn of our contemporaries what they know with little effort and almost through the pores of the skin. We catch it by sympathy, or as a wife arrives at the intellectual & moral elevations of her husband.[228]

↑The Gentleman.↓

There are people who are always in fashion; & style & fashion & aristocracy bends & fits itself to them, denies itself to be possessed of them[.]

[181] ↑Generalizing.↓

Every generalization ⟨supposes⟩ ↑shows the way to↓ a larger generalization. What is that game called which we play with children, piling hand upon hand? Generalizing? It is a trick very quickly taught.

↑March 24 [1846]↓

⟨I w⟩ Why should people make such a matter of leaving this church & going into that? They ⟨demonstrate⟩ ↑betray↓ so their want of Faith, or spiritual perception. ⟨On the instant when we converse with⟩ The[n] holy principles⟨, they⟩ discredit & accredit all churches alike.   God builds his temple in the heart on the ruins of churches & religions. It is not otherwise with social forms.[229] A. or B. refuses the tax or some tax with solemnity, but eats & drinks & wears & perspires taxation all day. Let them not hew down the state with axe & gunpowder, but supersede it by irresistible genius; huddle it aside as ridiculous & obsolete by their quantity of being. Eloquence needs no constable[.]

[182] The fault of Alcott's community is that it has only room for one.

---

[228] This paragraph, struck through in pencil and ink with vertical use marks, is used in "Uses of Great Men," W, IV, 26.
[229] "God builds . . . forms." is struck through in pencil with a vertical use mark; the first sentence is used in "Worship," W, VI, 204.

[183] Majorities, ⟨the reason of fools⟩ the argument of fools, the strength of the weak. One should recall what Laertius records ⟨‖ ... ‖⟩as Socrates' opinion of the common people, "that, it was as if a man should except against one piece of bad money, & accept a great sum of the same." [230]

Vice of the age that the integrating power which belongs to an idea is imputed by ⟨the⟩ ↑our↓ grossness ⟨of men⟩ to a multitude of men, & politicians cry, "a majority:" and Churchmen cry "The Church." Our skin heals at the first intention. We are made of hooks & eyes,[n] & do exceedingly coalesce & cohere. We were born to be educated & governed.[230a]

[184] One said, "if the hand had not been divided into fingers, man would be still a ⟨savage⟩ beast roaming in the desart." The like if the tongue had not been fitted for sharp articulation. Children cry & scream & stamp with fury unable to express their desires. As soon as they can speak & plainly tell their want & the reason, they become gentle. It is the same with adults. Whilst the perceptions are blunt, men & women talk vehemently[n] & superlatively, & overgo the mark. Their manners are full of desperation, their speech is full of oaths. As soon as a little clearness of perception is added, they desist from that weak & brutish vehemence, & accurately express their meaning.*[231] "I judge by each man's truth, of his degree of understand-

* Same weakness & want on a higher plane occurs in history of all interesting young men & women. "Ah you don't understand me;" and, "I have never met with any body that understands me," & so they sob & sigh, write poetry, & walk alone, fault of power to express their precise meaning. In a month or two they meet some one so related as to assist their volcanic estate and good communication ↑once↓ established they are thenceforward good citizens.

[230] Diogenes Laertius, "Socrates," *Lives of Eminent Philosophers*, Bk. ii, sec. 34.
[230a] See Journal W, p. [46] above.
[231] Emerson directed attention to his footnote by writing at the bottom of p. [184] the words "*note on p. 187"; on p. [187] the footnote is set off from the other entry on the page by a long rule and is prefaced by the notation "Note ↑to p 184↓."

ing;" said Chesterfield.[232] It is ever thus, the progress is to accuracy, to skill, to truth, [185] from blind force. Such is the history of Europe in all points, & s⟨o⟩uch in philosophy. Plato is the ⟨moderate accurate plain⟩ ↑articulate↓ speaker, who no longer needs a barbaric paint & tattoo & whooping, for he can define. He leaves with Asia the vast & superlative: he is the arrival of accuracy & intelligence. He is the unrivalled definer.

The men of whom we are to speak are all uplifted to this elevation of civility. Happy in this! happy the period in which this truly human force reaches its perfect extent, & has not yet gone over into fineness, and an excessive thought for surfaces.

There must be the Abyss, Nox, & Chaos out of which all come, & they must never be far off. Cut off the connexion between any of our works & this dread origin [186] & the work is shallow & unsatisfying. That is the strength & excellence of the people, that they lean on this, & the mob is not quite so bad an argument as we are apt to represent it, for it has this divine side.

There is a moment in the history of every nation when[,] ⟨the perceptive powers⟩ proceeding out of this brut⟨ish⟩e youth, the perceptive powers reach with delight their greatest strength & have not yet become microscopic, so that the man at that instant ⟨reach⟩extends across the entire scale, & with his feet still planted on the immense forces of night, converses ⟨with⟩ ↑by↓ his eyes & brain with solar & stellar [187] creation. That is the moment of perfect health, the culmination of their star of Empire.

Ah, let the twilight linger! We love the morning spread abroad among the mountains, but too fast comes on the broad noon blaze, only exposing the poverty & barrenness of our globe, the listlessness & meanness of the inhabitants.[233]

↑[On the difficulty of defining, see, Y 50]↓

[232] See p. [47] above.
[233] "One said, 'if the hand [p. [184]] . . . for surfaces. [p. [185]]" is struck through in ink with single vertical use marks; "Whilst the perceptions [p. [184]] . . . for surfaces. [p. [185]]" is struck through in pencil with single vertical use marks; "from blind force [p. [185]] . . . unrivalled definer. [p. [185]]" is struck through in pencil with two vertical use marks; "Cut off the connexion [p. [185]] . . . dread origin [p. [185]]" is struck through in ink with four vertical use marks; "& the work is [p. [186]] . . . Empire." is struck through in ink with single

[188] Every enemy turns to a giant.

Mr Savage had got as far as *M* in his antiquarian catalogue[.] [234]

Montaigne or Socrates would quote Paul of Tarsus & ⟨Moth⟩ Goody Twoshoes with equal willingness[.] [235]

Candor & hospitality to a thought   W 68

Plant corn & beans when the apple trees are in blossom[.]

Life in platforms reached by a winding stair

[189] The Questioners
The Coffee drinkers   See W 120
        the ridden & bestridden
or those who value philosophy as news & not for use.
                            Coffee house philosopher

Men are shopworn[.] [236]

Life on platforms. Montaigne good against bigots[,] as cowage against worms acts mechanically[.]
But there is a higher muse there sitting where he durst not soar.
A muse that follows the flowing power[,] a "Dialectic" that respects

---

discontinuous vertical use marks; "There is a moment [p. [186]] . . . Empire." is struck through in pencil with single vertical use marks; Emerson's footnote is struck through in pencil and ink with single vertical use marks. "One said, 'if the hand [p. [184]] . . . & intelligence. [p. [185]]" (omitting the quotation from Chesterfield), "There is a moment [p. [186]] . . . Empire.", and Emerson's footnote are used in "Plato; or, the Philosopher," *W*, IV, 45–47.

[234] The reference is probably to James Savage, the English antiquary, who died March 19, 1845. Between this and the preceding entry, "Montaigne", enclosed by two short rules, is erased.

[235] This and the following entry are in pencil.

[236] This line, and the five lines above it, were written first in pencil, then (with the exception of "Coffee house philosopher") copied in ink. Above "Men are shopworn" the notation "W 120" was written twice in the right margin and erased; below it, "Men are shop worn" was written and later erased.

results. And it requires a muse, as Hafiz expresses himself only in musical phrases, the hyphens are small unities not parts.[237]

[190] ↑Nov. 5, 1845.↓

Yesterday evening, saw Robert Owen at Mr Alcott's. His four elements are Production, Distribution, Formation of Character, and Local & General governing. His *Three Errors*, on which society has always been based, & is now, are, 1. That we form ourselves. 2. That we form our opinions. 3. That we form our feelings. The Three Truths which he wishes should replace these, are, 1. That we proceed from a creating power; 2. That our opinions come from conviction; 3 That our feelings come from our instincts.

The five Evils which proceed from our Three Errors & which make the misery of life are

    1 Religious perplexities

    2 Disappointment in affections

    3 Pecuniary difficulties

    4 Intemperance

    5 Anxiety for offspring.

[191] He also requires a Transitional state. *Fourier* he saw in his old age. Fourier learned of him all the truth he had, & the rest of his system was imagination[,] & the imagination of a banker.

You are very external with your evils, Mr Owen: let me give you some real mischiefs[:]

        Living for show

        Losing the whole in the particular

        Indigence of vital power

I am afraid these will appear in a phalanstery or in a tub[.] [238]

We were agreed, that Mr Owen was right in imputing despotism to circumstances & that the priest & poet are right in attributing

---

[237] A pencil version of these sentences, with "Life is on platforms." for "Life on platforms." and "Montaigne is good" for "Montaigne good", underlies the ink version. The pencil was later partially erased. "Montaigne good against . . . worms" and "But there is . . . soar." are used in "The Sovereignty of Ethics," *W*, X, 187.

[238] This entry is in pencil.

responsibility to men. Owen was a better man than he knew, & his love of men made us forget his "Three Errors."

His charitable construction of men, classes, & their actions was invariable. He was always a better Christian in his controversy with Christians, and he interpreted with great [192]²³⁹ generosity the acts of the Holy Alliance & Prince Metternich. "Ah," he said, "you may depend on it, there are as tender hearts, and as much good will to serve men, in palaces, as in cottages."

↑See Sequel, infra p. 204.↓

Plato discredits poets: he can afford to[,] just as all ↑fanciful↓ schemers say I am a man of business[.]

> Plato
> Extreme difficulty of the problem
> Proteus Y 32 ²⁴⁰

> Synthesis of the two elements
> Coin of Jove

It is as easy to be great as ⟨to⟩ small. Now came a balanced soul. Precisely as high as he soared so deep he dived. If he loved abstract truth he saved himself with the most popular of all principles[,] the absolute good which ⟨condemns the condemner⟩ ↑rules rulers↓ [and] judges the judge⟨s⟩. If he made transcendental distinctions above the vision of ordinary mortals he fortified himself by drawing all his illustrations from sources disdained by orators & conversers[:] from mares & soupladles, from cooks & criers, potters & shoemakers[.] ²⁴¹

[193]   Plato
        teaches realities & is an affirmer

---

²³⁹ The entries on pp. [192]–[194], with the exception of the entry concluded at the top of p. [192] and the note about Walden Pond at the top of p. [194], are in pencil. Two lines of erased pencil writing, struck through in pencil with a vertical use mark, underlie the ink entry on p. [192]: "These sentences are the culture[?] of nations[?] cornerstones of schools[?] reservoirs of literatures".

²⁴⁰ These three lines are struck through in pencil with a vertical use mark.

²⁴¹ This paragraph and the two short notations above it, struck through in pencil with a vertical use mark, are used in "Plato; or, the Philosopher," W, IV, 54–55.

Truth is good & ⟨not⟩ altogether wholesome, nutritious[.]

teaches
Dialectic
↑or↓ dry light or science for science's sake

Then morals or a higher science of Virtue
                              unteachable
                              Beauty

[194] Walden pond. greatest depth 10⟨4⟩2 ft. greatest length 2850 ft [242]

Plato grand; propriety, organized animal; Jove would speak;
    Plato various; almost as Shakspeare; he is a society
    ↑synthetic;↓
    circumspect; pious,   Y 68
    transcending;
                impossible to say what his system was
        he can be quoted by all parties,
        i.e. intellectual, practically dialectic, no coxcomb of a system
            grinder
        Follower of Nature. The ages
    precise; bold, bold, but not too bold; a Greek in love of bound-
        ary; rich in the discretion to select;
        the Definer [243]

literary; has finished his thinking [244]

[242] The source of these dimensions is probably Thoreau. In *Walden*, chap. 16, he notes that he surveyed the pond early in 1846, and the map he supplied with the first edition gives 102 feet as the greatest depth and 175 1/2 rods (2,895 3/4 feet) as the greatest length.
[243] "Follower of Nature . . . the Definer" is struck through in pencil with a vertical use mark. For the source of "bold, bold, but not too bold;" see p. [105] above.
[244] This line is struck through in pencil with two vertical use marks. See Journal W, p. [3] above.

poetic; invented names
adaptive: W 86 Y 56

[195]   Affirmative
Believe in the great & unweariable power of destiny.

⟨"I know that he can toil terribly."⟩[245]

Only life can impart life. Life is so affirmative, that I can never hear
of personal vigour of any kind, great power of performance, without
lively sympathy & fresh resolutions[.]

Any thing, child, that the mind covets, from the milk of a cocoa to
the throne of the three worlds, may be obtained by propitiating
Vishnu.[246]

No hope, ⟨so⟩how bright soever, but is the beginning of its
fulfilment. E 91 [247]

The belief of the Buddhist that no seed will die. Work on, you cannot
escape your wages.

Winter apples. Y 112

Every one gravitates to truth W 68

[196][248] His *synthesis* Sea shore. Y 110
                    Phercydes Syrus [249]
                    Ideas are the daemonic band that hoop in Unity
                    & Altereity

[245] In *JMN*, VII, 514, Emerson credits Robert Cecil, Earl of Salisbury, with
saying this of Sir Walter Raleigh. His source is probably Thomas Peregrine Courtenay's
article on Cecil in *Cabinet Cyclopedia: Lives of Eminent British Statesmen*, ed.
Dionysius Lardner, 7 vols. (London, 1831–1839), V, 16. The quotation, struck
through in ink with two vertical use marks, is used in "Uses of Great Men," *W*, IV,
14, and "Greatness," *W*, VIII, 311.
[246] See p. [123] above.
[247] See *JMN*, VII, 323.
[248] The entries on pp. [196]–[197] and [199]–[202] are in pencil.
[249] See Journal W, p. [2] above.

330

Caste & Culture
Asia & Europe
Nox & Boundary
Herein following Nature, jealous of partiality, if he
plants his foot here & says one thing, he is sure to plant
his foot there, & ⟨say⟩ make the counter-weight, resolved
that the two poles shall be manifest; the two poles still
appear & with him become two hands & grasp their
own[.] [250]

See W 36
In reading books keep his first thoughts.

[197]   Identity
              Coarse & fine W 62
              Liars also are true, & every false act reaches truth W 68

[198] [blank]
        [199] Platonic Errors

———

Literary

———

Misogynes

———

In the Republic admits the lye into government

———

He is charged with having failed to ⟨make the⟩ find the transition
from ideas to matter —

———

Popular in his doctrine of Immortality.

———

failed by being an Individual   Y 66

        [200] [251] Plato
General Excellence

[250] This paragraph, struck through in pencil with a vertical use mark, is used in
"Plato; or, the Philosopher," *W*, IV, 55.
    [251] This page is struck through in pencil with a vertical use mark.

Culture of nations
All but life itself
Vast range
  is Europe
  is American
    Genuineness
      Absorbed into himself all the learning of time
      Travelled & imported the other Element
        Quotation
We have to solve the problem how he came to stand so high

   ⟨Philosophy⟩
Articulate Europe
One sided juvenile systems of fire, water, this, & that,
Plato the Definer came

   Philosophy
   Difficulty of the problem. Proteus.
   The One
   The Other
   The human mind is always a partisan & adheres by religion or
by idolatry to the One,
or by intellect or senses to the Many

[201] *The One* [252]	*Many*
⟨Being⟩ ———————————	Intellect
Good	⟨Talent⟩
⟨Earnest⟩	⟨Trade⟩
Reality	⟨Pleasure⟩
Earnest	Culture
Inertia	Trade
⟨Caste⟩	⟨Pleasure⟩
religion	⟨Distribution⟩
Power ———————————	Distribution
Caste ———————————	Culture

[252] Most of the following contrasting terms are used in "Plato; or, the Philosopher," *W*, IV, 51.

King —————————————————— Democracy
Strength ⎫
  or   ⎬ —————————————— Pleasure
Health   ⎭
Earnestness ———————————— Knowledge
Genius ————————————————— Talent
Consciousness ————————— Definition
Rest ——————————————————— Motion
Necessity   Freedom
      European civilization triumph of talent W. 18 [253]

                                      ⎧ ⟨D⟩Instrumentality
Emancipation —————————⎨ Dominion
                                      ⎩ Deity
Substance   Form
Reality   Appearance
Good   Use

[202]   Europe & Asia illustrate the two tendencies
              Asia   Europe
              Unity   Variety
              Infinity   Boundary
              Fate   Freedom
              Caste   Culture

European civility the triumph of talent   W 18
The philosophers
Athens & Pericles had been doing that
Their philosophers were fast distributing & running into superfineness
Plato comes to join the two, more excellent in defining than any he
stands yet on the vast of Asia by taste & extent; ↑the excellence of↓
Europe & Asia are in his brain

    Metaphysics & nat. phil. seemed the genius of Europe[;] he
added the religion of Asia as the base.[254]

[253] This note is enclosed by a box.
[254] "European civility . . . base." is struck through in pencil with a vertical use
mark; "Plato comes to join the two," and "the excellence of . . . base." are used in
"Plato; or, the Philosopher," *W*, IV, 54.

[203] Law it is which is without name or color or hands or feet; which ⟨is⟩no acts affect; which is smallest of the least, & largest of the large; all; & knowing all things; which hears without ears, sees without eyes, moves without feet, & seizes without hands.[255]

"Only the law of God it is which has no antecedent, the law of God in which no change is to be discovered." *Koran.*[256]

[204] The moment a great man fails us as a cause, it is only to become more valuable & suggestive as an effect.[257]

The Owen & Fourier plans bring no *a priori* convictions. They are come at merely by counting & arithmetic. All the fine ⟨percepti⟩aperçus are for individualism. The Spartan broth, the hermit's cell, the lonely farmer's life are poetic; the Phalanstery, the "self supporting Village" (Owen) are culinary & mean.

Money plent⟨y⟩iful as rain
⟨a⟩economical as ants [258]

[205] Individualism
"Thy wisdom & thy science, it hath turned thee away; & thou hast said in thine heart, *I, & none else beside me*; & evil shall come upon thee, & thou shalt not know whence it cometh, & mischief shall fall upon thee, & thou shalt not be able to expiate, & vastation shall come upon thee suddenly, which thou shalt not know." Isaiah xlvii. 10, 11.

[206] [blank]
[207] Health is the obedience of all the members to the genius or character. As soon as any nerve, or muscle, or drop of blood, makes itself felt, it is disease.

"What is strength? The motion of the soul with the body." ↑*Socrates in Stob.*↓ [259]

[255] This paragraph, which is drawn from the passage on pp. [140]–[141] above, is struck through in ink with two vertical use marks and used in "Worship," *W*, VI, 221.
[256] See p. [86] above.
[257] This sentence, struck through in ink with three vertical use marks, is used in "Uses of Great Men," *W*, IV, 34.
[258] These two notes are in pencil.
[259] See p. [131] above.

Health must be a muse[.]

Magic. Life is only good when it is magical, a perfect timing & consent, & we know nothing about it.[260]   ↑See Y. 210↓

"All things are good & fair to those things wherewith they agree, but ill & deformed in respect of those things with which they agree not."
Socrates [261]

[208] Will not men let fall what tends to fall. Christianity is grown sentimental, and it is quite easy for those who are born a few years later, to stand free of traditions & tenets which embarrassed the Channings & Priestleys & Paleys. All that concerns the resurrection of the body of Christ &c[,] & in short all the miraculous history[,] the youth of today has no ears for.

[209] We are made of contradictions, — our *freedom* is *necessary*.

I cannot please but one at a time.

"The more the Lord is present so much the more free is man" Swedenborg

[210] There seems to be a certain vegetable principle pervading human nature also, (or, perhaps better, a vital power which the vegetable life illustrates,) ⟨t⟩which cannot be too much respected. It appears as if a good work did itself; as if whatever is good, in proportion as it is good, had a certain self existence & self creation or organism. ⟨It⟩ The good book grows whether the writer is awake or asleep[;] its subject & order are not chosen but preappointed him[.] [262]   ↑See p. 35↓

Perseverance
        "By always intending my mind"
                Newton [263]

[260] This sentence, struck through in ink with a vertical use mark, is used in "Works and Days," *W*, VII, 180.

[261] See p. [131] above.

[262] This paragraph is struck through in pencil with a vertical use mark.

[263] This quotation, struck through in ink with three vertical use marks, is used in

[211] The other thing I had to think of, was, that every man is the better for a streak of folly, inasmuch as it saves him from arrogance & monumental egotism.

I find it quoted ⟨to⟩ ↑from↓ Livy, "that the moment a man begins not to be convinced, he begins to convince." [264]

I had another experience in the coach, if I can recall it, that the reason why a man becomes intellectual & shuns practice, is reverential & religious, because action is so melancholy⟨; a noise & a fuss⟩.ⁿ Manliness seems to require something better than this desultoriness; &, as if out of selfrespect, & courtesy to the world, we withdraw from ⟨hubbub.⟩ ↑noise.↓ Skepticism has no such good argument as the irreligion of facts. We do not approach a man's house by his woodshed & offices but through his park & portico.

[212] The habit of society is an unprincipled decorum; and, in so many days & events as pass over him or her, it is rarely that the man or woman gets a chance to appear.[265]

——————

↑Life↓ [266]

We want all our power for every work; but, unhappily, the days' events come abreast, instead of coming in Indian file, so that we are compelled to extend, where we would so willingly concentrate.

⟨"the natural & the artificial foole one that did his kind, & the other who foolishly followed his own mind."

Nest of ⟨n⟩*Ninnies.*⟩ [267]

——————

"Power," *W,* VI, 75, where it is called Newton's answer to the question, "how he had been able to achieve his discoveries?" Cf. *JMN,* III, 200.

[264] This quotation is used in "Natural History of Intellect," *W,* XII, 25. A circled question mark is inserted after "Livy", probably by Emerson.

[265] "The habit of . . . decorum;", struck through in ink with a vertical use mark, is used in "Considerations by the Way," *W,* VI, 247.

[266] This word is added in pencil.

[267] Emerson's source is John Payne Collier's *Fools and Jesters: with a reprint of Robert Arnim's Nest of Ninnies, 1608,* Shakespeare Society no. 10 (London, 1842), p. 12. Nine of the Society's publications were loaned to Emerson by Longfellow in December, 1845 (*L,* III, 313).

Huts, huts, are safe[.] [268]

[213] [269] Shakspeare had good deliverance & so each play was new. Best tragedy can write best comedy. Plato also could make somewhat new, for he that could see so much in one direction could see as much in another direction. Each of them sufficed for the culture of a nation[.]

———

Plato's twice bisected line belongs to the doctrine of Representation[.] [270]

———

Greeley surprises by playing all the parts. Only possible in America[.]

We seem to need an ideal strength[;] if we adopt the ideal courses our flesh & heart fail us.

[214] [271] I would not be found far from the line of my tendency. I would not frisk[.]

Men purchase these enlargements by adamantine limitations[.] [272]

Great insight should have taught the equilibrium of the Universe, & that you cannot, if you would, dodge your reward[.]

Old plays were the property of the theatre, and the poet worked on them as the painter on the mythi of the Madonna or the Crucifixion[.]

Europe the deification of details

[268] This sentence is in pencil.
[269] The entries on this page, with the exception of the first, are in pencil. The first was written first in pencil, then in ink.
[270] Emerson quotes the passage from *The Republic*, VI, xx, dealing with the twice-bisected line in "Plato; or, the Philosopher," *W*, IV, 68–69. Cf. p. [243] below.
[271] The entries on this page are in pencil.
[272] See p. [220] below.

[215] ⟨C[harles] K N[ewcomb] thinks that we shall so surely have what we want that we should from the first aim high.⟩[n 273]

Reality bursting through all these men, through Plato, through Swedenborg, through Shakspeare[.] [274]

[216] Skepticism & gulfs of Skepticism; strangest of all that of the Saints. They come to the mount, & in the largest & most blissful communication to them, somewhat is left unsaid, which begets in them doubt & horrible doubt. 'So then,' say they, before they have yet risen from their knees, 'even this, even this does not satisfy: we must still feel that this our homage & beatitude is partial & deformed. We must fly for relief & sanity to that other suspected & reviled part of nature, the kingdom of the understanding, the ⟨play⟩ gymnastics of talent, the play of fancy[.]' [275]

Ah Lycurgus, old slyboots!

[217] [blank]
[218] [276] Lectures on men typical of permanent classes
Classes

Knower	Doer	Sayer
Philosopher	Hero	Poet
	Man of	Writer
	the world	

Mystic, overpowered by the moral & using the poetic solely to the moral.
Saint[,] overpowered by the moral & valuing action only as moral. No poetry.
Critic, body of truth without truth
Savant[,] truth without morals

[273] This entry, which was written first in pencil, then in ink, is struck through in ink with a vertical use mark and used in "Fate," *W*, VI, 47.

[274] This entry is in pencil.

[275] This paragraph, struck through in ink with a vertical use mark, is used in "Montaigne," *W*, IV, 174.

[276] The entries on this page are in pencil.

[219]   Absolutist *versus* Man of the World [277]

Then there is this monkey of Mesmerism or Momus playing Jove in the kitchen of Olympus.[278]

⟨When the ⟨E⟩ ilia dura [279] with their power of performance get well drilled at Oxford & then genius is added you get those masters of the world who have again & again appeared in England who combine the highest energy with the universal culture[.]⟩

[220] Locke said, "God, when he makes the prophet, does not unmake the man." Swedenborg's history confirms & points the remark. A poor little narrow pragmatical Lutheran for whom the heavens are opened, so that he sees with eyes & in the richest symbolic forms the awful truth of things, and utters again in his endless books the indisputable secrets of moral nature, remains with all these grandeurs resting upon him, through it all, & after all, a poor little narrow pragmatical Lutheran. His judgments are those of ↑a↓ Swedish polemic, and his vast enlargements seem purchased by adamantine limitations. He reminds me again & again of our Jones Very, who had an illumination that enabled him to excel every body in wit [221] & to see farthest in every company & quite easily to bring the proudest to confession: & yet he could never get out of his Hebraistic phraseology & mythology, &, when all was over, still remained in the thin porridge ⟨of Unitari⟩ or cold tea of Unitarianism.[280]

[222]   ↑*Influences*↓
We are candidates, we know we are, for influences more subtle & more ⟨exalted⟩high than those of talent & ambition. We ⟨should⟩ want a leader, we want a friend whom we have not seen. In the

[277] This line is in pencil.
[278] An erased pencil version of this entry is visible in the space between the ink version and the following entry. The sentence is used in "Demonology," *W*, X, 25.
[279] "tough stomachs" (Ed.).
[280] This paragraph is struck through in pencil and ink with vertical use marks; "Locke said . . . adamantine limitations" is used in "Swedenborg," *W*, IV, 136–137. For "his vast enlargements . . . limitations", see p. [214] above. For the quotation from Locke, see *JMN*, VI, 52.

company, & fired by the example of a god, these faculties that dream & toss in their sleep, would wake. Where is the Genius that shall marshal us the way that we were going? ↑There is a vast residue[,] an open account ever.↓²⁸¹

The great inspire us: how they beckon, how they animate, and show their legitimate power in nothing more than in their ⟨‖ ... ‖⟩power to misguide us. For, the perverted great derange & deject us, & perplex ages with their fame. Alexander, Napoleon, Mahomet. Then the evil genius of France at & before the Revolution, a learned fiend.

[223] Atmospheric influence.
Direct; such as that imputed by Calvinism to Christ
The great are ⟨our ⟨‖ ... ‖⟩Selves⟩
Our better selves, our selves with Vantages.²⁸²

I have thought that an error which misleads generations of men, some widespread federal insanity, is not traceable to any single commanding individual, but rather resembles an endemic disease, which, though it sometimes is communicated by contagion, is really in the atmosphere, & poisons all who are susceptible of it.

Direct
Atmospheric, Magnetic
Portal or introductory
Representative ²⁸³

"He is their god; he leads them like a thing made by some other deity than nature. That shapes man better."

[224]²⁸⁴ Off & on

---

²⁸¹ This inserted sentence was written first in pencil, with "unset" canceled before "open", then in ink. The paragraph, with the exception of this sentence, is struck through in pencil with a vertical use mark; "Where is the Genius . . . going?" is used in "Uses of Great Men," W, IV, 25.

²⁸² These four notes are struck through in ink with a vertical use mark.

²⁸³ These seven words are in pencil.

²⁸⁴ The entries on pp. [224]–[228], with the exception of "Men also representative." at the top of p. [227], are in pencil.

It is the largest part of ↑a↓ man that is not inventoried. He has many enumerable parts: he is social, professional, political, sectarian, literary, & of this or that set & corporation. But after the most exhausting census has been made, there remains as much more which no tongue can tell. And this ⟨part⟩ remainder is that which interests.[285] This is that which the preacher & the poet & the musician speak to. This is that which the strong genius works upon; the region of destiny, of aspiration, of the unknown. Ah they have a secret persuasion that as little as they pass for in the world, they are immensely rich in expectancy & power. Nobody has ever yet dispossessed this adhesive self to arrive at any glimpse or guess of the awful Life that lurks under it.

[225] For the best part, I repeat, of every mind is not that which he knows, but that which hovers in gleams[,] suggestions[,] tantalizing unpossessed before him. His firm recorded knowledge soon loses all interest for him. But this dancing chorus of thoughts & hopes ⟨are⟩is the quarry of his future, is his possibility, & teaches him that his man's life is of a ridiculous brevity & meanness, but that it is his first age & trial only of his young wings, but that vast revolutions, migrations, & gyres on gyres in the celestial societies ⟨ann⟩ invite him[.] [286]

[226]   Inward miracles.   Deliverances
That which so mightily annoyed & hampered us ceases utterly & at unawares. We wist not how or whence the redemption came. What so rankled at heart, & kept the eyes open all night, ⟨we have quite forgotten⟩ & which, we said, will never down; lo! we have utterly forgot it; cannot by any effort of memory realize it again, & give it importance. The crises in our history come so. Thus they steal in on us, a new life which enters, God knows how, through the solidest blocks of our old thoughts & mental habits, ⟨& holds⟩ makes them transparent & pervious to its subtle essence; sweetens & enlightens all, & at last ⟨holds them⟩ dissolves them in its new radiance[.]
The miracles of the spirit are greater than those of the history.

---

[285] "He has many . . . interests" is struck through in pencil with a vertical use mark.
[286] This paragraph is struck through in pencil with a vertical use mark.

[227]   ↑*Men also representative.*↓

Swedenb[org] & Behmen saw that things were representative. They did not sufficiently see that men were. But we cannot, as we say, be in two places at once. My doing my ⟨thin⟩office entitles me to the benefit of your doing yours. This is the secret after which the Communists are coarsely & externally striving. Work in thy place with might & health, & thy secretion to the spiritual body is made, I in mine will do the like. Thus imperceptibly & most happily, genially & triumphantly doing that we delight in, behold we are communists, brothers, members one of another[.] [287]

Mind thy affair, *ton metier*, says the Spirit. Coxcomb! would you meddle with the skies, or with other people? and so ↑on these terms,↓ the Spirit shoulders the adaptation or system[.] [288]

We are invited to an intellectual banquet[,] to a society of thought with them. We see them as illustrations[n] [228] incarnate & beautiful of the laws, the laws walking & speaking, but the ⟨invol⟩ direct service they render us is that of health & is above the region of thought & will.[289]

We are holden to the earth by self opinion[;] it is the conservative force & is animated by the deific energy which self covers[,] but it has its check or our feet would grow to marble like the princes in the Arabian tales.[290]

[229] Shakspeare's fault that the world appears so empty. He has educated you with his painted world, & this real one seems a huckster's shop[.]

[230] The transmigration must take effect; it is of no use to

---

[287] "Swedenb[org] & Behmen . . . men were." is used in "Uses of Great Men," *W*, IV, 8. For "members one of another", see Romans 12:5.

[288] This paragraph is struck through in ink with a vertical use mark; "Mind thy affair . . . people?" is used in "Uses of Great Men," *W*, IV, 8.

[289] This paragraph is struck through in pencil on p. [228] with a vertical use mark.

[290] This paragraph is struck through in pencil with a vertical use mark.

stand balancing there, first on one foot, then on the other. In he must, in to the new element, &, loth though he be, he must leave this ⟨clinging form he now wears⟩ ↑body which now clings to him↓, & cast it off like a coat. It is of no use to try to stay where he is, & speak or project poetry. No ⟨he⟩, his ⟨very self,⟩ ↑life↓ must pass out of him, — the gentleman, & be converted into it, — the poetry, ⟨an absolute transformation,⟩ or there is no poem.

"None any work can frame
Unless himself become the same."
↑See Y 16↓

[231] It is sad to see people reading again their old books, merely because they don't know what new books they want.

It does not content me if the coat only fits Montaigne; I go out into the street, & try it on the world.

Value of Skeptic is the resistance to premature conclusions. ⟨&⟩
If he prematurely conclude, his conclusion will be shattered, & he will become malignant[.]
But the Skeptic must limit himself with the anticipation of ^{n} ⟨law in the mutations;⟩ flowing law.   See *supra*, p. 106 [291]

[232] He is a lord & he is a goosy gander; and he is a lord in virtue of being a gander; & a gander again in virtue of being a lord. Let the saint say, I am a /scamp/rogue/, & I will trust his sanctity; but let him not try to come it over me by affecting to saint it all the time. If he harp on that string too much, & never loosen it, there is no music. I suspect the string is rotten. For I, who know the inevitable alternations, — if I see no relaxing of the sanctity, suspect at once that he ⟨is⟩has dishonest relaxations, — that the whole is rotten.[292]

[233] [blank]

---

[291] These three paragraphs are struck through in ink with two diagonal use marks in the shape of a V.

[292] This entry was written first in pencil, then "Let the saint say . . . is rotten." was rewritten in ink.

[234] Swedenborg
      Class I of men. See above p 83
      Too much form   Y 153
           fixity   124 [293]

[235] [blank]
   [236] [294] Every work needs a necessity
               a nature
               a material already existing, for motive to the poet & for credence to the people
Otherwise the work were fantastic
A man does not get up some fine morning & say I am full of life Lo I will build a cathedral[.]
But the church builds him & he builds it or he finds a war raging & he fights & conquers or he finds two counties or states studying how to get flour or lead from where it is produced to where it is wanted & he hits on a railroad[.]

S[hakespeare] like every genius found his material collected & his genius lay in that sympathy with the people[,] love of the material[,] & hence skill to use it. What an economy. All is done to his hand. The world has brought him [237] thus far on his way. Men, nations, poets, ships, all have worked for him. Choose any other thing, out of the line of tendency & national feeling & history, & he would have to do all, & one lifetime would not suffice[.]

Shakspeare came to plain open theatres which Scenepainting had not yet unpoetized. All was to be done for the imagination meantime. He had not to invent the play & say here is a new game: Try it, try to be amused. The people were resolute for it. They would have it. In vain the powers tried to put it down. Puritan could not, King could not.[n] It was ballad, epic, picture, newspaper.
   The plays were all in possession of the stage
The tale of Troy

[293] These four lines are in pencil.
[294] The entries on pp. [236]–[239] are in pencil. Those on pp. [238] and [239] are struck through in pencil with vertical use marks. Many of these passages found their way into "Shakspeare," *W*, IV, 190–198.

The Comedy of Errors
    King Lear
    King John
Wars of the Roses
Sir John Oldcastle
[238] Caesar
Antony
Coriolanus
Hereby holden fast to the people, supplied with ⟨re⟩ solid ground,
& left at leisure (which was inestimable) for the audacities of the
imagination[.]

    Gower eaten up by Chaucer
    Composition of Bibles
    Homer
    Cid
    Robinhood
    Saadi ↑See thus the inception & growth of the fable, or Iliad
    or Veda or Mythology, till the Genius arrives.↓
When this work is admirably done, all the contributors & hodmen
perish, & the memory of them[,] & the master stands alone & un-
accountable[.]

    [239] algebraically solved

    omnipresent propriety[;] has nothing particular but all duty;
great greatly, the small subordinately

    then he always rides,
    or never uses mechanical but ever poetical means   poem of
little poems

    [240] Swedenborg is a man of genius & served religion by
genius. He let in to the withered, traditional, positive, dogmatic
Church dealing out ancient results to men & only results, ⟨the⟩ nature
again. He let in nature again & the worshipper is overjoyed to find
himself a party again to the whole of his religion. He sees & knows.

It is a reality[,] it is a reason[,] & of universal application. Overjoyed, he turns it on every side, & finds it will fit, & open & raise & sweeten every part of his life, every work of his hands, every inconvenience, every delay, every

Hence all the members of the New Church find their intellect growing with the study of ⟨this⟩ his books.[295]

[241] How ⟨husky⟩ ↑chaffy↓ & external seemed now all the old creeds. When there is this sweet truth-seeking wide-ranging live-glowing religion, into which angels seem visibly to descend, how can men abide a day longer in their old frozen churches of chaff[?]

Well this is ever the effect of genius. But it must be content to serve us only as far as it is genius[,] & not the man of genius because he has been once faithful to the truth expect us to accept his infirmities & his limitations also. Though he were an angel, we will have only his wisdom, & take up not one of his infirmities[.]

[242] The distinctions of the national Church, the distinctions of the Jewish & Christian scriptures had, as he grew older, more than their due weight in his mind; & he loses the sympathy of the very minds he has won to him, by ⟨running himself insensibly in⟩ ↑attributing↓ to these local & temporary forms the ⟨same⟩ eternity [& universality] of the God who once spoke through them.[296]

[243] But that which he sought was the meaning of the world. It is strange that now that I come to this matter I am at a loss for any book in which the symbolical force of things is opened. Plato knew somewhat of it as is evident by his twice bisected line.[297] Bacon said ⟨Nat⟩ Truth & nature differed only as seal & print. Behmen implies it in all his writing. So do all poets but only playfully. But one would say that as soon as such a race as this is had once discovered

---

[295] This and the preceding entry, struck through in ink with a vertical use mark, are used in "Swedenborg," *W*, IV, 122–123.

[296] This paragraph is struck through in ink with a vertical use mark.

[297] Cf. p. [213] above.

or only so much as had a hint that the thing was so[,] that every material object subsists here not by itself nor finally to a material end but all as a picture language to tell another story of beings & duties[,] all other science would be put by & a science so grand & of such [244] magnificent presage, would absorb all competition & research.

But whether it is, that God does not wish this lesson to be learned intellectually, as if we ought not to discover that the ⟨means &⟩ materials we use are only means, lest we should throw them away, & no longer eat, & work, & beget children, it is certain that all men occupy themselves with the symbols as if they were the things signified.²⁹⁸

[245] How is it; I say in my bed, that the people manage to live along, so aimless as they are? After their ends (& they so petty) are gained, it seems as if the lime in their bones alone held them together, & not any worthy purpose. And how do I manage it? A house, a bargain, a debt, some friends, some book, some names & deeds of heroes, or of geniuses, these are the toys I play with, these intercept between me & heaven, or these are they that devastate the soul.²⁹⁹

[246] Every hose fits every hydrant[.] ³⁰⁰

———

Bacon on the analogy of matter & spirit
        Works: vol 1 p 95 [edition unlocated]

———

The profounder sort of wits are ever fond of this theme; but who has added a syllable to what Plato, Behmen, Bacon, Swedenborg have written concerning it?

²⁹⁸ These two paragraphs, struck through in ink with a vertical use mark, are used in "Swedenborg," *W*, IV, 116–118.
²⁹⁹ This paragraph is struck through in ink with a vertical use mark; "How is it . . . purpose.", struck through in ink with a vertical use mark, is used in "Worship," *W*, VI, 208.
³⁰⁰ This sentence is struck through in ink with a vertical use mark. See Journal W, p. [83] above.

The symbol always stimulates. Therefore is Poetry ever the best reading.

[247] Symbol
In the Egyptian emblems the ploughman & the ox indicate the natural society of wisdom & strength.

Students taking nitrous oxide gas[:] one would say the bladder was full of opinions.[301]

[248] Dear heart, take it sadly home to thee, that there will & can be no coöperation. Thy friends look so good & willing, that nothing seems of more reasonable Expectation than that they should ⟨work⟩unite with thee in the dearest enterprizes. All thy life hitherto has been only an earning of friends, a gathering of the holy ⟨fellow-ship⟩ ↑fraternity↓ that were to do the best of deeds. But ⟨you may as easily unite⟩ ↑so↓ the ↑remoter↓ stars ⟨of the sky —They too⟩ seem ⟨to the distant eye⟩ a nebula of united lights, ⟨but⟩ ↑yet↓ there is no group which a telescope will not resolve: And the dearest friends are separated by irreconcileable intervals. The cooperation is involuntary, and is put upon us by the Genius of Life, who reserves this as a part of his ⟨majesty, & never concedes it to our will⟩ ↑prerogative↓.[302]

[249] The other part of life is selfreliance. Love & it balance up & down, & the beam never rests. Thou wouldest fain not look out of the window, nor waste time in expecting thy friend. Thou wouldst be sought of him. Well, that also is in thy soul, and this is its law. The soul of man must be the servant of another. In its good estate, it is the servant of the Spirit of Truth. When it is abandoned to that dominion, it is great & sovereign, ⟨itself,⟩ & draweth friends & lovers. When it is not so, it serveth a friend or lover.

↑⌐ Is not p. 248 printed?↓ [303]

[301] See *JMN*, VII, 531, and p. [28] above.
[302] This paragraph is used in "Society and Solitude," *W*, VII, 8.
[303] This entry is in pencil.

[250] The other & third thing is this, that it is ever well with him who finishes his work for its own sake, & the state & the world is happy that has the most of such Finishers. ⟨Never fear but t⟩The world will do justice to such. It cannot otherwise; but never on the day when the work is newly done & presented. But forever ⟨& ever the man⟩ it is true that every man settles his own rate.[304]

See W 139

[251] Give up once for all the hope of approbation from the people in the street if you are pursuing great ends. How can they guess your designs? [n 305]

[252] Alcott says, that to Goethe he should say, Thou sawest God, & didʼst↓ not die.

Into the district school he goes, — clowns & clowns; a clown in the chair, & his clowns around him.

When one sees good men in any society or rule, he does not value the rule, but the good man, & feels him to be disadvantaged just so far as the rule ⟨r⟩works on him. Thus Myrick or Blanchard among the Shakers, Shakerism gains nothing by them, with the wise.
The Shakers also live for show, with buildings ostentatiously neat. They have good accommodation for strangers, but the stranger [253] should be accommodated as ourselves & not better.

⟨M⟩As I listened to the fine music, I considered the musicians, & thought th⟨e⟩at music seems to fall accidentally & superficially on most of its artists. They are not essentially musical[.]

[254] What confidence can I have in a fine behaviour & way of life that requires riches to bear it out? Shall I never see a greatness

---

[304] This paragraph is struck through in ink with a wavy vertical use mark; "who finishes . . . otherwise;" is used in "Worship," *W*, VI, 225–226.
[305] These two sentences, struck through in ink with a vertical use mark, are used in "Aristocracy," *W*, X, 61.

of carriage & thought combined with a power that actually earns its
bread, & teaches others to earn theirs? [n]

[255]   ↑Uses of great men.↓
The people make much ado of quitting this sect & entering that
& publish to the world a manifesto of reasons. ⟨The act only demon-
strates⟩ Great man, — good when he stands strong on his legs, good
when he is handsome, eloquent, & loaded with advantages. Better
he seemed to me yesterday, when he had the power to eclipse himself & all heroes by letting in the Divine element into our minds,
he himself a splendid nobody hiding himself[,] not like the cuttle
fish in ink, but like God in deluges of light[.] [306]

            ↑*Brook Farm*-ing↓ [307]
Our popular saxon system that I must be first. ↑[See W 76]↓ But
there is a rumour ⟨of⟩ ↑going from↓ the gods↑,↓ ⟨going,⟩ that a social
wellbeing is best[.]
        Eloquence lets in the social nature. Greatness of New England
consists in her confidence that slavery must end[.]

[256] Animal Spirits a low example of the fusion or blending[.]
                                                 ↑W 83↓

[257][308] Montaigne
        Skeptic is the considerer
        Is Montaigne *the* Book?

    We are natural believers; Connexion↑ists;↓ Causationists;
    We are dispirited by the destructionist
we like a lawyer as a connector
            a savant
            a conservative

---

[306] Erratic swirling lines in ink are struck through the extreme left portion of
the first sentence, perhaps to delete it. "Great man, — . . . of light" is struck through
in ink with a vertical use mark.
    [307] This heading, and the inserted words "going from" in the following paragraph,
are in pencil.
    [308] The entries on this page are in pencil.

We hate destructionists & their skepticism
But for that skepticism or consideration & pause
before assent, & resistance to the arrogance of
custom & tradition, the mind is no mind that is
without this skepticism

[258]　　　　　　　↑*Symbolism.*↓
The sonnets of the lover are insane enough, but they are as
valuable to the philosopher as the prayers of saints for their potent
symbolism. Love is a leveller and in the melodies of Hafiz, Allah
is a groom, & heaven but a closet[,] in his daring hymns to his mistress[.] [309]

　　　↑Belinda Randall↓
B R's music taught us what a song should be; how slight & thin its
particular meaning; you would not be hard & emphatic on the burden
of a song, as, Ti RA *li* ra &c
　　　Lilli burlero &c

The world is enigmatical, every thing said & every thing
known & done, & must not be taken literally, but genially. We must
be at the top of our condition to understand any thing rightly.[310]

[259] "Only poetry inspires poetry," said Schiller, "therefore we
ought to avoid affairs." —
True, if he use poetry in a liberal sense, but if he mean books of
poems, no. For, the test of the poet is, that he be able to read the
poetry of affairs.
　　　　　　　↑from W. 55↓

"Nature is likened to a female dancer exhibiting herself to soul as
to an audience. She desists when she has sufficiently shown herself: she
does so, because she has been seen. The spectator desists because he has
seen her. There is no further use for the world." Colebrooke p. 259.[311]

[309] This paragraph is struck through in ink with a vertical use mark. The first
sentence is used in "Poetry and Imagination," *W*, VIII, 10, the second in "Persian
Poetry," *W*, VIII, 249.
[310] This paragraph is used in "Works and Days," *W*, VII, 180.
[311] See pp. [95]–[96] above.

"All this world is but the transmutation of oblations" *Vishnu Pu[ráńa,* 1840, p. 100].[312]

[260][313] ⟨N⟩ Every symbol gives a new joy, as if it were a twirl of the world wheels.
That is the joy of eloquence;
and of Chemistry; Sir H. Davy's,
to know that here we have the same ⟨absolute⟩ matter, & not a vestige of the old form.
And of animal transformations, as in grub & fly; embryo & man[.]

⟨I⟩An example of it is in overpowering duration by other principles, & contracting or expanding durations at pleasure, as, in the story of the songs of the Hahas in Vishnu Purana[.][314]

/The/Every/ correspondence we observe in mind & matter, gives the same joy
suggesting a ⟨link⟩ thread older & deeper than either of these old nobilities[.][315]

"Apparent imitations of unapparent natures." Zoroaster[316]

[261] We see the law gleaming through like the sense of a half--translated ode of Hafiz[.]
The poet who plays with it with the most boldness best justifies himself. He is most profound & most devout[.][317]
Light thickens
Thought has its material side
Spirit is not all spirit but will be fluid, gas, solid ⟨presen⟩ already.

Nature seems to us like a chamber lined with mirrors, & look where

[312] See p. [130] above.
[313] The entries on this and the following page are in pencil.
[314] *The Vishńu Puráńa* . . . , 1840, p. 355: "When [Raivata] arrived, the quiristers Haha, Huhu, and others, were singing before Brahma; and Raivata, waiting till they had finished, imagined the ages that elapsed during their performance to be but as a moment." See *JMN*, VIII, 444.
[315] This entry is used in "Poetry and Imagination," *W*, VIII, 9.
[316] See Journal U, pp. [i] and [144] above and Journal O, p. [1] below.
[317] This entry to this point is used in "Poetry and Imagination," *W*, VIII, 9–10.

we will in botany, mechanics, chemistry, astronomy, the image of man comes throbbing back to us.

Each religion, each philosophy, each civilization, perhaps, is only the immense sequel of one exaggerated symbol: each, that is, is a mysticism. Example of this on p 127,

[262] Joseph Myrick really believed that God had his own way & would speed the right. He had not worn his clay coat or shuffled over the dreary floor in that asses' dance for nothing if he had learned that[.] [318]

↑Travelling↓ [319]
    Our education in Latin & Greek really mortgages us to Italy, & entitles us to go.
    Not go, if we had a commanding idea which concatenates our readings & doings[.]
    But we have not, why should we say we have.

[263] If you are abandoned to your genius & employment, be it never so special & rare, as engraving, or painting, — men will do you justice & not reproach you that you do not plough[.] [320]

The language is made, who has not helped to make it? [n] Then comes Milton, Shakspeare; and find it all made to their hand, & use it as if there never had been language before. We infer, how strictly lies greatness in the line of tendency; how near to greatness were all these insignificant cooperators[.]

    [264] Let every one mind his own. Hastings makes a good shoe because he makes nothing else. [321] ⟨Is it less true for the man of let-

---

[318] A partially erased pencil version of this entry underlies the ink version. The pencil version has "worn the coat" for "worn his clay coat" and omits "in that asses dance". The two sentences are used in "Worship," *W*, VI, 237.
    [319] This heading, and the three sentences that follow, are in pencil.
    [320] This entry is in pencil.
    [321] Jonas Hastings was a dealer in shoes "at the sign of the Big Boot on the Mill Dam" in Concord, according to advertisements in the Concord *Freeman*.

ters for the man of thoughts⟩ Let ⟨him⟩ not ↑the student↓ be above his business. ↑Let him↓ sedulously ⁿ wait every morning for the news concerning the structure of the world which the Spirit will give him. The merchants will say, If he was a practical man — A practical man can never do it. It needs a native student with all the armoury of learning & of inveterated habits of thought.[322]

[265] They who believe, & through their belief, delight in the preacher or poet, are not ignorant that he may fall away; that he has a salary, and, that if he should come to an estate, he might serve them with his eloquence less sedulously. ⟨B⟩ They know that, but they ↑also↓ know that ⟨the⟩ what they love & adore exists independently of its ministers; and they will hearken to him heedfully, as long as he speaks for it, & to another when ⟨he⟩ ↑their preacher↓ speaks for it no longer. They who put down chestnut posts ⟨are⟩ [266] know well enough that stone posts would last longer, but they have considered that these will last twenty years, & when they are rotten it will be cheaper to buy new ones than to set granite once for all.

> What creature slayeth or is slain?
> What creature saves or ⟨is⟩ saved is? ↑⟨brings or reaches
>   bliss?⟩↓
> ⟨Each loses or⟩
> His life ⟨each⟩ ↑will either↓ lose⟨s⟩ or gain⟨s⟩,
> As he ↑shall↓ follow⟨s⟩ ⟨good⟩harm or ⟨evil⟩ bliss.[323]

[267] [blank]
[268] [Index material omitted] [324]
[inside back cover] [Index material omitted]

[322] In the left margin beside "Let ⟨him⟩ not . . . business.", "Let him Sedulously . . . give him.", and "Let him Sedulously . . . of thought." are single vertical lines in ink.
[323] These lines are in pencil. For the wording of the quotation from *The Vishṅu Puráṅa* which Emerson is here versifying, see p. [167] above. Cf. "Brahma," *W*, IX, 195.
[324] A preliminary index in pencil covers this page. Additions in ink and pencil to the final index on the inside back cover occur in the right margin.

O

1846–1847

Journal O was begun in April, 1846, as the notation on the first flyleaf makes clear, and its last dated entry is February 15, 1847 — the same month in which Emerson began Journal AB, which follows it. It consists almost entirely of regular journal material, and provided passages for at least thirty lectures, addresses, and essays, most notably several lectures in the series on Mind and Manners in the Nineteenth Century, given in London in June, 1848, and several in the series Conduct of Life, given in Boston in December, 1851.

The covers of the copybook bear a green and brown mottled design and measure 17.5 x 21.5 cm. The spine strip and protective corners are of light brown leather. On the spine is the notation "1846 O"; on the front cover "O 1846", and on the back cover "O".

Originally there were 336 lightly ruled pages, plus two flyleaves at both front and back, but the leaves bearing pages 45–48, 59–68, 103–104, 187–188, and 347–348 are missing, and that numbered 31–32, once detached, has been re-attached with modern transparent tape. The leaves measure 17 x 20.7 cm. In his initial pagination, Emerson inadvertently omitted pages 215–244, and, after changing his mistaken 245 and 246 to 215 and 216, let the error stand; the present text retains his incorrect numbering to the end of the journal. Most of the pages are numbered in ink, but twenty-seven are numbered in pencil: 1, 5, 7, 9, 14, 15, 17, 19, 21–23, 27, 53, 84, 88, 92, 94, 96, 100, 101, 106, 114, 118, 120, 122, 126, and 296. Thirty-six pages are unnumbered: 2, 4, 13, 57, 69, 85, 93, 95, 105, 107, 113, 137–139, 141, 143, 147, 161, 171, 175, 201, 207, 272, 273, 285, 297, 301, 303, 309, 312, 313, 339, and 369–372. Twenty-one pages were first numbered in pencil, then in ink: 3, 11, 18, 25, 26, 50, 51, 80, 82, 86, 90, 97, 102, 110, 116, 124, 172, 182 (180 in pencil), 192, 202 (200 in pencil), and 206 (204 in pencil). Page 340 was originally numbered 390. Thirty-one pages are blank: ii, 13, 30, 93–95, 113, 119, 127, 129, 137–139, 141–143, 147, 156, 158, 161, 165, 170, 171, 175, 201, 207, 253, 272, 273, 286, and 313.

A calendar for 1846 is pasted to the top left-hand corner of the front cover verso. Laid in between pages 70 and 71 is a four-page sheet of white letter paper, bearing on the first side notations in Emerson's hand; it has been numbered 70a–70d. Pasted to pages 368–369 are three pieces of pale-blue paper bearing transcriptions, not in Emerson's hand, from the talk of Edward Waldo Emerson in September, 1846, when he was two years old.

[front cover]   O
                                1846

[front cover verso] [1] [Index material omitted]

                    Stoneham Friday Dec 4
                    ⟨Bangor October 6 Tuesday⟩
                    ⟨Waltham Nov. 7 Sat⟩
                    ⟨Newburyport Oct 30 Friday⟩
                    Salem Wednesday   sine mense
                    ⟨Beverly Tuesday 3 Nov⟩
                    ⟨New Bedford Oct 29 Thursday⟩
    N Merrill   Saxonville 17 December Thursd.
                    Beverly 8 December
                    Manchester 9 December
                    Cambridge 16 Dec. Wed.
                    Boston
↑Read Feb 1877↓   Lowell
                    New Bedford Monday Jan 4
                    Taunton   Jan 5?
                    Malden   12
                    Exeter   Jan 14

                    _____

[i] [Index material omitted]   R.W. Emerson
                                                April; 1846.

                            O

"Apparent imitations of unapparent natures." Zoroaster [2]

[ii] [blank]
[1]   "Oft have I heard & deemed the witness true,

----

[1] The entries on the front cover verso, which are in pencil, refer to lecture engagements for the 1846–1847 winter season. A calendar for 1846, measuring 5.1 x 8.5 cm and cut from a Boston newspaper, is attached to the top left-hand corner by a dab of red sealing wax.

[2] See Journal U, pp. [i] and [144], and Journal Y, p. [260] above.

Whom man delights in, God delights in too."
AD 1170   Pons de Capdueil.[3]

[2] Nature may be cooked into all shapes, & not recognized. Mountains & oceans we think we understand; — yes, so long as they are
contented to be such, and are safe with the geologist; but when they
are melted in Promethean alembics, & come out men; & then, melted
again, come out words, without any abatement but with an exaltation
of power — ! [4]

[3][5] To know the virtue of the soil, we do not taste the loam,
but we eat the berries & apples; and to mend the bad world, we do
not impeach Polk & Webster, but we supersede them by the Muse,

Intellect makes him strange among his house-mates. Every
person right[,] or to make him right needs only more personality[.] [6]

Demades surpassed all when he trusted to nature[.]

Every planet must get his living[.]
Every army must get its own living.
Want a fort, build a fort[.] [7]

Eloquence draws as the highest form of personal power.

Nature may be cooked into all shapes & not recognized. Mountains

---

[3] Emerson found these lines from the twelfth-century Provençal poet in *Lays of
the Minnesingers or German Troubadours of the Twelfth and Thirteenth Centuries:
Illustrated by Specimens of the Cotemporary Lyric Poetry of Provence and Other
Parts of Europe* . . . , [ed. Edgar Taylor] (London, 1825), p. 220, which he
withdrew from the Harvard College Library January 14, 1847. They are used in
"Success," *W*, VII, 306, and "Poetry and Imagination," *W*, VIII, 37. See p. [162]
below.

[4] "Mountains . . . power — !", struck through in pencil with a vertical use
mark, is used in "Poetry and Imagination," *W*, VIII, 16. See p. [3] below.

[5] The entries on this and the following page, with the exception of the first on
p. [3], are in pencil. In the top left-hand corner of p. [4] is a small crosshatched
square with a scroll-like border.

[6] See p. [17] below.

[7] For the first sentence, see p. [96] below; for all three sentences, see p. [17]
below.

& oceans we think we understand, but when they are melted in Promethean alembics & come out men, & then melted again & come out
words, [4] without any abatement, but with an exaltation of power??

x	Theodore Parker
x	W[illiam] H[enry] Channing
	Elizur Wright
x	J[ames]. F[reeman]. Clarke
	G[eorge]. Ripley
x	J[ohn] S[ullivan] Dwight
x	Charles Sumner
	Parker Pillsbury
x	J[ames] Elliot Cabot
	H[arrison] G[ray] O[tis] Blake
	John Brown
x	H[enry] D[avid] Thoreau
x	A[mos] B[ronson] Alcott
x	R[alph] W[aldo] E[merson]
	Edw[ard]. Bangs
x	T[homas]. T[readwell] Stone
x	J[ohn]. Weiss [8]

[5] The life which we seek is expansion: the actual life even of the
genius or the saint is obstruction.
What a contest between personality & universality! The man listens
to stoic, epicurean, or Christian, & acknowledges his mistakes. But
he was right; and a little afterward comes a new infusion of his own,

[8] Persons mentioned here not previously identified are: William Henry Channing, Unitarian clergyman and nephew of William Ellery Channing the elder;
Elizur Wright, editor of the associationist *Daily Chronotype* (Boston); George Ripley, founder of Brook Farm; John Sullivan Dwight, music critic and member of
the Brook Farm community; Charles Sumner, prominent Boston lawyer and later
leader of the antislavery forces in the U.S. Senate; Harrison Gray Otis Blake, Unitarian minister and schoolteacher in Worcester; John Brown, drygoods dealer of
Concord; Edward Bangs, Harvard '46, at this time studying for the law; Thomas
Treadwell Stone, liberal preacher from Maine and antislavery lecturer; and John
Weiss, Unitarian clergyman, who had been a classmate of Thoreau at Harvard. The
purpose of Emerson's list has not been established.

and he is triumphantly right again in his own way against the preju-
dices of the universe.*   ↑See p 17↓

What a dancing jacko'lanthorn is this estimate of our contemporaries. Some times I seem to move in a constellation. I think my
birth has fallen in the thick of the Milky Way: and again I fancy
the American Blight & English narrowness & German defectiveness
& French surface have bereaved the time of all worth.
↑That unlimited↓

[6] In your music, in your speech, in your writing, I am amused by
your talents; but ⟨if you are⟩ ↑in the presence of one↓ capable of
serving & expressing an idea, the finest talents become an imperti-
nence[.]

In nature every creature has a tail. The brain has not yet availed to
drop that respectable appendage. How odious is hunger! Well
enough in the animal, well in the citizen, but in the illstarred in-
tellectualist a calamity: he can neither eat nor not eat. If he could
eat an oak forest or half a mountain; I should like that; a good
Kurouglou;[9] supper for thirteen; but hunger for any dinner he is
likely to get, degrades him. If we cannot have a good rider, at least
let us have a good horse: now, 'tis a haggard rider of a haggard
horse.

[7] In Germany there still seems some hidden ⟨German⟩ ↑dreamer↓
from whom this strange genial poetic comprehensive philosophy
comes, & from which the English & French get mere rumours &
fragments, which are yet the best philosophy we know. One while
we thought that this fontal German was Schelling, then Fichte,
↑Novalis, then↓ Oken, then it hovered about Schleiermacher, &
settled for a time on Hegel. But on producing authenticated books
from each of these masters, we find them clever men, but nothing

[9] Emerson's knowledge of Kurroglou came from *Specimens of the Popular
Poetry of Persia, as Found in the Adventures and Improvisations of Kurroglou, the
Bandit-Minstrel of Northern Persia* . . . , trans. Alexander Chodzko (London,
1842), which he withdrew from the Harvard College Library September 2, 1846.

like so great & deep a poet sage as we looked for. And now we are still to seek for the lurking Behmen of modern Germany.

Hegel's philosopheme blazoned by ⟨Kant⟩Cousin, that an idea always conquers, &, in all history, victory has ever fallen on the right side, (a doctrine which Carlyle has, as usual, found a fine idiom for, that Right & might go together;) was a specimen of this [8] Teutonism. Something of it there is in Schelling; more in his quoted Maader; something in Goethe, who is catholic & poetic. Swedenborg had much; Novalis had good sentences; Kant, nothing of it. Kepler was "an unitarian of the united world." [10] Si non errasset, fecerat ille minus.[11]

↑*Scholar's society*↓

We ought to keep better company[,] you say[,] & ⟨our thoughts should⟩ we should see to it that our thoughts marry equally, as well as our daughters. ⟨But⟩ Now,[n] the company of each wise person is not wise, but gossiping. As Talleyrand[,] reproached with Madame T[alleyrand]., said, he found nonsense very refreshing.[12]

[9] Eloquence wants anthracite coal. Coldness is the most fatal quality. Phaedrus-horses, one winged, one not; there must be both. Burke had the high principles [in Chatham never a generalization]. Burke dragged them down to facts which he never loses sight of: he had mania, & yet also gives Mosaic accounts. You must speak ↑always↓ from higher ground. Webster does.

But give us the rare merits of impassivity, of marble texture, against which the mob of souls dashing is ⟨gr⟩broken like crockery falling on stone: the endurance which can afford to fail in the popular sense, because it never fails in ⟨the⟩ its own; it knows what it wants & advances today, & tomorrow, & every day, to that which belongs to it:[13]

---

[10] See *JMN*, VIII, 436, and "Blight," *W*, IX, 140.

[11] "Had it not erred, it had achieved less." Martial, *Epigrams*, I, xxi. See *JMN*, VI, 73.

[12] Cf. Villemarest, *Life of Prince Talleyrand*, 1834–1836, III, 233. The statement is used in "Considerations by the Way," *W*, VI, 269. See *JMN*, VIII, 324.

[13] A single vertical line in ink is drawn in the left margin from "the endurance" to "its own;".

We shall have to describe these arms in detail though the highest eloquence must combine them all. Kurouglou had seventeen weapons, & in personal combat was wont to try them all in turn.[14] One should have a great superseding personality[.]

[10] ↑Life↓

You must treat the days respectfully, you must be a day yourself, and not interrogate life like a college professor. Every thing in the universe goes by indirection. There are no straight lines.[15]

↑Life↓   *Too much Friction*

The proverb teaches that there is a pound of grindstone to a pound of cheese, but I think there are always many pounds of grindstone to an ounce of cheese. How much arrangement & combination & drudgery to bring about a pleasant hour, to hear an eloquent argument, or a fine poetic ⟨s⟩reading, or a little superior conversation, what rattle & jingle, how many miles must be ridden, how many woods & meadows[,] alder-borders & stone wall must be tediously passed!

[11] The beautiful is never plentiful.

Nothing is more rare in any man than an act of his own; but then how beautiful it is! [16]

What ⟨intense⟩ satisfactions in detecting now & then a long relation far over bounds of space & time in two parts of consciousness! Well, but we drop one thing when we grasp another. The least acceleration in our intellectual processes, and an increased tenacity, would constitute a true paradise.

[12] Alcott thinks that the happiness of old age consists in transforming the Furies into the Muses[.] [17]

---

[14] This paragraph is struck through in ink with a vertical use mark; "Kurouglou . . . turn." is used in "Eloquence," *W*, VII, 99.

[15] This paragraph, struck through in pencil with a diagonal use mark, is used in "Works and Days," *W*, VII, 180–181.

[16] These two sentences are in pencil.

[17] This sentence is struck through in ink with a vertical use mark; "transforming . . . Muses" is used in "Culture," *W*, VI, 166.

[13] [blank]

[14] Nov. 23. Burke a little too Latin in Debi Sing but what gradation! such opulence as permits selection. Webster too always has
senatorial propriety. I wish to see accomplished translators of the
world into language. I wish the leisures of the spirit. I please me with
I know not what accounts of Oriental taletellers who transport &
ravish the hearer & make him forget the hours of the day & the taste
of meat.

But our careful Americans blurt & spit forth news without grace or
gradation, parenthetically between the mouthfuls of their hasty
dining.[18]

[15] Swedenborg, how strange, that he should have persuaded
men & drawn a church after him[,] this enchanter with his mob of
dreams! It recalls De Foe and Drelincourt & Mrs. Veal,[19] the circum-
stantiality of his pictures, the combination of verity & of moonshine,
dreams in the costume of science.

The effect of his religion will be denied by his disciples, but
inevitable, that he leads them away from Calvinism, & under the
guise of allegiance to Christianity, supplants both Calvin & Christ.
When they awake, they have irrecoverably lost the others, & Swedenborg is not to be found.

Like a man with diseased eyes he carries *muscae volitantes*[20]
wherever he looks. He is a Prospero who travels with what a train!
All the kinds that went by pairs into Noah's ark surround this Æsop,
and furnish an appropriate mask for [16] every conceit of his brain.
The most fanciful of men[,] he passes for the most precise & mathematical.[21]

[18] These two paragraphs are in pencil. Emerson's reference to Burke involves
the Indian official Debi Sing, considered at length in *Speeches in the Impeachment
of Warren Hastings, Esquire*, Third Day, in Burke's *Works*, 7 vols. (Boston, 1826–
1827), in Emerson's library.
[19] Defoe's *A True Relation of the Apparition of Mrs. Veal* (1706) was written
to promote the sale of a book by the French Protestant divine Charles Drelincourt
(1595–1669) entitled *Les Consolations de l'âme fidèle contre les frayeurs de la mort*
(1651).
[20] The technical term for spots before the eyes.
[21] The word "capitulate," inscribed in pencil at some earlier time and later

I grow old, I accept conditions; — thus far — no farther; — to learn that we are not the first born, but the latest born; that we have no wings; that the sins of our predecessors are on us like a mountain of obstruction[.]

[17][22] Every person is right, or to make him right needs only more personality. ↑See p. 5↓

Intellect makes him strange among his housemates.[23]

Self help the law of nature.
            Every army must get its own living[.]
Every planet must get its own living[.]
Every planet must make itself, is nature's law. The river makes its own shores.
            Do you want a fort, — build a fort.[24]
                    See again in *AB* 92 [25]

We lie for the right. We affect a greater hope than we feel. We idealize character. We embellish the story[.] [26]

[18] Genius consists neither in improvising nor in remembering, but in both, ever trembles the beam of the balance in nature. Two brains in every man.[27]

_____

enclosed in parentheses to delete it, occurs between the last two lines of this entry. Between this entry and the next, half a line of pencil writing, first deleted and later erased, is still discernible.

[22] Erased pencil writing, consisting of a number of separate canceled entries, is discernible under the ink entries at the top of this page. The following significant words and phrases have been recovered: "Happy are the dumb"; "He quarries himself"; "Expression"; "The river makes its own shores" (also in ink); and "do I place intellectual natures". All of these also occur on p. [19].

[23] For this and the preceding entry, see p. [3] above.

[24] These six lines are struck through in ink with a vertical use mark. For the second, third, and sixth sentences, see p. [3] above; for the third, see also p. [96] below; for the fifth, see p. [19] below. Cf. "Fate," *W*, VI, 38.

[25] Journal AB will be published in a future volume.

[26] A pencil version of this entry underlies the ink version. There are no significant differences between the two.

[27] A pencil version of this entry underlies the ink version. The pencil version

Our power consists not in abolishing nor in creating, but in transference merely. I kill a worm, & another worm is hatched. I burn a
stick of wood, & a bud shoots from another oak.[28]

In any popular view of Christianity it must be said to have failed.
Jesus came to save the world, but it is ↑said to be↓ as bad as ever.

[19][29] Great satisfaction that the thing can be done

but to be voiceless
Expression is so much
To be a quarry & to quarry yourself

The river makes its own shores[30]

I place inferior natures
And rarely, with how much pleasure I place intellectual natures

Happy are the dumb

[20] But the dust is alive[,] is polar[.]
We cannot quite die. The old age & death are the approaches of sleep
by which we shall be refreshed[.]

Women waddle; men also do not make a straight but a zig zag path;
their essence is bifold, & undulates ↑or alternates↓[.] I see not how a
man can walk in a straight line, who has ever seen a looking glass.
He acts, & instantly his act is reflected to him by the opinion of men.
He cannot keep his eyes off of these dancing images; and that is the
death of glory, the death of duty in him. Safer, o far safer, is the

---

has "the balance the self equality of nature" for "the beam of the balance in nature."

[28] A pencil version of this entry underlies the ink version. The last sentence of
the pencil version shows Emerson's revisions: "I ⟨cut a bough from an oak⟩ ↑burn
a stick of wood↓ & a bud shoots from another ⟨stem⟩ ↑oak↓".

[29] The entries on this page and the next, down to "we shall be refreshed", are in
pencil.

[30] See p. [17] above.

reflection of his form that he finds in Zoology, in Botany, in Chemistry. Anthropomorphize them, — 'tis all well & poetical.[31]

[21] I cannot hope to make any thorough lights into the caverns of the human consciousness. That were worth the ambition of angels! no↑!↓ but only to make special, provincial, local lights? Yes, but we obey the impulse to affirm & affirm & neither you nor I know the value of what we say.[32]

Henry Thoreau objected to my "Shakspeare," that the eulogy impoverished the race. Shakspeare ought to be praised, as the sun is, so that all shall be rejoiced.

[22][33] That which is divine is to make an entire traverse from Deity to the dust, & it is indifferent whether it is in a book or in an institution[.]

O yes, he may escape from shackles & dungeons, but how shall he get away from his temperament? how from his hereditary sins & infusions? how from the yellow humours through which he must ever see the blue sky & the sun & stars? Sixty centuries have squatted & stitched & hemmed to shape & finish for him that strait jacket which he must wear.

[23]   ↑Croisement↓   ↑Mixture↓
Nature loves to cross her stocks.[33a] A pure blood, Bramin ⟨with⟩on Bramin, marrying in & in, soon becomes puny & wears out. Some strong Cain son, some black blood must renew & refresh the paler veins of Seth.

---

[31] Emerson first inscribed this paragraph in pencil, then copied it over in ink except for "Women waddle . . . alternates". There are no significant differences between the pencil and ink versions.

[32] Pencil versions of this and the following entry underlie the ink versions; the first is partially erased. There are no significant differences between the two versions.

[33] The entries on this page are in pencil.

[33a] This sentence is used in "Works and Days," *W*, VII, 162. Cf. the same thought in French in Journal U, p. [79] above.

What a discovery I made one day that the more I spent the more I grew, that it was as easy to occupy a large place & do much work as an obscure place & do little; and that in the winter in which I communicated all my results to classes, I was full of ↑new↓ thoughts.

[24] Queenie came it over Henry last night when he taxed the new astronomers with the poverty of their discoveries & showings — not strange enough. ⟨q⟩Queenie ⟨thought that for her they were better that they were not "strange," but only the most beautiful & astonishing discoveries.⟩ wished to see with eyes some of those strange things which the telescope reveals, the satellites of Saturn, &c. H. said that stranger things might be seen with the naked eye. "Yes," said Queenie "but I wish to see some of those things that are not quite so strange."

[25] The one good in life is concentration, the one evil is dissipation, and it makes no difference whether our dissipations are coarse or fine, whether they be property & ↑its↓ cares, friends, & a social turn of mind, or politics, or practicks, or music, or pleasure.

Everything is good which takes away one plaything & delusion more, & drives ⟨h⟩us home to do one poor indigent spartan thing. The book I read of lately, taught, that there are two brains in every man, as two eyes, two ears, &c. & that culture consisted in compelling the two to the entertainment of one thought.

Friends, pictures, books, lower duties, talents, flatteries, hopes, all are distractions which cause formidable oscillations in our giddy balloon, & seem to make a good poise & a straight course impossible.[34]

[26] Immortality
'Tis a higher thing to confide that if it is best we should live, then we shall live, — 'tis a higher thing to have this conviction than to have the lease of indefinite centuries & millenniums & aeons.[35]

---

[34] These three paragraphs, struck through in pencil with a vertical use mark, are used, with the omission of "The book I read . . . thought.", in "Power," *W*, VI, 73–74.
    [35] This sentence, struck through in ink with a vertical use mark, is used in "Worship," *W*, VI, 239.

"It is pleasant to die, if there be gods, and sad to live if there be none." [36]

Marcus Antoninus. [*Meditations*, II, 11]

"Vous direz ce serait mieux que nous aurions une vie éternelle. Bien. Je dis si ce serait mieux, cela viendra. Alors, je dis c'est une chose plus grande de confier que si ce serait mieux, cela viendra, — beaucoup plus grande que servit la promesse formelle du Createur que nous subsistérions pour tous les siécles." [37]

[27] We frigidly talk of reform, until the walls mock us with contempt. It is that of which a man should never speak, but if he have cherished it in his bosom, he should steal to it in ↑the↓ dark⟨ness⟩ as an Indian to his bride. Or, a monk should go privily to another monk, & say, Lo we two are of one opinion; a new light has shined in our hearts. Let us dare to obey it.

[28₁] I like people who can do things,

[29] "For Virtue's whole sum is to know & dare." [38]
[Donne, "To the Countess of Bedford," l. 33]

[28₂] Bardic sentences how few! Literature warps away from life though at first it seems to bind it. If now I should count the English Poets who have contributed aught to the bible of existing England & America[,] sentences of guidance & consolation which are still glowing & effective — how few! Milton, Shakspeare, Pope, Burns, Young, Cowper, Wordsworth — (what disparity in the names! Yet these are the authors) & Herbert, Jonson, Donne[.] [39]
↑Printed in "*Eng. Traits*"↓

[30] [blank]

[36] This quotation, struck through in ink with a vertical use mark, is used in "Worship," *W*, VI, 240, and "Immortality," *W*, VIII, 329.
[37] At the bottom of p. [27] is a pencil version of this quotation, struck through in pencil with a diagonal line, probably to cancel it. The pencil version has a canceled "jouerions" before the word "aurions" in the first sentence.
[38] Emerson connected these two lines, which appear at the top of their respective pages, by linking the long rules underneath them. See *JMN*, V, 341, VI, 386, and VII, 5.
[39] This paragraph is struck through in ink with a vertical use mark; "If now . . . how few!" is used in *English Traits*, *W*, V, 256.

[31]   ↑Printed in *"Society & Solitude."*↓

Is the picture beautiful, & was the man so great, and must so many Academies convene to settle the claims of the classic & the romantic schools? so many journeys & measurements, — Niebuhr, Muller, & Sir William Gell to identify the plain of Troy & tomb of Achilles?[n] And your homage to Dante costs you so much sailing & travel? And yet the Nile & isle ⟨of⟩ Phila remains unseen, Euphrates also, & the land of Zoroaster? Poor child, that flexile clay of which these old brothers moulded their admirable symbols was not Parian, or Persian, or Memphian, or Teutonic, nor local ↑at all,↓ ⟨no,⟩ but was oxygen & water & sunlight & the warmth of the blood & the heaving of the lungs; it was that clay which thou heldest but now in thy foolish hands & threw away to go & seek in [32] vain in sepulchres & mummy pits & old bookshops of Asia Minor, Egypt, or England. It was the ⟨wise⟩ ↑honoured↓ Today which all men scorn, it was the rich Poverty ⟨isolation⟩ (making isolation & concentration) which all men hate, it was the populous all-loving Solitude, which men quit for the tattle & gossip of towns.[40]

He lurks, he hides, he who is success[,] ⟨he-she-it,⟩ reality, joy, power, that which constitutes heaven, which reconciles impossibilities, atones for shortcomings, expiates sins, or makes them virtues, buries in oblivion the crowded historical Past, sinks religions, philosophies, nations, persons, ↑to legends;↓ reverses the scale of opinion, of fame; reduces sciences to opinion, and ↑makes↓ the thought of the moment the key to the [33] universe & the egg of history to come[.]

"Ah, ⟨c⟩si c'est égal, Monsieur." — It is all alike, astronomy,[n] metaphysics, sword, ↑spade,↓ pencil, ⟨hoe or spade,⟩ or instruments & arts yet to be invented, this is the inventor, the worth-giver, the worth,

This is he that shall come, or if he come not, ⟨c⟩nothing comes,[n] he that disappears ↑on↓ the instant that we go to celebrate him. If we go to burn those that blame our celebration, he appears in them.

---

[40] This paragraph, struck through in ink with a vertical use mark on p. [31] and three vertical use marks on p. [32], is used in "Works and Days," *W*, VII, 174–175, where it is followed by the opening words of the following paragraph, "He lurks . . . joy, power,".

The divine Newness.

Hoe & spade; sword & pen; cities, pictures, gardens, laws, bibles, are prized only because they were means he sometime used: so with astronomy, arithmetic, caste, feudalism.

[34] We kiss with devotion these hems of his garment. They ⟨turn⟩crumble to ashes on our lips.

Prophecy is not more sacred than is knowledge of the present.

Quantum scimus, sumus.[41]

Do not throw up your thought because you cannot answer objections[.] [42]

E 26 N 34 [43]

Health is good, — power, — life, — that resists disease, poison, & all enemies, & is conservative as well as creative. Here is great question whether to graft with wax or whether with clay, whether to whitewash, or to potash, or to prune, but the one point is the thrifty tree, & all the rest are indifferent.[44]

"Apollo is a god who defends or destroys, according to the nature of the case."   Muller. p. 195 [45]

[35]   *Imagination*
There are two powers of the imagination, one, that of knowing the symbolic character of things & treating them as representative; & [the other, Elizabeth Hoar thinks, is] ↑practically↓ the tenaci⟨ty⟩ousness of ⟨mind for⟩ an image, cleaving unto it & letting it not go, and, by the treatment, demonstrating that this figment of thought is as

[41] "We are what we know" (Ed.). Emerson's source was probably James Marsh's edition of Coleridge's *Aids to Reflection* (Burlington, Vt., 1829), p. 257, n. 10, where, however, it occurs as "quantum *sumus, scimus.*" See *JMN*, III, 164.
[42] This sentence is struck through in ink with a vertical use mark. See Journal Y, p. [74] above.
[43] These two references are in pencil. See *JMN*, VII, 281–282, and VIII, 260–261.
[44] This paragraph, struck through in ink with a vertical use mark, is used in "Power," *W*, VI, 60.
[45] Perhaps Johannes von Müller, *An Universal History, in twenty-four books*, 4 vols. (Boston, 1831–1832), in Emerson's library.

palpable & objective to the poet, as ↑is↓ the ground on which he stands, or the walls of houses about him. And this power appears in Dante & Shakspeare.

↑printed in P[oetry]. & I[magination]. p. 19, 20,↓
I should say that the imagination exists by sharing the ⟨cu⟩ ethereal currents. The poet is able to glance from heaven to earth[,] from earth to heaven, because he contemplates the central identity and sees it undulate & stream this way & that, with divine flowings [36] through remotest things &, following it, can detect essential resemblances in things never before named together. The poet can class things so audaciously because he is sensible of the celestial flowing ↑from↓ which nothing is exempt: his own body also is a fleeing ⟨image⟩ ↑apparition↓, his personality as fugitive as any type, as fugitive as the trope he employs. As one said, in certain hours we can almost pass our hand through our own bodies. I think the use or value of poetry to be the suggestion it affords of the flux or fugaciousness of the poet[.] [46]

[37]   ↑◰ All this probably printed.↓ [47]

[38] The caste of India, how shocking to your feelings, my dear democrat! uproot it with ax, stubhoe, & gunpowder, leave not a trembling ⟨r⟩fibre or radicle alive. And yet how could it not be, — close transcript or shadow as it is of the decagraded or centigrade [n] man? Each man is a scale of how many levels or platforms! [48] What a manifold many-chambered aristocracy is systematised or unexpanded in his structure, — king, senate, consistory, judiciary, Army, chorus of poets, tradesm⟨e⟩an, husbandm⟨e⟩an, mob, — room is found for them all in the brain & scope of each human form, & when we meet our neighbor, we inquire of his air & action which of all these rules the passing hour.

---

[46] This paragraph, struck through in ink on p. [35] with two diagonal use marks, is used in "Poetry and Imagination," *W*, VIII, 21. The word "apparition" is inserted in pencil. With "The poet is able . . . heaven,", cf. Shakespeare, *A Midsummer Night's Dream*, V, i, 12–13.
[47] This entry is in pencil.
[48] This sentence is struck through in pencil with seven diagonal use marks.

[39]⁴⁹ Talk with Brisbane   Times Newspaper   a capital machine but wants a conscience at the heart to make it grand[.]
Greeley has a conscience[.]
Chronotype has a victorious tone[.] ⁵⁰

Society is trying Fourierism in small pieces as the Union protective store; Clubhouses for the married; Boarding in Hotels; Book clubs; ⁵¹
It needs now only that a ⟨Un. S.⟩ Hotel Company should agree to build a palace for 300 families subscribing beforehand to rent suites of apartments for three years.

Fourier's 17 musical instruments taught him. His musical scale he applied with confidence to every part of nature[.]

[40] Life is the sleep of the soul: as soon as ⟨it⟩a soul is tired, it looks out for a body as a bed; enters into a body in the season of dentition, & sleeps seventy years.
Nobody is entitled to travel but such as have done their work. Whilst this world is in chaos, we shall not be allowed to leave it, & go into more harmonious systems. ⟨He⟩ Onlyⁿ the light characters travel. Who are you that have no task to keep you at home? ⁿ ⁵²
One thing more. Geoffroy St Hilaire gave a theory of monsters. There is never any new appearance but merely the joining of two normal forms that do not belong together[,] as part fish part man. It is right things out of place.⁵³
Well there is no moral deformity but is a good passion out of place. And no vice but somewhere or other has been bound up into a national

---

⁴⁹ The entries on pp. [39]–[41] are in pencil.
⁵⁰ Emerson had met Albert Brisbane, the American advocate of Fourierism, in New York in 1842 (L, III, 18). His references to newspapers are to the Boston *Times*, published from 1836 to 1857; Horace Greeley's New York *Tribune* (for which Brisbane wrote reformist articles); and the *Daily Chronotype* (Boston), an associationist organ founded in 1846.
⁵¹ Cf. "Historic Notes of Life and Letters in New England," *W*, X, 358.
⁵² The last two sentences are used in "Culture," *W*, VI, 145.
⁵³ This sentence, struck through in pencil with a vertical use mark, is used in "Considerations by the Way," *W*, VI, 258.

character, as assassination into Spain & Italy; theft into Sparta; adultery into France; concubinage into Turkey.

[41] "To see what money will buy"
Every step of civil & social advancement, of course, makes my dollar worth more. In Siberia, what could it buy, but wretched mitigations of suffering?[n] It would buy pain, want, & crime. In Rome it will buy beauty[,] magnificence. When I was born, a dollar would buy not much in Boston, now it will buy a great deal more, ⟨in t⟩ thanks to railroads, telegraphs, steamers, & the contemporaneous growth of New York, & the whole country.[54]

[42] The "Community" in its technical sense should exist, or our vulgar community should be elevated & socialized: There ought to be in every town a permanent proprietor which should hold library, picture & sculpture gallery, museum, &c. There are so many books that are merely books of reference that no man cares to buy, yet each should have access to; so much more with the elegances, nobilities, & festivities of pictures, prints, statues, music, it is much that I should have them sometimes. How often I think could I only have music on my own terms! Could I live in a great city, & know where I could go, whenever I wished ⟨to be⟩ the ablution & inundation of musical waves, that were a medicine & a /purification/bath/. [43] I do not wish to own pictures & statues. I do not wish the bore of keeping & framing & exhibiting. Yet I have to buy them, because no one is here to own them for me, no duke, no noble, no municipal or collegiate gallery. It does not help that my friend buys, if not permanent here. The best use by far of these comes when they are collected in one fit stately place, & their influence can be had occasionally as a strain of music, & to be the fitting decoration of public halls.[55]

[44] Tennyson & Browning, though full of talent, remind one of the catbird's knowing music[.]

---

[54] This entry, struck through in pencil with a vertical use mark, is used, without the opening quotation, in "Wealth," *W*, VI, 102.
[55] This paragraph is struck through in ink with a vertical use mark; cf. "Wealth," *W*, VI, 97–99.

Without their talent there is a certain dandy poetry[,] a certain dapper deftness & flourish[.] [56]

tea tray style

[45]–[48] [leaves torn out] [57]

[49] *Hymns* There are a great many excellent hymns in use in our Unitarian Churches. The best collection in the English language is no doubt Dr Greenwood's; [58] ⟨b⟩excellent in what he retained, in what he discovered & brought into use again from Cowper, Wesley, & the Moravians, &c & in what he sunk, as I had hoped, forever. But already the scribaciousness of our ministers has produced a number of pretended new collections; the Plymouth, the Cheshire, &c. All that is good in these they take from Greenwood. I will venture to say you cannot find one ↑good↓ piece in either of them that is not in his. But they have restored or added a great deal of trash. Their collections will pass away & his judicious book will come into lasting use.

[50] Have you ↑seen↓ Webster? Calhoun? Have you heard Everett, Garrison, Theodore Parker? Do you know Alcott? Then you may as well die. All conversation is at an end, when we have discharged ourselves of the five or six personalities that make up, domestic & imported, our American existence. Nor do we expect any⟨thing⟩body to be other than a faint copy of Napoleon, Byron, Goethe, Webster, Astor, Channing, or Abbott Lawrence.[59]

---

[56] This and the preceding entry are struck through in ink with a diagonal use mark.

[57] Emerson indexed p. [45] under Double Consciousness; p. [46] under Greatness and Marriage; and p. [48] under Character, Friendship, Love, Permanence, and Virtue.

[58] Francis W. P. Greenwood, *A Collection of Psalms and Hymns for Christian Worship* (1830), which Emerson had reviewed favorably, on its first appearance, in the *Christian Examiner*, X (March 1831), 30–34.

[59] Abbott Lawrence (1792–1855) founded and developed the mill city of Lawrence, Massachusetts. A pencil version of this entry, later erased, underlies the second entry on p. [51] and extends into the blank space below it. The pencil version has "to be anything but" for "to be other than". The paragraph, struck through in ink with two vertical use marks, is used in "Culture," *W*, VI, 135–136.

[51] Every word of Webster has passed through the fire of the intellect. The statement is always erect & disengaged.[60]

The non-resistants go about & persuade good men not to vote, & so paralyse the virtue that is in the conservative party. And thus the patriotic vote in the country is swamped in the legion of paddies. But though ⟨it⟩ ↑the non-voting↓ is right in the non-resistants, it is a patch & a pedantry in their converts, not in their system[,] not a just expression of their state of mind.

I did not write when I should how strongly I felt in one hour that the moral was the only [61]

[52][62] 31 July, 1846. Webster knows what is done in the shop & remembers & uses it in ⟨Congress⟩ ↑the Senate↓. He saw it in the shop with an eye supertabernal & supersenatorial or it would not have steaded. He is a ship that finds the thing where it is cheap, & carries it where it is dear. Knowledge is of some use in the best company. But the grasp is the main thing. Most men's minds do not grasp any thing. All slips through their fingers, like the paltry brass grooves that in most country houses are used to raise & ⟨pull⟩drop the curtain, but are made to sell, & will not hold any curtain but cobweb. I have heard that ideot children are known from the birth by the circumstance that their hands do not ⟨grasp⟩close round any thing. Webster naturally & always grasps, & therefore retains some thing from every company & circumstance.[n 63] [53][64] One of these tenacities, it is no matter where it goes. It gets an education in a shanty, in an alehouse, over a cigar, or in a fishingboat, as good as it could find in Germany

[60] A pencil version of this entry underlies the ink version. There are no significant differences between the two.

[61] This uncompleted entry is in pencil.

[62] Partially erased pencil writing covers the upper half of this page, of which only "I should only[?] write" and "& yet & yet" has been recovered.

[63] "But the grasp is . . . circumstance." is used in "Natural History of Intellect," *W*, XII, 48–49.

[64] Erased pencil writing, consisting of at least three separate entries, covers the upper half of this page. The following words and phrases have been recovered or conjecturally recovered: "Community is a"; "↑union than cannot but be;↓"; "↑union↓ of kings[?], that is production &"; and "Euth⟨r⟩yphron" (not erased).

or in Sais: for the world is unexpectedly rich, & everywhere tells the same things. The grasp is much, but not quite all; the juggle of commerce never loses its power to astonish & delight us, namely, the unlooked for juxtaposition of things. Take the peaches from under the tree, & carry them out of sight of the tree, & their value is centupled.[65]

Sex; the Sex of things, whose attractions work under all mutations.

1. You always carry a dirk under your shawl?
2. No, I always carry a heart under it, as the better weapon.[66]

ices into summer, fires into winter, & what new values! The child asked the other day, "Why do ⟨|| ... ||⟩huckleberries taste so much better with milk?" egg with salt

[54] ↑*Prints bought of Little & Brown   Apr 1846*↓ [67]

Sibilla Cumaea	single figure		1.75
Erithraea	do		1.75
Persi↑c↓a of Guercino	do		1.75
Libica of M. Angelo	with accessories		4.50
Persica of M A	with accessories		4.50
Four Sibyls of Raffaelle			6.00
School of Athens			6.00
Poesis			1.75
Justitia			1.75

29.75
The Daniel of M. Angelo was taken by C[aroline]. S[turgis]. 4.50

[65] This sentence is struck through in ink with three vertical use marks. See Journal Y, p. [142] above.

[66] This entry is in pencil.

[67] These prints, most of which can still be seen in the Emerson house in Concord, can be identified in order as follows: Michelangelo's "Cumaean Sibyl" and "Erythraean Sibyl," Guercino's "Sibilla Persica," Michelangelo's "Libyan Sibyl" and "Persian Sibyl," Raphael's four sibyls — "The Cumaean Sibyl, The Persean Sibyl, The Phrygian Sibyl, and the Sibyl of Tibur," "The School of Athens," "Poetry," and "Justice." A similar list occurs in *JMN*, VIII, 550. "The Daniel of M. Angelo was taken by C. S. 4.50" and "29.75" were written first in pencil, then traced in ink.

[55] Byron is no poet: what did he know of the world & its Law, & Lawgiver? What moment had he of that Mania which moulds history & man, & tough circumstance, — like wax? He had declamation; he had music, juvenile & superficial music. Even this is very rare. And we delight in it so much that Byron has obtained great fame by this fluency & music. It is delicious. All the "Hebrew Melodies" are examples.

"Warriors & Chiefs! should the shaft or the sword."
["Song of Saul before his last battle," l. 1]

How neat, how clever, how roundly it rolls off the tongue, — but what poetry is here? It is the sublime of Schoolboy verse. How many volumes of such ⟨poetry⟩ ↑jingle↓ must we go through before we can be filled, sustained, taught, renewed?

[56] ⟨Yet t⟩The office of poetry I supposed was Tyrtaean, — consoling, indemnifying; and of the Uranian, deifying or imparadising.

Homer did what he could, — & Callimachus, Pindar, & the Greek tragedians: Horace & Persius; Dante was faithful, & Milton, Shakspeare & Herbert.

But now shall I find my ⟨daily⟩heavenly bread in Tennyson? or in Milnes? in Lowell? or in Longfellow?
Yet Wordsworth was mindful of the office[.]

[57] Compare the music of Collins'

"Bubbling runnels joined the sound"
["The Passions: An Ode for Music," l. 63]

& Ben Jonson's "Drink to me only with thine eyes"
& Herrick
& Chapman's Homer
with the parlour & piano music of Byron & Scott, & Moore, & Mitchell.

"Who but he on the top wave was riding"

Neat versification without poetry is Cowper's Alex Selkirk

I am monarch of all I survey
My right there is none to dispute

From the desart all round to the sea
I am lord of the fowl & the brute

I am out of humanity's reach
I must finish my journey alone
Never hear the sweet music of speech
I start at the sound of my own
["Verses supposed to be written by Alexander Selkirk . . . ,"
                                          ll. 1–4, 9–12]

clever execution; but these are properly College exercises, not manly labors. No wind harp[.] [68]

[58] *Poetry*

   —   — ποντιων τε κυματων
  Ανηριθμον γελασμα   *Aeschylus*
                              [*Prometheus Bound*, ll. 89–90]
  O multitudinous laughter of the ocean billows!

"'Tis not clear" says DeQuincey "whether Æschylus contemplated the laughter as addressing the ear or the eye."

[59]–[68] [leaves missing] [69]
    [69] I see not how we can live except alone. Trenchant manners, a sharp decided way will prove a lasting convenience. Society will ⟨paw & paddle⟩ ↑coo & claw↓ & caress. You must curse & swear a little: They will remember it, & it will do them good. What if they are wise & fine people. I do not want ⟨their⟩your silliness, though you be Socrates, and if you indulge them, all people are babyish. Curse them.
Understand me when I say, I love you, it is your genius & not you. I like man, but not men. The genius of humanity is very easily & accurately to be made out by the poet-mind, but it is not in Miss Nancy nor in Adoniram with any ⟨adequateness⟩ sufficiency.

   [68] "Neat versification . . . wind harp" is in pencil.
   [69] Emerson indexed p. [60] under Fourier, Greatness, Heroism, and Permanence; p. [62] under Prints; p. [65] under Discontent, Egotism, Exigent Ideal, Greatness, and Ideal; p. [66] under Earnestness; and p. [68] under Inspiration. A few fragmentary words are visible on the stub of p. [68].

[70] I like man, but not men.

Instincts, tendencies, — they do no wrong; — they are beautiful, & may be confided in & obeyed. Though they slay us, let us trust them. Why should ⟨we pronounce & judge, we⟩ eggs, ⟨we⟩& tadpoles ↑talk↓? ⁿ All is mere sketch, symptomatic, possible, or probable, for us, — we dwellers in tents, we outlines in chalk, we jokes & buffooneries, why should we be talking? Let us have the grace to be abstemious.

The etiquette of society should guard & consecrate a poet; he should not be visited, nor be shown at dinner tables: too costly to be seen except on ↑high↓ holidays. ↑He should be relieved of visits ⟨trivi⟩& trivial correspondence. His time is the time of his nation.↓ ⁷⁰

[70ₐ]⁷¹ Fourier said "Indulge;" the Stoic said "Forbear." All great natures are lovers of stability or permane↑n↓ce as the type of the Eternal. The frivolous flutter & change. The hero is loved, draws warm & admiring affections around him, like a cloud of cherubs ⟨& cupids,⟩ but is pre-engaged ⁿ to his Destiny, & cannot bend or rove.⁷²

Are there any men now existing by whose death the civilization of their people would be retarded? But such men have appeared[:] Alfred, Roger Bacon, Columbus, Copernicus, and this age has its quota of power.⁷³

[70♭]–[70ᵈ] [blank]

[71] Yes, we want a poet, the genuine poet of our time, no parrot, & no child. The poets that we praise, or try to, ⟨the Brownings, Barretts, Bryants, Tennysons,⟩ are all abortive Homers; they at least show tendency, the direction of nature to the star ⟨L⟩in Lyra. Boys still whistle, & every newspaper & girl's album attest the ineradicable

⁷⁰ With "Though they slay us, let us trust them.", cf. Job 13:15. The added sentence was written first in pencil, then copied in ink and the pencil version erased.
⁷¹ Laid in loose between pp. [70] and [71] is a four-page sheet of white letter paper, each page measuring 11.5 x 17.8 cm. It has been numbered [70ₐ]–[70ᵈ].
⁷² The inserted "n" in "permanence" and the deletion of "& cupids," are in pencil. The first sentence is used in "Historic Notes of Life and Letters in New England," W, X, 354.
⁷³ See p. [73] below.

appetite for melody.[74] O no, we have not done with music, nor must console ourselves with prose poets, let Sampson Reed or Mr Stone think as they will.[75] We wish the undrawn line of tendency to be drawn for us. Where is the Euclid who can sum up these million errors, & compute the beautiful mean? We do not wish to make--believe be instructed; we wish to be ravished, ↑inspired,↓ & taught: we do not want prison melodies [72] nor modern antiques, nor Jim Crow songs, but the Godhead in music, as we have the Godhead in the Sky & in ⟨generation⟩ the creation.

↑Companions.↓

Men of thought who live in the same sphere, are poor company for each other, & say little. Each ⟨is⟩has access to the same fountain. Why should they speak? But bring to one of them an intelligent ⟨person, a⟩ stranger of quite another latitude, perhaps of a lower elevation, & it is as if you let off water from a cask or a lake, by cutting a lower basin; it seems a mechanical advantage. And a [73] great pleasure & ⟨|| ... ||⟩advantage it is to the speaker, as he can now paint out his thought to himself.[76]

↑See Uses of inferiors   CD p. 39↓

All sensible men have a hankering to play Providence, or assume to judge of law & fact.[77]

Are there any men now existing by whose death the civilization of their people would be retarded? But such men have appeared. Alfred, Roger Bacon, Columbus, Copernicus. ↑And this Age also has its quota of power.↓ [78]

[74] ↑1 May.↓ I was at Cambridge yesterday to see Everett

[74] "they at least show . . . attest" is struck through in pencil with a vertical use mark.

[75] Sampson Reed (1800–1880) was a Swedenborgian whom Emerson had known since his college days; Thomas Treadwell Stone (1801–1895) was a popular liberal preacher from Maine and an antislavery lecturer.

[76] This paragraph, struck through in pencil with a vertical use mark, is used in "Uses of Great Men," W, IV, 31. Journal CD will be published in a future volume.

[77] See p. [83] below.

[78] See p. [70] above.

inaugurated.[79] His political brothers came as if to bring him to the convent door, & to grace with a sort of bitter courtesy his taking of the cowl. It is like the marriage of a girl: not until the wedding & the departure with her husband, does it appear that she has actually & finally changed homes & connexions & social caste. Webster I could so willingly have spared on this occasion. Everett was entitled to the entire field; & Webster ↑came,↓ who is his evil genius, & has done him incalculable harm by Everett's too much admiration of his iron nature; — warped him from his true bias all these twenty years, & sent him cloud-hunting at Washington & London, to the ruin of all solid [75] scholarship, & fatal diversion from the pursuit of his right prizes. It is in vain that Everett makes all these allusions to his public employments; he would fain deceive me & himself; he has never done any thing there↑in↓, but has been, with whatever praises & titles & votes, a mere dangler & ornamental person. It is in vain for sugar to try to be salt. Well, this Webster must needs come into the house just at the moment when Everett was rising to make his Inaugural Speech. Of course, the whole genial current of feeling flowing towards him was arrested, & the old Titanic Earth-son was alone seen. The house shook with new & prolonged applause, & Everett sat down, to give [76] free course to the sentiment. He saved himself by immediately saying, "I wish it were in my power to use the authority vested in me & to say, '*Expectatur oratio in lingua vernacula*,'[80] from my illustrious friend who has just taken his seat."

Everett's grace & propriety were admirable through the day. Nature finished this man. He seems beautifully built, perfectly sound & whole, & eye, voice, hand ⟨perfectly⟩ ↑exactly↓ obey his thought. His quotations are a little trite, but saved by the beautiful modulation & falls of the recitation.

The satisfaction of men in this appointment is complete. Boston is contented because he [77] is so creditable, safe, & prudent, and the scholars because he is a scholar, & understands the business. Old

---

[79] After serving as governor of Massachusetts from 1836 to 1840 and as United States minister to Great Britain from 1841 to 1845, Edward Everett accepted the post of president of Harvard, succeeding Josiah Quincy, who had served since 1829.

[80] "We expect a speech in the common tongue" (Ed.).

'Quincy with all his worth & a sort of violent service he did the College, was a lubber & a grenadier among our clerks.

Quincy made an excellent speech, so stupid good, now running his head against a post, now making a capital point; he has motherwit, & great fund of honour & faithful serving. And the faults of his speech increased my respect for his character.

The Latin allusions flew all day; "Sol occubuit, nulla nox sequitur," [81] said Webster. "Uno avulso, non deficit aureus alter," [82] said Winthrop.

[78] It is so old a fault that we have now acquiesced in it, that the complexion of these Cambridge feasts is not literary, but some what bronzed by the colours of Washington & Boston. The aspect is political, the ⟨|| ... ||⟩speakers are political, & Cambridge plays a very pale & ⟨modest⟩ ↑permitted↓ part in its own halls. A man of letters — who was purely that, — would not feel attracted, & would be as much out of place there as ⟨in the Exchange⟩ at the Brokers' Board. Holmes's poem was a bright sparkle,[83] but Frothingham, Prescott, Longfellow, old Dana, Ward, Parker, Hedge, Clark, ↑Judd↓ the author of "Margaret," [84] & whoever else is a lover of letters, were absent or silent; & Everett himself, richly entitled [79] on grounds of scholarship to the chair, used his scholarship only complimentarily.

The close of Everett's Inaugural Discourse was chilling & melancholy. With a coolness indicating absolute skepticism & despair, he deliberately gave himself over to the corpse-cold Unitarianism & Immortality of Brattle street & Boston.

Everett's genius is Persian. The poetry of his sermons in his youth, his delight in Destiny, the elements, the colours & forms of things; & the mixture he made of physical & metaphysical, strongly recalls the genius of Hafiz.

[81] "The sun has set, yet no night follows" (Ed.).

[82] An adaptation of Virgil, *Aeneid*, VI, 143–144: "Primo avulso non deficit alter aureus" — "When the first is torn away, a second fails not, golden too." Robert C. Winthrop (1809–1894) was at this time a member of the U.S. House of Representatives from Massachusetts.

[83] "A Modest Request. Complied with after the Dinner at President Everett's Inauguration."

[84] Sylvester Judd (1813–1853), Unitarian clergyman, published his novel *Margaret* in 1845.

[80] People wish to be amused & therefore like to have the good natured man, the man of information, the "Uncle Isaac whose news is always true," or the Poet or the belle, come to their houses. But I do not wish to be amused, and the amusing persons are bores to me.[85] But if a man speak in public one right & eloquent word, like Gannett's once at some Bible society,[86] or Henry Ware's sometimes, or Lovejoy's lately over Torrey's dead body,[87] or disclose the least vestige of character, then is it pathetic to me, & I have a feeling of gratitude that would wash the feet of this benefactor.

[81] ↑*Hafiz*↓
Hafiz, whom I at first thought a cross of Anacreon & Horace, I find now to have the best blood of Pindar also in his veins. ↑Also of Burns↓ [88]

[82] Daguerrotype gives the sculpture of the face, but omits the expression, the painter aims at the expression & comes far short of Daguerre in the form & organism. But we must have sea and shore, the flowing & the fixed, in every work of art. On the sitter the effect of the Daguerrotypist is asinizing[.] [89]

[83] [90] Fales H. Newhall. Saugus, Mass. at Middletown ⟨Ct.⟩
↑Connecticut↓

walnut leaf

[85] "But I do not wish to be amused,", struck through in ink with a vertical use mark, is used in "Considerations by the Way," *W*, VI, 247.
[86] Ezra Stiles Gannett (1801–1871), Unitarian clergyman and coeditor of the *Christian Examiner*, had been a classmate of Emerson at Harvard.
[87] Charles Turner Torrey, the abolitionist, died in Maryland State Prison on May 9, 1846, while serving a term for aiding escaping slaves. The Reverend Joseph C. Lovejoy delivered the funeral service at the Tremont Temple in Boston on May 19th, after the directors of the Park Street Church, where the funeral was originally scheduled to be held, had withdrawn permission. With "But if a man . . . benefactor.", cf. p. [214] below.
[88] "Also of Burns" was added later in pencil.
[89] Emerson's attempts to get an acceptable photograph of himself are described in letters to Carlyle in May, 1846 (*CEC*, pp. 398 and 400).
[90] All the entries on this page, except the first, are in pencil.

co progress of chemistry & politics

⟨"the touch of the eye," said Alcott.⟩

↑The↓ man ⁿ that shoots a buffalo, lives better than he who boards at the Graham House[,] ⁹¹ said H.T[horeau].

fierce

disconsolate

All sensible men have a hankering to play providence, or assume to judge of law & fact[.] ⁹²

[84] Mystic labels & tickets one thing or two, Mystic who beholds the flux, yet becomes pragmatist on some one particular of faith, and, ⟨which⟩ ↑what↓ is the mischief, seeks to accredit this new jail because it was builded by him who has demolished so many jails. Is not the Mystic like a rogue who comes to an honest man & says, "by your accumulated character you could deal an immense stroke at counterfeiting." ⟨Your credit is so great.⟩ ⁹³

Swedenborg narrows the Scripture of nature to the wretched answers of the Swedish Catechism[.] ⁹⁴

[85] An artist took a sketch of the ⟨House of⟩ ↑Senate↓ of the U.S. at the moment of Henry Clay's resignation and to finish it procured Daguerre heads of all the members. Well such a picture as those grim fixtures would make does the piecemeal writer draw when he combines his sketches into one.

[86] Nature is always gainer, & reckons surely on our sympathy. The Russians eat up the Poles. What then? when the last Polander is gone, the Russians are men, are ourselves, & the Pole is forgotten in our identification with Russian parties.⁹⁵ A philosopher is no philosopher unless he takes lively part with the thief who picks his pocket and with the bully that insults or strikes him.

⁹¹ This sentence is used in "Thoreau," *W*, X, 463.

⁹² This sentence is erased. See p. [73] above.

⁹³ This entry is in pencil.

⁹⁴ Erased pencil writing, none of it recovered, underlies this sentence, which is struck through in ink with a vertical use mark.

⁹⁵ Cf. "Ode, Inscribed to W. H. Channing," ll. 90–97, *W*, IX, 79.

[87] American debility [96]

> To transmute crime to wisdom, & to stem
> The vice of Japhet by the thought of Shem.[97]

[88][98]   Eloquence
              Intellect   1 Method
                        2 Imagination
                          power of symbols
                          "rugged & awful crisis" [99]

Irish Eloquence of common people
example of the animal heat division
There must be spirit too

Language. Words borrowed from animals [100]
    to dog
    to raven
    to cow
    to ram
    to ape
    to horse
    to rabbit
    to snake
    to badger
    to worm
    to rat

[89] Memory⟨, what shall we say of that Presence, which⟩ performs the impossible for man, ⟨↑which↓ like a god⟩ by the strength of his divine arms holds together the Past & the ⟨Future⟩ ↑Present↓,

---

[96] These two words are in pencil.

[97] "Fragments on the Poet and the Poetic Gift," XXII, *W*, IX, 332. A pencil version of these two lines, later erased, is visible directly above the ink version.

[98] The entries on this page, down to "There must be spirit too", are in pencil.

[99] In *JMN*, VI, 165, Emerson quotes this phrase in context from an unidentified speech by William Pitt, Earl of Chatham.

[100] See a similar list in *JMN*, VIII, 288.

beholding both; existing in both; abid⟨ing⟩es in the flowing; ↑&↓
gives continuity & dignity to human life. ⟨Therefore⟩ ↑Hereby↓ only
a home is possible; hereby only a new fact has value; hereby am I
⟨truly a king⟩ lodged in a hall ⟨the most magnificent,⟩ filled with
pictures which every new day enhances, and to which every new
⟨march⟩ ↑step↓ of the Soul in her endless ⟨career⟩ ↑march↓ adds a
perspective more sublime.[101]

[90]   Wrote M. Fuller
American idea, Emancipation[,] appears in our freedom of intellec-
tion, in our reforms, & in our bad politics; has, of course, its sinister
side, which is most felt by the drilled & scholastic. But, if followed,
leads to heavenly places. The embarrassment of Boston-bred men is
the confusion of European & American culture. European & American
are each ridiculous & offensive out of his sphere. There is a Columbia
of thought & art which is the last & endless sequel of Columbus's
adventure.[102]

[91] A man who can speak well to a public assembly, I must respect,
and he is *ipso facto* ennobled. Like a great general ⟨he ma⟩or a great
poet, or a millionaire, he may wear his coat out at elbows, and his
shoes & his hat as he will. He has established relation, representative-
ness, that he is a good apple of his kind, proved by the homage of
the apples, and not merely like your lonely man of genius, that he
is an apple shaped like a cucumber. He is not a curiosity but capable
of yielding aid & comfort to men.

[92]   Oriental
_____

"Verily worlds on worlds can add nothing to him"
                                        Aklak y Jalaly [p. 301] [103]

"To him straw & mountains are alike" [104]

    [101] "Memory . . . has value;" is used in "Natural History of Intellect," *W*,
XII, 91.
    [102] This entry, which is in pencil, is used in "Boston," *W*, XII, 200–201.
    [103] See Journal Y, p. [82] above.
    [104] This quotation is used in the lecture "The Superlative in Manners and
Literature."

"His very flight is presence in disguise." [*Ibid.*, p. 364] [105]

"Verily the ground of Paradise is extension, & the plants of it are hallelujahs to God's praise." [*Ibid.*, p. 102] [106]

[93]–[95] [blank]
[96] ↑⟨Trust.⟩↓
                    Trust the rotation.

――――

"⟨There is⟩The mark of a great man is to succeed." *Cousin* [107]

――――

The man who is in the shirt can button it best.

――――

Autobiography & allo-biography go abreast; with every new insight we discover a new man.[108]

――――

The world is his who has money to go over it.[109]

――――

Every planet too must get its own living.[110]

――――

↑Prayer↓
'A man in danger importuned the priest to pray for him: — "No; you must pray for your self." So he said, "O Lord, thou knowest I never asked any thing of thee before, &, if thou wilt help me this time, I will never ask anything of thee again." '

Dr Allyne of D[uxbury]. prayed for rain, at church. In the P.M. the boys carried umbrellas. "Why?" Because you prayed for rain. "Pooh! boys! we always pray for rain: it's customary." [111]

――――

[105] See Journal Y, p. [83] above and p. [160] below.
[106] See Journal Y, p. [82] above.
[107] *Introduction to the History of Philosophy*, trans. Henning Gotfried Linberg (Boston, 1832), p. 306. This edition is in Emerson's library.
[108] This sentence is struck through in ink with a diagonal use mark.
[109] This sentence is used in "Wealth," *W*, VI, 95.
[110] See pp. [3] and [17] above.
[111] Emerson may have heard this story of the eccentric Dr. John Allyn, pastor of the Congregational church at Duxbury, Mass., from 1788 to 1833, from his brother-in-law Charles T. Jackson, who as a boy had been a pupil of the doctor.

[97] The symmetry & coordination of things is such that from any one creature ⟨[or fact of nature] truly⟩ ↑well↓ & inly known, any ⟨other⟩ & every other might be legitimately deduced. Palmistry, phrenology, & astrology rest on a real basis. It is certain that there is a relation between the stars & my wedding-day, between the lines of my hand & the works done by it, between the activity of my brain, & its outward figure; ⁿ there is a relation, but how to find it? [112]

Does not this belong to the Essay on
Nature (2d series)[?]

The world, the universe may be reeled off from any Idea, like a ball of yarn. Thus, if you please, it is all mechanical. The mental phenomena all admit very well of being solved so. Size is then a true difference & will be found to hold in men.   See above p. 60 & 72, or it is all electrical; or chemical; or moral. Suit yourself. [113]

[98] O'Connel in 1835, denounced Benj. D'Israeli as a humbug of the first magnitude, & wound up by referring to the origin of D'Israeli's family. He said, "he had no doubt, if his genealogy were traced, it would be found that he was the true heir-at-law of the *impenitent* thief who atoned for his crimes on the cross."

[99]   ↑Printed↓
"For my part," said Napoleon, "it is not the mystery of the incarnation which I discover in religion, but the mystery of social order, which associates with heaven that idea of equality which prevents the rich from destroying the poor. Religion is indeed a kind of vaccine inoculation, which, by satisfying our natural love for the marvellous, keeps us out of the hands of charlatans & conjurors. The priests are better than the Cagliostros, the

[112] A pencil version of this entry, later partially erased, underlies the ink version. The pencil version begins "I took[?] my pen[?] to say that the symmetry" and has "any creature" for "any one creature" and "truly & inly" for "well & inly". The added notation "Does not this belong to the Essay on Nature (2d series)" is in pencil only. The paragraph is struck through in pencil with a vertical use mark. Cf. "Nature," *W*, III, 182.
[113] A pencil version of this entry, later erased, underlies the ink version and extends onto the first two lines of p. [98]. There are no discernible significant differences between the two versions. The entry is struck through in pencil with a vertical use mark. See *JMN*, VIII, 447.

Kants, & all the visionaries of Germany." Napoleon's Speeches in Council.
Pellet. Basil Hall. p 258 [114]

[100] Double the dose.

The pale faces, the pale faces! We are tired of asking for a great
man, & now ask for a great deal of a man, somewhat satisfying;
Buonaparte, Webster, even Captain Rhynders.[115]

For we must have a success. It is not we that are in fault for not
being convinced, but you that cannot convince us. You should mould
us & wind us round your finger[,] so pliant & willing as we offer
ourselves. We know you are in the right, we are already half convinced. You should take the ground from under us if you had a
sliver of steel. Not only neutralize our opposition, that is a small
thing, but convert us into fiery apostles & publishers of your wisdom.
Good powder, but not a heavy charge enough.[116]

[101] The Muse demands real sacrifices, I wrote. You cannot
be poet & a paterfamilias & a militia captain[.]

One man thinks of
We live with such different velocity. We are not timed with
our contemporaries. We cannot keep step. One man is thinking of
Plato & his companion is thinking of lobsters.[117]

⟨The⟩What pity that the mother & child cannot change states. The
⟨m⟩child is always awake, & the mother is always asleep.

[114] Privat Joseph Claramond, Count Pelet de la Lozère, *Napoleon in Council, or,
the Opinions delivered by Bonaparte in the Council of State*, trans. Basil Hall (Edinburgh and London, 1837), withdrawn from the Harvard College Library November
18, 1846. " 'For my part,' . . . the poor.", struck through in pencil with a vertical
use mark, is used in "The Sovereignty of Ethics," *W*, X, 190. "Printed" is in pencil.
[115] A pencil version of this entry, partially erased, underlies the ink version. The
pencil version has "asking in vain for" for "asking for" and "Mr Rhynders" for
"Captain Rhynders." The heading "Double the dose." is in pencil only. Isaiah
Rynders was a United States marshal and Tammany leader in the poorer wards of
New York City.
[116] This paragraph is in pencil.
[117] This and the preceding entry are in pencil. Cf. p. [254] below.

[102] Webster. When he comes into the house astronomy & geology are suggested, the force of atoms. Here is the working nature. A spark also he has of the benignant fire that enables him to make an economy of his coals for the laboratory & for the altar which had otherwise been only a kitchen fire.

↑juvenes↓ Queis arte benigna
Et meliore luto finxit praecordia Titan.[n] [118]

So formerly I found him in the same category with Herr Driesbach & his cats. See R 26 [119]

[103]–[104] [leaf torn out] [120]
     [105] ⟨If it takes many Goethes to make a Washington, it takes many Washingtons to make a Goethe[.]⟩

     [106][121] Raphael found the material sufficiently ready & had all his heat for the main work[.]
     So Shakspeare[.]
     And the farmer & the mediocre man should find the road built, the orchard planted, the barns made,

     [107] M Angelo's designs teach us how near to creation we are; this man is of the Creator that made & makes men; how much of the original craft yet remains in him, & he a man.

     [108] Feb., 1847. It is now said, that the Mexican War is already paid for in the enhanced value of cotton & breadstuffs now ⟨in the⟩ to be sold by our people; & chiefly of cotton. Of cotton, a novelty, a single article on whose manufacture such immense mechanical powers have been concentrated that it takes the lead of all other

---

[118] A partially erased pencil version of "Webster . . . Titan," underlies the ink version, with "had been otherwise" for "had otherwise been" and with "juvenes" omitted. The Latin is from Juvenal, *Satires*, XIV, 34–35: "a youth . . . whose soul the Titan has fashioned with kindlier skill and of a finer clay." See *JMN*, VI, 21.

[119] See *JMN*, VIII, 362–363. Herr Driesbach was a wild-animal tamer who brought his menagerie to Concord on July 26, 1843 (*L*, III, 190).

[120] Emerson indexed p. [104] under Genius, Owning, and Rich.

[121] The entries on this and the following page are in pencil. Two erased letters are visible after "sufficiently ready" in the first entry.

articles of trade. Now I suppose this is mere ignorance. Not a single
plant, perhaps, in the whole botany, that is not also adapted to general
uses, & will not hereafter make the bread of millions, by its manufacture.[122]   ↑See *AB* 28↓

[109] Ward has aristocratical position and turns it to excellent
account; the only aristocrat who does. For the rest, this access to the
best circles of information is of no use, and they are trifling & tedious
company. But in reading Legaré's journal[,] who seems to have seen
the best company, I find myself interested that he should play his
part of the American Gentleman well, but am contented that he
should do that instead of me, — do the etiquette instead of me, as
I am contented that others should sail the ships & work the spindles.

[110] Feb. 15, 1847.
I find this morning good things in Legaré on Demosthenes[.] [123]
"Our experience," he says, "is conclusive, that in any assembly met to
discuss & do business, the speaker who really knows more about the
matter in hand than any body else & is at all in earnest about it, will
be sure to lead, in spite of every disadvantage in style & delivery."
He translates Ὑποκρισις, Demosthenes's famous receipt "Acting,"
not "action."

"Æschines describes Demosthenes as a magician or juggler in oratory, &
one whose passions are so much under his control, that, when occasion
demands it, he can cry more easily than others laugh."
Legare Vol 1 p 501

[111] The more it is considered, the more it will appear that Eloquence is an universal organ, valued because it costs the total integrity

---

[122] A single vertical line in ink is drawn in the left margin beside this entry to
"a single article".
    [123] Emerson's three quotations are from the essay "Demosthenes, the Man, the
Statesman, and the Orator," in *Writings of Hugh Swinton Legaré, late Attorney
General and Acting Secretary of State of the United States* . . . , 2 vols. (Charleston, Philadelphia, New York, Boston, 1845–1846), I, 457, 500, and 501. Emerson was reading this work in February, 1847 (*L*, III, 373). "I find . . . delivery.' "
is struck through in ink with three diagonal use marks; cf. "Eloquence," *W*, VII, 85.
For the second and third entry, see *JMN*, VI, 326.

of a man to produce it. The valour of the orator is not less indispensable than that of the general.

[112] Pillsbury said, that he found that people like to laugh, & he set himself to make them laugh at things which ought to be laughed down, such as the Church & Whiggism.

That parabola or hyperbola which is a curve that does not return into itself represents our bad population who never get convicted & punished in sight of men.

[113] [blank]
[114] The instincts appear in the society, in the individuals they are disobeyed, & hence the jangle of the individual.

↑Morals↓ [124]

We are easily great with ⟨the⟩ a loved & honoured associate; then the sentiments appear as new & astonishing as the lightning out of the Sky, & disappear as suddenly, without any sequel, leaving us among the market-men[.]

[115] The detachment of the Puritans without aristocracy, must be as great a gain to mankind, as the opening of that Continent. And though tender people may object to an aristocracy of wealth, if you think what that means, opportunity, free trade, & bringing all the powers to the surface, ↑—↓ it is what all aim at. Here the Englishman dislikes the dishonesty of primogeniture, & yet dislikes the democratic manners. [125]

↑From London.↓

"Tell E. that I often think there should be taken of each one of us, not a portrait, but a chart or plan, such as an engineer would draw of his mill, so many pounds of power, & so & so applied. Then it would be seen, that,

---

[124] This word is in pencil.
[125] This paragraph is struck through in pencil with a vertical use mark; "The detachment . . . Continent." is used in "Boston," *W*, XII, 201.

though the building was large, the engine was perhaps puny, & every
ounce wanted."

↑See *CD* 78
W 31↓

[116] Art acquaints us with the wonderful translations of the same
thought into the several languages of drawing, of sculpture, of music,
of poetry, of architecture, still further into scenery, into animals, that
express it or harmonize with it, and lastly into human form &
character.

[117] Bring any club or company of intelligent men together
again, after ten years, & if the presence of some penetrating & calm-
ing genius could dispose them all to ⟨self⟩ recollection & frankness,
what a confession of insanities would come up! How costly then
would the "Causes" appear, Abolition, Temperance, Socialism, Non
Resistance, Grahamism, ↑Romanism,↓ &c. What roots of bitterness,
what dragons of wrath! How dangerous & mischievous would every
man's 'talents' appear! It would seem as if each had been seized upon
in early youth by some delusion as a bird of prey which had whisked
him about, taken him out of his path, out of society, away from
fortune, from the truth, from the poets & God, — some zeal, some
bias, some bee in the bonnet, & only when he was now grey & nerve-
less, ⟨he⟩ was it relaxing its claws, & he [118] awaking to a sense
of his situation.[126]

[119] [blank]
    [120] The best is to be had.[127]

⟨The access⟩
The best is accessible, is cheap. Every man cannot get land or jewels,
but every man can get what land & money & rank are valued for, —
namely, substantial manhood, thoughts selfrealizing & prophetic of

---

[126] This paragraph, struck through in ink with a vertical use mark, is used in
"Culture," *W*, VI, 136.
    [127] This sentence is in pencil. See p. [181₂] below.

the farthest future, thoughts of which poetry & music are ⟨but⟩ the necessary expression.[128]

"The true coin for which all else ought to be changeable, is a right understanding of what is good." says Plato in Phaedrus.

αλλ ἢ εκεῖνο μονον το νόμισμα ὀρθον, ἀνθ᾽ ου δεῖ ἄπαντα ταῦτα καταλλάττεσθαι φρόνησις.[129]

↑See p 181 AB↓

[121][130]   "The neighbors keep about so"

Life is a pinch[.]
we eat our bread in anxious politics[.]

When summer opens, I see how fast it matures, & fear it will be short; but after the heats of July & August, I am reconciled, like one who has had his swing, to the cool of autumn. So will it be with the coming of death.

[122] A good invention was the Individual or Differential. Here are all the members of my body:—How they use & rely on each other, trust each other beyond all the fables of friendship, & yet without love of each other! Well, so live two young brothers or sisters, & have no good of their intimacy & use, because they know it not. Love never forgets the Differential.[131]

[123] "I will get you to mow this piece of grass for me," says the prudent mechanic, "for I can earn more in the shop:" And the poet replies in the same wisdom on a higher plane, to those who beg him to come in to the aid of the disturbed institutions:[n] I can best help them by going on with the creation of my own. I am a sad

---

[128] This paragraph, struck through in ink with a vertical use mark, is used, down to "farthest future,", in "Discourse at Nantucket."

[129] In *JMN*, VIII, 60, Emerson gives the source of this quotation as Heinrich Ritter, *The History of Ancient Philosophy*, trans. Alexander J. W. Morrison, 4 vols. (Oxford and London, 1838–1846), II, 412, where both the Greek and the English versions occur. The English version is struck through in ink with a vertical use mark.

[130] The entries on this page are in pencil.

[131] A pencil version of this entry, later erased, underlies the ink version. There are no significant differences between the two.

bungler at ⟨constitutions⟩ laws, being afflicted with a certain incon-
secutiveness of thought, impertinent association, & extreme skepticism; but I recover my eyesight & spirits, in solitude.

And the way to taste the soil is not to eat earth, but ↑wheat &↓ black-
berr⟨y⟩ies, and my way to help the govt ↑is↓ to write sonnets.[132]

[124] I can reason down or at least deny every thing except this perpetual belly. Feed he must, & will, and I cannot make him respectable.[133]

[125] ↑Costume↓ [134]
We must accept with↑out↓ ⟨little⟩ criticism or modification the costume of our times, & be glad we have one care less in our hands, —
dress, money, language, railroads, taxation, & the civilization generally. The custom of the country will do so much for us. Let it,
and be thankful. All the *materiel* is vanquished to your hand; now
for the triumphs of the *spirituel*.

Immortality. Is my future related to my ⟨past⟩present only as my
present to my past? say they all. The Universe suffers no detriment.
But for Cebes & Simmias — We wish to be certified that these dear
Johns & Henries, Anns & Marias, shall keep the traits that are most
their own, & make them dear.[135]

[126] Goethe ⟨insist⟩ treats nature as the old philosophers, say the
seven wise masters[,] did, & with whatever loss of French dissection
& tabulation, poetry & humanity remain to us; & they too must have
some doctoral skill. Eyes are better than telescopes or microscopes.[136]

Any thing that Goethe said, another might attain to say; but the
profusion of sayings, every one of which is good & striking, no man.
In these days we rather incline to sniff at men of talent, and at achiev-

[132] This sentence is in pencil.
[133] This paragraph, struck through in ink with a vertical use mark, is used in
"Montaigne," *W*, IV, 177.
[134] This word is in pencil.
[135] See Journal Y, p. [48] above.
[136] This paragraph is used in "Goethe," *W*, IV, 274.

ments, as if the artist cost too much; but when a man can do so many things, when achievment amounts to such a prodigious sum, it grows respectable.

Yet the Autobiography [*Dichtung und Wahrheit*] looks today like a storm of goldheaded canes & Ellery perceived the snuffbox.

[127] [blank]
[128] Men quarrel with your rhetoric. Society chokes with a trope, like a child with the croup. They much prefer Mr Prose, & Mr Hoarse-as-Crows, to the dangerous conversation ⟨per⟩ of Gabriel and the archangel Michael perverting all rules, & bounding continually from earth to heaven.

[129] [blank]
[130]   ↑*Walking one day in the fields I met a man.*↓
We shall one day talk with the central man, and see again in the varying play of his features all the features which have characterised our darlings, & stamped themselves in fire on the heart: ⟨we⟩ then, as the discourse rises out of the domestic & personal, & his countenance waxes grave & great, we shall fancy that we talk with Socrates, & behold his countenance: then the discourse changes, & the man, and we see the face & hear the tones of Shakspeare, — the body & the soul of Shakspeare living & speaking with us, only that Shakspeare seems below us. A change again, and the countenance of our companion is youthful & beardless, he talks of form & colour & the ⟨boundless⟩ riches of design; it is the [131] face of the painter Raffaelle that confronts us with the visage of a girl, & the easy audacity of a creator. In a moment it was Michel Angelo; then Dante; afterwards it was the Saint Jesus, and the immensities of moral truth & power embosomed us. And so it appears that these great secular personalities were only expressions of his face chasing each other like the rack of clouds. Then all will subside, & I find myself alone. I dreamed & did not know my dreams.

[132]   ↑Thine & Mine.↓
Be the condition what it may, you must support it, & by re-

sources native or c⟨r⟩onstitutional to you. Why then should I envy you, how brilliant soever your lot? I cannot support mine & yours. And if you really have yours, you cannot have mine; and I, if I really have mine, can well afford to spare yours, which I could not maintain. If you have not the spirit for your place, your place torments you, & nature is so avenged.

[133] ↑Mob↓
The boys kick & stamp for a noise when Abby Kelly & Stephen Foster speak, not for any good reason, but because it is understood that people are to yell & throw eggs when the Fosters speak.[137] 'Tis a regular holiday for the boys through the land, when these people go by; &, if they do not make the noise, who will? You cannot allow too much for the levity of men.

Inconceivable is the levity of men: Every body overrates their character. They have no meaning: they have heels, they wish to feel them, and it is the charm of noise *versus* the charm of eloquence.

[134]   ↑Individual↓   ↑Personality↓
The same thing which happens to us, would happen to the gods also; for if you come into the sweets of personality, you must accept its adamantine limitations.

[135] Whig.
The Whigs have only for their system the negative defence that they maintain it until something ⟨good⟩really good appears.

                                        ↑See also W 66↓ [138]

First come, first served, said the World to the Whig.[139]

[136]   A new commandment, ↑archly↓ said the Muse, ⟨receive⟩
             Thou shalt not preach, my dismal one,
             ↑Luther,↓ Fox, Behmen, Swedenborg grew pale

[137] Stephen Symonds Foster (1809–1881) and his wife, Abigail Kelley (1810–1887), were ardent antislavery lecturers.
[138] This notation is in pencil.
[139] See p. [255] below.

And rosier clouds upbore
Hafiz & Shakspeare with their happy choirs.[140]

↑Printed↓

_____

Alcott & Edward Taylor resemble each other in the incredibility of their statement of facts. One is the fool of his idea, the other of his fancy. When Alcott wrote from England that he was bringing home Wright & Lane I wrote ↑him↓ a letter, which I required him to show them, saying, that they might safely trust his theories, but that they should put no trust whatever in his statement of facts. When they all arrived here, he & his victims, — I asked them if he showed them that letter; they answered that he did: So I was clear.[141]

[137]–[139] [blank]
[140] We manage well enough with the elements, but when the elements become men, not so well; for they are no longer ⟨‖ . . . ‖⟩pure, but have such quantities of alloy as to make them of ⟨very⟩ questionable use. You can extract sunbeams from cucumbers, but there is more cabbage than sunlight; & phosphate from cows, but the chemical phosphate is better.   ↑Mignonette↓

[141]–[143] [blank]
[144]   The new man.
Neither Herodotus nor Hume have told the story as he knows it. None of the arts, no politics, no ↑extant↓ religion, no newspaper, no social circle or private friend quite represents him. Alphonso of Castille, it is too plain, was not consulted; might have given good advice.[142] I see nothing for it, but that yet his opportunity & theatre should ⟨for⟩once for all be expanded to his broad wish; let him make ⟨his⟩a little solar system of his own, let him play all the parts & sing all the songs.

_____

[140] "Ἀδακρυν νέμονται Αἰῶνα," W, IX, 297. This entry is struck through in ink with two vertical use marks.

[141] Although the text of Emerson's letter seems not to have survived, Rusk conjectures that it was probably written in July, 1842 (L, III, 76).

[142] Cf. "Nominalist and Realist," W, III, 238, and "Alphonso of Castile," W, IX, 25–28.

Don't bore him with your old France & Egypt, with Homer & Shakspeare, any longer.

His duties are to omit & omit, to show you the back of his hand, to do nothing as you would have him. His prudence is a new prudence, [145] his charity a new kind, his temperance original, his whole wreath of virtues are ⟨all⟩ undescribed varieties[.]

↑Where's the genius charm or stature
In our crowded highway shown↓ 143

Show me thy face, dear nature, that I may forget my own!

Come let us strew roses   ↑Hafiz↓
And pour wine in the cup
Break up the roof of heaven
And throw it into new forms

So soon the army of cares
Shed the blood of the true
So will I with the cupbearer
Shatter the building of woe

We will rosewater
In winecups pour
And sugar in the ⟨vase in⟩censer
Full of musksmell throw

Thy harping is lovely
O play sweet airs
That we may sing songs
And shake our heads

Bring Eastwind the dust of the body
To that great lord

---

143 These two lines are in pencil. Two diagonal lines in ink are drawn in the left margin beside the next entry.

That we also may cast our eyes
On his beauty [144]

[146]   The noblest Chemistry.

Sunshine from cucumbers. Here was a man who has occupied himself in a nobler chemistry of extracting honor from scamps, temperance from sots, energy from beggars, justice from thieves, benevolence from misers. He knew there was sunshine under those moping churlish brows, elegance of manners hidden in the peasant, heartwarming expansion, grand surprises of sentiment in these unchallenged uncultivated men and he persevered against all repulses until he drew it forth[.]

Now his ⟨boors are⟩ orphans are educated, his boors are polished, his palaces built, his pictures, statues, conservatories, chapels adorn them[.] He stands there prince among his peers[,] prince among princes[.] The sunshine is ↑out &↓ all flowing abroad over the world[.] [145]

[147] [blank]
[148]   ↑*Poetaster.*↓ [146]

No man deserves a patron until first he has been his own. What do you bring us slipshod verses for? no occasional delicacy of expression or music of rhythm can atone for stupidities. Here are lame verses, false rhymes, absurd images, which you indulge yourself in, which is as if a handsome person should come into a company with foul hands or face. Read Collins. Collins would have cut his hand off before he would have left from a weak selfesteem a shabby line in his ode.

Concord Mass

[144] These lines, which are in pencil, are Emerson's translation of a poem in *Der Diwan von Mohammed Schemsed-din Hafis*, trans. Joseph von Hammer, 2 vols. (Stuttgart and Tübingen, 1812–1813), II, 156. In Account Book 4, he notes the purchase of this work in April, 1846.

[145] These two paragraphs, but not the heading, are in pencil. For "Sunshine from cucumbers.", see p. [140] above.

[146] This word is in pencil. Emerson indexed p. [148] under Channing.

[149] ↑Rotation↓

The lesson of life lately is ⟨th⟩ a pretty rapid rotation of friends. Housekeepers say of a domestic who has been valuable, "She had lived with me long enough"; and as it happens that we are all tendencies, & none of us quite satisfying perform⟨ances⟩↑ers↓, it is better that we should touch & go, & catch the genius of life rather than drink the dregs.[147]

[150] At the funeral of Torrey,[148] it seems almost too late to say anything for freedom, — the battle is already won. You are a super-serviceable echo. Yet when you come out & see the apathy & incredulity, the wood & the stone of the people, their supple neck, their appetite[n] for pine apple & ice cream,

[151] Singular credulity which no experience will cure us of, that another man has seen or may see somewhat more than we have of the primary facts, as, for example, of the continuity of the individual; and eye for eye, object for object, their experience is invariably identical in a million individuals. In practical faculty there is great difference. ⟨Buonaparte⟩ No education can bring the grenadier to combine like Buonaparte.[n] But familiarity with a ⟨gr⟩ seer will accustom the dullest swain to contemplate the moral verities and the laws of life.   ↑See LM 52↓[149]

[152] It will not do to diminish personal responsibility: do not give money & teach the man to expect it. Do not give him a Bible, or a genius, to think for him. Break no springs, make no cripples & paupers. A fatal disservice does this Swedenborg or other lawyer who offers to do my thinking for me. Hold them to their manhood.

The Indians and the old monks chose their dwellingplace for beauty of scenery. The Indians have a right to exist in this world: they are, (like Monadnoc & the Ocean,) a part of it, & fit the other parts, as

---

[147] This paragraph, struck through in ink with a vertical use mark, is used in "Uses of Great Men," *W*, IV, 19.

[148] See p. [80] above.

[149] Journal LM will be published in a future volume.

Monadnoc & the sea, which they understand & live with so well, as
a rider his horse. The teamster, the farmer, are jocund & hearty, &
stand on their legs: but the women are demure [153] and subdued,
⟨& if you see the⟩as Shaker Women, &, if you see them out of doors,
look, as H.T[horeau]. said, "as if they were going for the Doctor."
Has our Christianity saddled & bridled us?

> "As I rode thro' sawder's wood,
> A possum passed me by, —
> He curled his tail, & served the Lord,
> But how he grinned at I."

These are the wretched verses which Carlyle seemed to like to repeat.

[154] There never was an eloquence: it is a fabulous power, as
I have said, concerning which men are credulous, because there is in
them all a tantalizing picture, which they would fain verify on some
personal history of Chatham or Demosthenes. Whoso assays to speak
in a public assembly is conscious instantly of this lambent flame en-
larging, elongating, contracting to a point, a Zodiacal light, a Jacko'-
lanthorn, evanescent, refusing to be an instrument. Ah! could he
confine that lambent fire! ⁿ once manage to catch & confine that wild
fire, — confine & direct it in a blowpipe, he would ⟨explode the
planet⟩ ⟨fuse⟩ ↑melt↓ or explode the planet. There is no despotism
like this clutching with one strong hand the master nerve which
carries all the pulsations from the brain to the heart of humanity.[150]

[155] Bust of Demosthenes, a face of ropes; all cord & tendon.

[156] [blank]
[157] Library
I find the same effect from looking over the budget of literary journals & newspapers which the steamer brings each month to the
Athenaeum, as from a visit to the Cambridge Library; ↑viz.↓ an
instant conviction that the best of it all is already in the four walls
of my study at home. The Library brings me back continually to
Burke, Johnson, Shakspeare, Plato, Demosthenes, & Company, and

[150] This paragraph is struck through in ink with two diagonal use marks.

to these it can afford ⟨b⟩only the most slight & casual additions. The Athenaeum lists ⟨o⟩& notices of new publications yield the fewest golden lines, whilst they invariably suggest my old fancy that every man should & some day will write all literature for himself[.] [151]

[158] [blank]

[159]   ↑Horoscope↓
The child should have a successful constitution, that tenacity of fibre & elasticity, at the same time, which warrant a good average, a good adjustment to this sophomore society. For the child must be one thing or the other to be well; either well knit & attempered to society, so as to work well with it, no odd one or speckled one; or else, must have inwardness & resources, being a poet or a saint.

                                        ↑See *Temperament*
                                          in *AB* p 95↓

[160] America
John Randolph is ⟨a⟩ somebody; & Andrew Jackson; and J.Q. Adams. ↑and Daniel Webster.↓

[161] [blank]

[162]   "Oft have I heard, & deemed the witness true,
              Whom man delights in, God delights in too."
                                        Pons de Capdueil.[152]

[163]   Criticism
The next generation will thank Dickens for showing so many mischiefs which parliaments & Christianities had not been strong enough to remove. Punch too has done great service. And Fourier & /other earnest teachers/Bentham/ whose direct teaching is rejected, render an oblique service of searching criticism on Marriage, Church, Courts,
Fourier, St Simon, Bentham, Louis Blanc, Owen, Leroux, and the Chartist⟨s⟩ leader, all crazy men & so they pound on one string till the whole world knows *that*.

---

[151] This paragraph is struck through in ink with a vertical use mark; "a visit to . . . additions." is used in "Books," *W*, VII, 193–194.
    [152] See p. [1] above.

[164] The Permanent in the Passing, the Old in the New,
⟨|| ... ||⟩the Philosophy of the Times.
1   Powers & Laws of thought
2   Relation to natural science
3   Tendencies & duties of ⟨man of thought⟩ ↑the Intellect↓ in XIX century.
4   Politics & Social spirit
5   ↑Poetry and↓ Eloquence
6   ↑The↓ Natural Aristocracy [153]

[165] [blank]
[166] Here are two or three things to be discriminated. *First*; the perception of one polarity impressed on all the universe, & on ⟨all⟩ the particles: As the whole has its law, so each has its genius. ⟨the⟩Obedience to its genius is the particular of Faith. Trust ⟨in the⟩ that the Tendency of the Whole is the good of the Individual,— is the Universal of faith. ↑Dignity & joy of being under law.↓ I stipulate for no private good. If truth live, I live; if justice live, I live.[n] Put men to death by principles, & they will not grumble:[154] the most generous extension of our private interest to the dignity & generosity of ideas. Do not truck for your private immortality. If immortality is best, you shall be immortal. If it is as good as the other things you see & hear of. That sky, that sea, ⟨both⟩the plants, the rocks,   chemistry, keep their word;   [167] morals⟨,⟩ will also.
Secondly, (if it be a *second*, & not a part of the same,) the perception that morals are geometrical,—that the flight of the moth is preordained, and all things go by number, rule, & weight. The moral of science is the transference to free agents of the trust felt in nature's admired arrangements.[155]

[153] Emerson's six lectures, under the general heading "Mind and Manners of the Nineteenth Century," were originally delivered at the Portman Square Literary and Scientific Institution, London, June 6–17, 1848. See p. [310] below.
[154] "Put men . . . grumble:" is a shortened version of a quotation from *The Chinese Classical Work* . . . , 1828, "Hea Mung," p. 166; see *JMN*, VIII, 410. The original version is used in "Discourse at Nantucket."
[155] "*First*; the perception . . . of faith.", "Do not truck . . . also.", and "The moral of science . . . arrangements." are used in "Natural History of In-

There is no escape but by virtue, ↑—↓ no succedaneum for that. AB 67
Time will not give the effect of electricity.

[168] Instinct the Totality
Inspiration its play & action
Newness its mark.

Religion
Mind has its bias   if he have not that, life
    its weapons   is a failure.
    its affinities
    its successes

[169] Inspiration will have this test also of advance, affirmation,
the forward foot, the ascending state. It will be an opener of doors.
This new wine makes the bottle new. Spirit is essentially motive &
ascending. Despair no muse.
At any pitch a higher pitch. O 120
What stream could fill
Transcendency O 176, 120, V 83
All history symptomatic

[170]–[171] [blank]
    [172] That none but a writer should write, & that he should
not dig.
Tell children what you say about writing & laboring with the hands.
I know better. Can you distil rum by minding it at odd times? or
analyse soils? or carry on the Suffolk Bank? or the Greenwich obser-
vatory? or sail a ship through the Narrows by minding the helm
when you happen to think of it? or serve a glass-house, or a steam-
-engine, or a telegraph, or a rail-road express? or accomplish anything
good or anything powerful in this manner? Nothing whatever. And
the greatest of all arts, the subtlest, & of most miraculous effect, you

---

tellect," *W*, XII, 87; "I stipulate . . . justice live, I live;" is used in "Immortality," *W*, VIII, 343; "the flight of . . . weight." is used in "Worship," *W*, VI,
220.

fancy is to be practised with a pen in one hand & a crowbar or a peat-knife in the other. All power is of geometrical increase.

And to this painting the education is the costliest, & mankind cannot afford to throw away on ditching or wood-sawing the man on whom choicest influences have been concentrated, its Baruch [173] or scribe. Just as much & just such exercise as this costly creature needs, he may have; & he may breathe himself with a spade, or a rapier, as he likes, not as you like: & I should rather say, bad as I think the rapier, that it were as much to his purpose as the other implement. Both are bad, are only rare & medicinal resorts. The writer must live & die by his writing. Good for that, & good for nothing else. A war; an earthquake, the revival of letters, the new dispensation by Jesus, or by Angels, Heaven, Hell, power, science, the Neant, — exist only to him as colours for his brush. That you think he can write at odd minutes only shows what your knowledge of writing is. American writing can be written at odd minutes, — Unitarian writing, Charlatan writing, Congress speeches, Railroad novels.[156]

[174] Hawthorn invites his readers too much into his study, opens the process before them. As if the confectioner should say to his customers Now let us make the cake.

[175] [blank]

[176] Truth indeed; we talk as if we had it, or sometimes said it, or know any thing about it: truth, that terrific reagent. That gun has a kick that will knock down the most nimble artillerist, and therefore is never fired. The ideal is as far ahead of the videttes & the van, as it is of the rear.[157]

Morals. We have never heard that music, it is that which is sung

---

[156] A pencil version of this long entry, partially erased, underlies the ink entry. The pencil version begins "That only a writer" instead of "That none but a writer", omits "or analyse soils?", "through the Narrows", and "or a steam-engine, or a telegraph,", has "or do[?] anything" for "or accomplish anything" and "under God's heaven[?]" before "in this manner?", and omits "Charlatan writing,". A single vertical line in ink is drawn in the left margin beside the second paragraph. "And the greatest . . . miraculous effect,", "And to this painting . . . costliest,", and "A war . . . for his brush" are used in "Art and Criticism," W, XII, 283.

[157] This paragraph is used in "Natural History of Intellect," W, XII, 78.

to the Fates by Sirens or by their mystic whirling wheel. ⟨A⟩That is what all speech aims to say, & all action to evolve. Literature, epics, tragedies, histories, are only apology, interlude, make-shift, in the absence of that. It is the basis of all the elements we know, and is as readily reached from one as [177] from another point. Anacreon, Hafiz, Horace, Herrick, come out on it from drinking songs, as easily as Newton from stars, & Jeremy Taylor from a Funeral Sermon. In the Delphin Juvenals, & other poets, they print the moral sentences in Roman capitals, and Pope asterisked Shakspeare, and, in early Greece, they carved the sentences of the seven Wise Masters on stones by the roadside, & the Christians inscribed the Churchwalls with the Commandments & Lord's Prayer.

I believe I must transcribe below some sentences I find on a stray leaf that seems to belong to some old lecture, which refer to this point[.]

"If I dared, I would summon a class to Lectures on Moral Philosophy: for, I well know that all real aid & inspiration which we can owe each other, is therein. It is really only so much moral [180][158] philosophy as enters into any ⟨one⟩ discourse or any action, — that is memorable, & gives value to the rest. All the rest is ↑overture or↓ interlude ⟨& farce, or flourish of trumpets before & behind,⟩ to fill the time, & make the company forget the absence of the great performer. But, on the instant when we rise so high as to see & affirm the ethical law in relation to our business, no apology is needed. ⟨Y⟩We feel that we have come together for a worthy purpose, & would have done so, though we had travelled hundreds of miles. If I am unworthy, if I am forbidden to pass within the paling, & to tell any secret of generosity & immortality, it is vain that I speak at all; I am only one pretender more. I hover still with inextinguishable hope about that mountain, ⟨happy⟩even in my exclusion happy to be in its neighborhood, [181₁] for, 'of divine things,' it is said, 'the confines are reverend.' "[159]

[158] Emerson directed attention to the continuation of this entry on pp. [180]–[181₁] by writing "turn to p. 180" at the bottom of p. [177] and "continued from p 177" at the top of p. [180].

[159] In *JMN*, VI, 29, Emerson quoted a slightly different version of this quo-

[178] The reason why I pound so tediously on that string of the exemption of the writer from all secular works is ⟨the frequent⟩ ↑our↓ conviction ⟨I have⟩ that his ⟨is⟩ work ⟨which⟩ needs a frolic health to execute. He must be at the top of his condition. In that prosperity he is sometimes caught up into a perception of means & materials, of feats & fine arts, of faery machineries & funds of poetic power, which were utterly unknown to him ⟨all his lifetime before,⟩ ↑hitherto,↓ & ↑of↓ which, if his organs are sufficiently subtle, he can avail himself, ⟨of, he⟩ can transfer to mortal canvas, or reduce into iambic or trochaic, into lyric or heroic rhyme. These successes are not less admirable & astonishing [179] to the poet, than they are to his audience. He has seen something which all the mathematics & the best industry could never bring him unto. And like our rich Raffaelle or Michel Angelo, it only shows how near man is to creating. Now at this small elevation above his usual sphere, he has come into new circulations, the marrow of the world is in his bones, the opulence of forms begins to pour into his intellect ⟨also⟩, & he is permitted to dip his brush into the old paint pot with which birds, flowers, the human cheek, the living rock, the ocean, the broad landscape, & the eternal sky were painted.[160]

[181₂] Nature never draws the moral; but leaves it for the spectator.
Neither does the sculptor, nor the painter, nor the poet,

The moral equalizes all, enriches, empowers all. It is the coin which buys all, & which all find in their pocket.[161] It makes doing & not doing alike; it is the law, it takes no heed of the flaws of the material, but fashions its cups & vases after its own divine model, alike of por-

---

tation, apparently from Bacon's *Fragment of the Colours of Good and Evil*. See *The Works of Francis Bacon . . .* , 10 vols. (London, 1824), II, 242, in Emerson's library.

[160] This paragraph, struck through in pencil with a vertical use mark, is used in "Poetry and Imagination," *W*, VIII, 40–41; "the opulence of forms . . . painted." is struck through in pencil with an additional vertical use mark. The inserted words "our" and "hitherto" are in pencil. For p. [180], see p. 406 above.

[161] This and the preceding sentence, struck through in ink with a vertical use mark, are used in "Worship," *W*, VI, 234.

celain, or of potter's earth, or of water, or of air, as you fetch it stock, or fetch it none. The best is to be had. (See p. 120) Under the whip of the driver, the slave shall feel his equality with kings; — the nothingness of all, the omnipotence of all, as they share the principle which [182] fashions suns & earths & the dreams of their dreamers, gossamer solid & gossamer in webs.

Morals is the science of results, it is that which the Oversoul is cognisant of, that which we communicate to another against our will, that which he cannot but hear, & we cannot but speak, though we shut up our mouths or pluck out our tongues.

[183] We can never be utterly demented. The very rancour of the disease denotes the strength of the constitution.[162]

[184] Wit has a great charter. Popes & kings ↑& Councils of Ten↓ are very ⟨fierce⟩ ↑sharp↓ with their censorships & inquisitions,[n] but it is ⟨for⟩ ↑on↓ dull people. Some Dante or Angelo, Shakspeare, Hafiz, Rabelais, Goethe, Beranger, Bettina, Carlyle, or whatever genuine wit, wit of the old & inimitable class, is always allowed. Kings feel that this is that which they ⟨themselves⟩ represent, this is no red-handkerchiefed redshirted rebel, but loyalty, kingship. But if the ⟨philosophers⟩ ↑metaphysicians↓ or learned German doctors mutter & analyse a little, the king cries with Diotima, "None of the gods philosophizes," & sends ⟨for⟩ the police to him.[163]

[185] All life, say the naturalists, is a superficial phenomenon. The animals crawl on ↑or fly over↓ the rind of the planet & the fishes & whales swim only at the surface of the water. You might skim the whole Mammalia with a kitchen dipper. In the deep sea, & under

---

[162] This entry is struck through in ink with a vertical use mark. Two lines of erased pencil writing, apparently poetry, underlie the entry. The words "citadel" and "lands which rose of eld[?]" have been recovered or conjecturally recovered. See *JMN*, VIII, 137.

[163] The reference to Diotima is to *The Six Books of Proclus . . . on the Theology of Plato . . .*, 1816, II, 40; see *JMN*, VI, 310. The words "themselves" and "philosophers" are canceled in pencil, and "metaphysicians" is inserted in pencil. The passages "or whatever genuine . . . kingship." and "class, is always . . . kingship." are struck through in ink with vertical use marks; "Wit has a great . . . kingship." is used in "Progress of Culture," *W*, VIII, 218.

the crust, all is still, nothing stirs. Human life & thought is not less external. Nobody is profoundly good or bad. Were they profound, they would satisfy. ↑History is superficial[.]↓ [164]

If a carpenter were a carpenter to the bone, or a painter or a blacksmith had a native predilection for his craft, they were objects of admiration; but now if they take off their coat, they take off the carpenter or smith, & ⟨have to⟩ ↑must↓ remember every morning what it was they did yesterday, in order to know what they shall do today.

↑Neither is Samuel Hoar, Samuel Hoar to the bone, but our politics, opinions, & way of living are deciduous. Our manifoldness is betrayed[.]↓

[186] Swedenborg was extraordinary: as happens in great men, there were twenty or a hundred in him,[n] like the ⟨st⟩ giant strawberries which are formed by the union of four or five blossoms.
⟨|| ... ||⟩Such a man could not measure tape, but goes ⟨to s⟩grubbing into mines & mountains, into chemistry & optics, into ↑physiology↓ mathematics & astronomy, to find something adequate for this Briarean brain.
With the like immense force of constitution he threw himself into theology, & is it that it was not pure force but only this composite force of many in one, that ⟨g⟩ brought into so distinguished a genius so large infusion of mere people's theology? [165]

[187]–[188] [leaf torn out]
[189]   ↑Swedenborg↓
instead of porcelain, they are potter's earth, clay, or mud.[166]

Swedenborg must have the credit of opening many new doors in what had been esteemed for ages dead wall, as Belzoni discovered chambers in pyramids. Then nobody knows his sources of informa-

---

[164] These three added words are in pencil.

[165] These three paragraphs, struck through in ink with a vertical use mark, are used, down to "threw himself into theology,", in "Swedenborg," *W*, IV, 98–99.

[166] This sentence, struck through in ink with a vertical use mark, is used in "Swedenborg," *W*, IV, 98.

tion. He exhibits an exotic culture as if he had had his education in another planet.

He was indebted to Malpighi, Wolff, Liewenhoeck, Heister[.] [167]

Malpighi said, "Cum tota in minimis existat natura[.]" [168]

[190] "St Peter a unitarian," 'Isaac Newton a unitarian[,]' that is neither here nor there, but if you will find the maple & elm, granite, slate, & lime, ↑to be↓ of your party & opinion, that were something. That ↑moral↓ nature ⟨is anti⟩ ↑abhors↓ slavery, & New England sides with moral nature against South Carolina & animal nature.[169]

[191] ↑Born with a public nature,↓ millions [n] of eyes seemed to rest on him. He could not live without attempting something worthy & memorable.

[192] The skeptics have got hold of Park street Church & will not let the body of the Martyr Torrey come into it, for fear the crowd will spoil their carpets.[170]
The skeptics have got into the Abolition society, & make believe to be enraged.
Fire fights fire, the larger faith the less. How shall I educate my children? Shall I indulge, or shall I controul them? Philosophy replies: [n] Nature is stronger than your will, and, were you ever so vigilant, you may rely on it, your nature & genius will certainly give your vigilance the slip, though it had delirium tremens, & will edu-

[167] This and the preceding sentence are struck through in ink with a vertical use mark. The first is used in "Natural History of Intellect," W, XII, 71; with the second, cf. "Swedenborg," W, IV, 104-105.
[168] This quotation, struck through in ink with a vertical use mark, is used in "Swedenborg," W, IV, 104, where it is translated "nature works in leasts." Another English version, "nature exists entire in leasts," occurs later in the same essay (W, IV, 114), and yet another, "Nature shows herself best in leasts," occurs in "Works and Days," W, VII, 176.
[169] The inserted words "to be" and "abhors" were written first in pencil, then in ink. With " 'St Peter . . . were something.", cf. "Poetry and Imagination," W, VIII, 13.
[170] For the circumstances of Torrey's funeral, see p. [80] above. The words "the crowd will spoil their carpets." are struck through in ink with a vertical use mark; see p. [195] below.

cate the children by the inevitable infusions of its quality. You will do as you can. Why then cumber yourself about it, & make believe to be better than you are? n [171]

[193]   ↑Plenum↓
No man can afford to want any thing. If there be any deficiency in his equipment, fling him out of the line; but it is by no means needful that he should have it in your form. Thus he must be rich, but not necessarily in money or lands, but with the riches of riches, with creative supplying power. He must be armed, and, seeing a musket or a pike, he must feel that he has ⟨also these or much more formidable artillery to oppose to these toyguns⟩ ↑better muskets & pikes↓ in his energy & constancy. To every man his own courage[,] new & peculiar[,] as much as his own voice. To every creature its own weapon. ↑See p. 199↓
To every one his own gratitude. O 282 [172]

[194] If I were a member of the Massachusetts legislature, I should ⟨vot⟩propose to exempt all ⟨person⟩ coloured citizens from taxation because of the inability of the government to protect them by passport ⟨or⟩ out of its territory. It does not give the value for which they pay the tax.
    Also I should recommend that ⟨no⟩the executive wear no sword, and the office of general ⟨& the⟩ be abolished & the whole militia disbanded; for if these persons do not know that they pretend to be ⟨some⟩ & to do somewhat which they are not & do not, ↑⟨Mr⟩ Hoar of Concord,↓ Walker of the branded hand,[173] Torrey the Martyr, knew that the sword of Massachusetts is a ⟨wooden⟩ sword ↑of lath,↓

---

[171] This paragraph, struck through in ink with a vertical use mark, is used in "Natural History of Intellect," *W*, XII, 75.
    [172] The heading "Plenum" is in pencil. The inserted words "better muskets & pikes" were written first in pencil, then in ink. "If there be any . . . toyguns)", "but it is by . . . toyguns)", and "but it is by . . . own weapon." are struck through in ink with vertical use marks; "he must be armed . . . constancy" and "To every creature its own weapon." are used in "Worship," *W*, VI, 224.
    [173] Captain Jonathan Walker, of Harwich, Mass., had the letters "S.S." ("slave stealer") branded on his right hand by a Southern court after trying to carry fugitive slaves from Pensacola, Fla., to the British West Indies. See Whittier's poem "The Branded Hand" (1846).

or a turkey feather. It gives me no pleasure to see the governor attended by military men in plumes; I am amazed that they do not feel the ridicule of their position.

[195] *Economy*
There is an ⟨E⟩economy that goes to bed to save oil & ⟨fire⟩fuel, and that will not let the people come into the Church⟨e⟩, for fear of soiling the carpet.[174]

[Abel] Brooks, the cowtroopial farmer,[175] see below, p. 293.

Socrates' domestic economy consisted in keeping his family at work. See CD 59 [176]

Economy must be system, or 'tis naught[.]
Y 40
See Οι ρεοντες RS 278 [177]

The custom of the country will do all[.] Y 109
The gods are severe with us on this point[.] LM 114

[196] New England is subservient. The President proclaims war, & those senators who dissent, are not those who know better, but those who can afford to, as Benton & Calhoun.[178]

---

[174] See p. [192] above. Cf. *JMN*, VIII, 471.

[175] The cowtroopial, or cowbird, is a small blackbird that frequently accompanies cows.

[176] In Journal CD, Emerson gives the source of this statement as "Boeckh": Augustus Böckh, *Public Economy of Athens, in Four Books; to which is added, a Dissertation on the Silver-mines of Laurion*, trans. Sir George C. Lewis, 2 vols. (London, 1828), I, 150. Emerson withdrew this work from the Harvard College Library March 30, 1847.

[177] The Greek can be translated "the flowing [ones]." Journal RS will be published in a later volume.

[178] Thomas Hart Benton and John C. Calhoun both had reservations about declaring war on Mexico, but neither voted against the Declaration in the Senate on May 12, 1846. This paragraph, struck through in ink with two vertical use marks, is used in "Power," *W*, VI, 63.

Democracy becomes a government of bullies tempered by editors. The editors standing in the privilege of being last devoured. Captain Rhynders tempered by Father Ritchie & O'Sullivan
"I'm as good as you be," the motto of Tammany Hall [179]

[197] ↑Oliver Wellington describes to me↓ Semanthe Crawford of Oakham, ↑who↓ thought & felt in such strict sympathy with a friend in the spiritual world, that her thought ultimated itself in a preternatural writing on her arm, and again ⟨on to⟩ into writing on a paper which seemed to float in at the open window, & alighted on her lap.

[198] ↑*Cunning.*↓
Shortsightedness of the mechanics is wonderful. To win from you an advantage of a few shillings or a few dollars, they will take the risk of the long discontent & heart-burning of the housemates, who will take in future any pains to avoid employing them again. Certainly it costs too much — those two or three dollars. Mirabeau said, "Madam, if there were no such thing as probity, it would be invented as a means of getting ⟨along⟩ ↑on↓ in the world." [180] The reason of this cheating, however, is plain; it is their inability to make good calculations; they have found themselves short, they had miscalculated, & they now go to piece the hide of the lion by the skin of the fox. [181]

[199] To every creature its own weapon, however skilfully concealed. I thought myself laid open without walls to the hoofs of all cattle, but found, many years ago, that the eyes of all comers respected

[179] These four lines are in pencil. Thomas ("Father") Ritchie (1778–1854), editor of the Richmond *Enquirer* and later the Washington *Union*, was a moderate who urged gradual emancipation of the slaves; John L. O'Sullivan (1813–1895), whom Emerson had met in New York in February, 1843 (L, III, 146), was editor of the *United States Magazine, and Democratic Review.* For identification of Isaiah Rynders, see p. 388, n. 115 above.
[180] See Journal V, p. [86] above.
[181] In *JMN*, VI, 34, Emerson credits this maxim to Lysander, as quoted by Plutarch in "The Apophthegms, or Remarkable Sayings of Kings and Great Commanders." See *Plutarch's Morals* . . . , 1718, I, 209.

some fence which I could not see. The very strawberry vines can hide
their berry from Fumble & keep it for Cupid.¹⁸²   ↑O 282↓

[200] The shopwindow
I got a large part of my education from the shopwindows.¹⁸³

[201] [blank]
[202] *Tending*
We never do nothing[,] or never need. When we know not how
to steer, & dare not hoist a sail, we can float, we can drift, ⟨&⟩ the
current knows the way, though we do not. When the stars & sun
come out, when we have conversed with other navigators who know
the coast, ⟨& have⟩ we may begin to put out an oar, ⟨to take hold of⟩
↑handle↓ the rudder, & ⟨to⟩ trim a sail.
        ↑This must have been printed, but I know not where[.]↓ ¹⁸⁴

One thing we have, though it is not of us, continuity. I live now
a little this way,—then a little that,—but nature, independently
of our mathematics, secures a consecutiveness which later we acknowl-
edge with pleased surprise.

Do you say, that the current goes down stream:—No, these are
ocean currents, and the currents of [203] that ocean I speak of, go
in all directions, up, down, sidewise, by exhalation, & by radiation.
The exhalation which we call death, is still in the current, and the
current knows the way.¹⁸⁵

Continuity of nature[,] not of us[.]

We have been baptized, vaccinated, schooled, churched, married
to one wife,¹⁸⁶

¹⁸² For "To every creature its own weapon,", see p. [193] above. For a longer
version of the last sentence, see *JMN*, VII, 228–229.
¹⁸³ This sentence, struck through in ink with three diagonal use marks, is used
in "Culture," *W*, VI, 142.
¹⁸⁴ This sentence is in pencil. The paragraph, which is enclosed by brackets in
pencil, is used in "The Sovereignty of Ethics," *W*, X, 196.
¹⁸⁵ A single vertical line in ink is drawn in the left margin beside the last
sentence.
¹⁸⁶ This uncompleted entry is in pencil.

[204] *Society.*
It is very slowly & late that I begin to question the value of the
fashionable circles. I have not suffered the emptiness of individual
fashionists to discredit the class. But it is only a self-protection against
the vulgarities of the "American House" & the "Marlborough
Hotel." It has no ideas or aims; is a clothesbrush & a laundry, not a
farm or a factory. Its negativeness starves.[187]

↑See p 33⟨7⟩3
the true man of the world↓

[205]   ↑*State*↓   ↑*Politics*↓
"Les routes sont elles sures la nuit? ———— 'O vraiment oui, les
brigands de ce pays-ci ne s'amusent pas à s'attendre les passants sur la
grande route; ils volent bien plus à l'aise dans les bureaux.' "

Democratie Pacifique [188]

[206]   *Intellect.*
An intellectual man has the power to go out of himself, & see himself
as an object; therefore his defects & delusions interest him as much
as his successes. He not only wishes to succeed in life, but he wishes
in thought to know the history & destiny of a man[.]
But the clouds of egotists drifting about are only interested in a
success to their egotism.[189]

[207] [blank]
[208] Secure the essentials.[190] Advertise the fabric if you will, but
have the fabric. Build the Church in Broadway, if you like; but a
religion will not hop into it by chance. Unitarianism is a manoeuvre
in N.Y.; & young Bellows ↑(the name is real)↓ⁿ has ⟨corr⟩swamped ⁿ
his best years in tending & managing this dangerous ostentation. — [191]

---

[187] This paragraph is struck through in ink with a vertical use mark.
[188] *Démocratie pacifique* was a daily paper published in Paris from 1843 to 1851.
[189] These two paragraphs, and the heading, are in pencil. The paragraphs are
used in "Goethe," *W*, IV, 286.
[190] See pp. [248] and [256] below.
[191] Henry Whitney Bellows (1814–1882), Harvard Divinity School '37, became minister of the First Unitarian Church in New York City in 1839, and later
of the Church of All Souls on Fourth Avenue. Emerson dined with him on February
11, 1843 (*L*, III, 144) after Bellows had helped arrange Emerson's lecture engagements in New York.

I believe the University of New York was another of these bubbles. "We must have numbers, a crowd, a building." You lose by every gain.

In the city of Makebelieve is a great ostentation bolstered up on a great many small ostentations. I think we escape something by living in the villages. In Concord here, there is some milk of life, we are not so raving-distracted with wind & dyspepsia. The mania takes a milder form. People go a fishing & know the taste of their [209] meat. They cut their own whippletree in the woodlot, they know something practically of the sun & the east wind, of the underpinning & the roofing of the house, of the pan & the mixture of the soils.

In the city of Makebelieve all the marble edifices were veneered & all the columns were drums.[191a]

[210]   ↑Scholar's expenditure.↓
A Scholar is a literary foundation. All his expense is for Plato, Fabricius, Selden, Bently. Do not ask him to help young grocers to stock their shops with his savings. That is also to be done, but not by such as he. How could such a book have come down as the Poem of Sextus, but for the sacred savings of scholars & their fantastic appropriation of them? We must not make believe with our money, but spend heartily, and we must buy *up* & not *down*.[192]

[211]   ↑Scholar↓
    Scholarship is our religion. We ⟨cannot⟩ attempt practice, urged by nature, & are swamped at once in the profane miscellany; and by religious instinct we recover the shore as quick as we can, & in fault of power to execute our thought, we console us at least with delineating the picture.

↑23 May.↓ In Carlyle's head (photograph), which came last night, how much appears! How unattainable this truth to any painter! Here have I the inevitable traits, which the sun forgets not to copy, & which

---

[191a] With "all the columns were drums.", cf. *JMN*, VII, 460, 461, and VIII, 8.
[192] This paragraph, struck through in ink with a vertical use mark, is used in "Domestic Life," *W*, VII, 110.

I thirst to see, but which no painter remembers to give me. Here
have I the exact sculpture, ⟨and o⟩ the form of the head, the rooting
of the hair, ↑thickness of the lip↓, the man that God made. & all
the [212] Lawrences & Dorsays will now serve me well as illustration.[193] I have the form & organism, & can better spare the expression
& color. What would I not give for a head of Shakspeare by the
same artist? of Plato? of Demosthenes? Here I have the jutting
brow, and the excellent shape of the head. And here the organism
of the eye full of England, the valid eye, in which I see the strong
executive talent which has made his thought available to the nations,
whilst others as intellectual as he, are pale & powerless. The photograph comes dated 25 April, 1846. ↑and he writes I am fifty years
old.↓ [194]

[213][195]   And I hope the virtues of my sons
                 Smack of the soil that fed them.

          The wood chuck ⟨ran along the wall⟩ ↑rolled like a ball↓
          ⟨Fat⟩ ↑Round↓ & plump along the wall
          The poet ⟨st⟩ watched him well
          But when the animal
          Saw ⟨himself⟩ the observer
          He stopped & sat   Quiet & fat   Perhaps he thought
                                                    of tanners
             ↑Mistook a poet's interest for a tanner's↓
          The ⟨poet said⟩ impatient poet said
          Good friend you have a weapon more
          Than ⁿ I knew of before
          ⟨For I set more value on my time
          Than you on yours.⟩
          For though I love the animals

[193] Samuel Laurence (1812–1884) had done a portrait of Carlyle in 1838 and
sketches in 1838 and 1841; Count Alfred D'Orsay (1801–1852) had done a portrait in 1839 (CEC, pp. 311, n. 1, and 263).
[194] Emerson used some of the same language in his letter to Carlyle on May 31,
1846, acknowledging receipt of the photograph (CEC, p. 400).
[195] The entries on this page are in pencil. The first two lines are struck through
in pencil with three diagonal use marks.

And to know their manners
It seems I set more value on an hour
Than you on yours
Part of the history of genius

[214] Boston or Brattle Street Christianity is a compound force or the best diagonal line that can be drawn between Jesus Christ & Abbott Lawrence.

I never hear an eloquent word in public like Gannett's once & Ware's & Lovejoy's lately over Torrey's dead body, without a feeling of gratitude that would wash the feet of the speaker.[196]

[245][197] I value the varieties & the extremes of literature for their certification of that which is real & central[.]
Thus Romaic, Scaldic, Ceylonese, Hindu, Lenapé

[246]   Superstition
The metre of poetic genius ↑is↓ the power to fuse the circumstance of today; not to use Walter Scott's superstitions, but to convert those of Concord & 1846 into universal symbols. Thus, it is boyish in Swedenborg to cumber himself with the dead scoriae & exuviae of the Hebrew & Canaanitish antiquity when the questions that were then alive & fraught with good & evil to men have vanished before the questions of property, of politics, of democratic life, which now prompt young men.[198]

How beautiful the manners of wild animals, the bird that trims herself by the stream, the habits of antelope & buffalo. Well[,] the charm of genius is the same. We wish man on the higher plane to

---

[196] This paragraph is in pencil. See p. [80] above.

[197] In his initial pagination, Emerson inadvertently omitted pp. [215]–[244]. The present edition retains his incorrect numbering.

[198] A pencil version of this entry, partially erased, underlies the ink version. There are no significant differences between the two. The paragraph, struck through in pencil with a diagonal use mark, is used in "Poetry and Imagination," *W*, VIII, 34–35.

exhibit also the wildness or nature of that higher plane but the biography of genius so thirsted for is not yet written[.] [199]

[247] I should say of the memorable moments of my life that I was in them & not they in me. I found myself by happy fortune in an illuminated portion or meteorous zone, & passed out of it again,— so aloof was it from any will of mine. Law of that! To know the law of that, & to live in it! o thought too wild! o hope too fond! [200]

We are roadsters & packhorses but turn pike is one thing, & blue sky another.

We educate & drill, we hotpress & polish, but the audacities of genius are one thing, & the skill of drill another.[201]

———

Superstition. We do not now make laws like our ancestors forbidding under ⟨c⟩severe penalties all persons whatsoever from transporting themselves through the air by night.

[248][202]   ↑Real↓
The English secure the essentials; [203] the French the finish or appearance. The English secure the essentials, after their light, and it falls, at present, on bodily good, health & wealth[.]

                "England shall never reign in France!"
↑Real↓
The Normans normanized England; the stockjobber drives his trade at the Bourse, & Anglicizes France. "The stockjobber," says the Granzbote, "and the cook." For, as the drayhorse of Flanders has

[199] This paragraph is in pencil.
[200] Pencil versions of this and the following entry, partially erased, underlie the ink versions. There are no significant differences between the two. In the first entry, "I should say . . . of mine." is used in "Inspiration," *W*, VIII, 279.
[201] A pencil version of this entry, never erased, underlies the ink version. It begins "Yet we educate . . . "
[202] The two headings "Real" and the line " 'England shall never reign in France!' " are in pencil.
[203] This statement is used in *English Traits*, *W*, V, 84. See *JMN*, VI, 351, and pp. [208] above and [256] below.

come into London, so it seems the English Cyclops of an operative ↑sent over to build railroad at Rouen in 1841↓ cannot subsist on food less solid than beef, & the French⟨m⟩ operative vying with him, cannot do but one third of the work done by his English brother, until he diets at the same table.[204]   ↑See p 2⟨48⟩56↓

English arrogance of the Times newspaper
One would think all the johnnycake in America came out ⟨that⟩ ↑of that↓ office.

[249][205] ↑England↓
The last adjective & highest praise the Englishman gives is, "So English."[206]

patriotism for a few holidays & summer evenings but cotton thread is the Union[.]
We ask the price of many things but some things each man will buy, as conveyance in cars & boats[.]
let him never buy anything else than what he wants[;] never subscribe for good things[;]
never give unwillingly.[207]

[250] "Fruitur fama,"[208] no never. The poet is least a poet when he sits crowned. The transcendental & divine has the dominion of the world on the sole condition of not having it.

It may be true what I had heard

[204] Emerson's information is drawn from the article "Roastbeef in Frankreich" in *Die Grenzboten. Zeitschrift für Politik und Literatur*, V (1846), ii, 1–7.
[205] Partially erased pencil writing is visible at the top of the page; it consists of the heading "Real" and the sentence "Cotton thread holds the union together, unites John C. Calhoun & ⟨|| . . . ||⟩ ↑Abbott↓ Lawrence" (see p. [263] below).
[206] This sentence, struck through in ink with two diagonal use marks, is used in *English Traits*, W, V, 145.
[207] These seven lines are in pencil. "We ask the price . . . good things" is struck through in pencil with two vertical use marks, and "We ask the price . . . unwillingly." is used in "Domestic Life," W, VII, 109–110; see pp. [251] and [261] below. For "patriotism for . . . the Union", see p. [263] below.
[208] "He delights in fame" (Ed.). See *JMN*, VIII, 528.

        Earth is a howling wilderness
        Truculent with fraud & force
Said I ⟨Yet⟩ strolling through the pastures
        And along the river side   [5]
        Caught among the blackberry vines
        Feeding on the Ethiops sweet
        Pleasant fancies overtook me
        I said aloud What right have I
        Elect to dreams so beautiful   [10]
        The vines replied And didst thou deem
        No wisdom went to our creation   [12]
        No wisdom to our substance went? [209]   [12]

[251]   The Age
Real superstitions & not Walter Scott's. Our poets seek something
American that resembles Scotland, & miss the real superstition which
was clouding their brow in this very hour.[210]
                              See also p 246 p 247 [211]

The Jewsharp has sounded long enough[.] [212]

↑Expenditure.↓ We ask the price of many things but some things each
man will buy, as conveyance in cars & boats. Let him never buy anything else than what he wants; [n] never subscribe for goodey things;
never give unwillingly.[213] See p 261

[252]   ↑Rus ruris↓ [214]
To the page on narcotics in "the Poet," is to be added the confession,

---

[209] "Berrying," *W*, IX, 41. These lines were written in pencil upside down on
the lower half of the page, and later erased.

[210] See *JMN*, VIII, 525.

[211] "p 246" was written first in pencil, then traced in ink.

[212] See *JMN*, VII, 352.

[213] This paragraph is struck through in ink with two diagonal use marks. See
p. [249] above. A line is drawn underneath and to the right of "Expenditure." to
set it off.

[214] In *JMN*, VI, 163, Emerson himself translates this as "the country of the
country." The Latin is used in the lecture "The Superlative in Manners and Literature." See *JMN*, VIII, 282.

that the European history is the Age of Wine. The^n Age of Water, the simpler & sublimer condition, when the wine is gone inward, or the constitution has powers of original chemistry & can draw the wine of wine from water, (as the earth from loam & water educes the orange, the pomegranate, plum, peach, & pine-apple,) is yet to be, is now in its coming.[215]

We shall not have a sincere literature, we shall not have anything sound & grand as nature itself, until the bread eaters & water drinkers come.

[253] [blank]

[254]   Different velocity.

It is a great social advantage[,] if it be not bought too dear, to be *timed* with our contemporaries. The misfortune of certain individuals seems to be that their pulse plays faster or slower than the general, so that they can never keep step with their companions. All the symptoms are anomalous. One is cold when all the rest are warm; full, when others are fasting. One is thinking of Plato, the other of lobsters.[216]

[255] We are slain by indirections. Give us the question of slavery, — yea or nay; Texas, yea or nay; War, yea or nay; we should all vote right. But we accept the devil himself in an indirection. What taxes will we not pay in coffee, sugar, &c but spare us a direct tax.

First come first served, said the world to the Whig.[217]

[256]   ↑See p 248↓

Frenchman wishes to know that he has dined scientifically, & has had several courses, does not then ask out of what refuse his ragout was procured, or what corruption is ⟨c⟩hidden under spice & condiments.

---

[215] For the reference to "The Poet," see *W*, III, 26–28. "European history . . . its coming." is used in the lecture "The Superlative in Manners and Literature" (see *W*, X, 547–548).

[216] See p. [101] above.

[217] This pencil entry is erased. See p. [135] above.

Englishman secures the essentials,[218] good beef, without curry or artichoke or spinnage.

To the fir tree by my ↑study-↓window come
the groundsparrow
 oriole
 cedar-bird
 common crossbill
 yellow bird
 goldfinch
 cat-bird
 parti-coloured warbler
 robin

[257] ↑France↓
There is pretty good example of French sentimentality in Cousin's Lecture X on Hist of Philosophy (Eng. Trans p. 325) in his account of his feelings with regard to Brutus! [219]

———

French have no word for *to stand*.[219a]

———

[258] Community
I remember often Greenough's fine eulogy of Phidias & his antique comrades who wrought together to make a ⟨sculptu⟩frieze or a statue, — for so intractable ⟨was⟩is the material of the sculptor that otherwise his heat is expended before his work is sufficiently forward to keep him in heart for it. How many things should a community exist for. I have already named the possession of pictures, maps, dictionaries, & apparatus, — as telescope, & galvanic battery, &c.[220]

Now I think of committees to read books, & on oath report of them. A scholar is crafty, & hides his reading; he is full of ends &

---

[218] See pp. [208] and [248] above.
[219] *Introduction to the History of Philosophy*, 1832: "I have not the courage to unveil all the instances of misconduct, and all the faults of the last of the Brutuses. They are not unknown to me, but an invincible tenderness for the man is at the bottom of my heart." See *JMN*, VI, 355.
[219a] See *JMN*, VI, 376, and VII, 365.
[220] See pp. [42]–[43] above.

reservations. I wish such report as a brother gives to brother, or a husband to a wife. I will read Boehmen, if you will read Swedenborg; and we will read it as generous gods, each for the [259] other. The committees must be as naked & liberal as gods in their agency. Here is Fourier with unsettled claims. Here is always Plato; even Livy, I want searched & reported on. ↑I will take one, if another who values his time as much as I, will take another book.↓

⟨W⟩There is, beyond this, ↑a↓ deeper stricter community. We converse as spies. Our very abstaining to repeat & credit the fine remark of our friend, is thievish. ⟨Well, e⟩Each man of thought is surrounded by wiser men than he, if they cannot write as well. Cannot he & they combine? Cannot they sink their jealousies in God's love, & call their poem Beaumont & Fletcher's, or the Theban Phalanx's? [n] The city will for nine days or nine years make differences & sinister comparisons. There is a newer & more excellent public that will bless the Friends.

[260] Yet is not Community the dream of Bedlam? In experience men are always less to us, signify less. I do not expect a sympathy with my thought from the village, but, I go with it to the chosen & intelligent, & find no entertainment for it, but mere misapprehension, distaste, & scoffing.

⟨And we⟩Men are so discordant & of unequal pulse. And excellence is inflamed or exalted individualism[.]

[261] We ask the price of many things, but some things each man will buy, as, letters at the post office; conveyance in cars & boats; tools for his work; books that are written to his condition; &c. Let him never buy any thing else than what he wants; never subscribe for goodies; never give unwillingly.[221]

↑printed somewhere↓

[262] If ⟨the⟩ capital punishment is abolished, private vengeance

[221] This paragraph is struck through in ink with a vertical use mark. See pp. [249] and [251] above.

comes in.[222] If England, France, & America, are forbidden war ⟨by public opinion⟩ with each other, by public ↑opinion,↓ they cut & hack ⟨|| ... ||⟩on the Sikhs, the Algerines, & the Seminoles or the Mexicans, & so get rid of their turbulent & piratical population. The nobles shall not any longer as feudal lords have power of life & death over the churls, but now as capitalists shall in all love & peace eat them up as before.   See the Granzbote

---

↑Idea & Fact↓

We are very imaginative creatures and are very much impressed by a fact, though the state of things that caused it has already long subsisted.

Why not say, then, very literal creatures? [n]

[263] Cotten thread holds the union together, unites John C. Calhoun & Abbott Lawrence. Patriotism for holidays & summer evenings with music & rockets, but cotten thread is the union[.] [223]

[264]   ↑Eloquence↓
We go to the bar, the senate, the shop, the study, as peaceful professions. But you cannot escape the demand for courage, no, not in the shrine of Peace itself. Certainly, there is no orator who is not a hero. His attitude in the rostrum requires that he ↑shall↓ counterbalance⟨s⟩ his audi⟨ence⟩tory. He is challenger & must answer all comers. The orator must always stand with forward foot in the very attitude of advancing. His speech must be just ahead of the whole human race, or it is prattle. His speech is not to be distinguished from action. It is the salt & electricity of action. It is action, as the General's word of command or chart of battle is action.[224]

---

[222] This sentence is struck through in ink with a vertical use mark. See p. [297] below.
[223] See p. [249] above.
[224] The inserted word "shall" is in pencil. A single vertical line is drawn in ink in the left margin beside the last sentence. The paragraph is used in "Eloquence," *W*, VIII, 115.

"The path of the gods is steep & craggy" said Porphyry,[225]

[265] I must feel that the speaker compromises himself to his auditory, comes for something;[n] it is a cry on the perilous edge of fight, or let him be silent. Pillsbury, whom I heard last night, is that very gift from New Hampshire which we have long expected, a tough oak stick of a man not to be silenced or insulted or intimidated by a mob, because he is more mob than they; he mobs the mob. John Knox is come at last, on whom neither money nor politeness nor hard words nor rotten eggs nor kicks & brickbats make the slightest impression. He is fit to meet the barroom wits & bullies[;] he is a wit & ↑a↓ bully himself & something more[,] he is a graduate of the plough & the cedarswamp & the snowbank and has nothing new to learn [266][226] of labor, or poverty, or the rough of farming. His hard head too had gone through in boyhood all the drill of Calvinism with text & mortification so that he stands in the New England Assembly a purer bit of New England than any, & flings his sarcasms right & left, sparing no name, or person, or party, or presence. The "Concord Freeman" of the last week he ⟨|| ... ||⟩held in his hand, (the Editor was in the audience,) and read the paragraph on Mexican War from it, & then gave his own version of that fact.[227]

What question could be more pertinent than his to the Church[:] "What is the Church for? if, whenever there is any moral evil to be grappled with, as Intemperance, or Slavery, or War, there needs to be originated an entirely new instrumentality?"

[267][228] Every man in the presence of the orator is to feel that he has not only got the documents in his pocket to answer to all his cavils & to prove all his positions, but he has the eternal reason in his head; and that this man does not need any society or Governor

---

[225] This quotation, struck through in ink with five diagonal use marks, is used in "Culture," W, VI, 163.

[226] "Eloquence" is centered at the top of the page.

[227] The first sentence of this paragraph has a single vertical line in ink drawn beside it in the left margin and is used in "Eloquence," W, VIII, 115–116. "Pillsbury, whom I . . . presence", struck through in ink with two diagonal use marks on p. [265] and a vertical use mark on p. [266], is used in "Eloquence," W, VII, 95–96.

[228] "Eloquence" is centered at the top of the page.

or Army for he has latent but really present in himself ın a higher form navy & artillery, judge & jury, farmer, mechanic, mob, & executioner. Danger is not so dangerous as he.[229]

———

Mr Ruggles ↑of Fall River,↓ whom I once heard in a conversation at the Lyceum[,] appeared to me a formidable debater. He had a strong personality which made nothing of his antagonists. They were baubles for his amusement. His light, scoffing, &, as it were, final dealing with them, seeming to weigh them & find them nothings, was exquisitely provoking.

[268] O yes, abolition, or abstinence from rum, or any other ↑far off & external↓ virtue that will divert attention from the all--containing virtue which we vainly dodge & postpone, but which must be met & obeyed at last, if we wish to be substance & not accidents.

Osman's friend thought the angels also made show-speeches, & men were ever inclined to patronize Providence, & talk a little better than their belief.
Osman replied that, ↑compared with him,↓ Pyrrho was orthodox. O⟨s⟩ur friend thought he had detected a little vanity in Nature too.[230]

What a blessed world of snivelling nobodies we live in! There is no benefit like a war or a plague. The poor-smell has overpowered the roses & the aromatic fern. Oil of vitriol must be applied. A good hell-cat, spiegato carattere, would stimulate the imagination & enforce the tardy virtue by reaction[.]

[269] The scholar's or poet's writing is expectant as the practice of physicians is[.]

[229] This paragraph, struck through in ink with a vertical use mark, is used in "Eloquence," *W*, VII, 96.
[230] No source for the name "Osman" is known. Emerson uses it to designate the ideal man and, more often, the ideal poet. As indicated by identifications in Index Minor[A], p. [162], Jones Very was sometimes a model for this figure. It also has autobiographical relevance, as is indicated in the index to Journal O, where p. [199] is listed under both Autobiography and Osman, although Osman is not mentioned on the page. This and the following entry are in pencil.

[270] Life is well enough, but we shall all be glad to get out of it, & they will all be glad to have us.[231]

Who cannot be famous, said Osman, since I am?

Life is a selection, no more. The ⟨garden is⟩ work of the gardener is simply to destroy this weed, or that shrub, or that tree, & leave this other to grow. The library is gradually made inestimable by taking out from the superabounding mass of books all but the best. The palace is a selection of materials; its architecture, a selection of the best effects. Things collect very fast of themselves; the difference between house & house is the wise omissions.

[271] A good success.[232]   Alvah Crocker
Sewel F. Belknap
Patrick Jackson
F C Lowell
Croton Water Commissioner
Upjohn
Wiley & Putnam
W H Eliot
Horace Greeley
W[illiam] L[loyd] Garrison
J[ohn] J[acob] Astor
Catlin

[231] This sentence, struck through in ink with a vertical use mark, is used in "Montaigne," W, IV, 154, and "Old Age," W, VII, 320.

[232] These three words, and the names which follow, are in pencil. Persons in this list not previously identified or easily recognizable are: Patrick Tracy Johnson (1780–1847), American textile manufacturer and railroad builder; Francis Cabot Lowell (1775–1817), his partner in the Boston Manufacturing Company, which built one of the earliest textile mills in America at Waltham, Mass., and after whom Lowell, Mass., is named; Richard Upjohn (1802–1888), architect, whose works include the gates to Boston Common, and Trinity Church in New York City; John Wiley and George P. Putnam, who made the publishing firm of Wiley and Putnam into one of the most successful and respected in America; and George Catlin (1796–1872), American traveler, author, and artist, who specialized in portraits and sketches of the Indians. The "Croton Water Commissioner" may have reference to the Croton Aqueduct supplying water to New York City, recently completed. Sewel F. Belknap and W. H. Eliot have not been identified.

Alcott a survivor of the institutions [233]

[272]–[273] [blank]
[274]   Superstition
Pillsbury[,] commenting on Beecher's precious distinction of *organic sins*, made, that is, by *law*, said that the ↑American↓ Church⟨,⟩ ought to adopt a new formula, & say, *I baptize thee in the name of the Governor, & of the Senate, & of the house of Representatives.*

⟨a⟩And really instead of Walter Scott's superstitions, the virtual ⟨p⟩superstitions now are the deference to a supposed public opinion; to a Parliamentariness, to which, for example, Governor Briggs has just now immolated the State of Massachusetts[.] ↑p 216↓ [246] [234]

parliamentariness, laws of property, (custom of painting & papering[,] carpeting[,]) genteel housekeeping

[275] [235] Alcott said that what ever could be done with the eye he could do; meaning gardening, architecture, &, I suppose, picture & sculpture[.]

He thought he would go to the Convention of Abolitionists as a survivor of the Institutions,[236] instead of a dead man with his head out of the coffin[.]

I look for poetry above rhyme, poetry which the inspirer makes & applauds. The orator & the poet must be cunning Daedaluses & yet made of milk like the mob.

[276] My friend said that ⟨eloquence⟩ ↑the orator↓ must have ⟨something devilish⟩ a dash of the devil in ⟨it⟩him to suit an audience: at least his rhetoric must be satanic.

[233] See p. [275] below.
[234] The notation "p 216" is in pencil. George Nixon Briggs, governor of Massachusetts 1844–1851, although opposing the Mexican War, cooperated in supplying the troops which the federal government asked Massachusetts to furnish. His proclamation calling for "one regiment of infantry" appeared in the Concord *Freeman* May 29, 1846. See p. [296] below.
[235] The entries on this page are in pencil.
[236] See p. [271] above.

There is also something excellent in every audience, capacity of virtue; it is expectant & greatly expectant. They are ready to be beatified also. They know so much more than the orators. And are so just. There is a tablet there for every line he can inscribe.[237] Archangels listen in lowly forms. ↑Archangels in satinette & gambroon.↓

So fleeting as it is, yet what is so excellent of present Power as the riding this wild horse of the People? ⁿ
I suppose we shall never find in actual history the orator: he is a fabulous personage. We know very well what eloquence is, but no [277] man was ever continuously eloquent. And our examples are private, felicities of colloquial energy. Webster never says any thing great to a popular assembly. At the bar & in the Senate he is good.

[278] The scrupulous & law-abiding become whigs, the unscrupulous & energetic are locofocos. The people are no worse since they invaded Mexico, than they were before, only they have given their will a deed.

Every reform is only a mask under cover of which a more terrible reform[,] which dares not yet name itself, advances. Slavery & Antislavery is the question of property & no property, rent & anti-rent; and Antislavery dare not yet say that every man must do his own work, or, at least, receive no interest for money. Yet that is at last the upshot[.]

↑Idea & Fact↓
We tolerate the Community. We talk with them, we do not upbraid their spirit, but when they do [279] that which the⟨y⟩ir faces & speech signified ⟨we⟩ long since, we scream.[238] Really it makes little difference whether we have it in the gaseous or in the solid form. The whigs cant, & the locofocos blaspheme.

The United States will conquer Mexico, but it will be as the man

---

[237] "There is also . . . inscribe.", struck through in ink with a vertical use mark, is used in "Eloquence," W, VII, 66.
[238] See p. [296] below.

swallows the arsenic, which brings him down in turn. Mexico will poison us.

⟨W⟩ The Southerner is cool & insolent. "We drive you to the wall, & will again." Yes, gentlemen, but do you know why Massachusetts & New York are so tame⟨,⟩? it is because we own you, and are very tender of our mortgages[,] which cover all your property.[239]

[280] The stout Fremont[,] in his Report of his Expedition to Oregon & California, is continually remarking on "the group," on "the picture," &c. "which we make." [240] ⟨It is⟩ Our secondary feeling, our passion for seeming, must be highly inflamed, if the terrors of famine & thirst for the camp, & for the cattle, terrors from the Arapahoes & Utahs, ⟨the⟩ anxieties from want of true information as to the country & the trail, & the excitement from hunting, & from the new & vast ⟨‖ . . . ‖⟩features of unknown country, could not repress this eternal vanity of *how we must look!*

[281] I play with the miscellany of facts & take those superficial views which ⟨are⟩we call Skepticism, but I know or might know, at the same time, that they will presently appear to me in their orderly order, which makes Skepticism impossible. How can a man of any inwardness not feel the inwardness also of the Universe? [n] If he is capable of Science & of moral sentiment, the masses of nature instantly undulate & flow. The world[,] the galaxy is a scrap before the metaphysical power.[241]

[282] There are so many ways of looking at the man. You call him ungrateful, because he does not flatter you who say ↑that↓ you conferred favors on him. He thinks that which ⟨you gav⟩ he took of

[239] This paragraph is struck through in ink with two vertical use marks. See p. [296] below.

[240] John Charles Frémont, *Report of the Exploring Expedition to the Rocky Mountains in the Year 1842, and to Oregon and North California in the Years 1843–'44* (Washington, D.C., 1845). In Account Book 4, Emerson notes the purchase of this work in May, 1846.

[241] "I play with . . . impossible." and "the masses . . . flow.", struck through in ink with two vertical use marks, are used in "Montaigne," *W*, IV, 183.

you, was no more yours than the air which he breathed in your house. He thinks that favours should be returned in kind & not in money; that is, that your strength should be returned by his strength, not by his weakness. You served, did you not, your genius, and the indications of nature & providence, as well as you could interpret them, in serving him? he will not be less generous in his ⟨reception &⟩ reciprocations. He ⟨also⟩ is grateful, but you must leave him to designate ⟨the⟩ who is the benefactor.

[283] June 27. There is an unwritten law of Criticism respected by all good scholars[,] this namely, that when a good book of poems has been once written, say Milton's Minor Poems, no man shall print anything thereafter in that kind less excellent.

⟨The pos⟩ ⟨When will⟩ The ⁿ Poet ⟨come who shall⟩ ↑should↓ instal himself & shove all ⟨these⟩ usurpers from their chairs by electrifying ⟨the⟩ mankind with the right tone, long wished for, never heard. The true centre thus appearing, all ⟨these⟩ false centres are suddenly superseded, and grass grows in the Capitol. Now & then we hear rarely a true tone, a single strain of the right ode; but the Poet does not know his place, he defers * 242 to these old ⟨us⟩conventions, and though sometimes the rogue knows well enough that every word of his is treason to all the ⟨govern⟩ [284] kings & conventions of the world, yet he says "It is only I," "Nobody minds what I say," and avails himself of the popular prejudice ⟨of⟩ concerning his insignificance, as a screen from the police.

We had conversation today concerning the poet & his problem. He is there to see the type & truly interpret it; ⁿ O mountain[,] what would your highness say? thou grand expressor of the present tense;

[285] * He defers. We defer. That is the mischief. We are out-voted, the Nays have it, and we let the Nays have it. We who should say, 'What is the majority but the strength of weakness, the reason of fools?' suffer a majority to be somewhat ⟨for us also.⟩ in our own eyes.

242 Emerson wrote "*note *over*" at the bottom of p. [283] and "*see p. 283" at the top of p. [285], where the note occurs, with a rule underneath it from margin to margin.

of permanence; yet is there also a taunt at the mutables from old Sitfast. If the poet could only forget himself in his theme, be the tongue of the mountain, his egotism would subside and that firm line which he had drawn would remain like the ↑names of↓ discoverers of planets, written in the sky in letters which could never be obliterated[.] [243]

[286] [blank]
[287] A man is entitled to pure air and to the air of good conversation in his bringing up, & not, as we or so many of us, to the poor-smell, & musty chambers, cats & paddies.
I told A.B.A[lcott]. that he resembled a steam-engine which should stand outside one of our new depots, & see hundreds of paddies with pick & shovel making small impression, and should say, Let me come in, I will give you all leisure.

[288] A man is caught up and takes a breath or two of the Eternal, but instantly descends, & puts ⟨its⟩his eternity to commercial uses. There is no other, no example of any who did not so.

But a pretty kettle of fish we have here, men of this vast ambition, who wish an ethics commensurate with nature, who sit expectant to be challenged to great performances, and are left without any distinct aim; there are openings only in the heavens before them, but no star which they approach; they have an invincible persuasion that the Right is to come to them in the social form, but they are aghast & desolate to know that they have no superiors in society. Society treats their conscience as it does men of [289] genius; the only compliment it knows how to pay a man of genius, is ↑to wait on him &↓ to ask him to deliver a Temperance Address. So it proffers to these holy angels wishing to save the world, some bead or button of ↑Communism,↓ an Antislavery Cause, Prison Discipline, or Magdalen Refuge, or some other absorbent to suck his vitals into ↑some↓ one ↑or other↓ bitter partiality, ⟨or another,⟩ & ↑anyhow to↓ deprive him of that essential condition which he prays for, adequateness.

---

[243] This paragraph is struck through in pencil with a diagonal use mark.

H.D.T. seems to think that society suffers for want of war, ↑or↓ some good excitant. But how partial that is! the masses suffer for want of work as barbarous as they are. What is the difference? Now the tiger has got a joint of fresh meat to tear & eat: Before, he had only bones to grind & gnaw. But this concerns only the tigers, & leaves the men where they were.[244]

[290] He points to the respectability of earnestness ⟨i⟩on every platform. Yes, but what avails it, if it be fatal to earnestness to know much?[n] The snails believe, the geniuses are constitutionally skeptical. I lament that wit is a light mocker, that knowledge is the knowing that we cannot know, that genius is criticism. I lament to have life cheap; that a great understanding should play with the world as he tosses his walking-stick & catches it again. I wish the years & months to be long, the days centuries, loaded, ⟨|| ... ||⟩fragrant: now we reckon them basely, as bank days, by some debt that we are to pay or that is to be paid us.[245]

Now if there were an affection, a friendship that ⟨w⟩could be sovereign, that would at once bridge over these volcanic craters & gulfs of inequality between the [291] doer & the task

Centuries of sunny days
My pleasant centuries shall pass[246]

[292]   ↑*Society.*↓
Society is a curiosity shop full of odd excellences, a Bramin, a Fakeer, ⟨an ogre⟩ ↑a giraffe↓, an alligator, Col Bowie, Alvah Crocker, Bronson Alcott, Henry Thoreau, Caroline Sturgis; a world that cannot keep step, admirable melodies, but no chorus, for there is no accord.

---

[244] See p. [296] below.
[245] "He points to . . . criticism.", struck through in ink with two vertical use marks, is used in "Montaigne," W, IV, 174; "I lament to have . . . paid us.", struck through in ink with a vertical use mark, is used in "Considerations by the Way," W, VI, 247.
[246] These two lines are in pencil.

The country people at New Ipswich offered their lands to Mr Hill; —"Wait till I get to you," he said, "then I'll trade with you." ↑he bought 45 deeds↓

[293] Yankeedom
Abel Brooks a farmer of the cowtroopial school.[247] ⟨Jonathan at New York boards at a French house, so as to learn parler Francais ⁿ between the mouthfuls. For Jonathan wishes to make moonlight useful.⟩ Etzler is a philosopher & Espy to suit him.[248]

There's nothing *to* him.
About so
Sounds purty
no put-out
"terrible sassy" [249]
truck & dicker,   salary & stealings

The Yankee means to make moonlight work if he can; & he himself, after he has spent all the business hours in Wall street, takes his dinner at a French boardinghouse that his soup & cutlet may not be quite unprofitable, but he shall learn the language between the mouthfuls.
      ↑I rode in the stage coach with a pedler;↓ "Mind the half cent," said my companion. "A man can about pay his shop rent by minding the half cent."

[294]   ↑Symbol↓
In the dance, some dance, & others stand still ⟨in⟩awaiting their turn

[247] See p. [195] above.
[248] John Augustus Etzler's *The Paradise within the Reach of all Men, without Labour, by Powers of Nature and Machinery* . . . , Part First (London, 1842), which advocated the harnessing of such sources of energy as the winds and the tides, had been reviewed by Thoreau in "Paradise (to be) Regained," *United States Magazine and Democratic Review*, XIII (Nov. 1843), 451–463. Emerson's other reference is to James Pollard Espy (1785–1860), American meteorologist. "⟨Jonathan at . . . mouthfuls." and "⟨Jonathan at . . . suit him." are struck through in ink with diagonal lines, perhaps to indicate use.
[249] These two words were written first in pencil, then in ink; the quotation marks are in ink only.

when the music & the figure comes to them. In the dance of God there is ↑not↓ ⟨n⟩one of the chorus but can & will begin to spin, monu-mental as he now looks, when ⟨the⟩ever the music & the figure reach his place & capacity.²⁵⁰

The only gift to men, the only event, is a new image, a new symbol. That satiates them, transports, alters; they assimilate themselves to it, they deal with it in all ways and it will last them five hundred years. Then comes a new genius & brings another.²⁵¹ Such is Plato, Menu, Mahomet, Zoroaster,
Think how many more eggs of that kind remain to be hatched when the under side of every stick & stone all round the [295]²⁵² lake is covered with them.

I would give all for a new knowledge. Can you not extend my kingdom a little? Now every body tells me what I knew before. The amount ↑of information I obtain↓ of these mesmerised, is, that my shoes are made of leather, that there is a mantelpiece & four windows in my chamber. Ah[,] a new perception avails much & always costs something. One perception costs me my orchard, another my wife, another my caste or social connexion, and another my body, & we are content to pay these prices.

Pomona complained of flies.

_____

↑Symbols↓ ²⁵³
"There is nothing existing in human tho't even though relating to the most mysterious tenet of faith but has combined with it a natural & sensual idea"   Arcana [Coelestia] W 3310   Swedenborg

[296]²⁵⁴ people no worse since the war; the thought became a deed; and no better; the tiger has got a joint of meat to tear

---

²⁵⁰ This paragraph is used in "Poetry and Imagination," W, VIII, 70. The in-serted word "not" is in pencil.
²⁵¹ "The only gift . . . another.", struck through in pencil with a vertical use mark, is used in "Poetry and Imagination," W, VIII, 13–14.
²⁵² "Symbol" is centered at the top of the page and deleted in pencil.
²⁵³ This heading is enclosed by two rules both above and below.
²⁵⁴ The entries on pp. [296]–[298] are in pencil.

but it is a business that concerns only
the tiger section of the population[.] [255]

the Southron said we drive you to the wall & will again
Northerner, Yes; but because we are very tender of our
        mortgages. We own you.[256]

When they do that which their faces signified long since we
scream[.] [257]

To parliamentariness Gov. Briggs has immolated the honor of Massachusetts[.] [258]

Calvinistic education

[297] Worcester to Worc[ester,] Plym[outh] to Plym[outh] send
peacetracts & war instantly follows[,] nay has not ceased[.]
What is the use of voting slavery damnable[?]
The people being wolfish will in one way or other have blood.   If
capital punishment is abolished ⟨It requires⟩ private vengeance comes
in[.] [259]

[298][260]   Heaven is alive   [x]
              Self commanded works   [5]

[255] See p. [289] above.
[256] See p. [279] above.
[257] See pp. [278]–[279] above.
[258] See p. [274] above.
[259] See p. [262] above.
[260] Partially erased pencil writing covers this page. The following significant
words, phrases, and sentences have been recovered or conjecturally recovered: "I
was struck with the tameness of the good people of Mass degraded in ‖ . . . ‖
observers[?] & a debating society. Are we such snivelling nobodies   But I think I
understand it better. There is a"; "braces the conservative half and tho' they are
men[?] with[?] good blood"; "very well able to give"; "never shoot their"; "ill
is paid"; "that we could hear[?] if we"; "and are not so tender of our";
"imagine[?] but we are very tender[?]"; "very willing to"; "the property"; "the
cabinet"; "other disruption of sale"; and "That for one part of the people. Opposition is paralysed   The other part is the barbarous part who love rum & blood &
animal excitement".

In vital circles well   [x]
By dint of being all   [x]
It meets no loss   [x]
Its loss is transmutation   [x]
Is no emblem to express   [x]
Its perfect stature youthful power   [x]
selfbuilt   [x]
⟨Grows by decay⟩   [7]
And thro' the arms of all the devils   [11]
Builds the firm seat of Innocence
Fears not the ↑craft of↓ undermining days   [6]
Grows by decays
And by the famous might that's lodged
In[n] Reaction and Recoil
Teach flames to freeze & ice to boil.[261]   [10]

[299][262]   Criticism.   Literature
We are a little civil, it must be owned, to Homer & Æschylus, to
Shakspeare & Dante, and give them the benefit of the largest interpretation. We must be a little strict also, & faithfully ask whether,
if I sit at home & do not go to Hamlet, Hamlet will come to me;
whether I shall find my tragedy written in his, and my wants &
pains & disgraces described to the life.[263]

[300][264]   Centre & periphery
   Mystic   ⟨We see⟩

[261] These lines are an early version of the epigraph to "Spiritual Laws," W, II,
129, and are further refined on pp. [309]–[310] below.
[262] Erased pencil writing covers this page. The following significant words,
phrases, and sentences have been recovered or conjecturally recovered: "Our This";
"is called"; "It is called"; "It is of no use"; "Old"; "with each other that does
not hinder"; "Algerians[?] Sikhs"; and "This ne We are very ⟨much⟩ imaginative creatures, very much impressed by a fact by an object The country is no
worse now than before War was so shabbily declared, only the boys throw up
their caps ⟨& this army of rowdy⟩ officered by this file of acid & profligate editors
who turn to a money account this leonine taste".
[263] This paragraph is used in "Poetry and Imagination," W, VIII, 67–68.
[264] The entries on pp. [300]–[301] are in pencil. Erased pencil writing covers
the middle of p. [300]. The following significant words, phrases, and sentences
have been recovered or conjecturally recovered: "Now I"; "as they cease to be";

Profile of the ball
Little know we

them
gem
phlegm
stem
hem
Methusalem
diadem

*Nature hating lines & walls   [x]
*Rolls her matter into balls   [1]
 Ah her wise ephemerals
 Nailed to surface & outside
 See⟨s⟩ the profile of the sphere
 ⟨Draw⟨s⟩ the moral bright & clear⟩   [x]
 ⟨Ah⟩ Knew they what that signified   [5]
 ⟨Another⟩ A new ⟨race⟩ genesis were here

[301]   Nature hates lines   [x]
           Rolls herself into balls   [1]
           And generates new   [x]
           Man who knows the most   [x]
           Is confined to surfaces outside   [3]
           And only learns the profile of the sphere
           Which is a circle   [x]

           Nature hating lines & walls   [x]
           Selfwilled rolls her into balls   [1]
           Generating satellites   [x]
           Ill observed by peeping man   [x]

"that which is not part but whole, & which not readily &"; "from[?] one man
as from the most numerous cooperation. I hope"; "those great men arise who like
the west wind bring the sublime with them those who do not defer as the men of
talent we know to the sublime nonsense of existing things but without an effort set
them aside & repudiate them because they are in the presence of those[?]"; and
"greater".

Very wisest of his clan   [x]
Anchored fast to the outsides   [3]
Half learns the profile of the sphere
Wise if he knew what that signified.[265]   [5]

[302] ⟨I⟩ Criticism is in its infancy. The anatomy of Genius it has not unfolded. Milton in the egg, it has not found. Milton is a good apple on that tree of England. It would be impossible by any chemistry we know to compound that apple other wise: it required all the tree; & out of ⟨a⟩ thousands of apples good & bad, this specimen apple is at last procured. That is, we have a well↑-↓knit, hairy, industrious Saxon race[,] Londoners intent on their trade[,] steeped in their politics, wars of the roses, voyages, & trade to the Low Countries, to Spain, to Lepanto, ⟨Vi⟩to Virginia, & Guiana, all bright with use & strong with success. Out of this valid stock ⟨get⟩ ↑choose↓ the validest boy, & in the flower of this strength open to him, ⟨open to this elixir of London⟩ the whole Dorian & Attic beauty [303][266] and the proceeding ripeness of the same in Italy. Give him the very best of this Classic beverage. ⟨Send him⟩ ↑He shall↓ travel⟨ling⟩ to Florence & Rome in his early manhood: he shall see the country & the works of Dante, Angelo & Raffaelle. Well, on the man ⟨thus⟩ to whose unpalled taste this delicious fountain is opened, ⟨now⟩ add the fury & concentration of the Hebraic Genius, through the hereditary & ⟨now⟩ ↑⟨no longer⟩already↓ culminat⟨ing⟩ed Puritanism — and you have Milton, a creation impossible before or ⟨si⟩again; and all whose graces & whose majesties involve this wonderful combination; — quite in the course of things once, but not iterated. The drill of the regiment, the violence of the pirate & smuggler, the cunning & thrift of the ⟨cou⟩ haberdasher's counter, ⟨&⟩ the generosity of the ⟨nob⟩ Norman earl, are all essential to the result.

[304]   Mixture
The whole art of nature ↑is↓ in these juxtapositions of diverse quali-

---

[265] The lines which Emerson here recast several times became the epigraph to "Circles," W, II, 299. The asterisks in the first version do not indicate footnotes.

[266] "Temperance", in pencil and centered at the top of the page, was written at some earlier time.

ties to make a lucky combination[,] as green & gold, ↑dry↓ oakleaves & snow enhance each other, & make a delicious mixture to the eye.

↑*Mixture*↓

Everything that makes a new sort of man is good; for though he is only a chemic dose in this generation, in the next, or next but one, he becomes a poet, & then the ⟨novel⟩ new metal becomes inestimable.

[305]   Mixture   [Chemical Combination]

People do not value raw material. The Laws of Menu, — Bhagavat, Behmen, Swedenborg, Alcott, Channing, & what not, I may have to myself: nobody to quarrel with me for these masses or particles. But when I have mixed these simples with a little Boston water, it makes what they call poetry & eloquence, & will sell, it seems, in New York & London.

[306] O Bacchus, make them drunk, drive them mad, this multitude of vagabonds, hungry for eloquence, hungry for poetry, starving for symbols, perishing for want of electricity to vitalize this too much pasture; &, in the long delay, indemnifying themselves with the false wine of alcohol, of politics, or of money. Pour for them, o Bacchus, the wine of wine. Give them, at last, Poetry.[267]

↑Test, opportunity.↓

Do they stand immoveable there, — the sots, & laugh at your socalled poetry? They may well laugh; it does not touch them yet. Try a deeper strain. There is no makebelieve about these fellows; they are good tests for your skill; therefore, a louder yet, & yet a louder strain. There is not one of them, ⟨I tell you,⟩ but will spin fast enough when the music[n] [307] reaches him, but he is very deaf, try a sharper string.[268] Angels in satinette & calico, — angels in hunting knives, & rifles, — swearing angels, roarers with liquor; — O poet, you have much to learn.   ↑See p. 294↓

---

[267] This paragraph is struck through in pencil with a vertical use mark; "O Bacchus . . . of money." is used in "Poetry and Imagination," *W*, VIII, 70.
[268] "Do they stand . . . string." is struck through in pencil with a vertical use mark.

Styles
There is the ⟨sl⟩Periclean & there is the slambang style[.]

O Carlyle[,] the merit of glass is not to be seen but to be seen through but every crystal & lamina of the Carlyle glass is visible[.] [269]

[308] Let the poet work in the aim to eliminate beauty; that is verily ⟨in⟩ his work; in that block of stone, in that rough verse, to free the noble conception, until it shall be as truly God's work as ↑is↓ the globe of the earth, or the cup of the lily↑.↓ ⟨is⟩

Metre of the Poet again, is his science of love. Does he know that lore? Never was poet who was not tremulous with love-lore.[270]

⟨As⟩ The [n] coral ⟨insect under⟩ ↑worm beneath↓ the sea
Mason planter spreads   Rock vegetable threads
For foundation of the isles
His colossal flowers [271]

[309]   Heaven is alive   [x]
             ⟨Self commanded works⟩   [5]
             Self built and quarrying itself   [x]
             ↑↑Up↓ builds [n] eternal towers↓   [4]
             Self commanded works   [5]
             In vital cirque   [x]
             By dint of being all   [x]
             Its loss is transmutation   [x]
             Fears not the craft of undermining days   [6]
             Grows by decays
             And by the famous might that⟨'s lodged⟩ ↑lurks↓
             In reaction & recoil
             Teach flames to freeze & ice to boil   [10]
             And thro' the arms of all the devils

[269] This sentence is in pencil.
[270] Emerson's quatrain "Casella," W, IX, 296, is a versified version of these sentences.
[271] These lines are in pencil.

Builds the firm seat of Innocence
Is no emblem to ⟨express⟩ measure   [x]
Its perfect stature youthful power   [x]
Youthful urgency   [x]
No lapse of memory   [x]
Betrays the Angel into unbelief   [x]
But in the beginning sees the time to come   [x]
⟨He sees the end⟩ And on the road his home   [x]
[310]   He cannot fear defeat   [x]
⟨And on the road he sees the goal⟩   [x]
Journeying thro' day & night to [272]   [x]

He who has no hands
Perforce must use his tongue;
Foxes are so cunning
Because they are not strong.[273]

Mind & manners in the XIX Century [274]
   1. Powers & Laws of Thought
   2. Relation to Natural Science
   4. Tendencies & duties of men of thought
   ⟨5. Natural Aristocracy⟩
   ⟨6⟩5. The Superlative in Manners & Literature — The
      Genius of the Eastern & Western Nations compared.
   6. The Natural Aristocracy.

[311]   ↑Longevity↓ [275]
I have often lamented the brevity of life, & yet it is easy [n] to see that
the⟨re⟩ stability of human beings depends on that consideration. Who
would stay in Concord, who had heard of Valencia, but that there
is not time to establish himself there, without too great a hazard of

[272] These lines are in pencil. A number of them occur in the epigraph to
"Spiritual Laws," *W*, II, 129. For an earlier version, see p. [298] above.
[273] "Orator," *W*, IX, 291. These lines are struck through in ink with two vertical
use marks. A pencil version, later erased, underlies the beginning of the next entry.
There are no significant differences between the pencil and ink versions.
[274] See p. [164] above.
[275] This word is in pencil.

his happiness in the few years that remain. Therefore we stick where we are.

[312]²⁷⁶ 〈That which〉 ↑Theme↓ no poet ↑gladly↓ sung
〈How parts are joined〉 ↑Dear to age↓ & foul to young
The love of parts
〈The〉 ↑And↓ articles of arts
And the grandeur of the sphere
〈By〉 Thanks the atoms that cohere

Theme no poet gladly sung
Fair to age & foul to young
Scorn not thou the love of parts
And the articles of arts
Grandeur of the perfect sphere
Thanks the atoms that cohere.²⁷⁷

[313] [blank]
[314] Build your prison walls thicker: it needs a firmer line of demarcation to denote those within from those without. What fetishes & Joshes we kneel unto! Great is paint! This poor child who has had no childhood, but a harsh hedgehog lot, talks of that grim farmhouse as the happiest days of her life.²⁷⁸ On the other side, all these martyrs of the pattypan school of unitarianism.—Is not America more than ever wanting in the male principle? A good many village attorneys we have, saucy village talents, preferred to 〈‖ . . . ‖〉Congress, & the cabinet,— Marcys, Buchanans, Walkers, &c., but no great captains.²⁷⁹ Webster is a man by himself of the great mould, but he also underlies the American blight, & wants the power of the initiative, the affirmative talent, and remains like the literary class, only a commentator,ⁿ [315] his great proportions only 〈making b〉 ex-

---

²⁷⁶ The entries on this page are in pencil.

²⁷⁷ These lines became the epigraph to "Prudence," *W*, II, 219.

²⁷⁸ This sentence is struck through in ink with three vertical use marks; cf. "Illusions," *W*, VI, 315.

²⁷⁹ In President Polk's cabinet, William L. Marcy (1786–1857) was Secretary of War, James Buchanan (1791–1868), Secretary of State, and Robert J. Walker (1801–1869), Secretary of the Treasury.

posing his defect. America seems to have immense resources, land, men, milk, butter, cheese, timber & iron, but it is a village littleness; —village squabble & rapacity characterises its policy. It is ⟨an⟩a great strength on a basis of weakness.

Perhaps the fairer picture of the permissive Destiny: we can see what it allows, what the vegetable nature grows to↑, if↓ unpruned; what fancies, what appetites are the crop of this plant↑, —↓*man*. What Destiny will⟨?⟩. "What's your wull?"

These rabble at Washington are really better than the snivelling opposition. They have a sort of genius of a bold & manly cast, though Satanic. They see, against the unanimous expression of the people, how much [316] a little well directed effrontery can achieve, how much crime the people will bear, & they proceed from step to step & it seems they have calculated but too justly upon your Excellency, O Governor Briggs. Mr Webster told them how much the war cost, that was his protest, but voted the war, & sends his son to it. They calculated rightly on Mr Webster.[280] My friend Mr Thoreau has gone to jail rather than pay his tax.[281] On him they could not calculate. The abolitionists denounce the war & give much time to it, but they pay the tax.

It seems now settled that the world is no longer a subject for reform: it is too old for that, & is to have custard & calves' jelly. We are no longer to apply drastic [317] or alterative pills, nor attempt remedies at all, but if we have any new game, or some fireworks or ice--cream, —if Jenny Lind come hither, or Fanny Elssler return,[282] it is all the case admits.

Boston is represented by Mr Winthrop whose ready adhesion to Southern policy outspeeds even the swift sequaciousness of his constituents.

---

[280] "These rabble at . . . Briggs.", struck through in pencil on p. [315] with a vertical use mark and in pencil and ink on p. [316] with vertical use marks, is used in "Power," *W*, VI, 65. For Governor Briggs's compliance in the Mexican War, see p. [274] above. "Mr Webster told . . . Mr Webster." is struck through in ink with a vertical use mark.

[281] Thoreau was jailed toward the end of July, 1846, for refusing to pay his poll tax as a protest against slavery and the Mexican War.

[282] Emerson saw Fanny Elssler, the Austrian ballerina, in October, 1841, during her American tour (*JMN*, VIII, 109–111).

The ⟨world⟩ ↑State↓ is a poor good beast who means the best: it means friendly. A poor cow who does well by you, — do not grudge it its hay. It cannot eat bread as you can, let it have without grudge a little grass for its four stomachs. It will not stint to yield you milk from its teat. You who are a man walking cleanly on two feet [318] will not pick a quarrel with a poor cow. Take this handful of clover & welcome. But if you go to hook me when I walk in the fields, then, poor cow, I will cut your throat.

Sparta & Christianity are two social things.

↑Printed↓ 283

Don't run amuck against the world. Have a good case to try the question on. It is the part of a fanatic to fight out a revolution on the shape of a hat or surplice, on ↑paedo-↓baptism or altar-rails ↑or fish on Friday.↓ As long as the state means you well, do not refuse your pistareen. ⟨But when⟩ You have a tottering ⟨case⟩ cause: ninety parts of the pistareen it will spend for what you think also good: ten parts for mischief. You can not fight heartily for a fraction. But wait until you have a good difference to join issue upon. Thus [319] Socrates was told he should not teach. "Please God, but I will." And he could die well for that. And Jesus had a cause. You will get one by & by. But now I have no sympathy.

The abolitionists ought to resist & go to prison in multitudes on their known & described disagreements from the state. They know where the shoe pinches; have told it a thousand times; are hot headed partialists. I should heartily app⟨ro⟩laud them[;] it is in their system. Good beastie help itself by reform & resistance as well as by law. But not so for you generalizers. You are not citizens. You are not as they to fight for your title to be churchmembers or citizens, patriots. Reserve yourself for your own work[.]

[320] A B A[lcott] thought he could find as good a ground for quarrel in the state tax as Socrates did in the Edict of the Judges.284

283 This word is in pencil.
284 Like Thoreau, Alcott in 1843 had refused to pay his poll tax, but it was paid for him by Samuel Hoar.

Then I say, Be Consistent, & never more put an apple or a kernel of corn into your mouth. Would you feed the devil? Say boldly "There is a sword sharp enough to cut sheer between flesh & spirit, & I will use it, & not any longer belong to this double faced equivocating mixed Jesuitical universe."

The Abolitionists should resist, because they are literalists; they know exactly what they object to, & there is a government ⟨to which⟩ possible which will content them. Remove a few speci⟨al⟩fied grievances, & this present commonwealth will suit them. They are the new Puritans, & as easily satisfied. But you, nothing will [321][285] content. No government short of a monarchy consisting of one king & one subject, will appease you. Your objection then to the state of Massachusetts is ⟨then absurd.⟩ ↑deceptive.↓ Your true quarrel is with the state of Man.

In the particular it is worth considering that refusing payment of the state tax does not reach the evil so nearly as many other methods within your reach. The state tax does not pay the Mexican War. Your coat, your sugar, your Latin & French & German book, your watch does. Yet these you do not stick at buying.

But really a scholar has too humble an opinion of the population, of their possibilities, of their future, to be entitled to go to war with them as with equals.
This prison is one step to suicide.

[322] He knows that nothing they can do will ever please him. Why should he poorly pound on some one string of discord, when all is jangle?

He goes for strong more than he goes for handsome[.] [286]

[323] 29 July. We do not care for you. Let us pretend or self deceived say what we will, we are always looking through you to the

[285] Page [321] is reproduced in Plate III.
[286] This sentence is in pencil.

speaker behind you. Whilst your habit or whim speaks, we civilly &
impatiently wait, until that wise superior shall speak again.[287]

Men also handsomer for some chromatic stains
⟨He⟩ ↑Arius↓ never explains himself

In the hot Friday almost froze to death;
Wore earthquake dresses every day;
Goes a-berrying in the night;
And makes ⟨a⟩ ↑this↓ will when he goes forth to ride.

[324] Astronomy of no use, if I cannot carry it into shops &
sittingrooms. A dollar in S. Carolina is not worth a dollar in Massachusetts. A dollar is ↑not value but↓ representative of value & at
last of moral values. A dollar is valued not for itself, but for the
corn it will buy, & not for the corn & houseroom, but for Athenian
corn & Roman houseroom, for the wit & probity & power which we
eat bread & enter houses to share & exert.
Mathematics leave the mind where they found it. Alas, so do all
things. Thought, whilst it lasts, is the only thing of value, & appears
of universal value, appears to hold central power. But we come out
of it pale sallow fellows, as if we had smoked cigars. No more social,
no more adapted, no more furnished than before. Poetry an excellent
art for a man of great strength & spirits, — heart & head ⟨rapidly⟩
supplying him copious material.[n] But for [325] a cold jejune person
of low pulse, no more unpromising employment suggests itself.[288]

We are an afflicted land, a people not strong in the knees.
⟨That⟩ ↑We make the↓ stunning discovery of the parallelism of the
lines, or concentricity of the arcs on which we move.[289] ↑We believe
in youth↓ that, world would play into world, there should be concert
& reaction, the practical on the poetical, the sphere of rapture on the

---

[287] This paragraph, struck through in ink with a vertical use mark, is used in
"Worship," *W*, VI, 228–229.
[288] "A dollar in S. Carolina . . . exert.", struck through in ink with a vertical
use mark, is used in "Wealth," *W*, VI, 103. "Mathematics . . . found it." is used
in "Montaigne," *W*, IV, 178; see *JMN*, VIII, 162.
[289] A single vertical line in ink is drawn in the left margin beside this sentence.

content. No government short of a monarchy consisting of one king & one subject, will appease you. Your objection then to the state of Massachusetts is (there absurd). Your true quarrel is with the state of Man.

In this particular it is worth considering that refusing payment of the state tax does not reach the evil so nearly as many other methods within your reach.
The state tax does not pay the Mexican War. Your coat, your sugar, your Latin & French & German book, your watch does. Yet these you do not stick at buying.

But really a scholar has too humble an opinion of the population, of their possibilities, of their future, to be entitled to go to war with them as with equals.
This prison is one step to suicide.

sphere of house & hearth, each exalting or solidifying the other. But they hate each other; their bloods will not mix in a basin. And the only means of keeping the peace of the skies is the assent of Pluto to the Compromise that Proserpine shall spend ↑alternately↓ a term with Ceres, and a term with him; no commerce therefore between Pluto & Ceres.

[326] Aug. 2⟨2⟩3, 1846.   ↑*Teachers.*↓
The teacher should be the complement of the pupil; now for the most part they are earth's diameters wide of each other. A college professor should be elected by ⟨taking from⟩ setting all the candidates loose on a miscellaneous gang of young men taken at large from the street. He who could get the ear of these ⟨people⟩ ↑youths↓ after a certain number of hours, or of the greatest number of these ⟨people⟩youths[,] should be professor. Let him see if he could interest these rowdy boys in the meaning of a list of words.

A poet is all we want. He acts on us like a thunder clap[.]
The poetry of the muse is to be readily discriminated from coffee poetry, or Hotel poetry, and that of *coups de force*, which is the best now going. All Hood's is of that kind.

[327] Channing thinks life looks great & inaccessible & constantly attacks us & notwithstanding all our struggles is eating us up.

A great design belongs to a poem and is better than any skill in execution; but where in modern ↑Eng.↓ poetry out of Wordsworth's Laodamia, Dion, & Ode, & the Plan of the Recluse, is any great design? [n 290] We shall come to value only that excellence of finish which great design brings with it[.]
Alcott's division of men was into three classes, ↑1.↓ those of aim; ↑2.↓ those of aim which they can hit; & ↑3.↓ the aimless. The second class are the poets.

[328] The world lies so in heaps that perhaps 'tis not strange

[290] This sentence, struck through in ink with a vertical use mark, is used in "Poetry and Imagination," *W*, VIII, 33.

that there should yet be ⟨no wonder there should be⟩ no painters, ⟨yet,⟩ no Homer of our thoughts, far higher than the Homer of Greek thoughts.

We are liberal to the Astors & Vanderbilts & Websters, & allow their barbarous & semi-beast life to pass, ⟨&⟩ though they give none to the Olympian & divine, yet we ought as equitably to reverence Pan in humblebee & cricket. One example of that would justify so much. — We talked of the old Baconian or Platonistic ⟨ru⟩canon. There is nothing in the globe of the world which is not in the crystal sphere. —[291] And our Parisian savant has discovered mathematically a new planet yet invisible.[292]

[329] ↑College Class of 1821↓

We have the less ⟨life⟩time to spend, for these many years since we met, & I must not detain you. We were here before, mere lambs & rams,[n] & we have come back solemn Abrahams; and on account of Mrs A. & the young *A's*, we had some ado to get here now; we that so ran & skipped . . . Scots like to come of "kenned folk," and there is an eminent use in having one's training in the public eye. But it is curious to see how identical we are. We can remember ourselves, about as good & bad as today, 25, 30, 40 years & more. In college, I had ⟨the same⟩ unpreparedness ⟨I⟩for all my tasks. I have the same unpreparedness ⟨today.⟩ at this moment. Who is he that does not remember the roots of all the habits of his chum & his set in ⟨their⟩ Dr Popkin's recitation room or in Commons Hall? [293] ↑We have had clients, pupils, patients, parishes.↓ We have had hay to make, horses to buy, ↑cargoes to manage,↓ estates to settle, ↑railroads to superintend,↓ ⟨cities to⟩ ↑banks to direct, cities to↓ preside over, states to govern, colleges to rule; but if we have done ⟨it⟩ ↑these things↓ well, as I doubt not, it was because we could carry ourselves

---

[291] In *JMN*, VI, 203, Emerson quoted this statement from *The Advancement of Learning* in *The Works of Francis Bacon* . . . , 1824, I, 200.

[292] In 1846, Urbain Jean Joseph Leverrier calculated the position of Neptune as a result of mathematical work on unexplained irregularities in the motion of Uranus.

[293] The Reverend John S. Popkin was professor of Greek during Emerson's undergraduate days at Harvard.

[330] ↑goodhumouredly ⟨& manly⟩↓ as boys. ⟨There is a good deal of bottom in the company⟩[294] With [n] a fair degree of speed, I think there is still more bottom in the company; and what pleases me best in the history of the class, is its good position & promise at this moment. Its strength is not exhausted: ↑our day has not been short; but↓ we are not yet thinking of going to bed, & being tucked up for the long night. I see ⟨a long & fair⟩ ↑an open↓ future before us; and I offer the ⟨⟨hope⟩sentiment The next twentyfive years shall be, God willing, as large a gain on the last as these were on the ⟨fifteen⟩ first score[.]⟩ [295]

The ⟨incessant⟩ ↑proceeding↓ education of ⟨our⟩ ↑the↓ [296] class: The next twentyfive years shall be, God willing, as large a gain on the last ⟨as⟩twentyfive as these were on the first score.

[331] 1846 Aug.   Wednesday
At Commencement met with the members of the Class of 1821. We counted nineteen present; Josiah Quincy presided: also present, [John] ⟨B⟩Angier, [Henry] Bulfinch, [Charles] Bunker, [Warren] Burton, [George M.] Dexter, [John L.] Gardner, [John B. or Joseph B.] Hill, [William] Hilliard, [John M.] Cheney, [Oliver H.] Blood, [Edward] Kent, [Francis C.] Lowell, [Benjamin T.] Reed, [Caleb] Stetson, [Charles W.] Upham, [William] Withington, [George B.] Moody, Emerson; a very cordial three hours' space we spent together, & made up at last a little purse of $82.50 for Henry Bulfinch.[297] Adjourned for five years.

At Phi Beta K. Sumner's oration was marked with a certain magnificence which I do not well know where to parallel.

He quoted Story, as saying, "Every man is to be judged by the horizon of his mind." "Fame," he said after Allston, I think, "is the

[294] This sentence is struck through in ink with three diagonal lines, perhaps to indicate use.
[295] This sentence is struck through in ink with three vertical lines, perhaps to indicate use.
[296] This word is inserted in pencil.
[297] In Account Book 4, under August, 1846, Emerson notes ten dollars as a "contribution for Henry Bulfinch." At the reunion of Emerson's class in 1841, when Bulfinch also was present, Emerson notes that "One poor man came whom fortune had not favored, & we carried round a hat, & collected $115.00 for him in two minutes" (JMN, VIII, 41).

shadow of excellence, but that which follows ↑him↓, not ↑which he↓ follows after." [298]

[332] ⟨In Ame⟩ All the notable Americans, ↑except Webster,↓ as I have said before, are female minds; Channing, Irving, Everett, Greenough, Allston, &c[.]
Ah the careful American faces
To the youth the hair of woman is a meteor.
I think that he only is rightly immortal to whom all things are immortal; he who witnesses personally the creation of the world; he who enunciates profoundly the names of Pan, of Jove, of Pallas, of Bacchus, of Proteus, of Baal, of Ahriman, of Hari, of Satan, of Hell, of Nemesis, of the Furies, of Odin, & of Hertha; — knowing well the need he has of these, and a far richer vocabulary; knowing well how imperfect & insufficient to his needs language is; requiring[n] music, requiring dancing, as languages; a dance, for example, that shall sensibly express our astronomy, our solar system, & seasons, in its course. —

[333]   ↑Greatness↓   ↑Man of the World↓
A man of the world[n] I wish to see, not such men as are called of the world who more properly are men of a pistareen, men of a quart pot, ⟨men of a wine glass,⟩ men of a ⟨champagne⟩ ↑wine↓-glass; whose report reaches about as far as the pop of a champagne cork, & who are dumb as soon as they stray beyond that genial circle.
But I wish ⟨men⟩ catholic ⟨& capable⟩ ↑men↓ who read ciphers which they see for the first time; who know the beauty of a quince-orchard; of a heron; of a wood pigeon; of ↑a↓ lonesome pasture. Men who see the dance in men's lives, as well as in a ballroom; & can feel & convey the sense which is only collectively or totally expressed by a population: men who are charmed by the beautiful Nemesis, as well as by the dire Nemesis; and wish to be its poets & dare trust their

[298] Sumner's address was "The Scholar, the Jurist, the Artist, the Philanthropist" — John Pickering, Joseph Story, Washington Allston, and William Ellery Channing the elder, respectively. Emerson recalls Story's remark accurately, but in the second combines remarks by Allston and Lord Mansfield. See *The Works of Charles Sumner*, 15 vols. (Boston, 1874–1883), I, 268, 283.

inspirations [334] for their welcomes.[299] Our poets have not the poetic magnanimity, but a miniminity rather; &, when they would go abroad, instead of inspecting their inward poem, they count their dollar bills.

The saints dare more, but I hate lampsmoke; I wish them to know the beautiful equality & rotation of merits, destroying their saintly egotism or prigism; let them worship the appletrees, the thistles, & their beautiful lovers the humblebees, ⟨&⟩ humming birds, & yellow butterflies, as they pass, & as I say, know the ⟨b⟩Beautiful Nemesis.

[335] All men are of a size, and true art is only possible on the conviction that every talent, trait, & property has also its apotheosis some where. ↑Fair play!↓ We are willing that Christianity should have its glories, & Greece its own, & India, & England; but we are inly persuaded that Heaven reserves an equal universe of good for each of us, & until we have produced our short ray unto the concave sphere of the heavens & beheld our talent also in its last nobility & exaltation we shall be malcontents[.] [300]

[336] Poets do not need to consider how fruitful the topic is, for with their superfluity of eyes every topic is opulent[.]

Spenser seems to delight in his art for his own skill's sake. In the Muiopotmos see the security & ostentation with which he ⟨still improves elongates⟩ ↑draws out &↓ refines his description of a butterfly's back & wings, of a spider's thread & spinning, of the Butterfly's Cruise among the flowers, "bathing his tender feet in the dew which yet on them does lie," [301] ————— it is all like the working of an exquisite loom which strongly & unweariedly ⟨does⟩ yield↑s↓ fine webs, for exhibition, & defiance of all spinners.

[337]   ↑*Destiny.*↓
Every thing will come home, & a man also. Where is his home? There, thither, where he is incessantly called. He will surely come home, and, if long delayed, the more fiercely.

[299] "but I wish . . . welcomes." is used in "Aristocracy," *W*, X, 39.

[300] This paragraph, struck through in ink with a vertical use mark, is used in "Uses of Great Men," *W*, IV, 31–32.

[301] "Muiopotmos, or the Fate of the Butterfly," ll. 181–182, misquoted.

Of the plenty of the world

————

Of a professor of reading

————

↑p 348↓   That men are individuals constructively

————

That speaking the truth is the little end of the great world

————

Of the use of the words 'dire' and 'silly.'

[338] The Age is ↑ocular,↓ facial; and is well symbolized by those sculptures of Palenque.[302]

[339][303] Concord Massachusetts

Rhyme well or rhyme ill
⟨Les⟩Lot of all that time will
⟨I guess b⟩By the color of the day
↑I judge↓ she[n] has made half her way
In fun he granted prayers
And made men heroes unawares

The Garden. Give a dollar for every weed. M examined the tree & discovered an insect from 5 to 6 f⟨t⟩eet long with large pocket-like processes that would hold half a peck[.]

Let others love the naked sun
My eyes are a little weak
I had much rather
Have some small medium
Like clouds or boughs of trees or plum⟨s⟩
Or clustering grapes

[302] In April, 1841, Emerson had seen plates by an unidentified French artist of the ruins of Palenque, one of the earliest excavated archeological sites in southern Mexico (*JMN*, VII, 425).
[303] Except for "Concord Massachusetts", the entries on this page are in pencil.

See him in his work
Know him by his fruits
Which ape their father
Peaches apples damsons

[340] Sunday, 20 Sept. Suffices Ellery Channing a mood for a poem. 'There, I have sketched more or less in that color & style. You have a sample of it. What more would you get, if I should work on forever?' ⁿ He has no proposition to affirm or support. He scorns it. He has, first of all Americans, a natural flow and can say what he will. I say to him, if I could write as well as you, I would write a great deal better.

[341] "As for beauty, I need not look beyond an oar's length for my fill of it." — I do not know whether he used the expression with design or no, but my eye rested on the ⟨beautiful⟩ ↑charming↓ play of light on the water which he was ⟨every moment⟩ striking with his paddle. I fancied, I had never seen such colour, such transparency, such eddies[:] it was the ⟨colour⟩ ↑hue↓ of rhine wines[;] ↑it↓ was jasper & verdantique[,] topaz & chalcedony[;]↓ it was gold & green & chesnut & hazel in bewitching succession & relief without cloud or confusion[.]

[342]   *Rhyme*
I know something more of rhyme, as all conversation with it strengthens the argument for it. I observe that it is the right material[;] as we do not enclose the face of watches in oaken but in crystal cases, so rhyme is the transparency that allows almost the pure architecture of thought to ⟨appear⟩ become visible to the reader. The genius of the sentence appears. There is great difference in mode & form. This artist presents like an enraptured boy a succession of rainbow bubbles, opaline, airborne, spherical as the world, and instead of a few drops of soul[,] soap suds.³⁰⁴
                    ↑Perhaps printed in *Letters & Social Aims*↓

³⁰⁴ This paragraph is used in "Poetry and Imagination," *W*, VIII, 52–53. "Perhaps printed in *Letters & Social Aims*" is in pencil.

[343] The scholar in the throng has two powers to hook him to the men he meets; viz. his thoughts; & his appreciation of thoughts. If there be any wit in all that company, how can it do without him?

<table>
<tr><td>Poems to [305]</td><td>[See ink list p 357]</td></tr>
</table>

LeBaron Russell
Mrs [Lydia Maria] Child
Mrs [Caroline Neagus] Hildreth
E[benezer] R[ockwood] Hoar
⟨M⟩ E[lizabeth] Prichard
M[ary] R[ussell] Watson
H[arrison]. G[ray]. O[tis]. Blake
N[athaniel] Hawthorne
E[lizabeth] P[almer] Peabody
W[illiam] Emerson   Bangor
W[illiam] Pope
E[liza Thayer] Clapp
J[ames] R[ussell] Lowell
Rebekah Haskins
Richard Fuller
W[illiam] A[llen] Wall
[C. G.] Fenner
J[ohn] M[ilton] Cheney
Mrs Cheney
H[orace]. Greeley
H[enry]. [Wadsworth] Longfellow
A[bel]. Adams
Dr [Oliver Wendell] Holmes

Mrs [Eliza Buckminster] Lee
Miss [Sophia] Foord
Prof. [Joseph] Lovering

[305] This list is in three columns, indicated by breaks. "LeBaron Russell" actually occurs above "Poems to", not below it. "Essex" and "Berkshire" are written above the last column, and "Middlesex" and "Suffolk" below it; the four are names of Massachusetts counties. All of the items are in pencil, except that the initial letter of the canceled "Rebekah G Haskins" is partially in ink.

M[ary] M[oody] E[merson]
C[aroline] S[turgis]
E[lizabeth] H[oar]
M[argaret] F[uller]
S[amuel] G[ray] W[ard]
W[illiam] E[llery] C[hanning]
H[enry] D[avid] T[horeau]
S[arah] C[larke]
A[mos] B[ronson] A[lcott]
G[eorge] P[artridge] B[radford]
F[rederic] H[enry] H[edge]
C[harles] T[homas] J[ackson]
L[ucy] C[otton] B[rown]
N[athaniel] L[angdon] F[rothingham]
G[eorge] B[arrell] E[merson]
W[illiam] H[enry] F[urness]
W[illiam] E[merson]
↑C[hristopher]. G[ore].↓ Ripley
A[bby] L[arkin] Adams
C[ornelius]. Mathews
Lucia Russell
⟨Rebekah G[reene] Haskins⟩

T[homas]. Carlyle
J[ohn]. [James Garth] Wilkinson
D[avid] Thom
Dr [Henry] M[a]cCormac
J[ohn] A[braham] Heraud

Essex
Berkshire
Middlesex
Suffolk

[344]   1846
Bangor, October 6, 7, 8 [306]
Three hundred townships good for timber & for nothing else. Palmer

[306] Emerson delivered five lectures from the Representative Men series in Bangor, October 6–15.

457

mills that I saw building, — the whole property was reckoned worth 60,000. before the freshet, but would not have been relinquished for that sum.

Pines a thousand years old.[n] Every year they must go farther for them: they recede, like beavers & Indians, before the white man.

Those Bangor men buy townships merely for the logs that can be cut on them, and add township to township. Some day a mine, a slate quarry, ⟨is⟩ good marble, or soapstone, or lime is found in them, or a new railroad is projected, the timber land becomes unexpectedly what is called a settling township, and the lumber merchant suddenly finds himself the lord of villages, towns, & cities, & his family established as great proprietors[.]

[345] My friend W[illiam]. E[merson]. at Bangor [307] told me that he thought "Judge Story might be a great man, O yes, a man of a good deal of talent & ⟨fame⟩ learning & fame," but he did not think so highly of him as a Judge, as many did; "that he had two failings as a Judge; first, in pint of judgment; & second, in pint of integrity; — you take my idea."

[346] The love of mesmerism is a low lust of structure & separated by celestial diameters from the love of spiritual truth.[308]

With his passion for facts, & his inability to draw them from the men of the world⟨,⟩ he fell in with, who were dumb to him, he came upon this expedient of mesmerism by way of suction-pump to draw the most unwilling & valuable mass of experience from every extraordinary individual at pleasure. It is not to be told with what joy he began to put this experiment in practice. The eyes of the man who saw through the earth the ingots of gold that were lying a rod or two under the surface, or of the diver who comes suddenly down full on a bed of pearl oysters, were not to be compared [347]–[348] [leaf torn out] [309]

---

[307] William Emerson, perhaps a distant relative, was a merchant whom Emerson had first come to know in July, 1834 (*JMN*, IV, 390).

[308] This sentence is used in "Demonology," *W*, X, 25–26.

[309] A few fragments of words are visible on both sides of the stub. Emerson indexed p. [348] under Individual and Vortex.

[349]   ↑*New England*↓

I think again of the true history of New England, & wish to see the just view taken with such grand sight as to omit all or almost all the chronologies & personalities which ordinarily constitute the tale. Now let us have only the aboriginal features, a god stepping from peak to peak nor planting his foot but on a mountain. Calvinism & Christianity being now ended, shall be ended. Their powerful contribution to the history shall be acknowledged. England shall be dealt with as truly. English conventions & the English public shall not have so much politeness from us. Neither shall ⟨our⟩ the forms of our government & that wearisome constitutional argument mislead us, as it has Whig parties and good-boy statesmen. But we will see what men here really wish & try to obtain, often against their professions. What New England gravitates toward.

[350] All the materialities should be freely received to refresh the picture; the ↑ice, the↓ lumber, ⟨the⟩ leather, ⟨the⟩ iron, & stone, and the cotton manufacture; and we should not spare to trace these facts to their grand home in the geology, and show the man the contemporary of pine, chestnut, & oak, ↑granite, ice, waterfalls,↓ & therefore a worker in them; & how his commerce brought him hides from Valparaiso & lead from Missouri.

The negative merit of the piece would be its resolute rejection of the faded or regnant superstitions, as ⟨our⟩of the Christian mythology, of the agricultural, commercial, & social delusions which pass current in men's mouths, but have long lost all reality.

[351] All of one kind. If the hand is grasping, so is the brain also only a finer hand, a modified hand, & grasps[.]

The world is saturated with deity or law[.]
                      See also Y 167

[352] ⟨I do not wish to see R. or P. or T.[,] who have no private character though they are good public orators, any more than I wish to see a cannon in the gunhouse which yet makes a fine figure on the musterfield[.]⟩

⟨I do n⟩ R. & [Edward] T↑aylor↓ & [Wendell] P↑hillips↓. are good orators, but I do not care to see them in private. The cannon, which made so good a figure on the musterfield, would be an uninteresting companion in the house.[310]

[353]   ↑*Tools*↓
What said you, that a half ounce of coal will draw two tons a mile? —[311]

[354] Dr. P↑arkman↓. told me yesterday 'twas 33 years since he was ordained; & he could not credit that he was as old as his predecessor, Dr Eliot, when he died. Dr E. was an old man, and *my* infirmity, said Dr P., is my extreme youth.[312] Whitfield's text after the death of his wife was "the creature was made subject to vanity."

———

"A little too much reality," said a young slip in the ferryboat yesterday ↑to his companion↓ coming in out of the snowstorm.

———

Care & coffee are rather dragonish[.]
I see men who seem to hear their ill-fames and I know one man who is always expecting stabs and always receiving compliments.

[355] The Emperor of Russia got tired one day of hearing of Atlantic & Pacific Ocean, & thought he would have the name changed, & call the former "My Ocean," so he gave Nesselrode instructions to make it a close sea[.]

Bonaparte projected making the Mediterranean a French Lake.[313]

[356] There is so much to say which only requires high health —

———

[310] This sentence is struck through in ink with a vertical use mark; cf. "Eloquence," *W*, VIII, 120.
[311] This sentence, struck through in ink with a vertical use mark, is used in "Wealth," *W*, VI, 87.
[312] The Reverend Francis Parkman (1788–1852), father of the historian, was pastor of the New North Church, Boston.
[313] This and the preceding entry, struck through in ink with a discontinuous vertical use mark, are used in "Works and Days," *W*, VII, 167–168. See Journal V, p. [93] above.

strength to the degree of frolic spirits, and not special, intellectual, or moral gifts.

One of the ingredients of eloquence then, is Health.

Another of my orator, is, that he should come ever from the high, from the highest ground[,] out of the azure & not from Change-
-Alley.[314]

↑To health every topic is opulent[.] p. 336↓

> W[illiam] M[ackay] Prichard
> E[dmund] Hosmer
> C[harles] C[reighton] Hazewell
> W[illiam] Pope
> E[liza] Clapp
> Mrs [Mary?] Larkin
> S[arah] M[argaret] Fuller
> ⟨G[eorge] P[artridge] B[radford]⟩
> Mr [Tristram Bernard] M[a]cKay
> ⟨Louisa [Snow] Jacobs⟩
> Miss Lydia Jackson
> ⟨Sarah Kendall⟩[315]

[357] I have sent copies of my Poems to the following addresses — [316]

> Rev S[amuel]. Ripley
> E. B. Ripley
> C[hristopher]. G[ore]. Ripley
> N[athaniel] Hawthorne
> LeBaron Russell
> Lucia Russell
> M[ary]. R[ussell]. Watson
> Mrs [Lydia Maria] Child
> Mrs [Caroline Neagus] Hildreth

---

[314] This sentence is struck through in pencil with a vertical use mark.

[315] These twelve names, presumably jottings for the list on p. [357], are in pencil.

[316] This list is in three columns, the first beginning with "Rev S. Ripley", the second with "My mother", and the third with "Edmund Hosmer". This page is reproduced in Plate IV.

Sam[ue]l Hoar Esq
E[benezer]. R[ockwood]. Hoar
Elizabeth Hoar
Fanny Prichard
H[arrison]. G[ray]. O[tis]. Blake
E[lizabeth]. P[almer]. Peabody
W[illiam]. Emerson, Esq.   Bangor
J[ames]. R[ussell]. Lowell
Rebecca G[reene]. Haskins
R[ichard]. F[rederic]. Fuller
W[illiam]. A[llen]. Wall
C. G. Fenner
J[ohn]. M[ilton]. Cheney
H[orace]. Greeley
H[enry]. W[adsworth]. Longfellow
Abel Adams
A[bby]. L[arkin]. Adams
O[liver]. W[endell]. Holmes
Mrs Eliza [Buckminster] Lee
Miss [Sophia] Foord
Prof. [Joseph] Lovering
George P[artridge]. Bradford
E. C. Goodwin
Mrs [Nathaniel?] Bowditch
Sarah Kendall
My mother
My wife
M[ary] M[oody] Emerson
H[annah]. U. [Haskins] Parsons
L[ucy]. C[otton]. [Jackson] Brown
S[amuel]. G[ray]. Ward
W[illiam]. E[llery]. Channing
A[mos]. B[ronson]. Alcott
H[enry]. D[avid] Thoreau
Caroline Sturgis
Sarah [Freeman] Clarke
George B[arrell] Emerson

462

Poems seem to have been published Dec 25 (Christmas)

I have sent copies of my Poems to the following
addresses—

#		
1	Rev S. Ripley	My mother
2	E. B. Ripley	my wife
3	C. G. Ripley	Wm. M. Emerson
4	N. Hawthorne	H. W. Parsons
5	Le Baron Russell	L. C. Brown
6	Lucia Russell	S. G. Ward
7	M. R. Watson	W. E. Channing
8	Mrs Child	A. B. Alcott
9	Mrs Hildreth	H. D. Thoreau
10	Saml. Hoar Esq	Caroline Sturgis
11	E. R. Hoar	Sarah Clarke
12	Elizabeth Hoar	George B. Emerson
13	Fanny Prichard	William Emerson
14	H. G. O. Blake	F. H. Hedge
15	E. P. Peabody	N. L. Frothingham
16	W. Emerson, Esq. Bangor	C. T. Jackson
17	J. R. Lowell	W. H. Furness
18	Rebecca G. Haskins	J. G. Palfrey
19	R. F. Fuller	C. Mathews Esq
20	W. A. Wall	C. B. Fairbanks
21	C. G. Fenner	E. Tuckerman
22	J. M. Cheney	J. E. Cabot
23	H. Greeley	Martha Bartlett
24	H. W. Longfellow	E. D. Robbins
25	Abel Adams	J. Williams
26	A. L. Adams	W. H. Channing
27	O. W. Holmes	Mrs Barlow
28	Mrs Eliza Lee	S. F. Haskins
29	Miss Foord	B. Frost
30	Prof. Lovering	A. W. Stevens
31	George P. Bradford	Elizabeth Burgess
32	E. C. Goodwin	B. Rodman
33	Mrs Bowditch	T. M. Brewer
34	Sarah Kendall	Anna Alcott
		Mary Willoughby
		Louisa Ann Jacobs
		W. W. Story

Edmund Hosmer
Charles Sprague
Lydia Jackson
John Chapman
Mrs Neilson
P. P. Hunt
W. H. Dennett
T Carlyle by E R Hoar
J. Chapman

Daily Advertiser
Chronotype
Transcript
Courier — Whipple
Harbinger
Atlas — Field

W C Bryant
N P Willis
Dr Parsons for Knickerb.
Southern Review
Christian Examiner
Phila.

1 copy for self
Sold 1 copy to L C B
1 to G P B
1 to Mrs Goodwin
2 to Miss Foord

Plate IV   Journal O, page 357   Text, pages 461–464

Recipients of Poems, *1846*

William Emerson
F[rederic]. H[enry]. Hedge
N[athaniel]. L[angdon]. Frothingham
C[harles]. T[homas]. Jackson
W[illiam] H[enry] Furness
J[ohn]. G[orham]. Palfrey
C[ornelius]. Mathews Esq
C. B. Fairbanks
E Tuckerman
J[ames] E[lliot] Cabot
Martha Bartlett
E. D. Robbins
J. Williams
W[illiam] H[enry] Channing
Mrs [Almira Penniman] Barlow
S[arah]. F[oxcroft]. Haskins
B[arzillai]. Frost
A W Stevens
Elizabeth Burgess
B[enjamin]. Rodman
T[homas]. M[ayo]. Brewer
Anna Alcott
Mary Willoughby
Louisa Snow Jacobs
W[illiam]. W[etmore]. Story
Edmund Hosmer
Charles Sprague
Lydia Jackson
John Chapman
Mrs Nelson [317]
B[enjamin]. P[eter]. Hunt
W[illiam]. H. Dennett
T[homas] Carlyle by E[benezer] R[ockwood] Hoar
J[ohn]. Chapman

[Boston] Daily Advertiser

[317] This name was written first in pencil, then traced in ink.

[Boston Daily] Chronotype
[Boston Daily Evening] Transcript
[Boston] Courier = [Edwin Percy] Whipple
[The] Harbinger
[Boston Daily] Atlas = [David Dudley] Field

W[illiam] C[ullen] Bryant
N[athaniel] P[arker] Willis
Dr [Thomas William] Parsons for *Knickerb[ocker]*.
Southern [*and Western Literary Messenger and*] Review
Christian Examiner
Phila[delphia].

1 copy for self
Sold 1 copy to L[ucy] C[otton Jackson] B[rown]
   1   to G[eorge] P[artridge] B[radford]
   1   to Mrs [E. C.] Goodwin
   2   to Miss [Sophia] Foord

[358] Alcott[,] among many fine things he said of my volume of Poems, said, the sentiment was moral and the expression seemed the reverse.

I suppose if ⟨I sh⟩ verses of mine should be compared with those of one of my friends, the moral tendency would be found impressed on all mine as an original polarity,[n] that all my light is polarized.

[359] Our system is one of poverty. 'Tis presumed that there is but one Homer, one Shakspeare, one Jesus, one Newton, not that all are or shall be inspired.[318] If every man wrote poems, there were no readers. But should we truly suffer social detriment, if the wit of all were exalted? No, surely, but rapid & magical methods of disposing of its food the Intellect knows & would employ.

[360] 1847, Jan. 10. Read Alfieri's Life: Who ⟨w⟩died the year I

[318] This and the preceding sentence, struck through in ink with two vertical use marks, are used in "Success," *W*, VII, 296.

was born, was a dear lover of Plutarch & Montaigne, a passionate lover of beauty & of study.[319] His rare opportunities & the determination to use them, make him a valuable representative. His temperament however isolated him, & he travels in a narrow track with high walls on either side. Yet he is most fortunate in his friendships, & at last in his love. The noble is seeking the same good as the republican, namely one or two companions of intelligence, probity, & grace, to wear out life with, & rebut the disparagement he reads in the sea & the sky. Gori, Caluso, & the Countess of Albany were sea & sky to him. One has many thoughts, in reading this book, of the uses of Aristocracy & Europe to the native scholar.

[361] The systems of blood & culture which we call France, Spain, Piedmont, &c must not be set down as nothing. There is a strong, characterised, ⟨individual⟩ resultant man, result of race, climate, mountain, sea, occupation, & institutions who is the Frenchman & appears well enough & acutely interesting to any one who has the opportunity of conversing with many of the best individuals of that nation; not recognized in any one man but well enough exhibited in the most distinguished French circles. In like manner there is a Spaniard, an Englishman, a Roman & the rest. This is plainer when we remember how fast Nature adopts art, & whatever form of life calculation leads us into for one or two generations Nature presently adopts into the blood, & creates men organized for that accidental & artificial way of [362] working. To be a noble is to have a ticket of admission to the flower of each of these races with their peculiarities exalted by nature & custom to the best degree. Also to be noble & rich, is to see the sea & take possession of it by sea voyaging,[n] to see the mountains, the Nile, Niagara, the desart, Rome, Paris, Constantinople, to see galleries, libraries, arsenals, navies, manufactories[.] [320]

The stoic sect[,] which are never far off[,] need not tell me that the

---

[319] *The Autobiography of Vittorio Alfieri, the Tragic Poet* . . . , trans. C. Edwards Lester, 2nd ed. (New York, 1845). The three persons Emerson names in this paragraph are Francesco Gori Gandellini, Alfieri's friend; Tommaso Valperga-Caluso, the Abbe di Caluso; and Louise Maximiliana Caroline Stuart, Countess of Albany, Alfieri's mistress.

[320] "To be a noble . . . manufactories", struck through in ink with a vertical use mark, is used in "Wealth," *W*, VI, 94.

man is all these & they are superfluous. No, grant the man divine[,]
he wants also a divine fact; and no man, let him be never so thoughtful, ever went to the sea shore, from an in-land home, without a
surprise, & a feeling that here was new invitation for somewhat
[363][321] that hitherto slept.

It appears too from this book that there are no large cities. Boston
is a little town, & if any man buys a loaf of bread, every other knows
where he had it; but so is Rome, & Italy, & England, each a little
province, in which gossip & the surveillance of a petty public opinion
is equally tyrannical.[322]

↑*Machiavelli*↓
I have tried to read Machiavelli's Histories but find it not
easy.[323] The Florentine factions are as tiresome as the history of the
Philadelphia Fire Companies, & the mobs of the ⟨l⟩Liberties of South-
wark and Moyamensing↑.↓ ⟨would be.⟩ The biography of Dante, of
Raffaelle, of Michel Angelo[,] to whom no word is spared, (excepting
a line twice to Dante) would be worth all this ⟨nonsense⟩ ↑noise↓ of
Signories & Gonfalonieri.

[364] H.D.T. wants to go to Oregon[,] not to London. Yes surely;
but what seeks he but the most energetic nature? & seeking that, he
will find Oregon indifferently in all places; for it snows & blows &
melts & adheres & repels all the world over.

Superlative
In Athens the Pelasgicon, a strip of land under the western wall
of the citadel, — a curse had been pronounced on any who should
tenant it and the oracle declared it "Better untrodden[.]"[324]

---

[321] "Alfieri . . . Machiavel" is centered at the top of the page.
[322] This paragraph is struck through in ink with a vertical use mark. Cf. "Worship," *W*, VI, 222.
[323] Emerson's library contains *The Florentine Histories*, trans. C. Edwards Lester,
2 vols. (New York, 1845). In Account Book 4, he notes the purchase of this work
in January, 1847.
[324] This entry, including the heading, and the two lines which follow it, are in
pencil. Emerson used both entries in the lecture "The Superlative in Manners and
Literature" (see *W*, X, 545).

On they came to the Dorian mood
Of flutes & soft recorders.
[Milton, *Paradise Lost*, I, 549–551, with changes]

[365] I live amidst dresses: — if I could live amidst persons —

The Chair is vacant, take it. The railroad is built and ⟨bu⟩ the builders see not why, but thou seest; use it: there is nothing in the depot
but frippery: thou hast the deposit for the depot.

Yes, the Zoroastrian, the Indian, the Persian scriptures are
majestic, & more to our daily purpose than this year's almanac or
this day's newspaper. Enlarge not thy Destiny. Let the Immortal
depth of your soul lead you.[324a]
But[n] these things are not to be said with the teeth & the end of the
tongue, & spoken as if out of the face, but they should come out of
the glow of the cheek & out of the throbbing heart. Friendship to
Friendship should give & take them. Solitude & Time should brood
& ripen them. Heroes should absorb & realize them[.]

[366] These are they which are not & cannot be held by ⟨printe⟩
letters printed on a page, but are living characters translateable into
every tongue & form of life. I read them on the lichens of rocks &
trees[;] I watch them on the waves at the sea beach[;] they creep on
the backs of worms. I detect them in the laughs & blushes & eye
sparkles of men & women[.]
These scriptures the missionary might well carry over prairie &
desart & ocean to Siberia, ⟨&⟩ Japan, & Timbuctoo. Now the poor fool
goes with his stupid tract & catechism & the snuffle of the Tabernacle,
carrying as he fancies somewhat portable. That which the true missionary carries journeys faster than he & greets him on his arrival
as long already there before him. The missionary must ⟨go to⟩ ↑be
carried by it &↓ find⟨, not to carry⟩ ↑it there↓, or he goes in vain.
[367] I ask whether there is any geography in these things. We call
them Asiatic[,] we call them primaeval. But perhaps that is only
optical; for Nature is always equal to herself & there are as good
pairs of eyes & as good ears in the planet now, as ever there were.

<hr>

[324a] Emerson quotes "Enlarge not . . . you." from "The Oracles of Zoroaster,"
The Phenix, 1835, in Journal E. See *JMN*, VII, 456.

Only these ejaculations of the soul are uttered one or a few at a time, at long intervals, & it ⟨‖ . . . ‖⟩takes millenniums to make a bible[.] [325]

In looking at Menu & Saadi & Bhagavat, life seems in the ⟨e⟩East a simpler affair, — only a tent, & a little rice, & ass's milk; & not as with us ↑⟨as⟩ what↓ commerce ↑has made it,↓ a feast whose ⟨ing⟩ dishes come from the equator & both poles[.]

[368] [326] Memoranda for Chapman [327]   Errata of Poems
                              Send copy to C[harles] Lane
                              Copy of Channing's Poems
                                    & Emerson's

Letter to A[lexander] Ireland
      to C[harles]. Lane
      to J[ames]. [John Garth] Wilkinson
      Herbert New
      J[ohn]. A[braham]. Heraud

  [369] Copies to J[ames] E[lliot] Cabot
             [Edward?] Tuckerman
             [Tristram Bernard] MacKay
             M[artha] Bartlett
             J Williams

---

[325] "Yes, the Zoroastrian [p. [365]] . . . a bible", struck through in ink with vertical use marks, with the exception of "I ask whether . . . optical;", is used in "Books," *W*, VII, 219–220.

[326] The entries on this and the following page are in pencil. Pasted to pp. [368]– [369] are three pieces of paper bearing what appear to be transcriptions of the talk of Edward Waldo Emerson at the age of two. Each of them is identified as coming from a "journal" — but this is hardly likely in view of Edward's age. With the exception of the notation "Eddie's Journal Sept 1846" on the first piece, none of the writing is in Emerson's hand. The first piece, measuring 8.5 x 20.2 cm, is attached to the bottom left corner of p. [368] and numbered "369"; the second, measuring 9.1 x 19.8 cm, is attached to the bottom right corner; and the third, measuring 10.2 x 12.7 cm, is attached to the top left corner of p. [369]. All the pieces are pale blue. The first and third are faintly lined on one side; the second is lined on both sides. Playing at journals was apparently an Emerson family pastime. In a letter from Bangor, Maine, October 12, 1846, where he went to lecture (see pp. 457–458 above), Emerson wrote to his wife: "Love to Nelly & Edie [Ellen and Edith]. Where are their journals?" (*L*, III, 356).

[327] John Chapman was Emerson's English publisher.

        E Robins
        B[arzillai] Frost
    x E[lizabeth] Burgess
    x E C Goodwin
        ⟨LeBaron Russell⟩
        ⟨Mrs [Ellen Sturgis] Hooper⟩
        Miss Lydia Jackson
        Mary H[owland] Russell
        Louisa Snow [Jacobs]
        Sarah Kendall

[370] [328]   Concord Lyceum 1846

           [John Albion] Andrew
Dec ⟨8⟩9   C[harles] F[rancis] Adams
    16
    23   H[enry]. [Norman] Hudson
    30
Jan   6 [Index material omitted]
    13
    20
    27
Feb   3
    10
    17
    24
Mar   3
    10
    17
    24
    31

[371] Channing's Poems
      Dec 20 Rec'd 5 copies
           1 to W[illiam] E[llery] C[hanning]

[328] Entries in pencil, some of them erased, underlie the ink entries and the index material on this page. They appear to be arithmetic and lists of expenses.

1 sold to G[eorge]. P[artridge]. B[radford].
1

Dec 28 Rec'd 2 copies
    1 sent by W[illiam] E[llery] C[hanning]
               to J[ohn] P Cushing
    1   do   do   J[ames?] Lawrence

[372] [Index material omitted] [329]
[inside back cover] [Index material omitted]

[329] A preliminary index, in pencil and erased, covers this page. The notation "43 cords 1 1/2 foot" is written in pencil one third of the way down the page to the left.

Textual Notes

6 man. **10** consciousness. | uphold-[13]er **12** or **15** s⟨‖ . . . ‖⟩end **17** organs, **20** evening — We **22** way — | bound. **25** this, **28** himself. **29** Character." **31** ruthless-[47]ness **34** other; **35** oil: **40** will, **43** Man, | population; **45** says; | head⟨,⟩!" **46** ⟨it[?]⟩& **47** Even **48** theirs. **49** sympathy: | joy: **50** v⟨‖ . . . ‖⟩ast ⟨‖ . . . ‖⟩as **53** colours; **55** comes **58** maxim; **62** no-church-, **63** are. | atmospherically, **66** If | ⟨of[?]⟩them **68** us. | ⟨to[?]⟩the **69** power. **72** assembly. **76** me, | wanted. **79** great. **80** cried. **82** by **83** specimen. **86** attack. | h⟨is[?]⟩e **89** last." **91** ear.

98 of. **101** fearless, **103** circle. | promisers; **109** it. | energy. **114** ⟨The[?]⟩fellow **115** re/ [not canceled] | condit-[42]ion **119** jury,⟨"⟩ | day:" **122** service. **123** g↑u↓aged **124** thin ⟨ex⟩nest **125** the **127** York, | need. | foun-[68]dation. | the⟨re⟩irs, **130** From | He | loved | a **132** daybreak; **136** not — **138** October. | man⟨."⟩-kind. **140** From **141** expression, **142** the **145** Putnam [canceled] **148** experiment. **150** face. **152** the [not canceled] **155** pu⟨tt⟩lling **156** articles **162** home. **165** When | led." **166** to | jingle | to **173** Napoleon,! **177** things. **178** it." | independence. | suprise | ⟨⟨a⟩In⟩ this **179** ⟨wa[?]⟩absence **180** ⟨at⟩

184 writings. | all." **187** fro' [not canceled] **191** Phoedrus **194** malcontents, **195** paints. **196** more, **199** warfare. | knife. **202** Berklely, **203** issue. | justified. **205** if **207** [Emerson wrote "peartree." then canceled "pear"] **209** Mr Briggs's [canceled] | is [not canceled] **210** prey, **212** interest. **215** modernness₂ perpetual₁, **218** knowledge, **221** spot." **222** month. **227** of **228** ⟨R[?]⟩Healed **229** skepticisms. **234** argu-[109]ment **237** he **238** weak ⟨day⟩ness **239** Have **240** these **244** we **246** frivolous. **247** alike — **248** English!, **252** Raffaelle; **253** world-books,

259 power" | with the security of a grenadier₂ into ⟨the most⟩ untried depths₁. **260** We | "Childe⟨,⟩ ↑Harold, — ↓ **262** everything **264** ⟨⟨fiv⟩a thousand⟩ | emerg-[19]ing | good **265** small. **267** ⟨⟨a⟩is⟩ **269** neighborhood. **270** sin, **274** ⟨te[?]⟩convulsed **277** But | Of **279** Variety. **280** his matter. [in brackets] **281** ancedotes **283** he **287** "If mankind were exactly on a [canceled] | faults [circled, not canceled] **288** lapse [circled, not canceled] **295** Be bold. | be bold. **296** ⟨&[?]⟩Plato **299** But | ↑⟨strength⟩↓ **301** possessions. **302** the [not canceled]

304 ⟨Y[?]⟩As 315 creation. | ⟨bo[?]⟩prompter's | us. 316 strata 320
⟨a⟩↑e↓nem⟨is⟩↑ies↓, 323 the 324 eyes. | vehemently₂ talk₁ 336 [semicolon not
canceled] 338 [canceled only through "have"] 342 illustra-[228]tions 343 of
[canceled] 344 not, 349 designs. 350 theirs. 353 it. 354 Sedulously

O

360 now, 368 Achilles. | astrono⟨m⟩nomy, | comes. 370 centigrade₂ or
decagraded₁ 371 only | home. 372 suffering. 374 circum-[53]stance. 378
tadpoles⟨?⟩ ↑talk↓. | pree⟨n⟩-engaged 383 Man 387 figure, 389 Titan, 393
institutions; 400 appetite, | Buonaparte; 401 fire⟨,⟩! 403 live; 408 inquisitions.
409 him. 410 Millions | replies; 411 are. 415 [editorial parentheses] |
⟨corr[?]⟩swamped 417 than 421 wants: 422 Wine⟨,⟩. ⟨t⟩The 424 Phalanx's.
425 creatures. 426 something, 430 People. 431 Universe. 432 the | it, 434
much. 435 Francois 438 in 441 mu-[307]sic 442 the | Builds 443 eesy 444
com-[315]mentator, 448 material — 449 design. 450 rams. 451 with 452
requiring, | world, 454 She 455 forever.' 458 old; 464 polarity. 465 voyag-
ing. 467 but

Index

This Index includes Emerson's own index material omitted from the text. His index topics, including long phrases, are listed under "Emerson, Ralph Waldo, INDEX HEADINGS AND TOPICS"; the reader should consult both the general Index and Emerson's. If Emerson did not specify a manuscript page or a date to which his index topic referred, the editors have chosen the most probable passage(s) and added "(?)" to the printed page number(s). If Emerson's own manuscript page number is an obvious error, it has been silently corrected.

References to materials included or to be included in *Lectures* are grouped under "Emerson, Ralph Waldo, LECTURES." References to drafts of unpublished poems are under "Emerson, Ralph Waldo, POEMS." Under "Emerson, Ralph Waldo, WORKS" are references to published versions of poems, to lectures and addresses included in *W* but not in *Lectures*, and to Emerson's essays and miscellaneous publications. Kinds of topics included under "Emerson, Ralph Waldo, DISCUSSIONS" in earlier volumes are now listed only in the general Index.

DATE DUE

SEP 2 9 2011